The Case Against Academic Boycotts of Israel

Edited by
Cary Nelson & Gabriel Noah Brahm

Preface by Paul Berman

MLA MEMBERS
for SCHOLARS' RIGHTS

Distributed by Wayne State University Press

MLA MEMBERS FOR SCHOLARS' RIGHTS
Chicago and New York

Cataloging-in-Publication Data has been applied for with
the Library of Congress

Library of Congress Control Number 2014021270

Nelson, Cary:
The case against academic boycotts of Israel / Cary Nelson
p. cm.
Includes bibliographical references.
ISBN: 978-0-9903316-0-5 (alk: paper)
ISBN: 978-0-9903316-1-2 (ebook)

Manufactured in the United States of America

10 9 8 7 6 5 4 3 2 1

Contents

Preface

The ancient Athenians used to ostracize anyone who was deemed to pose a political danger or was accused of a crime, and this custom was democratic and wise. Ostracism was democratic because the citizens were called upon to vote, and ostracism was wise because, by sending the troublemakers out of town, it kept the peace. Still, I have always loved the story that Plutarch tells about the illiterate fool who voted to ostracize Aristides the Just and, when asked why he would do such a thing, explained that he was sick and tired of hearing Aristides called "the Just." Plutarch was ever attuned to the human eccentricities, and he wants us to notice that low rancor and the occasional impulse to damage society enter sometimes even into the most thoughtful of customs. And he draws a moral. He knows that sooner or later we ourselves, his readers, will be solemnly requested to join in banning someone from civilized company. He wants us to pause and ask, "That famously stupid Athenian voter—that person couldn't be me, could it?"

The modern version of Athenian ostracism is known as the boycott. The word itself, "boycott," comes from nineteenth-century Ireland, where the Land League demanded that everyone shun a landlord's agent of ill repute who happened to be named Captain Boycott. But the concept and even the word—"boycotter" in French, "boicotear" in Spanish, and so forth—long ago ascended into universal acceptance. People organize boycotts in order to level accusations and mobilize their supporters. The ostensible purpose is to exert an economic pressure. But a boycott's larger purpose has always been to convey a sense of moral opprobrium, which, if enough people will only join in conveying it, may exert pressures of a deeper sort. To lose a few customers because someone has mounted a boycott against you and your business can be a misfortune. But to be shunned by people you respect, to be treated as a contemptible person, to discover that your equals and colleagues decline to enter into even the coolest and most professional of relations with you—this can be unbearable. And so, a popular and well-conducted boycott can end up wielding a mysterious power. Normally the effects take a while to become apparent. Boycotts are not supposed to go on forever, though. They are supposed to be practical. Either they work, or fail to work. They resemble labor strikes, in that respect. And yet, in the years since Captain Boycott, there is at least one example of a boycott that has failed to work, and, even so, has gone on forever, as if drawing on inexhaustible sources of rancor and rage.

This is the boycott against the State of Israel and its antecedent, the early Zionist settlements in Palestine, which has got to be, by now, the oldest continuous-running boycott in the history of the world—or, at minimum, the oldest boycott that has called itself a boycott. The anti-Israel boycott enjoys a further distinction. It appears to have been, over the generations, the world's most popular boycott, even if, from time to time, its popularity has bobbed up and down, now revitalized, now half-forgotten, in one region or another—the most popular of boycotts, judged by how many hundreds of millions of people appear to be its supporters even now. Still another distinction: the anti-Israel boycott has proved to be, ideologically speaking, the world's most adaptable boycott—a boycott that, without the slightest embarrassment, changes its costume every few years in order to present itself as Muslim, Christian, supernaturalist, right-wing, left-wing, liberal, secular, and sometimes all of the above, multi-striped, quite as if no single doctrine or philosophy or theology or geographical perspective, but only the lot of them ensemble, could possibly sum up the justifications for conducting the boycott, so various are Israel's sins. The several extraordinary traits that attach to this most singular of boycotts raise a question, which I will put here. To wit, do the exceptional aspects of the anti-Israel boycott, its duration, popularity, and ideological chameleonism, derive from the boycott's target—from an exceptionally evil or iniquitous quality that somehow inheres to Israel and its place in the world? Israel—does it deserve its fate? Or—the other possibility—do the peculiarities of the boycott reflect, instead, certain eccentricities of human nature that, if Plutarch were among us, might attract his bemused and disdainful attention?

The argument in favor of boycotting Israel and the Zionists has gone through, by my calculation, three main phases or waves, with a fourth phase presently floating in our direction. The earliest of these phases, back in the

1920s and '30s, was simple, practical, and Palestinian—an Arab boycott of the Jews, intended to put up a fight against the tide of Jewish refugees that was beginning to rival and outrival the Palestinian Arabs for control of the land. This was a boycott that, if anyone had been in a mood to work out a compromise between the two populations, might have conferred a much-needed negotiators' advantage on the Palestinian leaders. The spirit of the age did not smile on people who attempted negotiations, however, and the argument for a boycott entered its second phase more or less simultaneously with the first.

The second phase was more than regional. It was international, and it rested on supernaturalist doctrines about the Jews and their cosmic menace to the world. The 1920s and '30s were an era of anti-Jewish boycotts in several parts of the world, sometimes secular, sometimes Catholic, and in all of those places the analytic tendency underlying the boycotts ascribed to the Jews a sinister and not-quite human plan to dominate the world, as described in *The Protocols of the Elders of Zion* or sundry other documents with similar themes, unto *The International Jew: The World's Foremost Problem*, which was Henry Ford's American contribution to the literature. And the same supernaturalist interpretation of Jewish power and evil, except with an Islamic twist, took root among the Palestinian leaders, or at least the most influential of them, which proved to be a hugely unfortunate development for Jews and Palestinians alike. The anti-Jewish boycott in the Middle East, when it spread outward from Palestine to the wider Arab world—Cairo, 1936, the Muslim Brotherhood in command, riots in the streets—rested all too firmly on the supernaturalist argument, with its peculiar and fateful fusion of European conspiracy theory and Islamic tradition.

In the years after the Second World War, an anti-imperialist aspect within the boycott's justification began to loom a little more prominently. In this next phase of the argument, the old Nazi idea, which regarded Zionism as a plot against the Europeans, was turned upside down, and Zionism was accused, instead, of being a European plot, directed against everyone else for the purpose of maintaining the system of European imperialism. Third World solidarity, together with the need to protect Islam from the diabolical Jewish conspiracy, became the boycott's fundamental appeal, now under the administration of the Arab League. The anti-imperialist side of the new argument proved to be fairly convincing, too, here and there around the world, perhaps with a little help from the oil exporters. Only, in sketching these phases of the argument, I do not mean to ascribe too much simplicity or logic to the arguments or to the progress that led from one phase to the next. Certain of the supernaturalist arguments against Zionism and the Jews collapsed when the Nazis collapsed. Post-war Vatican reforms put an end to certain others. Some of the force in the anti-imperialist argument against Israel drained away when the Soviet Union drained away. The boycott itself, in its commercial aspects, went into decline.

And yet, as if to demonstrate that not every new step in the world of ideas is a forward step, the supernaturalist argument for a boycott of Israel underwent a revival, late-twentieth century. The Islamist revolution in Iran brought this about, and the revival grew stronger yet with the success of the Muslim Brotherhood, under the name of Hamas, among a portion of the Palestinians. It is daunting to consider that a document as barbarous as the Hamas charter, from 1988, could figure significantly in the political and cultural developments of our own moment—the Hamas charter, with its intermingled citations to *The Protocols of the Elders of Zion* and Islamic scripture and its call to murder the Jews. And yet, Hamas and its ideas do play a role in world affairs, and they play a role even in the politics of European book fairs and book prizes, and maybe they play more of a role in our own high-minded American debates than we like to imagine.

And just now has come the newest or fourth phase of the pro-boycott argument, which if you are a professor, has been filling your own mail slot at the office for the past few seasons. This is the argument that begins by likening Zionism to the old Afrikaner ultra-right in apartheid South Africa, and goes on to appeal to the liberal principles of human rights and the legacy of the anti-apartheid boycott of thirty or forty years ago. This newest of phases is the occasion for the book that you hold in your hands. And the newest of phases gives rise to still another question. This newest argument for the old boycott, as promoted by all kinds of bookish people and artists in the liberal countries and at the universities—can this newest argument be reliably distinguished from the older arguments? From a practical standpoint, can someone participate in the proposed new boycott without participating willy-nilly in the supernaturalist boycott, as well? Or does some fundamental accord underlie all of these arguments for boycotting Israel, which makes it impossible to disentangle the latest of arguments from its predecessors?

I note that, among the proponents of the anti-Israel boycott in its latest version, everyone seems to be obsessed with this question—with the need, from the boycotters' perspective, to distinguish their own call for a boycott from the still-vigorous arguments of the long-ago past. And everyone appears to have settled on a method for drawing the distinction. The method consists of proposing a partial boycott, instead of a total boycott. A nuanced boycott, instead of a blunt boycott. Only, the proponents have not been able to figure out how to define the nuance. No two boycott committees or leaders have been able to agree on this point. Some people advocate boycotting Israeli products manufactured in West Bank settlements, but not products manufactured behind the 1967 borders—a geographical nuance, which at least is easy to describe. Among the proponents of a strictly academic boycott, some people want to boycott the Israeli academic institutions, but not the individual academics who comprise the institutions—a puzzling nuance. At one of the American academic conferences, the boycott proponents decided to give up on boycotting altogether in favor of voting for a protest on the tiny question of Israel's travel visas and how they apply to academics. Some boycotters insist that, in favoring an academic boycott of Israel, they do not wish to restrict academic freedom per se, only the freedom of academics to associate with their Israeli colleagues. Some people favor boycotting Israeli academics who fail to make political statements that are deemed to be suitable, but do not wish to boycott Israeli academics who speak suitably—a dictatorial nuance. An argument has been advanced for boycotting Israeli university presidents, except for university presidents who agree not to invoke their university affiliations—a ridiculous nuance. The Presbyterian Church (to site a non-academic instance) has voted to divest from certain corporations that do business with Israel, but stipulates that, in divesting, the church has not joined the larger movement to divest—an organizational nuance. And so on, with further examples to be found among the essays in this book.

It is to laugh. Plutarch smiles. And yet, you can see what the people who draw these distinctions are hoping to do. They are trying to convince themselves or the world that, in coming up with their own contemporary and academic variations on the old anti-Israel boycott, they have found a way to pursue a campaign that is modern and progressive, and not a campaign that is disgraceful and retrograde. A good boycott, and not a bad one. Their search for the perfect nuance is commendable, though I have the feeling they will never get it right. In any case, as I run my eye down the list of proposed nuances and distinctions, it strikes me that even the people who are keenest on reviving the anti-Israel boycott appear to recognize that something about their own project is not quite what it should be and requires a bit of fine tuning. To which I respond by observing that, if even the people who favor the boycott feel a little uncomfortable about it, what do you suppose is the judgment of their opponents, who stand in adamant opposition?

The Case Against the Academic Boycott of Israel supplies the answer to this question. The twenty-five essays, together with the introduction, are shrewd and analytical, but they are also scathing. Certain of the essays are marvelously subtle and sophisticated in regard to specifically academic themes, as in the crucial discussion of academic freedom. One of the arguments, though, which crops up in different versions throughout the book, takes us outside the university gates, and, in doing so, makes its way to the heart of the controversy. This is the argument about holding Israel to a double standard—though I have discovered that anyone who even broaches the question of Israel and

A Boycotter: Double standards? Excuse me, this is the phony issue that is always raised when someone wishes to denounce a social wrong. I want to protest against Israel's unjust treatment of the Palestinians, and you reply by pointing to North Korea.

A Gentle Critic of the Boycott: But what is phony about observing that Israel is scarcely the worst place on earth?

Boycotter: It is because you can always point to someplace worse. "What about Congo? What about Tibet?" This should not prevent us from addressing injustice when we see it.

Gentle Critic: But the double standards that single out Israel are not anything routine or ordinary. Anti-Zionism is a madness. The worst crimes that have ever been committed against Arabs in the modern world, judged by any statistic you choose, have been committed by fanatics of the anti-Zionist cause: the Baath Party, the Islamists. Surely you see this. Look at Syria!

Boycotter: There you go again. If someone wishes to denounce violence in Syria, I applaud. Still, I have taken as my own concern the oppression of Palestinians by Israel.

Gentle Critic: But don't you see that, by joining so many millions of people all over the world in dwelling on this one issue, you have enrolled in a worldwide pathology. Ninety years of boycotts against Israel and Zionists and Jews—you don't see a problem there? Or never mind the boycott. Look at the United Nations General Assembly resolutions against Israel. At the ghastly United Nations Commission on Human Rights, which proved to be so obsessed with Israel it needed to be replaced with a Human Rights Council, whose obsessions turn out to be just as severe. Haven't you glanced at the resolutions of one political convention after another around the world during these last many decades, aimed overwhelmingly against a single country. Is the pattern really invisible to you? A maniacal harping on Israel.

Boycotter: Maybe those harpings have a point. Anyway, I do not have to accept responsibility for every disagreeable UN resolution that has ever been passed.

Gentle Critic: And your own comrades in promoting the boycott? Haven't you noticed that some of your comrades are a bit crazed on Zionist themes? Faintly medieval, if I may put it that way.

Boycotter: Your every remark is designed to deflect the valuable human-rights protest I wish to make. When you aren't pointing at Syria, you are pointing at the Middle Ages. You are the one who declines to look oppression in the face.

A more ferocious critic of the boycott breaks into the discussion.

Ferocious Critic: You speak about human rights, but your professed concern is a fake. The point about Syria is not a trivial point. One of the peculiar consequences of the anti-Zionist mania is to render invisible the vastest sufferings of the Arab people. Nor is anything in your campaign designed realistically to help the Palestinians. You even half-way recognize the oddity of your position, which is why you try so hard to distinguish your own proposed anti-Israel boycott from boycotts of the past. But your proposed boycott is merely a continuation of the old and the obscurantist. You are encouraging the world to remain mesmerized by a fear of terrible and supernatural forces plotting against Islam or the Arab world or whatever. And why are you doing this?

Boycotter: Yes, why?

Ferocious Critic: The Gentle Critic accused you just now of subjecting Israel to an unfair double standard—a forgiving standard for other countries, an exacting standard for Israel. I accuse you of no such paltry thing. I think you have launched your boycott against Israel because, somewhere in your thinking, you do believe that Israel is the world's most sinister and dangerous country. Israel's most extreme enemies are crazily fixated on their hatred, as if Israel were a cancer that needed to be rooted out—a characteristic phrase. And you, too, seem to be fixated. You have fallen into the ghastliest intellectual trap of the last hundred years. You and Henry Ford! Somehow you have concluded, along with Ford, that Jews, or at least the Jews of the Middle East, are, in Ford's phrase, "the world's foremost problem." That is why your boycott participates in the world's foremost boycott. There is no other logic to what you are doing. At minimum, you have been stampeded by the many millions of people who do accept the supernaturalist logic. Your own contribution consists of trying to put a sane face on an old insanity.

Boycotter: This is no longer an argument. This is name-calling. The purpose of your intervention, Ferocious Critic, is to shut me up. To silence me. And, by the way, I have noticed that anytime the proponents of a boycott against Israel open their mouths, the Zionist heavies go into action to stifle the debate. It is not just the Palestinians who are oppressed. It is the rest of us!

Ferocious Critic: I do not wish to stifle debate. I wish to open it up. In my opinion, the debate over boycotting Israel would be advanced if you and everyone else would agree to say, at last, what you really mean.

Just now I myself have said what I really mean. Why don't you do like-wise? Maybe you have already begun, with your theory that Zionists are trying to shut you up. If only you would lay out your true opinions in full, the sight of them might shock you into rethinking your position...

But I will not try to resolve the debate. Instead, I welcome you to *The Case Against Academic Boycotts of Israel*, edited by Nelson and Brahm, with contributions from a couple dozen other people, all of whom disagree with one another and with me on one point or another, and all of whom are admirable. ▪

CARY NELSON

Introduction

We live in an age in which millions of people are exposed daily to some variant of the argument that the challenges of the world they live in are best explained in terms of 'Israel.'

—David Nirenberg

The international Boycott, Divestment, and Sanctions (BDS) movement is the most influential current version of a long-term effort to delegitimate the State of Israel. Many of BDS's most prominent advocates support an agenda that would bring Israel's Jewish identity to an end by allowing the Palestinians who fled the new State of Israel in 1948 to return, along with their millions of descendants, thereby replacing the Jewish state with an Arab-dominated country. While BDS takes no official position on the Palestinian "Right of Return," the fact that BDS's key advocates, along with all major Palestinian groups, insist on honoring the principle means that all who join the movement are effectively promoting the dissolution of the Jewish state whether or not that is their intention. BDS's recruitment strategy opens with a demand for justice and the right for political self-determination for Palestinians on the West Bank, then migrates to the comprehensive rejection of Israel's right to exist, to its "ongoing, sixty-five-year theft of Palestinian land" (Abowd 169). As BDS advocate Steven Salaita announces, "Israel's soul died in the moment of its invention" (10). People may comfort themselves by supposing that references to "Palestinian land" refer only to the West Bank, but the fundamental claim is that Palestinians should control all of Palestine.

BDS's organizational incarnation and set of strategies originated in goals outlined in the summer of 2001 at the United Nation's World Conference Against Racism. Instead of focusing on problems of racism throughout the world, however, the event developed largely into a focused attack on Israel and promoted the claim that Israel was an "apartheid state" exercising racist policies against the Palestinian people. Though that actual language was withdrawn from the text approved by the conference, a parallel meeting of NGOs adopted language equating Zionism with racism, language that had been withdrawn from the main meeting when the United States, Israel, and other nations objected. Both meetings took place in Durban, South Africa, the first from August 31st to September 8, the second (the NGO forum) from August 28th to September 9th. Two days later, of course, more than 3,000 people died when the World Trade Center in New York City was destroyed, the Pentagon severely damaged, and an airliner brought down in Pennsylvania. Those events overshadowed the Durban meetings and limited the publicity they received.

The first BDS campaign in the US thus didn't begin until a February 2002 petition drive urging the University of California to sell (divest itself of) stock held in companies deemed as benefiting from their relationship with the Jewish state. That spring and fall divestment drives followed at Columbia, Harvard, MIT, Princeton, and elsewhere. They all failed, but the publicity generated helped fuel BDS in the long term. Both then and since, these drives are highly divisive, generating mutual antagonism, accusations, and acrimonious debate on campus. BDS supporters target universities because faculty and students can become passionate about justice, sometimes without adequate knowledge about the facts and consequences. Like other targeted institutions in civil society, universities also offer the potential for small numbers of BDS activists to leverage institutional status and reputation for a more significant cultural and political impact. Campus divestment campaigns were launched again in 2009 and 2010, among them another Berkeley effort. They continued through 2014 and are likely to be ongoing.

Students for Justice in Palestine (SJP), a national group that claims about 100 campus chapters, was established at Berkeley in 2001 to support the BDS movement, frequently by urging student government bodies to adopt divestment resolutions. The group has an activist history that includes not only organizing anti-Israel rallies but also organizing occasional building occupations and demonstrations that interrupt pro-Israel campus lectures. SJP has also been energetic in using social media to advance the BDS agenda. Their 2014 divestment campaigns included actions at DePaul University, University of California at Davis, University of Michigan, University of New Mexico, and University of Washington. Even when these campaigns fail, as most do to date, however, they typically succeed at attracting new student recruits to the BDS cause. Some of those students carry their anti-Israel convictions with them into their eventual careers.

Northeastern University banned SJP for a year in 2014 for actions that crossed the line between advocacy and intimidation. SJP's 2014 tactics included delivering fake eviction notices to Jewish students and others at an NYU dormitory to "draw attention to the reality that Palestinians confront on a daily basis" and a campaign to pressure candidates for student government office at UCLA to sign pledges not to take sponsored trips to Israel from organizations deemed pro-Israel. Jewish students of course felt especially targeted in the NYU case; the UCLA strategy amounted to a coercive personal and institutional blacklist, as well as an effort to limit academic freedom and freedom of association and to block student access to perspectives SJP dislikes. SJP also harassed two UCLA student government members by triggering a hearing to determine if their trip to Israel meant they should be disqualified from voting on a BDS resolution. Divestment campaigns have also focused on companies doing business in Israel, along with pension funds and financial institutions investing in Israel, urging them to cease doing so, once again because a prominent company name can leverage a great amount of publicity.

There is now more than a decade of international history behind these initiatives. The Palestinian Campaign for the Academic and Cultural Boycott of Israel (PACBI) was launched in Ramallah on the West Bank in April 2004 and joined the BDS campaign the following year, with incarnations worldwide, including the US Campaign for the Academic and Cultural Boycott of Israel (USACBI). In July 2004 the General Assembly of the Presbyterian Church in the US approved a divestment plan, but the membership as a whole rescinded the plan in a decisive vote (483 to 28) two years later. Efforts to revive the plan continue to the present day, with the Israel Palestine Mission Network of the Presbyterian Church publishing a fiercely anti-Zionist booklet, *Zionism Unsettled*, in 2014. In June of that year the Presbyterian Church's biennial General Assembly voted 310 to 303 to divest from stock in three American companies that sell Israel products used to implement administration of the West Bank. But supporters of the motion could only achieve their narrow victory by reaffirming support for a two-state solution, distancing themselves from the overall BDS agenda, and disavowing *Zionism Unsettled*. In July 2005 an alliance of 171 Palestinian organizations had called for BDS action against Israel, a date many BDS groups like to credit as their moment of origin, since it lets them claim they are answering a call from Palestinian civil society, even though the campaign was already four years old at that point. The Palestinian BDS National Committee (BNC) was inaugurated in Ramallah in November 2007 to coordinate BDS activities with Palestinian NGOs and networks.

The year 2005 also saw the emergence of "Israeli Apartheid Week," a mixture of rallies, lectures, exhibits, and film showings inaugurated in Toronto to support the BDS agenda and ideology. Now generally organized by campus groups and held in February or March, it may also include off-campus events. Locations in 2014 include over a hundred cities worldwide. MIT's Noam Chomsky has spoken at a number of Israeli Apartheid Week events, as has British historian Ilan Pappé. Some campuses, including my own in 2014, saw the erection of a huge "apartheid wall" in their central gathering space to highlight the week's events and their anti-Israel activism in a highly visible way. Although publicity for IAW events has often been limited to local coverage, the choice of the name was obviously designed to be provocative, disturbing, and a media draw.

The most difficult BDS goal to implement is the "S" in BDS, which refers to sanctions that nations or groups of nations might carry out against Israel. That requires considerable political clout. Far easier to pursue and often enough successful are cultural boycotts of arts and humanities events, which can be limited to pressuring one artist or speaker to cancel an Israeli tour, performance, or lecture. Those campaigns can be particularly brutal when they target a single person. The theoretical physicist Stephen Hawking canceled a 2013 visit to Israel following a public campaign to persuade him. Yet the poet Joy Harjo gave a reading in Tel Aviv despite considerable criticism from the Native American community. Elvis Costello and Roger Waters cancelled Israeli concerts, but Leonard Cohen, Elton John, Bob Dylan, Madonna, Justin Bieber, and the Rolling Stones refused to do so. The director Ken Loach pulled his film *Looking for Eric* from the Melbourne Film Festival in 2009 after discovering Israel was a cosponsor. In 2011 protestors disrupted a performance of the Israeli Philharmonic Orchestra at London's Albert Hall. In 2012 the American writer Alice Walker declined to authorize a Hebrew translation of her novel *The Color Purple*. In 2014, however, the actress Scarlett Johansson refused despite pressure to end her advertising relationship with the Israeli company Sodastream. But such BDS efforts are guaranteed to continue, in part because even failed ad hominem pressure campaigns gain publicity and lead other people to ask "Why?"

In 2014 PACBI organized protests against the joint Israeli-Palestinian project Heartbeat, which has used music to bring both peoples together and build trust. PACBI considers Heartbeat an unacceptable effort to normalize relations, which is so far the only argument specific to cultural boycotts that has been advanced. Most of those promoting cultural boycotts see no need to reflect on what is lost in the process, given that cultural boycotts can affect broad public audiences. Since there aren't any symphonies and art museums doing military research, the marginal arguments used to justify boycotting universities as complicit in state power do not apply to arts institutions. The humanistic outreach, vision, and aesthetic ambition central to the arts is simply expendable. In the end, like universities, they are basically targets of opportunity. A major BDS victory took place in January 2014 when the opening of a UNESCO-sponsored exhibition on the 3,500-year history of Jews in Palestine was cancelled after Arab nations lodged a protest against it. Organized by the Simon Wiesenthal Center in conjunction with the Canadian government, the exhibit had been curated and was ready to open in Paris. Cancelling such events means that opportunities for dialogue, mutual appreciation, and understanding are lost. So too are impulses to seek solutions that grow out of cultural contexts. Even the campaigns to cancel arts and humanities events can turn them into fraught political arenas, which is of course precisely the BDS intention.

Another BDS strategy, boycotts of Israeli industries and products, has a history long predating BDS itself, having been a concerted effort by Arab nations begun when Israel announced its statehood and continuing into the 1950s. And the first Arab boycott of Jews in Palestine, though on a much smaller scale, dates from 1921. Most boycotts have failed, but in recent years modest boycotts of West Bank products (or additional tariffs levied on them) have met with some success in the European Union and elsewhere. At the same time, *Buycott* campaigns urging people to purchase products targeted for boycotts have worked well. As we detail in this book, BDS's academic boycott campaigns began in Britain and migrated to the US.

Although nearly 300 college or university presidents issued statements opposing academic boycotts in 2007 and over 250 did so again in 2014—and although every major multidisciplinary academic organization that has addressed the issue opposes them as well—faculty members in at least some disciplines continue to approve them as a political strategy. Proposals to boycott universities continue to receive faculty support and publicity in the press, and have a potential impact on public opinion and perhaps eventually even on national policy. As the essays that follow will show, they have begun to shape the professional conduct of committed advocates.

Yet there remains no single place for higher education professionals or educated members of the general public to go to find either detailed scholarly essays critiquing boycott advocacy and the BDS movement of which it is a part. There is thus also no convenient place to go to find the appropriate background information relevant to informed reflection on boycott and

BDS opposition. We have edited this book to meet that need, in part by setting academic boycotts within the political and historical context of the broad BDS agenda. Doing so has generated a substantial volume that can serve as a lasting resource for all interested in what is certain to remain a contentious issue.

A number of recent pro-BDS books argue for the ultimate BDS solution—dissolution of the Jewish state. These include single-author books by Omar Barghouti and Judith Butler, along with such edited collections as the *Case for Sanctions Against Israel* (2012) and *Deconstructing Zionism* (2013), along with several of the essays in *The Imperial University* (2014). There are also a large number of general books either supportive or severely critical of Israel. But ours is the first collection of essays to critique the boycott campaign and the philosophy of the BDS movement.

We have not staged a pro and con debate about academic boycotts, though many of the essays here quote or summarize pro-boycott arguments and respond to them in detail. Our experience at many confrontational public boycott debates is that they produce polemical papers that generate more heat than light, hardening positions and too often promoting incivility. Longer essays written in a more scholarly style, we have found, can promote rational discussion. We have thus produced a book that people can both agree and disagree with but primarily by engagement with thoughtful and well-supported arguments.

That does not mean that our contributors do not have strong opinions. They do. When faculty members address divisive topics toward which they feel a significant responsibility or wish to help shape academic or public opinion, they may advocate for a particular position in their professional publications. Everyone in this collection is opposed to academic boycotts. That is part of what unifies the book. Should proponents of academic boycotts choose to edit a competing collection, adding to the pro-BDS books that already exist, they are certainly free to do so. That said, this book is not single-mindedly about boycotts. Some contributors are more broadly concerned with the cultural and political forces that have made boycott advocacy part of both academic life and contemporary culture. These essays provide context often absent in the polemics surrounding the BDS movement.

There is one and only one country, Israel, that is the object of an international effort to boycott its universities. That fact brings a significant number of nation-specific historical and cultural concerns into play, along with a considerable amount of factual information that is either explicitly or implicitly at issue in boycott debates. Once again, there is no one place to go to find the most important relevant information that should inform contemporary discussion. One might well argue that only a full bookshelf could fill that need.

Historical knowledge can always be pursued in greater depth. We have tried, however, to provide critical information, while directing readers where to seek further detail. Moreover, our list of online resources includes a number of pro-boycott papers and all major pro-boycott web sites so readers can easily access substantial pro-boycott material. References to pro-boycott books offer still further resources. This book provides a sound basis for discussing proposed boycotts of Israel as well as a model of what people should know if another country becomes the focus of an academic and cultural boycott campaign.

Our contributors, predictably, have varied takes on Israeli society, and they have different positions on elements of Israeli policy, as well as differences of opinion about the approaches that can and should be taken to limit the BDS movement's impact on American campuses. Not all, for example, would endorse legal remedies to limit speech that may produce a hostile environment. Some of the contributors are Israeli citizens. Others have spent considerable time there. Despite their differences, however, they are broadly unified in support of a two-state solution, both because they want Palestinians in the West Bank to be voting citizens of their own independent country, able to define their own society and shape their own destiny, and because they believe Israel cannot honor its democratic principles while it exercises control over a non-voting population. The book is also unified by a conviction that Palestinians will never be freed by efforts to promote one state with an Arab majority encompassing both Israel and the West Bank. BDS efforts to demonize and delegitimate Israel will only promote a hostile stalemate. The BDS agenda thus offers no realistic hope of freedom for West Bank Palestinians and no hope of return for those in the Palestinian diaspora.

BDS advocates, however, show no sign of either reflecting on or questioning their agenda and their tactics. Instead we are certain to see an increasing number of strategies put in place. Steven Salaita recently proposed a basic set of options for faculty BDS activism:

> One needn't be a firebrand or provocateur in order to support BDS. It's possible to maintain a low profile and still contribute. Here are some suggestions I hope accommodate the shy and brash alike:
> - Endorse the call to boycott from USACBI, the US Campaign for the Academic and Cultural Boycott of Israel.
> - Attend relevant events on campus. Ask questions. The mere existence of supportive people makes the work of BDS easier.
> - Encourage your students and colleagues to attend panels and presentations that might provide less conventional points of view about Palestine.

- Express support to student activists, even if only privately. They need faculty backing. They don't always receive it.
- Vote in the elections of scholarly associations. Various referenda about Palestine have been presented across numerous disciplines for member approval in the past ten years, with many more to come. A low percentage of membership traditionally participates in these elections. Voting is a virtually risk-free way to provide an impact. Also: help elect officers favorable to BDS.
- Propose a boycott or divestment resolution to your faculty senate. It might not get very far, but it will force acknowledgment of the university's complicity in the occupation and other Israeli abuses. You'll also be amused by breathtaking displays of indignant dissimulation.
- Work with the local Students for Justice in Palestine (SJP) chapter or its equivalent.
- Organize an event to generate better understanding of why BDS is an appropriate response to Israeli colonization.
- Investigate your school's study abroad program. If there is an arrangement with an Israeli university, it may contravene your school's anti-discrimination policies because Arab or Muslim students could be denied the opportunity to participate due to Israel's systematic discrimination at the borders it controls.
- Hold your university accountable to its inclusionary rhetoric as it pertains to the suppression of Palestinian voices.
- Write an article for your campus paper, or for a national publication. There is much interest in BDS these days.

Instead of encouraging faculty to challenge students to honor the standards of behavior that have guided the academy for decades, this program gives faculty a quiet way to promote antagonistic student activism. Meanwhile, Salaita assures BDS advocates that any effort to disagree with them should be read as suppression and a violation of their rights: "Israel's supporters, as they have illustrated for many decades, are perfectly content to rely on suppression as long as it can effectively preserve their colonial fetish, no matter how many constitutional rights they destroy."

We offer this book as a resource to bring reason, history, and sound information to campuses confronting this BDS agenda. The opening section of the book gathers contributions about the principles and motives at stake in academic boycotts, referencing the campaign to boycott Israeli universities as appropriate. Martha Nussbaum deliberately sets aside the Israeli example in order to look at relevant common principles and alternative possible boycott targets. Russell Berman asks what specific disabling contradictions are embodied in proposals to boycott universities and what damage to academic freedom can result if they are adopted. Cary Nelson documents the general complexity that both definitions and applications of academic freedom must confront before addressing some of the specific problems with academic boycotts. Gabriel Noah Brahm and Asaf Romirowsky ask us to reflect on what the real goals of the BDS movement must be, since its leaders must realize their stated aim of organizing effective boycotts is unachievable. BDS instead, they demonstrate, seeks broadly to delegitimate Israel, while encouraging its student followers to identify themselves as victims instead of learning critical analytical skills. Emily Budick, citing Emerson, calls for boycott supporters not only to inform themselves about the ethical and political implications of their position but also to reflect on their own country's human rights record; at the same time, she offers a detailed analysis of both BDS reasoning and Omar Barghouti's arguments in its favor. Throughout this section, indeed, issues of academic freedom or responsible professionalism predominate. The long-term risk in political efforts to constrain or compromise academic freedom is that our very definition of academic freedom will change as a result, with implications well beyond any potential impact on Palestinian and Israeli faculty members and institutions.

The second section concentrates on the most widely publicized academic boycott resolution to have been adopted to date, the resolution approved by the American Studies Association in December 2013. Sharon Musher gives a participant's chilling account of how the ASA struggle developed over time and how the vote unfolded at the organization's annual meeting. David Hirsch undertakes a careful point-by-point analysis of the ASA resolution. Michael Bérubé addresses the broader political implications of ASA's agenda.

The third section of the book looks closely at the segments of the American left that have joined the BDS movement, examining both aims and motives, and asking what has been gained and lost in political impact as a result. In an important essay from 2003, Ellen Willis observed that being "a surrogate for American power contributes to its [Israel's] symbolic importance as a target," a position that is now an overt part of BDS advocate arguments. At the time, Willis said that "the mainstream of contemporary political anti-Zionism does not oppose nationalism as such, but rather defines the conflict as bad imperialist nationalism versus the good liberationist kind." Some make that distinction explicitly, but for many others it remains an unacknowledged contradiction: they decry all nationalisms yet advocate for Palestinian statehood. In any case, as she adds, the "left animus toward Israel is not a simple, self-evident product of the facts," despite the BDS tendency to claim it is.

Increasingly, BDS tries to package opposition to Israel with other progressive commitments. Thus Gianni Vattimo announces in his 2013 contribution to *Deconstructing Zionism* that "by now anti-Zionism is synonymous with leftist world politics" (18). On the University of Minnesota Press website, Sunaina Maira, coeditor of *The Imperial University* (2014), declares that the ASA's academic boycott "resolution was not just a litmus test of where American studies scholars stood on the question of Palestine, but an index of the ASA's progressive politics and the intellectual shifts in the field to a more inclusive intellectual and political space . . . the support for the boycott emerged in the context of the growing centrality of antiracist and anti-imperial scholarship within the ASA." Having convinced people that all major progressive commitments are interconnected—that you cannot *be* anti-racist unless you are anti-Zionist—you then have to persuade people that an overall progressive agenda cannot move forward without first dismantling the State of Israel. Anti-Zionism becomes the necessary precondition of all other progressive commitments.

One problem that BDS faces in this regard is that a secure case can be made for what are obviously progressive elements of Israeli society itself, such as its gay friendly laws and the vibrant gay scene in Tel Aviv. Enter as a result the concept of "pinkwashing," meaning supposed efforts to whitewash Israeli West Bank practices by praising the freedoms gays have in Israel proper. Of course people regularly compare Israeli society's tolerance with the misogynist and homophobic character of a number of Arab cultures. Jasbir Puar argues that "the production of the 'Israeli gay tolerance/Palestinian homophobia' binary is a recognized discursive tactic" (286), which it certainly is, but that doesn't mean the binary isn't based in reality. Like all verbal formulations, it is necessarily discursively constructed, but it isn't a fabrication. Moreover, the argument that admiration for Israel's gay culture distracts us from Israel's violence against Palestinians collapses if you apply the same logic to other countries. Unless, for example, you think it is useful to say that praise for the US Bill of Rights distracts us from the ever more disastrous consequences of the war in Iraq. Comparisons between Israel and other area countries are an important and appropriate way of understanding both the individual nations and the differences between them. BDS would prefer to delegitimate all such comparisons.

Thomas Abowd celebrates BDS's "forged alliances with other struggles" (172). The outreach to leaders in the Native American and Indigenous Studies Association—who mistakenly identify with Palestinians as the only indigenous people in the area and see Israel as a colonialist power—has been successful, although there are dissenting pro-Israeli Native American voices as well, Ryan Bellerose (Métis), Jay Corwin (Tlingit), Kathy

Cummings-Dickinson (Lumbee), Santos Hawk Blood (Chiricahua), and Anne Richardson (Rappahannock) among them. The left in fact has not been universally converted to anti-Zionism, though there is reason for concern. Accusing BDS of anti-American bias will not, to be sure, discourage its growth on campus. However, while one can agree that all citizens are implicated in US policy, one might argue that those who object to US policies should oppose them by staging demonstrations, writing for publication, and promoting candidates for office who share their views, not by seeking to punish citizens of a foreign country that benefits from US policy.

Sabah Salih opens the section examining these trends on the left by reviewing the role that antagonism toward Enlightenment values plays in the opposition to Israel in the Middle East, and he asks whether reluctance to evaluate Islamic fundamentalism critically contributes to BDS support in the United States. He offers a capsule history of how the American left's values have developed over the last generation. Donna Divine offers a cautionary tale, describing what can happen when a campus debate, initiated by a traditional desire for dialogue, ends up being shaped by leftwing commonplaces rather than more probing analysis. Nancy Koppelman reviews the way movements for social justice have transformed higher education pedagogy, increasingly without promoting awareness of the historical contexts for and evolution of our concepts of human rights, limitations that have undermined the integrity of BDS debates. Tammi Rossman-Benjamin offers for the first time a statistical analysis of the prevalence of BDS advocacy in a variety of academic disciplines and then describes the specific campus strategies that BDS advocates have adopted. David Caplan looks at a key cultural context for boycott debates in the humanities: the changing representations of Jews in contemporary literature. Alan Johnson mounts a thorough and decisive analysis and critique of anti-Zionist ideology, meanwhile helping us see how it is constructed as an appealing basis for individual identity. Finally, in an essay made even more relevant by the rise of ISIS in Syria and Iraq, Richard Landes interrogates the apocalyptic ambitions that fuel radical Islam and how they bear on leftwing American opinion about Israel.

The fourth section of the book goes more deeply into Israeli history as well as the most pertinent elements of contemporary Israeli society. Rachel S. Harris uses a discussion of recent Arab Israeli novels written in Hebrew to present us with a subtle reading of the stresses and opportunities that shape the lives of Israel's non-Jewish citizens. She demonstrates the contradictory character of Arab assimilation while delegitimating the simple dichotomies that often dominate BDS debates. Ilan Troen tackles two different topics, first asking whether Israeli history justifies the claims that Israel is a fundamentally colonialist project and then describing representative forms of

Israeli/Palestinian collaboration presently taking place, all of which would be endangered by a boycott regime. Shira Wolosky describes her own experience teaching both Arab and Jewish students at an Israeli university to give us a more nuanced understanding of the character of the institutions the BDS movement seeks to boycott. And she describes the ways people from different cultures interact in her classroom, suggesting along the way that the Israeli academy promotes transnational identity formation. Rachel Fish traces the evolution of the concept of bi-nationalism from its generous, utopian incarnation in the first years of Jewish settlement in Palestine to its use as a political weapon today, concluding with a concise account of the grounds for its current purchase in the academy. Much of the material in this section challenges readers to consider what they should know about Israel before taking either a pro- or anti-boycott position. Faculty members especially should be willing to do the reading necessary to acquire at least a fundamental knowledge of relevant history and contemporary practices before taking stands urging public commitment from others.

Next we provide an essay-length history of Israel that offers background knowledge that many in boycott debates appear to lack. It corrects many popular errors and sets a minimum standard for what people seeking either to challenge or support Israel's institutions and its legitimacy ought to know if their politics is to be either factually or ethically grounded. Indeed many of the issues that shape the current struggle are historically grounded; some have been in contention for more than half a century. History always matters, but nowhere more than in the Middle East.

Throughout the book, one topic that returns repeatedly for intense reflection and analysis is the role of anti-Semitism in the BDS movement. As Willis commented, "it's impossible not to notice how the runaway inflation of Israel's villainy aligns with ingrained cultural fantasies about the iniquity and power of Jews; or how the traditional pariah status of Jews has been replicated by a Jewish State" or that "Palestinian victims are routinely used to stifle discussion of how anti-Semitism influences the Israeli-Palestinian conflict or the world's reaction to it or the public conversation about it." BDS advocates have so far largely addressed the issue by complaining that supporters of Israel assert that all criticism of Israeli government policy is fundamentally anti-Semitic. But that is not a common position in academia and, as Israeli control over the West Bank has continued and evolved, it is increasingly rare in public debate as well. Many of the contributors here have criticized Israeli government policy themselves and recommended basic changes in it.

That, however, leaves unanswered a series of more vexing questions: Does anti-Semitism help explain why Israel is singled out for especially severe international criticism when other states have much worse human rights records? Does anti-Semitism help underwrite demands that Israel literally be eliminated as a Jewish state and be absorbed into a larger Arab-dominated nation? Is the BDS movement as a whole contaminated by clearly anti-Semitic statements by some of its advocates? Are idealistic BDS advocates responsible for unintended anti-Semitic political and social consequences of the movement? These issues have not received adequate academic analysis to date. One of this book's major contributions, we hope, is to encourage sound discussion. At issue, we should emphasize, is not whether individual BDS advocates are anti-Semitic, though some surely are, but whether the history of anti-Semitic discourse informs BDS reasoning even if supporters are unaware of that. Readers interested in that issue might well begin with Kenneth Marcus's overview of definitions of anti-Semitism and his clear discussion of the criteria that should apply to evaluations of BDS's anti-Semitic status.

That said, what should no longer be in dispute is that BDS and other movements seeking to delegitimate the State of Israel gather anti-Semites into their fold. If you express solidarity with a large group of BDS advocates, you will likely be linking arms with some motivated by anti-Semitism. In a May 2014 piece in the *Chronicle of Higher Education*, Jonathan Marks quotes passages posted by Modern Language Association members on the website set up so they could comment on a resolution attacking Israel for the visa policies it has adopted to protect itself from terrorist violence.[1] Part of what is notable about the discussion is that all comments were automatically signed and that everyone was aware that 28,000 people could read what they said. Indeed much of the debate, with names included, was soon published on a publicly accessible website.[2]

Things took a turn for the worse after a recent Rutgers PhD opined that "This resolution rightly targets only Israel given the humongous influence that Jewish scholars have in the decision making process of Academia in general." Meanwhile, MLA Members for Scholars' Rights was concerned that MLA itself might not distribute the fact sheet opposing the resolution that Martin Shichtman had sent to his fellow Delegate Assembly members before their January 2014 vote. So we hired students to copy the 20,000 email addresses that members willing to receive email messages from other members had authorized the MLA to publish.[3] We emailed all 20,000 the fact sheet.[4] That triggered a series of agitated online messages from Stanford University faculty member David Palumbo-Liu, demanding that MLA investigate the matter.[5] "I do wonder how a small group of scholars marshaled the funds to hire enough students" to do the job of establishing "a shadow listserve." MLA Executive Director Rosemary Feal wrote to us, insisting that we reveal our finances, and suggesting, in effect, that we should have emailed each of the 20,000 to ask permission to email them. She copied a lawyer on her emails to us to add a bit of intimidation to her warning about needing to decide "what steps to take next." Echoing all-too-familiar accusations about Jewish money, Palumbo-Liu suggested that "an outside organization wishing to protect Israel from censure may well have donated the funds." At that point I was tempted to say Baron Rothschild had bankrolled the plot. After initially saying it was no one's business how we had funded the effort, I went online to say it had cost $670 to gather the emails and $150 to send them out and that an MLA member had written the check. To complete this little drama, I'll add that the person who wrote the check was me. As always, MLA sent its members the link to the discussion, along with the long anti-Israel memo the resolution's proponents had cobbled together from Palestinian activist web sites. The only supporting "evidence" all 24,000 MLA members received was thus that deceptive cut-and-paste packet advocating that they vote for the resolution. We were very glad we had done the work to counteract the organization's biased process and make sure that as many members as possible had access to evidence from the other side.[6] In June of 2014, MLA announced that the resolution was not ratified by the membership.

With the email episode mostly put to rest, the discussion returned to its roots. Elizabeth J. Ordoñez, formerly of Metropolitan State University of Denver, chimed in to regret how "moves to seek justice and opportunity for Palestinians" are "countered by Zionist attack dogs." Many members assumed that meant those of us who were criticizing the resolution. Not to worry. Basum L. Ra'ad of Al-Quds University came on board to reassure us that "'Zionist attack dogs' was probably used metaphorically." Exactly what Professor Ra'ad had in mind to suggest if the phrase were *not* metaphoric I cannot say. But that didn't prevent him from bewailing the pressure "exercised on universities by Zionist funders and lobby groups to quell any dissent."[7] But the dissent facing silencing efforts here was all dissent *from* the resolution. Its supporters were free to indulge themselves in a series of fantasy accusations. Much like the ASA boycott resolution's supporters, MLA's BDS advocates were crying foul every time someone disagreed with them. That tactic is now used nationwide.

We conclude this book with a "Boycott Dossier" that reprints the boycott resolutions endorsed by three academic associations, a letter opposing academic boycotts by members and former presidents of the American Studies Association, a sample letter to a university president asking for a public statement on academic boycotts, columns or online posts by Michael C. Kotzin, Jeff Robbins, and Robert Fine, and a list of online resources. Robbins, interestingly, is the brother of Bruce Robbins, one of the coauthors of the failed MLA resolution. These boycott debates not only divide friends and colleagues from one another; they also divide families.

Having quoted Ellen Willis several times, I am going to give her the last word:

> I'm not a Zionist—rather I'm a quintessential Diaspora Jew, a child of Freud, Marx, and Spinoza. I hold with rootless cosmopolitanism: from my perspective the nation-state is a profoundly problematic institution, a nation-state defined by ethnic or other particularist criteria all the more so. And yet I count myself an anti-anti-Zionist. This partly because the logic of anti-Zionism in the present political context entails an unprecedented demand for an existing state—one, moreover, with popular legitimacy and a democratically elected government—not simply to change its policies but to disappear. It's partly because I can't figure out what large numbers of displaced Jews could have or should have done after 1945, other than parlay their relationship with Palestine and the (ambivalent) support of the West for a Jewish homeland into a place to be. (Go "home" to Germany or Poland? Knock, en masse, on the doors of unreceptive European countries and a reluctant United States?) And finally it's because I believe that anti-Jewish genocide cannot be laid to rest as a discrete historical episode, but remains a possibility implicit in the deep structure of Christian and Islamic cultures, East and West.

Part of what has changed since 2003 is that Willis' position can no longer count as anti-anti-Zionist. In the current worldwide political landscape, with options for the international left over the Israeli-Palestinian conflict increasingly curtailed, it is simply Zionist.

We would like to thank Wayne State University Press for its support of this project, its good suggestions, and its enthusiastic decision to distribute the book. While this is not the place to name names, it needs to be said that there is an informal network of university presses unwilling to be associated with books sympathetic to Israel. Neither the editors nor the authors of the essays gathered here will receive royalties or other payment for their work. After costs are recovered, a portion of sales income will be donated to the Peres Center for Peace (www.peres-center.org). Founded in 1996 by President of Israel and Nobel Peace Prize laureate Shimon Peres, the Center is Israel's leading organization promoting peacebuilding between Israel and its neighbors, particularly between Israelis and Palestinians and Jewish and Arab citizens of Israel. It's mission is to promote lasting peace and advancement in the Middle East by fostering tolerance, economic and technological development, cooperation and well-being. Programs are designed to empower the populationsof the region to actively advance the creation of a real, effective, and durable peace. They are implemented in three core fields: Medicine & Healthcare, Business & Environment, and Peace Education. The center is a non-for-profit, non-governmental, non-political organization whose projects bring together thousands of people annually.

MLA MEMBERS FOR SCHOLARS' RIGHTS is a voluntary organization that stands for the universal principle of academic freedom. We oppose the unwarranted politicization of the academy. We believe in applying comparable professional standards to all countries, and thus we consider it discriminatory to single out one nation for criticism, including Israel, when others are not held to the same standard. The group was founded to analyze and organize opposition to efforts within the MLA to abridge academic freedom through boycotts and other means. While our efforts are focused on the MLA, as we are all members, we will comment when appropriate on problematic proposals or actions in other academic associations and offer other academic associations our assistance.

The editors are among the founding members. The group participated in a panel held off-site while the January 2014 annual MLA convention was taking place, and it has helped organize opposition to a resolution condemning Israeli travel policies. The group has no formal relationship with the Modern Language Association.

We want to thank the Israel Action Network for its support in the publication of this book.

Martha Nussbaum's "Against Academic Boycotts" (*Dissent*, Summer 2007, pp. 30-36) and Mitchell Cohen's "Anti-Semitism and the Left That Doesn't Learn" (*Dissent*, Winter 2008, pp. 47-51) are reprinted with permission of the University of Pennsylvania Press.

Note on documentation: We have given contributors some freedom in documentation style, so they can choose either endnotes or internal documentation. We have also chosen not to impose uniformity in spelling "anti-Semitism/ antisemitism" or to normalize transliteration protocols when a consensus does not already obtain. ■

Works Cited

Abowd, Thomas. "The Boycott, Divestment, ad Sanctions Movement and Violations of Academic Freedom at Wayne State University." In Chatterjee and Maira, eds. *The Imperial University,* 169-185.

Barghouti, Omar. *BDS—Boycott, Divestment, Sanctions: The Global Struggle for Palestinian Rights.* Chicago: Haymarket Books, 2011.

Butler, Judith. *Parting Ways: Jewishness and the Critique of Zionism.* New York: Columbia University Press, 2012.

Chatterjee, Piya, and Sunaina Maira, eds. *The Imperial University: Academic Repression and Scholarly Dissent.* Minneapolis: University of Minnesota Press, 2014.

Lim, Audrea, ed. *The Case for Sanctions Against Israel.* New York: Verso, 2012.

Marks, Jonathan. "'Zionist Attack Dogs'? The MLA's Debate on Israel Might Go Viral." *Chronicle of Higher Education.* May 21, 2014. Available at http://chronicle.com/blogs/conversation/2014/05/21/zionist-attack-dogs-the-mlas-debate-on-israel-might-go-viral/

Nirenberg, David. *Anti-Judaism: The Western Tradition.* New York: Norton, 2013.

Palumbo-Liu, David. "Why an Academic Boycott?" *Los Angeles Review of Books.* March 16, 2014. Available at https://lareviewofbooks.org/essay/why-an-academic-boycott

Puar, Jasbir. "Citation and Censure: Pinkwashing and the Sexual Politics of Talking about Israel." In Chatterjee and Maira, eds. *The Imperial University,* 281-297.

Ra'ad, Basem. *Hidden Histories: Palestine And The Eastern Mediterranean.* London: Pluto Press, 2010.

Salaita, Steven. *Israel's Dead Soul.* Philadelphia: Temple University Press, 2011.

Salaita, Steven. "How to Practice BDS in Academe." *The Electronic Intifada.* May 27, 2014. Available at http://electronicintifada.net/blogs/steven-salaita/how-practice-bds-academe.

Vattimo, Gianni, and Michael Marder, eds. *Deconstructing Zionism: A Critique of Political Metaphysics.* New York: Bloomsbury, 2013.

Willis, Ellen. "Is There Still a Jewish Question? Why I'm an Anti-Anti-Zionist." In Tony Kushner and Alisa Solomon, eds. *Wresting with Zion: Progressive Jewish-American Responses to the Israeli-Palestine Conflict.* New York: Grove Press, 2003, pp. 226- 232. Available at http://web.archive.org/web/20130618070828/http://contested-terrain.net/willis.

PART I.

OPPOSING BOYCOTTS
AS A MATTER
OF PRINCIPLE

On Academic Boycotts

In spring 2005, the Association's Committee A on Academic Freedom and Tenure, in response to a controversy that was roiling the British academic community, approved a statement condemning academic boycotts. The statement declared that

> since its founding in 1915, the AAUP has been committed to preserving and advancing the free exchange of ideas among academics irrespective of governmental policies and however unpalatable those policies may be viewed. We reject proposals that curtail the freedom of teachers and researchers to engage in work with academic colleagues, and we reaffirm the paramount importance of the freest possible international movement of scholars and ideas.[8]

We affirm these core principles but provide further comment on the complexities of academic boycotts and the rationale for opposing them, and we recommend responses to future proposals to participate in them.

The Controversy

In April 2005, the British Association of University Teachers (AUT) announced a boycott of two Israeli institutions: Bar-Ilan and Haifa universities.[9] The AUT asked its members to respond to the following call from some sixty Palestinian academic, cultural, and professional associations and trade unions:

> In the spirit of international solidarity, moral consistency, and resistance to injustice and oppression, we, Palestinian academics and intellectuals, call upon our colleagues in the international community to comprehensively and consistently boycott all Israeli academic and cultural institutions as a contribution to the struggle to end Israel's occupation, colonization, and system of apartheid, by applying the following: (i) refrain from participation in any form of academic and cultural cooperation, collaboration, or joint projects with Israeli institutions; (ii) advocate a comprehensive boycott of Israeli institutions at the national and international levels, including suspension of all forms of funding and subsidies to these institutions; (iii) promote divestment and disinvestment from Israel by international academic institutions; (iv) exclude from the above actions against Israeli institutions any conscientious Israeli academics and intellectuals opposed to their state's colonial and racist policies; (v) work toward the condemnation of Israeli policies by pressing for resolutions to be adopted by academic, professional, and cultural associations and organizations; (vi) support Palestinian academic and cultural institutions directly without requiring them to partner with Israeli counterparts as an explicit or implicit condition for such support.

The targeting of the two universities by the AUT reflected specific and different events at each of them. It was argued that these separate events were together representative of the ways in which these institutions were acting to further a state policy likened to apartheid and therefore in violation of the academic freedom of dissenting faculty and of Palestinians.

According to its website, under a section titled "Boycotts, Greylisting," the AUT "imposes or considers imposing an academic boycott on a university or college when we conclude that the actions of an institution pose a fundamental threat to the interests of members. . . . In publicly describing an institution as unfit to receive job applications, to engage in academic cooperation or host academic events, we recognize that it will cause significant damage to the university in its sphere of influence. In taking such a step, we would have to conclude that it was justified in the sense that it would be worse not to do so in the light of the circumstances." The AUT describes an academic boycott as a weapon of last resort, its use to be approved by a meeting of the association's full national executive committee. In recent years, the AUT called for boycotts of Nottingham University, for its refusal to honor a commitment to negotiate a pay and grading settlement; of Brunel University, because it threatened to dismiss thirty members of the academic staff and eventually dismissed two of them; and of higher education institutions in Fiji, following a coup in that country in 2000 and in response to requests for assistance from faculty in Fiji and academic unions in New Zealand and Australia.

When the AAUP learned of the 2005 call for a boycott, the Association's staff promptly drafted, and Committee A approved, a statement that condemned any such boycotts as prima facie violations of academic freedom. The statement, cited at the beginning of this report, singled out item four of the call (which exempted dissenting Israeli faculty) as an ideological test repugnant to our principles.[10] While a meeting of an AUT Special Council voted to drop its call for the boycott within a month's time of the initial decision and, therefore, no Israeli university was boycotted, we have been urged to give fuller consideration to the broad and unconditional nature of our condemnation of academic boycotts. We are reminded that our own complex history includes support for campus strikes, support for divestiture during the anti-apartheid campaigns in South Africa, and a questioning of the requirement of institutional neutrality during the Vietnam War. In what follows we engage with the tensions that exist within some of our own policies as well as with the larger tension between a principled defense of academic freedom and the practical requirements for action. Finally, we offer a set of guidelines to address those tensions.

AAUP Policies

The Association's defense of academic freedom, as explained in the "1940 Statement of Principles on Academic Freedom and Tenure," rests on the principle that "institutions of higher education are conducted for the common good . . . [which] depends upon the free search for truth and its free exposition." Although the statement says nothing about academic boycotts, plainly the search for truth and its free expression suffer if a boycott is in place. Legitimate protest against violations of academic freedom might, of course, entail action that could be construed as contradicting our principled defense of academic freedom. One such action is the Association's practice of censuring college or university administrations, which dates back to the early 1930s. The Association is careful to distinguish censure—which brings public attention to an administration that has violated the organization's principles and standards—from a boycott, by leaving it to individuals to decide how to act on the information they have been given. The AAUP engages in no formal effort to discourage faculty from working at these institutions or to ostracize the institution and its members from academic exchanges, as is the case in AUT "greylisting"; but moral suasion could have such results if faculty members were to decide to have no contact with an institution on the censure list.

AAUP censure differs from the AUT boycott in other important respects. Censure is preceded by an often lengthy effort to correct, and an investigation to document, violations of AAUP policies essential to academic freedom and tenure. Censure does not rest on a finding in regard to "member interests." Indeed, it is not required that faculty be AAUP members in order to have their complaints pursued by the organization. This is not to say, however, that the AAUP supports no practices that correspond to the AUT boycott undertaken in the interests of its members. Under AAUP policy, chapters that engage in collective bargaining can participate in a strike. Moreover, while AAUP policy states that strikes and other such actions are "not desirable for the resolution of conflicts within institutions of higher education," it also states that in certain cases "resort to economic pressure through strikes or other work actions may be a necessary and unavoidable means of dispute resolution."[11] A strike is an economic boycott (we will distinguish among types of boycotts below), but it often involves pressures that are not exclusively economic, such as the local faculty union's asking outside speakers not to come to a campus during a strike or the refusal of faculty elsewhere to attend conferences held on a campus where a strike is in process. So, while the AAUP insists on action that conforms to its principles, practical issues sometimes produce dilemmas that must be addressed.

AAUP History

In 1970, the AAUP published two conflicting commentaries on institutional neutrality; there followed an intense debate on the subject.[12] The context was the war in Vietnam, and the question was whether universities should take a position on the war. One side, by far the majority, argued that all ideas had to be tolerated within the academy, lest the university "become an instrument of indoctrination," and that therefore a university should not take a position on disputed public issues. The other side asked whether "perilous situations" called for extraordinary action: "It might be worthwhile to debate just how bad things would have to get before the principle of academic neutrality were no longer absolute." While this discussion about institutional neutrality led to no policy recommendation, it raised issues that have since surfaced in discussions about academic boycotts. Are there extraordinary situations in which extraordinary actions are necessary, and, if so, how does one recognize them? How should supporters of academic freedom have treated German universities under the Nazis? Should scholarly exchange have been encouraged with Hitler's collaborators in those universities? Can one plausibly maintain that academic freedom is inviolate when the civil freedoms of the larger society have been abrogated? If there is no objective test for determining what constitutes an extraordinary situation, as there surely is not, then what criteria should guide decisions about whether a boycott should be supported?

In 1985, the AAUP's Seventy-first Annual Meeting called on colleges and universities "as investors to oppose apartheid," to "decline to hold securities in banks which provide loans to the government of South Africa," and to favor divestiture of holdings in companies that did not adhere to the Sullivan principles. The meeting also urged similar action on the part of public and private pension funds serving higher education faculty.[13] Three years later, the Association's Seventy-fourth Annual Meeting urged TIAA-CREF to divest itself "of all companies doing business" in South Africa.[14] Although the resolutions did not apply to exchanges among faculty and, in this sense, did not constitute an academic boycott, some argued at the time that the indirect effect of disinvestment would be harmful to university teachers and researchers. Some individuals, publishers (University Microfilms), and organizations (the American Library Association, for example) did engage in an academic boycott, but the AAUP limited its protests against apartheid to resolutions of condemnation and to divestment, because it was considered wiser to keep open lines of communication among scholars in accordance with principles of academic freedom.

Throughout its history, the AAUP has approved numerous resolutions condemning regimes and institutions that limit the freedoms of citizens and faculty, but South Africa is the only instance in which the organization endorsed some form of boycott. Indeed, the Association has often called for greater freedom of exchange among teachers and researchers at the very time that the U.S. government has imposed restrictions on these exchanges, as occurred with the Soviet Union and is still occurring with Cuba. The Association has also disputed arguments of various administrations in Washington that the requirements of national security justify halting academic travel for bona fide academic reasons or scholarly communications.

Boycotts

Though often based on assertions of fundamental principle, boycotts are not in themselves matters of principle but tactical weapons in political struggles. Different kinds of boycotts can have different results. Economic boycotts can have a direct effect on a nation's economy; other forms of boycott are usually more symbolic. This is the case with sports boycotts, such as the exclusion from international competitions (the Olympics, for example) of a team that carries the flag of a nation whose policies members of the international community consider abhorrent. Cultural boycotts have a similar status, though they can affect the earning capacity of artists and writers who are banned from international events. Academic boycotts, too, although they certainly have material effects, are usually undertaken as symbolic protests.

In protesting against apartheid in South Africa, the AAUP carefully distinguished between economic and academic boycotts largely on matters of principle. Economic boycotts seek to bring pressure to bear on the regime responsible for violations of rights. They are not meant to impair the ability of scholars to write, teach, and pursue research, although they may have that result. Academic boycotts, in contrast, strike directly at the free exchange of ideas even as they are aimed at university administrations or, in the case of the AUT call for a boycott of Israeli universities, political parties in power. The form that noncooperation with an academic institution takes inevitably involves a refusal to engage in academic discourse with teachers and researchers, not all of whom are complicit in the policies that are being protested. Moreover, an academic boycott can compound a regime's suppression of freedoms by cutting off contacts with an institution's or a country's academics. In addition, the academic boycott is usually at least once removed from the real target. Rarely are individuals or even individual institutions the issue. What is being sought is a change in state policy. The issue, then, is whether those faculty or ideas that could contribute to changing state policy are harmed when communication with outside academic institutions is cut off and how to weigh that harm against the possible political gains the pressure of an academic boycott might secure.

This issue divided opponents of apartheid within South Africa. There, in the 1980s, many liberal academics argued against the academic boycott on principled grounds (it could not be reconciled with principles of academic freedom and university autonomy) and also on practical ones (it was vital to maintain channels of international communication). Even more radical groups opposed a total boycott and urged instead a selective boycott, one that would target supporters of apartheid but not its challengers. This position, like the Palestinian call for an academic boycott that the AUT initially endorsed, introduced a political test for participation in the academy.

The Academic Boycott as a Tactic

Addressing the African National Congress, Nelson Mandela stressed the need to choose tactics carefully. "In some cases," he wrote, "it might be correct to boycott, and in others it might be unwise and dangerous. In still other cases another weapon of political struggle might be preferred. A demonstration, a protest march, a strike, or civil disobedience might be resorted to, all depending on the actual conditions at the given time."[15]

Even from a tactical standpoint, as a way of protesting against what some see as the Israeli occupation's denial of rights to Palestinians, the academic boycott seems a weak or even a dangerous tool. It undermines exactly the freedoms one wants to defend, and it takes aim at the wrong target. Defenders of the Palestinian call for an academic boycott have argued that, as in South Africa, "the march to freedom [may] temporarily restrict a subset of freedom enjoyed by only a portion of the population." But this argument assumes that the ranking of freedoms as primary and secondary is the only way to accomplish the goals of "freedom, justice, and peace" and that the academic boycott is the best or the only tool to employ. Some argue that it is appropriate to boycott those institutions that violate academic freedom. But would we wish, for example, to recommend a boycott of Chinese universities that we know constrain academic freedom, or would we not insist that the continued exchange of faculty, students, and ideas is more conducive to academic freedom in the long run? Other kinds of sanctions and protests ought to be considered. Some of them are listed in the Palestinian call we cited at the beginning of this report, such as resolutions by higher education organizations condemning violations of academic freedom whether they occur directly by state or administrative suppression of opposing points of view or indirectly by creating material conditions, such as blockades, checkpoints, and insufficient funding of Palestinian universities, that make the realization of academic freedom impossible. These and similar actions may be more effective in obtaining better conditions for academic freedom. But if boycotts are to be used at all, economic boycotts seem a preferable choice, both tactically and as a matter of principle.

Colleges and universities should be what they purport to be: institutions committed to the search for truth and its free expression. Members of the academic community should feel no obligation to support or contribute to institutions that are not free or that sail under false colors, that is, claim to be free but in fact suppress freedom. Such institutions should not be boycotted. Rather, they should be exposed for what they are, and, wherever possible, the continued exchange of ideas should be actively encouraged. The need is always for more academic freedom, not less.

Summary and Recommendations

1. In view of the Association's long-standing commitment to the free exchange of ideas, we oppose academic boycotts.

2. On the same grounds, we recommend that other academic associations oppose academic boycotts. We urge that they seek alternative means, less inimical to the principle of academic freedom, to pursue their concerns.

3. We especially oppose selective academic boycotts that entail an ideological litmus test. We understand that such selective boycotts may be intended to preserve academic exchange with those more open to the views of boycott proponents, but we cannot endorse the use of political or religious views as a test of eligibility for participation in the academic community.

4. The Association recognizes the right of individual faculty members or groups of academics not to cooperate with other individual faculty members or academic institutions with whom or with which they disagree. We believe, however, that when such noncooperation takes the form of a systematic academic boycott, it threatens the principles of free expression and communication on which we collectively depend.

5. Consistent with our long-standing principles and practice, we consider other forms of protest, such as the adoption of resolutions of condemnation by higher education groups intended to publicize documented threats to or violations of academic freedom at offending institutions, to be entirely appropriate.

6. Recognizing the existence of shared concerns, higher education groups should collaborate as fully as possible with each other to advance the interests of the entire academic community in addressing academic freedom issues. Such collaboration might include joint statements to bring to the attention of the academic community and the public at large grave threats to academic freedom.

7. The Association recognizes the right of faculty members to conduct economic strikes and to urge others to support their cause. We believe, however, that in each instance those engaged in a strike at an academic institution should seek to minimize the impact of the strike on academic freedom.

8. We understand that threats to or infringements of academic freedom may occasionally seem so dire as to require compromising basic precepts of academic freedom, but we resist the argument that extraordinary circumstances should be the basis for limiting our fundamental commitment to the free exchange of ideas and their free expression. ■

MARTHA NUSSBAUM

Against Academic Boycotts

I do not plan to discuss the specific facts concerning boycotts of Israeli academic institutions and individuals. There are three reasons for this silence. First, I believe that philosophers should be pursuing philosophical principles—defensible general principles that can be applied to a wide range of cases. We cannot easily tell whether our principles are good ones by looking at a single case only, without inquiring as to whether the principles we propose could be applied to all similar cases.

Second, I am made uneasy by the single-minded focus on Israel. Surely it is unseemly for Americans to discuss boycotts of another country on the other side of the world without posing related questions about American policies and actions that are not above moral scrutiny. Nor should we fail to investigate relevantly comparable cases concerning other nations. For example, one might consider possible responses to the genocide of Muslim civilians in the Indian state of Gujarat in the year 2002, a pogrom organized by the state government, carried out by its agents, and given aid and comfort by the national government of that time (no longer in power). I am disturbed by the world's failure to consider such relevantly similar cases. I have heard not a whisper about boycotting Indian academic institutions and individuals, and I have also, more surprisingly, heard nothing about the case in favor of an international boycott of U.S. academic institutions and individuals. I am not sure that there is anything to be said in favor of a boycott of Israeli scholars and institutions that could not be said, and possibly with stronger justification, for similar actions toward the United States and especially India and/or the state of Gujarat.

I would not favor an academic boycott in any of these cases, but I think that they ought to be considered together, and together with yet other cases in which governments are doing morally questionable things. One might consider, for example, the Chinese government's record on human rights; South Korea's lamentable sexism and indifference to widespread female infanticide and feticide; the failure of a large number of the world's nations, including many, though not all, Arab nations, to take effective action in defense of women's bodily integrity and human equality; and many other cases. Indeed, I note that gross indifference to the lives and health of women has never been seriously considered as a reason for any boycott, a failure of impartiality that struck me even in the days of the South Africa boycott. Eminent thinkers alleged that the case of South Africa was unique because a segment of the population was systematically unequal under the law, a situation that of course was, and still is, that of women in a large number of countries. By failing to consider all the possible applications of our principles, if we applied them impartially, we are failing to deliberate well about the choice of principles. For a world in which there was a boycott of all U.S., Indian, and Israeli scholars, and no doubt many others as well, let us say those of China, South Korea, Saudi Arabia (on grounds of sexism), and Pakistan (on the same grounds, though there has been a bit of progress lately) would be quite different from the world in which only scholars from one small nation were being boycotted, and this difference seems relevant to the choice of principles.

The third reason why I shall speak abstractly is that I am not a Middle East expert. I have recently completed a book on the Gujarat genocide in India, after studying that incident and its history and context for five years, so I think I am equipped to speak about that case, and I propose to do so occasionally, because it sheds light on some of the issues before us. Above all, however, I shall be looking for general and defensible principles.

Some Distinctions

When people believe that a serious wrong has been done by some organization and its agents, there are a number of options open to those who want to express strong condemnation. Boycotts are not the only option. Quite a few others have been used effectively in comparable cases:

1.   **Censure.** Censure is the public condemnation of an institution, usually by another institution. Thus, for example, a professional association might censure an academic institution that violates the rights of scholars. Censure takes various forms, but the usual form is some sort of widely disseminated public statement that the institution in question has engaged in such and such

wrongful action. Professional associations have also censured governments, or government policies, such as the Iraq War.

Censure seems appropriate when the professional organization can reach a consensus about the badness of the actions in question and when it desires to place blame squarely on the institutions, whether academic or governmental, that perpetrated the wrongs, rather than to include all the individuals in those institutions. Censure does nothing to diminish the academic freedom or access of individuals: professors teaching at censured universities are actually helped in their attempt to secure their rights, and, in the case of government-directed censure, academics and citizens generally are not affected at all.

2. Organized Public Condemnation. Sometimes organized movements carry on campaigns to alert the public to the wrongful actions of an institution. Most of the international consumer protest movement against the apparel industry has taken this form. Thus, movement members will try to circulate documents to customers of the retail outlets where objects made by child labor are being sold and will try to make customers aware of the behavior of the corporation in question. The customers themselves can then choose whether to buy from the retail chain or not. This sort of public condemnation is very different from a boycott of the retail outlets, because it allows the individual consumer to choose and does not directly threaten the livelihood of workers. In her wonderful last book, on responsibility for global ills, Iris Marion Young studied the protest movement against the apparel industry, concluding that this approach was very fruitful, because it asks the individual consumer to act, thus promoting a sense of shared responsibility.

Another similar case, in which I am involved, is a movement to make food consumers aware of the conditions in which the animals they purchase for food have been raised. Professors and students at the University of Chicago Law School have designed a product label that will give consumers clear information about how the pigs and chickens are raised, leaving the choice to them, but hoping, obviously, that the informed consumer will make an ethical choice. This approach seems good partly because it is crucial to demonstrate that many consumers support decent treatment for animals, not just a small, highly organized group, as might be the case with a boycott.

Organized public protest is useful, then, in a range of cases, but particularly so when a movement is trying to get the wider public more involved and when the attempt is to target the institution and not its workers.

3. Organized Public Condemnation of an Individual or Individuals. When it is believed that certain individuals bear particular culpability for the wrongs in question, then it is possible to work for the condemnation of those individuals. Thus, if Martin Heidegger had been invited to the University of

Chicago, I would have been one of the ones conducting a public protest of his appearance and trying to inform other people about his record of collaboration with the Nazi regime. Again, in the approach I am considering, there would have been no attempt to prevent people from going to hear Heidegger: the emphasis would have been on informing, persuading, and promoting personal choice.

Organized public condemnation can lead to tangible results. Thus, when the Indian-American Hotel Owners Association invited Narendra Modi, governor of the state of Gujarat, to address a meeting in Florida, scholars concerned about Modi's leading role in orchestrating the violence against Muslims in that state wrote a letter of protest to the State Department asking that Modi be refused a diplomatic visa. Because Congress at the same time passed a resolution of condemnation, sponsored by Representatives John Conyers and Joseph Pitts, this attempt proved successful. Modi was denied a diplomatic visa, and his tourist visa was revoked. Revoking a visa seems appropriate in this case, because Modi orchestrated crimes against humanity; the case of Heidegger, who did not have criminal liability for what the Nazis did, would have been best served by allowing him to speak and encouraging people to inform themselves.

4. Failure to Reward. Some modes of interaction are part of the give and take of daily scholarly business; others imply approval of an institution or individual. Without going so far as to censure the institution or individual, people might decide (whether singly or in some organized way) that this individual does not deserve special honors. The debate resulting in Margaret Thatcher's being denied an honorary degree from Oxford University fits in this category. By conferring an honorary degree, a university makes a strong statement about its own values. Harshness to the poor and the ruin of the national medical system, not to mention then-Prime Minister Thatcher's assault on basic scientific research, were values that the Oxford faculty believed that it could not endorse. I would have been similarly opposed to many potential candidates for honorary degrees at my own institution—but for the convenient fact that Chicago never gives honorary degrees to politicians. However, one can imagine scholars whom one would oppose—Heidegger, for example, or Mircea Eliade, for whom an endowed chair has been named.

The failure-to-reward tactic can also be applied to academic institutions. There are institutional types of funding that reward unusually meritorious programs, and it has been pointed out, in some of the writing about Israel, that one might in some cases of competition for merit grants, refuse to reward Israel, without endorsing a boycott.

5. Helping the Harmed. Usually, when wrong has been done, some people have suffered, and one response would be to focus on helping those who have been harmed. Thus, many scholars concerned about the Gujarat genocide put aside their other engagements and went to help the victims find shelter, take down their eyewitness testimony, help them file complaints, and so on. Others occupied themselves in defending scholars who had been threatened with violence by the Hindu right, publicizing their situation and protesting it.

6.   Being Vigilant on Behalf of the Truth. Often, people who commit wrongs shade the truth in their public statements, and one thing that it is extremely important for scholars to do is to combat falsehoods and incomplete truths. Here again, the case of the Hindu right is instructive. It has its own cherished but quite false view of ancient and medieval history, according to which Hindus are always peaceful and Muslims are always villains. When they put this version of history into textbooks for public schools in India, there was a tremendous outpouring of scholarship showing exactly what was and is wrong with it. After the election of 2004, those textbooks were withdrawn, and the field of combat shifted to the United States, where the Hindu diaspora community is very involved with the Hindu right. The false history was written into textbooks proposed for children in California. Scholars from all over the United States devoted large amounts of time to fighting this, often despite threats of violence and much public vilification. I would like to single out Michael Witzel of Harvard for special praise in this regard. After a very difficult eighteen months, they prevailed with the school board, and the false narrative was withdrawn.

Boycotts

We now have five nonboycott alternatives before us. Let us discuss boycotts, which are very blunt instruments. Typically, they target all the members of an institution, as well as the institution itself. They suggest that all members of the institution deserve condemnation.

Before we can go further, however, we need to distinguish two different types of boycotts—the economic and the symbolic. Economic boycotts may contain a symbolic element, but their primary purpose is to have an economic impact. The boycott against Nestlé, begun in the late 1970s, was aimed at getting Nestlé to alter its policies about the marketing of infant formula in developing countries, which was clearly deleterious to child health, because it discouraged breast-feeding. The aim was to affect the company's profits. This strategy was combined with organized public opposition, but the boycott was significant, because organizers believed that only an economic impact would cause Nestlé to change policies. This boycott proved difficult to administer, as it turned out that Nestlé had a large number of subsidiaries that bore other names, and some of these manufactured products that were ubiquitous. Trying to organize this boycott at Harvard in 1980, I discovered that Del Monte, which made most of the sauces and ketchups used in Harvard's dorms, was a subsidiary of Nestlé; so our plan of getting the dorms to boycott Nestlé cocoa and a few other products with the Nestlé name left large numbers of actual Nestlé products untouched. An economic boycott is rarely a clear-cut proposition symbolically, and yet it can still have a serious economic impact, as this one did.

The most famous example of the economic boycott is that of South Africa. This boycott clearly had a strong symbolic aspect, especially the part of it devoted to divestiture of university stock holdings. But its primary rationale was economic, and that was how it intended to accomplish the goal of social change—by getting businesses that had not yet adopted the Sullivan principles (for corporate social responsibility) to change their actions. In my opinion, this boycott was successful.

Very different is the purely symbolic boycott. Here, the aim is not to have any tangible effect on people's lives, although there may of course be such effects. Instead, the purpose is to make a public statement about the wrongfulness of what a given institution has done, by encouraging people to shun not only the institution but all its members. The hope is, presumably, to persuade people of the wrongfulness of what has happened: if enough people join the boycott movement, others will see that the international community has a certain view, and they will then be encouraged to investigate the case and come to their own conclusions.

It is difficult to see what is accomplished by a symbolic boycott that cannot be more effectively accomplished by one of the alternatives, such as censure or organized public protest. Censure makes a clear statement of exactly who has done what wrong to whom, and it is also voted on by a group, in the typical case, so it is also very clear who supports it. Boycotts have neither type of clarity. It is not clear what the reason for the boycott is, and indeed each individual may join the boycott for different reasons. I suspect in the case of Israel it would not be easy to find a single account of the reasons behind the boycott that would command the agreement of its participants. Nor is it clear who is doing it: in this case there are journals, professional associations, and individuals, all forming a loosely linked movement, and nothing as crisp as a voted-on resolution of censure. Organized public protest also has a superior clarity, because each group involved issues its own public statements, signed by its own officers or representatives, and so we know both who is speaking and what they are saying.

Let me now turn to the case before us, though without arguing its specific facts. The proponents of the boycott movement hold that serious wrongs have been committed by the Israeli government. What they propose to do, however, is not to take direct action against the government or its members (as happened in the case of Governor Narendra Modi), but, instead, to target academic institutions and the individuals in them. The rationale for targeting academic institutions is, first, that these are public institutions, thus arms of government, and second, that some of them have engaged in questionable actions themselves. I would say that the first rationale is weak. The fact that a public university receives government funding does not confer complicity for all decisions of the government. Thus, the public universities of India and the United States cannot be held accountable for particular actions of the U.S. and Indian governments, actions most members of these institutions may strongly deplore.

The second rationale is something else. If a group of people believe that some Israeli universities have violated the civil rights of Arab students or engaged in some other questionable form of conduct, then it seems right to protest that specific wrongdoing. But censure and/or organized public protest would seem the means most appropriate to that goal.

Let me comment on one very alarming rationale that has been offered in this context. In some of the defenses of the boycotts, the wrongdoing alleged is failure to dismiss scholars who take political positions that the group of boycotters does not like. Here the principle of academic freedom becomes relevant in the most urgent manner. Surely the institutions in question should protect these people, unless they do something that counts as hate speech targeted at individuals, or some other form of criminal conduct. We all know what happened in the McCarthy era, when scholars were fired for political positions that a dominant group didn't like. As someone whose hiring, along with that of other "leftists," has been criticized on the editorial page of the *Wall Street Journal* (in a way that my dean, at least, took as tantamount to a McCarthyite call for my firing), I believe that if this principle is once breached, it will hurt most those whose positions go most against the dominant currents of governmental power: feminists, advocates of gay rights, whatever. Fortunately, academic freedom protects us feminists—although, I should add, it does not protect university administrators, who do not have tenure, and my university's president, the one who hired all those left wingers and feminists, was ultimately, in effect, the sacrificial lamb whose forced resignation (inspired by various factors, but among them this one) gratified the proponents of faculty firing or non-hiring. This is an ad hominem argument for readers on the left, but the principled argument is that nobody should be fired for a political position, left or right, short of threats, assault, sexual harassment—the legitimate reasons for dismissal from a faculty position.

Now, let me turn to the main force of the boycott, namely the boycotting of individual members of the academic institutions. This seems to me a particularly useless policy. If one has objections to the government of Israel, how could one suppose that it could be swayed in any way by imposing publication disabilities on some powerless young scholars? Boycotts are supposed to be a weapon of the weak against the powerful, and that is how economic boycotts have their success—by showing the powerful that a large number of people, weak in isolation, can make a difference to their business. It doesn't make practical sense to boycott scholars, typically among the most powerless of society's members, and it also doesn't make symbolic sense. These scholars have not been forming national policy (to say the least), and most of them would not even get a chance to publish their views on the op-ed page of a major newspaper, as we know from our own situation in the United States. And yet, the boycott can do very serious damage to the careers of young scholars especially.

In defense of the boycott, people say that scholars in Israel have not condemned the government as much as they might have. As a rationale for doing harm to them, this is both implausible and deeply repugnant to the core values of academic life. Usually, one aspect of being powerless is that one's voice is not heard in the corridors of power, and I would think that (a) lots of Israeli scholars do have critical views but these views just don't appear in the news and (b) that many are deterred from trying to write for newspapers for the same reasons that few Americans write for newspapers, namely that one almost never gets accepted there, and so it is a waste of time. Moreover, being a good chemist or classicist does not entail being a good writer of op-ed articles. Israeli scholars may well just be doing what they are good at doing. Whatever one says about this, I think one must, in all consistency, apply the same criticisms to scholars in the United States, who do not express their opinions much in public. (In India, where the media are much more interested in academics, it was quite easy for scholars to write something about Gujarat that would get published in a major newspaper, and many did so.

In general, I think that we can only debate this question in a philosophically respectable way if we first offer a principled account of the responsibility of scholars to engage in public debate. If we have such an account, we can at least say who is violating it, in a principled and impartial way. But what disturbs me about the proponents of the boycott is that they lack such an account, and certainly do not comment on the actions of scholars in the United States. vis-à-vis U.S. foreign policy, or the actions of Indian scholars vis-à-vis Hindu-Muslim relations in India, or the actions of South Korean or Pakistani scholars vis-à-vis the alarming levels of violence against women in those nations—and yet, lacking an account that they would be prepared to defend and apply impartially, they wish to impose damages on Israeli scholars.

An even more ominous suggestion on the part of the proponents of the boycotts is that scholars will be exempted from the boycott if they take public positions that the supporters of the boycotts approve. This is incredibly naïve, because it assumes that all scholars, young and old, no matter what their field, could publish something in the press if they tried to, a clearly false assumption. But it also violates a core principle of academic freedom, which is that the positions taken by scholars about political matters are not relevant to their academic employment.

There are limits to this, where the individual in question commits some crime—for example, assault or sexual harassment. But for a group to say that journals and academic conferences have a litmus test, namely a particular position on the actions of the government of Israel, is infinitely more threatening than if it simply boycotted all Israeli scholars alike.

Let me mention a case that bears this out. I was recently in India, at Jamia Milia Islamia, the one national Muslim university. Its current vice chancellor, or president, is the eminent historical scholar Mushirul Hasan. In 1989, when the fatwah against Salman Rushdie was announced and his book *The Satanic Verses* banned in India, Hasan wrote in defense of Rushdie, urging that the book not be banned and insisting that we need to protect the principle of the free exchange of ideas in a democratic society. At that time, he was a professor of history at the institution, and a dean. The students of the university immediately announced a boycott of him and his classes, and this boycott was joined by a substantial number of faculty. The students didn't stop there: in fact, a group of them assaulted him on his way to class, and the criminal charges that resulted from the serious injuries he suffered were only dropped in December 2006, about fifteen years later (justice is slow in India!), because Hasan himself decided that he did not want to ruin these young men's lives, denying them government jobs forever. Hasan consistently refused to change his position. He also refused to resign. So, for four years, boycotted and denied access to his own classrooms, he stayed at home and wrote books. After four years, he started going to the university again, and things slowly changed. After the pluralist government took over in the election of 2004, he was appointed to head the university that had once boycotted him. Now, when he addresses student groups, students stand and cheer.

I have mentioned this history because it suggests that boycotts of academic individuals deeply compromise the core values of a university, and that the current state of India's universities can be measured by the extent to which this boycott directed against an unpopular individual has gradually become unsustainable. The case also shows that deliberation and discussion about the purposes of the academy have led the students of Jamia Milia to a ringing affirmation of both academic freedom and the integrity of an individual who stood up for that principle—even though, even today, most of them would still differ strongly with him about Rushdie. I think that we should behave like today's Jamia Milia, and not like the Jamia of the Hasan boycott, showing respect for those whose positions are different from our own or even repugnant to us.

Scholars who have strong views about the Israeli government would be well advised, I think, to focus on the tactic of organized (nonviolent and nondisruptive) public protest, directed at the government and its key actors. If an academic institution in Israel has committed a specific reprehensible act, then censure is an appropriate tactic. If an individual member of an academic institution has committed reprehensible acts, then those acts should be publicized and criticized by anyone who wants to criticize them, and one might also oppose rewarding such an individual with an honorary degree. I have argued that any more negative action, such as firing the individual, should be undertaken only in a narrow range of time-honored cases, such as criminal acts or sexual harassment. Meanwhile, all involved should focus on stating the facts to the general public, and making good arguments about those facts. As for the academic boycott, it is a poor choice of strategies, and some of the justifications offered for it are downright alarming. Economic boycotts are occasionally valuable. Symbolic boycotts, I believe, are rarely valuable by comparison with the alternatives I have mentioned, and the boycott in this case seems to me very weakly grounded. ■

RUSSELL A. BERMAN

Scholars Against Scholarship:

The Boycott as an Infringement of Academic Culture

The call by the American Studies Association to boycott Israeli academic institutions has elicited a range of critical responses that provides a useful frame for understanding the implications for academic culture. On the one hand, more than two hundred American colleges and universities, typically through the office of their presidents, have denounced the boycott as inimical to the mission of higher education. Because it introduces a political constraint on academic activity—prohibiting certain forms of cooperation with the Israeli academic world on the basis of a set of political judgments—the boycott is viewed as interrupting the free flow of ideas within the international scholarly community, and this interruption of ideas is understood to be at odds with the expectation of an unencumbered pursuit of knowledge. The voluble chorus of denunciation from across the spectrum of institutions and their leaders indicates how the boycott and its proponents in the ASA stand outside the mainstream of higher education. The ASA deserves this criticism; by calling for a boycott of universities, it has broken faith with the scholarly community and betrayed deeply held academic values. There might be circumstances in which a boycott of material products would be plausible, but one should not boycott ideas or close off discussion, which is the real content of an academic boycott.

On the other hand, some opponents of the boycott have submitted proposals in various state legislatures and in Congress calling for reductions in funding to institutions that participate in any such boycott. While the wordings of these bills vary, their fundamental principle links government funding of institutions of higher education to specific political criteria, i.e. rejection of or participation in the boycott. As of this writing, no such law has been adopted; nonetheless, the very suggestion of establishing a political criterion for support for scholarship is worrisome and deserves to be opposed as a threat to academic freedom. Opening the door to political testing of scholarly behavior runs the risk of distorting scholarship and eroding free speech. (It is questionable whether the courts could even approve these proposals, given their first amendment implications, but merely opening this discussion endangers core assumptions about scholarly freedom.)

The anti-boycott legislation is dangerous because it imposes politics onto scholarship, threatening to sanction scholarly institutions due to certain political actions (i.e., participating in the boycott of Israeli universities). Subjecting scholarship to political evaluation can subvert the academic enterprise. For this reason, one should oppose these legislative proposals with no qualifications. Ironically, however, it was the call for the boycott itself, and especially the ASA endorsement, that established the current connection between politics and scholarship, introduced a political litmus test into the scholarly world, and thereby laid the foundation for the threatened legislative sanctions. The ill-advised ASA decision opened the door for the politicians' response: the repressive potential of state intrusion into academic affairs results directly from the underlying structure of the boycott, i.e., the appeal to impose political judgments (regarding Israel) on the behavior of the individual scholars who the ASA has encouraged to engage in various boycott practices. The politicization of scholarship began with the boycott call, not in the legislatures; it was the boycott call that began to bully others to conform to an ideological orthodoxy, and it is the boycott supporters who share the blame for this potential political repression of scholarship.

The alternative to this assault on academic values involves resisting the imposition of any political criteria on scholarship, whether the directives come from state legislatures or from professional scholarly organizations. Scholarship needs freedom of thought; scholars in the pursuit of knowledge should not face threats regarding funding cuts, nor should they face political denunciation or ostracism on the part of professional associations. Given the ASA boycott endorsement, scholars of American Studies who dissent and choose to work with Israeli institutions have become pariahs in their field, subject to implicit blacklisting and disdain. The ideological crusade against a political minority undermines core academic values, which should be defended against any such repressive agenda. Scholars should be free to pursue their research without regard to mandates of political correctness. To endorse that principle, however, would mean that one would have to renounce the boycott: definitely a desirable outcome, but one which the boycott adherents are unlikely to adopt: they—wrongly—want to claim the right to intimidate others with political tests but—rightly—resent submitting to political tests themselves. If only they would extend that same tolerance to their political opponents.

Of course, some defenders of the boycott think otherwise, believing that they can call for fellow scholars to boycott Israeli universities without in any way undermining academic freedom, infringing on academic culture, or impeding the free flow of ideas. They argue that their ends—ameliorating the conditions of Palestinians—justify their means: restricting others' academic freedom. This is an illusion: the boycott movement is poisoning debate in the US, and it aspires to eliminate connections between Israeli and American (and other) universities. It could therefore have a chilling effect on the world of ideas. By trying to limit what individual scholars do, what conferences they attend, and with whom they collaborate, the supporters of the boycott restrict academic freedom. These will be the real effects of the boycott, which is designed to dissuade scholars from activity in Israel or with Israeli institutions. It is remarkable and disconcerting that scholars who voted for the boycott were so prepared to endanger the foundational principles of scholarly work in the interest of pursuing a political agenda.

Still, some boycott proponents disingenuously reply that, on the contrary, the boycott does not restrict freedom because—and this now is the crux of their defense—it is directed exclusively against institutions and not against individuals: it prohibits cooperation with Israeli academic institutions, not with individual Israelis. The insistence on this focus on institutions is the basis on which the plausibility of the boycott is defended. Yet this differentiation between institutions and individuals is strange and untenable. Effective scholarship always depends on institutional support for individual scholars; individual scholars can thrive only because of their institutional contexts and the resources that institutions make available: colleagues, students, classrooms, libraries, laboratories, and of course financial support, including salary and research funding. Strip away the institution, and the individual scholar barely survives. However, the ASA boycott is premised on the strangely neo-liberal illusion that one can strip away that infrastructure without harming the individual scholar at all. Yet once one recognizes that the individual necessarily depends on the institution, then the distinction between the two, which is central to the argument that the boycott does not infringe on any individual scholar's academic freedom, melts away. A boycott of academic institutions is necessarily an attack on individual academics, no matter how much the boycott apologists implausibly assert the contrary. To pretend to welcome collaboration with Israeli scholars, while insisting that no funding come from Israeli institutions, is dishonest.

Some boycott advocates may be so ideologically committed to making an anti-Israel political statement that they blind themselves to the consequences of their own program, in particular the subversion of academic freedom through the proscription on institutional support. Others, however, are surely simply mendacious. To suggest that the boycott will not inhibit Israeli scholars from attending conferences abroad but only prohibits those scholars from utilizing institutional research funds is deeply cynical. Nonetheless, this is Judith Butler's understanding of the boycott: "The only request that is being made is that no institutional funding from Israeli institutions be used [...]."[17] Butler generously volunteers that such Israeli guests use their own personal funds, rather than rely on travel support from their own universities. Precisely how the ASA or Butler envisions monitoring the sources of travel funding is not addressed because it is not a realistic proposal. The real result of such a regime, in which Israeli scholars were somehow prohibited from relying on institutional support for conference attendance, would be a stifling of international travel and an impoverishment of the scholarly community. That is the logical consequence of the boycott, as explained by ASA and Butler; to claim that academic freedom will not suffer is erroneous.

The proposals for legislative sanctions, which represent a further consequence of this politicization of scholarly decision-making, offer another perspective on the question of individuals and institutions. If that binary distinction, individuals versus institutions, were credible in this alternative context, one could argue that the legislative threats do not endanger individual scholars (those who support the boycott); instead the legislation only endangers institutions that risk losing funding, and that therefore the legislation contains no threat to academic freedom since it refrains from targeting individuals. Yet such a suggestion that the legislative sanctions only threaten institutions and not individuals is as patently vacuous as the parallel claim regarding the boycott: one cannot separate individual and institution in either case. Once one begins to introduce political criteria that discriminate against certain scholarly practices—such as attending a conference at an Israeli university— the free flow of ideas and the intellectual latitude of individual scholars are reduced. A boycott is a version of a political litmus test, and establishing it will diminish academic freedom, no matter how much the ASA leadership claims the contrary.

The significant distinction in matters of the boycott is not the illusory separation between individuals and institutions but rather the genuine distance between the radicalism of the boycott rhetoric and the minimalism of it implementation parameters. This is particularly clear in the guidelines that the ASA has issued. For example, the ASA justifies its support of the boycott not on the basis of the occupation in the West Bank or the Israeli settlements but instead with a blanket condemnation of the substance of Israeli society as a whole: "As with South Africa, Israel's system of racial discrimination, at all institutional levels, constitutes apartheid [...]."[18] Support for the boycott depends on accepting the extremist credo that Israeli democracy is indistinguishable from South African apartheid, a myth that the ASA endorses thereby undermining its credibility as a scholarly organization. It is a fantasy that opportunistically trivializes the experience of apartheid in South Africa, while misrepresenting the reality of Israeli society. Nonetheless, support for the boycott requires the belief that the problem is not the unresolved Israeli occupation of parts of the West Bank but the existence of Israel altogether.

Yet against that radical backdrop full of heated rhetoric and the allegation of egregious conditions everywhere in Israel, the ASA chose to issue a call only for the tamest and most moderate action, indeed for hardly any action at all: "The ASA understands boycott as limited to a refusal on the part of the ASA in its official capacities to enter into formal collaborations with Israeli academic institutions, or with scholars who are expressly serving as representatives or ambassadors of those institutions (such as deans, rectors, presidents and others), or on behalf of the Israeli government, until Israel ceases to violate human rights and international law." This is an odd promise since, even without the boycott, the ASA was unlikely to collaborate formally with Israeli universities or invite its presidents to speak; at this point, the ASA threat sounds hollow: radical talk with no consequences—just an opportunity to flaunt political credentials while hoping to pay no price. (The isolation that the ASA now faces in the academic world and the reputational damage that it has incurred indicate that the whole episode was costly indeed: it will be a long time before the ASA can rebuild its credibility.)

However, matters become more complicated when one examines what the ASA asks of individual scholars. On the one hand, it claims, reassuringly, to ask nothing: "U.S. scholars are not discouraged under the terms of the boycott from traveling to Israel for academic purposes, provided they are not engaged in a formal partnership with or sponsorship by Israeli academic institutions." This leniency might seem to corroborate the claim that the boycott is not intended to infringe on individuals. Yet only a few paragraphs further, one discovers that "the boycott does oppose participation in conferences or events officially sponsored by Israeli universities." We should be clear what that statement means. The ASA has issued an explicit travel ban for its members, enjoining them from attending conferences in Israel, since academic conferences everywhere depend, one way or another, on institutional support. This prohibition on travel to conferences in Israel matches Judith Butler's reciprocal understanding of the boycott: "It also means that when Israeli scholars invite those of us who support the boycott to Israeli institutions, we decline, explaining that until those institutions minimally take a public stand against the occupation, we cannot come and support that silence, that status quo."[19] On this point, interestingly, Butler is less harsh than the ASA; at least, she suggests that the boycott of an institution might end if it were to take a public stand "against the occupation" (she does not clarify if she means the occupation of 1967 or Israel altogether as occupation). In contrast, the ASA refrains from indicating how an Israeli university could ever be removed from the list of prohibited venues. An untenured faculty member in a department chaired by a boycott supporter will risk his or her career by choosing to visit an Israeli university.

It is impossible not see the ASA prohibition as an attempt to curtail dialogue—although the ASA repeatedly claims the contrary—and therefore a restriction on the free flow of ideas. If one were to observe the ASA guidelines as quoted here, one should not attend an academic conference at an Israeli university, which would clearly constitute a limitation on the possibility of the thwarted visitor to share his or her scholarship, just as it would reduce the opportunity to develop scholarly collaborations with the Israeli (or other) scholars one might meet at the conference. While the ASA purports to claim that it does not intend to impair academic freedom, the consequences of its directives would inescapably have that result. The mere assertion by the ASA that it does not want to curtail academic freedom hardly means that its actions will do no harm. Indeed, the discrepancy between the unavoidable damage an implemented boycott will do to some scholar's academic opportunities and the ASA's stereotypical disclaimers is so large that one can only conclude that the ASA leadership, at least, knows full well that they will be trampling on free scholarship. They just pretend to hide this inescapable outcome of the boycott.

The hypocrisy of the ASA statement may in fact reflect an underlying political tension. The unified leadership that endorsed the boycott and the small number of members who chose to vote for it were clearly eager to make a political statement by articulating their critique of Israel in the radical terms of the apartheid criticism (rather than with moderate arguments that would have focused exclusively on the West Bank). However, the ASA linked its own verbal radicalism to a minimalist practice that in effect asks nothing of anyone: "In general, the ASA recognizes that members will review and negotiate specific guidelines for implementation on a case-by-case basis and adopt them according to their individual convictions." This proviso represents an open door through which any ASA member could with good conscience avoid any and all boycott directives that the ASA leadership might issue. By minimizing the expectations directed at members to participate in the boycott, the leadership effectively conceded that any more stringent understanding of the boycott might not have been adopted by skeptics in its membership. This dumbing down of the boycott must have been an intentional strategy to enable it to pass the membership vote. It allowed individual ASA members to cast their ballots for the boycott, while maintaining the illusion that academic freedom would not be infringed. Of course, it will be; the boycott will have a chilling effect on academic discourse, and it is disheartening that so many ASA members were evidently prepared to jeopardize academic culture in order to make a political statement. Even if one were to accept the ASA critique of Israel (which I do not), the choice of an academic boycott as a strategy was a bad one, since it undermines basic expectations of academic culture. One wonders if smarter alternatives were even considered within the ASA conclaves.

Yet that same proviso, which leaves the terms of the implementation up to the members, also has an alternative, ominous implication. By depicting Israel as the functional equivalent of apartheid South Africa, the ASA has borrowed from an incendiary rhetoric of vilification that casts Israel as the enemy of humanity. Against the backdrop of that stark verdict, the ASA also encourages its individual members to act in any way that is consistent with their "individual convictions." The organization's directives do not admonish members to respect others' academic freedom or their legal rights but only to implement the boycott however they see fit. The trial of Israel, in other words, has already ended, the guilty verdict is unambiguous, and in that context, the ASA appeals to its members to do whatever they like to the demonized enemy. The likelihood that some ASA members will take this invitation as an authorization to act more radically is considerable, as we know from the experience in the United Kingdom. Under the auspices of the boycott movement there, Israeli scholars were, for example, removed from the editorial board of a journal, merely on the basis of their nationality. In other notorious cases, an Israeli graduate student applicant was turned down for study in the UK because of previous service in the Israeli military, and a British scholar made a casual meeting with a visiting Israeli colleague contingent on the latter issuing a denunciation of Israeli policies. Every political movement has its fanatics who are eager to take the law into their own hands, and the ASA statement provides cover for such anti-Israeli vigilantism. Some extremists will take the boycott endorsement as license for extreme action, and nothing in the ASA directives cautions its members against extremism in the boycott. On the contrary, the apartheid rhetoric invites direct action with no limitations. The ASA "individual conviction" proviso represents an effort by the institution (the ASA) to shuffle responsibility onto the individual members, but here too the binary of institution and individual collapses: when the boycott turns into discrimination on the basis of national origin, as it surely will, the ASA and its leadership will bear responsibility for unleashing a logic of discrimination. The boycott has let the genie of bigotry out of the bottle. Boycott supporters whose positions are publicly known should understand that their participation in the regular processes of university governance—such as graduate student selection—will necessarily raise the question of bias, given their expressed hostility to Israeli institutions. Professional integrity dictates that they should recuse themselves, since their capacity to judge Israeli applicants objectively is now irreversibly in doubt.

This discrimination against Israelis is the structural racism inherent in the boycott, whose proponents typically attack their opponents rather than attacking their opponents' arguments. For Butler, critics of the boycott are "mechanical" and "shabby."[20] But her denunciatory rhetoric still belongs to a high road of moderation compared to what one finds elsewhere in the boycott camp. Following the low road through online comment sections or in social media, one finds boycott promoters quick to label their opponents as part of the "Zionist lobby." To dismiss a critic as part of a lobby means to deny him or her the right to independent thinking; defamation replaces argument. To treat lobbies as inherently corrupt betrays a simplistic view of modern liberal democracy, where lobbies, foundations, and other organizations fill the political landscape. (The boycott movement itself depends on extensive foundation support even as it pretends to represent Palestinian "civil society.") To use the term "Zionist" as the marker of ultimate vilification raises a difficult point, but one that it would be dishonest to avoid in this context.

Criticism of Israeli policies or Zionism is not necessarily anti-Semitic. However, it also holds, obviously, that the mere fact that one has anti-Zionist views does not prove that one is not anti-Semitic. It is a logical fallacy to assert that the presence of anti-Zionism proves the absence of anti-Semitism. That should not be difficult to understand. On the contrary, it would hardly be surprising to discover that individuals with pronounced anti-Semitic sentiments might be hostile to Israel and Israelis, and empirical studies have demonstrated just such positive correlations between accepting anti-Semitic stereotypes and anti-Zionist positions.[21] In particular in the Middle East and the public sphere of the Arab press, anti-Zionist politics often go hand in hand with anti-Semitic caricatures. Nonetheless, some boycott defenders would prefer to suppress discussions of anti-Semitism in their own ranks by complaining implausibly that they constantly face insinuations of anti-Semitism—when it is probably a whole lot less than "constantly." Their refusals to face anti-Semitism amount to an attempt to silence the Jewish community in the face of racism and adversity. What adversity? Leave aside the fantastic discourses in the Middle East, such as when President of Egypt Adly Mansour is imagined by his opponents to be Jewish in order to attack him. We can stay closer to home: In the *Electronic Intifada* in late 2013, Rania Khalek counts the Jews—not the Zionists, but the Jews—at *The Nation* and decides there are too many.[22] With that, the progressive camp has come around to Jew-counting with hardly a peep of protest, certainly not from the ASA or any more distinguished humanities association. Not all anti-Zionists fit this paradigm, but when boycott proponents automatically reject claims of anti-Semitism a *priori*, they undermine their own anti-racist credibility.

Yet pulling back from the contradictions of the ASA's directives, one can recognize how the boycott discussion involves a return to classic questions of scholarship and politics. The boycott represents a particularly acute version of this problem, however, since the boycott is not only a matter of scholars taking a political position but also one of pursuing a strategy that targets scholarly institutions: "scholars against scholarship" could be its slogan. It is akin to that moment in the 1960s when the student movement against the Vietnam War turned, self-destructively, against the universities, its home base, rather than against clearer political targets more directly responsible for the war. In the case at hand, the target is not the Israeli government or the Israeli military—remarkably, the ASA statement does not proscribe direct cooperation with those institutions—but the academic world, which it so happens is a hotbed of the Israeli peace movement. It is as if the real political agenda of BDS were intentionally to achieve a weakening of the peace camp. This agenda would of course be quite consistent with the content of the radical rhetoric: the goal is not peace between two sovereign states but the elimination of the State of Israel.

Had the ASA issued a statement of opinion on the Middle East, no matter how forceful, one might only have wondered why professional academic organizations feel compelled to have private foreign policies that stand in little relation to their core missions. Instead of merely declaring an opinion, however, the ASA chose to call for a specific action, the boycott, and no matter how its supporters try to minimize its implications, the aspirational goal of the boycott can only mean an isolation of Israeli academia and therefore a reduction in contacts between American and Israeli academic communities—and, of course, other countries too. Boycott supporters surely must have thought ahead at least this far to recognize this impoverishment of academic life as a potential outcome: limiting the free flow of ideas through the exclusion of other points of view. They chose to accept that result, and they should accept responsibility for the consequences. In this sense too, the boycott movement is destructive of academic values, and the boycott originators may well have intended it to be so. A hatred of knowledge and of reasoned argument pervades its prose.

Scholars—like everyone else—are members of political communities and, from the standpoint of civic virtue, one has to welcome political involvement, no matter the topic. Yet there is an enormous difference between a scholar's engaging in the public sphere in pursuit of political ends and a scholar bringing his or her political agenda into the university as the realm of scholarship. It is worth remembering that the boycott is directed at the full scope of Israeli universities, i.e., not just a few departments, and there are wide swaths of academic life, in universities in all countries, where this sort of politicization of scholarship is absent; i.e., the science, technology, engineering, and mathematics fields. In contrast, the boycott represents a sort of politicization of scholarship that is more common in parts of the humanities—such as the ASA—but that is an exception in the context of the full university. (The distinction between individual scholars and institutions might seem plausible in the humanities but makes no sense in the experimental sciences where collaboration is the norm.) The prominence of the humanities fields in the academic boycott indicates the marginality of those fields on the map of contemporary academic life.

Yet even in the humanities, so much more open to scholarly politicization than, for example, the medical schools, there remains a certain hesitation about the degree of politicization that is proper in a classroom. Even in a course that raises political topics, established academic values mandate that faculty members should not disadvantage a student who holds alternative political values. The classroom is not a political rally. The teacher's mission is not to inculcate one's politics but to enhance students' thinking. Yet given the extremism of the rhetoric of the boycott proponents, it is doubtful whether they will be able to maintain this fundamental distinction in their teaching. In its directives on the boycott, the ASA refrained from warning against politicization of the classroom. Therefore students and parents alike should expect some scholars, authorized to act on their own conviction, to continue with the politicization of the college classroom.

Humanists boast of a capacity to speak out, as scholars, on all sorts of political topics, even when specific expertise is lacking. The contrast between their disciplinary marginality in the contemporary university—which is everywhere largely a STEM enterprise—and their sense of self-importance is stunning. This is particularly the case in statements from professional associations, such as the ASA, or their leadership, who misuse their bully pulpits to pursue their idiosyncratic agenda, oblivious to the damage they do to the reputation of their associations, their disciplines, and the humanities in general. It is hardly a secret that the standing of the humanities in contemporary American culture is shaky at best. Even President Obama has come to dismiss humanistic study as a poor alternative to the STEM fields. Needless to say, it is unlikely that the professional associations of those disciplines that enjoy public respect will adopt boycott resolutions. Meanwhile, the call for the boycott by humanities organizations makes the humanities as whole appear even more bizarre to the public at large. Scholarly fields that take themselves seriously do not participate in empty gestures. ■

CARY NELSON

The Fragility of Academic Freedom

In the immediate aftermath of the American Studies Association vote to endorse an academic boycott of Israeli universities, Brooklyn College political scientist Corey Robin initiated an online dialogue about ASA's resolution. Robin supports the ASA's position. He also argues that, because ASA has no comprehensive enforcement mechanism and because compliance is partly up to individuals, its boycott is really more like an AAUP censure. The AAUP does leave it up to individual faculty to decide whether to accept employment or lecture at censured institutions. Robin consequently considers any distinction between a boycott and censure specious. But the AAUP doesn't urge faculty not to cooperate with a censured institution. Instead it issues a warning that the school may not honor the Association's widely accepted standards for academic freedom and shared governance. The AAUP also does not censure institutions as a whole, let alone their faculties. It censures university administrations. Moreover, the AAUP only censures university administrations one-by-one, after a detailed and lengthy investigation that includes opportunities for all involved to submit documents in evidence; an AAUP investigation also includes a campus visit by an investigating team to conduct interviews with all parties. For all these reasons, comparisons between academic boycotts and AAUP investigations are misleading and invalid.

As University of Oklahoma historian Ben Alpers responded to Robin, "trying to ban association with an entire nation's universities is the problem."

The AAUP did censure five Louisiana universities in the wake of Hurricane Katrina, but only after conducting five complete campus investigations, a massive undertaking that cost more than $100,000. ASA, of course, did no such investigations. Nor did the proposers of an MLA resolution that attacked Israeli travel policies affecting academics. Indeed, Richard Ohmann, one of the MLA resolution's cosponsors, protested at the MLA's 2014 annual meeting that it was outrageous to expect English professors to match the AAUP's investigative standards. But relying on unverified anecdotes, as Ohmann and Bruce Robbins did, produces unreliable results. Happily, MLA members chose not to ratify the resolution.

Echoing a misconception that Judith Butler had endorsed a year earlier, Robin went on to argue that "academic freedom is not merely about an individual's right to pursue a program of research or teaching, but also about material conditions and infrastructure that facilitate research and teaching." Given how few US universities actually provide significant research infrastructure, one would have to conclude that there is precious little academic freedom here. But in fact academic freedom does not in itself guarantee the infrastructure faculty need or want. Academic freedom gives them the right to pursue funding, but it doesn't guarantee success. Access to infrastructural support partly depends on the priorities set by campuses and funding agencies. Does a chemist or an engineer have more academic freedom than an English professor because chemists or engineers are likely to have greater resources at their disposal? As University of Bristol philosophy professor Chris Bertram responds, "I can't claim that my academic freedom has been violated because there isn't a world lecture tour organized for me!"

Has Israeli policy restricting movement on the West Bank limited the ability of Palestinian faculty to exercise their academic freedom? Yes. Have Palestinians themselves pressured West Bank faculty to conform to approved political opinions and thus restricted academic freedom? Yes. In a remarkable instance of blindness, Butler complains that Palestinian faculty had their academic freedom compromised in such years as 2002 and 2003, "which is why checkpoints are and should be an issue for anyone who defends a notion of academic freedom." But Butler never mentions that her examples are from the 2000-2005 Second Intifada, when Israel was facing suicide bombers infiltrating from the West Bank. The principle of academic freedom gives one no tools with which to evaluate the sort of lethal security threats Israel confronted, or to decide how academic freedom may reasonably be compromised as a result.

In response to arguments that academic boycotts are just matters of ethical choice for individual faculty, Hunter College English professor Sarah Chinn writes

Israeli universities have partnerships all over the world in various fields (not least of which is the new Technion/Cornell campus on Roosevelt Island). Boycotting Israeli universities means abandoning those partnerships, and depriving those scholars of the opportunity to work on research projects, denying students study abroad possibilities, and shutting down new transnational projects. These relationships are not just one-on-one, scholar-to-scholar, but require institutional support. It also means that scholars can't accept invitations to talk or teach at Israeli universities, which violates their freedom to disseminate their research and interact with students and scholars at other institutions.

Robin responds that this "requires you to say that any time a university shuts down a partnership with another institution—for whatever reason—it is violating the academic freedom of those who are engaged in the partnership." Hardly. Universities can curtail such partnerships because they discover fraud or ethical violations, or because funding has expired. But *not* for unrelated political reasons, which is what academic boycotts do—in violation of academic freedom.

The following month, in a post titled "The New McCarthyites: BDS, Its Critics, and Academic Freedom," Robin ramped up his rhetoric substantially. In *The Jerusalem Post* Edward Beck argued that faculty should not wait to fight organized BDS drives but rather be proactive; they should try to get anti-boycott principles adopted by academic associations beforehand. And he suggested that there should be sanctions for faculty who take boycott actions that compromise academic freedom. Russell Berman in a *Haaretz* interview warns that calls for academic boycotts damage higher education by promoting the view that ideas should be judged not by their quality but by a political assessment based on national origin. Misreading his sources, Robin decides this means that "the new line of march is that *mere advocacy* of the boycott is itself a violation of academic freedom" and that this "should tell us how far down the road of repression the opponents of the ASA boycott are willing to go—all in the name of academic freedom."

It has unfortunately now become standard for BDS advocates in the US to protest that their academic freedom is under assault whenever someone criticizes their arguments. Thus Noura Erakat falsely complains that "the recent response to the ASA boycott resolution has not challenged the allegations made against Israel, but has sought to shut down and censor the conversation altogether." This is nothing less than a disavowal of the principle of open debate that is the academy's fundamental sustaining value.

A few years ago, when I was trying to write some very basic documents for public outreach about the key concepts that govern academic life, I wrote a piece called "Defining Academic Freedom." It was published in *Inside Higher Education*. When I sent a draft to the staff of AAUP's Department of Academic Freedom, Tenure, and Shared Governance, they prefaced their suggestions with a droll caveat: "It's nice of you to try to educate the public, but faculty don't know these things either."

It's not surprising that BDS faculty often do not know much about academic freedom, since most of their colleagues don't either, but then most of their colleagues aren't making pronouncements about academic freedom. They simply persevere in quiet ignorance. BDS ignorance is, one may say, more proactive. It's out there, doing the hard work of spreading confusion and misinformation.

Consider what may seem a minor example. In a January 2014 issue of the *Chronicle of Higher Education*, BDS advocate and ASA activist Eric Cheyfitz tries to demonstrate his scholarly expertise by citing the AAUP's 1940 "Statement on Academic Freedom and Tenure" and describing it as "the gold standard." Unfortunately, it's not. The 1940 statement is a consensus document designed to get the critical components of a six-year tenure model widely accepted and to promote universal endorsement of academic freedom as the main pillar of faculty identity. If you take the trouble to read Walter Metzger's essay on the history of the 1940 statement, you will find that there was considerable debate over the wording. It was clear, for example, that brevity was key if organizations were to become cosigners. There were also some compromises necessary. A number of campuses incorporate the 1940 definitions into faculty handbooks. If asked, I advise otherwise. It may be a standard, but it is not gold. The 1940 text on academic freedom entails qualifications faculty should be reluctant to embrace.

The problem begins with brevity. Academic Freedom is an abstract principle that has to be applied to different questions and contexts. If the AAUP has a "gold standard," it is certainly our founding 1915 Declaration, but even that magisterial and still-inspiring document is colored by the historical context of its composition. As I've pointed out before, it portrays students as much more naïve and impressionable than they are now, a hundred years later, and it has language about faculty responsibility similar to the 1940 statement that is problematic. Nonetheless, the Centennial edition of the AAUP's Redbook collection of documents will open with the 1915 Declaration because much of it remains telling and relevant today. The problems with the 1940 statement include its avoidance of more nuanced explanation and its warning that faculty "should at all times be accurate, should exercise appropriate restraint, should show respect for the opinions of others." Is there any academic field that shows less adherence to this set of guidelines than Mideast Studies? We like to say that these guidelines are hortatory, not mandated, but putting them in a faculty handbook raises the specter of enforcement.

Enforcement is almost inevitably selective and often directed at politically controversial faculty. Cheyfitz himself protested the politically motivated firing of University of Colorado Professor Ward Churchill, as did I. In the current debates, one needs to be sensitive to the possibility that whichever group is politically empowered in the future—pro- or anti-boycott faculty—will use the strictures in the 1940 statement to punish their opponents. Honoring fundamental principles irrespective of political opportunities is the only sound policy either now or in the long run.

Yet the AAUP really has no one document that covers all elements of academic freedom. It never will have one, in part because the application of academic freedom is affected by technical innovations, new legal rulings, and new historical developments, and thus requires context-specific analysis. It is by no means easy to decide how academic freedom applies to new conditions. People have to work very hard at it. That said, if you want a concise definition, you might use the one from the organization's 2009 Garcetti report:

> Academic freedom is the freedom to teach, both in and outside the classroom, to conduct research and to publish the results of those investigations, and to address any matter of institutional policy or action whether or not as a member of an agency of institutional governance. Professors should also have the freedom to address the larger community with regard to any matter of social, political, economic, or other interest, without institutional discipline or restraint, save in response to fundamental violations of professional ethics or statements that suggest disciplinary incompetence.

The AAUP produced that definition in response to a US Supreme Court ruling that some district courts have applied to faculty speech about governance issues with deeply troubling results. What this definition most fundamentally emphasizes is that academic freedom covers faculty speech rights—in teaching, research, governance, and public commentary. It is partly a product of recent legal threats to those speech rights, but it remains nothing more than a clarification and shoring up of the specific terrain of speech and does not modify the fundamental principle at stake.

The AAUP is constantly engaged in rearticulating its core beliefs to the historical and political pressures of the day, which is different from either abandoning or dramatically expanding them. *Academic Freedom and National Security in a Time of Crisis* (2003) takes up the academic freedom implications of the Patriot Act. *Freedom in the Classroom* (2007) engages recent conservative efforts to limit academic freedom rights in classroom political speech. *Protecting an Independent Faculty Voice: Academic Freedom After Garcetti v. Ceballos* (2009) warned about the implications for shared governance speech of federal district court decisions following a key US Supreme Court case. *Ensuring Academic Freedom in Politically Controversial Academic Personnel Decisions* (2011) sets guidelines for preventing reprisals directed toward critics of Israeli policy, among other recent victims of efforts to curtail academic freedom. To say that the AAUP simply hews to an inflexible principle and ignores historical conditions is both ignorant and untrue. The unending record of the AAUP's policy work addressing the changing political and economic landscape—contained in these and other reports freely available on the AAUP website—decisively demonstrates otherwise. *The Journal of Academic Freedom*'s pro-boycott authors seem to think that only they realize that sustaining academic freedom requires constant struggle, whereas in fact the AAUP has been at the forefront of that struggle for a hundred years.

To offer another example of how changing conditions can make clarification of academic freedom necessary: universities have been very aggressively seeking to eliminate faculty patent rights since 2011. I've coauthored a new 2013 policy document, along with a book-length AAUP report (*Recommended Principles to Guide Academy-Industry Relationships*), detailing the AAUP's position that academic freedom covers not only the research you do but also decisions about how the fruits of that research are to be disseminated. Academic freedom doesn't end when you create something valuable; it covers decisions about how you want it to be shared with the rest of the world. Dissemination is once again grounded in speech.

Sometimes the AAUP decides that an earlier position on an application of academic freedom was misguided. Convinced that academic freedom does not assure confidentiality in a faculty member's financial dealings with outside agencies and companies funding research, I coauthored a complete revision of our policy on disclosure of conflicts of interest in 2013 as well. That said, the unending process of rearticulating the principle of academic freedom to emerging historical conditions does not mean, as David Lloyd and Malini Johar Schueller assert, that "academic freedom extolled by the AAUP is a geopolitically based privilege rather than a transhistorical right." As I have argued in print, transcendent notions are produced within history and exist in dialogue with social and political reality, but that does not mean they are useless. A principle that has been sustained over time and has survived legal and political changes can have significant cultural power. Indeed, more than one of the *JAF*'s pro-boycott authors urges that academic freedom be linked to universal, transhistorical understandings of human rights.

Apparently some transhistorical categories are more equal than others. Part of the work of rearticulation and clarification that the AAUP engages in is designed precisely to preserve academic freedom as a transhistorical principle. If it is not that, it is expendable to political expediency, which is exactly the status BDS is proposing for it.

BDS advocates regularly cite some of the American academics who have had their careers threatened or terminated because of their critiques of Israeli policy. In fact, it is the AAUP and its leaders that took up their cause, something for which the authors of these essays give the organization no credit. The AAUP went to extraordinary lengths to defend Sami Al-Arian. It flew a team down to Florida and made certain his leave was salaried. It demanded a full and fair hearing until the FBI took matters out of our hands. It had an investigation in place to defend Norman Finkelstein until he reached a settlement with DePaul University that prevented him from permitting the AAUP to pursue his case further. When David Robinson was under attack at UC Santa Barbara, I defended him as AAUP president. When Israeli faculty member Neve Gordon was attacked in both Israel and the US for his boycott advocacy, I defended him in "Neve Gordon's Academic Freedom," an essay published in *Inside Higher Education*, something for which both he and his family expressed their gratitude. These are the fruits of our "ahistorical" and "depoliticized" concept of academic freedom.

Bottom line: best not to pretend expertise on academic freedom unless you become a student of the subject. We all assume that one cannot speak confidently about microbiology or French poetry without studying them. Why do we assume academic freedom is a matter of common sense? It is not a concept to invoke casually, but rather one that requires serious reflection, careful application, and constant monitoring. Of course, I wish every faculty member would do just that. If Eric Cheyfitz were a student of academic freedom, he would know that his confident division between individual academic freedom and institutional rights is not so simple or so absolute as he thinks. My own "Defining Academic Freedom" essay lists a number of rights faculty often incorrectly think are guaranteed by academic freedom. But the AAUP also believes, I think regrettably, that collective faculty decisions routinely trump individual freedom regarding pedagogical choices. One might suggest that if you are a bit unclear about what academic freedom means in the US you might pause before trumpeting the need to boycott universities abroad.

Let me detail some of the additional misconceptions that guide BDS thinking. I'll concentrate for now on the 2013 essays published in the AAUP's *Journal of Academic Freedom*. The historical errors begin with the absurd claim by Lloyd and Schueller that "if there has ever been anywhere a systematic denial of academic freedom to a whole population, rather than to specific individuals or institutions, it is surely in Palestine under Israeli occupation." How many African, Asian, Eastern European, or Middle Eastern countries whose whole university populations are denied any semblance of academic freedom would one have to cite to discredit this hyperbole? Other curious assertions would include the bizarre statement that the AAUP "implicitly denies the freedom to criticize Israel to the US-based Palestinian students its policies so dramatically affect." As I stated above, the factual record demonstrates that the AAUP has repeatedly defended the right to criticize Israeli policy.

The conceptual errors are equally serious. Bill Mullen confidently declares that "academic freedom is a subset of political freedom," a claim the AAUP would dispute. The two are partly entangled in the US because of the Bill of Rights, but the legal status of academic freedom varies from country to country. Britain's libel laws, for example, limit the speech that academic freedom could protect there. Germany restricts Holocaust denial; we do not. In the US, however, we argue that academic freedom covers a very specific set of rights appropriate to the academy. Supreme Court decisions, for example, make it possible for employers to discipline you for public statements that affect a corporation's capacity to conduct business. Only academic freedom can offer broad protection against institutional reprisals for extramural speech. That doesn't mean we cannot recommend our laws and values to other countries. But no one so far as I know is urging a boycott of German universities because state law means academic freedom does not cover Holocaust denial. Here, unless you were, say, a professor of modern history or a member of another academic discipline for which knowledge of modern history was a prerequisite, academic freedom would protect you against campus reprisals for Holocaust denial.

Omar Barghouti attempts to parse a series of tests of academic freedom, and in almost every instance gets it wrong. He begins by suggesting that universities need to be able "to discourage academics from engaging in acts or advocating views that are deemed bigoted, hateful, or incendiary." Of course it is state and federal law, not university policy, that ultimately govern incendiary speech. Setting aside the problem of deciding what is objectively hateful, the AAUP, the ACLU, and FIRE (the Foundation for Individual Rights in Education) all urge the same solution: corrective speech, not restrictions on speech. Does Barghouti suppose there was no such incendiary speech on Palestinian campuses during the Intifadas? Then he goes on to ask whether an academic institution should tolerate, under the rubric of academic freedom, a hypothetical lecturer's advocacy of the "Christianization of Brooklyn." As former AAUP General Secretary Ernie Benjamin pointed out in response, the answer is very simple: Yes. Barghouti assumes this example is one that his readers would reject out of hand because he has virtually no reliable understanding of academic freedom. Finally, just to be sure we will all be scandalized and that Jewish critics of the BDS campaign for an academic boycott of Israel will be shown to have a double standard, he asks whether "academics who uphold Nazi ideology . . . enjoy the right to advocate their views in class?" While we would insist on students' right to disagree, the AAUP would again answer "yes." What Barghouti really endorses is getting the right people in power so they can suppress speech of which he disapproves. His goal is selective academic tyranny, not academic freedom. And yet he is honored as a shining spokesperson for judgments about how universities should do business.

BDS advocates almost all solemnly and bizarrely suggest that Israeli universities are unique in "systematically providing the military-intelligence establishment with indispensable research." Have they considered comparable research on American campuses? University research in the US, Israel, and many other countries serves the nation state in ways many of us find objectionable. The AAUP argues that no classified research should be done on campus, a principle that should apply in all countries. Such a prohibition would help reduce the military-oriented university research that so troubles Barghouti in his essay. But it would not completely prohibit American, British, French, or Israeli universities from doing military research.

Many BDS advocates persist in saying the AAUP is hypocritical in having raised no objections to a comprehensive *economic* boycott of South Africa while objecting to a targeted *academic* boycott of Israel. They simply repeat this comparison despite the fact that any student could understand the difference between an economic and an academic boycott. If you track the cynical and contradictory way that BDS advocates deploy the concept of academic freedom you eventually realize that to many of them it means very little. Their essays repeatedly invoke the concept because it means something to us, their readers. They feel they can win us over if they appear to respect it.

In the end, BDS is more than willing to sacrifice academic freedom to its political agenda. American and Israeli academic freedom must be set aside in order to seek justice for Palestinians. The underlying logic—the implicit message being sent—was most frankly expressed in a 2014 *Harvard Crimson* column by Sandra Korn, an undergraduate. Titled "The Doctrine of Academic Freedom," the subtitle makes its argument explicit: "Let's give up on academic freedom in favor of justice." Korn endorses BDS, but she also wants to extend its principles to all teaching and research:

Student and faculty obsession with the doctrine of "academic freedom" often seems to bump against something I think much more important: academic justice . . . . When an academic community observes research promoting or justifying oppression, it should ensure that this research does not continue . . . After all, if we give up our obsessive reliance on the doctrine of academic freedom, we can consider more thoughtfully what is just.

Sami Hermez and Massoun Soukarieh give the BDS take on the same critique of academic freedom, arguing that "this concept is serving US interests rather than those of local people's struggles, that it is supporting power rather than speaking truth to power." Actually, academic freedom protects the right to speak truth to power, but not if there is only one truth you want to have spoken. Contrary to the argument by Corey Robin that opened this essay, signs of a new McCarthyism are in evidence among BDS supporters.

Perhaps the most shameless advocate of a new McCarthyism is Steven Salaita. In classic Orwellian doublespeak, he recalls the academic community's failure to honor academic freedom in the 1950s, then argues for academic boycott sanctions against Zionists. In a 2014 post on the University of Minnesota Press website, he assures us that "only individuals who consciously participate in advocacy for the Israeli state would be affected. Boycott transfers responsibility to the individual, but never targets her for preemptive exclusion." The new BDS McCarthyism is organized around an implicit question: "Are you now or have you ever been a Zionist?"

Salaita also condenses BDS wisdom into a continuing series of sophomoric, bombastic, or anti-Semitic 2014 tweets (https://twitter.com/stevesalaita): "UCSCdivest passes. Mark Yudoff nervously twirls his two remaining hairs, puts in an angry call to Janet Napolitano" (May 28); "10,000 students at USF call for divestment. The university dismisses it out of hand. That's Israel-style democracy" (May 28); "Somebody just told me F.W. DeKlerk doesn't believe Israel is an apartheid state. This is what Zionists have been reduced to" (May 28); "All of Israel's hand-wringing about demography leads one to only one reasonable conclusion: Zionists are ineffective lovers" (May 26); "Universities are filled with faculty and admins whose primary focus is policing criticism of Israel that exceeds their stringent preferences" (May 25); "'Israel army' and 'moral code' go together like polar bears and rainforests" (May 25); "Keep BDS going! The more time Israel spends on it, the fewer resources it can devote to pillaging and plundering" (May 23); "So, how long will it be before the Israeli government starts dropping white phosphorous on American college campuses?" (May 23); "Even the most tepid overture to Palestinian humanity can result in Zionist histrionics" (May 21); "All life is sacred. Unless you're a Zionist, for whom most life is a mere inconvenience to ethnographic supremacy" (May 20); "I fully expect the Israeli soldiers who murdered two teens in cold blood to receive a commendation or promotion" (May 20); "Understand that whenever a Zionist frets about Palestinian violence, it is a projection of his own brute psyche" (May 20); "I don't want to hear another damn word about 'nonviolence.' Save it for Israel's child-killing soldiers" (May 19); "I stopped listening at 'dialogue.'" (May 27). The last example here presumably advises BDS students how interested they should be in conversations with people holding different views. More recently he adds, "if Netanyahu appeared on TV with a necklace made from the teeth of Palestinian children, would anyone be surprised" (July 19) and "By eagerly conflating Jewishness and Israel, Zionists are partly responsible when people say antisemitic shit in response to Israeli terror" (July 18). It is remarkable that a senior faculty member chooses to present himself in public this way. Meanwhile, the mix of deadly seriousness and low comedy in this appeal to students is genuinely unsettling. As Salaita says of his opposition in an accusation better applied to himself, he has found in Twitter "the perfect medium" in which to "dispense slogans in order to validate collective self-righteousness" (May 14).

Barghouti is less crude, but he is writing from the same set of convictions: "Without adhering to a set of inclusive and evolving obligations, academic institutions and associations have little traction to discourage academics from engaging in acts or advocating views that are deemed bigoted, hateful, or incendiary." Summarizing Barghouti's parallel line of reasoning, Stanley Fish writes sardonically that "when something truly horrible is happening in the world, the niceties of academic freedom become a luxury we can't (and shouldn't) afford . . . academic freedom, traditionally understood as the freedom to engage in teaching and research free from the influences or pressures of politics, is being declared an obstacle to—even the enemy of—genuine freedom." Butler worries that "debates on academic freedom constitute something of a displacement of political analysis" that should be focused on Palestinian rights. Ignoring the historical record, Salaita announces that "academic freedom is a byproduct (and progenitor) of deeply conformist institutional cultures." Mullen and Barghouti decry academic freedom's "casual fetishization" as "part of a liberal hegemony" that places it above basic human rights, but the AAUP and other advocates of academic freedom do not rank it in relation to, say, the right to health care or the right to trial by a jury. Mullen castigates "academic freedom as part of a liberal hegemony that provides ideological cover for brutal acts of intellectual and political terror by Israel." But no one argues that academic freedom covers military action or justifies political terror. Barghouti claims that, by asserting that academic freedom is of "paramount importance," the AAUP "sharply limits the moral obligations of scholars in responding to situations of serious violations of human rights." The reality is that the AAUP takes no position on our global responsibility to fight human rights abuses. Supporting academic freedom and protesting violations of human rights are perfectly compatible activities, but they are not necessarily linked. Academic freedom is a privileged concept in the context of higher education. The AAUP accepts no shame in its unqualified promotion.

Contrary to the argument that Rima Najjar Kapitan makes in her contribution to the *JAF* issue—that "academic freedom is fundamental to our social order partly because of its relationship to other fundamental rights and values"—academic freedom's role in facilitating other human rights is very limited. Certainly it helps protect other human rights on campus, and, in those countries that honor the protection academic freedom gives to extramural speech, the contributions faculty and students make to public advocacy and debate. At the same time, academic freedom cannot thrive in broadly repressive regimes like those historically in power in East Germany, Libya, North Korea, South Africa, the Soviet Union, Iran, and Syria, among others. Nor does it exist in comprehensively restrictive and undemocratic regimes like Saudi Arabia or Singapore. Israel is not such a country. Academic freedom is alive and well west of the green line.

Academic freedom is a specialized right that is not legally implicated in the full spectrum of human rights that nations should honor. The AAUP does not, as Barghouti claims, advocate "privileging academic freedom above all other freedoms." It simply is not an international human rights organization. Perhaps all AAUP members would endorse "the ultimate ethical principle of the equal worth of all human lives," but the AAUP's primary organizational mission is the state of higher education in the United States. When other countries violate the AAUP's fundamental higher education principles, the organization condemns them for doing so if it has conclusive evidence, but it does not pretend to investigate either academic freedom or human rights throughout the world.

On the one hand, Mullen, Barghouti, and other BDS leaders claim to be defending academic freedom, while elsewhere in the same essays they actually disparage it. Salaita declares himself "tepid about academic freedom as a right" and adds "the preservation of academic freedom as a rights-based structure, in other words, shouldn't be the focus of our work." Sunaina Maira bloviates, "the boycott enlarges academic freedom for all." Academic boycotts aim to kill academic freedom in order to save it, but academic freedom is more fragile than the mythical phoenix. It will not rise triumphant from the ashes of the State of Israel. ■

Works Cited

"Academic group won't consider Israel boycott, but its mere discussion raises hackles." *Haaretz* (January 8, 2014). Available at http://www.haaretz.com/news/diplomacy-defense/1.567561

American Association of University Professors. "Protecting an Independent Faculty Voice: Academic Freedom after *Garcetti v. Ceballos.*" Available at http://www.aaup.org/NR/rdonlyres/B3991F98-98D5-4CC0-9102-ED26A7AA2892/0/Garcetti.pdf.

American Association of University Professors. *Recommended Principles to Guide Academy-Industry Relationships.* Washington, DC: AAUP, 2014. Distributed by the University of Illinois Press.

Barghouti, Omar. "Boycott, Academic Freedom, and the Moral Responsibility to Uphold Human Rights." *AAUP Journal of Academic Freedom* (Vol. 4, 2013). Available at http://www.aaup.org/sites/default/files/files/JAF/2013%20JAF/Barghouti.pdf

Beck, Edward S. "The key to preventing academic boycotts' successes in the future." *The Jerusalem Post* (January 6, 2014). Available at http://www.jpost.com/Opinion/Op-Ed-Contributors/The-key-to-preventing-academic-boycotts-successes-in-the-future-337283

Benjamin, Ernst. "Why I Continue to Support the AAUP Policy in Opposition To Academic Boycotts." *AAUP Journal of Academic Freedom* (Vol. 4, 2013). Available at http://www.aaup.org/sites/default/files/files/JAF/2013%20JAF/Responses/Response-Benjamin.pdf

Butler, Judith. "Israel/Palestine and the Paradoxes of Academic Freedom." *Radical Philosophy.* (January/February 2006), pp. 8-17. Available at http://www.egs.edu/faculty/judith-butler/articles/israel-palestine-paradoxes-of-academic-freedom/

Cheyfitz, Eric. "In Protest of Indifference: Academic Freedom and the American Studies Association." *Chronicle of Higher Education* (January 2, 2014). Available at http://chronicle.com/blogs/conversation/author/echeyfitz/.

Erakat, Noura. "Structural Violence on Trial: BDS and the Movement to Resist Erasure." *Los Angeles Review of Books* (March 16, 2014). Available at http://lareviewofbooks.org/essay/structural-violence-trial-bds-movement-resist-erasure.

Fish, Stanley. "Academic Freedom Against Itself: Boycotting Israeli Universities." *The New York Times* (Opinion Pages, October 28, 2013) Available at http://opinionator.blogs.nytimes.com/category/stanley-fish/

Hermez, Sami and Mayssoun Soukarieh. "Boycotts against Israel and the Question of Academic Freedom in American Universities in the Arab World." *AAUP Journal of Academic Freedom* (Vol. 4, 2013). Available at http://www.aaup.org/sites/default/files/files/JAF/2013%20JAF/HermezSoukarieh.pdf

Kapitan, Rima Najjar. "Academic Freedom Encompasses the Right to Boycott: Why the AAUP Should Support the Palestinian Call for the Academic Boycott of Israel." *AAUP Journal of Academic Freedom* (Vol. 4, 2013). Available at http://www.aaup.org/sites/default/files/files/JAF/2013%20JAF/Kapitan.pdf

Korn, Sandra Y. L. "The Doctrine of Academic Freedom." *The Harvard Crimson* (February 18, 2014). Available at http://www.thecrimson.com/column/the-red-line/article/2014/2/18/academic-freedom-justice/?page=single

Lloyd, David and Malini Johar Schueller. "The Israeli State of Exception and the Case for Academic Boycott." *AAUP Journal of Academic Freedom* (Vol. 4, 2013). Available at http://www.aaup.org/sites/default/files/files/JAF/2013%20JAF/LloydSchueller.pdf

Maira, Sunaina. "The BDS movement and the front lines of the war on academic freedom." University of Minnesota Press web page. (April 9, 2014). Available at www.uminpressblog.com.

Metzger, Walter P. "The 1940 Statement of Principles on Academic Freedom and Tenure." *Law And Contemporary Problems* (Summer 1990) 53: 3, pp. 3-77.

Mullen, Bill V. "Palestine, Boycott, and Academic Freedom: A Reassessment Introduction." *AAUP Journal of Academic Freedom* (Vol. 4, 2013). Available at http://www.aaup.org/sites/default/files/files/JAF/2013%20JAF/Mullen.pdf

Nelson, Cary. "Defining Academic Freedom." *Inside Higher Education* (December 21, 2010). Available at http://www.insidehighered.com/views/2010/12/21/nelson_on_academic_freedom#sthash.BPgMip8u.dpbs

Nelson, Cary. "Neve Gordon's Academic Freedom." *Inside Higher Education.* (September 5, 2009). Available at http://www.insidehighered.com/views/2009/09/15/nelson#sthash.qvWqnWYu.dpbs

Robin, Corey. "Does the ASA Boycott Violate Academic Freedom? A Roundtable." (December 23, 2013) Available at http://coreyrobin.com/2013/12/23/does-the-asa-boycott-violate-academic-freedom-a-roundtable/

Robin, Corey. "The New McCarthyites: BDS, Its Critics, and Academic Freedom." (January 8, 2014) Available at http://coreyrobin.com/2014/01/08/the-new-mccarthyites-bds-its-critics-and-academic-freedom/

Robin, Corey. "But for the boycott there would be academic freedom." (February 6, 2014) Available at http://coreyrobin.com/2014/02/06/but-for-the-boycott-there-would-be-academic-freedom/

Salailta, Steven. "The definition of academic freedom, for many, does not accommodate dissent." University of Minnesota Press web page. (April 16, 2014). Available at www.uminpressblog.com.

GABRIEL NOAH BRAHM AND
ASAF ROMIROWSKY

Anti-Semitic in Intent
if Not in Effect:

Questions of Bigotry, Dishonesty, and Shame

I
t was a question of questions. Both asked and unasked. Answered and unanswered. And, most of all, questions answered badly—prompting more questions to be asked.

At the January 2014 annual gathering of the Modern Language Association (MLA) in Chicago, papers were given on the usual range of specialized topics in literary studies; candidates for jobs in English were interviewed; and the association of experts on modern language took extraordinary steps toward establishing a foreign policy. Starting small—presumably out of a sense of proportion indicated by modesty, given their lack of qualifications in this area—the professors of English, etc., prudently chose to begin with a proposal aimed solely at just one tiny country. As if to say, the more miniscule the target, the better—forgetting that although relatively small things may look easier to blast, they require better aim, even with big guns like national organizations the size of the MLA.

Yet not without precedent did the academic boycott lobby inside the MLA select their strategy of largely meaningless, if vociferous, denunciation of Israel in particular. Cleverly, like the United Nations itself in this way—no doubt the MLA activists were aware that three-fourths of all UN resolutions that single out a lone country for criticism by the General Assembly have been aimed at the Jewish state—the professors of various literatures knew just where to begin healing the world, by piling on with the "language." Moreover, not just the UNGA, but a smaller and less important MLA sister organization—the American Studies Association (ASA)—had also recently decided on a similarly cowardly course of action, and even went as far as voting to endorse the boycott of Israeli academic institutions. While the problems with a corrupt General Assembly are no secret (its motives for attacking Israel, mostly symbolically and out of all proportion, are well understood by that institution's observers), the ASA's weird decision to pick now to get in on the Israel-bashing phenomenon of many years raised a question. Why?

Which in turn gave rise to an answer.

As explained by ASA President, Professor Curtis Marez, in what quickly became an infamous joke—although/because he really was serious (he actually said it), "You have to start somewhere."

The inanity and appalling ignorance of this irresponsible statement aside, taken seriously (as meant) for the sake of argument, Marez's question-begging response begs the further question: Why not, then, simply "start" the American Studies scholars' campaign for justice in the world beyond America's borders a little more ambitiously—with the announcement of an even-handed policy, directed at the type(s) of injustice that the ASA membership presumably, rightly, abhors, wherever such wrongdoing rears its ugly head? Nor would a politically neutral, balanced, ethically universalist approach need to have been interpreted absurdly as mandating action everywhere all at once (as some of ASA's defenders have mockingly claimed), but would instead have served to clarify the organizations' mission and intent. Is it to help redress wrongs committed by the imperfect Jewish state alone? Or, do the professional Americanists, more reasonably and morally, have an interest in human rights and scholars' rights around the world, as these are imperiled daily by states far more imperfect than tiny, liberal-democratic, Israel, and with which the US also has strong ties?

Understandably, such questions begat more questions—until the whole ASA scheme and its aftermath came to seem…questionable, indeed. If, for example, because of the perceived wrongdoings of a government, an academic organization is going to boycott *fellow academics*—which was the ASA's "brilliant" strategy—and it wants to do so on the *basis of nationality* and in the name of *academic freedom*, well, is that not first of all itself a violation of academic freedom? And second, but no less important, an ethno-racist policy, too? Dubious enough tactics in general, right? Except it's worse than that—when one recalls that the supposed transgression under indictment by today's "progressive" academic organizations is precisely (what else?) Israel's own ostensible (purported) inhibition of *academic freedom* on *ethno-nationalist* grounds! Moreover, if any of that were the real issue with Israel (instead of a red herring, given Israel's vibrant and free academic culture) then why not at least (for appearances' sake if nothing else) shun as well the academics of China, Turkey, Russia, or even the United States? Since none of these countries are above criticism when it comes to what Israel gets branded with by its obsessed detractors—the violation of "human rights," "occupation," disrespect for "indigeneity," etc.—one would have thought that the *American Studies Association* might have found ample reason to boycott *itself* first of all, on these sorts of grounds.

But once you open up a can of worms, why not go further and question the policies of such model states as Iran, Syria or North Korea—places where, very much *un*like Israel, with its thriving civil society, there is *no academic or political freedom*? If, that is, you, with your can-of-worms opener, were serious about "starting somewhere" *appropriate* that made real sense, in a genuine campaign to better the world. Instead, the ASA chose to start with Israel—a country born heroically out of the national liberation struggle of a small minority of the earth's population, the Jewish people, in a movement to free itself from centuries of European endo-colonization, by renewing its ties to its own indigenous lands, and facing the kind of menace that turned out to include the only truly global-eliminationist genocide in history. Had Zionism succeeded in establishing a state by, say, 1933, would there have been a Holocaust? Questions, questions—Marez's "answer" about where to *start* just begs so many of them, it's hard to know where to *stop*!

For example, there is even the question (dare we say it? dare we not?) of *anti-Semitism* in the movement to boycott Israel. After all, when today's "new" anti-Semitism (as it's called) distinguishes itself qualitatively from just more of the same "old" kind, it does so largely on the basis of attacks against not only Jews but the Jewish state, some of which even go so far as advocating an end to Israel as a Jewish state. For this is the *sine qua non* of peace, freedom, and justice in the world. So, is not the very proposition of boycotts with the intent of helping to eventually wipe Israel from the map anti-Semitic by definition? While those in the academic boycotts movement (in this not unlike most Jew-haters around the world today) have disdain for the discredited, moldy old label, "anti-Semite" (even members of Hamas and its supporters reject the accusation), they proudly emblazon the term "anti-Zionist" upon their escutcheons (again, in line with virtually all kinds of resurgent anti-Semitism today). So there is a question here too. Has the world really forgotten what this reviled thing *Zionism*—which it is assumed to be so respectable to declare oneself openly "anti-"—really was and is? Namely, the movement for the self-preservation (only partly successful) and autonomy of a people no less beleaguered by oppression than any in history.

Questions, questions. Yet, with the ASA's previous blunder as recently established precedent, committed portions of the MLA were in no mood for a history lesson—but instead, activists in that organization merely followed suit, in a competition to see which organization could pass a more mindless resolution more thoughtlessly. Thus, at the January 2014 convention in Chicago, there came to be a "roundtable" discussion given over entirely to denouncing the Jewish state. Organized by a wing of the pro-boycotts, anti-Israel lobby internal to the MLA, it was a part of larger efforts to promote a "BDS" agenda (Boycotts, Divestments, and Sanctions against the Jewish state) within academia. And it offered no better justification for such an agenda than Professor Marez had given when queried—which tells you something. To wit: Professor Barbara Harlow, when asked from the floor a question similar to that put to the ASA President ("Of all the nations in all the trouble-spots on earth, why have you chosen Israel in particular for censure?"), responded blithely: "Why not?" It was symptomatic. It was gestures like that which tended to indicate that the MLA leaders of the academic and cultural boycotts movement might actually be as ignorant—if not, indeed, incurious—about the special object of their peculiar ire as the ASA as a whole seemed to be.

Which brings us to the question of yet another question: What else besides ignorance might this all be a sign of? Are such oddly unabashed, uncannily parallel expressions of indifference to the very issues ostensibly up for debate merely a random feature of this particular discussion? Or, are these symptoms symptomatic precisely of what often happens when self-styled scholar-activists voice opinions outside their fields of expertise, as (often poorly informed) activists rather than scholars per se? But if that were so (and while everyone's got a right to an opinion), then why should their— our!—scholarly organizations be allowed to be used as anyone's preferred organs of protest on matters outside of their field of study? Scholars stand for scholarship. Putting a scholarly seal on anti-Israelism isn't kosher.

Shamefully, it was after several more hours of such "answers" to the question of what was going on, most of them resembling Harlow's shrug, that at the end of the day (literally), the Delegate Assembly (DA) of the MLA approved a proposal to put a proposal critical of Israel before the full membership, a question to be voted on by the organization as a whole in the months ahead (as yet an undecided issue at the time of this writing). What this means is that much of what was said at the DA meeting in January to justify the MLA's considering a foray into foreign policy made no more sense than the hullaballoo that BDS supporters now routinely seek to stir up—as a way of casting aspersions almost as an end in itself. In fact, the MLA proposed resolution's chief architects—Professors Richard Ohmann, and Bruce Robbins—*as much as admitted defeat* of their original idea, in terms of any real substance their proposal might have ever been thought to have had. They had to, in order to try to save face, when it was quickly made clear that what they had spent god-knows how long drafting didn't make any factual or moral sense. And so it was that they themselves were forced to question—throw out—much of what they had planned to ask for an answer about, in the form of a vote, from members of the DA!

Thus: in response to criticisms from concerned fellow MLA members prior to any voting whatsoever, they—the proposal's chief advocates themselves—drastically cut portions that were easily shown to be manifestly absurd, leaving just a rump statement that was even crazier (more illogical) than the one they had thought was as good as any place to "start" from (because "why not?"). So: here's what happened. Instead of a resolution, as first formulated, protesting against Israel's policy toward those scholars wishing to visit Gaza (mention of which was excised soon after the would-be critics' critics pointed out that Israel hasn't occupied Gaza for years, and Egypt anyway controls its southern border-crossing, making the singling out of Israel in this regard even more problematic); instead of language condemning Israel for "arbitrary" denials of entry to the country (removed as well after other MLA members asked for evidence of arbitrariness, and the foes of Israel could produce none): instead, a significantly redacted resolution was finally put forward. But yet it still only passed by just seven votes out of 113 ballots cast!

Listen to this: The statement as finally forwarded had eliminated from it all reference to *either* Gaza *or* arbitrariness, which seemed fair enough. Except when one paused to recall that without the erroneous bits about *arbitrariness* and travel to *Gaza*, there was *nothing left* on which to base the original claim of the MLA's having a professional obligation to respond to a U.S. State Department Travel Warning—which, in point of fact, is a prudent warning that applies not to Israel at all but to Gaza, because it is governed by a terrorist organization. Hamas! Without the claim that Israel denies entry to its national territory "arbitrarily," in other words (just for fun, lacking reasons, because the Jewish state is a gang of fascists), there was nothing left of the original claim at issue. All the resolution finally "accused" Israel of was controlling its borders because of security concerns, as do the governments of all nations. Bizarrely, as the five and a half hour meeting of the Delegate Assembly dragged on, "Why not?" had morphed into "So what?" before the assembled delegate's eyes. And in order to avoid having to answer real questions such as those we have raised here. Questions some even tried to raise at the meeting itself, although it wasn't easy for Israel supporters to get a chance at the mic that day, for reasons that were reported on in *Inside Higher Education, The Chronicle of Higher Education*, and elsewhere.[23]

What it came down to was that, in spite of the emptiness of the resolution's final wording (or rather, precisely because of it!), there was a feeling in the room that had to be assuaged, stimulated by the committed BDSers in attendance (of which there appeared to have been about 60). The feeling seemed to be that Israel simply *had* to be deemed somehow uniquely to blame for something—and so it was. And so it was that a purely symbolic proposed resolution, void of content, logic, or substance, was approved by a slim margin to be put before the membership for a final vote later on in the year, with a clear intent of nothing more (or less) than stigmatizing Israel in the hopes of lending credence to the cause of those who question its very legitimacy, and would deny its right to existence as a UN member state.

So it was that Bigoted, Dishonest, and Shameful (BDS) *double-standards* aimed at *demonizing* and *delegitimating* Israel—Natan Sharansky's "3D Test of Anti-Semitism" in relation to the Jewish state—were firmly in place and fully in effect where one might naively have thought least to find them.[24] And, thus precisely it is that we believe BDS to be, in actuality, a movement that is anti-Semitic, first and foremost, *in intent*—if indeed, hopefully not, as it appears from the gutted resolution's meaningless wording, in effect. With apologies to Lawrence Summers for our inversion of his well-known formula to fit the absurd circumstances of the MLA's "postmodern" politics—a view of the world in which image is thought to be everything and reality nothing—it appears that it is in fact the intent to create an image that is, in this case, the only real effect.

Now let's be crystal clear: the BDS insistence on the Palestinian "right of return" and an end to the "greater occupation" of "all Arab lands" in a territory stretching "from the river to the sea" is the *antithesis of a call for peace* and reconciliation between two peoples in a compromise solution that would allow both a place in the sun, side by side in some kind of harmony.[25] Rather, it becomes painfully apparent that, for committed extremists of the academic and cultural boycotts movement, Palestinian identity is now conceived of as synonymous with three things—all non-starters in any peace negotiations with a chance of success, as everyone knows who is serious. For BDS trumpets: (1) the "right of return"; (2) the permanent, sanctified struggle with Israel until the bitter end, without genuine recognition of the Jewish state or real, meaningful compromise; and (3) perpetual recognition of the Palestinian's own status and *that of all their descendants until the end of time* as refugees, dispossessed of the land of Israel/Palestine with the connivance of the international community. More reasonably, however—since many, if not most, of the originally displaced victims of the 1948 *Nakba* would presumably be dead by now of old age or close to it—others have referred to the actual refugee problem as a diminishing, not growing, one. The actual refugee problem per se simply can't go on forever and becomes increasingly moot, ironically enough, due to what might be termed, albeit sadly yet inevitably, "facts in the ground." But Israel's haters won't mourn the dead and with that let their hatred die too, which they instead seek to keep alive and pass on from generation to generation.

To make matters worse, those stalwart BDSers, who know better, often seek to evade the "anti-Semitic" (because anti-Zionist) label, by resorting to ignoring or covering up what Palestinians say *in Arabic* about their political demands; the definition of their national identity; and widespread attitudes toward Israelis. While not unique to American "scholarly activism" (or is it "activist scholarship"?), this linguistic security fence is unfortunately often an obstruction to constructive American and European engagement with the Middle East—a structural feature of the rhetorical landscape that effectively forces meaningful discussion miles out of its way, thus avoiding the real issues at stake both inside academe and beyond. For, while the problematic phrase "right of return" is sometimes explained away as inherently symbolic by definition, rather than practical, just an element of the Palestinian "narrative" regarding the blameless circumstances of their diaspora; Israelis are in fact compelled in many ways to confront real demands along these lines, faced with interlocutors who insist both that they ("the Jews" or at most "the Zionist entity") accept the narrative in which they are the villains, and with it the possibility of a mass migration of Palestinians to Israel that would, by design, put an end to Israel as a Jewish and democratic state of all its citizens. Which is what it is.

These hardcore positions promoted by BDS, either blindly (in some cases perhaps) or with open eyes (as is plainly the case with others) are the opposite of any notion of a just settlement that both parties to a dispute over territory—two nations, one Palestinian and one Jewish—could ever possibly agree on. Tellingly, even liberal critics of Israeli government policies from within the Jewish community, such as Rabbi Chaim Seidler-Feller of UCLA Hillel, have concluded that this means, "*BDS is poison* and Omar Barghouti is a classic anti-Semite."[26] Did we mention that the same Omar Barghouti—the celebrity BDS spokesman, educated at Tel Aviv University, ironically—was on the "roundtable" with Barbara Harlow and Richard Ohmann? Well we should have. For he was!

And regarding Seidler-Feller's observation, we could not have said it better ourselves. Although we have both been saying more or less the same, in other words, for some time, along with others. Moreover, even the notorious Norman Finkelstein, who has gone so far as to accuse Jews in print of using the Holocaust for their own gain, has described the BDS movement as "a hypocritical, dishonest cult," led by "dishonest gurus" who want to "selectively enforce the law" by posing as human rights activists.[27] It is revealing, is it not, when not only radical critics of Israel, like the mad (former?) Professor Finkelstein, but even Palestinian "moderates," such as Mahmoud Abbas (aka Abu Mazen, who is, according to *Wikipedia*, both the "Chairman of the Palestinian Liberation Organization" and "President of the State of Palestine"), detach themselves from BDS and speak against it? Because BDS is poison. Even/especially those whom the movement claims to represent know it. Why, then, without the support of the Palestinian Authority even, does BDS push on?

Because, in spite of our questions, BDS supporters disingenuously claim that their brand of criticism of Israel is legitimate, even necessary, and that their positions are based in "real concern" for the well-being of the Palestinians. In fact, their strategy is clearly to target Israel and its advocates for stigmatization by nationality, holding citizens of the world's only Jewish state to a far different, unrealistically high, standard, set by rules not applied to other countries—including both miserable dictatorships and leading democracies in far less difficult circumstances. Amidst flowery "anti-imperialist" rhetoric, the movement sugarcoats its toxic medicine, misleadingly implying that merely ending specific Israeli policies, deemed "apartheid" practices in their intentionally inflammatory words, would satisfy its backers. In fact, BDS supporters envision the replacement of Israel as a Jewish and democratic state with a bi-national, majority Palestinian, entity—otherwise known as a greater Palestine in a world without Israel.

But the academic activists don't want people to know this. Thus, to try to help get the word out, one of us, Gabriel Brahm, among others (including specifically fellow authors of chapters in this book, Russell Berman, Cary Nelson and Ilan Troen) had to resort to joining a panel billed as the "alternative MLA" session in Chicago. This was organized by MLA Members for Scholars' Rights, and held *across the street* from the "real MLA," in response to the organization's decision to host an exclusively pro-boycott/anti-Israel roundtable which we have mentioned above). Brahm argued then and there on our behalf (with Romirowsky in the audience), and in no uncertain terms, that "*the stigma that properly attaches to anti-Semitism should adhere as well to anti-Zionism.*"

We conclude this essay therefore by *reiterating that claim here, unequivocally.* The latter incarnation of bigotry is but a species of the former. For, when a people is denied its right to self-determination, that's an attack upon that people, as a people. Moreover, there is no way that "debates" about a cultural blockade of Israel can fail to affect the Jewish residents of all countries disproportionately—given that for most of us, if not all, Israel is a distinctive marker of identity, no less important to Jews than the Koran, for example, is to most

Muslims. Denigration of anyone's ethnic identity—despoliation of a community's symbols—is incompatible with the values of multiculturalism and diversity, or what Hannah Arendt called more precisely the fact of "plurality" as a defining property of the human condition (see her famous remonstration of Adolf Eichmann for "not wanting to share the earth" with others in her controversial book, *Eichmann in Jerusalem*).[28] While certain so-called "stealth writers," like Professor Vijay Prashad, holder of the Edward Said Chair in American studies at the American University of Beirut, may choose to downplay, on occasion, for the purposes of public media consumption, the underlying genocidal intent of "mere anti-Zionism," it is both explicitly and implicitly there in the BDS movement. Frankly, we find it hard to imagine that any holder of an "Edward Said Chair" in anything (let alone American studies as it has come to be practiced) could fail to be aware of this fact, even if he doesn't bother to mention it when writing for a broad audience that could be expected to recoil from the full implications of Said's own explicit rejection of two states for two peoples.[29]

Moreover, with admiring/fawning students of Said (including, most prominently, the cultural theorist and *cult figure*, Judith Butler) at its philosophical core, the movement for academic and cultural shunning of Israel—the anti-Israel boycott lobby, understood as an outgrowth and organ of the "new anti-Zionist anti-Semitism"—is a movement against the Jews as a distinctive thread in the tapestry of humanity. It is a racist—anti-Semitism is a form of racism—movement. Anti-Zionism—anti-Zionism is a form of anti-Semitism—is immoral and, indeed, in its current guise as a campaign that proposes embargoing scholarship as a "place to start" since "why not," another self-inflicted wound to the reputation of today's university in crisis, or what one might term a "crime against the humanities." For it is no secret that anti-Zionism is the sort of prejudice that would see a Jewish state selectively excised from the map no less surely than the "old" anti-Semitism would like to have seen the Jewish people erased from the face of the earth. This must be faced, because if prominent individuals like Butler and others are allowed to dominate the scene in academia—if they succeed at shaping the kind of discussions happening on campuses regarding Israel—then extreme voices will have set the tone of a messed up discussion. MLA members like Ohmann and Harlow will carry the day. This must not be—for, how long before unchecked crimes against the humanities help inspire more crimes against humanity?

So! Questions, questions. Will scholarship carry the day on campus after all? Will the full membership of the MLA have the courage, decency, and good sense to vote down the proposed resolution put forth by its BDS inspired General Assembly? Or will debased excuses for real academic work continue to flourish in an age of declining literacy, leading to even greater ignorance and who-knows-what sort of outcomes down the line? The immensely learned doyen of Middle East Studies, Bernard Lewis, once explained the success of Edward Said's otherwise shoddy, theoretically incoherent and factually inaccurate proto-BDS primer, *Orientalism*, as residing centrally in its author's opportunistic cleverness, directed at transforming a single word, "orientalism"—a term that had always referred simply to an area of academic specialty, one focusing on societies and cultures of the Middle East, North Africa and Asia—into a term of abuse. As Lewis prophesied, upon its publication, Said's *Orientalism* began changing the face of Middle East studies across North America—as many Middle East classes began to present to students the Arab-Israeli conflict solely through a distorted lens of anti-Zionism. For to do otherwise would make one "orientalist."

Now, decades later, in a time when not just the study of the Middle East but the humanities and social sciences more broadly are under attack from a corporate America in quest of greater "efficiency" and profits—just as, probably not coincidentally, "functional" illiteracy is well on the way to becoming the "new normal" for nearly half the American population—the academic boycotters' retreat away from serious engagement of issues and into anti-intellectual demonology bears all the marks of what Richard Hofstadter long ago identified as the "paranoid style in American politics." As such, BDS's Manichean rhetoric offers the Israel-bashers of the world some old bottles, too—along with what's "new" about anti-Semitism today—into which they funnel the gasoline of their inchoate dissatisfaction with a much more complex reality. The yield is a fiery rag-stuffed cocktail of resentment, so easily and thrillingly hurled against readily identifiable stereotypes and made-to-order scapegoats.

In this context, if the MLA Delegate Assembly really wanted to do something "radical," it might consider a resolution not against Israel but against grade inflation on the one hand (a) and (b) the proletarianization of the professoriate on the other. Until then, imprudent, badly researched and unfair proposed resolutions like the ones approved lately in turn by the ASA as a whole, and the one put forward by the DA of the MLA (again, bearing heavily in mind that as this book goes to press the full membership of the latter still has to decide whether or not to endorse what its delegates have voted to put before them) will stand as glaring symptoms of our detractors' worst fears about us (we, the tenured, or, increasingly, untenured radicals on college campuses).

Which leaves us with just *one more* question: Why is it even a question? The "place [and time] to start" defending liberal values (academic freedom among others), by rejecting BDS demagoguery, is here and now. ∎

EMILY BUDICK

When a Boycott Is Not Moral Action but Social Conformity and the "Affectation of Love"

Boycotts, sanctions, and divestments are powerful political tools. When they work, they are highly preferable to violence and military intervention. Precisely for this reason it has to be very clear to anyone supporting such a strategy what a boycott is boycotting, and why. Since the BDS movement against Israel has emerged on the American scene as a stormy debate in several academic organizations and among intellectuals generally, the questions of when a boycott is a legitimate tool of political pressure and what it means to join such a movement have become inescapable issues, at least for those of us who wish to consider ourselves morally and ethically committed human beings.

Following is the BDS against Israel statement of purpose, as presented on its website and as repeated several times in co-founder Omar Barghouti's book *BDS: Boycott, Divestment, Sanctions—The Global Struggle for Palestinian Rights*. The statement, we are told, both on the site and in the book, represents the call of Palestinian civil society, and there is ample citation to confirm this claim. It also, we might note, follows closely on the position of the Palestinian Authority in its negotiations with the Israeli government concerning a peace agreement that might bring an end to the conflict. For these reasons, it is imperative to take the BDS platform with utmost seriousness. Here is the platform:

The call urges various forms of boycott against Israel until it meets its obligations under international law by:

1. Ending its occupation and colonization of all Arab lands occupied in June 1967 and dismantling the Wall;
2. Recognizing the fundamental rights of the Arab-Palestinian citizens of Israel to full equality; and
3. Respecting, protecting, and promoting the rights of Palestinian refugees to return to their homes and properties as stipulated in UN Resolution 194.

"Respecting, protecting, and promoting the rights of Palestinian refugees to return to their homes and properties as stipulated in UN Resolution 194" is nothing less than a call for the dissolution of the State of Israel as the homeland of the Jewish people. It is also the call for the dissolution of a fully constituted and recognized nation among nations, a nation that was established by an international vote in the United Nations and where eight million citizens now reside.

Of all the many things that might be said in opposition to the Boycott, Divestment, and Sanctions movement against Israel, the one I want to focus on (albeit not exclusively) is the failure of many of those who have signed on to its agenda to understand or, at least, to take seriously what that agenda is and how its ultimate objective is *not* what many supporters of the BDS suppose. The objective of the BDS is *not* the end of the military occupation by Israel of lands taken in the 1967 War between Israel and the Arab nations. It is *not* a two-state solution to the Israeli-Palestinian conflict. If that were not clear enough from point three of the platform, Barghouti's book leaves us in no doubt that the boycott is not about anything so finite and achievable as the restoration of lands taken by Israel in 1967 (some of them lands originally partitioned to Israel in 1948):

> For decades, but especially since the Oslo accords signed by Israel and the Palestine Liberation Organization (PLO) in 1993, Israel, with varying degrees of collusion from successive US administrations, the European Union, and complacent Arab "leaders," has attempted to redefine the Palestinian people to include only those who live in Palestinian territory occupied in 1967. The main objective has been to deceptively reduce the question of Palestine to a mere dispute over some 'contested' territory occupied by Israel since 1967, thus excluding the UN-sanctioned rights of the majority of the Palestinian people. (6)

And later in the book:

> Rather than focusing on the true objectives of the BDS movement—
> realizing Palestinian rights by ending Israeli oppression against all three
> segments of the indigenous Palestinian people—members of the Zionist
> "left" often reduce the struggle to ridding Israel of 'the occupation,' pre-
> senting BDS as a 'weapon' to *save Israel*, essentially as an apartheid, exclu-
> sivist state. . . . The heart of the BDS Call is not the diverse boycotting
> acts it urges but this rights-based approach that addresses the three basic
> rights corresponding to the main segments of the Palestinian people [:]
> Ending Israel's occupation, ending its apartheid, and ending its denial of
> the right of refugees to return (32-33)

I accept that the case against the existence of Israel or against any other
nation can be argued and counter-argued. In the case of the existence of the
State of Israel, I believe that the arguments for its destruction can be refuted,
especially since many of the BDS's accusations (such as Israel being a colonizer or an apartheid state) are patently untrue, as I shall show. My major point
in this essay, however, is that many of those who support the BDS movement
against Israel do not actually believe that Israel has any right to exist.

Therefore, I want to address the support of the Boycott, Divestment, and
Sanctions movement against Israel by prominent American academic groups
(such as the American Studies Association), through quotations from two
important philosophical figures: one the 19th-century American philosopher
so fundamental to everything Americans understand individualism and social
conscience to be: Ralph Waldo Emerson; the other the twentieth-century
writer who deals with a subject not unrelated to the existence of the State of
Israel and the boycott movement: Tzvetan Todorov. These are not easy writers. What both of them remind us is that nothing less than careful thinking
and moral courage are the prerequisites to whatever we understand ethical
action to be.

I quote first from the Emerson essay alluded to in my title, "Self-Reliance":

> Whoso would be a man must be a nonconformist. He who would gather
> immortal palms must not be hindered by the name of goodness, but must
> explore if it be goodness. Nothing is at last sacred but the integrity of
> your own mind. Absolve you to yourselves, and you shall have the suf-
> frage of the world. I remember an answer which, when quite young I
> was prompted to make to a valued adviser, who was wont to importune
> me with the dear old doctrines of the church. On my saying, What have
> I to do with the sacredness of traditions, if I live wholly from within? my

friend suggested,—"But these impulses may be from below, not from above." I replied, "They do not seem to me to be such; but if I am the Devil's child, I will live then from the Devil." No law can be sacred to me but that of my nature. Good and bad are but names very readily transferable to that or this; the only right is what is after my constitution, the only wrong what is against it. A man is to carry himself in the presence of all opposition, as if everything were titular and ephemeral but he. I am ashamed to think how easily we capitulate to badges and names, to large societies and institutions. (122-23)

I will continue with this passage in a moment, trying to explicate some of the complexity of Emerson's thought (and I apologize, in passing, for having to quote a gender-biased text; I'll return to this in a moment). First, however, I want to quote a related comment from Tzvetan Todorov in order to reinforce what I take to be the difference between the "integrity" of a moral position and "conformity" (122) with some sort of majority consensus that consists more of badges and names than the studied investigation of the good and the bad. To repeat: my argument in this essay is that there are too many folks simply jumping on the nearest bandwagon without bothering to ask where that bandwagon is headed and what it stands for.

So, here is Todorov in *Facing the Extreme: Moral Life in the Concentration Camps*, written in the aftermath of the Holocaust:

To denounce slavery constitutes a moral act only at those times when such denunciation is not simply a matter of course and thus involves some personal risk. There is nothing moral in speaking out against slavery today; all it proves is that I'm in step with my society's ideology or else don't want to find myself on the wrong side of the barricades. Something very similar can be said about condemnations of racism, although that would not have been the case in 1936 in Germany. (116)

The reference to slavery and anti-Semitism returns me to the Emerson passage I interrupted above, which continues in the vein taken up a century later by Todorov:

If an angry bigot assumes this bountiful cause of Abolition, and comes to me with his latest news from Barbadoes, why should I not say to him: "Go love thy infant, love thy woodchopper, be good-natured and modest: have that grace; and never varnish your hard, uncharitable ambition with this incredible tenderness for black folk a thousand miles off. Thy love afar is spite at home (123).

Both Emerson and Todorov point to two salient characteristics of moral thinking and action. One is the requirement that each and every one of us investigate the truth and examine for ourselves what constitutes "the good" and what does not. The other is the necessity for honesty in one's convictions, which is to say, also, the necessity of placing oneself, and not only the object of one's criticism, under suspicion. One cannot rail against slavery elsewhere, Emerson points out, if one tolerates it at home; nor, to cite Todorov, can one claim as moral *courage* taking a position with which everyone agrees, even if the position itself is moral. How many people today would argue for the morality of racism, anti-Semitism, slavery, or the occupation of other people's lands? To be sure, there are racists, anti-Semites, xenophobes, enslavers, and occupiers (colonial and otherwise). But the consensus, at least in the Western world, has shifted, and it takes neither courage nor particular erudition to argue against the deprivation of individual or communal rights. "Your good must have some edge to it," as Emerson puts it, "—else it is none" (123).

I eliminated sexism from my list of "isms" in order to get back to Emerson's gendered text. In being insensitive (to the point of giving offence in the 21st century) to the issue of women, even as he is arguing the case for African slaves in the United States, Emerson is doing no more and no less than speaking as a nineteenth-century man. My point here is not that we have to accept Emerson's gender bias. Quite the contrary. If we follow Emerson's idea of self-reliance, we have to oppose it. And that is the deep value of Emerson's philosophy: it doesn't just provide a catalogue of sacred laws or moral precepts. Rather, it constructs an enduring structure for self-conscious moral thinking. We are required by Emerson's logic to confront the contradictions of Emerson's own thought. We are also, however, required to apply to ourselves the same examination of contradiction, bias, and inattention that we level against him. What in our moral positions today, we must always be asking ourselves, constitutes, like Emerson's sexism, unexamined bias? What do we do about the fact that, insofar as we exist within a culture whose terms we accept, we likely cannot see our own prejudices until someone from outside or in the future reflects them back to us: our relationship to animals, for example. How will that seem several generations hence?

The issue of women is not irrelevant to a discussion of BDS and Israel, since sexist beliefs and even legislation are rampant in almost all the communities of the Middle East that stand so staunchly against the State of Israel and that are major players in the attacks against Israel, whether political (like BDS) or military. It might be noted that women of all the communities in Israel enjoy full rights by national law, although, of course, there is still gender imbalance in Israel (as elsewhere in the world, including the United States). This imbalance, it might be noted in passing, is most severe (it is also most violent) within *some* (by no means all) of the Arab and Bedouin communities in Israel, where bigamy and honor killings still exist and where Israeli law seems to these communities a violation of their cultural and religious rights. A major domestic issue facing the State of Israel is how to navigate between the rights of cultural difference and the law of the land, which defines honor killings and bigamy as criminal offenses.

According to Emerson, one cannot take someone else's word for who or what constitutes evil: integrity requires deciding that for oneself and acting accordingly. When Emerson says that no law can be sacred to him but that of his own nature, he is not suggesting that what he or any one of us believes is necessarily right. It is possible, he admits, that the voice of internal conscience that speaks to him emanates from the devil. Yet Emerson is quick to insert that he does not really think that this is the case. He would "write upon the lintels of the door-post, *Whim*, . . . hop[ing] it is somewhat better than whim at last," but also knowing that "we cannot spend the day in explanation"(123). For the sake of argument, Emerson is willing to play devil's advocate. "The doctrine of hatred," remarks Emerson, "must be preached as the counteraction of the doctrine of love when that pules and whines"—*counter-action*, we must note, not philosophical or ethical assertion, and only when the doctrine of love (the old doctrines of the church, as Emerson puts it earlier) is so much façade and hypocrisy (123). Emerson does believe that human beings have an innate moral sense, a position with which some might disagree. But he also believes that that conscience is far more than what he calls in the essay the "nonchalance" of boys (122). For this reason, Emerson begins an essay on the subject of self-reliance with quotations from other thinkers. Emerson is not advocating ignorance. He is, rather, here as elsewhere, advocating intelligent, philosophical, and moral thinking, and he will, if necessary, shock us into such philosophical and moral thought. Emerson is getting at what is finally a fairly obvious truth: that the only law that one can obey, the only law, therefore, that can acquire the status of a sacred law or a divine commandment is the one that comes from within and for which one can thereby assume personal responsibility. That law might well coincide with scripture. It also, however, might not. The individual has to figure this out for him or herself.

One does not have to be more than a casual student of history to observe that what seems moral to one generation or one segment of a population can seem immoral to another. To take, again, the example that both Emerson and Todorov cite: slavery before the Civil War was not only upheld by many American citizens as an actual moral good, it was defended on religious grounds. It was also accepted de facto by non-slave-holders (slavery is abolished in the northern states at the beginning of the 19th century) as the law of the land, a part of its Constitution. As philosopher Stanley Cavell has pointed out, Emerson's use of the word "constitution" in his text is no more casual than his reference to the valued advisor who speaks to him of the church's doctrines. Both nineteenth-century religious institutions and the Constitution supported slavery. Our "constitution" is not, therefore, for Emerson, simply the way we are built; it is not just "integrity" in a physiological sense. Rather, it is our "integrity" in a moral sense. And this "integrity" must make us question that other Constitution by which Americans are constituted, socially, politically, and economically. We humans, Emerson argues, need to recognize the degree to which we are constituted as individuals as much by our social and legal systems and our religious institutions as by anything we understand to be our inner moral lights. In nineteenth-century America, when Emerson is writing, citizens of the United States had to interrogate both their "Constitution" and their own personal constitutions, as participants in a slave-holding nation. The moral constitution of the nation itself and of all its citizens depended on it. The law of the land, Emerson makes clear, also includes those other "institutions" (including public opinion) that too easily, without scrutiny, command our consent, our conformity.

The difference between moral thinking and conformity as Emerson and Todorov present it is precisely the difference between informed political action and mindless capitulation to what Emerson labels "badges and names . . . large societies and institutions." It is not irrelevant to my argument that BDS co-founder Omar Barghouti introduces his book by citing, for forty pages, the organizations and individuals that have signed on to the movement, or that throughout the book he recurs to those who support BDS, as if consensus evidenced morality and accepting consensus were the equivalent of moral thinking. For anyone who has suffered slavery, sexual discrimination, racism, anti-Semitism, or any other form of discrimination (as have many Palestinians throughout the world), this is a highly fallacious and ultimately destructive equation. That half of the world's population believed that women were inferior and not entitled to the same rights as men did not make male domination an ethical position. The majority in any situation, even when democratically elected, as in Hitler's Germany, is not always right.

In the end, only the self can determine for itself what it believes; only the self can take responsibility for its actions. There is no guarantee, of course, that any of our moral positions, however deeply felt, are necessarily correct, only that the only position for which any of us can assume responsibility is the one that comes of one's own "nature." Self-interrogation is the key here; and it is self-interrogation, and therefore intellectual honesty, that seem to me lacking in many supporters of BDS against Israel.

I do not make this claim about such founders of the BDS as Omar Barghouti. I find his arguments full of distortion, misrepresentation, and rhetorical fancywork, as when he repeatedly calls the Israeli military incursion into Gaza in 2008 a "massacre" and conveniently ignores the eight thousand (8000!) rockets fired from the Gaza Strip into Israeli communities, which precipitated the Israeli military retaliation in the first place. War brings with it horrible consequences, not much different in the Gaza Strip from elsewhere in the world. But the Israeli army does not have a policy of disrespect for civilian rights, as Barghouti suggests. In fact, Israel gave prior notice to civilians in buildings that were terrorist bases and that were about to be bombed so that civilians (and terrorists, for that matter) could leave unharmed. It needs also to be recalled that the Gaza Strip was returned to the Palestinian people in 2005 through an un-coerced, unilateral withdrawal by Israel. Barghouti similarly ignores such facts as the terrorist attacks in Israel that were perpetrated by Palestinians from Gaza and elsewhere and that produced the conditions necessitating the security measures taken along the Gaza strip (including the checkpoints) and the construction of the security wall. Are the checkpoints and the wall unfortunate, unpleasant, abhorrent? However you characterize them, they do save Israeli lives being threatened by Palestinians. Barghouti also sidesteps the pertinent Jewish history preceding the Partition Plan and the establishment of the State. He doesn't deal with the Arab rejection of the partition. Indeed, the word "holocaust" enters the conversation insofar as the Holocaust, in Barghouti's view, is manipulated by Israel and is also the illegitimate excuse for support of Israel. The word holocaust is also used to describe Israeli actions in relation to the Palestinians. Barghouti quotes many anti-Israel accusations. What individual people say, even what individuals may do, cannot be taken as evidence that the State of Israel, its army, or its citizens are guilty of massacres, targeting civilians, racial cleansing, or starving Gazans into submission. I have shown Barghouti to be guilty of distortion, misrepresentation, and dishonesty. I do *not*, however, accuse him of hypocrisy. I quote him, because he is a co-founder of the organization that issued the call to which associations like ASA or MLA responded. Many of the points made in his book are made on the BDS website as well. Therefore, he can be taken as a trustworthy source of the BDS agenda. Barghouti has a coherent position and however difficult he makes it for his reader to grasp that position, intelligent readers may be expected to have understood what he, and thereby BDS, are actually calling for.

"The truth deserves to be spoken," Barghouti quotes Edward Said (34). So, what is the "truth" about the BDS movement that might interest morally thinking human beings, who are genuinely concerned with the plight of Palestinians? Many Palestinians (though by no means all) are indeed stateless, many are impoverished (wherever they live), and many are persecuted— indeed, in places other than Israel, and by others, not Israeli. I repeat the call to which many boycott supporters, including several American academic organizations, have responded with measures of their own. The platform begins innocently and unobjectionably enough, only to make demands on Israel that are anything but innocent and unobjectionable to most of us who care about what the call itself labels human "rights."

The call urges various forms of boycott against Israel until it meets its obligations under international law:

1. Ending its occupation and colonization of all Arab lands occupied in June 1967 and dismantling the Wall;

2. Recognizing the fundamental rights of the Arab-Palestinian citizens of Israel to full equality; and

3. Respecting, protecting and promoting the rights of Palestinian refugees to return to their homes and properties as stipulated in UN Resolution 194.

The BDS call begins with what is for most supporters of the boycott movement likely the major reason for answering the call of Palestinian civil society in the first place: an end to the occupation and the settling of lands seized in the June war of 1967. Boycott is urged against Israel until Israel (and not, we might note, the Palestinians) meets its obligations under international law, although both UN resolutions 242 (implied in point 1) and 194 (cited in point 3) pertain to *both* sides' obligations to the conflict. That is, both resolutions refer to *both* Palestinian and Israeli obligations. If the Israelis are in violation of international law, then, by the same logic, so are the Palestinians.

I will return to the ever popular and oft-cited UN Resolution 242 later, and deal for the moment with UN Resolution 194, explicitly referred to in point 3. Significantly, though unremarked on by the BDS, this is a resolution that goes back to 1948 and therefore has to do, not with boundaries post-1967 (which is where the platform, for obvious rhetorical reasons, begins), but with the more fundamental issue of whether or not a Jewish state has the right to exist. Historical context matters, and historical context is what is missing in the platform of the BDS (it is missing in Barghouti's book as well, in which, not only the circumstances that produced the establishment of the State of Israel following the extermination of six million Jews in Europe is conveniently ignored, but so is the history of the Jewish people in the place once and now again called Israel).

The 1948 U.N. Resolution, which calls for "respecting, protecting, and promoting the rights of Palestinian refugees to return to their homes and properties," was passed as part of an attempt to reach a peace agreement between or among the parties—a peace agreement that was not then and still has not been achieved between Israelis and Palestinians. This is so despite the peace treaties finally reached between Israel and Jordan and between Israel and Egypt *after 1967* (the post-'67 territories, we need to keep in mind, were seized from Jordan, not Palestine; the Gaza strip, now returned by Israel to the Palestinian Authority, was taken from Egypt). One of the several planks of Resolution 194 was the right of return for Palestinian refugees, which was *conditional* on the Arabs'/Palestinians' agreement to live in peace with their neighbors, a commitment hardly borne out by subsequent wars and acts of aggression against Israel, including the closing of the Suez Canal in 1956, the war of attrition in the 1960s, and the subsequent acts of hostility that resulted in the 1967 War and the Yom Kippur War. That the resolution was vetoed by all of the Arab states who were party to the conflict in 1948 suggests how citing this resolution today is a way of ignoring the historical events that culminated in 1967 and in the plight of the Palestinians from 1948 on, which was as much determined by the Palestinians' Arab allies as by their Israeli enemies. It also lays bare the real agenda behind the call for the return of Palestinian refugees to their homes and properties. The right-of-return is about the dissolution of the State of Israel as a homeland for the Jewish people. Establishing a Jewish homeland (alongside a Palestinian homeland) was the original intention of the Partition Plan, which the Jews accepted and the Arab nations, including the Palestinians, rejected, and which they still reject.

Now whether or not a state should officially be designated Jewish (or Catholic or Muslim or Palestinian or British or American); indeed whether or not there should be nation states at all, is an issue that can be debated. One can believe in the need to disband all nations and/or all national self-definitions, and one can foment revolution to that end. If one does that, however, then one is obliged as a moral human being, at very least, to lay bare that intention and, furthermore, to apply the same rule of a-nationalism to each and every nation on earth, including Palestine. BDS does not abide by that fundamental rule of moral integrity. Of course, for many individuals, the word "Jewish" seems to refer exclusively to a religious identity, such that a Jewish state is not analogous to a Palestinian state, in which there are at least two if not more religious groups: Muslims (who are the large majority) and Christians (who, we might note, are not only a minority within Palestinian society, but often experience themselves as a disadvantaged minority). Within the State of Israel there are, of course, also religious groups. In fact, the same religious groups that would exist in Palestine already exist in Israel, plus, of course, the Jews, who in the Israeli entity constitute the majority. Most likely in any national configuration some group will constitute the majority. But this is not my major point. More essential to the argument is that the Jewish people, like the Palestinian people, are a culturally and historically defined entity. They are a people, a nation (even when landless), and not simply a religion or, for that matter, a race. It was on the basis of their peoplehood, not their religion, that they were murdered in Nazi Germany. In Germany, and in Poland and Hungary, and throughout Europe, Jews were not asked to convert to Christianity, as if the issue were their religious beliefs. One did not have to be a practicing Jew to be slaughtered. Indeed, one didn't even have to be Jewish. One could be Christian and still be defined as a Jew for the purposes of extermination, if one had Jewish ancestry. One of the demands of the Israeli government is that the Palestinians recognize that Israel is the homeland of the Jewish people. This is a simple enough request, if what the Palestinian Authority wants from Israel is that they recognize a Palestinian homeland for the Palestinian people. This they refuse out-right to do. Nor is this what BDS advocates.

That Israel is a Jewish state (even if that were the equivalent of another state being Christian or Muslim rather than Arab or American, which, as I have suggested, it is *not*) does not have to mean that it is not a democratic state, for all its citizens. It can mean no more than that there is a majority population or culture within that nation, as is the case in almost every nation on earth. This immediately calls into disrepute point number 2 in the boycott platform: there is no need to compel Israel into "recognizing the fundamental rights of the Arab-Palestinian citizens of Israel to full equality." Such "full equality" by law, for all of it citizens, is already a part of Israeli law. Israeli Arabs (whether or not they identify themselves as Palestinians or Bedouin or Druze, Muslim or Christian or secular Israelis) do by law enjoy full civil rights: they are represented in the parliament, in municipal governments, in professions like medicine, law, and teaching; and at universities throughout Israel and so on and so forth. They own property. They run businesses. Any visit to an Israeli hospital or college campus dispels any notion of what BDS identifies on its home page as "Israeli Apartheid." As a former student of Tel Aviv University, individuals like Barghouti have to know this. Apartheid, as defined by BDS on its website, is "a social system that separates and discriminates against people based on race or ethnicity when that system is institutionalized by laws or decrees." It is, the statement continues, constituted by "acts committed in the context of an institutionalized regime of systematic oppression and domination by one racial group over any other racial group or groups and committed with the intention of maintaining that regime." However you want to characterize Israeli policy toward its citizens (and the Arabs are not the only minority in Israel), it is *not* apartheid. The boycott against South Africa took a position in relation to a country that, similar to the slave-holding and then the segregated American South, deprived human beings of their citizenship, their basic human rights, equality under the law, and equal access to national resources. This is *not* the case in Israel, despite BDS's and

Barghouti's claims to the contrary. Indeed, the analogy to South Africa, which pervades Barghouti's book, is not only a ploy for adducing sympathy for the boycott. More fundamentally, it is also another way of articulating the right for return for Palestinian refugees. The analogy (which is a false one) is that just as South Africa was a country of an African majority that was oppressed and marginalized by a white minority, so, according to BDS, is Israel a nation with a Palestinian majority (albeit many of them living outside of Palestine), which is being controlled by a Jewish minority. Yet, the State of Israel was established by international law as the homeland of the Jewish people in a place that already had, when the State was declared, a significant Jewish population, despite immigration restrictions imposed by the British, who were intent on preventing further Jewish immigration to British Mandated Palestine. The appeal to the example of the boycott of South Africa is nothing more than a rhetorical flourish, aimed at bringing the logic of one situation to come to bear on another very different situation, which requires a different set of terminologies and a different set of solutions.

Is there unequal distribution of wealth in Israel? Absolutely, and the Arab sectors of Israel are victims of this, disproportionately, in ways that are not to be tolerated by any of us. I have no wish to deny that. They are not the only communities in Israel that suffer such inequality, but they are certainly a major population whose needs and rights must be advocated. Some of the unequal distribution of wealth has to do with the ways in which socio-economic disadvantage tends to perpetuate itself wherever it exists. Israel did not, in the early days of the State, see the Arab population as among its priorities in terms of national development. That was a huge moral mistake, which needs to be corrected. And some of the continued disadvantage of Palestinians in Israel and Arab Israelis (let's let people decide how they want to be identified) surely has to do with the ways in which Israeli laws (like the laws in other countries) institutionalize discriminatory practices. The Israeli equivalent of the GI Bill, which gives demobilized soldiers moneys toward their continuing education, but which, therefore, excludes those segments of the Israeli population that do not serve in the army, is an example of such institutionalization. The inequality is not anti-Arab per se, but it is anti-Arab in consequence. Of course, one must also point out that Bedouin and Druze, who do serve in the army, are not excluded from these moneys; religious Jews who do not serve in the army are excluded. This is not a simple reality. But, and this is the important point vis-à-vis the boycott, these issues, especially in relation to Israel's Arab/Palestinian minority, are part of an on-going domestic debate in Israel, and progress is constantly being made, though not nearly fast enough, to be sure—in Israel as elsewhere in the world. There are many initiatives, public and private, such as scholarship programs, business incentives, and the like that aim to correct the imbalance in the distribution of public resources. These programs exist and have existed for quite some time, without any pressure from boycotts. In time, they, like similar projects in the United States and all over the globe, will hopefully erase socio-economic inequality wherever it exists, even if, as we all know, such processes grind painfully slow, much slower than any of us ought to permit. My point here is that the State of Israel and the majority of its Jewish majority know and are fully committed to the fact that the Jewish character of Israel cannot deprive non-Jewish citizens of their rights and liberties. This is absolutely clear. Boycotts are not necessary to pressure a nation into believing what it already believes or into doing what it has already undertaken to do.

Democracy does not depend on whether the majority in a particular nation is Catholic or Jewish or Muslim. It does not depend on whether the nation is called the United States of America or Palestine. The United States early on declared the separation of church and state. That did not prevent it from being a slave-holding nation in the 19th century, nor did it prevent segregation in the American south until the 1960s. Democracy depends on a nation's genuine attempt to insure equality for all its citizens. Most nations, including most of the nations in the Middle East, have failed in this endeavor, at least to some degree. Some nations, like Israel, continue to try to implement the fundamental principles of democratic government and society. The fact that Israel is a "Jewish" state rather than a Muslim or French state, is, contrary to what Barghouti believes, irrelevant. Therefore, "a unitary state based on freedom, justice, and comprehensive equality" is not the only or necessary "solution to the Palestinian-Israeli colonial conflict." This is Barghouti, declaring his advocacy of the one-state solution:

> While I firmly advocate nonviolent forms of struggle such as boycott, divestment, and sanctions to attain Palestinian goals, I just as decisively, though on a separate track, support a unitary state based on freedom, justice, and comprehensive equality as the solution to the Palestinian-Israeli colonial conflict. To my mind, in a struggle for equal humanity and emancipation from oppression, a correlation between means and ends, and the decisive effect of the former on the outcome and durability of the latter, is indisputable. If Israel is an exclusivist, ethnocentric, settler-colonial state, then its ethical, just, and sustainable alternative must be a secular democratic state, ending injustice and offering unequivocal equality in citizenship and individual and communal rights, *both* to Palestinians (refugees included) *and* to Israeli Jews. While individual BDS activists and advocates may support diverse political solutions, the BDS movement as such does not adopt any specific political formula and

steers away from the one-state versus two-state debates, focusing instead on universal rights and international law . . . . (51)

The "if" "then" "must be" formula is predicated on the claim that Israel is "an exclusivist, ethnocentric, settler-colonial state," which it is not. Therefore, "by steering away from the one-state versus two-states debates and focusing instead on universal rights and international law," Barghouti is not advancing democracy in the region. The one-state versus two-states solution is not, as Barghouti claims in an article in *The World Post* entitled "Why Is BDS a Moral Duty Today? A Response to Bernard-Henri Levi," "irrelevant." Indeed, it is as relevant as the question of whether a nation is Christian or Muslim or Jewish or not. Here again is Barghouti:

> While several leading BDS activists openly endorse the unitary state solution [Barghouti, we see from his book, is one of them], most of the members of the coalition leading the movement still subscribe to the two-state solution. *This is, however, an irrelevant issue,* as the BDS movement, being strictly rights-based, has consistently avoided taking any position regarding the one-state /two-states debate, emphasizing instead the three basic rights that need to be realized in any political solution.

Barghouti then goes on to cite the three principles I have already quoted from the BDS website and which appear in his book: "Ending the Israeli occupation that started in 1967 of all Arab territories, ending Israel's system of legalized and institutionalized discrimination against its own Palestinian citizens, and recognizing the UN-sanctioned rights of Palestinian refugees to return to their homes of origin." The alternative to the one-state solution (which some, like Barghouti, openly endorse) is a two-state solution in which, ipso facto, *both* states will have a Palestinian majority. What is eliminated is the possibility of the continued existence of Israel as it now exists.

The BDS call for the return of refugees in plank 3 of the platform, which seems little more than a defense of human rights, serves to eradicate all the history that has intervened between 1948 and now. It abolishes the rights of Jews to live in their national homeland as opposed to the homeland of the Palestinian people. It is also an historical misrepresentation that falsely accuses Israel of being in violation of international law. So is the allusion to UN resolution 242, in point 1. Resolution 242 concerns the territories occupied by Israel in the 1967 war. For most intellectuals and academics in the United States, Resolution 242 and the issue of occupied lands are central reasons for their criticisms of the Israeli government (say, as expressed by Thomas Friedman and Roger Cohen in their editorials in the *New York*

Times or by academic organizations like the American Studies Association of America expressing their support of BDS). I suspect that most of us would agree that the issue of lands taken in 1967 and the construction of Israeli settlements on that land is something that must be resolved. Yet, even here there are distortions in the presentation of what resolution 242 means. The resolution "affirms that the fulfillment of Charter principles requires the establishment of a just and lasting peace in the Middle East which should include the application of *both* [italics added] the following principles: (i) Withdrawal of Israeli armed forces from territories occupied in the recent conflict; (ii) Termination of all claims or states of belligerency and respect for and acknowledgment of the sovereignty, territorial integrity and political independence of every State in the area and their right to live in peace within secure and recognized boundaries free from threats or acts of force." This resolution, which, as Alan Dershowitz points out, for the first time in history ordered a nation to "return territories lawfully captured in a defensive war" (96), was accepted by the Israelis. It was accepted, however, in relation to "both" its directives: Israel agreed to withdraw from "territories" (not specified which or how many) on the condition that the state of belligerency ceased and that the sovereignty of the state of Israel as a Jewish homeland (meaning with its present Jewish character intact) was recognized. Israel is by no means more in violation of international law in holding on to territories, even conceived of as "the" territories, than the Palestinians. The Palestinian Authority is in violation of international law in not upholding its side of the bargain. Shall we boycott the Palestinian Authority into compliance? Insofar as those suffering the decisions of the Palestinian Authority and Hamas are the Palestinian people, such a boycott makes perfect sense. It makes at least as much sense as boycotting Israel, perhaps even more, since the Palestinian Authority and Hamas are clearly doing their own constituencies a severe disservice by not recognizing the State of Israel.

When BDS asserts falsely "that Israel was established by the Zionist movement over 60 years ago with the intention and effect of achieving the permanent removal en masse of the indigenous, predominantly Arab population of Palestine for the purpose of Jewish colonization and development of a 'Jewish state,'" what it is simultaneously exposing, in still another way, is the degree to which its objection is not to the occupation of Arab lands in 1967, nor even to the settling of this land (to which one might well object), but to the initial establishment of the state in 1948. For this crime of the Jews, of returning to their national homeland after millennia of persecution and the Holocaust, there can be for BDS only one reasonable solution: the dissolution of the State of Israel. *"Israel's current regime over the Palestinian people,"* writes Barghouti, *"should be characterized as a system combining apartheid, occupation and colonialism.* " "Occupation" is here only as the middle term linking two accusations that are also untrue—apartheid and colonialism. Furthermore, the "occupation" of the 1967 lands is only the most recent manifestation of the crime for which BDS is really asking redress—the creation of the State and its continued existence, for over sixty years, as a country like all other countries, with laws and communities and a national life. Keep in mind: the nascent State of Israel did not "occupy" Arab lands. It accepted a partition plan that the Arab states rejected.

In response to an essay that I published in *InsideHigherEd*, a fellow academic, Lloyd Alexander, took me to task, not for the content of my anti-BDS essay (with which he also happened to disagree), but (appropriately) for my failure to properly attribute to former ASA president Curtis Marez the larger context of his oft-quoted statement, as quoted in *New York Magazine* by Jonathan Chait, that he doesn't "dispute that many nations, including many of Israel's neighbors, are generally judged to have human rights records that are worse than Israel's [but] one has to start somewhere." That fuller context, as contained in the original interview in the *New York Times*, was that the support of the boycott was justified because Israel was receiving more money from the U. S. government than any other nation and also that the ASA was answering the call of Palestinian civil society to join the boycott. Of course, two questions immediately come to mind. The first has to do with whether moral action is a numbers game: the more money you get from the United States, the more the United States has the right to tell you what to do. The other is whether any and every civil call deserves a response. But putting both those issues aside, the particular civil call to which organizations like ASA responded was, as reported in Barghouti's book and as represented on their site, for the destruction of the State of Israel. That goal can in no way insure human rights, which are better protected in Israel, as Marez admits, than elsewhere in the Middle East. "In a historical moment of collective consciousness, and informed by almost a century of struggle against settler colonialism, the overwhelming majority in Palestinian civil society," writes Barghouti, "issued the Call for Boycott, Divestment and Sanctions (BDS) against Israel until it fully complies with its obligations under international law" (4). Curtis Marez's defense of the ASA agenda is not made less problematical by its being represented as a response to the Palestinian civil call. Indeed, it comes to seem much more deeply flawed, because the subtext of that call is not made clear by Marez or others defending and responding to that call.

I do not doubt that many people support the BDS out of genuine sympathy for the suffering of Palestinians, which is no fantasy. And I am sure there are those among the BDS supporters who, like members of the organization itself, believe exactly what the BDS is calling for, which is the destruction of the State of Israel as a nation and as a Jewish homeland. But I also suspect that there are many others who do not wish the extinction of Israel, either through its outright absorption into a new unitary state (Barghouti's position) or its de facto dissolution into an Israel in which there is a Palestinian majority. My essay is, therefore, addressed, primarily, to those individuals who object to the policies of the Israeli government vis-à-vis territories occupied in the 1967 War. It is addressed to any and all of us, on both sides of the conflict, who feel the need and the responsibility (as moral human beings) to question their own motives and allegiances. I count myself and my fellow Jews and fellow Israelis (Jewish, Christian, Muslim) among those who need always to interrogate our motives and examine our actions. I recommend that, after reading Omar Barghouti's rather mendacious book on BDS, they read Ari Shavit's critique of Zionist history: *My Promised Land: The Triumph and Tragedy of Israel*. Shavit pulls no punches in his critique of Israel. He shatters the optics through which many of us Jews and Israelis have heretofore viewed our own history. But he does so not to produce an equally distorted set of simplifications, reductions, and distortions, such as characterize Barghouti's book. Rather, he presents a picture of human suffering and frailty, in which desire sometimes overtook reason and a vision for the future frequently occluded the stark and very visible realities of the present. Human history, with the emphasis on the humanness of this, produced unforeseen and not necessarily wished for consequences. This is true for Israelis and Palestinians both, not to mention the other national entities (such as Great Britain, Jordan, Egypt, and the United States) which contributed to facts on the ground. There is a complexity to the history of the Palestinian-Jewish conflict. There are tragedies that preceded tragedies and that produced more tragedies in their wake. There are also triumphs of the human spirit and of the willingness to see beyond and beneath the historical facts. Those triumphs need to be brought back into view as the basis for change in the future.

Since I began this essay with two philosophers, let me conclude with a third. In his memoir *Little Did I Know*, Stanley Cavell asks the question that all of us—Israelis, Palestinians, Americans—must ask in the "global" world we inhabit. He is discussing the return of his good friend, philosopher Kurt Fischer, to the Austria that had, with the rise of Nazism, made of him a refugee, first in Shanghai, then in the United States. Fischer knows full well that he will now dwell among those very people who had ejected him, and that he is going to have to accept the human situation they now share. This is Cavell: "It takes an extreme case of oppression, which tore him from his home in his adolescence, to be posing the question every decently situated human being, after adolescence, either asks himself in an unjust world, or coarsens himself to avoid asking: Where is one now; how is one living with, hence counting upon, injustice?" (349)

BDS announces itself as a "global" movement. The idea of the global is, I suggest, a key term for all of us to keep in mind. In today's global world, there is no way we can claim ignorance of the thousands of acts of human abuse that occur daily. Read Nicholas Kristof in *The New York Times*. Watch CNN. Aside from the outright horrors of rape and slaughter and starvation and disease are the lesser but no less heart-rending facts concerning employment, education, and quality of life throughout the world. Anyone who buys an article of clothing manufactured (even by respected, top-name brands) in a factory in India or China that maintains substandard conditions; anyone who purchases a rug, however beautiful, tufted by the tiny fingers of six-year-old children is complicit in the extreme violation of human rights. The former president of ASA may have been quoted out of context by many, including me, but I now want to take his excerpted words that we have to begin somewhere and put them front and center, as issuing a call to all of us to begin with that somewhere that is each and every one of us. That challenge is the legacy of Ralph Waldo Emerson, which even a member of an oppressed minority, such as Ralph Ellison in the 1950s, before the end of segregation in the United States, held up as the essential principle of American democracy. Like others of his generation, Ellison believed that this legacy could be given back to American culture through precisely that community—the African Americans—who had been the victims of its occlusion. For Ellison, as for Emerson, self-reliance is the key.

Israelis and Palestinians can reclaim themselves if they take upon themselves not to boycott each other, but to reclaim each other by each and every one of us coming to understand a "truth" so obscured by rhetoric, political discourse, and historical accretions as to have almost faded from view. This truth is that we humans always exist in our contradictions and compromises and that only our willingness to see through the clouded optics of history and politics to a fundamental concern for others can begin to resolve the issues that separate us. "Truth," Emerson tells us, "is handsomer than the affectation of love." Perhaps the "affectation of love" is better than hatred. But the actualization, if not of love, then of respect, is better still.

At some moment, philosophizing and moralizing have to give way to action— political, economic, social, and otherwise. But to *act* morally, human beings have to also think morally. They have to examine every "truth" and determine if it is the "truth." Without this sacred law there is only conformity and a failure of moral courage. Without moral thinking there can be no such thing as moral action, either in relation to Palestinians or to Israelis, including those non-Jewish Israelis whose rights and wishes also need to be respected.

Without moral thinking we are all at risk of becoming victimizers. We are also all at risk of becoming victims. In this, we are all of us, all the time, in each other's keeping. ∎

Works Cited

Barghouti, Omar. *BDS Boycott Divestment Sanctions: The Global Struggle for Palestinian Rights.* Chicago, IL: Haymarket Books, 2011.

Barghouti. "Why is BDS a Moral Duty Today? A Response to Bernard-Henri Levi." *The WorldPost.* www.huffingtonpost.com. Jan. 2, 2011.

Budick, Emily. "Boycott Reflections." *Insider Higher Ed.* www.insidehighered.com Jan. 3, 2014.

Cavell, Stanley. *Little Did I Know: Excerpts from Memory.* Stanford: Stanford University Press, 2010.

Emerson, Ralph. "Self-Reliance." *Emerson's Prose and Poetry.* Ed. Joel Porte. Ithaca, New York: W. W. Norton & Company, 2001.

Shavit Ari. *My Promised Land: The Triumph and Tragedy of Israel.* New York: Spiegel and Grau, 2013.

Todorov, Tzvetan. *Facing the Extreme: Moral Life in the Concentration Camps.* New York: Holt, 1997.

http://en.wikipedia.org/wiki/United_Nations_Security_Council_Resolution_242

http://en.wikipedia.org/wiki/United_Nations_Security_Council_Resolution_191

PART II

THE AMERICAN STUDIES ASSOCIATION

SHARON ANN MUSHER

The Closing of the American Studies Association's Mind

O n December 16, 2013, the American Studies Association put into place an inequitable and discriminatory boycott against Israeli academic institutions. As worrisome to many of us who opposed the boycott was the method with which the resolution was implemented. One would think that a vote on such a contentious and politically fraught resolution—conducted by the premier professional association for those practicing American Studies—would come only after an open, multiple-sided, and carefully supervised discussion about the important issues at hand: What is America's responsibility to Palestinians in the light of its strong and continuing support for the Israeli government? How can we best preserve academic freedom for everyone? How can we promote peace and security for all in the Middle East? What is the proper role for us, as scholars of American Studies, in weighing in as a body about the Middle East? Instead, however, leaders who were seemingly ideologically pre-committed to the Boycott, Divestment, and Sanctions movement actively silenced oppositional points of view and railroaded the association into endorsing a resolution that marked a sharp departure from its professed goals: "the strengthening of relations among persons and institutions in this country and abroad ... and the broadening of knowledge ... about American culture in all its diversity and complexity." By endorsing a boycott against Israeli academic institutions, the ASA rejected complicated issues, offering instead, a simplistic good-evil binary. In showing contempt for a transparent procedure during the consideration of the resolution, the ASA's national council members showcased not only the closing of their own minds, but also the anti-intellectual spirit of the BDS movement as a whole.

In many respects, no one should have been surprised. The ASA's endorsement of a resolution to boycott Israeli academic institutions grew out of a tendency toward activism in the field. One of the key differences between American Studies and other fields is its attempt to link theory with practice, ideas with experiences, and scholarship with activism. Beginning in the late 1960s, one of the founders of the ASA's "Radical Caucus," Robert Meredith, encouraged those engaged in the field to devote themselves to "radical action—radical teaching, community organizing, [and] consciousness raising" rather than publishing.[31] While Meredith was reviled by the ASA's leadership at the time—many of whom subsequently resigned—he nevertheless provided a critical point of entry into the field for a new generation of scholars who viewed the ASA as more open to new subjects than traditional disciplinary ones and who pushed the association to take stances on women's issues, racial inequality, war, and pedagogy.[32]

More recent American Studies scholarship reinforces the connection between academic and political commitments. In *States of Emergency* (2009), Russ Castronovo and Susan Gilman argue that American Studies scholars should understand "objects" both as that which they study but also as verbs signifying scholar's objections or disagreements with dominant voices. Similarly, in the March 2013 issue of the *American Quarterly*, Barbara Tomlinson and George Lipsitz state that the "future of American Studies requires scholars to know *the work we want our work to do*…to insist that we infuse our ideas and activism with ethical judgment and wisdom…to acknowledge that our work speaks for us but also for others; and to recognize the dialogic and dialectically related nature of our views of American society."[33] For "ethical judgment and wisdom" to inform "ideas and activism," especially about controversial issues, scholars must be informed by careful scholarship, honest dialogue, and thoughtful consideration of the moral assumptions both contained within and resulting from them.

But little research and open discussion were in evidence as the ASA moved toward endorsing the boycott resolution. Instead, activist leaders from within the association redirected the process toward collective political engagement that, among other things, silenced dissent. The boycott represented both the "object of study" and the "work" that a disproportionate ratio of national council members wanted to do. More than half (ten out of eighteen) of the voting members of the council, including the sitting president, Curtis Marez, and the incoming one, Lisa Duggan, had earlier publicly endorsed the

US Campaign for the Academic and Cultural Boycott of Israel (USACBI).[34] Council members furthermore played leadership roles within the campaign. J. Kehaulani Kauanui was a member of its Advisory Board, and Sunaina Maira was on its Organizing Collective.[35] And they brought their politics to the range of professional associations to which they belonged, and in which they had assumed positions of authority. Maira proposed a boycott at the ASA's 2012 conference through its Academic and Community Activism Caucus, which she co-coordinated.[36] Another ASA council member, Karen Leong, presented a similar boycott resolution to the Association for Asian American Studies (AAAS), which passed it without objections or abstentions in April 2012.[37] And, in December, following the ASA's vote, Kauanui would go on to introduce a similar resolution to the Native American and Indigenous Studies Association, a professional organization she had co-founded eight years earlier.[38]

Within the ASA, support for the boycott came from the highest level. Marez endorsed an association-level boycott from the outset, and made advocating for it a key component of the 2013 annual conference.[39] He organized one of the featured events: an "ASA Town Hall: The United States and Israel/Palestine," which was a one-sided advocacy forum for the resolution rather than a traditional town hall. He also commented on a panel organized by the Academic and Community Activism Caucus, entitled "Activism: Boycott as a Non-Violent Strategy of Collective Dissent," and devoted a portion of his presidential address to promoting the boycott. There was no question where the vast majority of the ASA leadership stood on the issue of boycotting Israeli academic institutions and the intensity with which they embraced it and sought to carry it from one professional association to the next.

Given the political proclivities of the national council, it was unclear how those of us who opposed the boycott resolution might persuade the membership to vote against the boycott. After all, as the council states in its "Council Statement on the Boycott of Israeli Academic Institutions," the resolution's advocates had been lobbying and organizing around this initiative since 2006.[40] They had built support among ideologically like-minded cadres. But the great majority of the organization's members—who did not attend the few panels and caucus sessions dedicated to this issue—knew nothing about the boycott resolution, which the national council intended to deliberate at the 2013 meeting. Indeed, keeping the rank-and-file membership oblivious to the resolution might well have been the council's intention, given that there was no communication to members nor mentions of the resolution in the association's call for papers sent out a year before the conference, which is when most academics plan conference attendance and funding. Nor did the preliminary correspondence about the conference's schedule and calls to purchase tickets for conference events make any mention of the boycott resolution. Members wishing to read the text of the boycott resolution had to search actively to find it on the ASA's website by going to the "Academic and Community Activism Caucus" page and then clicking onto an area that read "Members seeking to support the resolution in favor of an ASA boycott may indicate their support here"—something no one would think to do unless he or she were already apprised of the impending resolution discussion.[41] Moreover, all of the hot-linked resources on the activism caucus's page supported the boycott; no opposing views were offered. Although there was space on the ACAC's website to comment on the resolution, it clearly was not a neutrally moderated space in which to engage in an open discussion about the proposed boycott or to post links.

Hence, even before the 2013 conference, the deck was clearly stacked in favor of the resolution. The handful of us who happened to be aware of the resolution and also opposed it needed to find one another and organize quickly. This goal, difficult under any circumstances, was made immeasurably harder because we had no formal structures to do so. None of us had submitted panels to challenge the resolution; and there existed no established ASA caucus for promoting academic freedom or scholars' rights. Thus, we had no ability to shape the ASA's Town Hall, which used "the theme of debt and dissent to encourage a discussion of historic and contemporary relationships between the U.S. and Israel/Palestine with a particular focus on their significance for American Studies," rather than focusing on whether or not the ASA should boycott Israeli institutions.[42] Furthermore, we had no space on the ASA's website and no access to a table at the conference.

Though not experienced in the methods of activism or organizational work, I began contacting colleagues in the early fall to try to develop a strategy. A few weeks before the annual conference, I found Simon Bronner of Penn State Harrisburg who, because he edits the *Encyclopedia of American Studies*, was an ex officio, non-voting member of the ASA's national council. Bronner also opposed the resolution. Indeed, the national council might have passed it at the May Executive Meeting if he had not raised problems with the proposal with the ASA's Executive Director John Stephens.[43] With a few other ASA members, we formed an impromptu committee, ASA Members for Academic Freedom, and began to draft a letter in opposition to the boycott resolution. The idea was to articulate a collective stance against the boycott and to begin to identify those who objected to it. Our letter encouraged vigorous discussion about the "Israeli-Palestinian conflict and how it should be resolved." We endorsed the American Association of University Professors' (AAUP's) 2005 statement opposing all academic boycotts on the grounds of academic freedom. As we put it: "the belief that scholars must be free to pursue ideas without being targeted for repression, discipline, or institutional censorship." We called for "constructive efforts to bring Israeli and Palestinian academics together on joint projects, including those that foster reconciliation and promote understanding and trust—all critical factors that will enable Israelis and Palestinians to coexist in peace and security. The call for an academic boycott of Israel," we continued, "is a destructive attempt not only to silence, but also [to] punish those involved in this important and potentially transformative academic work."[44] We circulated the letters among our colleagues and posted it to *change.org* for additional signatures (the Academic and Community Activism Caucus had previously posted its resolution on *change.org*).

We received considerable support, including from some of the field's most respected scholars, and we heard mortification and disbelief at the thought that the council might actually go through with such a resolution. Particularly striking was the number of senior Americanist scholars we recruited who had left the association—or never joined it—including Andrew Delbanco, Morris Dickstein, Richard Slotkin, Annette Kolodny, Laura Kalman, Jackson Lears, Kathy Peiss, and even former ASA president Karen Haltunnen.[46] Although sharing left or liberal politics, many of them explained their lack of affiliation as a result of the politicization of scholarship within the association. As Michael Kazin explained, "To be honest, I stopped attending the convention several years ago because so many of the panels were dedicated to elaborating the same beliefs about racial and gender oppression. I'm a leftist too, of course, but the ASA just got boring and predictable."[47] David Hollinger's assessment was even harsher. He had left the association about a decade ago because he "got fed up with the sandbox politics"; he described the ASA as "a shell of its former self, an apparatus being picked up and used as a vehicle by those who want to proceed in ideological overdrive."[48]

Over the past twenty years, there have been profound shifts in the association's membership as academics have left the field for specialized areas focused on technology, urban studies, Jewish Studies, and geography. Their departure opened the door for a new generation to enter the ASA, including those focused on topics that traditional disciplinary associations have often scorned, such as ethnicity, queer studies, prisoner studies, post-colonialism, and imperialism.[49] To reflect this transition, we created a second letter and collected the names not only of current ASA members who objected to the resolution but also of Americanists more broadly defined.[50]

One day before the conference began, I e-mailed both letters to the national council with signatures from 46 ASA members and 27 Americanists. Two hundred people had signed the change.org petition. In my e-mail to the national council, I argued, "As a member-driven organization, the council should respect that the resolution does not appropriately represent ASA membership."[51] Within two hours, one key ASA leader responded to my e-mail. In a back-and-forth exchange, which did not address any of the substantive issues we raised in the letter, she focused primarily on procedure. "You should correct the lie in your letters about our process," she wrote. "The caucus has a perfect right to put forward a proposal, and we are obligated to discuss and consider it. Period. Claiming otherwise, as your letters do, by claiming a 'vocal minority' is trying to 'force' anything on anyone, is highly irresponsible, and just wrong."[52]

But this was disingenuous. As I wrote in my resignation letter from the ASA, "Despite the national council's claims that it followed the association's deliberative procedures, anyone present could see that the conversation was organized well ahead of time to be one-sided. The association refused to share with its members information that might raise questions about the boycott."[53] The Academic and Community Activism Caucus had organized a pro-boycott table staffed by mid-rank to senior faculty to run throughout the conference. The table became a magnet for discussion precisely because a committed faculty member was always available to engage students and scholars alike. The table was laden with green "ASA Boycott Resolution Frequently Asked Questions" fliers with a Palestinian flag made out of butterflies in the background. There were several photocopied fliers and articles endorsing the boycott as well as a copy of the resolution, a sign-up sheet, and a bag of lollipops. An easel by the side of the table kept a rough count of how many members had endorsed the resolution. By the end of the weekend, it read "850+ signatures."

Our makeshift ASA Members for Academic Freedom group had no table, no bench of volunteers ready to leaflet throughout the weekend, no flags promoting Israeli-Palestinian harmony, and no lollipops. We did pull together an alternative FAQ sheet arguing against the boycott, but we did not manage to make copies before the ASA Town Hall on Friday afternoon. We pinned our letters opposing the boycott to bulletin boards next to the pro-boycott FAQ sheet and put stacks of the letters on two information tables with a folded sign on top of it that said "Oppose Resolution" to draw attention to the documents.

Empty-handed, we walked into the conference's featured ASA Town Hall. Organized by Marez, the supposed forum for an exchange of views was in fact a platform for promoting the boycott resolution. Kauanui was on the panel, giving the impression that the resolution had ASA approval. In addition, as I wrote in *Times of Israel*, "participants in the Activism Committee were pointed out to audience members, and the resolution was handed around the room of nearly 500 for signing (no comparable document opposing the resolution was distributed)."[54]

Common tropes articulated by the six speakers, included references to Israel as an "Apartheid state" and as engaged in "ethnic cleansing" and "settler colonialism." One speaker called for the "delegitimization of the Zionist project." Two panelists endorsed the US Campaign for the Academic & Cultural Boycott of Israel's call to 1) end the occupation, 2) recognize the rights of Arab-Palestinian-Israelis to full equality, and 3) honor the Palestinian's "right of return." In response to a rhetorical question about whether or not the right of return would end the Jewish state, a panelist attested, "if equality and justice would destroy Israel what does that say about the country?" Another speaker characterized the Holocaust as an "ur tragedy" that erased the plight of Palestinians and argued that American Studies outside of the U.S. "can't afford to respect this provisional perspective." "How," asked another speaker, "can a person of conscience reject boycotting?" As a different panelist contended, the boycott represented "a non-violent response within which a just solution might be imagined."

Beyond the one-sided, ideological perspective put forward by panelists, shoddy scholarship was also on display. To prove that Israeli institutions engage in surveillance on behalf of the state, a speaker put a single document on the screen from Tel Aviv University in 1972 that named students and categorized them as radicals. No broader context was offered for this document—where it was found, who created it, and under what circumstances—nor was additional evidence provided. "It's not a matter of liberal vs. conservative Israelis," the speaker insisted in describing surveillance in Israeli academic institutions, "it's a matter of principle, and these are the guiding ones that all Israelis subscribe to."[55]

When I described the Town Hall as a "vitriolic anti-Israel event" in *The Times of Israel*, I was not condemning people for criticizing Israeli policies.[56] Indeed, there was very little discussion of any specific policies and no debate about how Israelis and Palestinians might constructively work toward peace and toward improving the plight of Palestinians. Instead, opposition to the existence of a Jewish State was clearly and repeatedly articulated.

Some of the most telling exchanges came in the question and answer section when, for example, a British-Jewish scholar commented that she felt conflicted between the messages the speakers were conveying and her own Zionist upbringing, which had strengthened her especially in the context of the anti-Semitism she faced in London as a child. One panelist dismissively told her to "take it to her therapist."

Michael Rockland's question regarding where the balance was in this Town Hall met with snaps, hisses, and boos. I, who visibly shook throughout this session, read out loud an e-mail that Hank Reichman, Chair of the AAUP's Committee on Academic Freedom and Tenure, had sent to the national council. In it, he reiterated the association's opposition to academic boycotts, asking the council to dismiss this resolution and also to share the AAUP's stance with membership.[57] When I asked the panel why the national council had not done so, I was told that the AAUP discredited itself when it added a round of responses to the fall 2013 edition of the *Journal of Academic Freedom* without including any from a Palestinian perspective. The response, which was met with a round of applause, ignored the fact that six of the original seven essays advocated academic boycotts against Israel. In any case, all speakers were responding to was a snapshot of an issue in progress. Responses to the pro-boycott essays went online as they came in, followed by more pro-boycott responses to the responses, which went online as they came in. Responses were not solicited. Had Palestinians sent responses, they would have been published.

Following this travesty of a Town Hall came an award ceremony, celebrating Angela Davis, one of the Town Hall panelists who called for the ASA to endorse the boycott resolution. Afterward, Marez used his presidential address in part to advocate for the boycott. Whereas supporters of the resolution have referred to this event—and the eventual passage of the boycott resolution— as "historic" and "groundbreaking events in shattering what Edward Said called the 'last taboo' in the U.S. public sphere,"[58] opponents of the resolution described it as "like being in North Korea."[59] "I have not encountered anything like this," an ASA member wrote, "since I was involved with a bunch of people doing the EST training back in the 1980s."[60]

Saturday morning, our ASA Members for Academic Freedom group circulated our alternative FAQ sheet rebutting the main points of the resolution and pointing out its distortions and misinformation. We posted the FAQ sheets on bulletin boards and put them on the information tables. We also added to the bulletin boards articles opposing academic boycotts, letters sent to national council by those opposed to the boycott, including Hank Reichman's, our letters opposing the boycott, and a sign-up sheet.

Prior to the start of that afternoon's Open Discussion, we put both our FAQ sheet and letter opposing the boycott on each of the 500 seats in the room. Two members of the national council moderated the session. Avery Gordon had already publicly endorsed the U.S. Campaign for the Academic and Cultural Boycott of Israel;[61] Matthew Frye Jacobson, the second moderator, had not visibly articulated his stance. Shortly before the event, Gordon and Jacobson collected names into a hat. Jacobson opened the session by emphasizing that "tremendous care has been taken" in discussion regarding the boycott resolution. "We're all here," he continued, "because we all really care about the ASA." The moderators then called four people at a time and gave each two minutes to speak to the roughly 750 ASA members who were in the room. What became clear during the Open Discussion was the extent to which the assembled members appeared to agree with this resolution; also apparent was a racial and age divide between those supporting the boycott and those opposed to it. Approximately 45 members spoke in favor of the boycott and seven people spoke against it.

ASA members opposing the resolution spoke of the need for additional conversation and the poor scholarship inherent in portraying Israelis and Palestinians in purely black and white terms. Bronner, who identified himself as an Israeli academic—he is affiliated with Haifa University in addition to his appointment at Penn State—contended that Israeli universities are "the progressive institutions of change" and called for more, rather than less, dialogue with Israelis and Palestinians. Similarly, a professor from the American University of Beirut, who identified himself as opposing the occupation and favoring divestment, argued that a boycott was "too much," since educational institutions are part of Palestinians' culture and economics. Some opponents of the resolution pointed out Israel's liberal policies on homosexuality, its status as the only democracy in the Middle East, its protection of free speech, and its open access for Arabs to higher education. Another opponent of the resolution described herself as agreeing with many of the statements censuring Israel in the "whereas" section of the resolution, but rejected the boycott out of confusion: Would it prohibit faculty and students at her school from engaging in exchanges with those at Israeli academic institutions?

Many of those who spoke in favor of the boycott saw it as an extension of their own practice of American studies and anti-imperialist politics. Some explained that they had recently been drawn to the ASA because of this issue. A number of resolution advocates broadly equated Israel with subjugation and discussed the US's complicity in maintaining such oppression. As one person put it: "We are not bearing witness; We are a third party to this resolution." Another declared: "Our liberation is tied to this action." Many of them further contended that the resolution enabled them to act in solidarity with colonized and indigenous people and to enhance their free speech (ignoring the fact that Jews are also indigenous to Israel and that the boycott would stifle the speech of Israelis, including Jews, Arabs, Christians, Muslims, and Druze).[62] But the purging of guilt in this collective cathartic moment rang hollow. Rather than exploring specific measures to improve the lots of indigenous peoples, to challenge U.S. foreign policy, or to critique Israeli policies, ASA members endorsed a boycott that had few consequences for them. As Eric Aronoff of Michigan State University explained: "[B]oycotting Israeli universities is a cost-free way [for ASA members] to feel like they are 'doing something'—it requires no sacrifice on their part, will have no impact on their work, or the work of their colleagues. It is easy to do—much easier than taking radical political action or stands on the pressing social justice issues in what is our field of study—the massive amounts of injustice within the US, or (if they are consistent in their logic) of the 'complicity' of their own universities in those injustices."[63]

After the conference, the national council deliberated for eight days. On December 3—what would be the last day of deliberation—I was told that the council never received our letters opposing the resolution.[64] The next morning, I resent the original e-mail I had sent almost two weeks earlier and about which a senior ASA official and I had corresponded earlier. A few hours later, the council announced that it was opening the boycott issue to a vote of the entire membership (the overwhelming majority of whom had not attended the conference).

While it had been deliberating, the council made minor changes in the resolution, but primarily crafted its pitch in additional documents to explain the resolution to the wider ASA membership and the public. In "What Does the Boycott of Israeli Academic Institutions Mean?" the national council attempted to water down the resolution. The council claimed that it would only apply to Israeli academic institutions and not individuals, that ASA members are not obligated to follow it, and that it only relates to the virtually non-existent direct actions of the ASA "in its official capacities to enter into formal collaborations with Israeli academic institutions, or with scholars who are expressly serving as representatives or ambassadors of those institutions (such as deans, rectors, presidents, or others)."[65] But the council also explained that the boycott would stay in place until Israel honors the Palestinian right of return, among other requirements.[66] Even Noam Chomsky and Norman Finkelstein, sharp critics of Israeli politics themselves, agree that the BDS movement's support for a right of return implicitly calls for the destruction of the State of Israel.[67] Thus, the modified boycott, like the original one, challenged not only Israeli policies but also the very legitimacy of the Jewish state.

During the 10-day voting period, in the midst of final exams, we continued to gather signatures on our letters in opposition to the boycott, which by that point had been signed by more than 140 ASA members and non-member Americanists, including former presidents, prize winners, and lifetime members.[68] But neither the ASA nor the broader press would circulate or post our letters or any material that conveyed alternative perspectives. All of the ASA's official correspondence preemptively endorsed the boycott and included links to works that supported it. In addition to our letters, the council would not share an open letter to membership from the AAUP.[69] On its homepage, in a section designated "What's new in the community?," it posted only pro-boycott news and links. Moreover, in "What does the

Boycott of Israeli Academic Institutions mean for the ASA?," the national council referred to the AAUP in a way that ironically implied its support for the boycott despite its ongoing opposition. The document reads: "Like other academic organizations, including the American Association of University Professors (AAUP), the ASA unequivocally asserts the importance of academic freedom and the necessity for intellectuals to remain free from state interests and interference as a general good for society."[70]

On December 11, eight former ASA presidents who had signed our letter opposing the resolution issued a letter to the membership which attempted to make them aware of the case against the boycott and to urge them to vote. "Our task," they wrote, "is to open conversation, not to close it off, and to do so with those who reflect ideas (and support policies) with which many of us may strongly disagree."[71] They also expressed concern regarding the council's process. "That the membership vote is being undertaken with only one side of a complex question presented," the former presidents wrote, "seems to us to amplify the profound contradictions of the academic boycott strategy, and to compound its potentially pernicious consequences. This can only damage the ASA and further deflect attention from the serious moral and political issues proponents seek to raise."[72] But the national council was apparently unmoved by their pleas. Again, they refused to circulate or put on the ASA website the former ASA presidents' letter, a rebuff that one of the former presidents, Patricia Limerick, called "really quite breathtaking."[73]

The national council's silencing of boycott opposition grated on opponents of the boycott. "Let's remember," one former ASA president wrote, "that they will say they 'invited' comments to be posted on the website, and did not 'suppress' anything. They will have an answer for everything. They will claim that the Council acted as elected representatives of the members and simply turned to the members for endorsement because of the controversial nature of the issue (they did not need to do that, they will say, they had the authority to make the decision). We will be cast as poor losers (and worse). I hope the press takes this up so we won't have to be put on the defensive. It's ugly but unfortunately I think they will prevail with their story, and will maintain that the landslide vote vindicates their original decision. I'd love to be proven wrong."[74] Unfortunately, she was not. Others reiterated the view that a vote without access to multiple perspectives makes a mockery out of an ostensibly democratic process. As former ASA president Linda Kerber put it: "Even if there is a majority vote, I fear it won't be fully representative of the membership, who were communicated with primarily by email (and many people are off e-mail for extended periods of time) and given an overly short window. [I did not get a postcard urging me to vote until December 13, two days before the deadline, with an address label that did not include my member number, which I would have needed in order to vote. If I hadn't learned about this from you, I would never have taken that card seriously.]"[75] Compare this to the way that scholarly professional organizations normally conduct votes for, say, national offices—with ballots mailed out weeks or months ahead of time, options for electronic or paper voting, statements from all candidates provided—and the absurdity of the ASA's reckless, jerry-built procedure is all the more plain.

On December 16, the national council announced the election results, which hardly represented an overwhelming victory for BDS. Eight hundred twenty members voted in favor of the resolution (recall that more than 850 were said to have signed the resolution at the conference). Without any form of institutional support, without a caucus to promote academic freedom, without a table to distribute oppositional viewpoints at the conference, and with the national council's refusal to distribute or post on its website alternative perspectives, approximately 420 people either voted against the resolution or voted to abstain. The rest of the ASA's between 4-5,000 members cast no vote whatsoever. Of course the national council did not count those votes among its abstentions, since if it had the total number of votes for the resolution would clearly have been in the minority and, as a result, the council would presumably have rejected the resolution as promised. Instead, a front page article in the *New York Times* described the Council's unanimous decision as well as the results of the vote without mentioning the Presidents' letter or any other signs of opposition within the organization.[76] As Cynthia Ozick wrote to me, "So the miscreants won, malignity succeeded, filth washes over truth."[77]

The boycott met with significant backlash within academia. It was rejected by the American Council on Education, the Association of Public and Land-Grant Universities, the Association of American Universities, the American Association of University Professors, and the leadership of 250 universities and colleges. In perhaps the harshest statement of opposition, Catholic University President John Garvey asserted:

> The American Studies Association's recent call for a boycott of Israeli academic institutions is lamentable. The Association has appointed itself as a kind of inept volunteer fire department, aiming to put out the Israeli-Palestinian conflagration by throwing gasoline on the fire. That's not exactly right. *It has decided to pour gas not on the source of the fire but on bystanders, some of whom are trying to extinguish the flames.* No good can come of punishing academic institutions for the shortcomings, real and perceived, of their nations' leaders and policies.[79]

Within the ASA, seven American Studies departments dropped their institutional membership as a result of the boycott. An additional 12 American Studies departments denied that they were institutional members (the ASA apparently continues to print the names of institutions supporting the organization in its journal and website for at least six months after dues are in arrears.).[80] Two regional associations of the ASA, in California and the Eastern American Studies Association, refuted and refused to comply with the boycott.[81] Unsurprisingly, the "Academic Boycott and Related News" section of the ASA's website includes only one document that indicates any kind of dissent within the ASA from the resolution, an eloquent letter written by twelve recipients of the ASA's Turpie Award, the association's highest service award. There is no mention of departments that have dropped institutional support, members who have disaffiliated from the organization as a result of the boycott, or the regional associations' condemnations of the ASA's boycott.

Some organizations unadvisedly attempted to boycott the boycotters, a move that only further shuts down dialogue and strengthens support for the boycott on the left. The president of Indiana University cut Indiana's "Institutional Membership" in the ASA without consulting the faculty in American Studies. Rowan's president dropped the college's support for the EASA regional conference until EASA assured him that it was distancing itself from the ASA. And politicians in New York, Pennsylvania, Maryland, and Illinois labored to pass legislation that would withhold tax dollars from institutions of higher learning that used state money to fund attendance at conferences sponsored by associations engaged in a boycott or that directly participated in such a boycott. The ASA encouraged such misguided legislative efforts by using a watered-down boycott resolution to promote the greater BDS cause. "Having decided to boycott Israel, and even the idea of Israel," former ASA president Michael Frisch contended, "ASA now claims to be a surprised victim when Israel and its defenders respond by boycotting ASA."[82]

Representing itself as an embattled minority under seige by McCarthyesque forces given to legal bullying, the ASA has turned its own academic freedom into an organizing tool. Its website and Facebook page have become spaces for defending the right to boycott. The association has even developed a logo "Stand with the ASA" and a $100,000 fundraising campaign to defend the organization. The national council further asserted that it had attracted 700 new members, presumably many of whom were drawn to the organization explicitly because of its support for the boycott.[83] But in repositioning itself as a victim rather than an aggressor and accusing others of establishing litmus tests and blacklists, the ASA and other academic boycott advocates ignore their own complicity in silencing open discourse about the Israeli-Palestinian conflict.[84]

The ASA's boycott and the BDS movement more generally presume that ostracizing Israel will solve the ongoing crisis either by forcing Israel to make greater concessions at the bargaining table or by bringing about its elimination. But instead academic boycotts withdraw support for and isolate Israeli academia, one of the sectors in Israeli society where opposition to the occupation and inequitable Israeli policies is most vibrant. Unlike economic boycotts, which have historically been used productively to protest wrongful policies, boycotting ideas will only hinder the efforts of those who are at the forefront of a small and beleaguered peace camp to work toward coexistence.

Academic boycotts—symbolic or otherwise—have a silencing effect. Instead of deterring alternative perspectives, academic associations—even more than religious institutions, unions, and other professional associations—have an obligation to provide a big tent with room for open discourse and conversation, including disagreement. Rather than waving flags—either pro-Palestinian or pro-Israel—advocates of Palestinian-Israeli co-existence need to adopt what David Hirsch of the University of London calls a "politics of reconciliation."[85] Instead of boycotting Israeli academic institutions to end the occupation—and for some the Jewish state itself—academic associations, like the ASA, should seek to engage and enrich them and the academics associated with them. The ASA should create openings for Palestinian and Israeli scholars of American Studies to conduct research, attend conferences, and publish in American Studies journals, both individually and collaboratively.[86] Academic boycotts and other maximalist policies will only increase hostilities. Instead, we need more not less constructive dialogue to determine how to end the occupation and create a two-state solution that strengthens peace, security, and academic freedom for all. ■

DAVID HIRSH

The American Studies Association Boycott Resolution, Academic Freedom, and the Myth of the Institutional Boycott

Summary

1. The "institutional boycott" is likely to function as a political test in a hidden form. It would offer exemption from the boycott to those Israelis who are willing or able to disavow their own institutions or funding bodies.
2. An "institutional boycott," even if it did not in fact impact against individuals, would still be a violation of the principles of academic freedom.
3. In practice, the boycott campaign has been, and is likely to continue to be, a campaign for the exclusion of individual scholars who work in Israel from the global academic community. There is no general principle proposed for boycotting universities in states which have poor human rights records or which receive US aid or on the basis of any other stated criteria; there is only a boycott campaign against Israeli academia.
4. There are also foreseeable likely impacts within the boycotting institutions, or within institutions in which the boycott campaign is strong, which would be distinct from the impact against Israeli academia. The

violations of academic freedom which constitute academic boycott are likely to impact the boycotting as well as the boycotted institutions:

a. Academics in boycotting institutions, in subjects which specifically relate to Jewish or Israeli topics, would be cut off from the mainstream of their disciplines, for example Jewish Studies, Israel Studies, some theology, some archaeology, some history; and there is a more generic danger that scholars would be cut off from important colleagues in any discipline.

b. People who resist the characterization of Israel as apartheid or as Nazi or as essentially racist are likely to be characterized by the boycott campaign as apologists for apartheid, Nazism, or racism, and treated as such. People who "break the boycott" are likely to be treated as blacklegs or scabs. Social sanctions against opponents of the boycott or "strikebreakers" are likely to impact disproportionately against Jews. It is likely that some Jews will feel themselves to be under particular pressure to state their position on the boycott; it is likely that Jews will be suspected of opposing the boycott if they do not explicitly support it.

What the ASA resolution says[87]

The ASA resolution re-affirms in a general and abstract way its support for the principle of academic freedom. It then says that it will "honor the call of Palestinian civil society for a boycott of Israeli academic institutions." It goes on to offer guarantees that it will support the academic freedom of scholars who speak about Israel and who support the boycott; the implication here is that this refers to scholars who are opponents of Israel or of Israeli policy. The resolution does not specifically mention the academic freedom of individual Israeli scholars or students; nor does it mention protection for people to speak out against the boycott; nor does it say anything about the academic freedom of people to collaborate with Israeli colleagues.

What the ASA names "the call of Palestinian civil society for a boycott" is the PACBI "Call for Academic and Cultural Boycott of Israel."[88] The PACBI call explicitly says that the "vast majority of Israeli intellectuals and academics," that is to say individuals, have contributed to, or have been "complicit in through their silence," the Israeli human rights abuses which are the reasons given for boycott. There would be no sense in making this claim if no sanctions against individuals were envisaged. The PACBI guidelines state that "virtually all" Israeli academic institutions are guilty in the same way.

These claims, about the collective guilt of Israeli intellectuals, academics, and institutions are strongly contested empirically. Opponents of the boycott argue that Israeli academia is pluralistic and diverse and contains many individuals and institutions which explicitly oppose anti-Arab racism, Islamophobia, and the military and the civilian occupations of the West Bank. Israeli universities, they argue, are anti-racist spaces, where words are used rather than violence and where there is as much effort to eradicate discrimination against minorities as there is in other universities in democratic states.

These claims about the guilt of Israeli academia are also contested by those who hold that the principle of collective guilt is a violation of the norms of the global academic community and of natural justice. Opponents of the boycott argue that academics and institutions should be judged by the content of their work and by the nature of their academic norms and practices, not by the state in which they are employed.

The PACBI guidelines go on to specify what is meant by the "institutional" boycott. ". . . [T]hese institutions, all their activities, and all the events they sponsor or support must be boycotted." "Events and projects involving individuals explicitly representing these complicit institutions should be boycotted." The guidelines then offer an exemption for some other classes of individual as follows: "Mere institutional affiliation to the Israeli academy is therefore not a sufficient condition for applying the boycott."[99]

Summary of the ASA position[89]

- ASA is for academic freedom in general and for the academic freedom of critics of Israel and for boycott advocates in particular.
- ASA holds (via its endorsement of PACBI) that the vast majority of Israeli intellectuals and academics are guilty.
- ASA says (via its endorsement of PACBI) that virtually all Israeli academic institutions are guilty.
- ASA says (via its endorsement of PACBI) that individuals who are explicitly representing Israeli institutions should be boycotted.
- ASA says (via its endorsement of PACBI) that mere institutional affiliation at an Israeli university is not a sufficient condition for boycotting an individual.
- ASA does not mention any violations of academic freedom within Palestinian academic institutions other than those for which the Israeli state are responsible.

The "institutional boycott" functions as a political test by another name

Refusing to collaborate with academics on the basis of their nationality is, prima facie, a violation of the norms of academic freedom and of the principle of the universality of science.[90] It seems to punish scholars not for something related to their work, nor for something that they have done wrong, but because of who they are.

In 2002 Mona Baker, an academic in the UK, fired two Israelis from the editorial boards of academic journals which she owned and edited. Gideon Toury and Miriam Shlesinger are both well respected internationally as scholars and also as public opponents of Israeli human rights abuses, but nevertheless they were "boycotted."[91] In 2002 the boycott campaign in the UK supported Baker against those who were critical of her act of boycott, as implemented against individuals on the basis of their nationality.

The boycott campaign sought a more sophisticated formulation which did not appear to target individuals just for being Israeli.

In 2003, the formulation of the "institutional boycott" was put into action with a resolution to the Association of University Teachers (AUT), an academic trade union in the UK, that members should "sever any academic links they may have with official Israeli institutions, including universities." Yet in the same year, Andrew Wilkie, an Oxford academic, rejected an Israeli who applied to do a PhD with him, giving as a reason that he had served in the Israeli armed forces. The boycott campaign in the UK supported Andrew Wilkie against criticism which focused on his boycott of an individual who had no affiliation of any kind to an Israeli academic institution. If the principle was accepted that anybody who had been in the Israeli armed forces was to be boycotted, then virtually every Israeli Jew would be thus targeted.

In 2005 the boycott campaign aimed short of a full boycott of Israel, calling instead for the AUT to boycott particular Israeli universities: Haifa because it alleged the mistreatment of a professor, Ilan Pappé; Bar Ilan because of its links with Ariel College in the West Bank; and Hebrew University Jerusalem because it made the (contested) claim that HUJ was building a dorm block on occupied land. This was an attempt to try to relate the boycott to particular violations rather than just aim it at Israel as a whole.

In 2006 the boycott campaign took a new tack, offering an exemption from the boycott to Israelis who could demonstrate their political cleanliness. The other British academic union, NATFHE, called for a boycott of Israeli scholars who failed to "publicly dissociate themselves" from "Israel's apartheid policies." The political test opened the campaign up to a charge of McCarthyism: the implementation of a boycott on this basis would require some kind of machinery to be set up to judge who was allowed an exemption and who was not.[92] The assertion that Israel is "apartheid" or implements "apartheid policies" is emotionally charged and strongly contested. While it is possible for such analogies to be employed carefully and legitimately, it is also possible for such analogies to function as statements of loyalty to the Palestinians. They sometimes function as short cuts to the boycott conclusion, and as ways of demonizing Israel, Israelis, and those who are accused of speaking on their behalf. In practice, the boycott campaign attempts to construct supporters of the boycott as friends of Palestine and opponents of the boycott as enemies of Palestine.

The political test was implemented at the South African Sociological Association conference on August 28, 2012. An Israeli sociologist was required to disavow "Israeli apartheid." When he declined, the other participants in the panel left the room to give their papers elsewhere while his freedom of speech, it was claimed, was respected because he was allowed to give his paper to an empty room. Boycott can be as much refusal to listen as it is a prohibition to speak.

But long before 2012, the official boycott campaign had moved on from the political test, changing tactics again, calling for an "institutional boycott."

It is reasonable to assume that under the influence of the campaign for an "institutional boycott," much boycotting of individuals goes on silently and privately. It is also reasonable to assume that Israeli scholars may come to fear submitting papers to journals or conferences if they think they may be boycotted, explicitly or not; this would lead to a "self-boycott" effect. I offer an anecdotal example of the kinds of things which are likely to happen under the surface even of an "institutional boycott." An Israeli colleague contacted a UK academic in 2008, saying that he was in town and would like to meet for a coffee to discuss common research interests. The Israeli was told that the British colleague would be happy to meet, but he would first have to disavow Israeli apartheid.

The PACBI call, endorsed by ASA, says that Israeli institutions are guilty, Israeli intellectuals are guilty, Israeli academics who explicitly represent their institutions should be boycotted, but an affiliation in itself, is not grounds for boycott. The danger is that Israelis will be asked not to disavow Israel politically, but to disavow their university "institutionally," as a pre- condition for recognition as legitimate members of the academic community. Israelis may be told that they are welcome to submit an article to a journal or to attend a seminar or a conference as an individual: e.g., David Hirsh is acceptable, David Hirsh, Tel Aviv University is not. Some Israelis will, as a matter of principle, refuse to appear only as an individual; others may be required by the institution which pays their salary, or by the institution which funds their research, not to disavow.

An "institutional boycott" is still a violation of the principles of academic freedom

Academic institutions themselves, in Israel as anywhere else, are fundamentally communities of scholars; they protect scholars, they make it possible for scholars to research and to teach, and they defend the academic freedom of scholars. The premise of the "institutional boycott" is that in Israel, universities are bad but scholars are (possibly, exceptionally) good. Universities are organs of the state while individual scholars are employees who may (possibly, exceptionally) be not guilty of supporting Israeli "apartheid" or some similar formulation.

There are two fundamental elements which are contested by opponents of the boycott in the "institutional boycott" rhetoric. First, it is argued, academic institutions are a necessary part of the structure of academic freedom. If there were no universities, scholars would band together and invent them, in order to create a framework within which they could function as professional researchers and teachers, and within which they could collectively defend their academic freedom.

Second, opponents of the boycott argue that Israeli academic institutions are not materially different from academic institutions in other free countries: they are not segregated by race, religion, or gender, they have relative autonomy from the state, they defend academic freedom and freedom of criticism, not least against government and political pressure. There are of course threats to academic freedom in Israel, as there are in the US and elsewhere, but the record of Israeli institutions is a good one in defending their scholars from political interference. Neve Gordon, for example still has tenure at Ben Gurion University, in spite of calling for a boycott of his own institution; Ilan Pappé left Haifa voluntarily after having been protected by his institution even after travelling the world denouncing his institution and Israel in general as genocidal, Nazi, and worthy of boycott.

Jon Pike argued that the very business of academia does not open itself up to a clear distinction between individuals and institutions. For example the boycott campaign has proposed that while Israelis may submit papers as individuals, they would be boycotted if they submitted it from their institutions. He points out that

> papers that "issue from Israeli institutions" (BRICUP)[93] or are "submitted from Israeli institutions" (SPSC)[94] are worried over, written by, formatted by, referenced by, checked by, posted off by individual Israeli academics. Scientists, theorists, and researchers do their thinking, write it up and send it off to journals. It seems to me that Israeli academics can't plausibly be so different from the rest of us that they have discovered some wonderful way of writing papers without the intervention of a human, individual, writer.

Boycotting academic institutions means refusing to collaborate with Israeli academics, at least under some circumstances if not others; and then we are likely to see the re-introduction of some form of "disavowal" test.

In reality, the boycott campaign is an exclusion of individual Jewish scholars who work in Israel from the global academic community

In 2011 the University of Johannesburg decided, under pressure from the boycott campaign, to cut the institutional links it had with Ben Gurion University for the study of irrigation techniques in arid agriculture. Logically the cutting of links should have meant the end of the research with the Israeli scholars being boycotted as explicit representatives of their university. What in fact happened was that the boycotters had their public political victory and then the two universities quietly re-negotiated their links under the radar, with the knowledge of the boycott campaign, and the research into agriculture continued. The boycott campaign portrayed this as an institutional boycott which didn't harm scientific co-operation or Israeli individuals. The risks are that such pragmatism (and hypocrisy) will not always be the outcome and that the official position of "cutting links" will actually be implemented; in any case, the University of Johannesburg solution encourages a rhetoric of stigmatization against Israeli academics, even if it quietly neglects to act on it.

Another risk is that the targeting of Israelis by the "institutional boycott," or the targeting of the ones who are likely to refuse to disavow their institutional affiliations, is likely to impact disproportionately against Jews. The risk here is that the institutional boycott has the potential to become, in its actual implementation, an exclusion of Jewish Israelis, although there will of course be exemption for some "good Jews": anti-Zionist Jewish Israelis or Israeli Jewish supporters of the boycott campaign. The result would be a policy which harms Israeli Jews more than anybody else. Further, among scholars who insist on "breaking the institutional boycott" or on arguing against it in America, Jews are likely to be disproportionately represented. If there are consequences which follow these activities, which some boycotters will regard as blacklegging or scabbing, the consequences will impact most heavily on American Jewish academics. Under any accepted practice of equal opportunities impact assessment, the policy of "institutional boycott" would cross the red lines which would normally constitute warnings of institutional racism.

There was a case in the UK courts in 2007 in which Birmingham University decided to close down its department of Social Work in order to save money. It turned out that an unusually high number of the academics in this department were black. There was a challenge to the closure on the basis that it would have a disproportionate impact on black academics. The challenge was upheld by the UK employment tribunal. The tribunal found that the university ought to have carried out an equal opportunities impact assessment prior to its proposed closure. Nobody said that there was any racist intent or consciousness at Birmingham, only that there was a foreseeable institutionally racist outcome. Perhaps an institution which plans a boycott of Israel would have a similar responsibility to assess, in advance, whether there would be a disproportional impact against Jews, and whether there was any politically or morally valid justification for such a disproportionate impact.

The reality of the "institutional boycott" is that somebody will be in charge of judging who should be boycotted and who should be exempt. Even the official positions of ASA, BRICUP, and PACBI are confusing and contradictory; they say there will be no boycott of individuals but they nevertheless make claims which offer justification for a boycott of individuals. But there is the added danger that some people implementing the boycott locally are likely not to have even the political sophistication of the official boycott campaign. There is a risk that there will still be boycotts of individuals (Mona Baker), political tests (South African Sociological Association, NATFHE), breaking of scientific links (University of Johannesburg), and silent individual boycotts.

Even if nobody intends this, it is foreseeable that in practice the effects of a boycott may include exclusions, opprobrium, and stigma against Jewish Israeli academics who do not pass, or who refuse to submit to, one version or another of a test of their ideological purity; similar treatment may be visited upon those non-Israeli academics who insist on working with Israeli colleagues. There is a clear risk that an "institutional boycott," if actually implemented, would function as such a test.

While the boycott campaign offers the precedent of the boycott against apartheid South Africa as justification, there is a long history of boycotts against Jews, including exclusions of Jews from universities.[96] The boycott campaign is likely to resonate in Jewish collective memory in relation to these specifically Jewish experiences.

PACBI is the "Palestinian Campaign for the Academic and Cultural Boycott of Israel." What it hopes to achieve is stated in its name. It hopes to institute an "academic boycott of Israel." The small print concerning the distinction between institutions and individuals is contradictory, unclear, and small. It is likely that some people will continue to understand the term "academic boycott of Israel," in a common sense way, to mean a boycott of Israeli academics.

Appendix: Relevant excerpts from the ASA resolution and the PACBI documents to which the resolution refers.

The ASA resolution states:

Whereas the American Studies Association is dedicated to the right of students and scholars to pursue education and research without undue state interference, repression, and military violence, and in keeping with the spirit of its previous statements supports the right of students and scholars to intellectual freedom and to political dissent as citizens and scholars;

It is resolved that the American Studies Association (ASA) endorses and will honor the call of Palestinian civil society for a boycott of Israeli academic institutions. It is also resolved that the ASA supports the protected rights of students and scholars everywhere to engage in research and public speaking about Israel-Palestine and in support of the boycott, divestment, and sanctions (BDS) movement.[97]

The PACBI "Call for Academic and Cultural Boycott of Israel" states the following (which the ASA resolves to endorse and honor):

Since Israeli academic institutions (mostly state controlled) and the vast majority of Israeli intellectuals and academics have either contributed directly to maintaining, defending or otherwise justifying the above forms of oppression, or have been complicit in them through their silence...[98]

PACBI guidelines offer the following clarification (which the ASA implicitly resolves to endorse and honor):

...as a general overriding rule, it is important to stress that virtually all Israeli academic institutions, unless proven otherwise, are complicit in maintaining the Israeli occupation and denial of basic Palestinian rights, whether through their silence, actual involvement in justifying, whitewashing or otherwise deliberately diverting attention from Israel's violations of international law and human rights, or indeed through their direct collaboration with state agencies in the design and commission of these violations. Accordingly, these institutions, all their activities, and all the events they sponsor or support must be boycotted. Events and projects involving individuals explicitly representing these complicit institutions should be boycotted, by the same token. Mere institutional affiliation to the Israeli academy is therefore not a sufficient condition for applying the boycott.[99]

MICHAEL BÉRUBÉ

Boycott Bubkes: The Murky Logic of the ASA's Resolution Against Israel

T he American Studies Association is a relatively small professional association of scholars, but suddenly it has made an enormous impact on the public discussion of the Israeli–Palestinian conflict. On Dec. 16, 2013, the ASA endorsed an "academic boycott" of Israeli universities. It was a victory for what is known as the BDS (boycott, divestment, sanctions) movement, which began in 2005 but has been largely unknown in the United States until now.

The vote totals themselves were small: The ASA claims roughly 5,000 members, and the vote was 827 yes, 382 no, 43 abstaining. (By contrast, the Modern Language Association, of which I am immediate past president, has nearly 30,000 members.) But in an important sense the ASA vote has been productive, shattering an American taboo on discussions of whether to withdraw support for Israel. In another sense the vote has put everyone on the defensive: those who continue to support Israeli policies; those (like myself) who oppose academic boycotts in principle; and, not least, the ASA leadership itself, now experiencing a substantial (but entirely predictable) backlash in the press.

I do not see academic boycotts as a defensible strategy for pursuing social justice. But I also think it is imperative to address weak arguments against the ASA resolution.

The most important of these is the argument that the resolution is anti-Semitic—in effect if not in intent. For almost 50 years, supporters of Israeli policies have leveled the charge of anti-Semitism against critics. The charge is so familiar it is easy to miss how inflammatory and bullying it is, implicitly associating criticism of Israel or its policies with thousands of years of systemic oppression leading to the Holocaust itself.

I know and admire many BDS supporters in academe. They are not anti-Semites. The scholars known to me personally are people of principle and integrity, many of whom have been persuaded to their current position, in part, by pleas from the Israeli left. In 2009, for example, Neve Gordon of Ben-Gurion University published an op-ed in the Los Angeles Times in which he endorsed BDS on the grounds that there were no longer any political forces within Israel itself capable of creating the conditions for a viable two-state solution. Noting that nothing has stopped the building of settlements in the occupied territories, or indeed the steady rightward drift of Israeli politics, Gordon wrote, "I am convinced that (BDS) is the only way that Israel can be saved from itself."

One can argue that Gordon is mistaken; in the U.S., even Norman Finkelstein, a dedicated and sometimes inflammatory critic of Israel, wants nothing to do with BDS. But one cannot argue that Gordon is anti-Semitic. Like many Israelis who oppose the occupation, he speaks out of what he believes are the best interests of his country.

Critics of the resolution commonly ask why the ASA has singled out Israel when China, Russia, the U.S. and many other nations all violate human rights and international law. The standard response has been that the ASA merely (as its resolution states) "endorses and will honor the call of Palestinian civil society for a boycott of Israeli academic institutions." This leaves unaddressed—and perhaps dishonored—long-standing calls from Tibetan civil society for boycotts of China. BDS supporters counter that given the crucial U.S. economic, political and military support for Israel, U.S. citizens have a moral responsibility for Israeli policies that they do not bear for Russian and Chinese policies. I agree that the U.S. does have such a responsibility; but this reply does not explain why an academic boycott is being proposed, as opposed to, say, a more specific, targeted economic boycott of all products manufactured in the territories, or something more like an endorsement of the new European Union guidelines that prohibit grants, prizes or funding from the EU to the settlements in the West Bank, East Jerusalem or the Golan

Heights (and that, importantly, refuse to recognize those lands as part of the state of Israel).

The logic of the BDS strategy is based almost wholly on the analogy to South Africa. Even if one accepts the claims of some that Israel is an "apartheid state" (I would argue that this applies only to the occupied territories), one would still have to come to terms with the fact that no scholarly organization, anywhere in the world, ever endorsed an academic boycott of South African universities. Many people, myself included, supported boycotts, sanctions and divestment in response to the illegitimacy of South Africa's apartheid regime. Based on the analogy with South Africa, the logical strategy for expressing opposition to Israeli policies and conduct in the occupied territories would be an economic and cultural boycott of the occupied territories. The American Association of University Professors (on whose Committee on Academic Freedom and Tenure I serve) refrained from endorsing an academic boycott of South Africa, just as it refuses to endorse BDS today, on the grounds that such a boycott "undermines exactly the freedoms one wants to defend, and it takes aim at the wrong target."

The freedom the AAUP wants to defend, of course, is academic freedom; but academic freedom is not well understood, even by academics. It entails a delicate kind of intellectual autonomy, whereby professors are free to pursue knowledge independently of the dictates of other interested parties. Without it, academe as we know it (and should desire it) cannot function.

So does the ASA resolution infringe on academic freedom? The most common pro-BDS reply is that the resolution targets institutions, not individuals, and therefore harms no one's academic freedom. This is a meaningful but murky distinction. It would not countenance a situation like the one precipitated by British scholar Mona Baker in 2002, when she threw two Israeli scholars off the editorial boards of two journals simply because they were Israeli. At the same time, when it comes to the conditions in which scholarship is produced, it can be very difficult in practice to maintain the distinction between institutions and individuals. According to the guidelines promulgated by the Palestinian Campaign for the Academic and Cultural Boycott of Israel (PACBI), BDS covers "addresses and talks at international venues by official representatives of Israeli academic institutions such as presidents and rectors." But according to the literary scholar Judith Butler, a Columbia University professor and leading activist on behalf of BDS, any Israeli academic who accepts funding from his or her university becomes a "representative" of the institution: "Any Israeli, Jewish or not, is free to come to a conference, to submit his or her work to a journal and to enter into any form of scholarly exchange. The only request that is being made is that no institutional funding from Israeli institutions be used for the purposes of those activities." The ASA's "Frequently Asked Questions" page, by contrast, states that Israeli scholars are permitted to attend the ASA or visit any American campus even if they rely on Israeli university funding. And ASA President Lisa Duggan said that even presidents of Israeli universities may speak at the ASA if they are not representing their universities. So precisely where there should be clarity, there is murk: No two people agree on what "representative" means.

Clause 12 of the PACBI guidelines, by contrast, is crystal clear: BDS forbids "advising on hiring or promotion decisions at Israeli universities through refereeing the work of candidates, or refereeing research proposals for Israeli funding institutions. Such services, routinely provided by academics to their profession, must be withheld from complicit institutions." This is not targeted at any specific persons, but there is simply no way this provision would not affect individual scholars: If it were universally observed, anyone applying for a position or a promotion at an Israeli university, or anyone overseeing a job search or a tenure/promotion case at an Israeli university, would find him- or herself shut out of the system of peer review by the entire international scholarly community.

The uncertainty over who counts as "representatives" of Israeli institutions is troubling; but academic freedom is very clearly undermined by clause 12, insofar as it would prohibit important forms of scholarly communication between Israeli academics and the rest of the world. Nevertheless, BDS supporters argue that academic freedom is either (a) somehow enhanced for Palestinian scholars by boycotts targeting Israeli institutions or (b) not really all that important in the grand scheme of things, and never mind (a).

I have not seen any coherent explanation of how a boycott of Israeli institutions enhances academic freedom for Palestinian scholars. Much more has been said about (b), as when BDS founder Omar Barghouti writes, "By positing its particular notion of academic freedom as being of 'paramount importance,' the AAUP effectively, if not intentionally, sharply limits the moral obligations of scholars in responding to situations of serious violations of human rights," or when BDS supporter Sarah Roberts writes, "It is a peculiar sort of academic elitism that puts academic freedom, a somewhat abstract concept in itself, in a position of primacy before other types of very real and tangible physical freedoms."

It is remarkable how easily left-leaning professors can be cowed by the charge of "elitism." Academic freedom may be a freedom enjoyed only by the few, as Barghouti and Lisa Taraki charge when they write, "The march to freedom (may) temporarily restrict a subset of freedom enjoyed by only a portion of the population." But it is the raison d'etre of the American Association of University Professors, and it should be the raison d'etre of every principled academic. When it is subordinated to allegedly more exigent concerns, it simply dies. Whenever you make academic freedom contingent on something else, you violate the principle that academic freedom should not be subject to the dictates of church or state, political parties or boards of trustees, corporate funders or irate parents—or even activists in Palestinian civil society. Tellingly, BDS supporters tend to become aware of this (as Roberts does later in her essay) when they speak of reprisals against BDS supporters, which are real and intensifying, and which also threaten the academic freedom to discuss BDS. Academic freedom, in short, is the very condition of possibility for this debate.

And what, finally, are the goals of BDS? What would it take for the ASA to declare "mission accomplished" and end the boycott (nonbinding on individual members though it may be)? In the case of South Africa the purpose was clear: an end to apartheid and peaceful regime change. And thanks mostly to a determined South African resistance movement, it worked. But the BDS endgame is deliberately unclear. Barghouti, for his part, has made it clear that his desire entails, "at minimum, ending Israel's 1967 occupation and colonization, ending Israel's system of racial discrimination and respecting the right of Palestinian refugees to return to their lands from which they were ethnically cleansed during the 1948 Nakba." At the same time, he insists that the "BDS movement ... has consistently avoided taking any position regarding the one-state/two-states debate."

This allows BDS to practice a "big tent" politics, welcoming many different critics of Israeli policy. But it also puts moderate and liberal opponents of the occupation in the position of supporting radicals who define "occupation" as "the existence of Israel as a Jewish state." Just as handily, it allows those radicals to pretend that opponents of BDS are on the wrong side of history, supporters of Israeli crimes in the occupied territories and advocates of apartheid, when in fact many of us are simply proponents of the two-state solution who oppose the occupation as well as (to take a recent example) Israel's controversial "resettlement" of Bedouins in the Negev, which critics have called a form of ethnic cleansing.

Even if the goals of BDS were clearer, an academic boycott would still not constitute a defensible strategy for pursuing them. If supporters of BDS took their own South African analogies seriously, they would support targeted economic and political boycotts associated with specific Israeli actions and policies, not academic boycotts of Israeli universities. The fact that they do not—and that they misrepresent the ASA resolution as consonant with the AAUP's understanding of academic freedom—is revealing.

In this context, it is telling that the ASA refused to post on its website the AAUP's open letter opposing the resolution. The AAUP's *Journal of Academic*

Freedom had just published a number of pro-BDS essays (including one by Barghouti), because the AAUP, understanding the importance of academic freedom and open debate, welcomes and will publish critics of its positions and policies; the ASA, while claiming that the AAUP letter was misleading, could not bring itself to do so much as acknowledge a position contrary to its own. That, I think, is the difference between a scholarly organization that is firmly committed to the free and open exchange of ideas, and a scholarly organization that has—to borrow the immortal words of Dick Cheney—other priorities. I am proud to be a member of the first of these. ■

Note: This essay was first published in *Ajazeera America*. It is reprinted with the permission of the author.

DONNA ROBINSON DIVINE

The Boycott Debate at Smith

The American Studies Association's call to boycott Israeli academic institutions was denounced and rejected as antithetical to the theory and practice of academic freedom by over 200 College and University presidents across the United States, but for some, it struck a discordant chord that continues to reverberate through the halls of the academy. The tone and content of the statement drafted by Smith College's new President, Kathleen McCartney, and posted on the College website reflected the general thrust of the many statements published condemning the boycott; thus it also, unsurprisingly, triggered a typical kind of backlash:

> Smith College upholds the ideals of academic freedom and engagement with global scholarship, scholars, research and ideas. The college rejects the American Studies Association's proposed boycott of Israeli universities and will continue to support our students and faculty in pursuing opportunities in Israel and with their Israeli counterparts. In recent years, such opportunities have included hosting Israeli scholars on our campus for residencies in the U.S.; hosting summer Global Engagement Seminars for our students in Jerusalem; and running a thriving Jewish Studies program. Additionally, we are actively exploring the possibility of faculty and student exchanges with Israel.

What appeared reasonable to some faculty seemed problematic to others who raised objections both to the President's right to define the College's position without consulting the faculty and to the announced intention to expand rather than diminish ties with Israeli scholarly institutions. In response to critical emails she received, the President invited faculty on both sides of the issue to a dinner and discussion. Not everyone could attend, but nonetheless, all seated around her dining table said they were grateful for the opportunity to talk to the President about her statement. No one at the dinner actually expressed any support for an academic boycott although some suggested that economic pressure through divestment would be appropriate to bring Israel's occupation of West Bank lands to an end.

Partly because of student interest and a letter critical of the President's statement issued by the Justice for Palestine campus group, the Director of the Global Studies Center, Greg White, organized a noontime panel discussion of the ASA Boycott in a series called What is Happening Around The World, or WHAW, as it is known on campus. The current chair of American Studies, Michael Thurston, and Elliot Fratkin, from the Department of Anthropology, spoke. Because I teach Middle East Politics, including one on the history of the Middle East Conflict in the Department of Government, I was also asked to contribute to the faculty-led discussion. What happened at the Smith discussion may serve as a cautionary tale for those who wish to see the Middle East Conflict analyzed rather than politicized. Thomas Friedman may be correct in arguing that American campuses could very well become the staging grounds for the Third Intifada, but he may be incorrect in claiming for it the moral high ground or even the capacity to bring an end to this Conflict.

Michael Thurston began his remarks by noting that he was ambivalent about the call for the boycott, but that it was important to remember why the ASA passed its resolution. It was, he claimed, responding to "calls from Palestinian civil society" to protect the academic freedom of its scholarly community. He pitched his talk in what might be called the seductive language of human rights, drawing analogies between the apartheid regime of South Africa and what he seemed to take for granted as the politics of oppression practiced by Israel. He noted that charges were directed at Israel not only for violations of international law but also for abusing the academic freedom of Palestinian scholars. In response to the calls from a Palestinian academy presumably besieged by a strong Israel state, the ASA's decision could only be viewed as an attempt to advance the cause of ideals that stand at the very foundation of the American academy.

Thurston recalled, with nostalgia, his own participation in the 1980s in campus campaigns aimed at dismantling South Africa's apartheid system. Coming of age politically in that movement disposed him to identify the weak as possessed of a moral claim deserving of support. But while he stressed the impetus for freedom embedded in the ASA resolution, he never mentioned its backing for the Palestinian "right of return" which not only treats Israel as if the state possessed no sovereign legitimacy and hence no right to shape its own immigration policies but also offers support for a policy widely considered to constitute a demographic attack against the Jewish state. While the aim of making Palestine whole is presumably not intended to serve Palestinian interests but rather to advance the cause of human rights, it compacts within itself both a massive ambiguity and a language about the distribution of power, even if its flow is never fully acknowledged.

Thurston also never mentioned the percentage of Palestinian academicians actually asking for the kind of boycott endorsed by the ASA. Sari Nusseibeh, President of al-Quds University, opposes it and has forged all sorts of exchange programs with Israeli universities. (One might note that almost all Palestinian universities were founded after not before the Israeli conquest of the West Bank in June 1967.) Nor did Thurston provide evidence to suggest that Israeli occupation policies resemble the apartheid practices of South Africa. Repeating the charge without interrogating it ought not to strengthen its credibility.

Words matter, but so should facts, particularly in the academy where condemnation by analogy—without a shred of evidence demonstrating that the comparisons are apt and merited—ought to elicit skepticism, if not actual scorn, particularly if simply asserted and left without supporting documentation. Words like "apartheid" turn Israel into the equivalent of South Africa and an emblem of evil, injecting currency into a language that casts the Jewish state and justice as totally disjunctive. Like Mark Antony's funeral oration in Shakespeare's *Julius Caesar*, Thurston's remarks had to leave everyone wondering why he was even "ambivalent" about the boycott.

Invoking apartheid to describe Israel's West Bank policies, Elliot Fratkin dismissed as disingenuous my own attempts to explain how the Oslo Accords have divided political and security arrangements and restricted movements of both Israeli citizens and residents ruled by the Palestinian Authority. But while stating his opposition to academic boycotts, Elliot argued for a divestment campaign that would bring attention to Israel's occupation of Palestinian lands. Without ever mentioning its highly contested status—of which he was aware—he showed students a map endorsed by what many label an anti-Semitic organization, SABEEL, to show what could only be interpreted as a long history of Jewish thefts of Palestinian lands. Elliot went on to explain that he could not discuss the Middle East Conflict without becoming emotional because he was brought up in a Jewish household that stressed good deeds, and Israel's conduct with regard to Palestinian refugees embarrassed him as much as it humiliated this oppressed nation. Thus two of the faculty presentations left students with the impression that the moral issues are clear, but without the knowledge that this clarity could only come from a very selective rendering of the conflict's history.

My own presentation was brief and, although it preceded the others, it seems appropriate to summarize it as a way of showing the extent to which this conflict is more talked about than fully understood.

Like many activists, scholars increasingly view the Middle East conflict as enmeshed in longer historical processes, with Palestinians one of the many victims of global power politics and imperialism. My own approach focuses less on why the conflict occurred than on how it unfolded. The two perspectives lead in different directions. The question of "how" encourages an examination of interactions and decisions that produced outcomes at certain junctures, probing the many ways the available options were defined and accounting for why some were chosen and others rejected. By contrast, the search for the "why" of this conflict may have the appeal of identifying a single cause, but it risks the distorting effect of succumbing to political cliches as a way of rendering judgment and apportioning blame.

Thus, I began by dismissing one long widely held assumption about the Middle East Conflict: while it has existed for over a century since the 1880s, it has changed its dynamics, and sometimes dramatically. It was not always a Zionist/Palestinian confrontation, nor was it always clear that the fight against founding a Jewish state in Palestine was intended to replace it with Palestinian Arab sovereignty. Nor has the conflict remained static since the almost half century of Israel's occupation of the West Bank, nor even since the Oslo Accords nor, one might venture to say, in the last several years.

I turned, next, to reflect on the several questions that must be posed as a result of the ASA resolution. First, I argued that one must ask: what the boycott is trying to achieve? Second, I observed that it is important to consider whether a boycott focusing on Israel's educational institutions can achieve any of its stated objectives? Is a boycott of Israeli universities likely to contribute to establishing a Palestinian state? Is it reasonable to assume that harming the country's educational institutions will encourage Israelis or even force them to change their beliefs in Jewish sovereignty as critical to their security?

I noted that although Israel's universities operate with budgets from the government, they have been bastions of liberal political views. The Hebrew University's first president was Judah Magnes who helped organize the two binational movements during Great Britain's rule over Palestine. The university's most famous professor, Martin Buber, developed a liberating humanist discourse that still shapes core philosophical discussions. Martin Buber also attempted to establish a position at the university for peace studies just after the 1929 Riots in Palestine killed so many people and threatened an end to the development of a Jewish National Home. Buber lost the battle, leaving the designated professor—Hans Kohn—without an academic position until Smith College's History Department invited him to join its faculty. Leader of the BDS movement, Omar Barghouti, is enrolled in a doctorate program at Tel Aviv and the university has protected him against all sorts of calls for his ouster—because of its firm commitment to academic freedom.

Much would be lost in the study of the Middle East by shunning Israel's universities. There would be less knowledge of Palestinian society and history and certainly more ignorance about why Palestinians and Arabs lost their battles to prevent the establishment of a Jewish state. And here is what Smith would lose. One of our Global Studies Seminars on the Political and Religious History of Jerusalem (which I helped create and teach) could not have been taught without heavily relying upon Israel's university system.

Traditionally, there were two sides to the Middle East Conflict, but, currently only one—the Palestinian—receives the stamp of approval from a significant number of academicians who proclaim themselves and the causes they embrace as "progressive." In presenting their critiques, these academicians are asking people to discard past judgments about the national rights of the Jewish people as wrong-headed and for many, as inevitably implicated in the moral evils of an unjust global order where nation states constitute the legacy of once powerful but discredited empires.

For many in the academy, Israel has become shorthand for all manner of problems and especially for the suffering of the Palestinians. Zionism, the movement that founded the Jewish state and helped fashion its identity, has become an omnibus term of abuse.

Justice for Palestinians and Israelis has long been viewed as residing in the principle of two states for two peoples, a goal increasingly accepted in the region, across the globe, and, not incidentally, by most of the inhabitants of this overly promised land. However, because almost two decades of negotiations have not produced an agreement on how to divide Palestine, some academicians have mobilized around the idea of charging Israel with sole responsibility for the stalemate and for the reason Palestinians have not yet won their freedom. What is never mentioned is the number of times since 1936 Palestinians have rejected any proposal to share the land no matter the percentages offered them.

The occupation is an open wound for both Palestinians and Israelis, but like the conflict, itself, it has changed in the almost half century since the territories were conquered. There are many more Jewish settlements, but there is also a legitimate Palestinian authority dispensing justice and regulating the economy in the West Bank. And what should not be forgotten or discounted is that this is a region now engulfed by instability, with violence extending its reach to the very edges of the homes and lands of both these peoples.

Given these conditions we must ask: Can anyone guarantee that a Third Intifada driven by the BDS movement on European and American campuses will deem its goals fulfilled if it ends Israel's occupation of Palestinian lands and not Jewish sovereignty as it has repeatedly demanded? Does this, then, alter the moral calculus? Is it reasonable to believe a campus campaign can produce results that have eluded Palestinians and Israelis during their 20 years of negotiating? Finally, an important question for scholars is whether or not this kind of campus politics serves a useful purpose for the academy.

The feelings stirred up by the conflict between Palestinians and Israelis are so volatile that examining it without taking sides is difficult, even within the halls of the academy. But the terrible toll exacted by this hundred years' war should command intellectual analysis not political advocacy. Politicians posture and champion causes, teachers develop perspectives, generate critical and thoughtful scrutiny, open up conversation, and produce understanding. Properly practiced, the academic study of this conflict rights no wrongs, provides no political or social therapy, and configures no single moral compass for what to do outside of the classroom. The classroom should not become a battleground just as the lectern should not serve as a soapbox. The responsibility of an engaged intellectual is to bring clarity and substance to the issues probed. The deep attachment of Palestinians and Israelis to their national identities and societies has exacted a high price, and the task for academicians is not to condemn or praise one side or another but rather to explain why an overwhelming majority of both populations seem prepared to pay these costs and why Israelis and Palestinians cling so tenaciously to narratives that lock them so tightly into confrontation. WHAW missed an opportunity to demonstrate the importance of academic engagement with this conflict in all its many manifestations. Instead, the event mirrored the typical campus discussion on the Middle East in displaying more passion than analytic rigor. ∎

SABAH A. SALIH

Islamism, BDS, and the West

O n its website (www.bdsmovement.net) BDS offers this description of itself: "In 2005, Palestinian civil society issued a call for a campaign of boycotts, divestment and sanctions . . . against Israel until it complies with international law and Palestinian rights. A truly global movement against Israeli Apartheid is rapidly emerging in response to this call." Omar Barghouti, a Palestinian whose name has become closely linked with this movement, says in the *New York Times* of February 2, 2014, that Israel is now "as terrified by the 'exponential' growth of the . . . movement as it is by Iran's rising clout in the region." Writing in the *Washington Post* of January 25, 2014, another supporter of the movement, Vijay Prashad, cites last December's vote in support of BDS by the American Studies Association as further proof of the movement's growing success internationally. Israel may be irritated by BDS, but it is certainly not threatened by it. The American Studies Association, intellectually lightweight and politically toothless, is hardly the organization to have an impact in the ongoing Palestinian-Israeli conflict.

Nevertheless, BDS has managed to score a few propaganda victories against Israel. These days the ugly term "apartheid" tends to be mentioned frequently in reference to Israel, even though everyone knows it is a false comparison. In some circles, the linking of the two is now mandatory. Academic and journalistic discussions of Israel these days also seem to be dominated by just one theme: the Israeli occupation of Palestinian land and how this occupation continues to make life miserable for the Palestinians.

BDS propaganda may not sound like much, but as W. H. Auden realized in January 1937 during his seven-week stay in Spain, propaganda could be key in generating what he called the "intensity of attention" (qtd in Mendelson, xvii). Indeed, BDS has managed to put Israel on the defensive, at least in some academic circles. But the point here worth investigating is not so much what BDS does but how it benefits from a sea change in the West's intellectual life and its subsequent and recent colonization by Islamism.

Prashad says the movement's purpose is "to raise awareness of Palestinians' lack of academic freedom," but the movement's website demands a lot more; it wants Israel to comply with "international law and Palestinian rights." The implication of this last phrase is immense; in reality this means Israel cancelling itself out. Supporters of this movement in the West borrow from the language of democracy, human rights, and civil society to make their demands sound reasonable. The movement's supporters in the Middle East, however, see no need for such borrowings; they still cling to the prevailing belief in the region that Israel has to go; its elimination must be the ultimate goal. Barghouti and Prashad complain about the supposed "lack of academic freedom" for the Palestinians under Israeli control. People in the region outside Israel know this is false. They know who really is oppressed. The following passage is from Karima Bennoune's recent book *Your Fatwa Does Not Apply Here*; it offers a glimpse of what life is like in Gaza:

> This is all part of the Hamas social agenda. The group's violent acts against Israelis have gained it the most press; its coercion of Palestinians is much less discussed. Islamic clothing is required of girls in public schools, even for the dwindling number of Christians. This is accomplished, Naila recounts, not through Hamas written orders but rather through rumors and fear mongering. While the organization might "deny that it had given such an order, it is enough that Hamas would give a small indication here or there. Families would be afraid. The school administration would be afraid. The order is implemented accordingly." These fundamentalist tactics are repeated in many places. (115)

The situation described by Paul Marshall and Nina Shea is even grimmer; in their monumental 2011 book, *Silenced: How Apostasy and Blasphemy Codes Are Chocking Freedom Worldwide*, they document cruelties, impositions, and practices that make for sad reading. In Saudi Arabia it is forbidden to say "'amputation of a hand of a thief or stoning of an adulterer . . . is not suitable for this day and age (312).'" In October 2008, the Arab world's greatest poet, Adonis, was vilified by the Ministry of Culture, even called an "apostate" by some, for saying in a speech in Algiers that Islamists had no right to impose their religion on society. Today Iran is a country where one can be accused of a wide range of crimes, "including 'friendship with the enemies of God' and 'hostility towards friends of God,' 'fighting against God,' 'dissension from religious dogma,' 'spreading lies' and 'propagation of spiritual liberalism.'" Paul Marshal and Nina Shea continue, "In blasphemy cases in Iran, Saudi Arabia, Pakistan, and Sudan, the weight of testimony of a male Muslim is worth more than that of a non-Muslim, and even more again if the non-Muslim is a woman. On this basis, a simple accusation made against a non-Muslim by a Muslim can be enough to secure a conviction (313)." As horrifying as these examples are, they are of no concern to BSD people who, to borrow a phrase from Paul Berman from a similar context, seem to have learned "to avert their eyes from the accumulated consequences of Islamism in practice" (*Terror and Liberalism* 113). So the question that needs to be raised here is this: What makes this situation possible, where academics and even non-academics in the West become fixated on the so-called "Palestinians' lack of academic freedom"?

The answer can be gleaned from the reaction the late Christopher Hitchens got in an American institution several thousand miles away from America. In February 2009, Hitchens gave a lecture at the American University of Beirut. The topic, chosen by the university, was "Who Are the Real Revolutionaries in the Middle East?" Hitchens cited resistance to clerical rule in Iran, Egyptian secularists campaigning against Hosni Mubarak, and the Lebanese effort to put an end to the Syrian occupation of the country. He also lauded the long-suffering Kurds for moving in the direction of democracy and civil society in post-Saddam Iraq. Hitchens praised the then Palestinian Prime Minister Salam Fayyad for addressing the question of corruption in the Palestinian Authority seriously.

It was a packed hall of students, journalists, and academics; many were Americans. What was the response? "It was clear that a good number of the audience . . . regarded me as some kind of stooge," wrote Hitchens two years later in the introduction to his brilliant collection of essays *Arguably* (xvii). The Americans were adamant. Hitchens did not know what he was talking about. True revolutionaries, he was told, were groups like Hamas and Hezbollah; they alone in the region were prepared to fight back against Zionism and imperialism.

There is something revealing in that response, not just because it was made mostly by Americans at an American university; more important, because it bore all the hallmarks of an ideological shift that had been taking shape in the West since 1970s. It may have been started by the Palestinians, but the Boycott, Divestment, and Sanctions movement owes its rise in the West to this ideological transformation. You don't have to be an academic to know how the rest of this narrative goes, for it has by now penetrated deep into Western culture's collective thinking. We encounter it on television, in newspapers, in conferences, in high school and college class discussions, student organizations, professional associations, and sometimes even in town hall meetings. The real villain is the West, in particular the United States. Together with Israel, they are out to impose their hegemony on the world, especially in Arab- and Muslim-majority regions. As a colonial creation, Israel plays an indispensable role in this dirty effort. Globalization is just a continuation of that effort on the economic front. But the West is also employing a more sinister and potent weapon, one with the specific task of contaminating and colonizing and even obliterating non-Western cultures. This is called cultural imperialism—a subject whose time has come even in freshman composition classes. These people were telling Hitchens that resistance to Western domination was the only resistance that deserved to be called revolutionary; their examples, not Hitchens's, represented genuine voices of the oppressed. British journalist Robert Fisk, foreign correspondent for the *London Independent*, is a devoted fan of this view.

Fisk was in Afghanistan in December 2001 when the American-led effort to rid the country of the Taliban and al-Qaeda began. At a refugee camp, Fisk began with the Muslim greeting "*salaam u aleikum*." He was attacked instantly: "A small boy tried to grab my bag. Then another. Then someone punched me in the back. Then young men broke my glasses, began smashing stones into my face and head. I couldn't see for the blood pouring down my forehead and swamping my eyes." In the *Independent* of December 8, 2001, Fisk wrote, "My Beating by Refugees Is a Symbol of the Hatred and Fury of This Filthy War."

Fisk's fellow journalist Nick Cohen was not surprised in the least by Fisk's reaction. In his timely 2007 book *What's Left?* Cohen, columnist for the *London Observer*, writes, "Even when Fisk was on the floor, battered and bleeding and at his assailants' mercy, guilt rather than fear overwhelmed him" (272). Why guilt, not fear? Because the idea of guilt is central to the kind of thinking that Fisk has embraced. Fisk is in the grip of this thinking; it is his ideological blueprint for deciding what positions to take, what notions to support, who to attack, who to praise. Fisk saw in this little attack something big and ugly; instantly, he saw images of imperialistic hubris, of plunder, of cultural subversion and domination, of the white man waging aggression against a defenseless and brutalized people, and he needed no time to connect the dots to himself as a white man from the West and decide that he not only was implicated by the West's colonial past but also was responsible for it. Fisk saw in his own face the face of imperialism—a white face, a familiar face, a face that made him feel guilty because it was a white man's face.

Fisk's rationalization is emphatic about that: "I understood. I couldn't blame them for what they were doing. In fact, if I were the Afghan refugees of Kila Abdullah . . . I would have done just the same to Robert Fisk. Or any other Westerner I could find."

Western culture has always been in the healthy habit of looking at itself critically. One could argue that the whole project of modernism was just that: a prolonged and rigorous effort to subject the culture's values and practices to debate. Indeed, the best criticism of Western culture is made, not by its detractors, most notably Islamism, but by Western culture itself. Fisk's example, however, is not that kind of criticism, something dialectic and nonpartisan. Fisk's is a condemnation of the West. Fisk's criticism, if it can even be called that, is the product of a particular cast of mind, a cast of mind that today occupies center stage in the West's intellectual life. Undermining and undercutting the West is its priority. The result is that, as Terry Eagleton reminds us, the West has "disarmed [itself] in the face of those fundamentalisms, both within and without, which are too perturbed by other people's anti-metaphysical eagerness." The most the West can do now is offer "no more than a culturalist apologia for its actions—'this is just what we white Western bourgeois happen to do, take it or leave it'" (74). The achievements of the Enlightenment are now routinely the subject of ridicule and attack in academic and journalistic circles. Even the claim that "science and reason are somehow superior to magic and witchcraft," writes education historian Diane Ravitch, is now considered by many to be simply "the product of EuroAmerican ethnocentrism," whose aim has always been "to establish the dominance of European forms of knowledge" over non-Europeans (283). This revolutionary project that liberated humanity from the monarch and the feudal lord, from the tyranny of unverifiable claims, from fear of the unknown, and gave ordinary people a sense of dignity and revitalized society with such things as representative government, sexual freedom, gender equality, and the spread of scientific knowledge: this project is now generally derided in Christopher Hitchens's memorable words as "white" and "oppressive" (*Hitch 22: A Memoir* 280). Enlightenment, it is now argued, was a curse; rather than setting us free, it enslaved us. "The Port Huron Statement," the founding document of the 1960s left, reduced life in the West into a series of ugly paradoxes dominated by one theme: "men . . . [tolerating] meaningless work and idleness" (Hayden 562). The opening statement sounded the alarm and hinted at what was to come: "We people of this generation, bred in at least modest comfort, housed now in universities, look uncomfortably to the world we inherit" (561).

Reason and its accomplishments were now the problem. Where once culture was understood as an affirmation of universal values, and in Steven

Pinker's apt phrase "a tool for living" (68), it has now become an affirmation of tribal loyalties, more grandly called identity politics. Historian Niall Ferguson has shown that the reason why the Western way of life has become "a kind of template for the way the rest of the world . . . [aspires] to organize itself" is because for the last 500 years or so most major developments in science, politics, architecture, social life, and economy have come largely from the West, and that this domination has been accomplished "more by the word than by the sword" (5). But the view the universities promote these days is very different. Ignoring the fact that cultures when in contact shamelessly borrow from one another and that some cultures, in Pinker's words, "can accomplish things that all people want (like health and comfort) better than others" (67), our academic fundamentalists never seem to get tired of bashing Western culture. It is this dim-witted way of thinking that has been a major factor in helping BDS flourish in the West.

No book, to my mind, has been more instrumental in popularizing this form of fundamentalism than Edward Said's *Orientalism*. From the start, the book's sloppiness and weaknesses were there for everyone to see, as Robert Irwin has so meticulously documented in *For the Lust of Knowing: The Orientalists and their Enemies*. Clive James calls *Orientalism*, appropriately, "damagingly superficial" and makes this necessary corrective: "the great European students of foreign cultures were all humanists before they were imperialists, and often defended the first thing against the second, out of love and respect" (652). Nevertheless, the book went on to become an instant academic bestseller. The book was published in 1978. Three years later, I came to this country to pursue graduate studies in English. I have to say I had never seen anything like it. To borrow a phrase of Bernard Shaw's from another context, Orientalism was here, Orientalism was there, Orientalism was everywhere. In class discussions and conference papers, Said's book had the final say; its style of thinking was not to be questioned. Everyone seemed to proceed according to the book's blueprint: it was nearly mandatory for certain things to be said; it was also nearly mandatory for certain other things not to be said. The book had arrived at the right time. The 1960's rebels had now grown and entered the cultural sphere as shapers of ideas. Said's book spoke to them, vindicated their causes, helped them formulate their thoughts and positions better, helped them become a little more engaged with the world, even though their knowledge about the world remained abysmal. But then Said had told them knowledge was to be suspected, since its arrangements and accumulations were supposed to be mostly the result of Western exploitation and domination.

Had the book appeared, say, in the 1940s, it would have gone largely unnoticed. As Arthur Miller states in his autobiography *Timebends*, America was then a country where people had faith and confidence in its values and energies (184-85). But, in 1978, American intellectual life had all but lost faith in America. Leftism, which was now redefining itself as the Cultural Left, saw in Said's book a reflection of its own thoughts and positions. And Said's thesis helped Leftism enlarge its criticism. It wasn't just America that was the problem; it was the whole Western experiment in civilization. Because of its cultural and strategic ties to the West, Israel too came in for the same criticism.

Said described orientalism as "a Western style for dominating, restructuring, and having authority over the Orient." The book's purpose was "to show that European culture gained in strength and identity by setting itself off against the Orient as a sort of surrogate and even underground self" (3). Said even included this vulgar sentence: "It is therefore correct that every European, in what he could say about the Orient, was consequently a racist, an imperialist, and almost totally ethnocentric" (11). Said wrote these words in 1978—a time when the region he discusses the most as the victim of Western arrogance, the Middle East, was awash with nasty totalitarianism of both the Islamist and the Arab nationalist kind. This was a region where one could get executed, in public in some cases, simply for holding certain political beliefs. This was a region where most people were not allowed to have a passport, where censorship made sure no word from the outside came in, and where, in Saddam's Iraq, for example, one was not even allowed to own a typewriter. They were all nasty regimes, but Saddam's was the nastiest. Said, however, was not interested. As Kanan Makiya writes in his *Cruelty and Silence*, Said's Orientalism insisted one ought to be silent about the likes of Saddam; it also encouraged the Arab masses not to examine their own stereotypes of the West; Orientalism thus made "Arabs feel contented with the way they" were (319). They could now blame their failures on the West; they could now describe all criticism of their actions as a new form of colonial intervention. They could now put the West on the defensive. Even the Islamists in Anzar Nafisi's memoir, *Reading Lolita in Tehran*, know the value of quoting and appropriating Said (290). When in casual conversation Christopher Hitchens tried to find out how his one-time friend would fare under the Islamist or Arab nationalist rule, Said brushed the question aside; he simply could not bring himself to condemn Arab and Islamist cruelties as things in themselves. The United States was his ultimate horizon in all matters political and cultural; he could only condemn such cruelties if they could be blamed on America. So in Said's universe someone like Kanan Makiya, for daring to expose Saddam's cruelties, deserved to be attacked and called names. When at Hitchens's urging *The Nation* considered publishing Makiya,

Said called the editors to complain, implying that the Iraqi was "a paid agent, even a traitor" (*Hitch-22* 396).

Said's ideas were not new to me. In Iraq, where I spent the first 25 years of my life, the West was very much on everyone's mind. During the hey-day of Arab nationalism, the 1950s and 1960s in particular, the West, which invariably meant the United States, was depicted mostly in Said's favorite terms: imperialistic, hegemonic, and racist. Said could not bring himself to say anything bad about the Soviet Union. He told the visiting Hitchens, "I have never publicly criticized the Soviet Union. It's not that I terribly sympathize with them or anything—it's just that the Soviets have never done anything to harm me or us" (*Hitch-22* 386).

This was also the Arab nationalist line that was drilled into our heads at school, in the media, and even at the mosque. Up until the end of Saddam's rule, no one could pass a history or sociology or philosophy class without showing serious commitment to this totalitarian mindset; Saddam's Ba'thism even introduced us to the Leninist idea of political correctness. In public, everyone pretended to be on board, but in private there was no shortage of biting satire against the orthodoxy. One can easily imagine Said not to have been among the satirists.

Said's *Orientalism* and Western culture's war against itself shielded Arab tyrannies from criticism, but the book and the war also paved the way for something else: the intellectual colonization of the West by Islamism. That in turn boosted the fortunes of BDS. Terrible things would be said about Israel, but Islamism, much to its delight and disbelief, would be immune from scrutiny. It would be welcomed and championed as the voice of the oppressed and those opposing it—including non-Islamist Muslims—would be attacked as supporters of imperialism and racism. That Islamism did not believe in thinking for oneself, that Islamism was sexist through and through, that its agenda was totalitarian, that it was the sworn enemy of the life of the mind—none of that mattered. Leftism was ready to bestow its seal of approval upon it. The year 1989 was a watershed for Islamism: this was the start of a campaign that would in less than a decade give Islamism an important say in Western societies' internal affairs.

That year Salman Rushdie published a novel, *The Satanic Verses*. Islamism had been in power in Iran for nearly a decade, but what a decade! The Iranian Revolution started out as a non-religious revolution, both in character and direction. But, as so often happens with revolutions, this one too was soon hijacked. Islamists were eager to shed blood and managed the takeover with ease. Khomeini demanded the execution of "several thousands" and he wanted their executions to be carried out in public (Nafisi 93). Executions would become the country's national spectacle for weeks. By 1989, however, the Islamic Revolution had reason to worry. The war with Iraq had lasted eight years. Iranian dead were approaching a million. Scores of cities had been devastated. The country was on the verge of economic collapse. The situation in Iraq was not much better; the economy remained afloat only through a massive infusion of cash from Persian Gulf countries fearful of a Khomeini victory. Khomeini was desperate. The war was supposed to make him the Middle East's undisputed superpower; it was supposed to help export his revolution all the way to Israel and beyond; it was supposed to help topple Saddam Hussein. Now there was only defeat. He had to agree to a ceasefire with Saddam, even though this was, in Khomeini's own words, like drinking "a cup of poison" and losing "honor before God." Rushdie's novel could not have come at a better time. On February 14, 1989, Khomeini issued his infamous fatwa demanding the author's head.

This was a calculated strategic decision. It came at a time when the West was at its most vulnerable. Having lost confidence in itself, the West was in no position to defend itself. Luckily for Khomeini, Western Leftism was eager to lend a helping hand. The familiar excuses were made: Khomeini's was the voice of the oppressed. A great religion had been insulted. The West, with its history of aggression against Islam, was implicated in this one too. The Marxist journalist John Berger spoke for many, when he held Rushdie—not the Ayatollah—responsible for the deaths that followed. Others went even further, arguing that Rushdie had provided justification for racism against Muslims in the West. The late Susan Sontag, that year's PEN president, found some members not even willing to sign off on a resolution condemning the fatwa and reaffirming commitment to freedom of expression. Something new was in the making: Leftism had begun an alliance with Islamism.

Here was a reactionary cleric, not from the West and with no legal authority over any citizen of the West, demanding that a British subject be killed, not tried, for writing a novel. Khomeini lost the war against Iraq, but he was now poised to win the war against the West. At this juncture, the Shiite-Sunni split did not matter. Islamism needed a voice, and Khomeini provided it. In the years to come there would be other voices, but for now Khomeini's was sufficient.

Khomeini's fatwa was not just an Islamist attack on a single author. It was much more potent than that. It initiated a campaign that would eventually help Islamism become an important player in the West. The fatwa was an attack on the West, on the standards and beliefs that the West itself had been trying to undermine and discredit for some time. The fatwa was the first of many steps Islamism would take to put the West under a permanent state of self-censorship. The fatwa was issued in 1989. In February 2009, Christopher Hitchens would write in *vanityfair.com*, "a hidden partner in our cultural and academic and publishing and broadcasting world: a shadowy figure that has, uninvited, drawn up a chair to the table. He never speaks. He doesn't have to. But he is very well understood. The late playwright Simon Gray was alluding to him when he said that Nicholas Hunter, the head of London's National Theatre, might put on a play mocking Christianity but never one that questioned Islam."

In his best-selling 2010 book *The Flight of the Intellectuals,* America's foremost liberal intellectual Paul Berman examines how this particular cast of mind has found its way into mainstream US academic and journalistic discourse, and arrives, correctly I must say, at this bleak conclusion: "Here is a reactionary turn in the intellectual world—led by people who, until just yesterday, I myself had always regarded as the best of the best" (264). Berman cites in particular the joint effort by two well-connected liberal writers, Ian Buruma and Timothy Garton Ash, to discredit and vilify a liberal exile from Somalia, Ayaan Hirsi Ali. Why? Because she decided to write critically about tribal and religious cruelties in her native Somalia, just as Kanan Makiya did in 1993 about Iraq under Saddam. For that, Makiya found himself attacked by Edward Said in some very unscholarly and ungentlemanly ways. Said is not around anymore, but there is no shortage of people who had been persuaded by his ideas about Islam and the West. They are now attacking Ayaan Hirsi Ali in the same way Said attacked Makiya. Buruma and Garton Ash have called Ayaan Hirsi Ali "totalitarian" and "fundamentalist" and other such things; *Newsweek*'s Lorraine Ali has gone several steps further; in the February 26, 2007, edition, she calls Ayaan Hirsi Ali "a bomb thrower." In 2014, Brandeis offered, then withdrew, an offer for her to be the year's commencement speaker. In her book *Nomad,* Ayaan Hirsi Ali describes what it was like to grow up under a religion that preached violence against infidels and free thinkers. She says the West has its problems, but that she prefers the West to the world of Islam, citing in particular the West's respect for the life of the mind.

Now, contrast this contemptuous treatment of Ayaan Hirsi Ali with the highly favorable treatment the Islamist Tariq Ramadan regularly receives in the West. Here's a man who is in the grip of dogma, a man (though an academic) who trades in superstition, a man for whom any criticism of Islam, Allah, or the Koran amounts to an unpardonable offense against the faith, a man who has committed and subordinated himself totally to this faith, a man whose style of living and outlook on life is determined exclusively by this totality, a man who believes the Koran to be the literal word of God, a man whose father and grandfather were the backbone of the Muslim Brotherhood, a man who, as Berman states, "writes prefaces for the collected fatwas of Sheikh al-Qaradawi" (trn.com May 29 2007)—and yet, this man is

Buruma's kind of man; this man is Garton Ash's kind of man. Read just one page from Ramadan's book *In the Footsteps of the Prophet* and you will see how hopelessly out of touch this Islamist is with the life of the mind. Here is an academic at a Western university who is not troubled giving currency to Islamic absurdities, like angels performing two open-heart surgeries on Mohammed. Non-Islamist Muslims find such things too foolish even to joke about. It is a sad day for Western culture when its opinion shapers denigrate those who stand for secularism and rationality and applaud those who stand for damaging and obsolete ideas that, in Sam's Harris's words, "divide one group of human beings from another" (277).

Al-Jazeera television's Yusuf al-Qaradawi is Ramadan's idol. Consider what this spiritual leader of the Muslim Brotherhood is in the habit of saying. In July 2004, he tells a British television interviewer that Islam does "not require a war against . . . homosexuals." But on Al-Jazeera's Arabic service, commonly referred to in the Middle East as "The Brotherhood Channel," he describes gays as "sexual perverts" who must be punished harshly by being thrown from a high building (qtd. in Bennoune 17). In the West we are led to believe that this foul-mouthed cleric is the so-called Muslim world's most popular preacher. This is a myth. It is created by the likes of Ramadan and given second-hand currency by the West, especially by those who realize it is much safer to attack the likes of Ayaan Hirsi Ali than to be critical of Ramadan or Qaradawi. But in the Middle East the narrative is exactly the opposite. Ramadan and Qaradawi are considered to belong to the Middle Ages—people rendered obsolete by the spread of knowledge, representative government, civil society, and feminism. As one elderly woman in my family—and, yes, a Muslim—said recently, "These people have been trying to persuade the West that the majority of Muslims think of nothing else but their religion." She asked in disbelief, "Doesn't the West realize that most of us have no time anymore for religion except when tragedy strikes?" The common view is that Qaradawi and Ramadan are nativists whose views and ideas are simply too parochial and too limited to be of use in the modern world. Ayaan Hirsi Ali, not Tariq Ramadan or Qaradawi, is the big hero there. Buruma and Garton Ash and their compatriots need to realize that Muslim-majority countries are not a sea of mosque-goers or Koran readers. They also need to realize that challenging orthodoxy has always been part of their world. Here's the Middle East's most revered poet, Omar Khayyam writing in the eleventh century:

> The Koran! Well, come put me to the test—
> Lovely old book in hideous error dressed—
> Believe me, I can quote the Koran too,

The unbeliever knows his Koran best.

And do you think that unto such as you,
A maggot-minded, starved, fanatic crew,
   God gave the Secret, and denied it me?—
Well, well, what matters it! Believe that too.
          (stanzas 24-25)

  If today figures like Ramadan are in ascendancy in the West, it is because the West has put the likes of Khayyam and Ayaan Hirsi Ali under an embargo. Buruma and Garton Ash may think they are championing the oppressed, but in the Middle East they are seen as stooges of Islamism; some even accuse them of being part of a campaign by the West to impose Islamism on them. The understanding is that Islamism would be a lot easier for the West to handle than governments committed to fairness, accountability, and women's and minority rights. No doubt, by bestowing intellectual respectability upon the bearers of dogma, the West has allowed Islamism to prosper in the West; more important, this in turn has emboldened Islamism to try to invade the Middle East and market itself as the only viable alternative to bad government. Furthermore, the reactionary turn in the West's intellectual life has enabled Islamism to accomplish in the West what it has failed to accomplish in most Muslim-majority countries; it has managed to make virtually all criticism of Islam and Islamism unsayable. It is a very sad day for the world when one can subject Islam and Islamism to scrutiny in Muslim-majority countries but not in the liberal West. It is this ideological shift in the West's character, this intellectual assault on its achievements, this obsession with America as the world's ultimate villain that has led to the rise of Islamism and its surrogate, BDS. In 2006, Martin Amis returned to England after living in South America for two years. The most revolting change in his country, he wrote in the *Independent*, was "the sight of middle-class white demonstrators waddling around under placards saying, 'We Are All Hezbollah Now.'" Why are we not surprised? ■

Works Cited

Amis, Martin. "You Ask the Question." Independent.com. *Independent*, January 15, 2007. Web. February 27, 2014.

Ali, Ayaan Hirsi. *Nomad: From Islam to America*. New York: Free Press, 2010.

Ali, Lorraine. "A Bomb Thrower's Life." Newsweek.com. *Newsweek*, February 26, 2007. Web. Nov. 10, 2013.

Dennoune, Karima. *Your Fatwa Does Not Apply Here: Untold Stories from the Fight Against Muslim Fundamentalism*. New York: W. W. Norton, 2013.

Barghouti, Omar. "Why Israel Fears the Boycott." Nytimes.com. *New York Times*, February 3, 2014. Web. March 1, 2014.

Berman, Paul. *The Flight of the Intellectuals*. Brooklyn, NY: Melvillehouse, 2010.

—-. *Terror and Liberalism*. New York: Norton, 2004.

—-. "Who's Afraid of Tariq Ramadan? tnr.com. *The New Republic*, May 29, 2007. Web. February 24, 2014.

Cohen, Nick. *What's Left?* London: Harper Perennial, 2007.

Eagleton, Terry. *The Idea of Culture*. Oxford: Blackwell, 2000.

Ferguson, Niall. *Civilization: the West and the Rest*. New York: Penguin, 2011.

Fisk, Robert. "My Beating by Refugees Is a Symbol of the Hatred and Fury of This Filthy War." Independent.com. *Independent*, 8 Dec. 2001. Web. 1 February 2014.

Hayden, Tom. "The Port Huron Statement." *The American Reader: Words that Moved a Nation*. Ed. Diane Ravitch. New York: Harper Perennial, 2000. 560-63.

Harris, Sam. *The End of Faith*. New York: W. W. Norton, 2005.

Hitchens, Christopher. *Arguably: Essays by Christopher Hitchens*. New York: Twelve, 2011.

—-. *Hitch-22: A Memoir*. New York: Twelve, 2010.

—-. "Assassins of the Mind." Vanityfair.com. *Vanity Fair*, February 2009. Web. March 5, 2014.

Irwin, Robert. *For the Lust of Knowledge: the Orientalists and their Enemies*. London: Allen Lane, 2006.

James, Clive. *Cultural Amnesia: Necessary Memories from History and the Arts*. New York: W. W. Norton, 2007.

Khayyam, Omar. "From Rubaiyat of Omar Khayyam: A Paraphrase from Several Literal Translations by Richard Le Gallienne." In *The Portable Atheist: Essential Readings for the Nonbeliever. Selected* and with introductions by Christopher Hitchens. Philadelphia: DA Capo Press, 2007. 7-11.

Makiya, Kanan. *Cruelty and Silence: War, Tyranny, Uprising, and the Arab World*. New York: W. W. Norton, 2007.

Marshall, Paul and Nina Shea. *Silenced: How Apostasy and Blasphemy Codes Are Choking Freedom Worldwide*. New York: Oxford UP, 2011.

Mendelson, Edward. Ed. "Preface." *The English Auden: Poems, Essays, and Dramatic Writings 1927-1939*. London: Faber & Faber, 1977. xiii-xxiii.

Miller, Arthur. *Timebends: A Life*. New York: Grove Press, 1987.

Nafisi, Azar. *Reading Lolita in Tehran: A Memoir in Books*. New York: Random House, 2004.

Pinker, Steven. *The Black Slate: The Modern Denial of Human Nature*. New York: Penguin, 2003.

Prashad, Vijay. "Understanding the Boycott of Israel's Universities." washingtonpost.com. *Washington Post*, January 25, 2014. Web. March 2014.

Ravitch, Diane. "Multiculturalism: E Pluribus Plures." *Debating P.C.: The Controversy Over Political Correctness on College Campuses.* Ed. Paul Berman. New York: Laurel Trade Paperbacks, 1992. 271-98.

Said, Edward. *Orientalism.* New York: Vintage Books, 1979.

MITCHELL COHEN

Anti-Semitism and the Left
That Doesn't Learn

I.

A determined offensive is underway. Its target is in the Middle East, and it is an old target: the legitimacy of Israel. Hezbollah and Hamas are not the protagonists, the contested terrains are not the Galilee and southern Lebanon or southern Israel and Gaza. The means are not military. The offensive comes from within parts of the liberal and left intelligentsia in the United States and Europe. It has nothing to do with this or that negotiation between Israelis and Palestinians, and it has nothing to do with any particular Israeli policy. After all, this or that Israeli policy may be chastised, rightly or wrongly, without denying the legitimacy of the Jewish state, just as you can criticize an Israeli policy—again, rightly or wrongly—without being an anti-Semite. You can oppose all Israeli settlements in the occupied territories (as I do) and you can also recognize that Benjamin Netanyahu, not just Yasser Arafat, was responsible for undermining the Oslo peace process without being an anti-Semite or anti-Zionist. You don't have to be an anti-Semite or anti-Zionist to think that some American Jewish organizations pander to American or Israeli right-wingers.

The assault today is another matter. It is shaped largely by political attitudes and arguments that recall the worst of the twentieth-century left. It is time to get beyond them. But let me be clear: I am "left." I still have no problem when someone describes me with the "s" word—socialist—although I don't much care if you call me a social democrat, left-liberal, or some other proximate term. My "leftism" comes from a commitment to—and an ethos of—democratic humanism and social egalitarianism.

What I care about is the reinvention of the best values of the historical left—legacies of British Labour, of the Swedish Social Democrats, of Jean Jaurès and Léon Blum in France, of Eduard Bernstein and Willy Brandt in Germany, of what has always been the relatively small (alas!) tribe in the U.S. associated with names like Eugene V. Debs, Norman Thomas, Michael Harrington, and Irving Howe. It's not so much a matter of political programs, let alone labels, as it is of political sensibility. I care about finding a new basis for that old amalgam of liberty, equality, and solidarity, a basis that makes sense for our "globalizing age." But I also want a left that draws real, not gestural, conclusions from the catastrophes done in the name of the left in the 20th century.

There is a left that learns and there is a left that doesn't learn. I want the left that learns to inform our Western societies (a difficult task in George W. Bush's America) and to help find ideas that actually address poverty in what used to be called the third world—rather than romanticizing it.

After 1989, the left that doesn't learn was in retreat. It was hushed up by the end of all those wretched communist regimes, by images broadcast worldwide of millions in the streets demanding liberation from dictatorships that legitimized themselves in left-wing terms. You know who I mean by the left that never learns: those folks who twist and turn until they can explain or 'understand' almost anything in order to keep their own presuppositions—or intellectual needs—intact. Once some of them were actual Leninist; now they more regularly share some of Leninism's worst mental features—often in postmodern, postcolonial, or even militantly liberal guise. Sometimes they move about on the political spectrum, denouncing their former selves (while patting their moral backs). You can usually recognize them without too much difficulty: same voice, that of a prosecuting commissar, even if their tune sounds different. It's a voice you can often hear as well in ex-communists turned neoconservative.

Their explanations, their "understandings," often rewrite history or rei-magine what is in front of their eyes to suit their own starting point. Since their thinking usually moves along a mental closed circuit, it is also the end point. Sometimes it is an idea, sometimes a belief system (which they refuse to recognize in themselves), sometimes really a prejudice, and sometimes just ambition. Goblins were often part of the story for the older left that never learned, and so too is the case today. If things don't work out as you know they must, some nefarious force must lurk. After all, the problem couldn't possibly be your way of thinking, or your inability to see the world afresh, or that you got something very wrong in the past. No, it is much easier to announce that you, unlike anyone who could disagree with you, engage in 'critical' thinking. And if your critical thinking is criticized in any way, denounce your foe immediately for "McCarthyism." Pretend that your denunciation is an argument about the original subject of dispute. That's easier than answering any of the criticism.

Consider the collateral damage done by such cries of "McCarthyism" from professors with lifetime job security: their students will never understand the evils of McCarthyism. Consider how an understanding of the evils of McCarthyism is subverted when its characteristic techniques—innuendo, for example—are used by opinionated journalists in magazines with wide circulations. Take, for instance, the case of Adam Shatz, once literary editor of *The Nation* and now with the London Review of Books. He published an article half a year before the beginning of the Iraq war suggesting that people around *Dissent* were busy hunting for a "new enemy" following the end of the cold war, and that they found it in a combination of militant Arab nationalism and Saddam Hussein.

"Though rarely cited explicitly," Shatz also explained, "Israel shapes and even defines the foreign policy views of a small but influential group of American liberals" (*The Nation*, September 23, 2002). In other words, these liberals composed the Israel lobby within the left, and they sought the American war in Iraq for the sake of the Jewish state. True, Shatz didn't hold up a file and say, "I have a list of names of liberals who are really dual loyalists." Instead he pointed to Paul Berman "and like-minded social democrats," even though the overwhelming majority of *Dissent's* editorial board including co-editor Michael Walzer was opposed to the war.

Shatz didn't deign to engage any of Berman's actual points. And those Berman advanced in the actual run-up to the Iraq invasion did not focus on Israel, but on liberalism, democracy, and totalitarianism. Arguments made by the author of the words you now read, who was a left hawk (and is now an unhappy one), likewise had nothing to do with Israel and were different—significantly so—from those made by Berman. Nothing that appeared in *Dissent* before or after Shatz's article lends credence to his innuendos.

II.

History may not progress but sometimes it regurgitates. Over the last decade, a lot of the old junk has come back. The space for it opened for many reasons. They range from the sad failures of the social-democratic imagination in the era of globalization to the postmodern and postcolonial influence in universities to George W. Bush's ascendancy with its many, many miserable consequences (not only in Iraq). The left that never learns often became the superego of the twentieth century's left. Its attempt to play that same role in the twenty-first century needs to be frustrated.

Nothing exemplifies the return of old junk more than the 'new' anti-Semitism and the bad faith that often finds expression in the statement: "I am anti-Zionist but not anti-Semitic." The fixation on Israel/Palestine within parts of the left, often to the exclusion of all other suffering on the globe, ought to leave any balanced observer wondering: What is going on here? This fixation needs demystification.

In theoretical terms, anti-Zionism and anti-Semitism are pretty easy to distinguish. Anti-Semitism is a form of race or national prejudice that crystallized in the nineteenth century. In part, it displaced or reinvented anti-Jewish religious prejudice (although centuries of religious prejudice easily wafted into racial and national bigotry). Its target was clearly Jews, not simply "Semites." It also, for some, mixed matters up further by identifying Jews with capitalism. Sadly, this became a steady feature within parts of the left that would later, habitually, conflate Jews, capitalism, and Zionism. Oddly enough, that is also what Jewish neoconservatives have tried to do in recent decades.

Anti-Zionism means, theoretically, opposition to the project of a Jewish state in response to the rise of anti-Semitism. Let's be blunt: there have been anti-Zionists who are not anti-Semites, just as there have been foes of affirmative action who are not racists. But the crucial question is prejudicial overlap, not intellectual niceties.

Remember the bad old days, when parts of the left provided theoretical justifications of things like "democratic dictatorship." In fact, if you understood—especially if you bought into—all sorts of assumptions and especially Leninist definitions, the justification works. Any professor of political theory can construct it for you and it will make perfect theoretical sense. But if you lived in a "democratic dictatorship," it was intellectual poison. It was also poison if you were committed to the best values of the left.

They are again at stake when we ask: To what extent does much anti-Zionism replicate the mental patterns of anti-Semitism? And to what extent do demagogic articulations of anti-Zionism enhance anti-Semitism? There is a curious thing about anti-Semitism, and it was captured in a remark by British novelist Iain Pears that ought to be quoted and re-quoted these days: "anti-Semitism is like alcoholism. You can go for 25 years without a drink, but if things go bad and you find yourself with a vodka in your hand, you can't get rid of it." (*International Herald Tribune*, August 11, 2003).

Much may be gleaned from the fact that the recent campaign by some British academic unions to boycott Israel was thwarted because it was found to violate anti-discrimination laws.

Last year, Denis MacShane, British Labour Parliament Member, chaired a committee of parliamentarians and ex-ministers that investigated rising anti-Semitism in Britain and beyond. "Hatred of Jews has reached new heights in Europe and many points south and east of the old continent," he wrote recently in a very brave article in the *Washington Post* (September 4, 2007). He describes a wide array of incidents. "Militant anti-Jewish students fueled by Islamist or far-left hate" seek on campuses "to prevent Jewish students from expressing their opinions." There is "an anti-Jewish discourse, a mood and tone whenever Jews are discussed, whether in the media, at universities, among the liberal media elite or at dinner parties of modish London. To express any support for Israel or any feeling for the right of a Jewish state to exist produces denunciation, even contempt."

MacShane points out that this sort of behavior is distinct from specific disputes about this or that Israeli politician. Criticism, the investigatory committee "made clear," was "not off-limits." Rightly so; the same should be true with the policies and office- holders of every government on the globe. But MacSchane also warns that something else has been going on, that old demons are reawakening and that "the old anti-Semitism and anti-Zionism have morphed into something more dangerous." The threat, he says eloquently, doesn't only concern Jews or Israel, but "everything democrats have long fought for: the truth without fear, no matter one's religion or political beliefs."

What is "truth without fear" when we speak of the relation between anti-Semitism and anti-Zionism? Is it to be found in the late Tony Judt's declaration to the *New York Times* that "the link between anti-Zionism and anti-Semitism is newly created"? (January 31, 2007). How a historian—or anyone else—could assert this is astonishing. Consider what it airbrushes out of the twentieth century—the anti-Semitic binge of Stalin's later years, just for starters.

And surely Judt, who was based at New York University and took what turned into obsessive anti-Zionist campaigning to the École Normale Supérieure in ParisNYU's Remarque Center, which defines its goal as "the study and discussion of Europe, and to encourage and facilitate communication between Americans and Europeans" is opening a center there and Judt, its director, planned, according to its website, to inaugurate it not with an address European or French politics or transatlantic relations but rather: "Is Israel Still Good for the Jews?" recalls the arrests and assassinations of the leading Jewish cultural figures of Soviet Russia on the grounds that they were

"Zionist agents of American imperialism." Surely a historian of Europe like Judt—who was once a hard leftist but then rose to intellectual celebrity in the United States in the 1980s (that is, during the Reagan era) by attacking all French Marxists for not facing up to Stalinism—recalled the charges of "Zionist conspiracy" against Jewish communists who were victimized in the Czech purge trials in the early 1950s.

If he didn't recall them when he spoke to the *New York Times*, he might have checked them out in his own book *Postwar: A History of Europe Since 1945*. There he cites Stalin's secret police chief, Lavrenti Beria, urging Czech Communists to investigate the "Zionist plot" among their comrades. Surely a historian of Europe, especially one who referred to himself as an "old leftist," recalled the campaign in 1967 and 1968 to cleanse Poland of "Zionist" fifth columnists (I suppose they were the Israel Lobby of the Polish Communist Party). If Judt didn't recall it when he talked to the *New York Times*, he might again have looked at his own book, which cites Polish Communist chief Wladyslaw Gomulka's conflation of his Jewish critics with Zionists. Since he was a historian of Europe and not the Middle East, perhaps Judt hadn't noticed how "anti-Zionism" in broad swaths of the Muslim and Arab media has been suffused by anti-Jewish rhetoric for decades—rhetoric against "al-Yahud" not Ehud Olmert or Ehud Barak.

Remember how air-brushing was done in the bad old days? Trotsky (or someone else) would suddenly disappear from a photo. Lenin or Stalin and the cheering crowds would still be there. The resulting picture is not entirely false. Does all this make Judt an anti-Semite? The answer is simple: no. It does make his grasp of the history of anti-Semitism tendentious. And tendentious history can be put to all sorts of pernicious use.

Judt's political judgment complements his historical perceptions, especially when it comes to a declared concern about Palestinian suffering. Recall his article in the *New York Review of Books* (October 23, 2003) advocating a binational state to replace Israel. A Jewish state, he explained, is an anachronism. But since then, Hamas, a political movement of religious fanatics, won the Palestinian elections, and later seized power—by force—in Gaza. Israel, in the meantime, had withdrawn entirely from Gaza and torn down all Jewish settlements there in summer 2005. Yet if you follow Judt's logic, Israel should not have withdrawn but instead integrated Gaza into itself. Obviously this would have enabled a new, better life for Palestinians, perhaps even have prevented them from turning to Hamas. And it would have taken a first happy step toward saving Israel from its anachronistic status by affording Israelis, together with Palestinians, a domestic future of perpetual ethnic civil war—a feature of modern politics that farsighted historians, but perhaps not policymakers, who have to worry about real lives, will imagine is also an anachronism. Likewise, I suppose India can save itself from being an unfortunate anachronism by a reintegration with Pakistan.

A few years ago I sought to outline commonalities between anti-Semitic and anti-Zionist discourses in a scholarly journal. It is worth reproducing. Here are major motifs that inform classical anti-Semitism:

1) **Insinuations**: Jews do not and cannot fit properly into our society. There is something foreign, not to mention sinister about them.

2) **Complaints**: They are so particularistic, those Jews, so preoccupied with their "own." Why are they so clannish and anachronistic when we need a world of solidarity and love? Really, they make themselves into a "problem." If the so-called "Jewish problem" is singular in some way, it is their own doing and usually covered up by special pleading.

3) **Remonstrations**: Those Jews, they always carp that they are victims. In fact, they have vast power, especially financial power. Their power is everywhere, even if it is not very visible. They exercise it manipulatively, behind the scenes. (But look, there are even a few of them, guilty-hearted perhaps, who will admit it all this to you).

4) **Recriminations**: Look at their misdeeds, all done while they cry that they are victims. These ranged through the ages from the murder of God to the ritual slaughter of children to selling military secrets to the enemy to war-profiteering, to being capitalists or middlemen or landlords or moneylenders exploiting the poor. And they always, oh-so-cleverly, mislead you.

Alter a few phrases, a word here and there, and we find motifs of anti-Zionism that are popular these days in parts of the left and parts of the Muslim and Arab worlds:

1) **Insinuations**: The Zionists are alien implants in the Mideast. They can never fit there. Western imperialism created the Zionist state.

2) **Complaints**: A Jewish state can never be democratic. Zionism is exclusivist. The very idea of a Jewish state is an anachronism.

3) **Remonstrations**: The Zionists carp that they are victims but in reality they have enormous power, especially financial. Their power is everywhere, but they make sure not to let it be too visible. They exercise it manipulatively, behind people's backs, behind the scenes—why, just look at Zionist influence in Washington. Or rather, dominance of Washington. (And look, there are even a few Jews, guilty-hearted perhaps, who admit it).

4) **Recriminations**: Zionists are responsible for astonishing, endless dastardly deeds. And they cover them up with deceptions. These range from the imperialist aggression of 1967 to Ehud Barak's claim that he offered a compromise to Palestinians back in 2000 to the Jenin "massacre" during the second Intifada. These sketches of anti-Semitism and anti-Zionism, with

just some variation, were originally in Mitchell Cohen, "Auto-Emancipation and Anti-Semitism: Homage to Bernard-Lazare," Jewish Social Studies (Fall 2003).

No, anti-Zionism is not in principle anti-Semitism but it is time for thoughtful minds—especially on the left—to be disturbed by how much anti-Semitism and anti-Zionism share, how much the dominant species of anti-Zionism encourages anti-Semitism.

And so:

If you judge a Jewish state by standards that you apply to no one else; if your neck veins bulge when you denounce Zionists but you've done no more than cluck "well, yes, very bad about Darfur";

if there is nothing Hamas can do that you won't blame 'in the final analysis' on Israelis;

if your sneer at the Zionists doesn't sound a whole lot different from American neoconservative sneers at leftists;

then you should not be surprised if you are criticized, fiercely so, by people who are serious about a just peace between Israelis and Palestinians and who won't let you get away with a self-exonerating formula—"I am anti-Zionist but not anti-Semitic"—to prevent scrutiny. If you are anti-Zionist and not anti-Semitic, then don't use the categories, allusions, and smug hiss that are all too familiar to any student of prejudice.

It is time for the left that learns, that grows, that reflects, that has historical not rhetorical perspective, and that wants a future based on its own best values to say loudly to the left that never learns: You hijacked "left" in the last century, but you won't get away with it again whatever guise you don. ■

CARY NELSON

The Problem with Judith Butler:
The Political Philosophy of BDS and the Movement to Delegitimate Israel

The millennium in which national differences will disappear, and the nations will merge into humanity, is still invisible in the distance. Until it is realized, the desires and ideals of the nations must be limited to establishing a tolerable modus vivendi.

—*Leo Pinsker (1882)*

When American Studies Association president Curtis F. Marez gave his absurd "one has to start somewhere" answer to a *New York Times* reporter's question as to why one should single out Israel's universities for a boycott, one might have thought he had set the gold standard for empty boycott advocacy. But soon a still more vacuous contestant arrived. At the pro-boycott session on January 9 at the Modern Language Association's 2014 annual meeting, University of Texas professor and panelist Barbara Harlow offered her own concise answer to the "Why boycott Israel?" question: "Why not?"[100]

With advocates like these, one might think the Boycott, Divestment, and Sanctions (BDS) movement against Israel would need no opponents. Certainly the public image of the humanities is not enhanced by remarks of this sort. But in truth many boycott supporters do not look for adequate reasoning. They want their existing passions inflamed still further. Palestinian BDS entrepreneur Omar Barghouti, who lectures regularly on US campuses, is adept at generating moral outrage in susceptible audiences. But the BDS movement also has more sophisticated spokespersons at its disposal. Judith Butler, who has become the movement's premier philosopher and political theorist, is perhaps the foremost among them. Her work, which carries signif-icant authority among humanists, helps us get to the heart of the movement's guiding principles. The critique I will offer thus addresses the theoretical framing of the whole BDS movement by way of Butler's approach to Israel and the Arab-Israeli conflict. She has complained that pro-BDS arguments do not receive detailed analysis. I will make every effort to provide that here.

I think it appropriate to preface an analysis of Butler's work by stating clearly that I believe she is sincere in advocating for the positions she has taken. In that light I set aside the somewhat artificial humility front-loaded into her influential 2013 talk at Brooklyn College ("I am not even a leader of this movement") as a technical distinction. And I completely believe that her journey toward boycott advocacy has been a trying one. That is especially convincing in her testimony in the 2013 Bruce Robbins film "Some of My Best Friends Are Zionists" (http://www.bestfriendsfilm.com), though by the time she gets to the point of condemning Israel as "a pernicious colonialism that calls itself a democracy" one may reasonably conclude that rage has supplanted trauma.[101] As she suggests, she's an independent advocate, not a member of the BDS governing committee. But an intellectual leader in the broader sense she surely is. Her studied denial of virtually any persuasive intent ("I am not asking anyone to join a movement this evening") I count as merely performative. In view of the objectionable and misguided campaign to prevent her and Barghouti from speaking at Brooklyn College, a campaign that violated academic freedom, she had warrant to try to disarm the audi-ence. Yet one does not need to carry a picket sign to join a movement. One can also participate by making a public intellectual and political commitment and writing on its behalf, as Butler herself has. She also gently assured the Brooklyn College audience that, for both her and Barghouti, "achieving una-nimity [of opinion] is not the goal." She urged the audience to judge their arguments dispassionately, even though Barghouti's incensed recitation of purported Israeli crimes and violations of human rights encourages not dis-passionate evaluation but self-righteous anger. Butler herself also finds such litanies of crimes—of "inequality, occupation and dispossession"—appealing. After all, she was not there just to expose the audience to ideas. She was there to persuade, and litanies of purported crimes can be persuasive.

The BDS Movement and the Academy: The State of Play

At the core of the BDS debates, unacknowledged contradictions abound. A standard BDS claim is that a university president who speaks out against academic boycotts is intimidating those faint faculty hearts on campus that would beat to a different drummer. In this age of administrative timidity, a presidential defense of academic freedom may be uncommon, but it remains part of the job; many have consequently stood up against academic boycotts (http://legalinsurrection.com/2013/12/list-of-universities-rejecting-academic-boycott-of-israel/). As Jonathan Marks points out in a January 2014 Commentary piece ("Academic Boycotters Talk Academic Freedom") the same BDS advocates who lauded Brooklyn College President Karen Gould when she quite properly defended her political science department's right to bring Barghouti and Butler to campus to speak have not adequately reflected on the fact that she is now among more than 250 college and university presidents opposing academic boycotts on the same ground: defending academic freedom. The irony goes unnoticed among BDS acolytes.

One central BDS claim is that a boycott of Israeli universities targets institutions, not individuals. Yet in his Modern Language Association panel presentation, Barghouti conceded that individual faculty members would pay a price in an academic boycott. He simply said the price was worth it. It is disappointing then that Butler in a December 8, 2013, column in *The Nation* ("Academic Freedom and the ASA's Boycott of Israel") retained the mantra of denial, again asserting that "BDS targets institutions and not individuals." It may well be that Butler believes this. She has friends who teach in Tel Aviv—including a progressive photographer and a filmmaker who focus on West Bank subjects—so it is unreasonable to imagine she wants to undermine their inter-collegial relationships, their mechanisms for professional advancement, or their academic freedom. Yet that is exactly what an academic boycott resolution will do. Her December column, the lecture she gave at Brooklyn College—the text of which appeared in the February 7, 2013, online issue of *The Nation*—her 2012 book *Parting Ways: Jewishness and the Critique of Zionism*, and a 2004 essay "Jews and the Bi-National Vision" are her major pro-boycott pieces and will be my focus here, though I will cite other pieces as appropriate.

Although Butler says a boycott would deny Israeli faculty the right to use Israeli university funds to travel to conferences in the United States, she reassures us they would be free to "pay from their own personal funds." This is hardly a realistic option for most of them, given that many have relatively low salaries. Indeed academic salaries in Israel are so low that universities provide funds for overseas travel in compensation. The fact that Israeli faculty would still be free to make the trip without financial support enables her to announce solemnly "that the only version of BDS that can be defended is one that is compatible with principles of academic freedom." Unsurprisingly, American Studies Association (ASA) leaders object to any effort to prohibit universities from funding US member travel to ASA meetings. Both the American Association of University Professors and I strongly agree and consider such prohibitions to be violations of academic freedom. Either one honors this principle comprehensively, opposing any political litmus test on scholarly travel, or it will not be honored at all. At the very least, those legislators or pro-Israeli organizations advocating ideological restrictions on state-funded faculty travel should realize that, as political winds shift, these punitive measures may target their own constituencies in turn.

Travel is not the only serious limitation faculty would face. A significant number of American, Israeli, and Palestinian faculty are involved in inter-institutional research projects funded both by their own universities and by grants they administer. These critical collaborations would collapse under a boycott regime. Butler says she has "no problem collaborating with Israeli scholars and artists as long as we do not participate in any Israeli institution or have Israeli state monies support our collaborative work." Refusing such financial support is a good deal easier for a philosopher than a scientist or an engineer who requires lab space, equipment, and staff to carry out research. Academic freedom includes the right to pursue the research of your choice, including collaborative research, and the right to pursue the funding necessary for that work. Butler dismisses the limitations a boycott would impose as a mere "inconvenience," but faculty members who find their collaborative research projects on desalinization or solar energy torpedoed are certain to use stronger language.

Then she generates an unnecessary contradiction when she claims, "Academic freedom can only be exercised when the material conditions for exercising those rights are secured, which means that infrastructural rights are part of academic freedom itself." Academic freedom protects your right to seek infrastructural support, but it does not guarantee you will get it. A physicist who cannot find the money to buy a linear accelerator has not had his or her academic freedom violated. The allocation of infrastructural support is determined by disciplinary, institutional, and political priorities, as well as available resources. Butler can certainly plead for more infrastructural support for Palestinian faculty, but it is a misunderstanding of academic freedom to make it the issue.

Fairness may well be an issue, but her dismissive "inconvenience" remark about available resources refers to constraints on Israelis, whereas her claim for the extension of academic freedom to funding addresses constraints on

Palestinians. Israelis, meanwhile, are to be selectively denied one of the most common forms of infrastructural support: travel funds. Butler frequently fails to apply a principle in an evenhanded fashion or to distinguish between an abstract statement and its practical effects, a problem, as we shall see, that infects all of her writing about Israel and that makes the political appeal of the BDS movement problematic at best.

Butler and other BDS loyalists in the United States also seem not to understand that you cannot control the consequences of a political movement by putting a couple of sentences in a resolution or a manifesto. Some faculty in the United Kingdom have already felt morally and politically driven to put a "symbolic" or nonbinding boycott resolution into practice by boycotting individuals rather than only institutions. In May 2002 University of Manchester faculty member Mona Baker removed two Israeli academics, Miriam Shlesinger and Gideon Toury, respectively, from the boards of her journals *The Translator and Translation Studies Abstracts* because of their institutional connections to Israeli universities. Despite strong academic records, they were removed on the grounds of nationality and academic affiliation. Ironically, both are also committed human rights activists. Andrew Wilkie made news in June 2003 when he rejected an Israeli student who had applied to Oxford University because the student had served in the Israeli army. In May 2006, Richard Seaford of Exeter University refused to review a book for an Israeli journal saying, "I have, along with many other British academics, signed the academic boycott of Israel." These events and more are covered by David Hirsh in his "Anti-Zionism and Antisemitism: Cosmopolitan Reflections." Some US university administrators are likely concerned about liability as a result of faculty or departmental actions that would count as discriminatory, especially admissions decisions made following a boycott endorsement. An academic boycott of Israeli institutions should be called out for what it is: a selective anti-faculty, anti-research, and anti-student agenda.

Although Butler endorses an academic boycott of Israeli universities, it is important to note that she also endorses a very broad boycott that would extend to all Israeli

> cultural institutions that have failed to oppose the occupation and struggle for equal rights and the rights of the dispossessed, all those cultural institutions that think it is not their place to criticize their government for these practices . . . . When those cultural institutions (universities, art centers, festivals) were to take such a stand, that would be the beginning of the end of the boycott.

It is important to remember that most faculty members in the United States expect their universities *not* to take political positions. Doing so jeopardizes their tax status, but institutional neutrality in political matters also protects the right of individual faculty and students to take positions that differ from one another and avoids any implication that the university speaks for its students and faculty on political matters. Butler expects all these Israeli institutions to endorse the comprehensive right of Palestinian return that would abolish Israel as a Jewish state, dissolving the very government that funds those institutions.

Meanwhile, although Butler, Barghouti, and other key BDS spokespersons have unequivocally endorsed a Palestinian right of return, they insist that the movement currently has no "official" position on the matter and thus that people who sign on to BDS petitions or otherwise endorse the movement are free to adopt their own stands. This amounts to a bait and switch operation, as people are hailed by calls for justice and then drawn into a movement whose past history and current advocacy in fact supports a more radical agenda.

A political litmus test for cooperating with Israeli universities, theater groups, symphonies, and art museums is bad enough, but their individual cooperation with this impossible demand would only *begin* the process of ending the boycott. It would continue, Butler writes, until "conditions of equality are achieved." Then the boycott would be "obsolete," but then there also would be no Israeli institutions left to boycott. In case this leaves anyone anxious, she reassures us the BDS movement "seeks to use established legal means to achieve its goals." Just what the legal mechanisms are for dissolving a nation she fails to say. Meanwhile the continual drumbeat of Butler's references to "rights" and "justice" helps blind her audience to her real agenda. Those who do follow the implications of her words might reasonably conclude they amount to war by other means.

While the assertion that only established legal means would be required to dismantle the existing Israeli state may comfort US audiences, no such plausible route actually exists. Having supported their country through a series of wars, Israeli citizens are not likely to rise up in nonviolent revolution, Eastern European style, to overthrow it. An Israeli vote to dissolve the state would require a constitutional provision to do so and is equally improbable. A flotilla of US warships enforcing a comprehensive economic blockade is not a sound bet either.

Nonetheless, the nonviolence assurance has helped the movement. Boycott advocacy has now been enhanced by a series of pro-boycott or related resolutions introduced by other faculty associations. In addition to the ASA, the Asian American Studies and Native American and Indigenous Studies associations endorsed academic boycotts of Israel in 2013. Resolutions may be introduced in other academic associations during the 2014-15 academic year. Whether the BDS wagon train is gaining momentum is impossible to say, given that in November 2013 the American Public Health Association rejected a resolution that had attacked Israel for its medical practices toward Palestinians. But BDS is certainly getting more visibility. The MLA's Executive Council decided in February 2014 to call on its 23,900 members to vote on a Delegate Assembly resolution condemning Israel's history of handling visa applications for American faculty seeking to teach or do research in the West Bank. And it discussed whether to take up a rejected call to express solidarity with the ASA by decrying intimidating notes, emails, or blog posts directed toward its members. Indeed the rhetoric of BDS presentations, documents, and essays does not always make it easy to be civil. Lack of empathy for the other side is a basic impediment to both campus debates and Arab-Israeli negotiations. As it happened, the MLA's Delgate Assembly failed to forward the resolution supporting the ASA, and the visa policy resolution went down to defeat in a vote by the membership.

Butler and the Holocaust

Butler herself draws on a number of philosophical traditions in her attempt to construct the ideal identity and form of subjectivity for Jews worldwide, especially for Israelis. My concern is not so much with whether her readings of Emmanuel Levinas, Walter Benjamin, Martin Buber, Hannah Arendt or others are accurate but rather with what she extracts from them in the service of her project to reform Israeli identity and her still more troubling goal of convincing readers that the State of Israel should be dissolved. As abstract, metaphysical speculation, her spiritual and argumentative journey toward what she considers ideal Jewishness would have no real significance. But it makes no sense—and it is more troubling—to claim it, as she does, as a mandate for personal, social, and political change.

That said, her *Parting Ways* chapters on individual writers have definite virtues. The chapter on Primo Levi, for example, offers challenging reflections on motivations for Holocaust survivor suicide. Those passages are of interest whether or not Levi actually took his own life. Her analysis of the dynamics of Holocaust memory and representation is both sound and useful. She appropriately quotes Hayden White to the effect that Holocaust metaphors sometimes have "the effect of actually producing the referent rather than merely pointing to it" (193). That can help us understand Holocaust poetry's potential for impact. Her primary motive in writing the chapter, however, is not to explicate Levi, but rather to use his doubts about Holocaust discourse to delegitimate the Israeli state. In an odd way, this turns Levi, the author of *The Drowned and the Saved*, who was a moral witness against injustice to Palestinians, into a voice warning us that Israel's founding rationale and continuing existence are corrupt, even though Butler acknowledges that "in actuality he was taking a public stand against some Israeli military actions, not Israel itself" (187) and "he clearly valued the founding of Israel as a refuge for Jews from the Nazi destruction" (186). Her bottom line is that Levi "asserts the 'I' that would not instrumentalize the historical memory of the Shoah to rationalize contemporary military violence against Palestinians" (188).

Who indeed could disagree that "it will not do to call upon the Shoah as a way of legitimating arbitrary and lethal Israeli violence against civilian populations" (187)? As in all such matters, the most intense debates about the meaning and influence of the Holocaust in contemporary life occur in Israel itself and amongst Israeli citizens and authors alike. The two books Butler cites in support of her claim that Holocaust allusions are used to justify Israeli policy are Idith Zertal's Israel's *Holocaust and the Politics of Nationhood* (2005) and Avaham Burg's *The Holocaust is Over: We Must Rise from Its Ashes* (2008). Both are Israeli authors. Zertal demonstrates that Holocaust references were widely used during Israel's founding (when their relevance is a historical fact), during the 1948 war (when the fledgling state felt militarily threatened), and that they have returned with every subsequent war. In my view, such allusions are again warranted today as the world faces the risk Iran will acquire nuclear weapons. Burg's claims are more inflammatory; he argues the Holocaust is used to justify every government policy and has permeated Israeli culture as a whole. Certainly Holocaust references do occur in political discourse, but they do not overwhelm Israeli policy making. I can find no evidence that the Holocaust is routinely invoked to justify every policy in the West Bank. There remains as well a chilling antisemitic, anti-Israel discourse among some Arabs and Europeans alike that invokes the Holocaust as unfinished business. We should recall, moreover, that in the first decade after Israel's founding about a quarter of the population were Holocaust survivors and many more had been powerfully affected.

That said, as Dina Porat points out in "From the Scandal to the Holocaust in Israeli Education," a 2004 essay in the *Journal of Contemporary History*, the Holocaust was not front and center in Israeli public life in the country's first years. Nor did it play a significant role in Israeli education for decades. The country wanted to promote collective strength and pride, which made a story of mass slaughter counterproductive. When the Holocaust came up at all, it was often to celebrate moments of resistance like the Warsaw Ghetto uprising. The picture began to change with the Eichmann trial in 1961, which emphasized victim testimony, after which Holocaust commemoration became a more visible part of public life. Yet it was not until after the

Yom Kippur War in 1973 and a heightened sense of national vulnerability that young Israelis took a major interest in the darkest period of Jewish history. That was finally reflected in the country's educational curriculum after 1980, and trips to Auschwitz became common. Before that, the Holocaust was consistently marginalized in Israeli high schools, which means that most senior Israeli politicians missed the Holocaust in their education.

The claim that young Israelis and the political culture are now obsessed with the Holocaust, however, is unsupportable. Is it the Holocaust that governs Israel's relations with European countries complicit in the Shoah? Is it the Holocaust that led Israel to cede territory to Egypt? The fact that some Israeli constituencies overuse and misuse Holocaust references does not justify condemning the entire state on that basis, as Butler would have us do. Menachim Begin, dead 30 years, used Holocaust allusions repeatedly to justify and build support for Israeli policies and actions, but Begin does not represent all Israeli politicians, then or now. Burg himself is a former Knesset Speaker. As a shorthand way to distinguish between history and current policy, I would say that the Holocaust helps justify Israel's founding but not building settlements on the West Bank.

Although Butler herself does not detail these arguments, the complaints about Holocaust references usually assert that they are used to exempt Israel from all moral responsibility for its policies and actions. As a homeland for history's ultimate victims, Israel's security needs consequently trump the rights at once of its neighbors and the Palestinians in the West Bank. According to anti-Zionist arguments, Israel's security thus falsely functions as a higher morality. Yet the very incommensurability between the Holocaust and the myriad local decisions required to maintain Israel's security should be enough to suggest that the Holocaust would not be routinely invoked whenever policies are being formulated or being put into place. Indeed, invoking the Holocaust would make most policy debates unintelligible. When the founding of the Israeli state is under discussion, however, the Holocaust is part of the historical record.

As Seyla Benhabib has written in a detailed and thoughtful March 2013 essay review of *Parting Ways* in *Constellations*, "Had it not been for the Holocaust, the small community of idealistic dreamers in Palestine would have held the sympathy of the world Jewish community, but sooner or later they would have disappeared as a separate political entity" (158). On the other hand, as Dina Porat writes in Alvin H. Rosenfeld's 2013 collection *Resurgent Antisemitism: Global Perspectives*, "Had there not been a 600,000-strong Yishuv (the Zionist Jewish entity that resided in pre-State Israel) the 360,000 survivors would not have found a shelter" (477). For Butler, as she argues in "Jews and the Bi-National Vision," such accounts of the relationship between the Holocaust and the founding of Israel are not historical facts but merely "founding narratives." She thus adopts a radical post-structuralism that denies any irrevocable relationship between historical fact and its inevitable narrative conceptualization. While one never gets past narrativity to arrive at absolute facticity, that does not mean there are no actual events and circumstances to be narrated. But for Butler it is imperative to "rethink and rewrite the history of the founding of the Israeli state" so as to "unlink the way in which the Nazi genocide continues to act as a permanent justification for this state."

Half a century and more of debates about the meaning of the Holocaust have left an immensely complex legacy that doesn't merit Butler's reductive summary. Butler characterizes Holocaust references as a "cynical and excited recirculation of traumatic material—a kind of traumatic spree." Since she has come up with that abusive language, one may fairly ask whether she, Barghouti, and others are doing anything else themselves with their litanies of anti-Palestinian violence? It was theologians and poets who first warned us that what the Holocaust teaches us about human beings leaves doubts about the meaning of life itself. Butler would have been better served by consulting Israeli philosopher Elhanan Yakira's important *Post-Zionism, Post-Holocaust: Three Essays on Denial, Forgetting, and the Delegitimation of Israel* (2010). One conclusion we can draw from Holocaust testimony and Holocaust literature is that it casts a shadow over everything we say and do. That is the burden, among other texts, of Primo Levi's utterly unsparing poem "Shemá."

Justice as an Ahistorical Abstraction

Foremost among Butler's strategies in all her pro-boycott work—and central to her appeal and success—is the deployment of an abstract, universalizing concept of "justice" detached from any serious contextual challenges. In "Deconstructing Israel," a January 2014 review first published in German in *Jungle World* and then translated, Stephan Grigat points out that her main strategy is to mobilize an abstract and ahistorical universalism against all the historical particularities of Zionism. The main particularities she does cite are Israeli-imposed injustices suffered by Palestinians. But she does nothing to historicize the concept of justice itself in her work on the Middle East.

I have trouble accepting that this abstract version of justice is being deployed by the author of *Gender Trouble* (1990), a book I have long admired, have taught repeatedly, and whose model of gender as socially and historically constructed (and thus learned and performed) I have pretty completely internalized. While gender and justice are concepts that operate in different registers, both are socially and historically constructed. An abstract notion of justice can serve as a social good and can hail people's sense of identity and patterns of behavior, but it has no place in discussions of the Middle East without historically-based qualifications. Like other BDS advocates, Butler takes political self-determination as an unqualified good for Palestinians, an end result that then becomes a sine qua non for any acceptable resolution of the conflict. Anything less than that, she believes, will not constitute justice. And Americans, especially on the left, like to believe they stand firmly on the side of justice.

Like other BDS proponents, she avoids any serious reflection on what would constitute political self-determination for Israelis, save for the implication that Israeli hearts can never really be at peace until Palestinians have secured all their wishes. That, however, is precisely what cannot be achieved in a "just" resolution of the conflict. For too many Palestinians "justice" means Palestinian sovereignty throughout the land between the Mediterranean and the Jordan River, a dream that perhaps too many Israelis share in reverse, in the form of ambitions for a "Greater Israel," though it is not a majority view. The main Israeli constituency for that perspective is those far right West Bank settlers who believe they have a divine mandate to be there. If peace is to be achieved, many on both sides will have to relinquish a model of justice designed to benefit only one party to any negotiations. So would Butler if she were to imagine a solution adapted to political realities.

Everyone will have to settle for less than they imagine "justice" to entail. For neither the Palestinians nor the Israelis will give up their ambitions for sovereignty. Both sides will have to settle for less land over which their sovereignty will reign. The territorial compromises will have to include some way of establishing a Palestinian capital in East Jerusalem. For some Jews, that is a betrayal of a legacy at once religious and historical, a betrayal therefore of their notion of justice. Yet Jerusalem has evolved into a city with interwoven working relationships between Arabs and Jews and with public services that crisscross any conceivable boundaries. Some local cooperation will be necessary. We thus get nowhere by holding aloft a lantern called justice and letting it blind us to complexities of culture, history, and national desire, along with the realities of economic and social integration. That lantern also blinds Butler to the diversity of Palestinian experience and desire. As Benhabib writes,

> The number of Arab youth who are now perfectly bi-lingual is grow-ing and, along with it, their political capacity to engage Israeli society directly. Many Palestinian Arabs living in occupied East Jerusalem would much rather become Israeli citizens in an open and gender-egalitarian society than live under the Islamist rule of a party. (159)

That is at least one reason why Butler cannot simply assert without proof that non-Jewish Israeli citizens fundamentally feel unhappily bound "to a specific and controversial, if not contradictory, version of democracy." As a literature scholar, I might add this: does anyone imagine that the Palestinian novelists and poets who write in Hebrew would choose to dismantle the state of which they are citizens?

Butler's decontextualized, abstract notion of justice also helps her give strong literal endorsement to the Palestinian "right of return" to reside in Israel. They could choose compensation instead, she acknowledges, but compensation could not be the exclusive option. "People who have been made stateless by military occupation," she remarked to *Open Democracy*, "are entitled to repatriation." Yet an unqualified right of return policy means the end of the Jewish state. I believe it may be possible to endorse a qualified right of return as an abstract principle, not as a way literally to return to Israel, but as a way to regain something of what was lost, to acknowledge that wrongs were done, and so to confirm some version of belated compensation, while fully admitting that actual physical return cannot possibly be put into practice. Affirmation of the principle then becomes symbolic, a form of historical witness. Butler, however, cannot reliably negotiate distinctions between an abstraction and the complexities of social life. In truth many Palestinians want the right of return as a way to leverage the demographics of the Israeli state, so the symbolic statement would work only if it were clearly accepted as such in a negotiated agreement.

Again, Butler leaves the specifics of how the right of return would be put in place to speculation, but her conviction that Israel is an illegitimate state creates impediments. Is every existing deed to Israeli land to be voided? How can an illegitimate state issue new deeds that would be valid? Or are we to wait until the incorruptible Palestinian Authority can assign ownership? Perhaps an Oklahoma-style land rush can be scheduled, with Palestinians lined up on the border waiting till the starting pistol signals the chance to claim a homestead.

"It is not possible," Butler argues, "to restrict the problem of Palestinian subjugation to the occupation alone." Some confidently claim that if Israel unilaterally abandoned much of the West Bank—a solution I think may not only be morally and politically necessary but also inevitable if Israel is to save the soul of its democracy by freeing itself of an internal subject population— BDS would lose its raison d'etre and would quickly wither away as an organization. But everything Butler says argues for the opposite outcome. So long as the children and grandchildren and extended families of Palestinians who once lived within Israel's 1948 borders cannot return to surviving homes, she believes, so long as they cannot return to rebuild villages razed in 1948 or later, justice will not be served. Indeed, as early as her 2004 essay "Jews and the Bi-National Vision" she called for "the just reallocation of arable land" in Israel proper.

Contrary to Butler, it is entirely *possible*, politically possible and logically possible, to confine the problem of Palestinian *subjugation* to the West Bank. She doesn't like that possibility, but that does not make it logically or politically impossible. Subjugation, moreover, hardly describes the status of Palestinian citizens within Israel proper. Whatever inequalities affect Israel's Arab citizens could be more readily resolved if the threat of a Palestinian majority were taken out of the equation. But Butler and too many other BDS supporters insist that threat of a Palestinian majority must become a reality, just as it remains a sacred principle for some Palestinian political groups.

Unilateral Israeli withdrawal from the West Bank is not likely to involve abandoning all the settlements, because it would be politically impossible to do so absent an agreement, but it should be possible to withdraw from at least 90 percent of the West Bank. Complete withdrawal would leave Palestinians no incentive to negotiate further and thus no way to agree on territorial swaps. Israel would also face serious security risks, not the least of which is fear of a Hamas takeover on the West Bank. In the end, real peace cannot be achieved without an agreement that provides for Israeli security. Nor would partial withdrawal relieve Israel of all international pressure. But it would involve abandoning all settlements (including Hebron) except those close to the border and thus separate Israel from large numbers of Palestinians, which would change the nature of and basis for international protest and undercut the popular left claim that Israel is a colonialist power.

If most of the West Bank were free of an Israeli presence, it would in effect be a preliminary Palestinian state, one achieved without resolving the most difficult problems, but one that would give the two-state solution significant inertial force. It would also eliminate many of the oppressive features of West Bank Palestinian life, or at least those that are consequences of Israeli policy, an outcome that must occur sooner rather than later. In numerous publications Peter Beinert has pioneered the use of the term "nondemocratic Israel" to describe conditions on the West Bank. That seems a useful way to distinguish the West Bank from the robust democracy that prevails in Israel proper. If current negotiations fail, I believe Israel has no choice but to abandon its undemocratic zone. Support for that deadline could help pressure the current Israeli government to negotiate in good faith.

Internal resistance to unilateral withdrawal has increased because many Israelis feel the withdrawal from Gaza has been less than a rousing success, given what Gaza has become. Israelis have faced the culmination of the struggle between Fatah and Hamas in a Hamas victory in 2007, a continuing series of rocket attacks on Israel, and such cultural changes in Gaza as the imposition of limitations on women's rights—none of which the BDS movement has seen fit to criticize. Nor has Butler. In a 2006 Q&A at a UC Berkeley teach-in, Butler remarked that "understanding Hamas, Hezbollah as social movements that are progressive, that are on the Left, that are part of a global Left, is extremely important," that despite their official state department classification as terrorist groups. Her remarkably modest qualification—"that does not stop us from being critical of certain dimensions of both movements"—does not really undercut her basic claim.

In a 2012 *Mondoweiss* piece Butler backtracked by saying "those political organizations define themselves as anti-imperialist, and anti-imperialism is one characteristic of the global left, so on that basis one could describe them as part of the global left" and repeated her rejection of state violence, but still could not quite bring herself to condemn Hamas explicitly. If asked to comment on a particular suicide bombing with named civilian casualties, Butler would presumably repeat her standard "I reject violence" rejoinder. Actually naming a specific terrorist attack and condemning Hamas for it is apparently unpalatable for her. Nor is she inclined to admit that Hamas is a fundamentally antisemitic organization. Nonetheless, in my view, despite Hamas's ascendency, Israel is still better off without Gaza than with it, though Gaza certainly needs to be demilitarized. Ari Shavit in his recent *My Promised Land: The Triumph and Tragedy of Israel* (2013) acknowledges that but suggests the experience of withdrawing from Gaza may recommend a more staged withdrawal from the West Bank. The *Jerusalem Post* reported similar recommendations by Amos Yadin, a former Israeli chief of military intelligence, in an article by Herb Keinon published on January 27, 2014.

Anti-Semitism and Butler's Agenda for Jewish Identity

The context for Butler and others in the United States is different from that for Palestinians and Israelis. She is not prey to a desire to live in an ancestral family home in Tel Aviv, clinging instead to a distinctly American politics based on an idealist fantasy of historical possibility. She holds out the ideal of "a just and peaceable form of co-existence," of "a place beyond war." But that place for her has a name, Greater Palestine, and it has a people in command, Palestinians. This peaceable kingdom fantasy, of a binational state in which everyone just "gets along," has great appeal to the American left, which partly explains Butler's immense political appeal. It is an abstract, idealist solution— underwritten by Edward Said's equally unrealistic observation that Israelis and Palestinians are both diasporic peoples whose parallel histories should generate compatibility—that neither Middle Eastern politics nor history can deliver. Are Jews who have lived all their lives in Israel supposed to have inherited their diasporic souls genetically? Or did they acquire this identity by listening to stories of their grandparents' lives? Presumably an observation like that Yossi Klein Halevi makes in *Like Dreamers* about "the rapidity with which the rerootedness of the Jews had occurred" in a kibbutz in the 1960s may simply be dismissed, since it does not fit the theory: "In a single generation . . . the kibbutz had created young people who seemed to lack even a genetic memory of exile" (14).

There are of course traditions of assigning common psychological identities to racial, ethic, sexual, and religious groups, but that has hardly been an admirable enterprise. One may cite Otto Weininger's immensely popular *Sex and Character*, published in Vienna and Leipzig in 1903, as an example. Its main point was to argue that women have no souls, but in the 13th chapter, "The Jewish Character," Weininger points out that the Jews are a "feminine race" and thus have no souls either. Nor, he adds, do they play sports or sing. Jews, he advised, need to resist their fundamental nature. Butler of course wants Jews to succumb to what she supposes is theirs, and she thinks it a virtue, not a flaw, but this reopens the territory to less positive and fundamentally racist speculations about Jewish identity. This game cannot be controlled once the play begins. Jews have a collective shared history as a people, but that does not install a uniform character in people with different life histories and nationalities.

Butler's fantasy notion that Israeli Jews would willingly submit to Arab rule is grounded in yet another hypothetical piece of invented diasporic psychology: "one of the most important ethical dimensions of the diasporic Jewish tradition, namely, the obligation of co-habitation with those different from ourselves." In *Parting Ways*, as Benhabib points out, Butler develops her distinctive notion of cohabitation as an ethical imperative from a reading of Hannah Arendt: "This is a strange attempt to interpellate Arendt for Butler's own social ontology via the use of terms, such as 'cohabitation' that are not Arendt's at all" (154). It is an effort "to tease out what she calls a 'principle' out of Arendt's text." "This may be Butler," Benhabib concludes, "but it is certainly not Arendt. Arendt writes of 'plurality' and not of 'plural cohabitation.'" Most importantly, Arendt considered plurality part of the human condition, not something particular to the diasporic experience of Jews.

It is remarkable that Said himself believed this tenuous level of identity could sustain a shared national allegiance, especially given that the Palestinians blame the Israelis for their diasporic condition. But perhaps, as Butler suggests, Said was just conducting a thought experiment. Of course there is a certain kind of theorist who does not readily distinguish between a thought experiment and a policy proposal. Butler's own analysis does not embody a responsible account of history; instead it is divorced from history and presents a grave danger were it to become the centerpiece of US foreign policy. Meanwhile, it represents a delusional form of false consciousness for American students and faculty. Butler is marketing a very unhealthy drug to her readers. But they love the high it gives them, grounded in a confident and absolute division between good and evil and a vision of transcendent justice that justifies the absolute victory of the former over the latter.

There is a signal moment in Butler's 2013 *Nation* essay, easy to overlook, when we can see the price a frustrated idealist can exact when real bodies embedded in history are subjected to the idealist gaze. It is when she engages those "smaller forms of binational cultural communities in which Israeli Jews and Palestinians live and work together." There have been local realities of this sort repeatedly over the last century in Palestine, and they persist in some places and in some contexts today, despite the wave of nationalist sentiment that swept through Palestinian communities in the 1920s and 1930s and that transformed the conflict thereafter.

What is astonishing and disturbing in Butler's analysis is that she finds the lives of such people inadequate and unacceptable unless they take on the larger oppositional agenda she wants to promote. Ten years ago, in "Jews and the Bi-National Vision," she was comfortable hoping that "modes of civil and economic cooperation would lead organically to a form of government that would be based on a shared way of life between Arabs and Jews." She imagined then that "such alliances could provide the foundation and the model for collaborative associations seeking non-violent and just solutions to conflicts that appear intractable." Now she displays the impatience that frustrated utopians on the left and the right have shown many times when people in local communities are satisfied to live their lives as they see fit. "The only question," she writes, "is whether those small communities continue to accept the oppressive structure of the state, or whether in their small and effective way oppose the various dimensions of subjugation and disenfranchisement." Coexistence is insufficient, misguided, lacking, unless it matures to join "solidarity struggles." "Co-existence becomes solidarity when it joins the movement that seeks to undo the structural conditions of inequality, containment and dispossession." Of course, then it is likely to cease being coexistence. Discontent with those uninterested in reshaping their lives to fit an overarching political agenda not infrequently produces intolerance and violent strategies—leaving millions of dead in the USSR in the 1930s and again, decades later, in Cambodia. What is one to do in the end when people just will not listen to those who know better? They will need to be reeducated. It will require a cultural revolution.

Butler makes much of the nonviolent character of the BDS movement. It is "the only credible non-violent mode of resisting the injustices committed by the state of Israel." I suppose she believes that because BDS works through discourse and protest. And it is nonviolent as a fantasy structure. Butler invokes this fantasy when she protests that the "BDS is not the same as Hamas." Of course they aren't the same. BDS is a political movement, though one that offers no real prospect of improving the lives of the Palestinians it proposes to speak for, and Hamas is at least partly an armed terrorist group, though its role in Gaza has led it to provide social services as well. Like it or not, however, the BDS movement and Hamas share the same goal, the elimination of the Jewish state, and Hamas has hardly embraced nonviolence. BDS and Hamas are conceptually and politically linked, even though Butler and BDS assume a peaceful transition to majority Palestinian rule is plausible. The Jews give up the state of Israel and with it all their religious and political commitments and submit to a Palestinian majority. I have not heard the related left fantasy for some years, for obvious reasons, but before suicide bombers visited Israeli cities and crude Qassam rockets arrived from Gaza, leftists sometimes characterized Palestinians as uniquely peace-loving and gentle among all the peoples of the earth. We like to project our fantasies of extra-human virtue onto political victims, but doing so makes them something other than what they are.

Nonetheless there is a remnant of that celebratory left dichotomy in what Benhabib describes as Butler's "simple equivalences between rationalism, the sovereign subject, Eurocentrism, and Zionist colonialism" (157). Opposed to this outdated epistemology of mastery is what Butler sees as a blameless anti-colonialist Palestinian resistance movement, but, as Benhabib adds, "We know that anti-colonial movements are not always emancipatory and that political action in the name of oppressed peoples can also carry the seeds of oppression within it." Butler, she concludes, "seems beholden to an anti-imperialist jargon of the politics of purity" (157).

Butler sustains the relative purity of the opposition in part by minimizing its antisemitism. "Some forms of Palestinian opposition do rely on antisemitic slogans, falsehoods, and threats," she writes, and "all these forms of antisemitism are to be unconditionally opposed." Thus she reduces Palestinian antisemitism to a rhetorical strategy, trivializing its significance, and discounting what Israelis know to be true: that antisemitism sometimes represents deep-seated conviction. Even the most vocal of Israel's internal critics acknowledge the level of local and regional antisemitism Israel faces. Thus Israeli faculty member Eva Illouz, a fierce critic of Israeli policy, writes "Some Palestinians are virulently antisemitic and are supported by even more violent antisemites in the surrounding Arab countries." It does little good for Butler to denounce slogans confidently—though also, oddly, often in the passive voice—when what Israel is actually confronting is long nurtured hatred and resentment, as if Palestinians, by censuring their language could reform their feelings and beliefs as well. Part of what we now know in full detail, courtesy of Jeffrey Herf's 2010 *Nazi Propaganda for the Arab World*, is that German antisemitic radio broadcasts in Arabic in the 1930s and 1940s helped prepare the ideological ground for opposition to Israel and the first Arab-Israeli war.

Nor does it help to address antisemitic impulses within BDS philosophy by defensive denial—countering that "it would appear that no oppositional move . . . can take place without risking the accusation of antisemitism." Israel is surrounded by undemocratic regimes intolerant of religious diversity. While it may be a conflicted democracy with serious problems, Israel proper remains a remarkably free society by any comparison with its neighbors, so one may fairly wonder why American BDS followers single it out as a rogue state. Is one left with the flippant "Why not?" response? Dialogue with anyone who argues that any criticism of Israeli policy amounts to antisemitism may be impossible, but a defense of the BDS movement that defends its challenges to Israel's existence with a blanket denial of antisemitism is no better than its more extremist opposition.

In the end, one of the key cultural and historical traditions that makes it possible to isolate Israel conceptually and politically from all other nations is antisemitism. It is the long and abiding international history of antisemitism that makes Israel not only available to be singled out but also always already singled out—*othered*, set apart. Antisemitism is a fundamental condition of possibility for unqualified opposition to the Israeli state. It is certainly not the only impulse underlying opposition to Israel. Some feel betrayed by conditions on the West Bank because they long championed Israel as an example of liberal democracy. But opposition to Israel also provides antisemitism with its contemporary intellectual and moral credibility. Anti-Zionism is thus antisemitism's moral salvation, its perfect disguise, its route to legitimation. Absolute opposition to Israel's existence increases antisemitism's cultural and political reach and impact. Arguments about whether a given opponent is or is not antisemitic are thus necessarily at least in part irrelevant. If you augment and empower antisemitism unwittingly, it may not matter what is in your heart. In that light, denial of antisemitism among those who reject Israel's right to exist counts only as affirmation. Thus Barbara Harlow's seemingly idiotic answer "Why not?" actually speaks to the existential reality. Why not single out the country that already stands alone in our minds? Indeed it stands alone in the minds of Jews and non-Jews alike.

Some Jews, including some who testify in the Bruce Robbins film, experience an overwhelming need to expel Israel from themselves, to convince both themselves and everyone else that they do not harbor it—to use a Derridean metaphor—encrypted within. That helps explain the intensity with which some Jews reject the very existence of an Israeli state. And yet for Jews Israel always seems to be encapsulated, warded off within, so their passion for expelling it escalates. It is a dynamic and progressive process. The well-known accusation of Jewish self-hatred is thus a simplification and a slander. They hate and fear but part of themselves. Asked why they are determined to condemn Israel for practices comparable to those many other nations engage in, some Jews claim their right to do so as a birthright. At public events, most recently at MLA in 2014, Bruce Robbins always responds to the "Why Israel" question by answering "because I am a Jew, and I object to what Israel is doing in my name." He delivers the statement with enough anguish and vehemence so as to forestall further discussion. As I suggest in *No University is an Island: Saving Academic Freedom* (2010), I have heard some opponents of Israel speak with such uncontrolled venom that I am convinced that they are antisemitic whether they know it or not, but I would not say that of either Butler or Robbins.

Yet antisemitism, it is critical to realize, is an inescapable, enabling condition underwriting the possibility of castigating Israel on grounds on which it is the same or similar to other countries, not different from them. Worse still, Israel's sameness actually applies not to fact-based comparisons but rather to the programmatic invocation of cultural and political categories: Israel discriminates against segments of those under its control; Israel is a religious state, and we object to religious states on principle; Israel's warrant to exist as a nation state implicates power dynamics, not some inevitable destiny; other populations believe they have equal or greater right to the land; Israel's borders have not remained the same since its founding; Israel's human rights record in areas over which it exercises control is imperfect. All these concerns are less applicable to Israel than to more than a score of other countries in the Middle East and elsewhere, yet BDS advocates consider Israel alone a pariah among nations. It is no surprise, moreover, that BDS advocates discount both past and future violence against Israel and that antisemitism makes it possible to do so. Everything that might be done to a group of Jews has already been done, has already happened. Such violence is not a risk; it is a historical given.

In the context of celebrating BDS nonviolence, Butler dismisses as categorically absurd the accusation that BDS rhetoric is a form of hate speech. She also rejects the argument that her and other BDS arguments have "spawned a set of variations" that include "hate speech directed against either the State of Israel or Israeli Jews." Certainly we must agree that rational arguments against Israeli policy do not constitute hate speech. There can be no meaningful political dialogue or debate unless people are free to criticize a nation's policies. The problem arises with Barghouti's, Butler's, and BDS's intense and unqualified rejection of the Jewish state and with all the moral outrage they direct toward Israel. That moral outrage is not directed toward

Israeli policy alone. It is an existential and political rejection of Israel's right to exist. It is filled with hostility. And it does encourage still more inflamed rhetoric that crosses the line into hate speech. Hate speech can and does promote violence.

Suffice it to say that there is no nonviolent way to transition to Judith Butler's peaceable kingdom and no reason either to suppose the kingdom would end up being peaceable. "Is it possible," she asked in Brooklyn, that words might "bring about a general ethos of non-violence?" As a political theory, that speculation and the BDS goal she offers for Palestine has no relation to reality. It is a fantasy that could only play out in violence. However nonviolent the fantasy is in intent, therefore, it could only be violent in effect. That said, I am convinced Butler believes this nonsense. While she may have been merely performative in her lead-in to *The Nation* piece, I believe she had drunk her own Kool-Aid by the end: "My wager, my hope," she writes, "is that everyone's chance to live with greater freedom from fear and aggression will be increased as those conditions of justice, freedom, and equality are realized." At that point feelings of ecstatic self-love sweep over the American audience and the applause rises. They can imagine themselves to have entered that "ec-static relationality, a way of being comported beyond oneself, a way of being dispossessed from sovereignty and nation" that Butler repeatedly invokes in *Parting Ways* (9). Of course that illusion of a move beyond nation is one that American exceptionalism and power has itself made possible for its citizens. It would not find such a warm reception in the Middle East. Indeed there is no evidence that either Palestinians or Israelis in general *want* to live together.

Although those who have not read basic histories of Israel may not realize it, Butler does invoke the right context for discussions of the origins of the Arab-Israeli conflict. She realizes that the incompatible "claims of 1948" still underlie positions today. Unfortunately she overlays those competing claims with the absolutist moral stance that dominates BDS discourse. Instead of acknowledging competing claims for national identity and sovereignty over the land, she contrasts the "Israeli demand for demographic identity" to "the multivalent forms of dispossession that affect Palestinians." In other words, what are in fact parallel but competing nationalist and religious ambitions are transformed into a simple binary of Israeli dominance and Palestinian subservience.

Such binaries permeate BDS ideology. Israel is a state; the Palestinians are a people. Israelis assert privileges, whereas Palestinians seek rights. Israel is a monolithic and authoritarian state oppressing a pluralistic people. The conflict embodies an opposition of wealth versus poverty, white European colonialism versus brown indigeneity, and finally the demonic versus the saintly.

The history of the Jewish people in the land of Israel, the land's connection to Judaism, all this has no meaning for her. She simply "eschews the Zionist linkage of nation to land" (15). Instead of seeing the conflict as one between two peoples with indigenous ties to the land, she credits only one. Justice is thus all on one side, and the conflict is to be resolved by granting the Palestinians everything they wanted from the outset, from the moment that war broke out on November 30, 1947. In *Parting Ways* Butler explicitly lists "the massive dispossessions of Palestinians in 1948" (2) as one of the wrongs that must be righted. Indeed she goes on to say misleadingly that "Israel has been built on a series of land confiscations that preceded 1948" (205). A very frank account of violence on both sides may be found in Benny Morris's *1948: The First Arab-Israeli War* (2008). Ari Shavit's powerful and disturbing chapter "Lydda, 1948" has also convinced many for the first time that they need to recognize why that year was a tragedy for the Palestinians. For Butler, importantly, not only are the 1967 borders illegitimate. There are no legitimate borders. She believes that a fully ethical Judaism would lead one to reject the whole existence of a Jewish state, not just its policies. Does she really think she can preach that sermon to Jews worldwide with a commitment to a Jewish state, let alone to Israelis themselves? If not, what is her audience for that argument, and what would their motives be for endorsing it?

Butler disparages "the football lingo of being 'pro' Palestine and 'anti' Israel." "This language is reductive," she adds, "if not embarrassing." But what her decontextualized and ahistorical notion of justice allows her to do is to duplicate exactly that dichotomy by way of a moral economy of right and wrong. Repairing all the components of Israeli "injustice" then becomes the one priority and the only goal for the region. And we are assured that the result "might one day become a just and peaceable form of coexistence," that is, if we create a state with a Palestinian majority, a state that by its very nature grants "justice" to only one of the parties to the equation. But Butler in fact maintains that justice only inheres in the Palestinian cause. For her there is no valid case to be made for Israelis as citizens of a Jewish state. In the rhetorical economy of her work there are no competing arguments. It is a conflict between truth and error. That model provides no basis for either negotiation or compromise. It foresees only a basis for continuing struggle and eventual Israeli capitulation.

Whatever willingness Butler herself might have to discuss these matters, moreover, does not carry over to the BDS movement as a whole. They accept the logic that transforms parallel claims into a moral opposition of right and wrong, infecting BDS discourse with a presumptive sense of moral superiority that need not be examined further. If you sign on to BDS discourse, you sign on to its conclusions. Indeed you may take refuge in its slogans and its rallying cries—"justice," "colonialism." BDS converts sometimes do not need to think any further. That is why Butler's Brooklyn College invitation to a dialogue is in reality somewhat disingenuous. The BDS movement is not interested in reflection or conversation. The fraction of the American left that has adopted the BDS mantra thus revels in the confidence that they are in the right, whereas the only real hope for peace lies in a cold recognition that the opposing forces can only be accommodated by stable, negotiated forms of partition. If you are committed to promoting solutions, then slogans will not suffice. That gives BDS an advantage with impressionable students hungry for a cause to embrace.

BDS discourse can only sustain this moral absolutism by erecting a series of prohibitions, prohibitions against speaking the words that must be spoken if honest discussion and debate are to proceed. There is first of all the virtual prohibition against mention of Palestinian violence. Butler gives no attention to (and shows no concern about) the effect on Israelis of a series of suicide bombings whose victims have included both Jews and Palestinians, along with continuing threats from Arab and non-Arab states in the region, Iran being the most worrisome. If she talked to someone who escaped an explosion at a favorite café by a few minutes, she might feel differently. Then there is the prohibition against granting any legitimacy to the concept of a Jewish state, along with the prohibition against admitting what the fate of Jews would be in an Arab-dominated state. And finally there is the "third rail" of all US debate over opposition to Israel, the role of antisemitism. As Robert S. Wistrich writes in his contribution to Rosenfeld's *Resurgent Antisemitism*, "Even to raise the issue is often considered by leftists and some liberals, too, as an act of Zionist 'intellectual terrorism' primarily designed to silence justified opposition toward Israel" (411). In an effort to counter this strategy, faculty here and abroad have been working to turn the issue of antisemitism in anti-Israel groups from a prohibited topic into a valid academic subject for research and analysis, and they have made notable progress. As I suggested above, it is not that "any and all criticism of the State of Israel is antisemitic" (*Parting Ways* 2), the sad defensive position that Butler unnecessarily debunks, but that any solution that involves dismantling the Jewish state is antisemitic in effect and fueled at least obliquely, as Butler seems not to understand, by antisemitic traditions that make the needs of a long dispossessed people, the Jews, either secondary or expendable. Many BDS advocates simply become agitated when the subject is broached, especially in conversation, branding suggestions that Jews would fare poorly indeed under Arab nationalism and Muslim fundamentalism as themselves irrational.

Ever since Larry Summers, then Harvard president, argued in 2002 in response to the campus divestment movement of the time, that it was among the anti-Israel causes he found "anti-Semitic in their effect if not in their intent," Butler has taken this to mean that many irrationally regard all criticism of Israel as antisemitic. In fact, virtually no serious commentators do so, and thus Butler is essentially torching a straw man in making this argument. Her detailed response to Summers occurs in "No, it's not anti-semitic," a 2003 essay published in the *London Review of Books:* "Summers's distinction between effective and intentional anti-semitism cannot hold." "The only way to understand effective anti-semitism," she argues, "is to presuppose intentional anti-semitism: the effective anti-semitism of any criticism turns out to reside in the intention of the speaker as retrospectively attributed by the listener." This is a very odd piece of logic that is completely divorced from any understanding of human behavior, since people routinely make statements without understanding the effect they might have. Statements about Israel and international politics in general, moreover, are commonly naïve, misinformed, or ignorant. Indeed people often have no idea what cultural traditions their statements echo, revive, or help mobilize for the present. The distinction between effective and intentional anti-Semitism is thus both realistic and useful.

Helen Fein's widely cited 1987 definition of antisemitism describes it as "a persisting latent structure of hostile beliefs towards Jews as a collectivity" (67). The European Union Monitoring Center on Racism and Xenophobia notably observed that antisemitism could be embodied in verbal attacks that "target the State of Israel, conceived as a Jewish collectivity." Butler's other strategy is to insist she is "holding out for a distinction to be made between Israel and Jews." Fair enough. But that does not give her license to imagine dissolving the state of Israel would be either neutral or beneficial for the six million Jews living there, the largest population of Jews in the world. Calling for the end of the Jewish state has antisemitic effects even if Butler's professed intent is redemptive and utopian. While Butler, finally, complains that nothing tells us how to differentiate between criticism of Israel that is and is not antisemitic, that is simply not the case. Criticism that pressures Israel to improve its laws and practices, that helps Israel see its way toward a negotiated solution, that would lead to withdrawal from the West Bank—while reaffirming Israel's right to exist as a Jewish state within secure borders—is not antisemitic. Claims that Israel has no right to exist as a Jewish state, that it was an illegitimate colonialist enterprise from the outset, are indeed antisemitic in effect.

In addition to its prohibitions, BDS has its epithet of choice: Zionist. Butler helps solidify that epithet, as Alan Johnson points out in a January 2013 review of *Parting Ways* in *Fathom*, by creating

> what Marx would have called an 'ahistorical, eternal, fixed and abstract conception' of the history of Zionism and Israel from which is missing actual experience and real emergence, from which has been erased all concrete differences (between periods of Israeli history, between different wings of Zionism, between different political parties within Israel, between different Israeli social classes).

There are other Zionisms in her account, but not constitutive of the monolithic Israeli state she has constructed. Indeed, although she acknowledges "the singular history of Jewish oppression" (29), her theory of Jewish identity relies on the same unitary model of Jewish history, homogenizing it as a rich broth exhibiting multiple forms of cohabitation with non-Jews. That leaves all Jews, though some would be surprised to learn it, with identities founded in "an impurity, a mixing with otherness . . .an ineradicable alterity" (31).

Ineradicable? What on earth is Butler thinking? She attributes the concept of "an ineradicable alterity" to Continental philosophy, but then decides herself it is "constitutive of what it is to be a Jew" (31). So Jews can never be truly assimilated. They never have been and never will be. Even though Butler wants to celebrate the post-nationalist consequences of this otherness as a virtue, it remains as well a burden. And despite her decision to affirm her and my alterity, it remains a racist construct. For how can a relativist poststructuralist sustain alterity as a transhistorical culturally constructed category? For the Nazis, it was race. And for them it was a feature of the eternal Jew, "*Ewige Jude.*" Now with Butler the eternal Jew returns to disavow Zionism. Of course one hears echoes in Butler's insistence on a unitary and transhistorical Jewish identity based on otherness and exile of the antisemitic myth of the "Wandering Jew," "*le Juif errant,*" that first was popularized in the Middle Ages and spread through Europe in the Renaissance. Long thought the punishment for the supposed crime of killing Christ, it is now to be fulfilled as the punishment for the Naqba.

Of course this primal crime means there can be no redemptive element to Zionism. Butler makes the absurd demand, in fact fully in play for over a century, that "the historiographical presumption of progressive history that supports the idea of Zionism as the unfolding realization of an ideal can and must be countered by a critique of that form of progressivism" (99). Has she read any reliable histories of Israel? She could start with Anita Shapira's

Israel: A History (2012). The history of Zionism is complex and different and never without self-critique. Zionists often had competing and contradictory aims and beliefs, but now it seems mere belief in the validity of a Jewish state can be belittled as a Zionist obsession, often with the implied slander that Zionism equals racism. That is certainly where a portion of the American left, including a segment of the Jewish left, now stands. American Jews young enough to have grown up feeling fully assimilated find the controversy over Israel increasingly uncomfortable. It sets them apart, others them within the left in ways they have never experienced before. And so they seek sometimes to rejoin their comrades by paying the only price that is acceptable: defining the occupation as the very existence of the Jewish state and implicitly advocating its delegitimation and dissolution. Butler gives them the arguments they need to persuade themselves that process could be nonviolent. In clinging to that illusion they join a long and troubled tradition of Jews who flee their heritage out of fear and a desire for acceptance.

In *Parting Ways* Butler makes it clear that for Israeli Jews this would entail an "obligatory passage beyond identity and nation as defining frameworks" (5) so as to conceive "complex and antagonistic modes of living together" (4). Palestinians, a subjugated people, are apparently not required to abandon nationalism. Toward the end of *Parting Ways* she poses this as a question: "Do we want to oppose the nationalism of those who have yet to see a state, of the Palestinians who are still seeking to gather a nation, to establish a nation-state for the first time" (205)? So until a Palestinian state fully embodies nationalism's inevitable limitations and value distortions, Palestinian nationalist ambitions should remain intact and uncriticized. Tony Judt notoriously declared nationalism to be an anachronism in his influential 2003 *New York Review of Books* essay "Israel: The Alternative," but now, more than a decade later, ethnic nationalisms remain alive and well in Europe and elsewhere. At times the international anti-Zionist left muses that all nationalisms are on their way to being abandoned, but the exceptionalist opposition to Israel in practice means that all national aspirations are valid except that of the Jews.

What Butler, in a gesture of extraordinary arrogance, actually means is that binationalism requires Israeli Jews not only to cease being Israelis but also to cease being Jews. The history of both European and Arab antisemitism, we will remember, includes no few examples of such advice delivered in more violent rhetoric. In that light, Butler's demand for "an indefinite moratorium on the Law of Return" (209) that gives Jews worldwide the right to immigrate to Israel may seem almost modest. Since Israel is not a legitimate state, why should it have a right to an immigration policy? Stripped of its drama, that's really all the Right of Return is: an immigration policy with a religious preference established by a state with a large religious majority in which religion and nationality are entwined—a state, however, in which other religions flourish.

Some of Butler's critics have no difficulty labeling her antisemitic. I claim no knowledge of what is in her heart, but the accusation gets in the way of countering her specific arguments. The point she has difficulty address-ing is that her positions have antisemitic consequences and lend support to antisemitic groups and traditions. She says two things in response: first, that opposition to the very existence of the state of Israel is not equivalent to anti-semitism, since Jews should be ready to give up an outdated, fundamentally un-Jewish nationalism; second, that she is indebted to an alternative Jewish philosophical tradition that is more true to the heart of Judaism than the politics that drive her opponents. But it is to a significant degree a tradition she has had to construct, not one she has clearly inherited. And, in any case, that supposed intellectual loyalty has no purchase on political advice that would have disastrous consequences.

One State and the Right of Return

Where Butler is correct—and painfully so—is in asserting that there never was a possibility for a Jewish state in Palestine without the dispossession of Arab lands. What she does not trouble herself to confront is the fact that Jews purchased land prior to 1936 that was owned by wealthy Arabs, and that some tenant farmers lost their right to live there as a result. As Asher Susser writes in *Israel, Jordan, and Palestine: The Two-State Imperative* (2012), "Until 1948 the Zionists, as opposed to classical colonial movements, did not con-quer the land, but bought it on the market from local as well as nonresident landowners." Jews also owned land in the region before the nineteenth cen-tury, and much of the land in the area fell under Ottoman administrative rule, rather than being in private hands. Nor in confronting the genuine tragedy of 1948 is she much interested in acknowledging that the Arab states launched a war against Israel that year. But the fact remains that Palestinians lost their homes and saw their communities destroyed. Displaced Palestinians should have been offered reconstruction of their villages on other Arab lands at the time. The United States should have offered to cover much of the cost. But that option has been swallowed in the sands of time. Also missing—at least from Butler's account—is the fact that a comparable number of Jews were forced out of their ancestral homes in Arab lands as a consequence of the establishment of Israel; they and their descendants make up the majority of Israeli Jews today. I trust readers will understand why Jews are not demanding a Right of Return to Iraq, Egypt, Syria, or other Arab countries.

Does one find BDS supporters sympathizing with Jews from Arab lands who lost their homes, their lands, and their businesses? Not so far as I know.

Do they call on Arab governments for reparations? Why is it that "justice" does not include full justice for those displaced Jews? For many Jews from Arab lands it was not the Holocaust they had to flee but rather the risk of a similar fate at Arab hands. If the creation of Israel intensified Arab antisemitism, it also gave Jews from Arab lands a haven and a home. Justice for them would not be enhanced by dismantling that home.

What can be made available as part of an agreement without destruction of the State of Israel is fair financial compensation to Palestinian families displaced in 1948. As part of its commitment to creating two viable states in the region, the United States can shoulder most of the cost, with Israel contributing according to its ability. While few seemingly like to admit it, the relevance of a literal right to return has diminished as Palestinian adults living within Israel's 1967 borders have aged and died. It is likely that fewer than 10 percent of those who fled or were expelled in 1948 remain alive. Many of those were very young children at the time. The right of later generations to return to a home they have never seen or to a village that no longer exists seems at best chimerical. The principle is less a human right than a political weapon. Its emotional valence, to be sure, has been sustained by prolonged life in the refugee camps, during which people felt they had no home with a future. As Amira Hass, an Israeli critic of her country's policies, has acknowledged in an essay published in Marianne Hirsch and Nancy K. Miller's collection *Rites of Return: Diaspora Poetics and the Politics of Memory* (2011), "With the passing of the years, as many first-generation refugees age and die, the return home becomes increasingly transtemporal, metareal" (183). The sense of loss is thus metaphysical, not material, and can be unlearned, especially if other benefits and possibilities accompany it. But a Palestinian state would be free to adopt its own immigration policy. Does anyone doubt that such a policy would give preference to returning Palestinians, as one would properly expect it to?

Once again, Butler deploys her abstract notion of justice to decry the contradiction between a right of return denied for Palestinians and a Law of Return affirmed for Jews. It is a contradiction, but it is one that Israel must sustain if it is to remain a Jewish entity. As United States history might have led Butler to acknowledge when she states in *Parting Ways* that "no democratic polity has the right to secure demographic advantage for any particular ethnic or religious group" (210), democratic polities have done precisely that; such rights are partly a function of historical circumstance and relative power. As Alexander Yakobson and Amnon Rubinstein point out in their comparative *Israel and the Family of Nations: The Jewish Nation-State and Human Rights* (2008), democratic polities in fact not infrequently seek demographic advantage. The Scandinavian countries have immigration policies that grant preferential treatment to other Scandinavians. Germany gives preferential treatment to ethnic Germans. Those are only two examples among many. BDS advocates typically either sidestep such detailed comparisons with other nations' policies and practices or they accept only irrational and unsupportable comparisons with some of the most odious states in modern history, namely Nazi Germany and white-dominated South Africa.

Butler claims that a UN resolution affirms the Palestinian *right* of return, but then a UN resolution established the State of Israel as well. That said, UN Resolution 194 does not actually speak of a right of return. What it says is that "refugees wishing to return to their homes and live at peace with their neighbours should be permitted to do so." As Asher Susser writes, "the resolution spoke of a permission that ought to be granted rather than an inherent right to return." Given that Resolution 194 came but a year after Israel was founded, it is reasonable to conclude that "living at peace" with one's Jewish neighbors did not entail opposing the state whose creation the Jews had just celebrated. The resolution was also part of a peace plan indexed to the conditions of the moment. There is no reason to suppose it stated a principle that should not be modified to reflect conditions more than half a century later. Ben-Gurion might well have been advised at the time for both moral and pragmatic reasons to make the return of refugees conditional, rather than refusing to accept any.

The opportunity for that solution has now passed. Divested of a demilitarized West Bank now, however, Israel could make certain that no forms of discrimination persist within its borders. Israeli politicians should find the resolve now to do what a majority of Israelis want, for example, and make provision for civil marriages to be carried out within Israel itself. Legal means are readily available to bar discrimination in areas like housing, employment, and municipal services, and Israel must strengthen them to protect its Jewish minorities as well as its Palestinian citizens. Enforcement requires commitment, but that is not unimaginable either. Symbolic issues (the flag, the national anthem) will still mark difference, but the benefits of a democratic society can counterbalance them. Yakobson and Rubinstein add that Israel should also grant formal recognition to its Palestinian minority in its constitution. In other words, if what Butler actually wants is "that the State of Israel consider undertaking formal acts by which equality might be more inclusively allocated and contemporary forms of discrimination, differential violence, and daily harassment against the Palestinian people [be] brought to an end" (33), then Jews need neither ground their identities in diaspora nor dissolve their nation. They need to reform their laws to foster equality internally and abandon the bulk of the West Bank so the Palestinians living there can govern themselves. To be a refugee, to be stateless, is an unacceptable condition, but that does not mean Palestinian refugees need to live in Tel Aviv.

Despite these problems with Butler's unreservedly idealist agenda, I want to conclude by acknowledging that I am convinced she believes in her "single state, one that would eradicate all forms of discrimination on the basis of ethnicity, race, and religion." The problem is that no major players in the Middle East believe that goal is realistic and most have no interest in it. When Palestinian political groups announce that they acknowledge the existence of Israel, they refer to a place where Jews and Arabs live. They do not typically intend to affirm Israel's right to exist as a Jewish state. That is not surprising, given that endorsing Israel's Jewish identity conflicts with the goal of implementing a massive return of diasporic Palestinians that would turn Jews into a minority. Over time, the Naqba (the flight and expulsion of Palestinians in 1948) and the right of return have become the central features of the Palestinian historical narrative. Indeed, as Benny Morris argues in *One State, Two States: Resolving the Israel/Palestine Conflict* (2009), Palestinian insistence on the right of return is "code for the elimination of Israel and the conquest of all of Palestine" (172).

Other than wishful thinking, Butler really has no answer to the challenge Morris offers to happy-family prospects for the Middle East:

> What Muslim Arab society in the modern age has treated Christians, Jews, pagans, Buddhists, and Hindus with tolerance and as equals? Why should anyone believe that Palestinian Muslim Arabs would behave any differently . . . ? (168-69)

In *Israel and the Family of Nations*, Yakobson and Rubinstein offer equally pertinent observations about why one state embodying all of Palestine would cease to have any Jewish character and would not be hospitable for its Jewish residents:

> In order to believe that such a state would in fact be binational, a number of wildly implausible assumptions need to be made: that the Arab-Palestinian people would agree over the long term that its state—the only state it will have—would not have an Arab character and would not be regarded as part of the Arab world; that it would agree to be the only one among the Arab peoples whose state would not be officially Arab, would not be a member of the Arab League and would not share, by declaration, the aspirations for Arab unity; and that the Palestinian people would agree to make this concession—a declared relinquishing of Palestine's 'Arabness,' something which no Arab nation has agreed to do in its own state for the sake of the non-Arab native minorities—for the sake of the Jews, widely considered 'foreign intruders' and 'colonialist

invaders' in Palestine, whose very claim to constitute a nation is no more than 'Zionist propaganda.' (10)

Meanwhile the troubling results of the Arab spring confirm Morris's tough judgment that "the Palestinian Arabs, like the world's other Muslim Arab communities, are deeply religious and have no . . . tradition of democratic governance" (170) doesn't mean Arab countries cannot develop democratic institutions over time, but it does mean that a minority Israeli population will have reason to fear that neither their rights nor their physical security would be guaranteed in the critical first years of a binational state's existence. Does anyone actually think Israelis would willingly sign on to that risk? Is that what installing their diasporic history in their identities is supposed to do for them?

By addressing only the most apocalyptic warnings about the risks of violence in calls for the abolition of the Jewish state, Butler is conveniently able to dismiss all lesser but still consequential risks of violence. If a BDS proponent argues that Israel is not a legitimate state, she complains, "that is taken to be a genocidal position," a "wish to see a given population annihilated." She can then come neatly to the conclusion that "no thoughtful discussion about legitimacy can take place under such conditions" (19). Except for her idiosyncratic theory that Jews should so thoroughly internalize their diasporic history that they are led to embrace statelessness, however, there is little hope that anything but a bloodbath would follow upon an attempt to dissolve the Jewish state. BDS advocates protest that that is an alarmist or "hysterical" response to a one-state proposal, but I believe instead that it is coldly realistic.

Given that Butler's diasporic identity theory is phantasmatic at best, one may reasonably ask why she invokes it. Perhaps, although she gives no sign of being willing to admit it, it is because she realizes at some level that the BDS movement is fundamentally and exclusively coercive. We might call it coercive non-violence, since it relies on the prospect of international pressure forcing the Israelis to do something they are otherwise powerfully disinclined to do. Thus she wants to offer them a route to delegitimation based on self-realization and inner transformation. Otherwise as Hussein Ibish writes in *What's Wrong with the One-State Agenda?* (2009), the idea that they would "let bygones be bygones, forego their national identities and independence and join the vanguard of enlightened humanity transcending the most fundamental of modern identity categories" (58) is equally improbable. Unfortunately, Butler thus presents us with a twofold utopian model: first, Jews will take diaspora into their hearts, then Palestinians will choose not to dominate a state politically, ethnically, culturally, and religiously that they will certainly dominate numerically.

In a July 2013 interview with *Open Democracy,* Butler implies that Jews and Palestinians would learn to control "whatever murderous rage" they have, but I doubt if many outside the United States find that reasoning reassuring. In any case, it is hardly reliable to extend standards of familial and interpersonal relations to interactions between hostile political movements and nation states. Not that relations between heavily armed family members always work out well either.

There is also a broader lesson to be learned here. Butler's mystical journey toward diasporic inwardness should lead us toward serious examination of the relationship between abstract theoretical speculation and the responsibilities entailed in making policy recommendations. Becoming enamored of a thought experiment, however elegant and internally logical it may seem, does not in and of itself justify either advocating or mandating its application to real world politics.

What Butler's BDS-style one-state solution would actually produce is a Muslim Arab-dominated state devoted to ethnic cleansing of the Jewish population. But Israelis would not go peacefully into that dark night. They would fight. At best a civil war recalling the civil war following the Arab rising of 1936-39 would ensue, leading now to untold deaths of Jews and Palestinians and serious regional economic and humanitarian disasters. Of course we have Syria as a model for how much worse a civil war would be now. I do not accept a Holocaust analogy for the prospect, but I do believe at the very least we would see both general clashes and innumerable local acts of revenge. Butler's claims of a nonviolent route to a single state are thus at best naïve and at worst genuinely dangerous. They bear no relation to reality. They demonstrate what happens when a brilliant theorist turns to real world politics she does not or will not comprehend. The binationalism she advocates, she acknowledges, "is not love, but there is we might say, a necessary and impossible attachment that makes a mockery of identity, an ambivalence that emerges from the decentering of the nationalist ethos and that forms the basis of a permanent ethical demand" (53). Good luck with that. Does she think millions of Arabs and Jews are mere clay she can mold to fit her fantasy ambitions for them?

Those who question where Butler's heedless pursuit of an abstract logic of justice would take us should read very carefully the sometimes oblique sentences she crafts. In 2004 in "Jews and the Bi-National Vision" she simply declared that "the institution of a Palestinian state will not by itself nullify the claims to the land or the petition for restoration" and added "I don't believe that the Israeli state in its current form should be ratified." Now, toward the end of *Parting Ways* she suggests that any *relationship* with a Jewish state is morally and politically unacceptable. "Palestinians who have been forced to become diasporic" should not have to contemplate even a "colonial power" that "stays in place and out of sight" (216). According to her, the two-state solution would be psychologically and politically corrupted by the past. Palestinians would be living in juxtaposition with the embodiments of their former oppressors. "If coexistence requires working within the disavowed framework of colonial power, then colonial power becomes a precondition of coexistence" (216). This parallels Barghouti's argument, in a 2009 *Electronic Intifada* interview with Ali Mustafa, that coexisting Palestinian and Israeli states would create an unacceptable appearance of moral equivalence: "I am completely and categorically against binationalism because it assumes that there are two nations with equal moral claims to the land."

Following this logic, the establishment of a Palestinian state will do nothing to stop the ongoing tragedy of the Naqba (the catastrophe of Palestinian expulsions), for a Palestinian state would still bear within itself, be the product of, that foundational and eternally intolerable expulsion. Butler's reasoning is quite strange at points. "As the homogenous nation moves forward," she writes, "it continues to spit out and pile up those who are no longer supported by a history that would establish them as subjects. They are, rather, expelled from the nation as so much debris, indiscernible from a littered landscape" (102). Quite apart from her indifference to those of Israel's Arab neighbors who have far more homogenous societies than Israel, Butler's meaning here presumably cannot include the claim that Israel would expel its own Arab citizens in the wake of a formal two state solution. Presumably what Butler means is not only that those who fled in 1948 continue to live as victims of expulsion, that the present time continues to reenact the past, but also that any Palestinian who doesn't have free access to and choice of residence throughout Palestine lives in an intolerable condition of exile. Butler's solution: "the undoing of Israeli colonial power and military force" (217). Setting aside her appalling tendency to forget that Israel includes millions of human beings, not just the mechanized colonialist entity she has constructed in her mind, one may say simply that Butler has crafted a recipe for war.

A certain studied indifference to Israel's citizens also informs Butler's last abstract claim. Following the standard (and explicit) BDS effort to *delegitimate* the Israeli state, she argues, as Elhanan Yakira points out in his own contribution to Rosenfeld's *Resurgent Antisemitism* collection, "that Israel either never has been 'legitimate' or that it has lost its legitimacy by its allegedly criminal behavior" (53). What is odd about this argument, as Yakira elaborates, is that a nation's legitimacy is first of all established and sustained as a pact between a government and its citizens, and the citizens of Israel overwhelmingly want the Jewish state to persevere. From Butler's perspective, Israel's legitimacy can only be established by the true citizens, the Palestinian descendants of those who once lived there, most of whom do not live there now. The numbers are such that Israeli Jews would have no say in their own country's future. For Butler, Israel would merely be "changing the foundations of its legitimacy," the latter concept being Butler's contribution to the political logic of Mideast peace.

In reality, Butler's and the BDS movement's first goal is to maximize international hostility toward Israel, a project destined to harden positions, not move the peace process along. In the real world, moreover, contrary to Butler's utopian fantasy, history offers no guarantees.

If what we actually seek is peace in the Middle East we need to accept the need for Palestinian rights to self-determination *within* agreed-upon borders, to fair compensation to families displaced in 1948 or 1967, and to secure borders for a Jewish state. We can then work back from that goal to see what steps are most likely to lead there. As Kenneth Walzer observed in his May 2010 "Arguing With Judith Butler," distributed in Scholars for Peace in the Middle East's Faculty Forum, "She says nothing about how we might get from here to there." What vague hints she offers, as in "Jews and the Bi-National Vision," where she invokes a future "decided through radically democratic means by all the inhabitants of these lands," is once again not reassuring. What she seems to be advocating—and here she is, I believe, being willfully unclear for tactical reasons—is a "democratic" vote by Israelis, West Bank residents, and *the entire Palestinian diaspora* to decide the future of Palestine. That radical, indeed apocalyptic, plan offers no achievable benefit to any of the parties. Perhaps that is what David Lloyd, a cofounder of the US Campaign for the Academic and Cultural Boycott of Israel, means in his 2014 *Los Angeles Review of Books* essay when he writes

> it is not the armed resistance of Palestinians that poses the greatest danger to Israel, but the nonviolent claim to legal and political equality. The greatest challenge to the state that often preposterously claims to be the only democracy in the Middle East turns out to be the demand for democracy.

What will not help move us from here to *any* there is a BDS-inspired effort to demonize and delegitimate the State of Israel. But perhaps the worst thing about one-state fanaticism is that it offers no realistic route for political independence and full citizenship for Palestinians. Israel will certainly not accede to these radical demands. The practical effect is thus that Palestinians would remain in their powder keg limbo. BDS offers nothing whatsoever to the Palestinians it purports to champion. All it offers is a way to mobilize hatred as a political identity in the West.

If Butler is the best BDS can offer in the way of a rational case for their cause, and her work is fundamentally flawed by its unmitigated hostility toward Israel, American academics instead might begin their own education by reading what Israeli historians and journalists have to say about their own country, a country and situation they know and understand. It is a country whose politics cannot be reduced to simple platitudes within an ahistorical frame. Educated Americans should encourage respect for all parties, enhanced empathy among those who lack it, and come to the recognition that no one can win everything in Palestine. ■

Works Referenced

Benhabib, Seyla. (2013) "Ethics without Normativity and Politics without Historicity: On Judith Butler's *Parting Ways: Jewishness and the Critique of Zionism.*" Constellations 20:1, pp. 150-63.

Burg, Avraham. (2008) *The Holocaust is Over: We Must Rise from Its Ashes.* New York: Palgrave Macmillan.

Butler, Judith. (1990) *Gender Trouble: Feminism and the Subversion of Identity.* New York: Routledge.

Butler. (2003) "No, it's not anti-semitic." *London Review of Books.* 25:16 August 21, 2003, pp. 19-21.

Butler. (2004) "Jews and the Bi-National Vision." *Logos: a journal of modern society and culture.* Winter 2004. Available at www.logosjournal.com/butler. htm.

Butler. (2006) "Judith Butler on Hamas, Hezbollah & the Israel Lobby." *Radical Archives.* March 28, 2010. Available at http://radicalarchives. org/2010/03/28/jbutler-on-hamas-hezbollah-israel-lobby/.

Butler. (2012) *Parting Ways: Jewishness and the Critique of Zionism.* New York: Columbia University Press.

Butler. (2012) "Judith Butler responds to attack: 'I affirm a Judaism that is not associated with state violence." *Mondoweiss: The War of Ideas in the Middle East.* August 27, 2012. Available at http://mondoweiss.net/2012/08/judith-butler-responds-to-attack-i-affirm-a-judaism-that-is-not-associated-with-state-violence.html.

Butler. (2013) "Judith Butler's Remarks to Brooklyn College on BDS." *The Nation.* February 7, 2013. Available at http://www.thenation.com/article/172752/judith-butlers-remarks-brooklyn-college-bds.

Butler. (2013) "Academic Freedom and the ASA's Boycott of Israel: A Response to Michelle Goldberg." The Nation. December 8, 2013. Available at http://www.thenation.com/article/177512/academic-freedom -and-asas-boycott-israel-response-michelle-goldberg.

Fein, Helen. (1987) "Dimensions of Antisemitism: Attitudes, Collective Accusations, and Actions," in Fine, ed. *The Persisting Question: Sociological Perspectives and Social Contexts of Modern Antisemitism.* New York: Walter de Gruyter, pp. 67-85.

Filar, Ray. (2013) "Willing the impossible: an interview with Judith Butler." *Open Democracy.* July 23, 2013. Available at (http://www.opendemocracy .net/transformation/ray-filar/willing-impossible-interview-with-judith-butler.

Grigat, Stephan. (2014) "Deconstructing Israel." *Jungle World.* January. The German original is available at http://jungle-world.com/ artikel/2014/03/49173.html. An English translation is available at https:// axis-of-goodness.com/2014/01/29/deconstructing-israel/.

Halevi, Yossi Klein. (2013) *Like Dreamers: The Story of the Paratroopers Who Reunited Jerusalem and Divided a Nation.* New York: HarperCollins.

Hass, Amira. "Between Two Returns." In Marianne Hirsch and Nancy K. Miller, eds. *Rites of Return: Diaspora Poetics and the Politics of Memory.* New York: Columbia University Press, pp. 173-84.

Herf, Jeffrey. (2009) *Nazi Propaganda for the Arab World.* New Haven: Yale University Press.

Hirsh, David. (2007) "Anti-Zionism and Antisemitism: Cosmopolitan Reflections." New York: Institute for the Study of Global Antisemitism. Available at http://eprints.gold.ac.uk/2061/1/Hirsh_Yale_paper.pdf.

Ibish, Hussein. (2009) *What's Wrong with the One-State Agenda?* Washington, DC: American Task Force on Palestine.

Illouz, Eva. (2014) "47 years a slave: A new perspective on the occupation." *Haaretz.* February 7, 2014. Available at http://www.haaretz.com/news/fea-tures/.premium-1.572880.

Johnson, Alan. (2013) "Parting Ways." *Fathom.* January 31, 2013. Available at http://www.fathomjournal.org/reviews-culture/parting-ways/).

Judt, Tony. (2003) "Israel: The Alternative." *New York Review of Books.* October 23, 2013.

Keinon, Herb. (2014) "Yadlin: Israel should consider 'coordinated unilateral' action if peace talks fail." *Jerusalem Post.* January 27. Available at http://ivarfjeld. com/2014/01/28/yadlin-israel-should-pull-back-behind-the-security-fens/.

Levi, Primo. (1988) *The Drowned and the Saved.* Trans. Raymond Rosenthal. New York: Simon & Schuster.

Lloyd, David. (2014) "What Threatens Israel Most? Democracy." *Los Angeles Review of Books.* March 16, 2014. Available at http://lareviewofbooks.org/ essay/threatens-israel-democracy.

Marks, Jonathan. (2014) "Academic Boycotters Talk Academic Freedom." *Commentary.* January 24, 2014.

Morris, Benny. (2008) *1948: A History of the First Arab-Israeli War.* New Haven: Yale University Press.

Morris. (2009) *One State, Two States: Resolving the Israel/Palestine Conflict.* New Haven: Yale University Press.

Mustafa, Ali. (2009) "Boycotts work: An interview with Omar Barghouti." *The Electronic Intifada.* May 31, 2009. Available at http://electronicintifada. net/content/boycotts-work-interview-omar-barghouti/8263).

Nelson, Cary. (2010) *No University is an Island: Saving Academic Freedom.* New York: New York University Press.

Pinsker, Leo. "Auto-Emancipation: An Appeal To His People By a Russian Jew." In Arthur Hertzberg, *The Zionist Idea: A Historical Analysis and Reader.* Philadelphia: Jewish Publication Society, 1997.

Porat, Dan A. (2004) "From the Scandal to the Holocaust in Israeli Education." *Journal of Contemporary History.* 39:4, 619-36.

Porat, Dina. (2013). "Holocaust Denial and the Image of the Jew, or: 'They Boycott Auschwitz as an Israeli Product.'" In Rosenfeld, ed. *Resurgent Antisemitism,* pp. 467-81.

Rosenfeld, Alvin H. Editor. (2013) *Resurgent Antisemitism: Global Perspectives.* Bloomington: Indiana University Press.

Shapira, Anita. (2012) *Israel: A History.* Waltham, MA: Brandeis University Press.

Shavit, Ari. (2013) *My Promised Land: The Triumph and Tragedy of Israel.* New York: Random House.

Susser, Asher. (2012) *Israel, Jordan, and Palestine: The Two-State Imperative.* Waltham, MA.: Brandeis University Press.

Waltzer, Kenneth. (2010) "Arguing With Judith Butler II." Forum. Scholars for Peace in the Middle East. May 31, 2010.

Weininger, Otto. (1906) *Sex and Character.* New York: G. P. Putnam's Sons.

Wistrich, Robert. (2013). "Anti-Zionist Connections: Communism, Radical Islam, and the Left. In Rosenfeld, ed. *Resurgent Antisemitism,* pp. 402-23.

Yakira, Elhanan. (2010) *Post-Zionism, Post-Holocaust: Three Essays on Denial, Forgetting, and the Delegitimation of Israel.* Trans. Michael Swirsky. New York: Cambridge University Press.

Yakira. (2013). "Antisemitism and Anti-Zionism as Moral Questions." In Rosenfeld, ed. *Resurgent Antisemitisms,* pp. 42-64.

Yakobson, Alexander, and Amnon Rubenstein. (2009) *Israel and the Family of Nations: The Jewish Nation-State and Human Rights.* New York: Routledge.

Zertal, Idith. (2005) *Israel's Holocaust and the Politics of Nationhood.* New York: Cambridge University Press.

NANCY KOPPELMAN

"When you want to *do* something, join us!":
The Limits of the Social Justice Mandate in American Higher Education

E ach fall after the academic year begins, a student representative from a local citizen advocacy organization asks to visit my class to recruit new members. I'm always glad to host. After explaining the group's work, the student usually says something like, "When you get tired of just reading and thinking and you want to *do* something, join us!"[102]

This formulation of the link between reading and thinking on the one hand, and "doing" on the other, suggests that social justice efforts can bypass or even supersede thoughtful judgment. They can't. Thinking is a kind of doing, and all other kinds of doing, especially in college, ought to be based on it. Nevertheless, colleges and universities have made "doing" as distinct from reading and thinking into a necessary feature of education by implementing a social justice mandate.

The social justice mandate holds that higher education should both foster humanist values and support students' efforts to put those values into practice. Initiatives include community-based learning, volunteer work, and internships. A mandate is an official order or commission to perform an ongoing action or work toward a goal. Mandates enact conclusions. They cause people to do things.

Higher education is supposed to be in the business of questioning, disrupting, and sometimes defeating conclusions, as well as shaping new ones which will also be tested. The solutions of one era become the problems of the next; today's expert knowledge is moot tomorrow. This dynamic of intellectual renewal is the very essence of higher education. When colleges enact the social justice mandate, they mobilize conclusions and implicitly condone actions that take place under their auspices.

Some social justice efforts enact conclusions that enjoy a broad consensus. For example, initiatives to alleviate hunger, provide literacy services, protect natural resources, assist the homeless, and support at-risk youth contribute to the public good. They link theory to practice and create bridges to students' post-graduate ambitions. They are valuable opportunities for students to experience responsible citizenship by contributing to their communities. They feed and water habits of service that foster a thriving democracy. American higher education has long promoted social change efforts such as these, but today's activities are much more popular than they used to be. Undergraduate programs informed by the social justice mandate are embraced nationwide as fully in keeping with the goals and commitments of higher learning. They enjoy the stamp of approval from accrediting bodies that certify that curricula meet widely shared institutional standards.[103]

In contrast, some academics claim that direct political activism—the kind that citizens do on their own time—can also be legitimate expressions of the social justice mandate. In so doing, they reach well beyond the standards that make higher education what it is and use their institutions as weapons to fight for their own hotly contested causes. This is precisely the case with the Boycott, Divestment, and Sanctions movement (BDS). Some faculty who are critical of Israeli policy weigh in on the Israel/Palestine conflict by mobilizing BDS, not in their own names and on their own time, but under the broad banners of higher education and the fields of study in which they claim expertise. When they do, they reveal that their allegiance to firm conclusions that they share with political allies is stronger than their commitment to cultivate their students' skills and critical capacities. They blur activism and inquiry, thus erasing what W.E.B. DuBois took to be the university's purpose: "above all, to be the organ of that fine adjustment between real life and the growing knowledge of life, an adjustment which forms the secret of civilization."[104] They attempt to deploy education and critical thinking on behalf of a highly controversial political orthodoxy. They undermine the aims of education by shutting down discussion and thought and turning inquiry into moral one-upmanship. The message to students is that they need not bother with the difficult intellectual work of understanding culture and history for themselves. They can join a movement instead. Academics who champion BDS are not concerned about distorting genuine inquiry in this manner. To the best of their ability, they proudly captain their institutions and professional organizations to sail with the current of BDS.

The reason for this moral certainty is not that they are right. Their activism is based on two conclusions which have come to undergird scholarship in the humanities and social sciences: a commitment to human rights and anti-colonialism. On the face of it, this seems as uncontroversial as feeding the hungry. Who in American academia, or nearly anywhere else, would fail to either condemn colonialism or value human rights? Here is where the social justice mandate rubs against the grain of a well-worn postmodern groove from which conclusions about human rights and colonialism have issued. Concepts of truth, fact, and certainty have been eclipsed by theories of social constructionism and contingency. Yet in spite of embracing contingency and constructionism as guiding principles, some academic activists make rather bold certainty claims about the Israel/Palestine conflict. These certainties are quite dissonant with what appears to be a stalwart skepticism fundamental to their intellectual culture. The BDS enclave is an outcome of this development.

For the last two decades, many scholars working in the humanities and social sciences draw their credentials from fields now shaped by this shift in emphasis.[105] They have produced countless conference papers and doctoral dissertations that unwittingly illustrate this same irony: they are *sure* that all knowledge is *uncertain*. If all our perceptions of the world and all the ideas in our heads are socially constructed, then where does this uncharacteristic certainty come from?

The people who express it cannot say. According to Mark Bauerlein, the theory of contingency is replete with self-congratulation, so this contradiction tends to elude the awareness of the people who embody it. Those who truck this approach as a given (and as a good), he writes, believe that "the constructionist premise [is] a cornerstone of progressive thought and social reform." Bauerlein has observed that the tendency of up-and-coming academics to parrot this "party line" acts like "tribal glue distinguishing humanities professors from their colleagues in the business school, the laboratory, the chapel, and the computing center, most of whom believe that at least some knowledge is independent of social conditions."[106] Loyalty to contingency is their common coin and contradicts their favorite exception to their own rule: their certainty about the Israel/Palestine conflict.

Given these theoretical leanings and the way the idea of human rights informs the social justice mandate, what kind of knowledge do academics who advocate boycotting Israeli higher education institutions rely on to undergird their certainties about colonialism and human rights? Can they be trusted to make sound judgments and enact conclusions about the Israel/Palestine conflict that are in keeping with the mission of higher education?

The answer to the latter question is "no." The knowledge—or more properly the lack of it—that academics in the BDS movement rely on to justify their activism reveals an ignorance of the history of human rights and a failure to engage deeply with the disturbing insights that a historical understanding of colonialism yields. Due to how they frame their scholarly interests, they do not know how ideas in history intersect with post-Enlightenment institutions and social formations, and why this knowledge matters to social justice efforts. More disturbing still, they would keep their students away from this kind of understanding by tightly controlling the discourse about the Israel/Palestine conflict.[107]

For a host of reasons, a better approach to social justice than boycotts, and particularly academic boycotts, is partnerships with collaborative Israeli/Palestinian organizations creating alliances on the ground. This slow and patient work depends on knowing how to do archival research, engage in and lead institutions, collaborate across significant differences, and work within hard-won, fragile, but enduring social and political structures. In other words, it presupposes the very institutions that BDS undermines. Although the idea of human rights is an attractive rallying cry, in the case of the Israel/Palestine conflict effective efforts toward social justice are not promoted simply by thrusting one's fist in the air. The idea of human rights is a blunt instrument. An evaluation of its meaning and history, and of how the idea of human rights intersects with colonialism, will illustrate its strengths and limitations for the social justice mandate.[108]

★

The idea of human rights embodies high moral principles that stand outside the vagaries of history. For example, when Referendum 74 was passed in Washington State in 2012, I heard a King County clerk say on the radio that she was glad our state now recognizes "the right to marry that gay people *have always had*, even though those rights were not honored" (emphasis mine). The clerk's comment illustrates perfectly the timeless standard of human rights. Likewise, an ahistorical orientation informs academic efforts to lay claim to the social justice mandate under the BDS banner.

Consider the flocks of well-educated anti-universalists who gather beneath the universalist concept of human rights. The contradiction they embody cannot be resolved. People around the world are increasingly

challenged to embrace universalist principles while simultaneously understanding contingency, recognizing the constructed dimensions of perception
and of the social world, and living intelligently and justly with cultural diversity. It matters, though, whether people live in this tension while aspiring to
understand its historically potent dimensions.

The branch of philosophy that studies the nature and meaning of history
can clarify what "historically potent" means. First, contradictions are integral
to the very fabric of our shared forms of life. This idea was central to both
Hegel's and Marx's philosophies and has guided the development of modern
historical scholarship. The idea of contradiction deeply informed the field
of the "new" social history which has flourished since the late 1960s. This
field documents and interprets the thoughts and experiences of everyday
people. New social historians found the search for contradictions wonder-
fully fruitful. They argued convincingly that across time and place, intelligent
and reasonable people often unknowingly act against the very interests they
hold dearest. History shows the folly of expecting a perfect match between
conscious intention and outcome.[109]

Second, although historians can show that dimensions of experience
are socially constructed, all facts cannot be deconstructed and reconstructed
willy-nilly into alternative outcomes that genuinely might have come to pass.
As Jonathan Prude patiently instructed his graduate students in an American
social history seminar over twenty years ago at Emory University, "The Civil
War is not a text." The war was an event in time and place that had material
reality. It was produced by and generated specific lingering legacies which are
still with us. That Professor Prude needed to say this at all illustrates the presence and power of theories of constructivism in the 1990s. Understanding
what facts are and what it means to live with them is a feat of mature historical understanding. Facts can pressure self-appointed judges who preside over
the court of retrospection to question the stability of their certainties.

Third, in any given historical moment, future ideas are not available for
people to think. While this may seem so obvious that it doesn't need to be
said, rampant use of "human rights" to apply to everyone who ever lived
implies exactly that. People take the concept as a matter of course, reflecting
a contemporary habit of mind and not a timeless truth about its actual presence in the fund of ethical ideas. The history of the concept of human rights
sheds welcome light on the social justice mandate in higher education.

(A caveat: in the spirit of the Annales School, this analysis considers history quite broadly. A sweeping approach to historical interpretation fell out of
favor with the rise of postmodernism, but the transhistorical generalizations
in the concept of human rights must be tested against a range of intellectual
developments across eras. The analysis is somewhat schematic in order to

provide insights about changes in worldviews over long time spans, and necessarily leaves out a good deal more than it explains. Yet this method makes salient the character of the human rights idea as embodied in the social justice mandate, yielding an illustration of what Greg Mullins has called the "cultures of human rights" over time.[110])

The idea of human rights calls to mind a better world than ours. It's a world where fairness and equality reign and a comprehensive social justice has been realized. In contrast with philosophical insights about history sketched above, in such a world people need not live with unresolvable contradictions. Pressures that create such tensions are peacefully alleviated or have ceased to exist. Intractable conflicts of earlier times are rendered transparent by final insights. Structured by the value of human rights, the world no longer needs new ideas about justice. The search is over. We have reached "the end of history."[111]

Actual study of the past interrupts this wishful portrait of the world we want by providing a sobering account of the world we actually have. The work of deeply learning history imposes a simple but weighty truth: humanity existed long before human rights did. The problem isn't just that this wonderful world doesn't exist now; it never has, and no one knows if it ever will.

A brisk walk through the centuries, tracing the etiology and development of the idea that collective human actions can be ethically causal in nature, can illustrate this fact. For millennia, many causes of suffering did not mean what they do today. Hurricanes, earthquakes, plagues, famines, and the invasion of enemies were interpreted as tests or punishments from mystifying higher powers. Shooting stars, strange coincidences, and all manner of unexplainable events could be signs from the almighty. Oracles were honored because they predicted the future; through them, people might align their expectations with fate.

Ideas about justice did not stand *outside* these beliefs, but were *expressions of* them. The outer limits of justice were defined by what could be imagined as a cause. Ineffable powers of spirits, gods, or God were, in nearly every situation, the only causes with final authority. Even nowadays it is not unknown for interpreters of natural disasters to claim, for example, that Hurricanes Katrina and Sandy were payback for America's sins. Any conception of justice presupposes a socially constructed and historically specific fund of causal explanations to conceptualize with and make sense of the world.[112]

Yet countless innocent people have suffered for reasons that are quite difficult fully to accept on faith. God is characteristically stingy about letting us in on the plan. Explanations for suffering must either let higher powers off the hook or keep them enigmatic. Sometimes all one can do is surrender with awe and fear in Job-like resignation. Lives are either unlucky or blessed and governed by forces that people cannot comprehend.

Since the Greek tragedians invented theater in the 8th century B.C.E., people have documented and collectively grappled with the causal explanation that fate is a function of divine will. Attempts to figure out what on earth *isn't* fated predate Aristotle. For centuries, efforts to understand tendencies in the material world were quite fruitful. In contrast, the world of human affairs is abidingly unpredictable and difficult to map over time and place. Even the compassion endemic to monotheistic religions did not, and could not, inspire the development of a broad cross-cultural awareness of human beings as agents of justice.

For hundreds of years, university education was dominated by religious instruction, but this began to change in the Middle Ages with the discovery of Aristotle's lost works. Aristotle was a keen empirical observer. His works demonstrated a brilliant mind discovering patterns in the natural world and among people, and speculating what these observations taught and meant. From then on, university education gradually transformed as religious education came to embrace new questions about the relationship between the Word and the insights that empirical observation can yield. By the Early Modern period, this shift began to have earth-shaking implications. Copernicus introduced the idea that the earth revolves around the sun rather than vice versa, and Galileo enabled people to see the rotation of planets with their own eyes through a telescope. Newton posited the universality of laws of motion and gravitation. Natural laws were a lot more predictable than those of the almighty—indeed, they were so constant that they could be considered true. Discoveries multiplied apace and demonstrated not the mysterious doings of God, but material structures that were so reliable as causes that they inspired whole new fields of endeavor and accomplishment.

In later years, Jean Jacques Rousseau, Adam Smith, Immanuel Kant, and Karl Marx, among many others, considered the wider meanings of natural law. They hypothesized that causal reliability might be evidence of a new category of knowledge more broadly conceived. Perhaps laws or law-like tendencies were innate not only in the material realm. Natural law might also govern social, political, economic, and even ethical relationships. Perhaps the universalism suggested by breakthroughs in physics, chemistry, biology, and mathematics could also illuminate features of the human condition, and particularly how people understand their own causal properties.

These efforts coincided with the tremendous reach of European colonialism to Africa, Asia, and the Americas. Colonialism always expressed the hubris typical of many insular pre-modern societies: the belief that one's own way of life is the gold standard. What we call "ethnocentrism" today was commonplace all over the world. The first work of documentary history, Herodotus' *The Histories* recorded in the 5th century B.C.E., set the terms for interpreting foreign peoples by assessing differences in power as evidence of divinely ordained entitlement. Yet the ideas generated during the Age of Reason enabled new interpretations of domination. They were many and contradictory, reflecting the broad intellectual crisis regarding the place of human agency in the causal explanations that rocked the educated world.

For example, many imperial colonizers believed their Christian duty was bringing salvation to "heathens" even by force, as was the imperative to make the land "useful" as their own world view defined that concept. These ethical beliefs were integral to their greed. Others genuinely thought their ability to conquer was proof of their superiority, and that their power bespoke a responsibility to control "inferiors." This is neither an apology nor an excuse for their thoughts and actions, but rather a description of the limits of their ability to imagine themselves as causes in an arena of justice that had yet to be invented.

As historian Richard White noted in his account of the "would-be *conquistadores*" of sixteenth-century southwestern North America, who were actually lost, "The Spanish had unleashed changes of a depth and magnitude that they neither fully comprehended nor controlled." Many of their ultimate victims also practiced their own forms of domination, competition, and conquest. Quite a few enacted brutalities equal to what they suffered under the blade and gun of European imperial powers. All these causal interpretations and culture clashes coexisted, and together were colonialism itself.[113]

Recall for a moment the anti-colonial bent of many contemporary humanities scholars. Their current habits of mind reduce colonialism to simple matters of European cruelty and power. In fact, a much more disturbing mix of people with different understandings of themselves as causes presses students of history to understand complexity—that is, if thought is as relevant to the past as it is to the present. The ideas in the heads of pre-modern colonizers, and their conception of themselves as causes, developed from material conditions that were worlds apart from our own.

If ideas such as these are meaningfully related to material conditions, Jared Diamond's Pulitzer Prize winning book *Guns, Germs, and Steel: The Fates of Human Societies* offers a most unsettling insight to social constructionists. Thousands of years ago, geographical conditions created unequal opportunities to create wealth and social stability. Thus, the dice were loaded in favor of people in some places and against people in other places. The outcome was imbalances of power, some of which have lasted for generations and shaped the culture of competition between peoples, including the causal explanations for those imbalances. Empire-driven colonialism across centuries is but one expression of these abiding disparities.[114]

Clashes of cultures were inevitable and revealed diverse forms of social organization. Violence continued apace, yet horrors and breakthroughs alike grew from competing pressures and interpretations which tested natural law theory. Eventually, these tests took the form of new epistemologies, the *human* sciences, which may be said to begin with Hume's work in the 18th century and attempted to reveal and explain patterns in minds and souls.[115] New fields of knowledge developed and, by the 19th century, became organized international efforts at human self-understanding. Academic disciplines came to be housed in the world's universities and colleges and cultivated authority by employing standards of evidence originally drawn from the hard sciences. In important ways, rationalism was winning out over faith.

University-trained experts in the humanities and social sciences shared with their colleagues in the laboratory the familiar premise that reliable knowledge issues from agreed-upon methods that reveal new truths. These efforts produced viable understandings about how human beings tick individually and in families, tribes, communities, states, and nations, and through the arts and categories of identity that became politically salient in the modern world. Even after Gramsci, subaltern theory, and the Foucault/Spivak critique that Western knowledge is a collection of "epistemologies of violence," disciplines and fields in the humanities and social sciences continue to share the bedrock premise that rational inquiry and tested methodologies are the vehicles to defensible knowledge. Presumably, one must still make a good argument backed up by sound evidence in order to earn a Ph. D.[116]

The implications for morality and ethics were profound. An important conceptual turning point was Immanuel Kant's moral theory. In the late 18th century, Kant argued that morality has law-like features and is therefore rational. He posited the idea that if a person possesses a good will, she or he can be moral regardless of material circumstances. The "categorical imperative" also assumed that individual human beings have equal value as "ends in themselves, and not merely as means," and that one can test the moral content of one's actions a *priori* by imagining those actions universalized. Universalist ideas were written into both the Declaration of Independence and the Declaration of the Rights of Man and Citizen. These political documents would govern the lives of millions over many generations. But material conditions, coupled with the inertia of what Raymond Williams called "structures of feeling," prevented any international politics of human rights from emerging.[117]

Over the next 250 years, religious and secular thinkers, some in positions of power who were friendly to the skepticism implicit in the scientific method, began to imagine that whole peoples should not have to accept all human-generated forms of suffering, both within and between cultural groups, as expressions of divine law. They believed it might be possible to enter into such situations and actually shape them. These political awakenings were coterminous with religious awakenings in British North America and Protestant Europe in the 18th and 19th centuries. The Christian embrace of the idea of the sanctity of every human soul informed principles of political freedom. The association of justice not with fate, but with fairness engineered by human intentionality and applied quite broadly, has been rare across time and among diverse peoples in conflict. While the idea of progress has long been a target of penetrating critique, it could also consist of a hope that people can and should attempt to shape the course of history—that is, to strive for social justice whether their motives and justifications are religious or secular.

While all this sounds quite promising, ambitious ideas about universal justice met a world that was perpetually fractured, conflicted, unpredictable, and unimaginably diverse in ways that the ideas themselves could not effectively address. Moreover, many of these hopeful ideas issued from the outcomes of colonial impulses and actions, thus illustrating a natal moment of contradiction between universalism and contingency in modern thought. This contradiction pulses in the heart of academic social justice efforts today, and has shaped the emergence of human rights as an organizing ethic of our time.[118]

Like all rights, human rights are conceptual in nature and depended on new ways of seeing in order to be real to people. According to historian Lynn Hunt, a belief in human rights powerful enough to make a dent in public practices depended on a collective emotional sea-change. Hunt argues that "[h]uman rights are difficult to pin down because their definition, indeed their very existence, depends on emotions as much as on reason." Emotions were collectively awakened and educated in Europe and Britain in the 18th century, she argues, by literature. Epistolary novels confronted readers with emotional interiority in a uniquely compelling way. Gustavus Vassa's late eighteenth-century autobiographical account of slavery, published and read widely in London, likewise touched a deep moral nerve. New forms of literary culture promoted empathy and compassion among the emerging middle class. Awareness of the suffering of others reached an apex when torture, long an acceptable and often public form of discipline, began to be called into question. Readers experienced the new universalism, Hunt claims, when they simultaneously encountered the suffering of characters in imagination. In the United States, the publication of Harriet Beecher Stowe's *Uncle Tom's Cabin* did similar cultural work; the genre of sentimental fiction both expressed and created new emotional bonds with injustice. Collective emotional engagement transformed vicarious experience in such a way as to engender a collective sense of empathy for real people, broadening the imaginative reach of compassion and the idea of human rights.[119]

Decades later, a sudden shift in the collective imagination that Hunt describes occurred due to sheer accident. Tendencies of mass empathy coalesced in a shocking moment of failure to respond to an emergency when the Titanic sank in the hours before dawn on April 15, 1912. The Titanic had been hailed as an unsinkable triumph of modern ingenuity. Although disasters of its scale and worse had occurred before, such as the Johnstown Flood of 1889 (2,209 dead) and other large shipwrecks, an analysis by the historian Stephen Kern suggests that the Titanic tragedy was a turning point in modern moral sensibilities. Kern notes that within hours, news of the disaster went round the globe by wireless telegraph. A shift in awareness that no one engineered on purpose was brought about by a technological innovation that transformed the fundamental experiences of time and space. A machine primarily intended for use in war united humanity (at least those whose minds or lives could be touched by the information) in an unprecedented outpouring of worldwide empathy, awe, and mourning. According to Elaine Scarry, knowing how to think and what to do in an emergency depends first on developing habits that embody an understanding of particular kinds of crises. No one knew just *how to think*, much less what to *do*, in this kind of emergency.[120]

Before the Titanic's maiden voyage, producers of its reputation crafted its cutting-edge attractiveness in order to wow the public. The Titanic disaster inspired a mortifying assessment of the cocky confidence associated with modernity. Like the emotions inspired by eighteenth- and nineteenth-century fiction, this was only a baby step, but the practical and public implications were worlds apart from what Hunt's readers felt while reading novels in their parlors. Large-scale responses to this new kind of knowledge and experience took decades longer, but immediate reactions anticipated a wider orbit for universal concepts about the world's people. For example, two days after the accident, a *London Times* commentator noted that the telegraph "enabled the peoples of many lands to stand together in sympathetic union, to share a common grief." A month later, Michigan state senator Alden Smith wrote in an investigation of the disaster, "when the world weeps together over a common loss, when nature moves in the same directions in all spheres," circumstances demand new standards for safety. The Titanic disaster thus marks a turning point on the timeline of what kind of suffering was possible for people around the world to imagine simultaneously—the beginning, perhaps, of a challenge to practice "thinking in an emergency" on a larger scale than ever before.[121]

Still however, no international politics of human rights was conceivable until 1948 when the Universal Declaration of Human Rights formalized some of these ambitious values and was adopted by the United Nations, itself only three years old. This occurred a month after Israel declared its existence, following more than six decades of legal settlement by European and Russian Jews, most of them fleeing pogroms. After the establishment of the state of Israel, hundreds of thousands of Jews from Algeria, Iran, Iraq, Morocco, the Soviet Union, Tunisia, Turkey, Yemen, and from all over Europe moved there as well, many of them fleeing from hostile conditions.[122]

Yet even these post-war events did not inspire an outpouring of human rights efforts. That took nearly three more decades. In 1961, Amnesty International was founded in London but remained largely unknown until 1977, when the organization received the Nobel Peace Prize and made news throughout the American and British press. The idea of human rights was looking better on paper, but still had no international leverage to speak of.[123]

Place these undeconstructable facts beside the idea's universalist aspirations—timeless and unchanging—and the contemporary commitment to human rights must be considered in a whole new way. That commitment is not usually informed by a keen awareness of its recent place in the available supply of ideas about injustice, or an appreciation of just what a strange and unusual idea it really is in light of the intellectual history traced above. The theorist George Mosse offers a disturbing perspective based in a careful study of centuries of European intellectual history. Given the funds of knowledge that our predecessors had to think with, coupled with the abiding material demands of everyday life which tightly drew the contours of survival for most people, he argues that racism and anti-Semitism, and by extension many other forms of human-generated suffering, were going to exist in this world no matter what.[124] And even when universalist ideas about human beings began to spread around the globe, they met realities on the ground that the ideas could not effectively or quickly challenge. One need not embrace Hegel's hypothesis that history is a progressive, goal-oriented process through which God expresses his will in order to grasp its practical implications. Persistent study of history reveals the compelling weight of Hegel's characterization of "history as the slaughter-bench at which the happiness of peoples, the wisdom of states, and the virtue of individuals have been sacrificed," whatever else it may also have been thus far.[125]

Whether suffering and injustice are the necessary costs of making progress toward a better world is not at all clear, although Lenin thought so and Stalin bypassed the problem of injustice altogether. In any case, the idea of human rights has only recently intersected with a simultaneous and geographically accurate picture of the forms of human suffering that the idea itself aims to address. That intersection arguably began just over 100 years ago with the advent of the wireless telegraph. Until then, what we call "human rights violations" today were unstoppable features of history caused by relations of power set in motion by random conditions launched by geography. People have been unable to produce meanings and effective politics to address their knowledge of the ensuing inequalities because the modern commitment to social justice emerged directly from conflicts that the universalist idea of human rights professes to tackle.

Recall for a moment Kant's idealism, which posits a standard for morality both rational and universal. "Universalism" is a socially constructed idea, the outer limits of which are prefigured by what can count, in a given time and place, as what exists and is possible in the universe. Kant could not mobilize understandings that he thought were ethically right. Born in 1724 in Königsberg, Prussia, he was raised and lived and died in the same town, never traveling more than ten miles from his home. He did not have access to a wireless telegraph, and neither did the important intellectuals and politicians who took his ideas seriously. No one did. For most of human history, people didn't think like Kant, and they didn't, in part, because they couldn't.

This approach to the idea of human rights assumes that, in Louis Menand's deft shorthand for American pragmatic philosophy, ideas are a lot like the wireless telegraph: they are tools. If a tool hasn't been invented yet, it can't be used to perform the task for which it will someday be made.[126] For example, our distant ancestors can't be faulted for making their children till the fields or failing to send them to school. Phillip Ariès's path-breaking work suggests that the idea that youth should be a carefree time in life devoted to education is a concept that emerged only in the 19th century.[127] The "tool" of this particular idea of childhood is now in every home that embraces middle-class values, but for most of human history no home possessed it, just as no home possessed, say, a manufactured stove. In other words, people can think and act only with the conceptual tools—the ideas—that they have. They can't "think outside the box" if they don't even know they're in the box. The social sciences showed that, to some degree, people are in that box in perpetuity. As dramatic as that insight is, even when universal rights were declared emphatically in the late 18th century, or when positive laws did change as during the Civil Rights era, minds and actions did not quickly follow. Reality tends to lag behind epoch-making ideas. Again, such ideas don't meet a unified and simple world, but a diverse and complex one.

★

In light of this depressing news, what are college and university faculty and their students supposed to *do*, here and now, about the injustices we know about that tear the world? Do the foregoing insights about the ideas of human rights and colonialism have anything to offer to the social justice mandate?

First, the social justice mandate enables scholars in many fields to easily make contemporary human suffering a serious concern of their intellectual work, and to draw institutional approval for channeling their expertise in support of social change. But actions that enjoy endorsement from higher education should always be informed by the most persuasive and ethically sound insights that such work offers: for example, historical knowledge of the abiding contradictions of the human condition, the persistence of unde-constructable facts, and the lack of an ability to think with future ideas and thereby know what the "right" side of history ever means. Many academics who have joined the BDS movement and attempt to turn institutions toward its demands exemplify the opposite habits of mind, as illustrated by the closed-door character of the recent American Studies conference at NYU, mentioned earlier in this essay.[128]

For another example, consider Curtis Marez, former president of the American Studies Association, defending his leadership of the organization's December 2013 boycott of Israeli institutions of higher education. In an editorial in the *Chronicle of Higher Education*, Marez wrote, "One day, after the tide turns, boycotts against Israel and the apartheid regime it has instituted will be viewed in the same way" as the boycotts of South Africa in the 1980s, which "history proved … right."[129] Unfortunately, history tends to yield not proofs and certainties, but puzzles. Academic and cultural boycotts of South Africa were controversial at the time, even among those who were in favor of economic boycotts. Academic boycotts never dominated the anti-apartheid movement.[130] The Israel/Palestine conflict is a puzzle that badly needs bold, brave, and informed engagement among parties who disagree. But the BDS movement generously expresses intense compassion for one of the contending parties, while showing spectacular indifference to the other. Academics who speak for this movement profess the conclusion that there is a quite simple solution to the conflict—just end the occupation, preferably today—which is naïve at best and ethically irresponsible at worst when proffered by intellectuals who ought to know better how international politics actually works—"not like the nursery," as Hannah Arendt once wrote. By extension, they claim that students who really care about social justice—who want to *do* something—will embrace this conclusion, happily provided by their wiser elders, and make it their own.

Second, academic boycotts in support of social justice illustrate a lack of understanding for how vulnerable and scarce institutions of higher education are. If their central values are to be stewarded and protected, they cannot be compromised without damaging the very goods that social justice advocates seek.[131] Their lifeblood is people who can take the intellectual risk of studying the world rather than being "directly caught up in the practical business of production and power," in Christopher Lasch's words. BDS principles aim toward an outcome that is already known by its adherents, based on an analysis of causes that they do not think they ever need to question again. This conclusion-driven approach threatens the wide range of emergent work by Israelis and Palestinians alike who are collaborating, often against terrible odds, to address the decades-long conflict plaguing their people even as geography undeniably ties their fates, like their histories, tightly to one another.[132]

Third, even some of Israel's staunchest high-profile critics express serious doubts about the BDS movement. For example, in 2010 Noam Chomsky said he was deeply troubled by how the BDS movement enflames the most reactionary constituents of Israeli society, worrying that "a call for an academic boycott on Tel Aviv University [for example] will strengthen support for Israel and US policy." Chomsky realistically assessed political activism with an eye to its effects. In reaction, Jeffrey Blankfort, former editor of the *Middle East Labor Bulletin*, reluctantly criticized Chomsky's failure to promote everything the BDS movement does, writing that because "of the viciousness and consistency with which Chomsky has been attacked by his critics on the 'right,' one ventures cautiously when challenging him from the 'left.'"[133] An organization that champions itself a paragon of critical engagement should not hesitate to welcome differences of opinion within its ranks. Ultimately, Blankfort chose not to deal with Chomsky's critique but to shame him instead, accusing him of "intellectual dishonesty" among other trespasses. This is not a real debate between people who aim toward the same goal, but an effort to keep lines between "us" and "them" stubbornly drawn even if doing so means rejecting a stalwart associate.

Likewise, in 2012, Norman Finkelstein noted the "cult"-like features of BDS, calling into question the usefulness of its political analysis and the integrity of its leadership. *Mondoweiss*, a prominent pro-BDS website, cynically accused him of using his public platform to "[fashion] his own persona as a cult leader."[134] Again, this response illustrates that the BDS movement can't abide second thoughts, even from allies like Chomsky and Finkelstein. This fact alone should raise a red flag in the mind of anyone who is paying attention to the Boycott, Divestment, and Sanctions movement, and who cares about higher education. Second thoughts, and third and fourth and hundredth thoughts, are what education is all about, and from which the scope of justice actually grows.

★

Susan Sontag once wrote, "There are ways of thinking that we don't yet know about. Nothing could be more important or precious than that knowledge, however unborn. The sense of urgency, the spiritual restlessness it engenders, cannot be appeased…"[135] Certainly college and university faculty are trusted to steward the discovery and invention of "ways of thinking that we don't yet know about." This stewardship is only possible if professors don't betray students' trust by giving up on inquiry. Students must be able to confront ways of thinking from the past that they don't know about, and ways of thinking held by people whom they don't identify with or fully understand. As educators, this is supposed to be what we're good at helping students do. When we're at work, the value of inquiry should stubbornly trump other values, even and perhaps especially our own politics. If higher education is to participate in aiming effectively for social justice, the structures and institutions that nurture the habits of mind through which the very outlines of justice can be debated, developed, revised, and ultimately mobilized must be protected even from within.

These insights could influence the way the social justice agenda unfolds in higher education. They could inspire appreciation for the practical limits of universalist, idealistic aspirations and how to pursue them. They could turn on a cautionary yellow light, illuminating the seductions of simple solutions to complex problems. When colleges and universities enact the social justice mandate, they are trusted, to put it simply, to know what they are doing. Questioning certainties takes time, patience, commitment, and trust that is deserved: a more demanding set of factors than it takes to recruit political allies and maintain their loyalty. For all these reasons, academic boycotts corrupt higher education's *raison d'être,* which is not primarily to enact the social justice mandate, but to promote careful thinking and a continual exploration and revision of what justice is and might be in the future. ■

TAMMI ROSSMAN-BENJAMIN

Interrogating the Academic Boycotters of Israel on American Campuses

I. Introduction

Boycotts of Israeli universities and scholars are among the newest expressions of academic anti-Zionism and antisemitism. In the U.S., more than 1,000 scholars on more than 300 college and university campuses across the country have endorsed an academic boycott of Israel,[136] as have a number of American academic organizations, including the American Studies Association (ASA),[137] the Association for Asian American Studies,[138] and the Native American and Indigenous Studies Association.[139]

Academic boycotts of Israel have included the boycott of academic events such as conferences convened or co-sponsored by Israeli institutions,[140] institutional cooperation agreements with Israeli universities,[141] and study abroad programs in Israel.[142] The academic boycott of Israel has also been invoked to bar the participation of Israeli scholars from academic conferences[143] and academic publications.[144]

Like virtually all anti-Israel Boycott, Divestment, and Sanctions (BDS) campaigns within the last several years, the academic boycott was established in response to the Palestinian political call to join the BDS movement against Israel.[145] That call[146] was issued by 171 Palestinian Non-Governmental

Organizations in 2005. The first and primary signatory of the Palestinian BDS Call was the Council of National and Islamic Forces in Palestine, which was founded by Yasser Arafat at the start of the Second Intifada in 2000 for the purpose of "organizing a unified effort among major Palestinian factions to oppose Israel and coordinate terror attacks."[147] The Council includes among its constituent organizations Hamas, the Popular Front for the Liberation of Palestine (PFLP) and PFLP-General Command, all three of which are on the U.S. Department of State's list of Designated Foreign Terrorist Organizations[148] and are committed to the elimination of the Jewish state through violent means. Omar Barghouti, founder and most vocal advocate of the Palestinian Campaign for the Academic and Cultural Boycott of Israel, has publicly described his desire to "euthanize" the "Zionist project,"[149] and his American counterparts, the academic founders of the U.S. Campaign for the Academic and Cultural Boycott of Israel (USACBI),[150] have all publicly expressed their opposition to the Jewish state.

The recent controversy over the ASA's adoption of a resolution boycotting Israeli universities and scholars has focused considerable attention, predominantly negative, on the topic of academic boycotts. The ASA has been subjected to scathing criticism by several prominent academic associations, including the American Association of University Professors, more than 250 university presidents, state and federal legislators, and virtually every mainstream Jewish organization.[151] These groups have argued that a boycott of Israeli universities and scholars violates the tenets of academic freedom and is discriminatory towards Israelis and the Jewish state.

Despite the attention that the ASA and its boycott resolution have received to date, little attention has been paid to the individual faculty members who support and promote the academic boycott of Israel, nor has there been an assessment of the negative impact these academic boycotters have had on the universities where they teach. For example, since the passage of the ASA resolution, events promoting the academic boycott of Israel, organized by faculty who themselves are founders of academic boycotts and sponsored by multiple academic departments, have taken place on several university campuses, including New York University,[152] San Francisco State University,[153] University of California, Riverside,[155] and University of California, Davis.[155] In all of these cases, the departmentally-sponsored events and their faculty organizers have been directly linked to student anti-Israel divestment campaigns on these campuses, as well as to student complaints about anti-Jewish hostility and harassment.

In order to understand how the academic boycott of Israel has taken root and flourished on many American college and university campuses and its deleterious consequences for the campus community, this paper will address the following questions:

- Who are the academic boycotters: With what academic departments are they affiliated? What ideologies motivate them?
- How have boycotters used their university positions to promote the academic boycott of Israel?
- How has the university allowed efforts to promote the academic boycott of Israel to flourish on campus?
- What are the effects of academic boycott efforts on college and university campuses?
- What can be done about the problem of faculty who use their university positions and university resources to promote a boycott of Israel?

II. Who are the Academic Boycotters of Israel?

The following analyses are based on a set of data that includes the institutional and primary departmental affiliations of 938 faculty members in 316 American colleges and universities, who have signed or endorsed one or more of 15 statements calling for an academic boycott of Israeli universities and scholars.

Divisional and Departmental Affiliations of Boycotters

Of the 938 boycotting faculty, the vast majority— 789 (86%)— were in the Humanities (453 or 49%) or Social Sciences (336 or 37%). Only 61 (7%) of the boycotters were affiliated with departments in Engineering and Natural Science, and only 38 (4%) were affiliated with departments in the Arts division. See Figure 1 for boycotters' divisional affiliations.

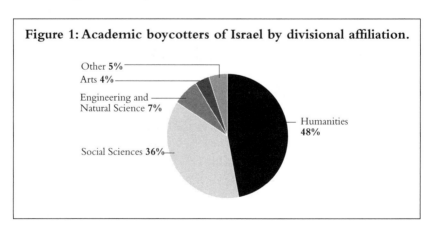

Figure 1: Academic boycotters of Israel by divisional affiliation.

Other 5%
Arts 4%
Engineering and Natural Science 7%
Social Sciences 36%
Humanities 48%

The departments with the largest numbers of boycotters were English or literature (192 or 21%), followed by ethnic studies (96 or 10%), history (68 or 7%), gender studies (65 or 7%), anthropology (53 or 6%), sociology (44 or 5%), linguistics or languages (43 or 5%), politics (39 or 4%), American studies (33 or 3%), Middle or Near East studies (32 or 3%). See Table 1 for the top ten departmental affiliations of the boycotters.

Table 1—Top 10 Primary Departmental Affiliations of Academic Boycotters.	
Department	**Number of Boycotters**
N = 938	
English or Literature	192 (21%)
Ethnic Studies	96 (10%)
History	68 (7%)
Gender Studies	65 (7%)
Anthropology	53 (6%)
Sociology	44 (5%)
Linguistics, Languages	39 (4%)
Politics	53 (6%)
American Studies	33 (3%)
Middle or Near East Studies	32 (3%)

Ideological Motivation of Boycotters

The above data clearly suggest that a boycotter's field of study is related to his or her endorsement of an academic boycott of Israel. But why is this so? Why would a faculty member in the Humanities be far more likely to endorse an academic boycott of Israel than one in the Sciences or Engineering? Why would a professor of English be more likely to be a boycotter than a professor of history, linguistics, philosophy, or psychology?

In order to investigate this question, we looked more closely at 143 boycotters whose primary departmental affiliation was English. We did this not only because of the surprisingly high proportion of boycotters in English and literature departments—more than 1/5 of the total number of boycotters, a proportion which is significantly higher than the proportion of English faculty to total faculty in any university —but also because there is no obvious connection between the discipline of English and the Israeli-Palestinian conflict. Therefore, we reasoned that any difference in research focus between those English professors who have endorsed an academic boycott of Israel and those who have not could be an indicator that ideological factors are at play in a professor's choosing to endorse an academic boycott of Israel.

In examining the on-line descriptions of the research interests of several English professors who have endorsed the academic boycott of Israel, we discovered four recurring themes:

1. **Class**: including terms such as Marxism, Critical Theory, Class
2. **Gender**: including terms such as Feminism, Gender, Sexuality, Queer
3. **Race**: including terms such as Ethnic, Race, Native, Indian, African, Black, Indigenous, Asian
4. **Empire**: including terms such as Post-Colonial, Empire, Imperialism, Subaltern, Alterity

A comprehensive analysis of all 143 professors of English who endorsed the academic boycott of Israel reveals the following:

- 92% have research interests that include one or more of the above four categories.
- 63% have research interests that include Race.
- 46% have research interests that include Gender.
- 39% have research interests that include Empire.
- 26% have research interests that include Class.
- In order to ensure that the predominance of these research themes among boycotting English faculty was not simply a function of departmental affiliation—in other words, perhaps 92% of *all* English faculty, irrespective of whether they have endorsed an academic boycott of Israel, have research interests that include these four categories—we conducted a survey of the research interests of all of the faculty in English departments at 21 American universities where one or more members of the English department had endorsed a boycott of Israel.[158]

We found the following:

- 40% of the total English faculty (N = 866) at the 21 universities surveyed have research interests that include one or more of the four research areas above, with the smallest percentage found at Bates College (10%) and the largest percentage at the University of Chicago (73%).
- 23% have research interests that include Race.
- 22% have research interests that include Gender.

- 9% have research interests that include Empire.
- 11% have research interests that include Class.

Table 2 provides a comparison of the research interests of those English faculty who have endorsed the academic boycott of Israel and of all English faculty on 21 university campuses with respect to the categories of Race, Gender, Class or Empire. As can be seen, boycotters are significantly more likely to be engaged in research in these four areas than their departmental colleagues, suggesting that these areas of study may predispose faculty members to endorse an academic boycott of Israel.

Table 2—A Comparison of the Research Interests of Boycotting English Faculty and All English Faculty in 21 University English Departments.			
Research Interests	English Boycotters N = 143	Total English Faculty N = 866	Statistical Significance
Race, Gender, Empire or Class	132 (92%)	326 (38%)	$x^2 = 147; p < .0005$
Race	92 (63%)	201 (23%)	$x^2 = 101; p < .0005$
Gender	67 (46%)	198 (22%)	$x^2 = 35; p < .0005$
Empire	57 (39%)	80 (9%)	$x^2 = 100; p < .0005$
Class	38 (26%)	91 (11%)	$x^2 = 30; p < .0005$

This conclusion is supported in part by the fact that faculty whose primary affiliation is in ethnic studies or gender studies show the second and fourth highest rates of academic boycotting, respectively, despite the fact that these two departments are, in general, significantly smaller than other departments on most campuses.

These data beg the question: What, if anything, do these four areas of study have in common, and why might they predispose a faculty member engaged in studying one or more of them to boycott Israel?

One possibility is that all four areas represent ideological paradigms which divide the world into oppressed and oppressor along the lines of Race, Gender, Empire, or Class, making it a short ideological leap to seeing the Palestinian-Israeli conflict in the same binary terms, casting the Palestinians as the oppressed and the Israelis as the oppressor. Moreover, these areas of study all grew out of, and to some extent continue to have ties to social movements such as the civil rights movement, feminism, anti-imperialism, and Marxism, which were established to pursue "social justice" for the oppressed by combating the "evils" of the racist, sexist, colonialist, capitalist oppressor, a fact which makes for the blurring of the lines between scholarship and activism. The linkage between scholarship and activism inherent to the study of Race, Gender, Empire, and Class not only helps to explain the disproportionate number of English faculty among the academic boycotters of Israel, it also helps to explain why some faculty feel justified in bringing their anti-Israel activism onto their campuses and into their classrooms.

III. How Have Faculty Promoted the Academic Boycott of Israel on Their Campuses?

Here are seven examples of the diverse ways in which founders and organizers of the academic boycott of Israel have used their university positions and the university's resources to promote the boycott:

1. As Part of the Course Curriculum

David Lloyd is a Distinguished Professor of English at University of California Riverside.[159] He is also a founder of USACBI. In January, he organized on his campus a lecture by Omar Barghouti, the founder and most vocal advocate of the Palestinian Campaign for the Academic and Cultural Boycott of Israel. The talk was funded and sponsored by the College of Humanities, Arts, and Social Sciences along with the Department of Ethnic Studies, a third of whose faculty have endorsed the academic boycott of Israel, including the department chair.[160] Students in eight courses were required to attend and listen to Barghouti's talk, which consisted of anti-Israel propaganda laced with classic antisemitic tropes used to promote the academic boycott of Israel.

2. At an Academic Conference

Lisa Duggan is a professor of Social and Cultural Analysis at New York University.[161] She is also the 2014 President of the American Studies Association and was an organizer and vocal advocate of the ASA's resolution to boycott Israeli universities and scholars. A few months after the ASA's membership approved the boycott resolution, Duggan helped to organize the annual conference of NYU's American Studies Program, entitled "Circuits of Influence: U.S., Israel, and Palestine." The conference, which was co-sponsored by three other NYU departments, included talks by 21 BDS-supporting academics and activists focusing on "using boycotts as a tactic and substantive challenge to systems of injustice" that include Israel's "racialization, empire, and settler colonialism". The conference also featured workshops on how to boycott Israel, run by representatives of virulently anti-Zionist organizations such as Adalah-NY, Students for Justice in Palestine, and Jewish Voice for Peace.[162]

3. On the University Website

David Klein is a mathematics Professor at California State University, Northridge, and the faculty advisor for CSUN Students for Justice in Palestine.[163] He is also a founder of USACBI and organized a petition to boycott the Israel Abroad program on CSU campuses in solidarity with the academic boycott of Israel.[164] For more than four years, Klein has been using his university's server to promote his web page entitled "Boycott Israel Resource Page," calling for the economic, academic, and cultural boycott of Israel. His university-hosted web page contains a litany of false and inflammatory statements and photographs intended to incite hatred and promote political activism against the Jewish state, particularly boycott.[165]

4. Through Departmental Sponsorship of a Student BDS Event

Sunaina Maira is a professor of Asian American Studies and Middle East/South Asia Studies[167] at University of California, Davis, as well as a founder of USACBI and an organizer of the ASA's academic boycott resolution. About a month after the ASA vote to boycott Israel, Maira helped the UC Davis Students for Justice in Palestine (SJP) to organize an event featuring Omar Barghouti and three other anti-Israel activists, who demonized and delegitimized the Jewish state and encouraged students to engage in activism against it, particularly boycott.[168] The event, which was used by the SJP group to kick off their campaign to pass an anti-Israel divestment resolution in the student senate in the spring, was co-sponsored by four academic units, including Maira's Asian American Studies department, more than half of whose faculty has endorsed an academic boycott of Israel.

5. By Advising Pro-Palestinian Students

Rabab Abdulhadi is a professor of Ethnic Studies and senior scholar of the Arab and Muslim Ethnicities and Diasporas Initiative at San Francisco State University,[169] a founder of USACBI, and the faculty advisor of the General Union of Palestine Students (GUPS) at SFSU. As a featured speaker at student-organized events, Abdulhadi has advocated overthrowing the "settler colonial" occupation of Palestine by any means, including by armed violence and BDS. She has also posted messages on the GUPS Facebook page promoting BDS. In her role as GUPS faculty advisor, Abdulhadi helped the

GUPS students organize an event in November 2013 that featured an image of PFLP terrorist Leila Khaled holding a rifle with the caption "resistance is not terrorism,"[171] and another with the words "My Heroes Have Always Killed Colonizers."[172] Abdulhadi was also the personal mentor of former GUPS president Mohammad G. Hammad,[173] who was expelled from SFSU in January 2014 for numerous violent social media postings glorifying terrorism and threatening to kill Israelis and their supporters.[174]

6. In the Academic Senate

Manzar Foroohar is a professor of history at California Polytechnic State University San Luis Obispo[175] and a founder of USACBI. She has also served as the chair of Cal Poly's Academic Senate Faculty Affairs Committee since 2002 and currently serves as the chair of the CSU Faculty Affairs Committee. Foroohar has used her leadership roles in the campus and state-wide academic senates to advance her anti-Israel positions, as well as to silence criticism of herself and other faculty who use the university's name and resources to promote anti-Israel activism, including boycotts of Israel. After Foroohar and two other CSU faculty members were criticized by a community organization and many members of the public for using their university affiliations and resources to host talks by Ilan Pappé, a well-known advocate of the academic boycott of Israel, in February 2012,[176] Foroohar drafted an academic resolution condemning "appalling attempts by political pressure groups to quell academic freedom on campuses and to impose their political agenda on our educational institutions."[177] Her resolution was approved with slight revision by the Cal Poly Academic Senate Executive Committee and adopted by the Cal Poly Academic Senate. Later that year, Foroohar volunteered and was appointed to chair the state-wide faculty senate committee charged with implementing the "Governor's Task Force on Tolerance and Anti-Semitism Training," apparently in an attempt to subvert that committee's charge.[178] In January 2014, at a meeting of the statewide Academic Senate Plenary that took place in the Office of the CSU Chancellor Timothy White, Foroohar criticized White for his public statements condemning the ASA's academic boycott of Israel, which she claimed inhibited "faculty and student advocacy for Palestinian organizations."[179]

7. Using a Faculty Advocacy Group

Sondra Hale is Professor Emeritus of Anthropology and Women's Studies at UCLA[180] and was the previous co-director of the UCLA Center for Near Eastern Studies. She is also a founder of USACBI and helped organize a petition calling for the boycott of the Israel Abroad program on University of California campuses in solidarity with the academic boycott of Israel.[181]

In 2009, Hale and three other California-based co-founders of USACBI established California Scholars for Academic Freedom, and most of that organization's membership consists of California faculty who have endorsed the academic boycott of Israel, including David Lloyd, Sunaina Maira, David Klein, Rabab Abdulhadi, and Manzar Foroohar. Although the organization describes itself as a group of more than 100 academics whose goal is to protect California scholars from violations of academic freedom,[182] their primary focus has been protecting the rights of California faculty who wish to promote the academic boycott of Israel and engage in other anti-Israel activism on their respective campuses. To this end, they have written numerous letters to UC, CSU, and state legislative leaders defending California faculty who have been criticized for engaging in anti-Israel activism in their classrooms and conference halls,[183] censuring a UC report[184] and State Assembly resolution[185] that documented and condemned antisemitism on California campuses, and disparaging the CSU president's statement condemning the ASA's academic boycott of Israel.

IV. Institutional Factors that Allow Faculty to Promote the Academic Boycott of Israel on Campus

The above examples demonstrate how academic boycott leaders have not only promoted anti-Israel campaigns on their respective campuses but have sought to stifle all criticism of their behavior. To a large extent their efforts have been successful. This is primarily the result of three conditions that exist on many university campuses today.

1. Academic Departments That Encourage Political Activism

A number of academic departments devoted to the study of race, gender, class, or empire explicitly or implicitly encourage their faculty to engage in political advocacy and activism, including against the Jewish state. For example, the following departments, one or more of whose affiliated faculty have endorsed the academic boycott of Israel, have incorporated the promotion of political activism, especially the pursuit of "social justice," into their mission statements:

- San Francisco State University Ethnic Studies: "The College of Ethnic Studies aims to actively implement a vision of social justice focusing on eliminating inequalities motivated by race and ethnicity."[187]

- University at Albany: "Women's, Gender, and Sexuality Studies is an interdisciplinary field of study that recognizes excellence in research, teaching, and service in three important ways...Social Justice, a commitment to dismantling sexism, racism, classism, and other oppressive practices in our research, teaching, and service to different communities."
- University of California, Santa Barbara: "[T]he sociology department has a strong tradition of mixing scholarship with activism and concerns for social justice."
- University of Illinois at Urbana-Champaign, Asian American Studies: "Faculty, staff, and students associated with the department are expected to contribute to this mission not only through teaching, research, and service activities, locally and nationally, but also through active participation in social, intellectual, and political endeavors."[190]

Some departments even consider the anti-Israel activism of their faculty as a valued aspect of academic service and mention it on their departmental websites. For instance, in her official faculty biography on the website of the UCLA Center for Near Eastern Studies, Emeritus Professor Sondra Hale is described as "an activist academic" who is "co-founder of the U.S. Committee for the Academic and Cultural Boycott of Israel."[191]

In light of such departmental emphasis on political and social activism, a faculty member's on-campus promotion of the boycott of Israel is more likely to be applauded by his or her departmental colleagues than condemned.

2. The Vagueness and Malleability of Academic Freedom

The use of university affiliation and resources to promote the boycott of Israel has been publicly challenged as an abuse of academic freedom in the cases of all seven of the academic boycott founders and organizers cited in the previous section. However, in each case, university administrators, who themselves have condemned the academic boycott of Israel on the grounds that it violates the tenets of academic freedom and is antithetical to the mission of the university, have declared that the behavior of these professors is absolutely protected by academic freedom—even the behavior of mathematics professor David Klein, who has used his university's web server to post his "Boycott Israel Resource Page," whose contents are totally unrelated to his field of scholarly expertise.

This raises the question of what, exactly, academic freedom denotes, a question which becomes even more complicated when we consider that academic freedom has been so confidently invoked in each of the following contexts:

- Academic boycotters claim that the academic boycott is being imposed on Israel as a response to Israel's violation of the academic freedom of Palestinian scholars.
- Critics of the academic boycotters claim that the imposition of such a boycott violates the academic freedom of Israeli scholars and those American scholars who would choose to work with them.
- Academic boycotters claim that their academic freedom to champion the academic freedom rights of Palestinian scholars is being violated.
- Critics of the academic boycotters claim that boycotters are stifling their academic freedom to complain about the boycotter's violation of academic freedom.

In fact, the answer to the question of what academic freedom denotes has been so distorted and misrepresented by BDS advocates, and the concept as a result applied in such contradictory ways, as to disable its use in many discussions about academic boycotts of Israel and their advancement by faculty on campuses. Until clarity is restored to the concept and better education regarding guidelines established for its use promoted, claims of academic freedom will continue to provide cover for faculty who wish to promote an antisemitic boycott of Israel at their college or university.

3. The Unwillingness of Administrators to Enforce University Policies and the Law

In contrast to the vagueness and malleability of academic freedom, university policy and state and federal laws provide objective standards of behavior for faculty, and several of them seem to clearly apply to the case of faculty who promote an antisemitic boycott of Israel on campus:

- University policies that protect the academic mission of the university from political indoctrination: For example, the University of California Regents Policy on Course Content provides that "Misuse of the classroom by, for example, allowing it to be used for political indoctrination... constitutes misuse of the University as an institution."[192]
- Laws that prohibit state and federal monies from being used for purposes not consistent with the educational mission of the university: For example, California Government Code 8314 prohibits the use of public resources for political or personal purposes.[193]
- Laws that prohibit discriminatory boycotts: For example, New York Human Rights Law section 296 prohibits boycotts based on national origin,[194] and the Ribicoff Amendment of the Tax Reform Act of

1976 makes it a federal violation to "participate or cooperate with an international boycott."[195]

- Laws that prohibit the harassment of and discrimination against Jewish students: For example, Title VI of the 1964 Civil Rights Act, which prohibits discrimination against students on the basis of race, color, or national origin, and has included Jewish students since 2010.

Although university policies and careful use of laws such as these could provide a means of protecting the campus community from the harmful effects of faculty bringing the boycott of Israel onto campus, university administrators have been loath to acknowledge, let alone enforce, these policies and laws.[196]

V. Effects of Academic Boycott Efforts on Campuses

Faculty members' unbridled use of the university for promoting the boycott of Israel has had three primary negative consequences for the universities at which they are being carried out.

1. Corruption of the academic mission of the university

The political nature of the campaign to promote a boycott of Israel damages the educational endeavor that is at the heart of the university. In a 2012 report of the California Association of Scholars entitled "A Crisis of Competence: The Corrupting Effect of Political Activism in the University of California,"[197] the authors detail the extent to which UC campuses have been harmed by the politicization of their academic programming. They conclude that when the focus of a professor or department is political advocacy, the quality of teaching and research is compromised. One-sided partisan teaching also limits the access of students to vital information about complex topics of global importance, and it violates their fundamental right to be educated and not indoctrinated.

2. Creation of a hostile environment for Jewish students

Professors who use their university positions and university resources to promote campaigns to harm or dismantle the Jewish state and who encourage students to do the same, can contribute to the creation of a hostile and threatening environment for many Jewish students, who report feeling emotionally and intellectually harassed and intimidated by their professors and isolated from their fellow students. Moreover, in light of the fact that no other racial, ethnic, or religious group is currently being subjected *by faculty* to such pervasive harassment and intimidation, Jewish students experience this flagrant double standard as a kind of institutional discrimination that is antisemitic in effect if not in intent. Unfortunately, Jewish students who feel emotionally or intellectually threatened as a result of their professor's anti-Israel advocacy are often afraid to come forward and confront the professor or to complain to an administrator, because they are concerned about potential retaliation. In addition, students who do try to speak up about faculty harassment and intimidation risk being accused of violating their professors' academic freedom and subject to further harassment and intimidation.

3. Giving academic legitimacy to global campaigns to harm Israel

American college campuses have become a critical front in the war of ideas being waged against the Jewish state. The language and imagery used to demonize Israel and portray the state as worthy of destruction, as well as the BDS campaigns intended to be the first steps towards that end, are the main weapons of this "war by other means," and they have caused significant harm to the reputation of Israel and her supporters, both on and off campus, in America and around the world. Moreover, when antisemitic tropes and campaigns are promoted by faculty in their classrooms and at departmentally sponsored events, a cloak of academic legitimacy attaches to them, considerably enhancing their ability to flourish on campus and well beyond, and contributing to the growth of global antisemitism.

VI. Conclusions

As the foregoing analysis has demonstrated, faculty members on hundreds of university campuses across the country have endorsed an academic boycott of Israeli universities and scholars. Predominantly hailing from the humanities and social sciences, many of the academic boycotters are involved with the study of race, gender, class, or empire, and seem to be motivated by ideologies which divide the world into oppressed and oppressor and are linked to social movements which pursue social justice for the oppressed by combating the perceived oppressor, in this case Israel.

Academic boycotters have found multiple points of entry for advancing the boycott of Israel on their campuses, including in the classroom, conference hall, and campus square, on the university website, and through the academic senate. Faculty boycotters have also created advocacy groups to defend the right of faculty to continue using university resources to promote BDS. The boycotters' efforts have been facilitated by the activist focus of some departments in the social sciences and humanities, the lack of clarity about (and misrepresentation of) academic freedom, and the unwillingness of administrators to enforce university policy and state and federal laws that would curb the behavior of the boycotters. The net result is that many universities are at risk of becoming bastions of political hatred directed against Israel, and inhospitable to Jewish students who identify with the Jewish state.

The problem is a serious one and worsens with each campus-based boycott effort that goes unchallenged. But what can be done to stem the tide of virulent hatred directed against the Jewish state and its supporters? In the absence of a willingness on the part of faculty and administrators to address the problem, pressure must be brought from outside of the university. Such pressure could be applied in the following ways:

- **Public Pressure**—Information about BDS and other antisemitic efforts on campuses, as well as the names and affiliated departments of faculty members who endorse them, should be published and circulated widely. Then, university consumers and stakeholders—students, prospective students, alumni, parents, donors, and taxpayers—should be encouraged to express their outrage at the university's collusion with an antisemitic campaign to eliminate the Jewish state. Potential loss of student or donor revenue and the erosion of the goodwill of the taxpaying public send a compelling message to university administrators to address the problem.

- **Legal Pressure**—When the behavior of faculty, students, or administrators violates state or federal law, legal action, or the threat of legal action, may prove effective.

Among the founders of the US Campaign for the Academic and Cultural Boycott of Israel, Lara Deeb (Scripps College), Nada Elia (Antioch University, Seattle), Cynthia Franklin (University of Hawaii at Manoa), Sondra Hale (University of California, Los Angeles), Salah D. Hassan (Michigan State University), David Klein (California State University, Northridge), Dennis Kortheuer (California State University, Long Beach), Sunaina Maira (University of California, Davis), Fred Moten (University of California, Riverside), and Edie Pistolesi (California State University, Northridge), signed a letter to President Elect Barack Obama which, among other things, argues for elimination of the Jewish state. David Lloyd (University of California, Riverside) wrote the letter. He has stated that Israel is "an apartheid state, whose self-declared constitution as a 'Jewish State for a Jewish People' should have no more international legitimacy than South Africa's 'white state for a white people' or Northern Ireland's 'Protestant State for a Protestant people,' both of which finally fell to a combination of military and civil resistance and international opprobrium." Elia, Franklin, Klein, and Kortheuer also signed a petition for "Palestinian Right of Return and a democratic state throughout historic Palestine—'From the River to the Sea'—with equal rights for all," as did Sherna Berger Gluck (California State University, Long Beach).[198]

Rabab Abdulhadi (San Francisco State University) signed a petition stating that "the rights of the Palestinian people—and our land, the entire land of Palestine—are not for sale or bartering at the negotiations table."[199] She has argued for "a liberated Palestine" that is "an inclusionary alternative to the exclusionary strategy of Zionism."[200] Manzar Foroohar (California Polytechnic State University, San Luis Obispo) signed a petition calling on Israel to end its "occupation and colonization of all Arab lands," which is clearly referring to all of Israel.[201] She signed a statement calling Israel's treatment of Palestinians a "crime against humanity" which "symbolizes a regime rooted in more than six decades of piracy, ethnic cleansing, racism, and apartheid against Palestinians and other indigenous people of the region."[202] Jess Ghannam (University of California, San Francisco) co-founded Al-Awda: Palestinian Right of Return. The organization "unequivocally supports the fundamental, inalienable, historical, legal, individual, and collective rights of all Palestinian refugees to return to their original towns, villages, and lands anywhere in Palestine from which they were expelled," "supports the struggle for the liberation of Palestine and views it as a struggle against all forms of colonialism," seeks "the dismantlement of the exclusionary and racist character of 'Israel,'" and "[t]he formation of an independent, democratic state for all its citizens in all of Palestine."[203] Hale signed a petition opposing the Geneva Accord since it "provides a Palestinian-Arab cover for the exclusive nature of the Israeli polity as a 'Jewish State', thus abrogating the national character of the Palestinian people within 1948 borders. It therefore fails to recognize the right of the 1.2 million Palestinian citizens of Israel to live in a democratic state for all its citizens: Jews and Palestinians."[204] Academic activist Steven Salaita has stated: "My hope is that in the end, we'll let lie Israel's dead soul and examine its destruction of actual minds and bodies instead."[205] He adds: "I would urge you not to limit your critique of Israel only to its errors of judgment or its perceived excesses; it is more productive to challenge the ideology and practice of Zionism itself . . . I am not arguing that Americans should reassess their level of support for Israel. I am arguing that Americans should oppose Zionism altogether."[206]

The problem is not with these faculty taking such public positions, something they are entitled to do both as US citizens and as faculty members engaged in the extramural expression of their political opinions. The problem arises when such political convictions become so fanatical that classroom instruction becomes coercive, students' rights to express alternative views are compromised, or discussion becomes bullying or intimidation. That is a problem universities need to face with a level of courage and honesty little

SAMUEL M. EDELMAN AND
CAROL F. S. EDELMAN

"When Failure Succeeds": Divestment as Delegitimation

Since 2005, student legislative bodies at universities across the US, Canada and Europe have considered resolutions calling for universities to divest from Israel. Debates on these resolutions are well attended sessions, more crowded than the usual student council meetings. In addition to the student legislators, other students, faculty, and staff who are concerned with this issue and local community members from both sides and the press attend. BDS groups devote huge resources to defending their proposals while anti-BDS groups are equally committed to fighting these resolutions. The discussions are rancorous, emotional, and usually go on for hours, sometimes even lasting till sunrise the next morning.

These marathon BDS debates have been going on for 10 years. We might logically expect that the continued use of this strategy is because it's so successful, but surprisingly, nothing could be farther from the truth. While it's happening on more and more campuses, the movement is not getting universities to divest from either Israeli companies or multi-national companies that do business with Israel or getting universities to boycott Israeli products. For example, in the 2013-2014 academic year, 15 divestment resolutions were introduced at universities in the U.S. Of these, only two passed. In the previous academic year, 2012-2013, the record for BDS supporters was superficially better. Of the 13 resolutions introduced in universities across the U. S., 6 were actually passed by the student government. That's an almost 50% "success" rate, unheard of in most of the years this has been going on.[207]

But let us consider "success" in more depth. What happened on the 6 campuses where student organizations voted in 2012-2013 to support a BDS resolution (Earlham, Oberlin, UC Berkeley, Swarthmore, UC Irvine and UC San Diego)? Not one of these campuses boycotted, divested, or sanctioned Israel. It seems that few student governments have any power over the investment policy of their campus. They can pass resolutions but they cannot act on them. They can only call on the financial officers and/or trustees to divest. The three University of California campuses (Irvine, San Diego, and Berkeley) passed the same resolution calling for a boycott of companies that do business with Israel, but not one of those campuses instituted such a ban. The only resolution in 2012-2013 that impacted the campus was at Earlham College in Richmond, Indiana. The impact was trivial and brief; the food service stopped serving Sabra hummus in the dining halls for a short time, an insignificant action that had no discernable economic impact.

So we have a movement that for 10 years has seen less than 50% of their resolutions passed and, even worse, virtually none of those passed had any impact on university policy. Clearly, this strategy is not working. Yet Students for Justice in Palestine, Jewish Voice for Peace, and the American Friends Service Committee, along with other like-minded groups continue to pursue this strategy with determination and dedication. They continue to devote time, energy, and money promoting resolutions that will go nowhere. Why? That is a critical question for pro-Israel, anti-BDS groups to contemplate; they are winning many battles on university campuses but are they winning the war? Is there a BDS goal beyond resolutions and banning Sabra hummus?

At a conference held at UC Hastings Law School in the spring of 2011, Gwynne Skinner, plaintiff lawyer for *Corrie vs. Caterpillar*, and Professor Jules Lobel of the Center for Constitutional Rights (CCR), argued that winning legal cases and divestment and boycott efforts are not and should not be the end goal of the BDS movement.[208] Instead, they said, the goal should be to change the opinions of young Americans about Israel. Similarly, over the last two years members of organizations supporting BDS have argued in the same fashion at similar conferences, workshops and training camps about BDS campaigns.

There is data to support Skinner's and Lobel's assertion that the attitudes and opinions of young people, including college students, are open to influence. The Brand Israel Group and the Conference of Presidents of Major American Jewish Organizations co-sponsored a study of Americans attitudes toward Israel in 2010. In their report released in 2011, they concluded: "This research confirms all recent polling data that shows that while there is a solid base of core support for Israel in the U.S. (comprised of Jews, Evangelicals, older Americans, and the political right), there are key segments "at-risk": younger Americans, college students, the political left and, to a lesser degree, women and minorities." The study reveals major differences in perceptions of Israel/Israelis among the core vs. at-risk groups on almost all key measurements. Particularly given the advancing age of core supporters, if we don't alter our approach to more effectively broaden our reach, we are at risk of losing the next generation.[209]

Advocates of BDS understand that the movement's success is not measured by the resolutions themselves. The resolutions are a means to a larger end. "From an organizing perspective, the tactics of BDS provide a common platform and points of unity for people in the United States to start working on," said Yaman Salahi, a member of the Students for Justice in Palestine group at Yale University, where he is a law student. "BDS provides a concrete way for students and people outside of campuses to directly connect with the issues . . . and it also provokes a discussion that is often difficult to provoke."

Supporters also argue that the movement has had an impact on how people think about and discuss the conflict. "It's been great in affecting the discourse and just mobilizing people," said Balzer. "Suddenly the discussion on campus is, do Israel's atrocities merit divestment? Which is a very different question than, is Israel angelic?"[210]

The resolutions create discussion, generate publicity, and attract attention. The discussion of Israel's alleged human rights violations starts months and years before the vote will take place. School newspapers, community newspapers, and social media spread the word. They engage students in an issue that most know very little about. Two of the campuses passing divestment resolutions, University of California, San Diego and Oberlin College, are representative of the approach taken by pro-BDS activists in setting the scene for divestment resolutions while also spearheading a public relations/propaganda campaign focused on the delegitimation and demonization of Israel.

UC San Diego's student government's passage of an anti-Israel resolution took four years. Over all those years, the campus experienced a barrage of anti-Israel films, speakers, panels, editorials, and faculty presentations portraying Israel as a human rights violator, as a racist nation espousing apartheid-like policies against an oppressed, occupied Palestinian people. Students for Justice in Palestine's use of Jewish pro-BDS students and speakers from outside of campus enhanced their own credibility, showing that this issue was not just an SJP issue. Counter programing by Hillel with the help of the Israel on Campus Coalition, pro-Israel student groups and faculty as well as strong relationship building with student government leaders enabled the narrow defeat of the anti-Israel resolutions for three years. But the weight of three years of constant demonization of Israel and Israelis, as well as a successful political campaign seeding pro-BDS people into student government, eventually led to the resolution's passage. BDS supporters were adept at using editorials, op ed's, letters to the editor in the *Daily Californian*, a Twitter campaign and a Facebook campaign to keep the issue alive on campus and encourage sympathetic faculty to address the issue in their classes. Social media, especially Twitter, was used to stop any amendments that might water down the resolution; the BDS advocates used Facebook and Twitter to push supporters on the senate to block other senators' attempts to alter the resolution and make it palatable to all sides.

In the year preceding the successful vote, SJP mounted events around the prosecution of the Irvine 11, had a number of boycott teach-ins for the campus community, sponsored a presentation on Christmas in Occupied Palestine from Al Jazeera, brought the former mayor of Birzeit to speak on campus, had showings of "Occupation 101" and "5 Broken Cameras," and had presentations and distributed articles and statements from Ben White, Nasser Barghouti, and Hatem Bazian, all major BDS supporters, just to name a few. They were also able to get endorsements from the AW Local 2865 student workers union, the coalition of South Asian peoples, the Sustainability Collective, Jewish Voice for Peace, Groundwork Books, Pakistani Student Organization, and the Sikh Students. A lot of effort went into publicizing this issue on campus; Israel was portrayed negatively over and over again.[211] On March 14, 2013, at 1:28 am, the final resolution passed in a secret ballot after five hours of rancorous heated debate and numerous attempted amendments, 20 in favor, 12 against and 1 abstention. Later that same morning the Chancellor of UCSD, Dr. Pradeep K. Khosla, released the following statement:

> Last night, the Associated Students Council at UC San Diego approved a divestment resolution that cites the Israeli-Palestinian conflict and calls for the University of California to divest of holdings in a list of companies . . . The UC Regents set investment policy for the ten-campus system, including UC San Diego. The UC leadership has reiterated its decision that such divestment is not the policy of the University of California and that a divestment resolution will not be brought before the Regents.[212]

The students in student government knew that the Chancellor would respond in this way. Students for Justice in Palestine knew it as well. Nevertheless they all proceeded as if the resolution would indeed do something. The reality is that it did do something. It made Israel and Israelis look bad in the eyes of the students on campus who witnessed these events from the sidelines.

The Oberlin College divestment drama played out in a slightly different way. Oberlin was already a fertile ground for BDS activities. Students for a Free Palestine already had cemented a strong relationship with student government leaders. Oberlin College's Students for a Free Palestine pursued a divestment proposal requesting that the university's finance committee divest from Caterpillar, Hewlett Packard, Group 4 Securicor, SodaStream, Elbit Systems and Veolia because those companies were Israeli owned or did business with Israel.

Again the divestment campaign was preceded with years of work in portraying Israel in a negative light with speakers, panels and films. In the few months leading up to the vote, Students for a Free Palestine used facebook and Twitter campaigns to drum up interest. They got seven editorials published in the *Oberlin Review* supporting divestment and demonizing Israel. An ongoing program called Divestment 101 was created to educate students and student leaders on divestment issues. They also brought to campus Alice Rothchild, a Jewish obstetrician-gynecologist turned anti-Israel activist, who spoke in support of BDS. In addition to all that activity, in the weeks preceding the vote, a twitter campaign and a Facebook campaign through OberlinDivest and Facebook Oberlin Divest was going strong. No wonder that, after only a three hour discussion, the divestment resolution passed with a majority vote.[213]

The resolution was non-binding and ultimately ignored by the college investment committee. Once again, as in the case of UCSD, Oberlin College's divestment resolution was understood from the beginning as a meaningless effort in that it would have no real impact on the investment committee of the college. As a vehicle for attitude change for Oberlin students witnessing these events it can only be viewed as a successful campaign to demonize and delegitimize both Israel and Israelis. The *Cleveland Jewish News* reported after the vote that "Rabbi Shimon Brand, Jewish chaplain at the college, said the resolution is not a cause for great concern." In trying to downplay what happened on campus, Rabbi Brand continued:

It's a sad thing, but not a significant thing," said Brand, director of Hillel at Oberlin College. The Oberlin College Student Senate is not a representative of the student body. It's a minor organization on campus. The Student Senate does not have a clue about Israel; they know nothing about it. This also has no reflection on Oberlin College's investment policies. The (college's) investment committee will not pay attention to it. It won't affect the administration on its investments.[214]

Rabbi Brand was only partially correct in his assessment of the BDS effort at Oberlin. He was right that passage of the divestment resolution was sad and not significant; it did not result in any action on the part of the university. He was right that the BDS efforts at Oberlin and UCSD and other universities fail badly at getting any divestment, sanctions, or boycott against Israel going even when a resolution is passed by the student legislators. His remarks focused on the immediate event, the resolution—whether it passed or not and then whether it was implemented or not. This is a perspective common in the pro-Israel, anti-BDS communities. If the resolution does not pass, or if it passes but is not implemented, those individuals and groups that fight BDS believe that the BDS effort has failed. Contrary to Rabbi Brand's perspective, what happened at Oberlin was indeed very significant for the BDS movement. Focusing only on the resolution and its possible implementation is too narrow. It ignores so much of what has taken place on campus. What BDS did not fail at was weeks, months, and even years of constant attacks against Israel, portraying it as a pariah nation, an occupier, a human rights violator, a racist nation, and a denier of Palestinian rights. That is significant.

Young college-aged men and women, the "at risk group" identified in the Oppenheim study, now have been exposed over time to repeated anti-Israel rhetoric. These include many young people who have little or no knowledge of the Middle East, really don't care that much about the issue, and have no affinity to one side or the other, who now have a kernel of doubt about Israel planted in their minds. Now Israel is connected with the important negative buzzwords for this cohort—racism, apartheid, occupier, and human rights violator. We can't predict what attitudes this "at risk" generation will have in the future but, as an evil master of propaganda often said, "something always sticks."

A proponent of this kind of win-by-losing strategy comes from prewar Nazi Germany. In 1924, Julius Streicher, editor of the *Der Stürmer* newspaper, began a campaign of anti-Jewish invective, diatribe, and hate. Streicher embarked on a long-term campaign of vilification against German Jewish community leaders and organizations, social democrats, and labor leaders. He attacked individual Jewish leaders with the most outrageous accusations. Using his weekly magazine he published half-truths, outright lies, misquotes and quotes out of context, and every fallacy of argument under the sun to vilify not only these individual Jewish leaders but also the Jewish community as a whole.[215] These community leaders and organizations sued Streicher in court dozens of times and won every verdict. Each trial took place in the public eye and was covered by the news media all over Germany. Each time, Streicher paid the fine or served the time, and laughed that, "Something always sticks." "Something always sticks" became his unofficial motto. Each time the Jewish victim of his outrageous accusations walked away feeling tainted by the experience, because even though they won the court case, their reputation was tarnished.

The Streicher story is an illustration of the possibilities of potential long-term strategies both pro-BDS and anti-BDS forces might take. We have tried to show in this article that the pro-BDS forces have understood in some fashion the concept of "something always sticks" and have effectively used it for the purpose of long-term attitude change in a new generation of potential leaders. The BDS efforts in Europe, Canada, Australia, and the United States have had years of spreading anti-Israel propaganda without a similarly effective countervailing rhetoric. Another way to conceptualize this is that while the BDS movement is losing most of the battles on the various college campuses, they may still possibly win in the future because of their propaganda campaign.

If that weren't bad enough, the anti-BDS forces have too often focused on the short term and often minor victories of beating down a BDS initiative without seeing that by focusing just on the refutation of BDS accusations they are once again repeating the very thing that stuck in the beginning. Refuting individual accusations, repeating the terminology of the BDS accusers, reacting to activities and events generated by the BDS people are strategies with the unintended consequence of enhancing and reinforcing the negative arguments of the BDS and making them more memorable.

The "something always sticks" approach can also work in favor of the anti-BDS forces in two ways. First, rhetorical strategies which demonstrate the propagandistic nature of the BDS effort; which show their use of fallacies of argument, half truths and emotional appeal can lead to negative attitudes in response to BDS activities. The BDS movement has created an aura of doubt about Israel. It is in that doubt that the long-term seeds of delegitimation of Israel are set in place. The anti-BDS forces need to delegitimize the pro-BDS side's propaganda strategies. Second, and maybe more importantly, taking a more positive approach, using the research like that of the Oppenheim research referred to earlier, which identified the issues that impact college-aged men and women, those who oppose BDS need to create positive yet realistic messages about Israel. We need to think about what it is we want our audiences to remember about Israel after they have forgotten everything else.

In the end, we cannot permit ourselves to forget that any one boycott, divestment, or sanction initiative contains within it long term seeds of doubt about Israel and Israelis that left to fester might have consequences far beyond anything we can imagine today. We have no idea of the future impact of the constant drip, drip, drip of accusation and portrayal of Israel as evil on the minds of students who have witnessed BDS activities on their campus. We can only hope that by providing students with a realistic and truthful understanding of the complexity of Israel and the Middle East we can make sure that they will remember ideas and images important to them that will enable them to be thoughtful and effective decision makers in the future. ■

KENNETH L. MARCUS

Is the Boycott, Divestment, and Sanctions Movement Anti-Semitic?

Is the movement to boycott, divest from, and sanction Israel (BDS) anti-Semitic?[216] To some readers, the question may seem rude, counter-productive, or poorly framed. As we will see, however, the question must be asked if we are to properly address the dangers that this movement poses. As a political and human rights campaign, the BDS campaign appears at first blush not to be a form of discrimination. The use of boycotts to advance legitimate political objectives has been well established since American patriots boycotted British goods in the years leading up to the Revolutionary War. But the line between political movements and psychological prejudice may be more permeable than it seems, as modern anti-Semitism emerged as a nineteenth-century political ideology and movement. Nor would this be the first time that a systematic boycott of the Jewish people was rationalized as a response to alleged Jewish crimes. Indeed, such justifications have been a distinctive characteristic of anti-Jewish boycotts since 1933. When seen in historical perspective, the BDS campaign is the latest in a series of efforts to resist the normalization of the Jewish people. But determining whether BDS is anti-Semitic is a difficult question requiring more than historical research.

As this author has argued elsewhere, there are four grounds on which anti-Israel hostility may properly be considered anti-Semitic, which have been identified as the *Intentionality, Tacitness, Memetics, and Jewish Trait* principles.[217] In a nutshell, hostility to Israel is anti-Semitic when it is based on:

(i)   conscious hostility toward Jews (Intentionality),

(ii)   unconscious hostility toward Jews (Tacitness),

(iii)   transmission of negatively coded cultural myths, images, or stereotypes (Mimesis), or

(iv)   irrational ethnic trait discrimination (Jewish traits).

In other words, the BDS movement is anti-Semitic if its proponents are consciously motivated by anti-Jewish bigotry, driven by unconscious anti-Semitism, immersed in a climate of opinion that is increasingly hostile to Jewish people, or engaged in irrational ethnic trait discrimination.

Some commentators prefer to avoid the anti-Semitism question alto-gether. To ask the question is to raise hackles. The very inquiry may impede the search for common ground. Worse, the debate can quickly coarsen into an exchange of aspersions. And then one tends to lose sight of important issues, such as the facts underlying the various claims made by Israel's defend-ers and critics, or the possible solutions to conflicts bedeviling Israel and its neighbors. Moreover, if one identifies a movement as anti-Semitic, then one is vulnerable to various counter-charges. For example, one will be accused of exaggerating one's claims, or crying wolf, or improperly playing a race card. In some cases, one will be subjected to the so-called "Livingstone formula-tion," which argues that anti-Semitism claims are bad-faith efforts to distract public attention from the manner in which Israel treats Palestinian Arabs.[218] All of these risks may be averted by avoiding the question of anti-Semitism and focusing instead on lower-stakes arguments against BDS, such as its hypocrisy, false claims, or violations of academic freedom.

Despite these hazards, the question must be asked. In order to know how best to address BDS, one must know if the appearance of human rights advocacy masks a form of bigotry. If it is only the former, then it may be fully addressed by arguments regarding the validity and veracity of its claims. It would be appropriate to conduct debates between those who favor BDS and those who oppose it as, for example, *The New York Times* and *Los Angeles Review of Books* have done in their respective pages. But if it is the latter, then it is no more a matter of proper debate than, for example, the putative inferiority of certain racial groups. To focus only on the truth or falsity of its claims, while ignoring the question of prejudice, would be as inappropriate as to examine, for example, the accuracy of claims historically made about the physical ugliness or bodily odors supposedly associated with many minori-ties (including Jews). The proper inquiry is to ask why these groups have been construed, during certain times and places, with particular stereotypical appearances, sounds, or odors, rather than to nose around to discern whether the racist assumptions are in fact correct.

In similar fashion, questions about academic freedom loom larger or smaller depending on the answer to this fundamental question. If BDS is not anti-Semitic, then one might properly ask whether BDS, as applied to academic institutions and scholars, advances or retards the scope of academic freedom. But if BDS is anti-Semitic, then its damage to academic freedom would be, at least by some standards of value, a matter of secondary importance. When the American Studies Association (ASA) endorsed a boycott of Israeli academic institutions, scores of institutions, including over two hundred and fifty university presidents, distanced themselves from the ASA's actions. Some did so in strong language. But almost all framed their argument in terms of the ASA's encroachment upon the sphere protected by the doctrine of academic freedom. This criticism has great resonance within academic communities. Moreover, it incurs little political cost, in the sense that exaggerated claims of academic freedom rarely elicit stinging rebukes. Nevertheless, if BDS is in fact anti-Semitic, then criticizing it for its violations of academic freedom have something of a busting-Al-Capone-for-tax-evasion quality to them. That is to say, the arguments may prevail, but they are rather beside the point.

The Origins of BDS

Anti-Jewish boycotts emerged from the Enlightenment as a resistance to the legal equality that Jews received in France, following the French revolution, and then throughout Western Europe. Jewish emancipation, or legal equality for European Jews, carried with it a notion of normalization: Jews would no longer be subjected to special legal disabilities or enjoy special legal protections.[219] Yet this emancipation placed Jewry in a double-bind. Those Europeans who embraced modernity, such as Voltaire, often disdained the Jews, seeing them as zealous and parochial, and thus a potential enemy of mankind.[220] Other Europeans, especially in German and Austria-Hungary, resisted Jewish emancipation, despising the Jews as a visible, alien, and inassimilable emblem of modernization, and opposing normalization of the Jewish people.[221] The latter responses ultimately led to anti-Jewish riots, physical attacks, expulsions, and then calls to boycott Jewish businesses in various parts of Europe during the late nineteenth century and into the early twentieth century. As Theodor Herzl observed, equality before the law had become meaningless when Europeans, *inter alia*, mounted "attempts to thrust [Jews] out of business" that urged: "Don't buy from Jews!"[222]

These sporadic efforts were formalized and systematized a few decades later in Germany. On April 1, 1933, two months after coming to power in

Germany, the Nazis set the pattern for future anti-Jewish boycotts when they conducted, as their first nationwide action against Jews, a temporary boycott against Jewish businesses and professionals.[223] As Lucy S. Dawidowicz has observed, Adolf Hitler's contribution was to formalize, rationalize, and channel the impulses behind hooligan attacks on stores owned by German Jews, into "meaningful' political action."[224] It is important to recall that the Nazis did not justify the Nazi boycott on Jewish racial or religious issues, any more than their successors did. Rather, they justified the boycott, in the rhetoric of their era, as a response to the anti-German propaganda that Jewish people, as well as foreign journalists, were allegedly spreading in the international press.[225] For this reason, German soldiers insisted they were defending Germans from Jewish aggression, rather than attacking Jews for racial reasons, which is why the Stormtroopers' battle-cry was, "Germans! Defend yourselves! Do not buy from Jews!"[226] This ushered in the Nazi's nationwide campaign against the entire German Jewish population. Just a week later, for example, the Nazis passed a law barring civil service employment to non-"Aryans."[227] Like the yellow star that Jews were later forced to wear, the Nazi boycott was the first systematic national socialist mechanism to strip Jews of the "normalization" that had come with emancipation. Poland also passed and adopted a number of measures throughout the 1930's to exclude Jews from various trades and professions and established a mass boycott of Jewish shops from 1936 to 1939.[228] The culmination of European anti-Jewish campaigns was the program of systematic extermination.

From 1933 to 1945, Nazi propagandists transmitted anti-Semitic propaganda to Arabs and Muslims in the Middle East and North Africa.[229] This included Arabic language shortwave radio programs broadcast seven days per week during this period, as well as millions of printed items.[230] This propaganda combined selective readings of the Koran, Nazi critiques of Western imperialism, and anti-Jewish themes in Islam. Evidently, Nazi officials considered anti-Semitism and anti-Zionism to be the best means of entrance into Arab and Muslim hearts and minds.[231] Nazi ideology would continue to influence both Arab nationalists and religious extremists throughout the Middle East, including Palestinian leaders, for decades afterwards.[232]

In 1945, the 22-nation Council of the Arab League, founded the previous year, called for an economic boycott of Jewish goods and services in the British controlled mandate territory of Palestine: "Jewish products and manufactured goods shall be considered undesirable to the Arab countries."[233] All Arab "institutions, organizations, merchants, commission agents, and individuals" were called upon "to refuse to deal in, distribute, or consume Zionist products or manufactured goods."[234] At the time, the League was "filled with ex-Axis collaborators."[235] Three years later, following the war establishing

Israel's independence, the League formalized its boycott against the state of Israel, broadening it to include non-Israelis who maintain economic relations with Israel or who are perceived to support it.[236] During this period, affinity for National Socialism in the Arab world continued unabated.[237]

Although formally a boycott of the State of Israel, the Arab League boycott has been, during at least some periods, also a more general boycott of Jews. Indeed, Bernard Lewis has remarked that "the way in which the boycott of Israel, operated by all member states of the Arab League, was put into effect" is "[p]erhaps the clearest indication of the way in which the war against Israel was generalized to be a war against the Jews."[238] This can be seen, for example, in various examples in which Arab states canceled cultural events or rejected ambassadorial credentials based on Jewish rather than Israeli or Zionist connections.[239] Some Arab League member states and entities have formally withdrawn from the boycott, or at least some aspects of it, either through peace treaties, or other diplomatic agreements, or as a result of diplomatic relations, e.g., Egypt (1979), the Palestinian Authority (1993), and Jordan (1994).[240] Today, Lebanon enforces the old primary, secondary, and tertiary boycotts, although enforcement is now uneven.

The anti-Jewish boycott movement was reinvigorated at the turn of the new millennium, as failed hopes in the Oslo Accord helped to fuel a Second Intifada and global animus against Israel. The World Conference Against Racism, Racial Discrimination, Xenophobia, and Related Intolerance, held in Durban, South Africa, in late 2001 (Durban I) helped to re-launch the boycott movement on a new ideological basis. The main platform to criticize Israel and the U.S. was the NGO Forum, held in Kingsmead Stadium in Durban, and attended by 8,000 representatives from as many as 3,900 NGOs. The Durban Conference's NGO "Meeting in Solidarity with the Palestinian People" yielded an NGO plan of action that called for "complete and total isolation of Israel as an apartheid state as in the case of South Africa, which means the imposition of mandatory and comprehensive sanctions and embargoes, the full cessation of all links (diplomatic, economic, social, aid, military cooperation and training) between all states and Israel."[241]

This was followed by numerous calls to boycott or divest from Israel, including Palestinian boycott calls in 2002, 2003, and 2004.[242] By October 2002, more than 50 campuses were circulating divestment petitions.[243] On July 9, 2005, over 100 Palestinian organizations issued the "Palestinian Civil Society Calls for Boycott, Divestment and Sanctions against Israel Until it Complies with International Law and Universal Principles of Human Rights." This "Call" was justified on Israel's supposed history of ethnic cleansing and racial discrimination. Its three explicit objectives were to end Israel's "occupation and colonization" of "all Arab lands" (presumably including all pre-1967 lands, although BDS leadership has equivocated on this), recognizing the equal fundamental rights of Israel's Arab-Palestinian citizens, and promoting a proposed Palestinian right of return to their former homes and properties.[245]

Like Hitler's Nazi boycott, the Durban I and Palestinian Call formalized, systematized, and attempted to justify the sporadic individual boycotts and anti-Jewish attacks that preceded them. The primary strategy of BDS leadership is to reject Israel's "normalization," defined as the treatment of Israel as a "normal" state with which business as usual can be conducted.[246] PACBI's leadership insists they oppose normalization on political rather than racial grounds. Indeed, their public statements speak of resistance to putative Palestinian oppression, rather than of any essentially malevolent characteristics of the Jewish people. Nevertheless, this anti-normalization effort echoes prior anti-Jewish boycotts. It also provides a dark rejoinder to the early Zionist thinkers, who had argued that a Jewish state could solve the problem of anti-Semitism by giving the Jewish people, who had been haunted by their statelessness, a sense of normalcy.

Human Rights Campaign or Bigoted Double Standards?

Despite the ugly history of anti-Jewish boycotts, the BDS movement appears at face value to be based on human rights objectives rather than racial, ethnic, or religious bigotry. To be sure, these demands are framed in terms of the Palestinian narrative. Terms such as "occupation" and "colonization" are politically contested, as is the putative right of Palestinian return. One might argue that neither term is apposite to the current situation in Israel. Yet the decision to frame this issue in a manner advantageous to one side of the dispute may be based on strategic and political considerations, rather than ethnic animus. In the same way, the Call's reference to UN resolution 194 is highly contested but not necessarily driven by animus. Some Jewish leaders argue the proposal for a Palestinian right of return is anti-Semitic. They point out that if all Palestinians were to return to their families' pre-1948 homes, the demographic shift within Israel could destabilize the Jewish state, with uncertain consequences for Israeli Jews.[247] Whatever the merits of this analysis, it does not prove that the underlying claim is anti-Semitic. Simply put, the Palestinian people may seek a right of return for reasons that have less to do with a hatred of Jews than with a desire for their own collective advancement.

Many commentators have argued that BDS is anti-Semitic based on some version of Natan Sharansky's well-known 3-D test, according to which anti-Israel hostility may be anti-Semitic if it demonizes Israel, delegitimizes the Jewish state, or applies double standards.[248] For example, the Statement of Jewish Organizations on Boycott, Divestment, and Sanctions (BDS) Campaigns Against Israel argues that the campaign is anti-Semitic on the grounds that it "demonizes Israel or its leaders, denies Israel the right to defend its citizens or seeks to denigrate Israel's right to exist."[249] Sharansky's test is brilliant as a short-hand guide even if it lacks the rigor required for either practical or academic purposes.[250] Both the U.S. Department of State's definition of anti-Semitism and the EUMC Working Definition of anti-Semitism are built on the framework that Sharansky's test provides.

The problem with applying any of these iterations is that they establish presumptions rather than bright-line tests. For example, the BDS movement's pervasive use of double standards for Israel surely requires explanation, but they do not automatically prove that BDS is in fact anti-Semitic. It is far too glib for Israel's critics to respond that all political argument relies upon double standards, since the use of this practice within the BDS movement is exceptionally pervasive. Based on empirical research, sociologist Sina Arnold has identified five distinct double standards employed by American progressives in their criticisms of Israel:

- The "double standard of *salience*," by which Israel's conflicts garner vastly more public attention than other comparable international disputes;
- The "double standard of *state foundation*," by which Israel's establishment is characterized as violent and hostile, while violence in the early history of other nations is downplayed;
- The "double standard of *state formation*," by which Israel's political arrangements are portrayed as archaic while similar structures are not;
- The "double standard of *self-understanding*," which criticizes Israel's ethno-religious characteristics while disregarding similar characteristics among other states; and, finally,
- The "double standard of *self-determination*," which recognizes a right of self-government for Palestinians but not necessarily for Israelis or, alternatively, which recognizes the validity of Palestinian feelings of frustration or anger under the present political circumstances while declining to recognize the validity of such feelings among Israelis.[251]

Moreover, the most important double standard has been the double standard of *punishment*, which singles Israel out for boycotts, divestment, and sanctions that are not urged upon other states that have substantially worse human rights records. Nevertheless, if a person applies double standards to Israel, and that person turns out to be a rabbi, the anti-Semitism accusation may be unwarranted if the rabbi merely believes that all religious leaders should hold their own community to higher standards than they apply to others. Similarly, if a Palestinian civic society organization applies more stringent standards to Israel than to other countries, its motivations may have more to do with ethnic conflict, political rivalry, or personal experience than with psychological prejudice. Sharansky's test yields important presumptions, but it is often not dispositive. For this reason, it is important to examine underlying principles.

Ultimately, the question boils down to whether the BDS movement is animated by hostility towards Jews or just towards Israel. It is not enough that Israel happens to be a Jewish state, indeed the only Jewish state. If the BDS movement were based, as its leaders argue, only on Israel's actions rather than its Jewish character, then we would not call it anti-Semitic. For this reason, anti-Semitism is frequently defined as hostility towards Jews as Jews, *i.e., because* they are Jews, or because of their (actual or perceived) *Jewish* identity.[252] In one important formulation, Charles Glock and Rodney Stark define anti-Semitism as "the hatred and persecution of Jews as a group; not the hatred of persons who happen to be Jews, but rather the hatred of persons because they are Jews."[253] This formulation has been widely influential, because it serves the important conceptual function of screening out certain hostilities faced by Jews that are not anti-Semitic. The question then is whether BDS arises from hostility to Jews despite its leaders' contrary protestations. As this author explains in a forthcoming volume on *The Definition of Anti-Semitism*, there are four grounds on which anti-Israel hostility may properly be considered anti-Semitic: the *Intentionality, Tacitness, Memetics*, and *Jewish Trait* principles.

The *Intentionality Principle* provides that critics of Israel sometimes consciously use Israel as a pretext to express anti-Jewish animus. There seems to be widespread agreement that conscious antipathy toward Jews fuels at least some of the growth of the BDS movement. There can be little question of anti-Jewish animus, for example, when BDS activists call Jewish American college students "kike" and "dirty Jew" or spit on them for wearing a Star of David necklace.[254] Similarly, it is unquestionably anti-Semitic for BDS activists to engage in or support Holocaust denial, as some have done.[255] These are unquestionably anti-Semitic. There is scarce agreement, however, on how widespread this phenomenon may be. Yet, unquestionably, much support for BDS is not based on any such conscious hostility to Jews.

The *Tacitness Principle* provides that other critics of Israel, who may not be consciously aware that they harbor negative attitudes towards Jews, nevertheless denigrate Israel to express unconscious resentment of Jews. It is well established in the psychological literature that white Americans harbor far more prejudice toward minority groups than they are willing to admit even to themselves. This is true for anti-Semitism but it also applies to anti-black racism and other forms of bias.[256] In North America and Western Europe, such prejudice is often repressed because it is socially stigmatized.[257] In an important Rutgers University study of college students, researchers confirmed that hostility to Israel often reflects unconscious anti-Semitism.[258] This is consistent with the results of a prior Yale study that had found a strong correlation between anti-Semitism and hostility towards Israel among 5,000 people in ten European countries.[259] A smaller study, which examined the attitudes of Arab Muslims, Arab Christians, and non-Arab Muslims in the United States and Canada, similarly found a high statistical correlation between anti-Semitism and anti-Israeli sentiment.[260] A 2004 German study found that 90 percent of Germans who criticized Israel also endorsed anti-Semitic statements.[261] Unfortunately, no studies specifically examine the incidence of unconscious anti-Semitic views among members of the BDS movement. Based on the existing research, however, it is fair to extrapolate that unconscious anti-Semitism is substantially higher among BDS advocates than among the general population. At the same time, the empirical studies also confirm that some virulent critics of Israel are not motivated by anti-Semitism, whether consciously or unconsciously.

The *Memetics Principle* provides that some hostility to Israel is anti-Semitic in the sense that arises from a climate of opinion that is hostile to Jews, regardless of the conscious or unconscious beliefs of individual speakers. Whether BDS advocates are aware of it, either consciously or unconsciously, they often spread anti-Jewish stereotypes, images, and myths. For example, BDS advocates within Protestant church groups sometimes equate Palestinians with Jesus Christ's suffering, *e.g.*, referring to the so-called "Israeli government crucifixion system."[262] Such tropes may be understood as a revival of the anti-Semitic deicidal accusation that Jews killed Jesus. Even Judith Butler acknowledges that some criticisms of Israel "do employ anti-Semitic rhetoric and argument and so must be opposed absolutely and unequivocally."[263] In some cases, the cultural transmission of these memes colors the social environment in substantial ways. Bernard Harrison, the English philosopher, has cogently explained that anti-Semitism often permeates what he calls the "climate of opinion," even when those most in its thrall are unaware of its influence. In Harrison's writing, a climate of opinion is not the work of an individual mind, either conscious or unconscious. Rather, it is formed from a "multitude of spoken and written items—books, articles, news items, . . . lectures, stories, in-jokes, stray remarks—of equally multitudinous authorship."[264] Individual speakers buy into it, rather than developing it themselves.

When enough people in a subculture buy into a climate of opinion, that climate becomes dominant in the subculture.[265]

Finally, the *Jewish Trait Principle* provides that certain forms of hostility towards Israel are anti-Semitic in the sense that they cause foreseeable harm to Jews based on a trait that is central to Jewish identity. Regardless of intent, bias, or mimetics, some abuse of Israel by the BDS campaign is profoundly offensive to Jews because of the intimate relationship between a person's Jewish identity and that person's sense of attachment to Israel. Indeed, for many Jews, a commitment to Israel is so intrinsic to their religious belief as to be the paradigmatic case of a characteristic that a people should not be required to change. For those Jews who embrace Israel as a part of their Jewish identity, the commitment may be of multi-generational duration, shared historically by many members of the group, inscribed centrally in the group's common literature and tradition, and pervasive of the culture. The *Jewish Traits* argument provides that a sense of connectedness to Israel is of such fundamental importance that Jewish persons should not be required to disavow it. This does not imply that all Jews share this sense, nor even that all Jews should share it. Moreover, it certainly does not imply that Jews (or others) are precluded from criticizing Israeli policy. People often most vigorously criticize those to whom they feel closest, including family members.

The BDS Response

Needless to say, BDS leaders reject the notion that their movement is anti-Semitic, going so far as to insist that it is anti-Semitic to oppose them. The argument proceeds through three claims: (i) BDS cannot be anti-Semitic because BDS criticizes Israel, and criticizing Israel is not the same as criticizing all Jews; (ii) not all Jews identify with Israel, and Israel should represent Jews and non-Jews equally; and (iii) some Jews actually support BDS, so it is actually anti-Semitic to say that BDS is anti-Semitic. Each of these claims contains a kernel of truth, but all of them distort that truth. It is true that criticizing Israel is not the same as criticizing all Jews, that many Jews do not identify with Israel, and that some Jews enthusiastically support BDS. But none of these propositions supports the conclusions that BDS' supporters draw from them.

Omar Barghouti cogently expresses the first claim, *i.e.*, that BDS cannot be anti-Semitic unless all Jews and Israel are one. "Arguing that boycotting Israel is intrinsically anti-Semitic is not only false," the BDS movement's principal spokesman argues, "but it also presumes that Israel and 'the Jews' are one and the same."[266] Barghouti likens this to the notion that boycotting a self-defined Islamic state like Saudi Arabia, because of its horrific human rights record, would of necessity be Islamophobic. We will put aside the obvious problem with Barghouti's example, which is that no one boycotts Saudi Arabia because of its horrific human rights record, even if they insist on boycotting Israel for its much stronger human rights record, and this application of double standards may itself be anti-Semitic. At a deeper level, Barghouti misunderstands the argument that he tries to refute. No one argues that BDS is anti-Semitic on the grounds that Israel and "the Jews" are the same. Those who argue that BDS is anti-Semitic typically observe that BDS uses double standards to denounce Israel, while demonizing and delegitimizing Israel as anti-Semites traditionally tried to do with the Jewish people. The argument is not that Israel and the Jewish people actually are the same but rather that hateful misperceptions of Israel reflect prior misperceptions of the Jewish people.

Judith Butler articulates the second claim, i.e., that BDS cannot be anti-Semitic because some Jews do not identify with Israel:

> Only if we accept the proposition that the state of Israel is the exclusive and legitimate representative of the Jewish people would a movement calling for divestment, sanctions and boycott against that state be understood as directed against the Jewish people as a whole. Israel would then be understood as co-extensive with the Jewish people. There are two major problems with this view. First, the state of Israel does not represent all Jews, and not all Jews understand themselves as represented by the state of Israel. Secondly, the state of Israel should be representing all of its population equally, regardless of whether or not they are Jewish, regardless of race, religion or ethnicity.[267]

Butler is unquestionably right to assert that some Jews do not consider themselves to be "represented by the state of Israel." Indeed, many Jews do not identify with Israel even in the weaker sense that they consider Israel to be their homeland. But no one argues to the contrary. And it would be too much to expect this of any ethnic traits argument. To say that a sense of connection is a deeply held Jewish trait is not to imply that every Jew shares the same sense of conviction. This can be seen by analogy to the sort of ethnic traits claims that are made on behalf of other groups. Those who attack Spanish language speakers harm Hispanics, even if many Hispanics do not speak Spanish and many Spanish speakers are not Hispanics. The same is true of the harm that hostility to Israel inflicts on Jews. In both cases, the animus is directed at a trait that is, as an American court has characterized such socially immutable traits, "so fundamental to the identities or consciences of its members that members either cannot or should not be required to change it."[268]

The U.S. Campaign for the Academic Boycott of Israel articulates the third claim on its website, i.e., that BDS cannot be anti-Semitic because many Jews support it and second that it is anti-Semitic to identify Jews with Zionism:

> Zionism is a political movement that is by no means supported by all Jews, many of whom support and advocate for boycott, divestment and sanctions and the end of Zionism itself. Indeed, what is really anti-semitic is the attempt to identify all Jews with a philosophy that many find abhorrent to the traditions of social justice and universality that Judaism enshrines.[269]

Some BDS proponents add that this sense of connectedness is inconsistent with forms of political expression to which they feel compelled by their own sense of Jewishness. This criticism also misconstrues the Jewish Traits Argument. Consider that deafness is now considered an immutable trait even where the disabled person could eliminate the trait through surgery. This is because members of the relevant group consider the trait to be closely connected to their identity. There may be some disabled people who disagree, and some may undertake surgery to eliminate the condition. The presence of some dissenters within the group is altogether conventional and does not, without more, deny the existence of an immutable ethnic group trait.

Jewish Anti-Zionism

Many who dispute the connection between anti-Semitism and anti-Zionism observe that many of Israel's sharpest critics are Jewish.[270] The presence of these Jewish anti-Zionists has been used to rebut accusations of anti-Semitism on the purported ground that a Jewish person cannot be an anti-Semite.[271] This argument has been described as "Jew Washing," referring to the enlistment of Jews to provide cover for activities that would otherwise be seen as anti-Semitic.[272] In fact, the presence of Jewish participants within the BDS movement does not disprove its anti-Semitic character.

Their presence can be partly explained on the ground that some Jews absorb anti-Israel and even anti-Jewish attitudes tacitly as a function of their choice of ideologies. Like anyone else, Jews often adopt broad ideologies that resonate with them across a range of issues and then maintain views and behavior that follow from these over-arching ideologies.[273] If they choose to embrace certain progressive ideologies, they may adopt the positions on Israel that come with the package, even if these positions are based upon anti-Jewish stereotypes. Moreover, insofar as anti-Israel attitudes have become part of this "package deal," they have become a cultural code marking their adherents as belonging to a particular subcultural milieu.[274] Sina Arnold has argued that this "collective identity" approach best explains anti-Zionist attitudes among progressive Jews because it averts the need for psychological and speculative concepts such as "Jewish self-hatred."[275]

A full treatment of this issue, however, cannot ignore the reality that Jews, like members of other persecuted groups, sometimes embrace the perceptions of their group that circulate within the larger society. Just as there are Jewish anti-Semites, there are many Jewish critics of Israel, including some whose criticisms are devoid of anti-Semitism and others whose criticisms are not. The concept of Jewish self-hatred is now considered impolitic in some circles, just as there are other circles in which its existence is beyond question. Sander Gilman has persuasively argued that "self-hatred" is a valid term for a form of self-abnegation that has existed among Jews since ancient times.[276] The power of common prejudices, the "persuasive wisdom of what 'everyone knows,'" can cause members of any minority group to believe even the worst that others say about them.[277] Gordon Allport explained self-hatred as a "subtle mechanism" through which a victim comes to agree with his persecutors and to see his group through their eyes. He observed, for example, that a Jew "may hate his historic religion . . . or he may blame some one class of Jews . . . or he may hate the Yiddish language. Since he cannot escape his own group, he does in a real sense hate himself—or at least the part of himself that is Jewish."[278] Indeed, members of persecuted groups have powerful incentives to reject the markers of their otherness. In anti-Semitic environments, this has generated efforts to deny or escape from Jewish origins in environments that attach stigma or inferiority to Jewishness.[279] In such cases, Jewish self-hatred reflects a persecuted group's identification with its aggressor.

In many cases, Jewish dissidents have stressed their Jewish origins in order to support projects hostile to the Jewish people. In this way, they have responded to an assimilationist fantasy, whether in medieval Spain or on contemporary California university campuses: "Become like us—abandon your difference—and you may be one with us."[280] Thus, for example, Jews were among the first medieval polemicists to write against Judaism, and they stressed their Jewish origins in doing so.[281] Indeed, many of the Jewish people's greatest persecutors throughout history have been rumored to be converted Jews, although historians have cast doubt on some of these rumors.[282] Over the centuries, anti-Jewish polemicists within the Jewish community have used the authority of their Jewish background to legitimize virtually every anti-Jewish canard, from blood libel to international Jewish conspiracies.[283]

At the end of his classic treatise on *Jewish Self-Hatred*, Sander Gilman writes that "one of the most recent forms of Jewish self-hatred is the virulent opposition to the existence of the State of Israel."[284] Jewish progressives and intellectuals are often responsible for some of the most virulent criticism of Israel. Noam Chomsky, Norman Finkelstein, Ilan Pappé, and Jacqueline Rose, for example, have been among Israel's most unrelenting critics. It should not be surprising that some leading supporters of the BDS movement, including Judith Butler, are Jewish as well.

Conclusion

Commentators tend to draw opposite conclusions from BDS' ugly history and noble-sounding goals. Some assume that it is nothing more than a continuation of its Arab League and Nazi predecessors, while others deny that a human rights movement could be prejudiced. Neither argument is particularly strong. The pre-Nazi, Nazi, Arab League, and BDS boycotts all share common elements: they seek to deny Jewish legitimacy or normalcy as a punishment for supposed Jewish transgressions. The BDS campaign, like its Nazi predecessor, rationalized and justified sporadic efforts that had preceded it. To be sure, these various campaigns began at very different times, places, and cultures. While there are continuities among them, there are also discontinuities. It is as simplistic to assume that they form one undivided whole as it is to deny the commonalities among them.

Rather, it is more reasonable to identify these boycotts, like other campaigns against Jewish people, as a repetitive series of incidents that serve the same underlying function, *e.g.*, a low-risk expression of anxieties about modernity's destabilizing tendencies. This is as true of the Arab League Boycott and the Palestinian BDS Call as it was for their Nazi antecedent. The fact that the contemporary BDS movement is dressed up in the language of human rights does not differentiate it so radically from its predecessors, which also used the rhetoric of their respective times to establish the common theme.

In assessing BDS, it is not sufficient to observe that its advocates apply double-standards in order to impose a boycott on the world's only Jewish state, while ignoring the substantially greater transgressions committed by other nations. The pervasive use of such double standards should indeed create a presumption that something other than mere political criticism is at play. But there may also be legitimate explanations for the application of such double standards. At any rate, when such explanations are provided, they deserve to be carefully examined on a case-by-case basis to examine their validity vel non.

In the last analysis, the BDS campaign is anti-Semitic, as its predecessors were, because some of its proponents act out of conscious hostility to the Jewish people; others act from unconscious or tacit disdain for Jews; and still others operate out of a climate of opinion that contains elements that are hostile to Jews and serve as the conduits through whom anti-Jewish tropes and memes are communicated; while all of them work to sustain a movement that attacks the commitment to Israel that is central to the identity of the Jewish people as a whole. This does not imply that all or even most of BDS' proponents are anti-Semites. That is a different question. Based on the best available empirical research, it appears that some of Israel's critics are not motivated by prejudice. Rather, they oppose Israel's actions for legitimately non-discriminatory reasons. Their reasons may be good or bad, convincing or unconvincing, logical or illogical. But they are not anti-Semitic.

Nevertheless, it ought to give them pause to realize that, for whatever reasons, they are participating in a boycott that has deeply unsavory roots and ramifications. It is not coincidental that the world's only Jewish state is subjected to greater scrutiny and pressure than most of the world's other nations. Nor is it coincidental that current efforts to boycott the Jewish State resemble the nearly constant efforts that have been made to boycott Jewish businesses since well before Israel's establishment. The historical record is clear that many and perhaps all of these efforts have been based, in no small part, on the basest forms of human bigotry. Some BDS advocates may be ignorant of this history, but this only makes them unwitting agents in a process by which hatred articulates itself across time. Moreover, they are allying themselves with people who consciously seek to undermine Israel for reasons of sheer bigotry.

The most apt metaphor may be to the poll tax. Poll taxes were implicit pre-conditions on the exercise of the ability to vote. Like boycott resolutions, poll taxes were sometimes described in race-neutral terms. Nevertheless, these taxes emerged in the late nineteenth-century American South as part of the Jim Crow laws. Some white Southerners intentionally adopted poll taxes to disenfranchise African Americans; others purported to support the tax for race-neutral reasons, such as revenue-raising, but were at least unconsciously prejudiced against blacks; still others acted upon and reinforced a racist climate of opinion, regardless of their personal mental states; and all of them acted to sustain a system that disenfranchised black voters. Under these circumstances, it would be possible to describe the poll tax as a neutral revenue-raising scheme and to emphasize the pure motives on which some of its proponents acted. One might even abhor the false or exaggerated claims of discrimination that have been made against some of these proponents. But this would miss the point of the taxes, which were a peculiarly effective means of marginalizing and delegitimizing an entire people. The institution was racist, through and through, whether all of its supporters were themselves racists or not. ■

ALAN JOHNSON

Intellectual Incitement:
The Anti-Zionist Ideology and the Anti-Zionist Subject

It is a peculiarity of every *ideological* conception . . . that it is governed by "interests" beyond the necessity of knowledge alone ... [and] takes its meaning from the *current* interests in whose service it is subjected. —Louis Althusser.[285]
I want to devote my energies to delegitimising the state of Israel. —Ilan Pappé.[286]

Introduction

In early 2014 I spoke against a boycott resolution at the National University of Ireland, Galway. Anti-Israel student activists tried to break up the meeting by banging on the tables, using the Israeli flag as a toilet wipe, and screaming at me, again and again, "Fuck off our fucking campus you fucking Zionist!"[287]

Writing about the experience shortly afterwards, I blamed their (intellectual) parents who had educated them to think of Zionism—the movement to establish a Jewish homeland in part of Palestine—as a kind of Nazism.[288] Their heads were filled with the common sense of intellectual circles in Europe—Zionism is racism, the Zionists "ethnically cleansed" the natives from the land in 1948, Israel is an "Apartheid State," Israel is

259

committing a slow genocide against the remaining Palestinians, and so on. In short, they were in thrall to an *Anti-Zionist Ideology* that had turned them into *Anti-Zionist Subjects*.

I extend that argument in this essay. "An ideology," wrote Louis Althusser, "is a system of notions that can be projected socially . . . ideology begins only at this point."[289] In this chapter I focus only on the *system of notions* of the Anti-Zionist Ideology (hereafter AZI), not the social and political practices and institutions through which those notions are "projected socially" and so come to "subjectivize" individuals.[290]

Four ideological "notions" constitute the system of the AZI—Zionism is racism, Israel is a crime, the dichotomous understanding of "Natural Palestinians / Cultured Israelis," and the political program of vindictive one-statism. They constitute the anti-Zionist Imaginary and they distort reality. This does not mean, of course, that the AZI is simply an error. As Althusser pointed out, "no ideology is purely arbitrary" but rather "an index of real problems, albeit cloaked in the form of misrecognition and so necessarily illusory."[291] I seek here to begin to map the ways in which the underlying "problematic" of the AZI—i.e. its systematic structure, including not only the system of notions but the field of problems that the ideology can (and cannot) confront, the questions it can (and cannot) pose, its evasions and silences as well as its explicit claims—misrecognizes the conflict and offers only illusory solutions to it.[292] The AZI does not provide genuine *knowledge* of Zionism as a movement, or Israel as a State, but only a kind of *intellectual persecution* of both, being shaped decisively by what Althusser calls its "practico-social function"[293]—in this case the political project of delegitimizing Israel.

Notion One: Zionism is Racism

As a "notion" within the AZI, Zionism is an ideology and movement of "racial superiority and supremacy"[294] with a relation of "inherent contradiction" to democracy and liberalism,[295] and which is, anyway, based on a calculated fabrication of peoplehood. This conception of Zionism renders it homogenous; all is essentialized, all is simplified. Judith Butler, for example, reduces Zionism to nothing but "a violent project of settler colonialism," while Yitzhak Laor attacks the "fundamentally intolerant nature" of a movement that "has no source of legitimization except the old colonial discourse."[297] For Jacqueline Rose, Jewish nationalism is racism, separatism, and exclusivism.[298] The Nobel laureate José Saramago tells us that "the great majority" of Israeli Jews exhibit "a contempt and an intolerance which, on a practical level, have led to the extreme of *denying any humanity* to the

Palestinian people, at times *denying their basic right to existence.*"[299] Zionism, then, is understood as a *genocidal* ideology and movement which "expelled, massacred, destroyed, and raped" in 1948, conducting an "ethnic cleansing" of the Palestinians. And which could do no other: "Zionist ideology" is an "ethnic ideology" that seeks a "total cleansing" of non-Jews from the land to make possible the complete "Judaisation of Palestine."[300] Israel, Pappé claims, is "preparing an ethnic cleansing in the West Bank and a genocide in Gaza," only leaving the Strip in 2005 so it could "bomb freely."[301]

Zionism, then, is understood in a philosophically *idealist* fashion, with what Karl Marx called an "ahistorical, eternal, fixed and abstract conception."[302] Hirsh complains of the tendency of left-wing anti-Zionism to "explanatory flattening" and "methodological idealism": "In a departure from the method of historical materialism, their analyses of Zionism tend to focus more on Zionism as an idea than on the material factors which underlay its transformation from a minority utopian project into a nation state."[303] The AZI does not engage with those material factors but only with Zionism as an Idea, conceived autonomously from history. In place of Marx's "logic of actual experience and real emergence" there is Pappé's breezy idealism: "This book treats Zionism as a discourse" and Shahak's conviction, quoted approvingly by Rose, that "the real issue [is] the racist character of the Zionist Movement and the State of Israel and the roots of that racism in the Jewish religious law [Halakha]."[305] The anti-Zionist philosophers Vattimo and Marder define Zionism as "a metaphysically inflected ideology and political worldview."[306]

In the mid-19th century Karl Marx began to talk about "the German Ideology" as a way to reassert the earthy claims of materialism against the airy idealism of German philosophy. I think we should talk about the anti-Zionist Ideology so that we can reassert the claims of earthy material history in the story of Zionism and Israel. The AZI reduces the complex history of a people (the Jewish people) and the nature of a state (Israel) to the *simple expression* of a Bad Idea ("Zionism") and the Bad Men and Bad Women who pursued it ("the Zionists"). That distorts reality because it excludes key actors other than "the Zionists"—not least non-Jewish Europeans, Palestinian Arabs and the surrounding Arab states—and factors other than "the Zionist idea"—not least the storm that Herzl saw approaching: the collapse of European liberalism, the failure of European socialism, the victory of Stalinism, Fascism, and Nazism, and the radicalization of antisemitism culminating in the Holocaust.

The AZI refuses to let that history *irrupt* within our thinking because to do so would not serve the interest of delegitimizing Israel. As David Hirsh noted about a 2013 collection of essays which largely *recapitulated* the Bundist and Bolshevik thinking of the early 20th century, "The truth, which is not confronted in this book, is that all the strategies adopted against antisemitism failed. Bundism was eradicated in the Nazi gas chambers. Bolshevism failed to stop the Shoah and, while it did succeed in gaining state power over a third of the world, it did not do so by defeating antisemitism but by adopting it in its anti-Zionist variant." The political consequences of this refusal of history by the AZI are huge. Not least, as Hirsh points out, "Before 1939 anti-Zionism was a position in debates amongst Jewish opponents of antisemitism. After 1948 it became a programme for the destruction of an actually existing nation state."

The abstract universalism of the AZI

Why was the AZI unable to adapt to the mid-century rupture that transformed the political *meaning* of "anti-Zionism"? In part, because it still saw Zionism as it had in Tsarist Russia, as a political rival. In part, because it was in thrall to abstract universalism. In the 19th century, most of the Left decided that *assimilation* was the only acceptable Jewish response to modernity and antisemitism. Lenin—employing the "Good Jew / Bad Jew" dichotomy still found in parts of the Left today—wrote that "the best Jews have never clamored against assimilation."[308] This Left mostly disapproved of the survival of *Jewishness*—of the Jews as a *people* with the right to national self-determination, as opposed to individuals with civil rights. It dreamed of the dissolution of Jewish peoplehood in the solvent of progressive universalism. The proletariat, understood as the universalist class par excellence, was to make a revolution that would solve "the Jewish question" once and for all. This abstract universalism came at a price, however. The political theorist Norman Geras has pointed out that Karl Marx's 1844 essay *On the Jewish Question* "deploys some well-known negative stereotypes, according to which: the mundane basis of Judaism is self-interest, egoism, or, as Marx also calls it, 'an anti-social element'; the worldly religion of the Jew is huckstering; and the Jew's jealous god—'in face of which no other god may exist'—is money. The emancipation of the Jews is said by him to be equivalent to the emancipation of mankind *from* Judaism." Geras calls that kind of universalism "spurious" because it singled out the Jews as "special amongst other groups in being obliged to settle for forms of political freedom in which their identity may not be asserted collectively; Jews must be satisfied, instead, merely with the rights available to them as individuals."[309]

It is true that, in the 19th century and the early 20th century, many European Jews were attracted to both universalism and assimilation; it was the name of their desire too. *But when world history went another way, Jewish history went with it*; the Shoah left the appeal of assimilationism and universalism in tatters and, in response, the Jews insisted on defining their own mode of participation in universal emancipation: Zionism and support for the creation of the state of Israel. Whether individual Jews moved to Israel or not, that was the choice of all but a sliver of world Jewry.

The failure on many parts of the Left to respond to this great rupture in history *for* the Jews had profound consequences for the Left's relationship *with* the Jews. As Moishe Postone, the anti-Stalinist Marxist, has observed, "After the Holocaust and the establishment of the state of Israel . . . the abstract universalism expressed by many anti-Zionists today becomes an ideology of legitimation that helps constitute a form of amnesia regarding the long history of European actions, policies and ideologies toward the Jews, while essentially continuing that history. The Jews have once again become the singular object of European indignation." Postone goes on: "The solidarity most Jews feel toward other Jews, including in Israel—however understandable following the Holocaust—is now decried. This form of anti-Zionism has become one of the bases for a program to eradicate actually existing Jewish self-determination. It converges with some forms of Arab nationalism—now coded as singularly progressive."[310]

The teleology of the AZI

The AZI has a teleological structure. In other words—the words of Gregory Elliot summarizing Louis Althusser's critique of teleological forms of Marxism—a complex, contradictory, and *contingent* history is read "through the grid of [its] purported realization," while the present is read as the inevitable expression of an essential founding moment. In the AZI, Zionism is treated as a simple and expressive totality, Israel as nothing but its epiphenomenal form. All concrete differences between Zionists are "no sooner posited, than negated, by the totality's internal principle, of which they are merely so many moments."[311] Left/Right, Socialist/Revisionist, Secular/Religious, Two-Statist/Greater Israelist—all these differences are not really allowed their status as differences at all, but flattened out until all are mere moments in the ineluctable unfolding of the undifferentiated and "simple essence" of genocidist Zionism. In this way, the "complexity of a concrete historical process" is erased in favor of "an evolutionary schema in which the goal is present in germ at the origin."[312]

As a result the AZI goes nowhere. It is trapped, performing a "repetitive revolution in an ideological circle" closed off to "pertinent problems and their rigorous solution," lacking a capacity for "(self-) rectification and development."[313] Not for the AZI, then, the chastened reflection of Trotsky's biographer Isaac Deutscher who wrote in 1954: "I have, of course, long since abandoned my anti-Zionism, which was based on a confidence in the European labor movement, or, more broadly, in European society and civilization, which that society and civilization have not justified. If, instead of arguing against Zionism in the 1920s and 1930s I had urged European Jews to go to Palestine, I might have helped to save some of the lives that were later extinguished in Hitler's gas chambers. For the remnants of European Jewry—is it only for them?—the Jewish State has become an historic necessity. It is also a living reality."[314]

The AZI refuses to face the challenge of *the way history went*. For example, Azoulay and Ophir reject the two-state solution because they see no need for the Jews to have one place in the world in which they exercise sovereignty as a people. "But why would the ethnic nation need sovereignty that requires its political separation from other ethnic nations?" they ask, genuinely incredulous.[315] In similar vein, Jacqueline Rose applauds Marcel Leibman's rejection of Zionism on the grounds that "the answer to racism is to denounce it, not to flee behind a defensive, self-isolating barrier of being—and being only—a Jew." A few lines later Rose passes on Liebman's war-time memory of the total abandonment of the Jews in Europe: "When the announcement was made expelling all Jews, there was not a word of comment or protest," he recalls.[316] Rose does see that the short, hard, material second sentence challenges the abstract-universalist anti-Zionism of the first. Plainly, it was *not* enough to "denounce racism." Plainly it was *Zionism*, not Liebman, that was correct about the need for the "defensive barrier" i.e. a Jewish state. And while Shlomo Sand does admit that Zionism's "appreciation of history was later revealed to be justified," he literally entombs that inconvenient truth *within* brackets, thus allowing it no analytical weight or explanatory power.[317] As Zeev Sternhell has pointed out, even an anti-Zionist book of high caliber and general culture such as Gabriel Piterberg's *The Returns of Zionism: Myths, Politics and Scholarship in Israel* does not avoid "the usual faults of the genre," not least idealism. For example, although the 1947-49 war was "launched by the Arab states against the founding of the Jewish state," as Sternhell reminds us, Piterberg can only see "the 'logic' of an ideology." He misses the ugly rise of 19th century volkish Europe ("Half a century before the Shoah, Europe began to vomit up its Jews," Sternhell comments), mid-century European fascism, the defeat of world revolution (and with it the hopes of the Bundists and the anti-Zionist left) and the Arab war against the Jewish state. None of this counts. *The only factor given any weight by Piterberg is (murderous-from-inception) Zionist ideology.*[318]

And because the AZI spurns a properly materialist analysis of Zionism (by which I do not mean a narrowly economistic approach), embraces an abstract universalism targeted only at the Jews (even after the Holocaust), codes Arab nationalism as progressive (even when it is antisemitic), and remains trapped within teleological and idealist modes of thought that leave it unable to face the weight of history or the duty of self-criticism, it has a tendency to indulge various forms of *magical thinking*.

In her wild psychoanalysis ("learnt from books," as Freud put it) Jacqueline Rose puts Zionism in treatment as an analysand.[319] Rose plays the part of the analyst and comes to a speedy diagnosis: the traumatized patient exhibits symptoms of "resistance" which have "blocked the passage of the psyche into freedom." This "defense mechanism" has protected the patient "from the pain and mess of the inner life," but at a steep price: an inability to face the pain of either Holocaust survivors or Palestinians. Rose argues that the former were not just "used" and "hated" by Israel, which exhibited a "willed blindness" towards them, but that this "shameful treatment" was "constitutive of the state." As for the latter, the "destruction of the entire infrastructure of Palestinian life," no less, is acceptable to Israel because it lacks any sense of the shared vulnerability of peoples, having chosen to promote "omnipotence as the answer to historical pain."[320]

The AZI also drinks deep at the well of conspiracism, including wildly inflated estimates of the power of the "Jewish lobby." John Mearsheimer's and Stephen Walt's 2007 book *The Israel Lobby* gave a stamp of academic legitimacy to conspiracism, by claiming to prove that only the power of the Israel lobby to shape US foreign policy could explain the US decision to invade Iraq—a war Israel did not think wise, as it happens.[321] A shiny new Ivy League stamp of approval was given to the smelly old idea that hidden Jewish power pushes states into wars and revolutions to serve Jewish inter-ests.[322] In this vein, Pappé claims that in 1947 "the Truman administration was probably the first ever to succumb to the power of the Jewish lobby"[323] and today's US policy in the region is "confined to the narrow route effec-tively delineated . . . by AIPAC."[324] More: "In the United States today," Pappé writes, "one cannot ignore the level of integration of Jews into the heights of American financial, cultural and academic power" nor "the exploitation of the fruits of successful integration into American society for the benefit of a foreign country."[325] He doesn't quite call American Jews a fifth column, but he is getting there.

The *Haaretz* commentator Carlo Strenger has expressed his frustration at Judith Butler's conspiracist view of Zionism, but he might have had the entire AZI in his sights. "Judging from [Butler's book] *Parting Ways*," he writes, "you might think that Zionism was a unitary ideology run by some politburo. At no point would you recognize how complex the history of Zionism is, and how different its various shades can be. You would not guess that there are committed liberal Zionists who argue for a secular constitution for Israel that would give full equality to Arabs and lead to a complete separation of religion and state." He went on: "Quite remarkably, Butler, whose life's work is about nuances, unquestioningly accepts simplistic premises about Zionism."[326]

Another indication that the AZI is dominated by the "practico-social function" of delegitimizing Israel is its addiction to what we might call the Higher Ad Homenism. Pappé dismisses historiography which offers an alternative interpretation of Zionism or Israel as craven ("to satisfy the powers that be") or an "intentional fabrication," nought but "the scholarly scaffolding for acts of repression, oppression and discrimination," written by people of bad faith who occupy "the tribal space."[327] Norman Finkelstein trashed the social democratic Zionist and political philosopher Michael Walzer in those terms, comparing him unfavorably to inter-war fascist thinkers.[328] Shlomo Sand indicts Zionist intellectuals *per se* as calculating little entrepreneurs of political identity, wily but "dominant agents in the development of . . . the national imagination," mere peddlers in "foundation myths", "docile in their acceptance of the cult of the State" who have embraced "an exclusive holist State identity that only Jews can participate in."[329] Former Matzpen leader Tikva Honig-Parnass incites her readers against the "Zionist Left intellectuals" on the grounds of their "failure to warn their readers against (sic) ethnic cleansing, which makes them complicit to the growing discourse of 'transfer' in Israeli society."[330]

Zionist literature fares no better than Zionist historiography. Laor's *The Myths of Liberal Zionism*, a short bilious polemic, indicts the novelists David Grossman (ultimately) and A.B. Yehoshua and Amos Oz (enthusiastically, with genuine loathing) as dishonest practitioners of "hasbara," i.e. propaganda. Although each is a proponent of the two-state solution, Laor trashes them all as "prophets of a new xenophobia" who have been "marketed" to European audiences as "fetishes of progress" but who are really the creators of a genre of writing—"Israeli writing in the west"—that is kitsch, written in defense of racism and "the return of the colonial," and marked by "that obsessive hatred towards anything which is 'impure.'"[331]

Notion 2: Israel is a crime

The second "notion" of the Anti-Zionist Ideology is that the state of Israel created in 1948 is a *crime against humanity*. In the imaginary of the AZI, Israel is an illegitimate nation, born through an "ethnic cleansing"; it is an "Apartheid state" that is pursuing "genocidal" policies in defense of a militarist and expansionist "ethno-democracy."

A Genocidist State

"Among all the harms produced by Hitler's politics and the Holocaust," suggests the Heideggerian-Communist philosopher Gianni Vattimo, "one can also list the creation of Israel as a Jewish state in 1948."[332] Once it was the "devilish Jew," notes David Hirsh; but now, for the AZI, it is Israel doing what the devilish Jew used to do: "standing in the way of world peace, of being responsible for stirring up wars, of being uniquely racist or apartheid or dangerous in some other way." Jewish nationalism, he points out, is now viewed as "essentially different from all other nationalisms ... nothing at all but a mode of exclusion ... more like a totalizing and timeless essence of evil than a historical set of changing and variegated beliefs and practices."[333]

For example, Yitzhak Laor claims that Israel Defense Force "death squads" are guilty of "indiscriminately killing," and of acts of "sadism," including "mass starvation."[334] Omar Barghouti claims Israel has an "insatiable appetite" for "genocide and the intensification of ethnic cleansing."[335] (One is reminded here of those inter-war cartoons of gigantic Jews looming over and eating up the world.) According to Shenhav's *Beyond the Two-State Solution*, Israel is "built on the ruins of the indigenous people of Palestine, whose livelihood, houses, culture, and land had been systematically destroyed"; the country is "an aggressive war machine," pregnant with genocide; Israel's "violence-generating mechanisms" drive it into "killing Arabs regularly," the 1956 Kafr Qasim massacre, for example, being not an exceptional event but "the political model of Jewish sovereignty." Israel, seen through the lens of the AZI, is on course to achieve "the annihilation of the Palestinian people."[336]

The unhinged portrayal of Israel as a genocidist state often takes the form of what has been called "Holocaust Inversion."[337] Four forms can be identified. First, the depiction of Israelis as the new Nazis and the Palestinians as the new Jews; an inversion of reality. As Klaff notes, "We see headlines like 'The Final Solution to the Palestine Question,' references to the 'Holocaust in Gaza,' images of Israeli IDF soldiers morphing into jackbooted storm troopers, or of Israeli politicians morphing into Hitler, or of the Star of David morphing into the Swastika."[338] Noam Chomsky described the IDF as "those who wear the jackboots,"[339] while Jacqueline Rose falsely claimed that the IDF "provided a guard of honour" at the tomb of Baruch Goldstein, the Jew who massacred 29 Arabs in Hebron in 1994.[340] Shenhav quotes approvingly from the testimony of a person who "describes the wrongs forced upon the Palestinians in the territories as 'Sabra and Chatilla times a million.'"[341]

Second, the Zionist ideology and movement is made to appear in the AZI as *akin to Nazism*, or is considered alongside of, or in comparison to, or even collaborating with Nazism. For example, Honig-Parnass finds in the socialism of the early Zionists "a local version of National-Socialism that retained the main tenets of organic nationalism."[342] A theme in Shlomo Sand's work is "[t]he relative inaction and indifference of Zionist leaders towards the annihilation of European Judaism,"[343] while other anti-Zionists such as Lenni Brenner radicalize the notion of "indifference" and claim there was active "collaboration" between Zionists and Nazis during the Holocaust.[344]

Third, the Holocaust is turned into a "moral lesson" for, or a "moral indictment" of the Jews—an inversion of morality. Rose argues that after "escaping the horrors of Europe, the Jews are in danger of transporting their own legacy of displacement, directly and perilously, onto the soil of Palestine ... the displacement of one history of suffering directly onto another."[345] The AZI writers Hazem Saghiyah and Saleh Bashir are perhaps the most candid in treating the Holocaust as laying a special moral burden on the Jews. They write: "The dissociation between the acknowledgment of the Holocaust and what Israel is doing should be the starting point for the development of a discourse which says that the Holocaust does not free the Jewish state or the Jews of accountability. On the contrary, *the Nazi crime compounds their moral responsibility and exposes them to greater answerability.*"[346]

Fourth, *Holocaust memory* appears within the AZI only as a politicized and manipulated thing, a club wielded instrumentally, with malice aforethought, by bullying Jews, for Jewish ends. Pappé devotes a chapter of *The Idea of Israel* to lambasting the "official and collective manipulation" of Holocaust memory by the Israeli state, praising the work of Idith Zertal because there "one encounters Israel as a necrophilic nation ... [o]bsessed and possessed by death ... yet quite able to use and abuse [Holocaust] memory for the sake of its political aims."[347] Gianni Vattimo goes further. The Shoah is not just used as "an all-encompassing justification for all the actions of Israel." Israel is guilty of "much more than a simple and cynical political expediency." And what is this "more"? It is a "radical and vindictive executionism."[348] With Vattimo, it is clear, the AZI is brought (hardly kicking and screaming, it has to be said) to the very threshold of antisemitism.

A racist in-gathering

But surely Israel is also a *raft-state*, as Isaac Deutscher put it? Surely, when Europe was a burning ship for the Jews, they had the right, as Amos Oz believes, to jump? Was the creation of a Jewish homeland not an "existential necessity" as the left-wing Zionist intellectual historian Zeev Sternhell argues?[349] Not according to the AZI, which relentlessly frames the Jewish in-gathering as a racist and colonial project and Jewish sovereignty as criminal. While *Palestinian* ethnocentrism is praised as the foundation of a "beautiful resistance"—as the Vicar of St James Church in London wrote, justifying the staging of an eight metre high replica of "the Apartheid Wall" in the church courtyard during Christmas 2013—[350] the Jewish in-gathering is treated by the AZI as a dirty and clannish affair, driven by supremacism and racism. "Israeli Jews are . . . pied noirs . . . [we are] part of you as long as we are here," writes Laor.[351]

The Jews, and only the Jews, are held to the *universalist* standard; only *their* pursuit of national self-determination is condemned: "[e]thno-racial separation lies at the very core of the Jewish social-democratic worldview," sneers Shenhav.[352] The political program of the left for every other oppressed people in history—the right to national self-determination as a necessary stage prior to universalism, necessary for "clearing the decks for the class struggle," as Lenin put it—is denied to just one group, the Jews, who must embrace universalism; and not in the socialist future, but *now*.[353]

But what of the 700,000 or so Jews who were driven or emigrated from the Arab lands after 1948 and found refuge in Israel? Don't *they* complicate the picture of Zionism and Israel found in the AZI? They are not allowed to. They are rigorously denied the status of victims or refugees, for a start. A prettifying language of free will is draped over their experience of being abused, stripped of their property and possessions and driven out. To the AZI, they simply "entered the country" (Yiftachel),[354] or "emigrated from Arab countries" (Honig-Parnass),[355] or are described neutrally as "Jewish immigrants from Arab countries" (Rose).[356] However, the moment they arrive in Israel the AZI treats them as victims . . . *of Zionism.* Exemplary in this regard is Pappé, for whom the Mizrachi Jews were "enslaved" by Zionism and its racist Ashkenazi ideology of supremacism.[357]

Notion 3: "Natural Palestinians / Cultured Israelis"

The third "notion" of the AZI is buried but active within its problematic (or systemic structure), so it must be, as Althusser puts it, "dragged up from the depths." It takes the form of the unexamined assumption, a dichotomy in thought: "Natural Palestinians / Cultured Israelis."[358] In other words, when it comes to identifying actors with *agency, responsibility, and choice*, the AZI has a dichotomous approach: Palestinians (and Arabs per se) are absent, while Israelis are (massively and exclusively) present. The unarticulated assumption of the AZI is that Palestinians are a driven people, dominated by circumstances and moved by emotions; qualities associated with the world of *nature*. Israelis are the opposite; masters of all circumstances, rational and calculating; qualities associated with the world of *culture*.

Reactionary Anti-Imperialism

The dichotomy is an integral aspect of a mind-set: the *reactionary anti-imperialism* that became dominant on much of the Left from the late 1960s. Whereas anti-imperialism had previously been only "one value amongst a whole set—democracy, equality, sexual and gender liberation, anti-totalitarianism," it was now raised to an altogether higher status: "the central value, prior to and above all others." The world was divided into two "camps": imperialism versus anti-imperialism. Soon enough, and rapidly after the 1967 war and the occupation of the West Bank and Gaza, Israel was reframed as "a key site of the imperialist system."[359] Since 1989 and the collapse of Communism, campism has remained the dominant intellectual framework for many parts of the Left. Reducing the complexity of the post-cold-war world to a single Great Contest—"Imperialism" against "the resistance," or "Empire" against "the multitude"—many on the Left became gripped by the same Manichean world-view and habits of mind that dominated during the Stalinist era; from apologia to denial, from cynicism to grossly simplifying tendencies of thought, from the belief that "my enemy's enemy is my friend" to the abandonment of all who get on the wrong side of the "anti-imperialists." For example, by defining Radical Islamism as part of the anti-imperialist "resistance" to imperialism, parts of the left *redefined itself* as a (not very) critical supporter of Radical Islamism. AZI theorist Judith Butler, for example, insisted the eliminationist antisemites of Hamas and Hezbollah were "social movements that are progressive, that are on the Left, that are part of a global Left."[360]

Pascal Bruckner's essay *The Tyranny of Guilt* traces the rise of this mentality ("the whole world hates us and we deserve it") and this post-communist politics (a "Third Worldism of introspection") in which guilt-ridden intellectuals, even as they enjoy all that Western liberal democratic society has to offer, retain a deep personal need to feel wholly oppositional to a "fallen culture." So they *turn in on the West itself*, which must now be as bad as the East was once good. Now we "hate ourselves much more than we love others." Look around, says Bruckner: "one applauds a religious revolution, another goes into ecstasies over the beauty of terrorist acts, or supports a guerrilla movement because it challenges our imperialist project." Israel, in this world-view, is part of the imperialist West. This campist framing shapes how the conflict is perceived: we end up "pursuing our own mythologies in a foreign theater." Bruckner again: "People who support the Palestinians are not hoping to aid flesh-and-blood human beings but pure ideas … not so much engaged in inquiring into a specific antagonism—a real estate dispute involving two equally legitimate owners as Amos Oz puts it—as in settling accounts with Western culture."[361]

While 19th century universalism and assimilationism gave the socialist left a predisposition to be hostile to the Jews as a people, the 20th century accretion of reactionary anti-imperialism, identity politics, and Occidentalism added a predisposition to view Israel as a state beyond the pale and the Palestinians as the embodiment of victimhood. And this dichotomy is absolutely central to the AZI. It underpins the radical decontextualization of history, the discounting of Israel's security fears and their reframing as Zionist frauds, the infantalization of the Palestinians as a people without responsibility and beyond judgment, and the evasion of Arab and Palestinian antisemitism. In toto, these tendencies of thought frame Israel rather as a corrupt police officer would frame a suspect for a crime.

One-sided History

Granting only one side agency and responsibility, the dichotomy distorts key events of the conflict (e.g. the war of 1948, the collapse of the Camp David peace talks in 2000, Gaza after the 2005 disengagement). The Palestinians are cast as passive victims; a compelled people (Laor claims the second intifada was "instigated" by . . . Israeli policy); a duped people (Honig-Parnass writes of "Barak's pre-planned collapse of the Camp David talks in October 2000");[363] and a *people beyond the reach of judgment* (Rose views Palestinian suicide bombers as "people driven to extremes" and thinks Israel has "the responsibility for [the] dilemma" of the suicide bomber.[364] In a particularly stark example of the poverty of dichotomous thinking, Shenhav's account of 1948 has no Arab rejection of the UN Partition plan, no massed Arab armies on the borders, no coordinated Arab invasion, no desperate Jewish self-defense, no ethnic cleansing by Arabs of Jews in every place they won battlefield victories. There are only Zionist "massacres" and "forced expulsions" and "ethnic cleansing"; all caused by a Zionist "transfer ideology" that the Zionists successfully "realized in that war." Shenhav dismisses alternative accounts of 1948 as "denial"—a kind of academic crime against humanity.[365] Similarly, Pappé's portrait of "the ghetto of Gaza," where Palestinians are "incarcerated in a huge megaprison" by cruel Israelis, is missing only disengagement, rocket attacks, the anti-Semitic Hamas Charter, and Iranian-supplied Fajr 5 rockets with a 70km range (not to mention the Egyptian border).[366]

Bracketed security fears

The dichotomous understanding of "Natural Palestinians / Cultured Israelis" also shapes how the AZI understands Israel's security. In short, the threats Israel faces are *discounted* and the security measures taken by Israel in response are reframed as examples of "apartheid." Zionists, claims Pappé, are "[c]ompelling a nation to be constantly at arms" by stimulating "continual angst" through the abuse of Holocaust memory.[367] Sand argues that Zionism falsely "portray[s] itself as a persecuted innocent" and it is this portrayal, not any actual threats, that "have given Israeli society . . . a well of deep-seated collective anxieties."[368] Pappé dismisses the "useful fabrications about Israelis suffering under intense rocketing" as a "fantasy of apologists."[369] Honig-Parnass rolls her eyes at "warmongering by the Israeli security and political establishments against Iran," *placing beyond judgment* the Iranian regime, its pursuit of a nuclear capability, its threats to wipe Israel from the pages of time, and its Holocaust denial.[370] For the AZI, Israel's concern with security (like its approach to Holocaust memory) is either a pathology (a psychological condition Israelis cannot break out of) or—contradictorily, though the AZI does not seem to notice the contradiction—a politically-manipulated instrumentalism (a political ploy used cynically).

Infantalizing Palestinians

The third consequence of dichotomous thinking about the nature of the two peoples is the infantalization of one of them. Nothing can ever be expected or demanded of the Palestinians, who remain perpetually below the age of responsibility; the source of their behavior is always *external* to themselves, always located in Israel's actions.

For example, when Amos Oz complained that incitement by Arafatesque intellectuals is one major reason why so many Palestinians are "suffocated and poisoned by blind hate," Yitzhak Laor responded by accusing Oz of "incitement" against the Palestinians. Oz's temerity in *seeking to hold the Palestinians* to account was enough to condemn him in Laor's eyes.[371] Jacqueline Rose issued a barely disguised apologia for the Palestinian suicide bomber as a person *compelled*, then admonished Israel a few lines later for failing to take note of Freud's warning that "the forcefulness with which a group builds and defends its identity was the central question of modern times."[372] She also described Palestinian suicide terrorism as "tragic," a term which, as the late political theorist and ethicist Jean Bethke Elshtain pointed out, *brackets* human agency and responsibility, falsely assimilating a conscious human act (terrorist murder) to a mindless act of nature (such as a flood).[373] Of course, Rose then indicts the Israeli state as "the agent" that is responsible for the terrorism, and for "plac[ing] Jews in Israel . . . at risk."[374]

When the AZI infantalizes the Palestinians, it politically disorientates *itself.* One example: Shlomo Sand expresses his disgust at those Jewish Israelis who opposed Saddam Hussein during the first Gulf War. Given Saddam was firing Scud missiles at Israeli civilians, why does Sand feel disgust? Because *the Palestinians* felt "joy" at this "Arab" show of force." And *that* is what is decisive for Sand. So he, a socialist, ends up uncritically celebrating the brutal invasion of Kuwait by a genocidal dictator. Another bitter fruit of the AZI.[375]

Evading Arab and Palestinian Antisemitism

A final consequence of the dichotomy is that when faced with Arab anti-semitism, the AZI tends to minimize it, rationalizing, bracketing, and render-ing invisible, or just plain falsifying.[376] For example, in Pappé's *The Idea of Israel*, one would never know that the Palestinian leader Al-Husseini was so supportive of the Nazis that he formed a Muslim SS Unit. Pappé pres-ents this as just "an episode" in the "complex" life of a nationalist; a "foolish flirtation" that should only be of interest to the reader because it has been exploited by Zionists to "demonize" the Palestinians and "made it easy for Israeli historiography."[377] Al-Husseini, you see, was "forced" into the alliance with Hitler because the British had expelled him from Palestine after the Revolt of 1937. Similarly, the antisemitism of Al-Qassam is lawyered away by Pappé and the antisemitic British foreign secretary Ernest Bevin is retouched as a "pragmatic and sensible" figure. More seriously, Pappé flirts with the notion of Jewish responsibility for antisemitism. Discussing the 17th century pogroms against the Jews in Eastern Europe, Pappé invokes the "heresy" of Israel Shahak in order to argue that Jews must acknowledge "some degree of Jewish responsibility" for those pogroms; it was the "lack of empathy or iden-tification with the oppressed peasants" on the part of the Jews that led to their targeting. Pappé urges the reader to ignore those Zionist textbooks that say Jews were attacked "because of who they were and not because of anything they did." Pappé then tells us that the "same explanation"—antisemitism is, at least in part, about what Jews do—can be applied "to the hatred and aggres-sion of the Arabs or Palestinians against Israelis."[379]

Pappé also claims that the exodus of Jews from the Arab lands after 1948 had no anti-Semitic component. After all, the Jews of the Arab lands were enjoying "organic cohabitation ... in Arab and Islamic societies ... a life of integration and coexistence" until Zionism "reintroduced this schism in modern times."[380] Similarly, for Azoulay and Ophir, the "long positive his-tory of coexistence shared by Jews and Arabs in various countries, includ-ing Palestine until the end of the British Mandate" are "played down" by "the Zionists," while "shows of anti-Semitism are magnified out of all proportion."[381]

And when Jacqueline Rose erases the distinction between the Palestinian suicide bomber and his Israeli civilian victim, *uncritically* passing on to the reader the view of the Hamas leader Abdul Aziz al-Ratansi ("If he wants to sacrifice his soul in order to defeat the enemy and for God's sake—well, then he's a martyr"), are we not reminded of Moshe Postone's observation about the "Orientalist reification of the Arabs and/or Muslims as the Other, whereby the Other, this time, is affirmed?"

Notion 4: Vindictive One-Statism

The fourth "notion" of the AZI is a utopian political program: *vindictive* one-statism. *One-Statism*: the resolution of the conflict by denying the right to national self-determination to *both* fiercely nationalist peoples. *Vindictive*: its primary interest is ending Israel rather than birthing Palestine.[383]

Vindictive One-Statism versus the Israeli people

Vindictive one-statism seeks to end Israel by rewinding the film of history and undoing 1948. "Nationhood is not a right . . . self-determination is a myth" says Rose.[384] Omar Barghouti, a founder of the BDS movement, rejects any expression of Jewish self-determination because "by definition it infringes the inalienable rights of the indigenous Palestinian to part of their homeland."[385] The leading one-stater, Ali Abunimeh of *Electronic Intifada*, writes that "self-determination ... cannot apply to Israelis as a separate group due to the settler colonial nature of Zionism."[386] Gabriel Piterberg, notes Zeev Sternhell, "holds that Israel can only obliterate the original sin of its birth by disappearing."[387] More: the idea of *conquest* lies just beneath the surface of vindictive one-statism. Coercion is necessary, implies Shenhav, because Israel is an example of what Herbert Marcuse called a one-dimensional society, that is, a "pseudo-democracy" in which all critical thought has been "paralyzed."[388] Saree Makdisi, an English professor at UCLA, is blunter still. "No privileged group in the history of the world has ever voluntarily renounced its privileges," he says, so "the Israelis will never relinquish their privileges until they are *compelled* preferably by non-violent means ... to accept the parameters of a single democratic state."[389]

Vindictive One-Statism versus the Palestinian people

The program of vindictive one-statism also pushes the Anti-Zionist Subject into trying to play the role of the conscience of the Palestinian national movement, policing it from the left, attacking Abbas as a "sell-out" and prettifying Hamas as "the resistance." It all makes for a ludicrous spectacle. Judith Butler, the booster of Hamas and Hezbollah as "part of the global left," wags her tenured Berkeley finger at the Palestinian president Mahmoud Abbas, rallies opposition to the two-state solution he seeks to negotiate, and charges him with "abandon[ing] the right of return for diasporic Palestinians."[390] The *London Review of Books* routinely denounced the two-stater Salam Fayyad, when he was prime minister of the Palestinian Authority, as a collaborator. "Fayyad's critics," wrote Adam Shatz, "call him a 'good manager of the occupation,' a 'builder of apartheid roads,' 'the sugar daddy who got us hooked on aid,' and it's all true."[391] Pappé simply defines the entire Palestinian Authority as a bunch of hopeless "collaborators."[392] The US-born Palestinian academic Saree Makdisi expressed his disdain for "those Palestinians who cling to what is manifestly an outmoded form of political thought … centered on the nation-state."[393] Honig-Parnass spits at the "collaborative" PA as a "police force to keep Palestinians under control."[394] Noam Chomsky spits at the PA as "nothing but a quisling regime."[395] Makdisi spits at the PA because "its main function is to facilitate the ongoing occupation and colonization of the West Bank."[396] Pappé spits at the Oslo traitors . . . *of Fatah*, because they have embraced "a concept of peace that altogether buried 1948 and its victims."[397] Shanhav is just glad Israel does *not* have a partner for peace, because the two state solution is "immoral."[398] And so on.

The AZI, in short, encourages Palestinian rejectionism and maximalism, echoes the obstructionism of the pro-Iran Hamas, stokes the fantasy of a full untrammelled right of return for every last Palestinian refugee, and can find no place in its heart for the right of the Jewish people to national self-determination.

The utopianism of vindictive one-statism

Vindictive One-Statism is therefore utopian in the sense Marx and Engels used that term in the *Communist Manifesto* to describe those socialists who imagined that "historical action [will] yield to their personal inventive action, historically created conditions of emancipation to fantastic ones" and who span a "politics of dreaming" without a "real basis." For example, Azoulay and Ophir's book *The One-State Condition*, while being a serious (if one-sided) analysis of the Israeli occupation of the West Bank, is utopian when it turns to a solution to the conflict. "Imagine a state in which . . ." begins their conclusion, worryingly. They go on to describe a state without borders, in which categories such as "illegal alien" have been abolished and people are, instead, "rapidly naturalized," all belonging and living together in partnership. Significantly, they admit that "[i]n order to imagine such a regime, three main features of the commonly accepted conception of modern democracy must be given up" by Israel. These are (a) "the idea that the state is a closed, given entity that dictates the borders of the political system and maintains relations with similar closed entities" (i.e. the international state system); (b) "the idea that national sovereignty is tested by the state's military might and its willingness to exert it occasionally" (i.e. the right to self-defense); (c) the distinction between citizens and non-citizens (i.e. the basis of political obligation and right). But what would the state *be*, after these three disavowals? It would be the "ever-changing product" of "power relations and political struggles." They accept that many will think their proposal "utterly naive" but they are undaunted because "utopian discourse cannot be measured in terms of its applicability."[399]

We find this same (symptomatic) demand—to be exempted from the criteria of applicability—in Judith Butler's *Parting Ways*. The "one-state solution," she writes, rather optimistically, would "eradicate all forms of discrimination based on ethnicity, race, and religion" as Jews and Palestinians "converge to produce a post-national polity." Noting that Edward Said thought this "an impossible task," Butler adds that it is "for that reason no less necessary."[400]

Azoulay and Ophir at least pose the question of whether a one-state solution might lead to civil war and repartition, but they do not allow it to detain them for long. That danger, they swiftly conclude, can easily be "dealt with by organizations of civil society alongside state mechanisms that bear an equal responsibility to both nations destined to live together, and with sufficient means to address the separate national matters and the contradictions they embody." The only problem is that those words—read them again, slowly—mean precisely nothing.[401] Shenhav's program is even cloudier: a "post-Westphalian sovereignty that is, in essence, porous, non-continuous, and multiple." He "assumes the existence of cross and joint sovereignties organized in a complex manner in different spheres of a common spatial region." He seeks "the redivision of the space and the decentralization of sovereignties" and the creation of "new spheres of overlapping political, communal, municipal, and theological sovereignties." Again, mere words enclose an empty space.[402]

Honig-Parnass's words do mean something concrete, but they hark back to a political fantasy. She thinks the solution lies in a "radical anti-imperialist perspective": an "anti-capitalist globalization" and a "democratic transformation of the entire region, which would lead to a socialist Middle East."[403]

Conclusion

As a system of "notions" that direct thought—Zionism is racism, Israel is a crime, Natural Palestinians / Cultured Israelis, and vindictive one-statism—the AZI has made "Israel" and "Palestine" into a *screen* onto which western activists like those I met at NUI Galway can project their "radical" political identity. To pull off this performance of identity, the "Palestinians" are required to be the *pure victims* of the wicked Israelis. That is why Palestinians being starved by Assad hold no interest. Nor do Palestinians being thrown from rooftops by Hamas members. Nor the Palestinians doing the throwing, for that matter. That is why, when Salam Fayyad was building up the basis of a Palestinian state, the BDS activists and *Guardian* editorialists yawned, or denounced him as a collaborator. As for "the Israelis," well, they must be reduced to "the fucking Zionists"—a continuation of Afrikaner racism or Nazism.

There is more than a threat to scholarship at stake here. David Hirsh—the most useful critic of the AZI writing today—helps us to see that the road from intellectual incitement to physical violence against Jews is not a long one.[404] That journey begins with denial. "One could confront the reality; that history had forged a Hebrew speaking Jewish nation on the Eastern shores of the Mediterranean, or one could deny it." It continues with the adoption of the *reactionary political program* of ending Israel: "the hope that the film of history could be unwound, and Israel could somehow be made to disappear." It ends in *violence* because (Hirsh again), "To call Israelis 'The Zionists' is to cast them as a political movement rather than as citizens of an existing state; and a political movement can be right or wrong, can be supported or opposed, while a nation state can only be recognized as a reality. And if 'the Zionists' are characterized as essentially 'racist' or 'apartheid' or 'Nazi', then Israeli Jews can be treated, once again, as exceptional to the human community."

Consider, for example, Gianni Vattimo's editorial introduction to *Deconstructing Zionism*, a collection of essays written, note, by "some of today's leading philosophers." "When I continue to recite, in the Latin breviary, certain Psalms like the 12th, (*Cum reduceret Dominus captives Sion . . .*)" writes Vattimo, "I increasingly feel its literal more than its allegorical sense: this is . . . a song of jubilation for the military victory of one people over another." In other words, Vattimo thinks he is digging up the roots of a violent tribal Jewish essence and he is disgusted by what he finds: here is "the feeling of a nomadic people with whom I have nothing in common." More: "To speak of Israel as an 'irredeemable sin' is therefore not so excessive." And he has had enough of the Holocaust being used as a litmus test, "a type of Nuremburg trial before which all thinkers are brought in order to be judged." As for those "Nazi hunters who never seem to get enough of justice-vengeance"—well, enough of them, too. Vattimo suggests we listen less to "the Zionists" and more to the former Iranian President Ahmadinejad who has had the courage to "question the very legitimacy of Israel's existence." Passing in silence over Ahmadinejad's threats to erase Israel from the page of time and his Holocaust denial, Vattimo praises the former Iranian leader in terms that should give us pause: "When Ahmadinejad invokes the end of the State of Israel, he merely expresses a demand that should be more explicitly shared by the democratic countries that instead consider him an enemy."[405]

In such terms is devotion to the intellectual program of the delegitimization of the state of Israel now beginning to legitimize the practical program of the physical destruction of the Jews.[406] ■

Works Cited

Althusser, Louis and Etienne Balibar. *Reading Capital*, London, Verso, 1970.

Althusser, Louis. *Philosophy of the Encounter*. London: Verso, 2006.

Azoulay, Ariella and Adi Ophir. *The One-State Condition: Occupation and Democracy in Israel/Palestine*. Translated by Tal Haran. Stanford: Stanford University Press, 2013.

Ben Noah, Gerry. "Brenner on the Nazi Massacre," in *Arabs, Jews and Socialism*, ed. John O'Mahony. London: Alliance for Workers Liberty, 1993, 37-38.

Butler, Judith. "The End of Oslo," *London Review of Books Blog*, 25 September 2011. http://www.lrb.co.uk/blog/2011/09/25/judith-butler/the-end-of-oslo/

Butler, Judith. *Parting Ways: Jewishness and the Critique of Zionism*. New York: Columbia University Press, 2012.

Cohen, Steve. *That's Funny You Don't Look Antisemitic*. London: Beyond the Pale Collective, 1984. http://www.engageonline.org.uk/ressources/funny/contents.html

Chomsky, Noam and Ilan Pappé. *Gaza in Crisis: Reflections on Israel's War Against the Palestinians.* London: Penguin, 2010.

Elliot, Gregory. *Althusser: The Detour of Theory.* London: Verso, 1987.

Fine, Robert. "The Lobby: Mearsheimer and Walt's Conspiracy Theory," *Engage.* 21 March 2006. Accessed April 24, 2014. http://www.engageonline.org.uk/blog/article.php?id=310

Finkelstein, Norman G. *Image and Reality of the Israel-Palestine Conflict.* London: Verso, 1995.

Geras, Norman. "Alibi Antisemitism," *Fathom Journal* 2 (2013). Accessed April 24, 2014. http://www.fathomjournal.org/policy-politics/alibi-antisemitism/

Hirsh, David. *Anti-Zionism and Antisemitism: Cosmopolitan Reflections.* Working Paper, Yale Initiative for the Interdisciplinary Study of Antisemitism, Yale University, 2007.

Hirsh, David. "Hostility to Israel and Antisemitism: Toward a Sociological Approach," *Journal for the Study of Antisemitism*, 5 (2013) 1401-1422.

Hirsh, David. "Rebels Against Zion," *Fathom Journal* 5 (2014). Accessed April 24, 2014. http://www.fathomjournal.org/reviews-culture/rebels-against-zion/

Honig-Parnass, Tikva. *False Prophets of Peace: Liberal Zionism and the Struggle for Palestine.* Chicago: Haymarket Books, 2011.

Johnson, Alan. "More Palestinian than the Palestinians," *World Affairs* (blog) 16 October 2012. http://www.worldaffairsjournal.org/blog/alan-johnson/judith-butler-more-palestinian-palestinians

Johnson, Alan. "BDS bullies at Galway University." *Times of Israel* (blog), March 10, 2014, accessed April 24, 2014. http://blogs.timesofisrael.com/bds-bullies-at-galway-university/

Johnson, Alan. "On Israel, the intellectuals are driving the students mad". *The Daily Telegraph* (blog), 13 March, 2014. Accessed April 24, 2014. http://blogs.telegraph.co.uk/news/alanjohnson/100263386/on-israel-the-intellectuals-are-driving-the-students-mad/

Johnson, Alan. "This barrier stops fascists: A response to Bethlehem unwrapped," *The Times of Israel* (blog), 8 January 2014. http://blogs.timesofisrael.com/this-barrier-stops-fascists-a-response-to-bethlehem-unwrapped/

Johnson, Alan. "What a one-state solution really means," *Jewish Chronicle,* 17 October 2012. Accessed April 24, 2014. http://www.thejc.com/comment-and-debate/comment/86919/what-a-one-state-solution-really-means

Klaff, Lesley. "Holocaust Inversion", *Fathom Journal* 5 (2014). Accessed April 24, 2014. http://www.fathomjournal.org/policy-politics/holocaust-inversion/

Klaff, Lesley. "Political and Legal Judgment: Misuses of the Holocaust in the UK," *Social Science Research Network*, 8 May 2013. Accessed April 24, 2014. http://papers.ssrn.com/sol3/papers.cfm?abstract_id=2284423

Lappin, Shalom. "The Question of Zion." *Democratiya* 6 (2006): 11-36.

Lappin, Shalom. "A Question of Zion: A Rejoinder to Jacqueline Rose." *Democratiya* 7 (2006). Accessed April 24, 2014. http://www.dissentmagazine. org/democratiya_article/a-question-of-zion-a-rejoinder-to-jacqueline-rose

Laor, Yitzhak. *The Myths of Liberal Zionism*. London: Verso, 2009.

Lewis, William. ed. *The Stanford Encyclopedia of Philosophy*. Stanford: 2014 Edward N. Zalta (gen ed.) http://plato.stanford.edu/archives/spr2014/entries/althusser/

Loewenstein, Anthony and Ahmed Moor. eds. *After Zionism: One State for Israel and Palestine*. London: Saqi Books, 2012.

Mead, Walter Russell. "Jerusalem Syndrome: Decoding The Israel Lobby", *Foreign Affairs*, November/December 2007. Accessed April 24, 2014. http://www.foreignaffairs.com/articles/63029/walter-russell-mead/jerusalem-syndrome

Mearsheimer, John J. and Stephen M. Walt. *The Israel Lobby and US Foreign Policy*. London, Penguin, 2007, 229-262.

Morris, Benny. "The Liar as Hero", *The New Republic*, March 17, 2011. Accessed April 24, 2014. http://www.newrepublic.com/article/books/magazine/85344/ilan-pappe-sloppy-dishonest-historian

New Left Review. ed. *Western Marxism: A Critical Reader*. London: Verso, 1983.

O'Mahony, John. "Lenni Brenner's Fake Internationalism," in *Arabs, Jews and Socialism*, ed. John O'Mahony (London: Alliance for Workers Liberty, 1993), 52-54.

Pappé, Ilan. *The Idea of Israel: A History of Power and Knowledge*. London: Verso, 2014.

Piterberg, Gabriel. *The Returns of Zionism: Myths, Politics and Scholarship in Israel*. London: Verso, 2008.

Postone, Moishe. "Zionism, anti-semitism and the left: an interview with Moishe Postone," *Workers' Liberty*, 5 February, 2010. Accessed April 24, 2014. http://www.workersliberty.org/story/2010/02/05/zionism-anti-semitism-and-left

Rose, Jacqueline. *The Last Resistance*. London: Verso, 2007.

Rose, Jacqueline. "The Question of Zion: A Reply to Shalom Lappin." *Democratiya* 7 (2006): 94-115.

Saghiyeh, Hazem and Saleh Bashir. "Universalizing the Holocaust: How Arabs and Palestinians relate to the Holocaust and how the Jews relate to the Palestinian victim." *Palestine-Israel Journal*, Vol. 5 Nos. 3 & 4, 1998. http://www.pij.org/details.php?id=382

Sand, Shlomo. T*he Words and the Land: Israeli Intellectuals and the Nationalist Myth*. Los Angeles: Semiotext(e), 2011.

Shatz, Adam. "Is Palestine Next?", *London Review of Books*, 14 July 2011. Accessed April 24, 2014. http://www.lrb.co.uk/v33/n14/adam-shatz/is-palestine-next

Shenhav, Yehouda. *Beyond the Two State Solution: A Jewish Political Essay*. Cambridge: Polity Press, 2012.

Sternhell, Zeev. "In Defence of Liberal Zionism." *New Left Review* 62, 2010.

Vattimo, Gianni and Michael Warder., eds. *Deconstructing Zionism: A Critique of Political Metaphysics*. London: Bloomsbury, 2014.

Winkett, Lucy. "Bethlehem Unwrapped is about 'beautiful resistance,' not taking sides," *Guardian Comment is Free*, 2 January 2014. http://www.theguardian.com/commentisfree/2014/jan/02/bethlehem-unwrapped-not-taking-sides-israel-security-wall

YouTube, "BDS Bullies at NUI Galway." posted by "Legal Insurrection." March 12, 2014. http://www.youtube.com/watch?v=1gkiGUBAM7g

Imaginary Jews

Expendable as Jews
—Derek Walcott[407]

In Sharon Olds's "The Window," the poet's daughter criticizes her for a poem she wrote. Announcing *"I am mad at you,"* the daughter explains the reasons for her anger:

You said in a poem that you're a survivor,
that's O.K., but you said that you are
a Jew, when you're not, that's so cheap. You're right,
I say, you're so right.[408]

The daughter accurately paraphrases a poem that Olds did in fact write. "That Year" describes a social studies lesson devoted to the Holocaust. The non-Jewish speaker, who suffers from parental abuse, identifies with the Jewish Holocaust victims so completely she declares herself to be—as the daughter later witheringly notes— "a Jew":

The symmetrical piles of white bodies,
the round white breast-shapes of the heaps,
the smell of the smoke, the dogs the wires the
rope the hunger. It had happened to others.
There was a word for us. I was: a Jew.[409]

The daughter does not object to the explicit, perhaps even lewd, description of the corpses, "the round white breast-shapes of the heaps." Instead, she declares her mother's self-identification as "a Jew" to be "cheap," that is, in aesthetic and moral bad taste. Tellingly, the mother neither objects to nor defends herself from the charge. Her quick agreement validates it.

"That Year" is hardly the only poem in which an American non-Jewish author declares him- or herself to be Jewish. Instead, it follows a number of poems and short stories with similar pronouncements, written by American poets. "That Year" is notable mainly for its belatedness. First collected in 1980, it arrives late in a well-established tradition that had lost much of its power. By the 2002 publication date of the second poem, two decades had discredited the metaphor. To borrow the daughter's insult, it had been cheapened. Accordingly, "The Window" addresses a mistake. The poem also suggests a broader shift, as Olds feels the need to apologize for an identification that she once sought. Olds adjusts to what Vivian Gornick has called (in a slightly different context) "the end of the Jew as metaphor."[410] The rise and fall of the non-Jewish Jew echoes this larger development. It marks shifting attitudes towards Jews in literary culture, changes which inform current thinking about Jews and their place in the world. It offers one useful context to recognize how intellectuals understand Jews and the limitations of their thinking. Attention to it clarifies our historical moment; we have discarded a troubling metaphor for a more dangerous position.

The most famous example of an American non-Jewish poet identifying as Jewish remains John Berryman's story, "The Imaginary Jew," based on an incident in Berryman's life.[411] The story depicts a Southern gentile living in New York City, who takes exception when a street debater denounces Roosevelt as "a goddammed warmonger."[412] An argument ensues, during which the street debater accuses the speaker of being Jewish. The speaker responds that he is Catholic, "or I was born one, I'm not one now. I was born a Catholic":

"Yeah?" said the Irishman. "Say the Apostles' Creed."

Memory went swirling back, I could hear the little bell die as I hushed it and set it on the felt. Father Boniface looked at me tall from the top of the steps and smiled, greeting me in the darkness before dawn as I came to serve, the men pressed around me under the lamps, and I could remember nothing but *visibilum omnium . . . et invisibilium?*

"I don't remember it."

The Irishman laughed with his certainty.

The papers in my pocket, I thought them over hurriedly. In my wallet. What would they prove? Details of ritual, Church history: anyone could learn them. My piece of Irish blood. Shame, shame: shame for my ruth-less people. I will not be his blood. I wish I were a Jew, I would change my blood, to be able to say Yes and defy him.[413]

Originally published in 1945, the scene recalls the street harassment many American Jews faced in the 1930s and 1940s. In his memoir *Boston Boy*, Nat Hentoff recalled how eight Irish-American teenagers surrounded him when he was alone. One "strapping" member of the group challenged Hentoff, "You Jewish, kid?" "I'm Greek," replied Hentoff. Unlike the nar-rator of "The Imaginary Jew," Hentoff used his wits to defuse the situation. Told to "say something in Greek," he recited the opening of the *Odyssey*, which he had learned in school.[414]

Significantly, though, Berryman's version blurs the distinction between Jew and non-Jew, victim and persecutor. Hentoff presents the triumph of Jewish intelligence over anti-Semitic brawn whereas Berryman shows how the non-Jew's imagination collapses these boundaries. Reflecting on his experience, the narrator presents the same self-characterization Olds will later offer, "I was: a Jew":

> In the days following, as my resentment died, I saw that I had not been a victim altogether unjustly. My persecutors were right: I was a Jew. The imaginary Jew. I was was as real as the imaginary Jew hunted down, on other nights and days, in a real Jew. Every murderer strikes the mirror, the lash of the torturer falls on the mirror and cuts the real image, and the real and the imaginary blood flow down together.[415]

In the last line, the rhetoric surges as the story rises from the particular incident it details to a grander truth. In this movement, "the real and imagi-nary" blend together and the Jew and the non-Jew turn indistinguishable. This shift does not suggest that Jews have been assimilated into American culture. On the contrary, the "Jew" retains his outsider status; or, to be more precise, the metaphor of the Jew signifies an outsider status. No actual Jews appear in Berryman's story. All remain "imaginary." The speaker's putative gesture of solidarity excludes actual Jews. The imagined state of Jewishness allows the speaker to escape the safety of his own situation, to experience persecution, to face "the lash of the torturer" and of being "hunted down." To do so, the narrator sets aside the lived reality of Jewish experience. Instead, Jewish history—namely, the real lives of actual Jews—exists mainly to stimu-late the non-Jewish imagination.

Many authors and readers found this position to be immensely attrac-tive. Berryman's story appeared in the *Kenyon Review* in 1945 and won the

Kenyon Review-Doubleday Doran Contest. It was reprinted in the British journal *Horizon* and translated into German.[416] The story's admirers included Ezra Pound.[417] Part of the story's success arises from the fact that it eloquently expressed a familiar aspiration of post-war American literary culture as non-Jewish authors claimed real or imaginary Jewish "blood" in order to assume the virtues they associated with Jews. To find one's Jewishness is to access modern humanity's most profound essence. "[T]he Jew becomes everywhere Everyman the outsider," R.P. Blackmur wrote, "and in each of us, in the exiled part, sits a Jew." A certain shared logic guides such pronouncements. If "exile" and suffering define the modern era, Jews serve as the era's exemplary figures. To claim the status of an imaginary Jew is to elevate one's importance. It gives significance to the traumas one endures—whether petty street harassment (in Berryman's story) or parental abuse (in Olds's poem). "I think it would be better to be a Jew," Anne Sexton observed, anticipating Sylvia Plath's more dramatic and controversial pronouncement, "I may be a bit of a Jew."[419] Though Plath's line inspired intense debate about its propriety, including heated denunciations,[420] it also served as a kind of model. Midcentury American literary culture featured the odd ritual of non-Jewish authors proudly claiming rather obscure Jewish ancestry so they would not feel (as Robert Lowell put it) "left out in a Jewish age." "Do I feel left out in a Jewish age?" Lowell rhetorically asked before reassuring his interviewer, "Not at all. Fortunately, I'm one-eighth Jewish myself, which I do feel is a saving grace."[421] The language Lowell employs underscores his position's oddity. Using a term from Christian theology, "saving grace," he boasts that his ancestral connection to Judaism qualifies as a credential. Lowell descended from two distinguished Yankee families: the Winslows, who arrived in America on the Mayflower, and the Lowells, considered one of Massachusetts' "first families."[422] Collected in *Life Studies*, his prose memoir "91 Revere Street," though, emphasizes his tenuous Jewish connection, opening with a fairly extensive description of Lowell's great-great-grandfather who "has no Christian name."[423]

Berryman recognized Lowell's ancestral maneuvering as strained; still, he envied the claim. Like the speaker of Plath's "Daddy," he too wished he were "a bit of a Jew." Berryman's posthumously published novel *Recovery* includes notes for an unfinished section. Titled "The Jewish Kick," one chapter refers to Lowell's nickname of "Cal" in order to note Berryman's "resentment of Cal's tiny Jewish blood."[424] This "resentment" follows a certain associative logic. In a late interview, Berryman described his view of how creativity works: "I do strongly feel that among the greatest pieces of luck for high achievement is ordeal . . . My idea is this: The artist is extremely lucky who is presented with the worst possible ordeal which will not actually kill him .

.. I hope to be nearly crucified."[425] On one hand, Berryman's story describes "the real Jew" and non-Jew as equally "real": "The imaginary Jew I was was as real as the imaginary Jew hunted down, on other nights and days, in a real Jew." On the other hand, when writing of his "resentment," Berryman acknowledges that distinctions exist between "the real and the imaginary blood," between Jews and others mistaken for Jews. If "ordeal" inspires creativity, suffering offers artists "great pieces of luck." After the Holocaust, then, Jews are "extremely lucky" as history has presented them with "perhaps the worst possible ordeal which will not actually kill" all of them. The Holocaust intensifies this association, but it extends across historical periods (as in the example of Lowell's distant ancestor). This close association of Jews with the prized quality of suffering fuels Berryman's envy. No matter how small, "Jewish blood" gives Lowell, his poetic rival, a creative advantage.

Increasingly, though, American poets shied away from, if not rejected, such contorted ways of understanding Jews, suffering, and creativity. Tess Gallagher's poem "The Women of Auschwitz" describes a friend shaving the speaker's head as she faces the effects of chemotherapy treatments. The title, "The Women of Auschwitz" spills over to the first line, "were not treated so well as I,"[426] as the title unexpectedly forms the subject for the opening sentence. "This device," Paul Fussell scoffed, surveying the technique, "seems by now almost obligatory in a certain kind of enjambed free verse which aims at wit."[427] Gallagher's poem, though, "aims" less at "wit" than hesitancy. The poem compares the speaker's suffering as a cancer patient to what the "women of Auschwitz" endured but expresses reservations about the comparison even before the poem offers it. Instead of rushing into a forced identification with Jews, the poem qualifies it.

Several poems in Sherman Alexie's 1996 collection, *The Summer of Black Widows*, work similarly. "Inside Dachau" describes the poet's visit to the concentration camp. Pointedly titled, "*big lies, small lies*," the opening section describes the speaker's "plan" to write about the trip by imagining the experience of a Jewish victim and imaginatively assuming his identity: "I would be a Jewish man who died in the camp. / I would be the ideal metaphor."[428] The speaker, however, quickly castigates himself for what he calls his "selfish" "earlier plans": "What could I say about Dachau / when I had never suffered through any season // inside its walls?"[429] Another section, "*after we are free*," returns to the essential difference between the speaker's and the Jewish victims' lives. The section consists of nine couplets. In each, the opening line poses a question, starting with, "If I were Jewish," and the second line opens, "I am Spokane." For example, the first couplet presents the following question and response, "If I were Jewish, how would I mourn the dead? / I am Spokane. I wake."[430] The first line asks the speaker to imagine life as a

Jew. Instead of answering the question, the second line sets it aside. "I am Spokane," nine times the poem insists. The couplet structure brings the two identities into close proximity, but the syntax asserts the need to respect their essential difference. "Let's say I am a Jew," another poem in the collection supposes before firmly declining its own invitation, "No."[431]

So far I have stressed the limitations of the genre of "Imaginary Jews," in which non-Jewish authors identify themselves as Jewish. Many of the works share a similar logic. The Jews remain metaphoric; as such, they allow the non-Jewish authors to elevate themselves and their own situation. The authors do not concern themselves with understanding the lives that Jews lead, with the particular challenges and historical forces they encounter. Instead, the authors wish to appropriate Jewish identity without thinking much about actual Jews. In blunt terms, the Jews exist to serve the Christian imagination and do so largely by suffering.

Randall Jarrell's "Jews at Haifa" forms a notable exception. Originally published in the September 1947 issue of *The Partisan Review*, the poem describes Jewish immigrants barred from entering Israel and placed in camps in Cyprus:

Here on the edge

Of the graves of Europe
We believe: we are not dead;
It seems to us that hope
Is possible—that even mercy is permitted
To men on this earth,
To Jews on this earth . . . [432]

In the face of the "knowledge: / That all men wish our death," the poem pleads for "hope" and "mercy." "Ours. // Ours," the Jews "whisper," and the poem celebrates their quiet determination.[433] In fact, the poem's identification with the Jews is so complete that the poem repeats their vow as it if were its own. The poem joins their cause.

One striking difference between Jarrell's poem and the other works I have discussed is that Jarrell tries to understand the Jews' plight, not simply adopt it as a metaphor for his own situation. When Berryman and Lowell express their ambitions, whether boasting of a Jewish "saving grace" or expressing a "hope to be nearly crucified," their language remains markedly Christian. In contrast, Jarrell seeks to recognize the specific situation the Jews face. When the speaker wishes "that even mercy is permitted / To men on this earth," he quickly adds the relevant sub-category, "To Jews on this earth." Instead of subsuming "Jews" into all humanity, the poem recognizes difference.

Several reasons exist for the decline of the genre of the "Imaginary Jews" in American literature. In one respect, this development echoes the decline in prestige of Jewish-American literature, as factors including changing political attitudes to Israel, greater assimilation, and the receding of the Holocaust into historical memory made the Jewish-American experience seem marginal to the contemporary moment.[434] The Jew no longer serves as "the ideal metaphor" or "Everyman." One might hope that a more accurate and balanced understanding might take the metaphor's place, that the culture might develop a more enlightened way of thinking about Jews. Instead, an uglier, rawer tendency has found expression and, to a disturbing extent, legitimacy.

Terry Eagleton offers an illustrative example of how certain thinking about religion, Jews, and Israel bleed into each other. The Distinguished Professor of English Literature at Lancaster University and the Excellence in English Distinguished Visitor at the University of Notre Dame, Eagleton maintains a considerable presence on both sides of the Atlantic, in part because of his ability to balance wit and polemic when addressing the latest subjects in cultural and literary studies. The subject of Jews, though, tests the limits of his urbane sophistication.

In *Reason, Faith, and Revolution: Reflections on the God Debate*, which collects revised versions of the talks he delivered as the Dwight T. Terry Lectures at Yale University, Eagleton observes that his book's purpose is to expose how little agnostic critics know about religion. He writes, "It is with this ignorance and prejudice that I take issue in this book." "[T]he agnostic left," he observes, "cannot afford such intellectual indolence when it comes to the Jewish and Christian Scriptures." Only a few pages later, however, Eagleton offhandedly offers a rather startling admission: "I should also confess that since the only theology I don't know much about is Christian theology, as opposed to those kinds I know nothing at all about, I shall confine my discussion to that alone, on the grounds that it is better to be provincial than presumptuous."[435] The obvious contradiction does not trouble Eagleton; he freely espouses his own ignorance while berating others for that particular failure. His own "intellectual indolence" does not embarrass him. The reason arises from the question of what counts as necessary knowledge. When considering the subject of religion, Eagleton feels no need to study the insights of Jewish theologians or the Jewish tradition. They do not require his attention. Eagleton calls his own position "provincial," but it is more accurate to say it is bigoted. Jews need not be listened to, even when a scholar reflects on "the God Debate."

Setting aside self-deprecating gestures, Eagleton's tone turns aggressive when he applies his particular theology to address contemporary political realities. In 2011, Occupy London constructed a protest camp outside St. Paul's Cathedral. Much public debate ensued as politicians, church officials, and media considered whether police should evict the protestors from their camps that were partially built on Church of England property. The fact that the incident involved a Christian Church, Christian clergy, and a secular political movement did not dissuade Eagleton from viewing it from a certain perspective. Writing in the *Guardian*, Eagleton evoked the incident of Jesus confronting the Temple money lenders in order to understand the protests outside St. Paul's Cathedral:

> The fracas Jesus created in this holiest of places, driving out the money changers and overturning their tables, was probably enough to get him executed. To strike at the temple was to strike at the heart of Judaism. This itinerant upstart with a country-bumpkin background was issuing a direct challenge to the authority of the high priests. Even some of his comrades would probably have seen this astonishing act of defiance as nothing short of sacrilegious.
>
> We are not told whether the riot police (temple guards) dragged him off, but they would surely have felt fully justified in doing so. Some members of the Jewish ruling caste would have been searching for an excuse to shut the mouth of this populist agitator.[436]

A classic anti-Semitic strategy is to draw parallels between tendentiously interpreted passages in the Christian Bible and contemporary events. Eagleton retells an incident in the Christian Bible that anti-Semites have historically found particularly useful, Jesus "driving out the money changers." As a historian of the field notes, they are "key anti-Jewish phrases."[437] Eagleton plays only a slight variation on this well-established theme. The Jesus he praises "strike[s] at the heart of Judaism," fighting the "Jewish ruling caste." Menacing, violent, money-grubbing, and, yes, villainous, Jews both belong to the power structure and serve as its violent enforcers. As if updating a medieval Passion play, Eagleton assigns Jews the role of the violent suppressor: the Jew quashes "populist" uprisings. Drawing from familiar stereotypes, Eagleton needs only a parenthetical aside to evoke old hatreds: "the riot police (temple guards)."

Eagleton employs such phrases so economically because he draws from a distressingly familiar vocabulary and set of ideas. Three days after the *Guardian* printed Eagleton's column, its reader's editor, Chris Elliott, noted that the newspaper faced "an increase in complaints of antisemitism within the last few months" and offered a highly qualified apology, worth quoting in some length:

For antisemitism can be subtle as well as obvious. Three times in the last nine months I have upheld complaints against language within articles that I agreed could be read as antisemitic. The words were replaced and the articles footnoted to reflect the fact. These included references to Israel/US "global domination" and the term "slavish" to describe the US relationship with Israel; and, in an article on a lost tribe of Mallorcan Jews, what I regarded as a gratuitous reference to "the island's wealthier families".

Two weeks ago a columnist used the term "the chosen" in an item on the release of Gilad Shalit, which brought more than 40 complaints to the *Guardian*, and an apology from the columnist the following week. "Chosenness", in Jewish theology, tends to refer to the sense in which Jews are "burdened" by religious responsibilities; it has never meant that the Jews are better than anyone else. Historically it has been antisemites, not Jews, who have read "chosen" as code for Jewish supremacism.[438]

Addressing what he admitted were anti-Semitic "references to Israel/ US 'global domination' and the term 'slavish' to describe the US relationship with Israel," Elliott did not mention, let alone apologize for, Eagleton's writings. However, Eagleton affirms similar ideas in his writing, both in the newspaper and elsewhere, framing them with religious imagery. "The Jewish ruling class," he darkly reminded readers of his book, *After Theory*, "handed him [Jesus] over to the Roman colonial power."[439] In *Reason, Faith, and Revolution: Reflections on the God Debate*, Eagleton thunders, "No middle ground is permitted here: the choice between justice and the powers of the world is stark and absolute." Again the "powers" who threaten both the ancient and modern world—that is, the enemies of Jesus and right-thinking people—are coded as Jewish. A Biblical parallel clinches the point, "Neither would he [Jesus] go down well on Wall Street, just as he did not go down well among the money changers of the Jerusalem temple."[440] The implied word, "Jewish," whispers through this sentence. A contemporary Jesus would drive off the Jewish Wall Street bankers, just as the historical Jesus drove off the "money changers of the Jerusalem temple."[441] "*Guardian* reporters, writers and editors must be more vigilant about the language they use when writing about Jews or Israel," cautioned Elliott, suggesting that a certain linguistic carelessness was at fault.[442] Of course another, perhaps more plausible possibility exists: the language the writers used accurately reflects their views of Jews and Israel.

It is dismaying that such positions might be called "moderate," more tempered than other representations that leading intellectuals offer. In his widely-praised novel, *Freedom*, Jonathan Franzen describes a dinner party held by a Jewish family—"A house full of Jews!," as a character sarcastically calls it. Repeatedly Franzen emphasizes the characters' Jewishness. "[O]ne of the bald uncles" "regaled" the host's son's friend, Joey, "with an account of his recent vacation-slash-business-trip in Israel." Joey was starting to "long to be more Jewish—to see what this kind of belonging might be like." On cue, the host starts to speak:

> The turkey-like cords in his neck were more noticeable in the flesh than on TV, and it turned out to be the almost shrunken smallness of his skull that made his white, white smile so prominent. The fact that such a wizened person had sired the amazing Jenna seemed to Joey of a piece with his eminence. He spoke of the "new blood libel" that was circulating in the Arab world, the lie about there having been no Jews in the twin towers on 9/11, and of the need, in times of national emergency, to counter evil lies with benevolent half-truths. He spoke of Plato as if he'd personally received enlightenment at his Athenian feet. He referred to members of the president's cabinet by their first names, explaining how "we" had been "leaning on" the president to exploit this unique historical moment to resolve an intractable geopolitical deadlock and radically expand the sphere of freedom. In normal times, he said, the great mass of American public opinion was isolationist and know-nothing, but the terrorist attacks had given "us" a golden opportunity, the first since the end of the Cold War, for "the philosopher" (which philosopher, exactly, Joey wasn't clear on or had missed an earlier reference to) to step in and unite the country behind the mission that his philosophy had revealed as right and necessary. "We have to learn to be comfortable with stretching some facts," he said, with his smile, to an uncle who had mildly challenged him about Iraq's nuclear capabilities. "Our modern media are very blurry shadows on the wall, and the philosopher has to be prepared to manipulate these shadows in the service of a greater truth."[445]

Set in the privacy of the neo-con's home, the scene reveals the truth that his media image hides: what is "more noticeable in the flesh than on TV." He is lying, manipulative, and barely human, small skulled with "turkey-like cords in his neck." Well-healed, he profits on human misery, boasting, "Our fundraising's been off the charts since the attacks."[446] The ugliness of the Jews' physical appearances matches their moral ugliness; "the fact" that one fathered an attractive daughter is presented as startling. To decry Bush Neo-Conservatism, the scene sets aside any moderating wit or novelistic charm. The word "Jewish" keeps reoccurring: it appears ten times in five pages. To borrow a phrase from Eagleton, Franzen exposes what he sees as the workings of "the Jewish ruling caste."

When imagining themselves as Jews, many midcentury non-Jewish authors sought to develop more generous representations than the slurs the previous generation offered, whether Eliot's image of "the jew squats on the window sill, its owner" or Pound's various anti-Semitic rants in poetry and prose.[447] However, they slighted the group they wished to honor. A more direct hostility and condescension has replaced this complicated mix of arrogance, envy, and appreciation. Berryman's imaginary Jew argued with an anti-Semite; Franzen puts the anti-Semite's accusations into a Jewish character's mouth.

Such gestures reinforce a broader cultural logic. If Jews seem unwilling to play their assigned role as sufferers, they no longer are respected. They are a failed metaphor. If their ideas depart from this old narrative, they are told their ideas are not worth hearing or they have no ideas at all. The current movement to boycott Israeli academics, to silence them, is one manifestation of this tendency. When Israeli Ambassador Michael Orin attempted to deliver an invited lecture at the University of California, Irvine, protestors decided not to hold a counter-event or picket the talk. They shouted him down. Of course more sophisticated tactics exist to accomplish similar ends: to banish Jews from the realm of intellectual debate, to pretend they do not or should not exist because their ideas differ from what the others want from them. "I'm the last Jewish intellectual. You don't know anyone else. All your other Jewish intellectuals are now suburban squires. From Amos Oz to all these people here in America. So I'm the last one," explained Edward Said.[448] ■

RICHARD LANDES

Fatal Attraction:
The Shared Antichrist of the Global Progressive Left and Jihad

Summary: In the aughts, the "global, progressive, left" (GPL) adopted a secular version of the Jihadi apocalyptic scapegoating narrative in which Israel and the U.S. are the "great and little Satan" (or vice-versa). This overlap between two ostensibly completely different value systems has served as the basis for mobilizing a common struggle against the U.S. and Israel over the last decade or so. In so doing, the Left has welcomed, within its "anti-imperialist" mobilization, one of the most ferociously imperialist movements in the long and dark history of mankind, one which opposes not merely Israeli and American "imperialism," but also targets the very culture of progressive values—human rights, peace, tolerance for diversity, human freedom—that GPL champions. BDS is a flagship (and symptom) of this self-destructive disorientation wherein progressives join forces with their worst enemies.

Prologue

This essay is not written to persuade the reader that Boycott, Divestment, and Sanctions is a movement unworthy of support by anyone committed to progressive principles. Anyone who compares Israel's human rights record—even the Palestinian version—with the behavioral norms of Arab political culture could not possibly endorse the Arab insistence that Israel be put on the global docket for human rights violations. This is all the more true when one scrutinizes the list of accusations made against Israel and realizes how many accusations are not only false, but in some cases, indicate the exact opposite of their claims.[449] This essay is written rather to explain how such an inversion of moral and empirical reality could have made so much headway in the Western public sphere.

I write this essay as a scholar of millennialism who has been studying the emergence in the last fifteen years of an active, cataclysmic, apocalyptic movement (the most dangerous kind). I also write it as a Jew who began his academic career believing in a self-sustaining, self-critical, democratic public sphere and assuming the fundamental maturity and commitment of its participants. I write in defense of that sphere: for the maturity (and now, courage) of the academic community and, not coincidentally, in defense of my people who are being (successfully) slandered. To those who believe they should listen to the "other," I formally request an audience.

Imagine all the people...

> Imagine there's no countries
> It isn't hard to do
> Nothing to kill or die for
> And no religion too
> Imagine all the people
> Living life in peace ...
> You may say I'm a dreamer
> But I'm not the only one ... (John Lennon, 1971)

And now,
> Imagine there are no countries
> It isn't hard to do
> Something to kill and die for
> And one religion too
> Imagine all the people
> Living life under our peace...
> You may say we're dreamers
> But we're not the only ones...

Welcome to the 21st century.

The Jihadi Apocalyptic Narrative: World Conquest and the Great and Little Satan

An apocalyptic narrative is a cosmic/global story, or scenario, about how, at some point in the future, the forces of good and evil will enter into a final stage of conflict and the good will emerge on the other side to live and share in a just, abundant, peaceful society, while the bad are cast out. The most destructive form of apocalyptic narrative sees a massive battle between the forces of good (us) and evil (them). In the Book of Revelation, for example, the battlefield is littered with the corpses of the slain, upon which the birds of carrion feast—from kings to slaves. In passive apocalyptic scenarios (e.g. Revelation) divine forces carry out the destruction, not humans; in active scenarios, the believers themselves become the divinely appointed agents of that cataclysmic violence. In these latter "active" scenarios, the "them"– the apocalyptic enemy—embody evil; and their elimination brings redemption. Historically, when movements with such violent apocalyptic scenarios gain power, they have proven capable of wholesale massacre and genocide. In the worst cases (five in the last two centuries), this has produced mega-death in the tens of millions of human lives.

Despite the spectacular attacks on the West, most Westerners have little familiarity[451] with the *Jihadi* narrative that animates the movement across a broad range of groups, a narrative that made its first "real-world" appearance in Khoumeini's Iran. It varies significantly in some ways from traditional Muslim apocalyptic thought, which focused on a Last Judgment at the end of the world. Instead, this apocalyptic scenario focuses on a *this*-worldly *millennium* (messianic era) envisioned as the global victory of Islam: when all of Dar al-Harb becomes *Dar al-Islam*.[453] Those who join this movement fight in an apocalyptic battle in which the Jews will be slaughtered and the rest of the harbi would be subjected, either by conversion or by accepting the *dhimma* contract of submission[454]: a "Second Global Islamic Kingdom."[455] Globally, in the battle, no mercy should be shown to those who resist Islam's dominion. Everything to kill and die for: suicide martyrs go straight to heaven; their victims, straight to hell.

Muslim apocalyptic believers hold that virtually all traditional great and small "signs of the end" have been fulfilled in our day with the advent of modernity. The power of the godless West has grown so great that it threatens Islam with annihilation. With its progressive values of tolerance and equality for all, including women, the West incarnates the rebellion against Allah's will, the triumph of diabolic forces, including women misbehaving.[456] And is not that one of the most fatally poisoned "gifts" of a gender-transgressing modernity?

But behind the scenes of this global battle with a modernity that aggressively presses for a civil, tolerant, global community of universal "human rights" lies a second more important battle. The U.S. and the rest of Crusader Christianity (i.e. European West) are mere pawns in a cosmic drama where the Jews have duped and manipulated them. They now serve the Jewish conspiracy to degrade and enslave all of humankind. First the Jews got the Christians to take the tendered bait (democracy), and now they bow to every Jewish whim. And now these Jews, with their duped Crusader Christians, want to similarly degrade Islam:

> the Zionist world government, which governs the entire world . . . the Zionist American government . . . the United Nations and the Security Council . . . the Zionist world government, which are managed from behind the curtain by the Antichrist and Satan, just as the book of Revelation points out.[457]

While this "apocalyptic enemy" working to destroy Islam takes many forms, from military invaders to the NGOs spreading the gospel of "human rights" and "women's equality," none of the enemies loom so central to contemporary Muslim apocalyptic imagination as the Jews. Israel constitutes the most unbearable of the mortal insults to Islam of the modern world. It is an unbearable blasphemy—an independent *dhimmi* state in Dar al-Islam, a beachhead of Western decadence (including women's liberation), an infuriatingly small group of (historically cowardly, i.e. unarmed) Jews who hold their own in wildly asymmetrical fight with Arab might and honor, the headquarters of the conspiracy to exterminate Islam.

But Israel itself is only the visible tip of a vast Jewish conspiracy to enslave mankind, which has already subjected and degraded the Christian World:

> Thus the Jewish slap on the faces of the Christians continues, who apparently enjoy and allow this sort of humiliation and attack, and give them their other cheek so that the Jew can continue to slap the Christians— just as we see—ruling them in Europe through the Masons who dig the grave of Western civilization through corruption and promiscuity. The Crusader West continues like a whore who is screwed sadistically, and does not derive any pleasure from the act until after she is struck and humiliated, even by her pimps—the Jews in Christian Europe. Soon they will be under the rubble as a result of the Jewish conspiracy.[458]

And having accomplished that, the Jewish conspiracy now manipulates Christians into inflicting the same subjection on the Muslim world. Israel is the "Great Satan."

Traditional Muslim apocalyptic writing has few references to the Jews since, for most of Islam's fourteen-century-long existence, the Christians presented the military foe. With the advent of Israel, however, everything changed: for Muslims the world over, and especially for Arab Muslims neighboring her, Israel posed the most terrifying threat. The embodiment of a modernity that has repeatedly eluded the other countries in the Middle East, tiny Israel has managed to win war after war with a vastly more powerful enemy. The humiliation, on a global scale, embodies the catastrophe (Naqba) of history gone wrong.

Muslim apocalyptic literature responded with a previously rarely invoked hadith that declared that the Day of Judgment (i.e. the Day of Vindication for the true followers of Muhammad and Allah) will not come until Muslims kill every last Jew:

> The day will not come until the Muslims fight the Jews, and the Jews will hide behind rocks and trees, and the trees and the rocks will say, "*O Muslim, O servant of Allah, there is a Jew behind me, come and kill him.*"

Hamas cites this hadith as a call to action in its charter (¶7); and its theologians developed the justification for "Shahid operations," even though Sharia forbids suicide, as a sacred duty in the apocalyptic battle.[459] Most recently, a Hamas official has expressed his dual preference for the fate of the Jews: dead in Palestine, dhimmi elsewhere:

> We must massacre [the Jews] . . . to prevent them from sowing corruption in the world . . . We must restore them to the state of humiliation imposed upon them . . . They must pay the jizya security tax while they live in our midst . . . However, in Palestine, where they are occupiers and invaders, they cannot have the status of *dhimmis*.[460]

In short, Jihad views its path to global domination via a genocide against Jews in Israel.

Nor will Allah abandon his faithful in this time of need. He only asks that those faithful take up Jihad and strive with every fiber of their being for the promised victory: the global Caliphate. Now is the time when one must fight back. Now is the time to destroy the conspiracy. Now is the time to restore Islam to its rightful place, dominating the world.[461] Indeed, the very process of modern globalization that has so terribly humiliated Islam will become the vehicle for Islam's global domination. Western global hegemony is the *Praeparatio Califatae*.[462] The day will come when Muslims will have uprooted Israel, when the green flag of Islam will fly from the White House, when the Queen of England will wear a burkah.

The current generation of apocalyptic Jihadis agree that virtually all preliminary signs of the Last Days have been fulfilled in our day.[463] They live in apocalyptic time; and they have identified the apocalyptic enemy against whom they fight in this final war of extermination. The overwhelming choice in the literature—to the point of monotony—is some combination of the U.S. and Israel: "the Great and Little Satan."[464] And it is the sacred task of the Jihadis to destroy that enemy in order to redeem the world by the global imposition of Sharia.

Implementing Jihad while Militarily Weak: Cognitive Warfare

But world history abounds with dreamers, some haters, some lovers, who *saw* the brave new world on the other side of present excruciating suffering, and never got beyond the suffering. Rather, they ended up amplifying it. Millennial studies is littered with the cases of believers suffering tribulations at the hands of their enemies that they had, only recently, so confidently predicted *for* their enemies.[465] Jihadi plans, however compelling, however desirable for some, were more than a tall order. In the 20th century, when the West dominated the globe, it seemed a ludicrous quest. It meant conducting an asymmetrical war of conquest in which you must convince your enemy, whom you could never defeat in an open fight, to surrender without using his vastly superior strength. For a movement with so appalling an ideology to succeed in a world committed to human rights for all seemed improbable, indeed unthinkable.

Thus, looking into the future from the 1990s (1410s AH), when global Jihad was still on the margins of even the Muslim world (if only because it was so implausible), a Jihadi warrior, intent on destroying the godless West and imposing a Sharia-ruled *Dar al-Islam* on the world was just a dreamer, if not the only one. Practically speaking (from the Western point of view), no asymmetrical conflict could be more lopsided than the one Jihadis waged against them, and Westerners reacted with amusement if not disdain at the news of Jihadi intentions.

So, at least in its initial stages, the Jihadi strategy in the West had to be circumspect. It was far too soon for any kind of military invasion. Global Jihad had first to conduct a cognitive war that convinced the infidels whom they invaded not to use their superior power and resist, not to fight back, but to submit, to act like *dhimmi* ("protected" infidels) even before the conquest, to cooperate with the Jihadi occupation of their lands. In Jihadi terms, this is *Da'wa* or "summons" to convert or submit to Islam without the necessity of conquest. As one of the major figures in Islam today, Sheikh Yussuf al-Qaradawi, put it: "We will conquer Europe, we will conquer America! Not through sword but through Da'wa."[466] Thus, were the Jihadi in the year 2000 to formulate a prayer of beseeching to Allah to further His divinely appointed global mission, it might have run as follows.

Jihadi Prayer to Allah for Useful Infidels

"Oh Allah, the all Merciful, give us enemies who…

…help us to disguise our ambitions, even our acts of war, blinding themselves to our deployment targeting them.

…accept those of us who fight with da'wah as "moderates" who have nothing to do with the violent "extremists."

…choose these false "moderates" as advisors and consultants in intelligence and police services, and as community liaison.

…verbally attack anyone, including Muslims, who criticize Islam as Islamophobes.

…believe that, "except for a tiny minority," the "vast majority" of Muslims are moderate and peaceful; that we are a "Religion of Peace."

…adopt our apocalyptic enemy as theirs, so that they join us in an attack on one of their key allies.

…legitimate our terrorism as "resistance" and denounce any recourse to violence in their own defense as "terrorism."

…respect the dignity of our beliefs even as we heap disdain on theirs.

…believe us when we invoke human rights to defend Jihadis and attack them.

…introduce our intimidating "Street" in the heart of their capital cities.

And may those who so act, play prominent roles in their public sphere."

On the face of it, it's hard to imagine that such an implausible prayer could be answered. Granted there have been "useful idiots" in the West—indeed some of the West's greatest minds, like Shaw and Sartre—but they were blinded by the dazzling promise of freedom and equality proffered by Marxism. They fought for a progressive dream however twisted by the totalitarian impulse implementing it. Surely now, after both the Holocaust and the revelations of the tens of millions of people killed by Communism, any sane progressive would refuse the demand to empower another, even cruder, round of people aspiring to mega-death wars and Jewish genocide.[467] And were there some such useful infidels among the progressive left, surely they'd be a tiny minority, not a critical mass capable of promoting and adopting suicidal policies that played into the hands of so terrible an imperialist enemy.

And yet, beginning in the new century, from October 2000 more specifically, there emerged a widespread, programmatic "anti-imperialist," "anti-war" alliance between the Global Progressive Left and the Global Jihadi Right.[468] This alliance displayed itself most prominently in massive global demonstrations denouncing the U.S. and Israel, in journalism, in academia, in international NGOs, and in the various forums of UN sponsored globalization.[469] BDS is one of the more sustained initiatives of this alliance in which, while progressives imagine they stand shoulder to shoulder with other global anti-imperialists in opposing war, racism, and xenophobia, their Jihadi comrades in arms cannot believe how easily they convince progressives to support their imperialist war: the 21st century Jihadi does indeed face the foe of his dreams and prayers.[470]

When Bin Laden struck the Twin Towers, for example, Jean Baudrillard, French post-modern intellectual and theorist, spoke for many who rejoiced at the blow to an American hegemony, so oppressive, so suffocating:

> the prodigious jubilation engendered by witnessing this global superpower being destroyed; better, by seeing it more or less self-destroying, even suiciding spectacularly. Though it is (this superpower) that has, through its unbearable power, engendered all that violence brewing around the world, and therefore this terrorist imagination, which—unknowingly—inhabits us all. . . . In the end, they did it; we wanted it.[471]

Rather than what many (especially in the U.S. and Israel) thought, namely that the attack would lead to a strengthening of the transatlantic alliance and a resolve to oppose Jihad, 9-11 actually produced widespread anti-Americanism and anti-Zionism,[472] which only grew stronger over the course of the decade,[473] including the spread of conspiracy-thinking about 9-11 that literally absolved the Jihadis and indicted the US and Israel as participants in a right-wing plot.[474]

By the time the collective voice of global morality, in the tens of millions world-wide, protested Bush's war in 2003, the image of the GPL's Antichrist had taken shape: a combination of Nazism, Capitalism, US Imperialism, and Zionism.

Antichrist of the Left: San Francisco "Anti-War" Rally, 2003.

Some years later, Judith Butler, reigning queen of post-modern theory, mistook imperial anti-Americanism for anti-imperialism and, despite being a pacifist, agreed that Hamas and Hizbullah belonged on the GPL. And by 2009, speakers and protesters of the IDF's "Operation Cast Lead" in Gaza, shouted "We are Hamas!" Had you told a signer of the paranoid, genocidal Hamas Charter in 1988 that, within twenty years, anti-war Western infidels would march in the streets of European capitals shouting "Victory to Hamas!"[475] he would have laughed out loud.

But, you object, this is only the crazy left, the most extreme "revolutionaries." And in its most absurd formulations, as above, that may be true. The problem arises from the use of the word "only." While most disavow the more extreme formulations, they have nonetheless been drawn into the orbit of a more powerful vortex, either by sins of commission or omission. As Norman Cohn noted:

> It is a great mistake to suppose that the only writers who matter are those whom the educated in their saner moments can take seriously. There exists a subterranean world where pathological fantasies disguised as ideas are churned out by crooks and half-educated fanatics for the benefit of the ignorant and superstitious. There are times when this underworld emerges from the depths and suddenly fascinates, captures, and dominates multitudes of usually sane and responsible people, who thereupon take leave of sanity and responsibility. And it occasionally happens that this underworld becomes a political power and changes the course of history.[476]

How and when does this happen? How do such unsound—and deeply destructive—beliefs surge from the primordial muck of human ambition and hatred and move to the center of a public sphere? In the aughts, Jihadis invaded the West most successfully via its soft underbelly: Anti-Zionism.

Anti-Zionism, the Soft Underbelly of the West: Lethal Narratives, Moral Schadenfreude, and Radical Disorientation

For the West, especially for the anti-imperialists, nothing could be more catastrophic than a Jihadi victory over Israel. For Jihadis, Israel's demise would signal a victory of immense symbolic power, far greater than taking over Iran or chasing the Russians from Afghanistan. It would decisively change the direction of sacred and global history.[477] The destruction of Israel would revive Arab pride and Muslim confidence that their religion will dominate, even as it would reveal the weakness of the West, which, in failing to defend Israel, sacrificed an ally to curry favor with an enemy. It would sound a clarion call to the whole world that Jihad was "the strong horse." It would encourage a new round of recruiting, a new round of intimidating public behavior targeting infidel civilians, a new round of terrorist attacks, be they planned or rogue outbursts. And this increased aggression would target a weakened West.

Getting the West to adopt so self-destructive a policy would not be easy. While the Jihadis may have made friends with some of the more radical elements in Western culture, there were still important areas of resistance, where the right of Jews to exercise sovereignty and not depend on the good will of others, was a mainstay of the moral political order. Where Europeans felt a debt of guilt to a people they had despised and violated for over a millennium, anti-Semitism was one of the worst accusations one might throw at a public figure. And America both politically and socially supported Israel in profound ways.

The Jihadi had to succeed in two ways: first, convince Westerners that they were neither anti-Semitic nor aggressors; second, convince Westerners to embrace a narrative in which the conflict was entirely Israel's fault, and peace impossible without its elimination. Without affecting decision-making elites, who, in democratic countries, would need the support of an important body of public opinion, Jihadis could not expect the West to sacrifice Israel in an effort to curry Arab favor, especially as Arab behavior became more aggressive. Somehow, they had to convince more moderate progressives and liberals to abandon Israel, if not in one fell swoop, at least in salami tactics that fatally weakened her. A tall order.

And yet, in the course of the first years of the 21st century, the Jihadis won signal victories in this anti-Zionist battle, victories whose momentum continues to carry them forward, largely unopposed. The mechanics (or dynamics) of those victories work along the following lines: Western journalists working in the Middle East, responding to the stick of intimidation on the one hand and the carrot of advocacy journalism on the other, repeatedly mainstreamed, *as news*, Jihadi war propaganda against Israel—framed in the post-colonial narrative of the aggressive, imperialist Israeli Goliath against the plucky, resisting Palestinian David.[478] Some of this propaganda had an electric effect: angry demonstrations repeatedly filled the streets of Western and Muslim capitals denouncing Israel in lurid terms and affirming solidarity with its Jihadi enemies. International "human rights" NGOs supplied journalists with lethal narratives, who in turn amplified their harsh criticisms. Academics pressed the conflict into the procrustean bed of post-colonialism, in which Israel was the last remnant of racist Western imperialism. And Jews, even Jews claiming to be "pro-Israel," made loud protestations of their horror at Israeli behavior. Western intellectual elites showed an almost insatiable appetite for stories about Israel behaving badly.

The key moment when the GPL lost its moral bearings was in late 2000. A voice that had previously had limited impact on the larger discussion now came suddenly and powerfully to the fore, to the center of the discourse: virulent Anti-Zionism. While some marginal voices on the extreme edges of both right and left had adopted the Palestinian claim that they were the new Jews and the Israelis the new Nazis,[479] and while under combat conditions, journalists found it tempting to liken Israel to Nazi Germany (however unsupportable the comparison),[480] not until the new century did the narrative that Israel was a racist, Nazi state bent on the genocide of the Palestinian people find much traction in the Western public sphere.

There is nothing intrinsically apocalyptic about the image of Muhammad al Durah, a twelve year old boy allegedly shot to death in the arms of his father by IDF troops at Netzarim Junction in the Gaza Strip on September 30, 2000.[481] As a piece of war propaganda, designed to stir hatred and a burning passion for revenge, it was well played and skillfully manipulated by Palestinian authorities. Palestinian TV played the footage with martial music in the background, spliced tape of an Israeli soldier firing a rifle into the footage just before Muhammad al Durah dies, thus identifying the IDF criminal targeting the boy.[482]

The image, however, rapidly took on mythical proportions in the Muslim public sphere: a symbol of the Al Aqsa Intifada and a fabulous recruiting device for global Jihad. Music videos by the most popular singers and poets called on other children to join the boy in martyrdom. Poets sang the martyr's praises. Osama bin Laden seized upon the tale as a central element in his recruiting video for global Jihad, thrusting before the viewer the images, even as a tremulous voice recited poetry condemning the Jews for the death, and excoriating Arab rulers for failing to take vengeance.

Jihadis seized this war propaganda and made it into a blood libel: "In killing this child, the Israelis have [revealed their intention to have] killed all the children in the world," Bin Laden declared.[483] Muhammad's "murder" offered a warrant for apocalyptic genocide. The first suicide terrorists invoked his vengeance, and their approval ratings among fellow Palestinians shot from 30% to 80%. Even "moderate" Imams who forbade suicide martyrdom granted its legitimacy against Israel. During the Jenin operation against that all-out terror campaign, Sheikh Ibrahim Mahdi referred to the genocidal hadith of "the rocks and trees":

> We believe in this Hadith. We are convinced also that this Hadith heralds the spread of Islam and its rule over all the land . . . Oh Allah, annihilate the Jews and their supporters . . . Oh Allah, raise the flag of Jihad across the land . . . Oh beloved, look to the East of the earth, find Japan and the ocean; look to the West of the earth, find [some] country and the ocean.

Be assured that these will be owned by the Muslim nation, as the *Hadith* says, 'from the ocean to the ocean.'[484]

From genocide of the Jews to conquest of the world.[485]

The most surprising, most powerful symbolic response, however, came not from Muslims, but from Europeans who enthusiastically embraced this tale as true and deeply meaningful, as the emblem of Palestinian suffering and merciless Israeli killing of the innocent. Indeed, completely independently of the real conflict, the Al Durah icon had the mythical power to reshape the historical narrative. It "proved" the substitution theology whereby the Israelis are the new Nazis and the Palestinians the new Jews, and permitted progressives in the West to shift allegiance fully to the side of the subaltern, to help him disseminate propaganda for a war in which they themselves were prime targets.

It explained everything: why Muslims hated Jews and why Jews deserved that hatred; what the problem was—Israel—and how to fix it. Perhaps precisely because it was under the apocalyptic radar, dressed up as a news item about something that really happened, and something that "fit" perfectly into the post-colonial paradigm, it played so pivotal a role in mainstreaming the most virulent anti-Zionism among the Western GPL. In Paris, organizations with progressive names like Mobilization against Racism (MRAP) joined groups of North African immigrants waving Hamas and Hizbullah flags and holding aloft a great banner using al Durah to equate Israel with the Nazis, and shouted "Death to the Jews!" for the first time in Europe since the Nazis. The leftist participants neither distanced themselves from that genocidal cry, nor did they denounce the wave of attacks on European Jews that followed.

AUTHOR'S COLLECTION

Paris: Place de Republique, October 6, 2000.

Were one to use the language of medieval religious movements, "le petit Mohamed," as the French call him, was the patron saint of a secular replacement theology in which Israel became the new Nazis (for post-war Westerners, the embodiment of evil), and the Palestinians the new Jews. Nor did such extravagant symbolic rhetoric remain on the fringes. Catherine Nay, respected Europe 1 news anchor, spelled out the meaning of that graphic: "This death," she intoned "replaces, erases, the picture of the boy in the Warsaw Ghetto." Thus the image of a child reportedly killed in a war zone replaced an image that symbolized the deliberate murder of one million children. Despite the staggering disorientation involved in such a moral judgment, Nay spoke for many.[487]

One can find no single incident, no single symbol more apt to identify the folly of Europeans embracing this *icon of hatred*. Even as they repeatedly waved the image, a "get out of Holocaust guilt" card, before their audiences on TV, they unwittingly waved the flag of Jihad before the eyes of their restive Muslim immigrant population. Within years, their streets were filled with rioters who firebombed churches, synagogues, and cars yelling "Allahu Akhbar," and their prisons filled with Jihadis whose first call to arms came when they saw images of Muslim suffering run on Western TV.[488] How often in history have nations energetically disseminated the war propaganda of their deadliest enemies, much less warmly embraced them? How often have civilizations adopted an apocalyptic narrative that targeted them?

Lines of Diffusion: From Durban to BDS

One of the key elements in this tale is the role of "human rights" NGOs. In August of 2001, the UN held a global conference dedicated to combating racism and other forms of discrimination in Durban, South Africa. The conference rapidly descended into an orgy of hatred directed not at the world's current practitioners of slavery and genocide, but at the USA and Israel who, inundated with hostility, withdrew from the conference rather than accord it legitimacy. Yasser Arafat brought Jamal al Durah with him in his personal jet, and Al Durah, paraded in effigy, presided as patron martyr of the gathering.

At Durban, NGOs from the West and the third world gathered to denounce Israel as a racist state, and although the final drafts of resolutions watered down some of the most extreme language, they resulted in "the Durban Strategy":

> The Durban conference crystallized the strategy of delegitimizing Israel as "an apartheid regime" through international isolation based on the South African model. This plan is driven by UN-based groups as well as non-governmental organizations (NGOs), which exploit the funds, slogans and rhetoric of the human rights movement.[489]

At Durban the two unlikely allies, progressive Westerners and Jihadi imperialists, agreed upon a global strategy to destroy Israel. Knowingly or not, the GPL had adopted the Jihadi Dajjal as *their* enemy.

One group that formed in the immediate aftermath of the Al Durah incident, half a world away at the University of California, Berkeley, home to a (near) venerable tradition of radical politics, called themselves "Students for Justice in Palestine" (SJP). They and their allies would serve on campus as the cutting edge of the Jihadi cogwar: spreading destructive narratives about Israel, mobilizing support for its ostracization, allying with other radical Islamic groups, a strategy which took on new proportions with the inauguration in 2004 of Israel Apartheid Week. They subsequently spread to every major college campus, and constituted the most militant segment of the BDS movement. They are the ones whose latent violence keeps hostility focused on the Israelis, even among some who find themselves in the middle of a movement that is being hijacked, yet fear, with good cause, to say something. They are the violence lurking behind the "summons."

And the key to their success is *moral* outrage over Israel: Israel is so evil, so beyond the pale of moral discussion, that even to defend her is heinous and blameworthy. Shout down such terrible creatures.[491] This attitude, which first appeared in more radical circles in the early aughts (from Al Durah 2000 to Durban 2001), rapidly went mainstream. In 2002 the BBC's equivalent of Larry King had a discussion on the topic: "Whether Israel is a morally repugnant society."[492] Now, on campuses across the country, the answer is in: it is so repugnant that no one should dare try and defend her.

This is, of course, the Israel of Palestinian war propaganda disseminated and amplified as real news by hostile journalists—the child murderers, the slaughterers of civilian populations, the ruthless enemies of mankind, the *Dajjal*. This moral outrage targeting a scapegoat is classic fascism (in the sense of what was worst about the fascists). One should not appease such demands, *especially* in the case of scapegoating the Jews. Given the long and complex history of the West's handling of the Jewish "other,"[493] one might expect some circumspection here before leaping to such conclusions. Indeed, one might expect enough people to be courageous enough to challenge those making that leap.

Alas, this narrative about an evil Israel beyond the pale has been fully adopted and tirelessly purveyed by the GPL over the last fifteen years: the ruthless, colonial, racist imperialists, the post-colonial Antichrist.[494] If one wants to gauge how deeply the Israel=Nazi=Dajjal apocalyptic trope has penetrated the Western public sphere, look for the degree to which this loud, incensed moral indignation dominates the BDS discussion, justified in the name of "freedom of speech": after all, who could defend the Nazis.[495] Here, the civic guerrilla tactics of the sixties operate in alliance with, or in the service of, the worst enemies of civil society imaginable. These progressives, who think that by bringing Israel low they can then move on to further "human rights" victories, actually empower their enemies. Once Israel is eliminated, *they* are the low-hanging fruit, not the rest of the world's human rights abusers and racists.[496] In a remarkable and terrifying way, at least where Israel is concerned, the GPL has turned into the *dhimmi* soldiers of global Jihad.

On Jewish Self-Criticism

Of course, no Jewish text written for a larger audience, especially a text critical of non-Jews, can go out without some words of criticism for Jews. So let me identify one of the greatest contributors to the ability of the Jihadis to enlist the progressive left in their ranks, one that permits the false consciousness of good intentions—this is for *peace*! —to operate far longer than it should among people who unintentionally but consistently contribute to war. In leadership positions both within the BDS movement and supporting it from without, there are a host of Jewish progressives who want to show their commitment to world redemption by accepting the lethal narratives about Israel, and thus *prove* their bona fides. Scholars have extensively chronicled this old and disturbing phenomenon that goes back at least a millennium.[497]

In the wake of Al Durah, for example, a new contingent of such Jews cropped up with particular vigor in France, people who had made careers as successful if invisible Jews, all of a sudden feeling they must, "as a Jew…" denounce the crimes of the Israelis. These "alter-juifs," as their critics call them, dominated public discussion in the aughts.[498] In Anthony Julius' apt phrase, they're "proud to be ashamed to be Jew."[499] Anyone who had the slightest whiff of *communautarisme* (partisanship) got sidelined.[500] Among such Jews, we find Judith Butler, who applies her most stringent standards of pacifism to Judaism (thou shalt not exercise sovereignty) even as she accepts Hamas and Hizbullah into the "anti-imperialist" global progressive left.[501] Indeed, one might even identify an actual *religious* movement among such Jews, a *tikkun olam* (repairing the world) that believes that in sacrificing Israel, Jews will contribute to global peace.[502]

This is a messianic syndrome, a kind of masochistic omnipotence fantasy, in which, since everything is *our* (we Jews') fault. If only we could change, we could fix everything. It invokes the prophetic tradition to insist on moral perfectionism, although the prophets did not write their scathing (and rhetorically inflated) criticism for a non-Jewish audience. It's not enough for these Jewish critics that Israel matches or surpasses every marker of the most "advanced" armies in respect for enemy civilian lives, for the civic and human rights of populations in wartime, for tolerance of criticism. No. Israel must live up to its own exalted standards. And anything short of that standard deserves public denunciation in the most uncompromising rhetoric.[503]

We end up with a post-modern moral inversion. If the tribal attitude is "my side right or wrong," and the civil attitude is "whoever's right, my side or not," then one current position has become, "their side right or wrong." Some Jews have become leaders in the poisonous marriage of pre-modern sadism—"you, the imperialist, racist whites are evil and we must kill you"—and post-modern masochism—"you, the subaltern indigenes, are right; we deserve it." Hence, Jews, even Israelis, who compare their own people to Nazis.

Of all the Western answers to the Jihadi prayer for allies, none have proven so valuable: they gave legitimacy to his master narratives even as they attack as "Israel-firsters" those who resist. Of all the people duped by Jihadis,

PART IV

THE ISRAELI CONTEXT

ILAN TROEN

The Campaign to Boycott Israeli Universities:
Historical and Ideological Sources

Introduction

The Arab/Israeli conflict has taken many forms, including the current call to boycott Israeli higher education. This movement is part of a continuing challenge to the legitimacy of a Jewish state and even a Jewish presence in *Eretz Israel* (The Land of Israel). It is based not merely in opposition to specific policies of different governments. Rather, it has deep cultural and ideological roots that have been expressed repeatedly in various tactics over the past century. At its core, it is the legitimacy of a Jewish state and the idea that Palestine should contain a "Jewish" homeland that are at issue.

The sources of opposition have been varied but often complement each other. The common thread is that Jews are foreign to a country that belongs only to Arab "natives" who are viewed as the sole people indigenous to the country. Zionism is thereby rejected as irrevocably and permanently Western and but another form of colonialism. The current furor over an academic boycott is but the most recent ploy camouflaged as an appeal to human rights by fabrications of the reality on the ground. Stated differently, alleged human rights abuses are not the issue; Israel's existence is under attack.

I will first review the history of boycotts against the Jews of Palestine and Israel. I will then examine where denying the authentic Jewish connection to the land has infiltrated various academic disciplines. This will explain how false accusations have gained such traction in recent decades. Tracing this development is important for understanding the current moves to delegitimate the Zionist project. Until recently, this account of the Jews' right to a homeland was unquestioned in scholarship and in world politics. Otherwise, Zionism would not have won international approval for a Jewish state.

The Beginning of Arab Boycotts

Boycotts of Jews and of Israel are not new to the Arab/Israeli conflict. They first occurred in 1922, 26 years before Israel's formal establishment. At that time, the League of Nations issued a Mandate for Palestine. It included a legal basis for the right of the Jewish people to establish a homeland in Palestine and the recognized right of Zionist institutions to become the official instrument for Jewish settlement. These first boycotts targeted Jewish merchants in Jerusalem as well as Arab businesses that engaged in commerce with Jews. This ineffective gesture became a precedent during the countrywide Arab uprising in 1929 against the British Mandate and the developing Jewish presence in Palestine. During the 1930s, further sporadic attempts were made. These too were ineffective since Jewish physicians, hospitals, and businesses were essential to the functioning of the country and served both the Arab and Jewish communities.[505]

The boycott movement advanced beyond Palestine in 1945 when Middle Eastern states created the Arab League. They called for an economic boycott, declaring that "Jewish products and manufactured [goods] in Palestine shall be undesirable in the Arab countries" since their purchase could lead "to the realization of the Zionist political objectives." The successful defense of the UN partition plan by Palestine's Jews and the creation of the State of Israel led to a further expansion of the Arab League boycott. Arab states called upon the world community to avoid economic and political relations with Israel. Nevertheless, Israel became a member of the United Nations. Here, too, the boycott had limited practical effect. Israelis drank Coca Cola and purchased French cars rather than Pepsi Cola and Japanese automobiles when these foreign companies succumbed to Arab pressure.[506]

In subsequent decades, the Israeli economy enjoyed one of the highest growth rates in the world. By 1980, an ineffective boycott movement began to crumble as major actors in the Arab/Israeli conflict decided to accommodate to Israel. In the course of signing peace treaties with Israel, Egypt in 1979, the Oslo Accords with the Palestinian Authority in 1993, and then agreement with Jordan in 1994, these three entities ended cooperation with the boycott movement, and additional countries soon followed. At present, Israel has significant if unpublicized relations with many Arab and Muslim countries if not through direct commerce then through transshipment of goods. The ultimate futility of the boycott is manifestly demonstrated by Israel's acceptance into the OECD (Organization for Economic Co-operation and Development), the elite club of economically advanced and politically progressive states, in 2010.

An academic boycott is likely to be equally futile. Israel has the most advanced system of higher education and modern scientific research in that part of the world. Its relationships with the centers of world science are deep and mutually beneficial. The number and amount of grants and academic partnerships with Israeli higher education may well be unparalleled for a society of its size. Thus the call for an academic boycott is rather a gesture intended to pressure Israel. By questioning Israel's legitimacy it casts Israel as a pariah state. As demonstrated elsewhere in this volume, Palestinian Arabs in Israel are themselves major participants in Israeli higher education. Moreover, there are extensive relations between students, faculty, and researchers in both Israeli and Palestinian institutions. Given that the call to an academic boycott would surely be fruitless and injure Palestinians themselves, it behooves us to uncover and address the real sources of such persistent anti-Israeli activity.

The Ideological Roots of the Contemporary Boycott

For all the practical and public success Israel has achieved, it has been rhetorically branded a pariah of the world community. In 1975 the United Nations General Assembly Resolution 3379 infamously associated Zionism with colonialism, racism, and apartheid. In 1991 the United Nations repealed this canard. Despite the retraction, the charge is repeated. It has continued to echo in various United Nations organs and committees, most notably in the Durban conference of 2001 and in successor gatherings where collections of NGOs repeat the "Zionism is racism" mantra, ostensibly in an effort to advance human rights.[507]

This accusation is the fundamental basis for justifying BDS. It is noteworthy that the US, western states, and others boycotted these conferences in protest at the hijacking of an important UN initiative for a narrow and noxious Arab-inspired agenda. This fault line between supporters and opponents of Israel has become an all-too-common source of upheaval in international relations.

The assault on Israel's legitimacy draws on several different and even contending sources that coalesce to make common cause against Zionism. There is an odd alliance of Muslim Fundamentalists, secular Arab nationalists, leftist intellectuals (including some from Israel), and even self-styled "progressive"

Jews who privilege nationalism for other peoples while denying this right to fellow Jews. They all agree that Jews are not "natives." They belong elsewhere. Only the Arab is a true native and entitled to dominance in the country.

We should begin with a brief exposition of Zionist claims and why they trumped the opposition for much of the past century. This will make sharper the paradigm shift when we examine the litany of anti-Zionist and anti-Jewish claims that have taken hold in the academy since the 1970s.

Affirming the Jewish Connection to Eretz Israel

Zionists who made *aliyah*—or immigrated into Palestine—from the end of the 19th century yearned for a natural and direct connection with the country. The phrase employed in the 1922 League of Nations Mandate for Palestine and repeated throughout the discourse on the relationship of Jews to the country reflects what once had been common wisdom. The Mandate's preamble thus asserted that "recognition has thereby been given to the historical connection of the Jewish people with Palestine and to the grounds for *reconstituting* [my emphasis] their national home in that country."[508] "*Re*-constitution" had a shared meaning found in other key concepts widely employed in describing Zionism: *re*-turn, *re*-claim, *re*-build, *re*-store. The reiterated "*re*," or "again," was crucial. It reiterated that the relationship between *Eretz Israel* and Jews had never been lost and that it was now being renewed. The sense of recapturing identity with the Land of Israel has been brilliantly detailed in Neumann's *Land and Desire in Early Zionism*. Pioneers were at one with a land where they had come to invest their sweat, tears, joy, and blood. Termed "sabras"[the cactus fruit found in much of the countryside] by the 1930s, their offspring were natives, the natural realization of the longing to return to build and be rebuilt in their historic homeland.[509]

In this view, Jews were a people, entitled to a state located in the land where they had originated, where they had been resident continually for millennia and in the region where they still constituted a vital presence in proximate areas of North Africa and throughout the Middle East.

Such formal recognition by international bodies was bolstered by evidence of reconstitution that solidified the argument for legitimacy. It was on this basis that in November 1947 the United Nations recommended partition of Palestine into an Arab and a Jewish state. Perhaps the most manifest or visible evidence was the revival of Hebrew; marking the landscape with a Jewish identity as well as working it with their own labor; and the development of an indigenous culture with roots in the ancient past. For most observers, it looked like Jews really belonged and fit in with the landscape.

Cultural Reconstitution

Notice that Zionism created a society unlike other European colonies or "imagined communities."[510] Zionists explicitly distanced themselves in crucial ways from the exile they left behind. They never imagined their polity tied to a European state nor did they aim to transplant European culture whole. Rather, they consciously and overtly sought independence from the European past in their effort to restore Jewish and Hebrew culture. A prime example is the singular success of making Hebrew into a living spoken language with a vibrant popular literature, modern media, scientific scholarship, commerce, and politics. No other ancient language has been so revived in the modern world and reconstructed for everyday purposes. In fact, more people—the Jewish and Arab citizens of Israel—speak Hebrew as a living modern language than many contemporary languages spoken in European states. A Nobel Prize was awarded to a modern Hebrew author (Agnon), world class science is written in the language, and award winning films are made in Hebrew. In Zionist praxis, cultural production in Hebrew has become a large-scale, conscious, and well-publicized enterprise with the object of transforming immigrants into natives.

Zionism also set out to "re-imagine" or "re-constitute" the landscape. The process had begun with Christian explorers, archaeologists, and bible scholars from Europe and the United States who visited Palestine from the mid-19th century when the country was under Turkish rule. They recognized contemporary Arab names as adaptations or corruptions of ancient designations found in Hebrew sacred texts or other historical sources. Zionist settlers continued the process not merely to recapture the Holy Land of Scriptures but, in a deeply personal attempt, to re-imagine themselves in the land of their ancestors. As a consequence, in Israel there is no New Vilna, New Bialystock, New Warsaw, New England, New Amsterdam, New York, or Oxford, Cambridge, Paris, Berlin and so on. Instead, Zionists celebrated the return to history of Biblical Rehovoth and Ashkelon. Jerusalem, of course, did not require a new name. They recalled Jewish history and celebrated local flora in naming streets, public squares, and the landscape, with signs in Hebrew everywhere. All this made manifest that it was native sons and daughters returning from exile who established the settlements as part of a national revival.[511]

The return to the land succeeded. It was this hard won success that convinced a large portion of the world community that Jews were entitled to independence within that portion of the country they had so distinctively marked and worked. This appreciation predates the tragedy of the Holocaust and continued beyond it. The Zionist cause was recognized as an expression of the vital Jewish connection to Palestine, a land that could serve as a home-land as no other venue could.

De-Judaizing *Eretz Israel* in the Academy

Contemporary moves to identify Zionism with colonialism originated in debates over the disposition of Palestine after the British Mandate. These debates, outside the academy, began in the 1930s. George Antonius, a leading Lebanese Christian intellectual, scholar, and public servant who served under the British in Palestine and spent much time in London, blatantly denied the validity of Jewish "reconstitution." He systematically set forth his views in the period's most influential pro-Arab volume, *The Arab Awakening* (1938). The work begins with an historical analysis of how the Arabs emerged in history, and concludes with a survey of their situation after World War I. An attack on the validity of Zionist claims is the closing chapter.[512]

Antonius argues that the Arabs of Palestine have deep roots in the land. Their unbroken connection far precedes the Muslim conquests of the 7th century and actually extends to the Canaanite period before the invasion of the Hebrews. In sum, he claims Palestine has been Arab since time immemorial, absorbing one conqueror after another. Moreover, Arabs are the only authentic, long-resident, and indigenous population. Wresting them of their land, Antonius warns, invites active and justified resistance. Importantly, this definition can be applied to both Christian and Muslim Arabs, and is so understood by both. Jews are another matter. The Hebrews' connection to the land was interrupted and lapsed. The ancient Hebrews no longer exist; contemporary Jews are merely members of a religious confessional community. While Judaism survived, the Jewish people did not. They have disappeared.

Some context is necessary to clarify how this redefinition of Jews countered the Zionist program. In the post-WWI world, "people" enjoy the right to claim a state. Wilson's "Fourteen Points," the creation of the League of Nations and of the United Nations reflected the belief that peoples are essential actors in history and are thereby entitled to states. This idea is rooted in European thought after the French Revolution. Freedom and liberty could not just happen. They had to be implemented by political communities organized around distinct peoples. In this context, nationalism was a progressive ideal that would promote the Enlightenment's highest political values.

To remove the Jewish people from history as a way to fight Zionism was not merely a technique of Arab writers. It may have reached its largest audience through the work of Arnold Toynbee, another former British official and intellectual familiar with Antonius. Toynbee, in a particularly offensive if stunning phrase, described Jews as "fossils," thereby vitiating the Zionist claim for *restoration* —his term for *reconstitution*. It was this charge that occasioned well-publicized debates in the 1950s and 1960s between Toynbee and Abba Eban as well as leading Jewish scholars.[513]

The view championed by Antonius and Toynbee is a staple in Arab public documents and debates over the future of Palestine. It underlies anti-Israel discourse throughout the Arab world. The PLO's National Charter of 1968 echoes Antonius in the often cited paragraph 20: "*The claim of historical or spiritual links between the Jews and Palestine is neither in conformity with historical fact nor does it satisfy the requirements for statehood. Judaism is a revealed religion; it is not a separate nationality.*" That is, Judaism as a religion exists, but Jews as a people do not. Similarly, the Hamas Charter of 1988 endorses this view and wraps it in Islamic theology so that the anti-colonial war becomes *jihad*. Whatever the discourse, secular or religious, detaching Jews from their nationality has become integral to justifying violence and the destruction of a Jewish state.

Anti-Zionism in the Contemporary Academy

Probably the most significant contemporary scholarly corpus that advanced Palestine's de-Judaization is Edward Said's work. Said, another Christian intellectual, identified himself as Arab—in this case a Palestinian—although he grew up in Egypt and lived most of his life in the United States.

Said took up Antonius's complaint that western scholarship is biased against Arabs and charged that, furthermore, it has served colonialism.[514] Like Antonius, he set out to provide a corrective to the idea of "reconstitution." For example, in *Blaming the Victims: Spurious Scholarship and the Palestine Question*, he contends that Palestine was home to a remarkable civilization "centuries before the first Hebrew tribes migrated to the area."[515] Moving far beyond his acknowledged expertise in literary criticism, he assessed conventional biblical and archaeological scholarship as merely "retrojective imperialism" complicit in the dispossession of Arabs or, again, in Said's phrase, "passive collaboration" in that injustice. Allying with the recent scholarship of biblical "minimalists" and revisionist archaeologists, Said offers a "retrojective" identification of the ancestors of contemporary Muslim and Christian Palestinians. They are the long-resident, indigenous inhabitants; Jews are usurpers. (I shall soon comment on this use of politically-motivated biblical research.)

Said identifies Jews only with the Christian European establishment, and its alleged Orientalist framework. He fails to relate that Jews were considered outsiders in Christian Europe, indeed often identified as Asian outsiders. However, as Ivan Kalmar and Derek Penslar have shown in *Orientalism and the Jews*,[516] Jews were, in fact, "orientalized" or marginalized in Christian Europe. The key term is *Christian* Europe, for in speaking of European Orientalism without its Christian tradition Said avoids a pertinent reality. This would make Jews simultaneously European Orientalists and targets of European

Orientalism. Said resolves the contradiction by removing Jews from the Orient while maintaining their European identity intact. He can comfortably conclude that Jews are perpetrators, not victims. They may therefore be foreign Europeans intruding in Arab Palestine.

The removal of Jews as actors in history is, of course, a familiar theme in supersessionism or replacement theology and so it has been cast within Saidian discourse. For example, Palestinian apologists enlist Liberation Theology, whose principles were first articulated by Third World clerics committed to anti-colonialism and Marxism, to conflate theology with history and politics. The best known exemplar is Naim Ateek, a leading Christian clergyman living in Israel who claims to trace his ancestry to pre-Islamic Palestine—indeed to the time of the Savior. He maintains that Christianity should support the Palestinian cause since Jesus not only heralded a successor religion but dispensed with the divine promises made to the ancient Hebrews. He does not reiterate the promises of national return and national redemption for the *Jews*. Rather, Jesus spoke in a universal language, thereby indicating that any special promises to the Jews have been abrogated. Not surprisingly, Ateek approves Toynbee's historical judgment that Jews have exited the stage and are no longer actors in history. In other words, Jewish claims based on the Old Testament have lapsed.

The same sacred texts, however, are vital and valid for Palestinians. Thus Ateek uses the Old Testament narrative of the Exodus to illuminate the current position of Palestinians who, in the name of historical justice, must be returned to their Promised Land. Like Antonius, who opposed the Peel Plan of 1937 for partition, and Said who opposed Arafat when he recognized Israel through the Oslo Accords, Ateek claims that full justice would require the dissolution of the Jewish state. Nevertheless, deferring to pragmatism, he proposes a temporary federation between a Jewish and an Arab state—a federation he anticipates will dissolve when Jews ultimately leave the country.

The current academic support for Said and Ateek did not exist when Antonius wrote *The Arab Awakening*. New interpretative frameworks have since developed to endorse the de-Judaization of the Holyland: "Minimalist" biblical scholarship and revisionist archaeology. Neither provides evidence to corroborate the Palestinian claim to being the indigenous natives and only rightful citizens of the land. Yet it seems to satisfy Zionism's critics that they question the historic Jewish presence. Since the mid-19th century, a sophisticated scholarly tradition has demonstrated that it is possible to be critical of the Bible as history without refuting that the Hebrews existed and played an important role in the history of humankind. The value of sound evidence-based criticism is not the issue here. Rather I want to expose how this ideologically driven scholarship is employed in the Arab/Israeli dispute.

An anti-Israel approach is endemic in the minimalist school of biblical criticism. Also known as "the Danish School," it originated in Copenhagen around 1970, spread to England, centering in Sheffield, and has flared out from there. The common thread is that the Old Testament is an intricate and complex deception invented by Hebrew scribes some two and a half millennia ago during the period of Persian and Hellenistic influence over Judea. Out of scattered echoes of a distant past, an ancient and manipulative clerical establishment created foundation myths and historic narratives to lend credence to their theology and to serve their immediate political purposes. This required fabricating details and exalting the Davidic line and its connection to Jerusalem. In sum, from the patriarchs through the exodus and the Davidic dynasty the Bible is replete with purposeful deceit and calculated fantasy.[518] The number of scholars involved in this approach is relatively small, but their claims have reached a wide audience in popular and scholarly journals, and not surprisingly, have been enthusiastically endorsed by Palestinian supporters in the Arab/Israeli dispute.

The politicization of biblical scholarship is readily apparent in the work of Keith Whitlam, a recognized leader of the minimalist approach. Significantly, his claim for scholarly authority derives not merely from textual analysis but from invoking Said and Saidian terminology. Whitlam berates conventional biblical scholarship as mere "Orientalist discourse" designed to erase the Palestinians from history. He goes on to declare that "Biblical studies has formed part of the complex arrangement of scholarly, economic, and military power by which Palestinians have been denied a contemporary presence or history." To use a favorite phrase, reminiscent of both Said and Antonius, there is a conspiracy to "silence" Palestinian history.[519]

Anti-Zionism in the Social Sciences

Yet another part of the academy contributes to denying the Zionist enterprise. The regnant, if not hegemonic, analysis of sociologists, historical geographers, and political scientists construes the Jewish state as founded on the injustices of a "colonial-settler society." While Zionist settlement was supported and even celebrated by an earlier generation of social scientists, it is now viewed as a destructive phenomenon whose negative consequences demand correction. In large measure this view is a product of choosing a radically different historical paradigm.[520]

Probably the best known though not the first such analysis is found in Gershon Shafir's *Land, Labor, and the Origins of the Israeli-Palestinian Conflict, 1882-1914*.[521] Shafir's approach is comparative and he begins by identifying multiple types of settler societies in the 400 years of colonialism that began with Columbus and ended with Zionism. Relying on the insights of historians of western imperialism, he and his colleagues review Jewish settlement to determine which of the various colonial models fits Zionism best. The comparative framework based on European colonialism as the sole explanatory instrument inevitably faults Zionism by definition. That is, since he compares the Jews to the Portuguese, Spanish, Dutch, French, and the English and views them exclusively in the European historical framework, Zionist settlement may be more or less benign, but it is always guilty of being colonialist. To borrow a phrase: one cannot be a little pregnant. Shafir posits no additional or alternative model and ignores the possibility that the Jewish case is an anomaly.

The universal reference point for all of such critical or revisionist scholarship is the seminal work of D. K. Fieldhouse, a British scholar whose writings continue to influence generations of researchers. Written during the heyday of de-colonization, with which he identifies, and on the eve of one of the great flashpoints of the Arab/Israeli conflict, the 1967 Six-Day War, Fieldhouse's 1966 *The Colonial Empires: a Comparative Survey from the Eighteenth Century*[522] is a magisterial and comprehensive work that contains no mention of Zionism. Except for a passing reference to the Balfour Declaration of 1917, Jews and Zionists are totally absent from his work.

Fieldhouse concentrates on an economic and materialist approach to colonialism that derives from the early twentieth-century work of J. A. Hobson and V. I. Lenin even though his conclusions are markedly different.[523] Zionism plays no role in this far-reaching account of European colonial expansion and in the world where empires establish colonies. Contemporary critics, who consistently reference Fieldhouse to support their claim that Zionism is an outrageous and vexing form of colonialism, willfully or carelessly distort his definition of "settler society" when they apply it to the Zionist case.

Why did Fieldhouse exclude Jewish settlement that had already been in process for more than eighty years from his research on "settler society" and colonialism? A likely explanation is that it did not fit his definition, based on the rubric he established for the Dutch, British, French, Spaniards, Portuguese, Germans, and Italians. Jewish colonization during its first forty years took place in the Ottoman Empire; it was certainly not part of the process of imperial expansion in search for power and markets. It was also not a consequence of industrialization and financial interests. Indeed, as numerous scholars have noted, Jewish settlement was so unprofitable that it has been pronounced economically irrational.[524] In sum, Fieldhouse's exactingly developed analysis does not fit the Zionist case. Revisionist scholars have wrenched it out of context to describe an entirely distinct historical experience to serve their own ideological purposes. At the same time, their interpretations served pro-Palestinian apologists.

Zionism did not establish plantations or other large units of capitalistic agriculture. Instead, Jews created small truck farms or modest-sized collective colonies. These were more naturally suited for homogeneous communities and totally unlike the large plantations managed by European settlers operating with a significant force of native labor. Small landholders and collective communities did not need native labor. For ideological as well as practical reasons, Jews worked the land themselves.

Ironically, this self-reliance and determination to engage personally in hard work has provided yet another reason to blame the Zionist enterprise in its entirety. The economic and cultural separation between Jews and Arabs is decried as the sole responsibility of Zionist ideology and praxis. The contemporary indictment of Israel as an "apartheid state" is a natural, albeit absurd, outgrowth of this charge.

A contextualized and more nuanced analysis would note that for centuries Muslims had separated themselves from Jews who they defined as *dhimmis*, tolerated but second-class members of the community. Moreover, separation between Jews and Muslims was the norm throughout the Arab Muslim world and imposed by the Muslim Turks and their predecessors since the rise of Islam in the 7th century. Is it reasonable to castigate a handful of Jews living in remote agricultural colonies under Turkish rule because they failed to overturn such deeply engrained and accepted practices? Faulting them for not implementing the kind of egalitarian and integrated civil society that had yet to be actualized even in the United States is an exercise of imagination that borders on fantasy. Yet, that has become this generation's operative paradigm. Worse, Israel is blamed for instituting this system, one maliciously defined with the epithet "apartheid."

The misuse and abuse of Fieldhouse's "settler society" distorts in another crucial way. Fieldhouse viewed British "settler societies" as intended "replicas" of the home society and "true reproductions of European society."[525] The same was true of French colonies: "The French imperial mission was to mold their colonies into replicas of France and eventually to incorporate them into the metropolis." In the case of Algeria, the French even tried to incorporate the colony into the home country.[526] In marked contrast, as we saw above, Zionist settlements were at once deliberately distinct from Europe and different from Arab society. This distinction was at the core of the idea of "reconstitution." European and American technology, political ideas, and other aspects of modern culture were transferred to Palestine and also transformed; Zionist society was consciously recast into a unique mold dedicated to creating the "new Jew."

Thus, there is a pernicious use of rhetoric that underlies this discourse. Casting Zionists as colonizers represents them as usurpers who occupy a land in which, by definition, they do not belong. Palestine is home to the one and only indigenous people; there cannot be two. In what must be an extreme anomaly in the history of colonialism, this new scholarship posits Palestine as occupied by two imperial powers—the British and the Jews. In view of the multitudes who desperately sought entry into Palestine prior to independence, this characterization of Jewish imperial power appears as a cruel joke at best.

Accusation by Misappropriation: The Palestinian as Indigenous

The concept of indigenousness is the latest weapon in the arsenal of attempts to de-Judaize Israel/Palestine. The insistence that only Arabs are the indigenous is ubiquitous in recent discussions of academic boycotts. It is the most recent version of a concept that Palestinian academics inside Israel use in arguing for transforming Israel from a Jewish state into a "state of all its citizens." Consider the opening statement of the *Future Vision of the Palestinian Arabs in Israel* (2007): "We are the Palestinian Arabs in Israel, the *indigenous* [my emphasis] peoples, the residents of the States of Israel, and an integral part of the Palestinian People and the Arab and Muslim and human Nation."[527] This assertion has become the basis of a claim that Jewish settlement is illegitimate. It supports the right and indeed the imperative to oppose a Jewish state in the 1948 war, even if defeat resulted in a *nakba* [catastrophe]. It upholds demands for far-reaching autonomy in a Jewish state and the right of Palestinians to return to anywhere in the State of Israel even as the legitimacy of Jewish settlement nearly everywhere is questioned.

This morphing of "native" into "indigenous" is not accidental. Since the 1960s, the idea of indigenous rights has become increasingly part of an international legal system. First initiated by the International Labor Organization to protect Indian tribes in Central and South America, it quickly came to embrace Australian Aborigines and Canadian First Peoples as well as American Indians in the Southwest. In the original and pristine meaning, indigenous referred to peoples like the Aborigines whose claim of continued presence for 35,000 to 40,000 years in Australia is unchallenged. That certainty is rare in less isolated areas of the world where there are all manner of records for the last 3,000 or 4,000 years. It was for admittedly more ancient and unprotected populations that in 2007 the UN issued a Declaration on the Rights of Indigenous Peoples. The US and Canada ultimately signed this convention but only with the expressed reservation that indigenous rights do not trump those of the modern sovereign state. It had become apparent that assigning newly constructed rights to rectify ancient injustice could cause contemporary mischief. This potential was exploited by Palestinian activists who in the1990s adopted it as a new tactic in the campaign against Israel.[528]

The first practical challenge to the authority of the State of Israel was made by the Bedouins in a case brought before Israeli courts concerning ownership of lands in the Negev. Their case failed due to lack of evidence: they provided no valid documents verifying ownership at any time since the Ottoman period nor proof of residence in the area prior to the 19th century. The latter assertion to ancient presence was an attempt to claim the rights of the indigenous. Indeed, how does a Christian Arab prove that he is a "living stone" (1 Peter 2:5) and descended from forebearers who were present at the time of Jesus? How, too, does a Muslim Arab substantiate descent from Jebusites, other Canaanites, or any pre-Israelite peoples or, for that matter, anyone from but a few centuries previous?

The historic reality is that Palestine had no more than 250,000 inhabitants from the Jordan to the Mediterranean in 1800. It was a vastly underpopulated area that had had many times that population in the ancient world, but in the 20th century the country became a magnet for Jewish and non-Jewish immigration. Indeed, the Albanian, Mehmet Ali, moved to Egypt to become its leader in the second quarter of the 19th century and sought to extend Egyptian control into the country. Egyptian settlers entered the area in significant numbers in the 19th century. Circassians arrived in Palestine from the Caucasus in the 1870s. From the Turkish coast to Beirut and on to Jaffa and Alexandria, the entire eastern Mediterranean littoral of the Ottoman Empire attracted migrants to a region poised for development as it became incorporated into the European economic system. This migration included Jews both from former Ottoman territory and from Europe who now constitute the country's majority with more than 6,000,000 inhabitants. It is not obvious why all others could become natives except Jews.

The claim of "indigenousness" is a political issue everywhere. Few peoples have such status in Africa and Europe. In the Middle East and Northern Africa, for example, only the Marsh Arabs south of Basra in Iraq and the Berbers of North Africa are generally considered authentically indigenous peoples in UN registries. Nevertheless, the push to include Negev Bedouins and Palestinians in general in this category is an integral part of the campaign to discredit Jews as foreigners and colonial-settlers.

Conclusion

As this brief survey makes clear, long before Israeli higher education became a target of boycott under the pretext of alleged abuse of the rights of educators, Palestine's Arabs and their supporters had marshaled a set of arguments opposing the existence of the Jewish state. They had also employed boycotts in the past. Their fundamental claim was and still is that Palestinians have the exclusive right to sovereignty in the land. A thin veneer of human rights language attempts to mask this unyielding rejection of the Jews. The rhetoric of BDS websites and of information distributed in support of boycott resolutions at the meetings of professional academic associations is replete with accusations of racism, apartheid, and colonialism urging[529] readers to embrace the polemic of Palestinian victimhood and align themselves with human rights by shunning and dispossessing the Jews.

Into this vortex of self-referential claims and justifications, old and new arguments are spun to the same end. For secular leftists who oppose imperialism and colonialism, Zionism is a contemporary example of both. For those who draw on long-held theologies found in Christianity and Islam, Judaism is a usurper and has established a state that is a theological impossibility. For the historically inclined who believe that the antiquity of a relationship to territory provides exclusive rights, invented narratives blithely deny Jewish peoplehood and presence. For advocates of the exploited and endangered indigenous, valuable legal concepts are hijacked and misapplied to disenfranchise Zionists, of whatever origin.

In sum, any argument will do, no matter how specious, and any ally is welcome, no matter how different or even conflicting their agenda may be on other issues. The broadest possible coalition is made to achieve a single end. In tracing the evolution of these fronts dedicated to the denial of Jews, their history and their rights, we find that the discourse can be conveniently adapted to different audiences. In the current case of a call for an academic boycott of Israeli higher education, what passes for new scholarship in different disciplines may be mobilized from Said's orientalist approach, minimalist biblical scholarship and archaeological revisionism, analyses of the political economy of settlement, and from the anthropological and human rights interest in the native and indigenous.

Whether or not Israel actually impedes the education of Palestinian students is in fact irrelevant; the claim is made without regard to evidence. Assertions and anecdotes are enough. So, too, are unexamined petitions and accusations emanating from groups within and without Palestine who oppose the Jewish state.

The most curious aspect of the current campaign is that it will have no practical effect. Biblical scholars and archaeologists will not stop visiting the Holy Land; scientists engaged in hi-tech and health sciences will not stop their collaborations; researchers committed to the world-wide effort of combatting desertification will not desist from learning what Israeli science is creating; and so on through the academy. In effect, the call for a boycott, whatever votes it might garner in one professional association or another will have, at most, limited practical effect. As we have seen, this has been the case with the economic and political boycott of Zionism, Jews, and Israel.

But this apparent failure of the campaign is also irrelevant. That is because the real purpose of BDS is not immediate success. It is part of a long-term effort to defame and discredit the state. It is a cynical and corrosive effort that is designed to gradually undermine the rights of Jews to a state of their own and simultaneously perpetuate the case for Palestinian victimhood. Detractors of Israel are engaged in a form of warfare with means other than conventional weapons and on a battlefield distant from the actual conflict. Boycotters now seek to enlist scholars with an arsenal drawn from diverse academic disciplines and encased in the language of human rights. In the course of this campaign of slander and distortion, the ultimate object is to delegitimize the Jewish state. This long-term battle is being waged with persistence and opportunism. When the battle over the boycott is over, the larger struggle will continue and move to yet another front. Since Palestinian rejection is fundamental to this continuing conflict, its resolution will require shifts in attitude and position that are similarly basic. Acceptance of a Jewish state is the necessary starting point for mutual accommodation. The boycott campaign can only delay reaching that beginning. ■

RACHEL S. HARRIS

No Place Like Home:
Arab-Israelis, Contemporary Fiction, and an Arab-Hebrew Identity

Proponents of academic and cultural boycotts often attribute a monolithic character to Israeli society; they assume it is entirely Jewish, generally conservative, and that the only minority is a disenfranchised Palestinian population. In fact, Israel is a vibrant and diverse multicultural society. To claim that Israel's Arab citizens all feel decisively alienated toward the Jewish state and consequently yearn for a one-state solution to the Israeli-Palestinian conflict is to assume that Israeli-Arabs exist in isolation within Israeli society. The boycott camp wants to exchange this supposed Israeli reality for a monolithic Palestinian polity that would, to their mind, justly represent Arab values and identity. The reality is a good deal more complicated. Within the Arab population of Israel there are cultural and generational differences and tensions that reveal major fissures within Palestinian and Arab-Israeli society. A new generation of fiction writers has used this social conflict as a creative source, demonstrating that Arab-Israeli citizens are increasingly integrated into Israeli society, while rejecting time-honored and patriarchal Arab social systems. This essay explores the increasing Hebraization of Israeli-Arabs whose mastery of the Hebrew language and the codes of Israeli culture—accompanied by an increasing alienation from the values of traditional Palestinian society—is leading to a new hybrid generation of Arab-Israelis who are creating a third way; neither Zionist nor Palestinian nationalist, but integrated within the complexities of contemporary Israel.

The Hebrew language unified Jews from disparate countries and ethnic backgrounds as part of Israel's nation-building process; consequently, linguistic mastery of the Jewish language served as the *sine qua non* of social mobility. Arab citizens living within the new state were caught in this wide net; knowing Hebrew and becoming familiar with secular Jewish-Israeli culture were preconditions for advancement and integration.[530] In time, Arab writers like Emile Habiby would write in Hebrew, while some Jewish writers in Israel continued to write in their mother-tongue, Arabic. That confronts what Lital Levy describes as the conventional binaries of Israel: "Hebrew Arabic, Arab and Jew." By disrupting these traditional dichotomies, writers "engage translation inside their texts as a creative alternative to barking, as a mode of resistance to the authority that has displaced them from their pasts and their homes."[531] This binary division has traditionally assumed that Arab means Palestinian, and is separate from Israeli, which implies Jewish; but two young writers, the prolific and widely known Sayed Kashua, and the first-time novelist Ayman Sikseck, offer a new hybrid identity in which the Arab-Israeli (non-Jewish Arab citizen of Israel) casts off the polar division the two options represent, and instead presents a third path.[532] Rejecting the isolated position of the Arab within Israel, and arguing for increasing assimilation in the twenty-first century through mastery of language, integration within the education system, changing social values and economic status, as well as a radical reformulation of political values, the hybrid identity offers ways in which a generation of Arabs coming of age within Israel have staked out a cultural and intellectual space that confounds previous categorizations.

The history of Arab writers using Hebrew has been viewed within a framework of post-colonial criticism in which writing in Hebrew is deemed an act of protest. Arab-Israeli writers are considered to produce minor literature: literature by a minority in the language of a majority. This position assumes, as Hannan Hever has shown in his study of Anton Shammas's novel *Arabesques*, that Arab-Israeli authors de-familiarize and de-territorialize Hebrew by separating it from its Jewish identity while simultaneously opening up space within Hebrew for the Arab-Israeli. Writers such as Shammas and Habiby satisfy the criteria of writing minor literature that Gilles Deleuze and Felix Guattari consider an act of dissent by the colonized protesting against established hierarchies of power.[534] Arab-Israeli writers, moving between Hebrew and Arabic in poetry, prose, political writing, and journalism have established Hebrew as a space of "otherness," creating a distance within self-representations.[535] In an Israeli context, Hever has argued that Arab minor literature, in Hebrew, "invades and subverts the majority culture,"[536] whereby Arab writers, as Lawrence Silberstein elucidates, "problematize and subvert the dominant Zionist/Israeli conception of Hebrew literature as Jewish literature and Israeli culture as Jewish culture."[537]

In inscribing the Arab's story in Hebrew, Arab-Israeli writers have called attention to identities that remain separated within the otherwise Jewish social space. Nonetheless, writing in Hebrew is not only a political act against the Jewish/Zionist elements of Israeli culture, as Hever and Levy claim. It can also, as Yael Feldman contends in discussion of *Arabesques*, release the Arab-Israeli from the constraints and taboos of his own Arab language and culture: "[F]or Shammas the Hebrew language has become the language of liberation that set free the forbidden story of an internal Arab conflict."[539] Scholars view the dichotomy of Arab-Hebrew writing from multiple perspectives. Rachel Feldhay Brenner has claimed that an Israeli Arab uses Hebrew as a "relational act that accepts the status of second class citizens and appeals against it at the same time," and Hever has described the use of Hebrew by Arab writers as an "Achilles' heel," attacking Hebrew culture from within. Catherine Rottenberg, who argues in reference to the writing of Sayed Kashua that the Arab subject is not a "free agent" and is not affirmed as the "Arab citizen," rejects Brenner's emphasis on the aspect of dialogue and communication but supports "Hannan Hever's assertion that a certain kind of authorial voice on the part of the Arab writers can *force* Jewish readers to take a fresh look at their cultural assumptions and expectations."[540] Thus, scholars have interpreted the act of Hebrew writing from Arabs as a form of cultural attack against Jewish cultural hegemony, a mode of free expression for Arabs who are censored within Arab culture, and an opportunity to highlight the treatment of Arabs in Israel.

Mapping this binary of Jewish/Arab onto a colonial dichotomous model of black/white that characterizes post-colonial discourse belies the complex social hierarchies in Israeli society. Differences between the native and foreign interloper that this scholarship depends upon, as embodied in physical characteristics, food, and domestic landscapes, do not translate onto the racial or ethnic differences in Israeli society, while the assumed divisions between Arabs and Jews obscure the complicated origins of Jews (including Arab Jews) which offers its own black/white issues. Among Jews from different sites of migration, color difference is less socially significant, since European Jews can be dark-skinned and dark-eyed while Jews from other places including the Middle East and Asia can be light-skinned with blue or green eyes. Though some measurable differences do exist (between Russian and Yemenite Jews, for example), this has led to symbolic rather than real color divisions and an importing of racial politics from other cultural spaces. Moreover, Palestinians can also be dark- or light-skinned with dark or light eyes, and may more closely resemble Jews than some Jews resemble one another. Even the stereotypical Western conventions used to describe "Semites," such as dark or almond eyes, dark curly hair, or large noses, cannot be employed to distinguish between ethnic or religious groups in Israel. Just as Jews from Arab countries, and Jews who have settled in the Middle East have come to see the regional food as their own (falafel, tomatoes, olives, couscous, humus, et cetera) Arabs in Israel have also come to share the globalization of cuisine, and may be found eating pasta, schnitzel, sushi, matzoh, and ice cream. While hierarchical divisions exist, they do not necessarily accord neatly with the conventions of post-colonial theorizing. Moreover, as Orna Sasson-Levy and Avi Shoshana have shown in regards to Jewish intra-ethnic distinctions, "the hegemonic discourse in Israel denies the existence and importance of ethnicity and does not acknowledge social inequality."[541]

Subtle variations of ethnicity notwithstanding, cultural representations of the divisions between different groups within Israeli society have been undermined through depictions of "passing" that serve to highlight the flimsy boundaries of difference. In her examination of Israeli cinema of the 1980s and 1990s, which examines characters "passing" in the film's text and actors from one background "passing" in roles identified with a different group, Carol Bardenstein claims that most instances of social "passing" take place between those closest to one another along a spectrum of social mobility. Unlike other Middle Eastern cultures in which there is a binary division (fellah/urbanite, black/white, Christian/Muslim), she argues that Israeli culture has a scale of identity—Ashkenazi Jews, Mizrachi Jews, Arab-Israelis, Palestinians[542]—which leads to a greater degree of fluidity in the process of acculturation, but often means that "the majority of the enactments of identity boundary crossings in these films take place between the subjectivities of Mizrachi Israeli Jews and Palestinians with Israeli citizenship and the rest shift between points on the spectrum that are similarly in close proximity to each other in the social hierarchy."[543] Therefore "passing," in the Israeli-Palestinian cinematic context, can be seen as an adoption of those social codes and linguistic markers that are not entirely dissimilar from those already known and experienced, thus the process of masquerade is already partially complete before the "passing" ever takes place. Yet Bardenstein's contention that Israeli cinema represents characters usually playing an ethnic and social position one step apart on this spectrum (Mizrachi as Israeli Arab, Ashkenazi as Mizrachi) is not comparable to the literary model. In Hebrew, Arab writers have represented Arab characters (often Palestinians from Gaza and the West Bank) passing as Jewish Ashkenazim.

But what is meant by "passing" here? Passing "can be understood at the most basic level as an attempt to control the process of signification."[544] Its association with the performative nature through which identity is constructed is a key element in thinking about the ways in which Kashua and Sikseck challenge the expectations of what Arab-Israelis should be within Jewish and Palestinian society. In the Israeli context, passing is embodied in a history through which Arabs passing as Jews already repeats an earlier process by which Mizrachi Jews sought to pass as Ashkenazi Jews. The treatment of passing in American and Caribbean literature was situated within a racial context with implications of racial mixing that emerged out of a culture of slavery, discrimination, and miscegenation. Its formation against a background in which interracial sex and interracial marriage were forbidden—and a racist society in which a "drop" of black blood (the claim that a person had any black ancestry) meant they were socially and legally black, even when their "white" looks might allow them to "pass" undetected in white society, but could lead to imprisonment, slavery, or death—bears little relation to the distinctively separate Israeli identities of Arab and Jew. Instead, "passing" in Israeli culture is more closely allied with Homi Bhabha's postcolonial notion of "mimicry," meaning the imitation of the colonizer by the colonized. As a form of subversion, the adoption of modes of behavior that enable the colonized access to power works to undermine the system by suggesting both the ease of infiltration and the performativity of colonial authority. Defining "passing" in Israel as "mimicry" remains problematic, since Bhabha's framing depends on determinations of racial (and color) differences which in this context are absent.

Accepting a reading of "passing" that draws on models of the undetectable Jew within Christian society (or the homosexual passing as heterosexual) assumes overlapping and shared identities that threaten society's divisions and its supposed heterogeneous (or heteronormative) values, offering a temporary disguise which may be, at any moment, cast off. While the Arab may "masquerade" as a Jew, pretending to be that which he is not in order to avoid detection as an Arab, this term implies no permanent physical transformation and only a temporary adoption of Jewish mores. While writers such as Habiby have played with this pretense, the transformation of the characters in Kashua's and Sikseck's work is a subtle and usually permanent process.

To define "passing" in the Hebrew context most accurately, it is perhaps wisest to think of it within the frame of the Hebrew term *lehitashknez* ("to become Ashkenazi"), which is used to denote adopting cultural values, dress, tastes, language, social etiquette, etc., of the historic—and symbolically, if not actually—white, socialist, ruling elite, and was originally used to indicate the assimilation of Mizrachi Jews to Ashkenazi Jewish cultural norms. This "mimicry" in its historical Jewish frame is not subversive but manifests the country's determined melting-pot aspirations that framed the immigration of Jews from many countries of origin as an "ingathering of exiles." Though issues of racism and cultural superiority were an element of this process, it cannot be viewed within the usual post-colonial terms of minority/majority, or powered/disempowered, since fiction and cinema, key sites of Israeli culture, resolve these conflicts in harmonious scenes of weddings and births across Jewish ethnic groups, rather than emphasizing cultural separateness.[545] Likewise, this term is not employed by the Ashkenazi to denigrate the Mizrachi who adopt behavior and modes of discourse assumed to be Ashkenazi, as mimicry is viewed in other contexts. In recent years it has become a term of vilification used by Mizrachim, deployed to attack those who assume the adoption of certain behaviours associated with Ashkenazim as part of a process of self-empowerment; thus the in-group/out-group binary conventions of colonial discourse are disrupted in the Arab/Israeli context. Moreover, the condemnation of *hitasknezut* (process of becoming Ashkenazi) as social critique implies the abandonment of a particular and specific ethnic tradition, culture, and value set, and is a legacy derived from the local variant of black culture politics, "The Israeli Black Panthers," that emerged in the 1970s, thereby allying Arab/Israeli passing with national inter-ethnic political discourse rather than with post-colonial discourse.

In the Israeli context, in which Mizrachim have already worked to become the "right" kind of Jew, for Arabs to pass as Jews in Israeli society as is not simply to mimic Jewish behavior, which is itself ethnically and culturally diverse, but to become Ashkenazi, subsequently facing censure within the Arab community for doing so. Arguing that Arab writers are working subversively within Hebrew by creating characters whose Arab origins are undetected by Jewish characters is to apply a post-colonial reading that loses the cultural specificity of the term *lehitashknez*, by substituting for it the racially implicated term "passing." More complex cultural politics are at work. Moreover, reading the Arab character as a figure playing out the colonizer/colonized literary paradigm imposes a Western literary reading that obviates Arab literary traditions already present, such as that of the trickster. In this essay, though I use the term "passing," I define it within the specific cultural framing of *lehitashknez*, showing that mastery of Ashkenazi conventions represses the Arab's "Arabness," thereby enabling free movement within Jewish spaces. Yet it also serves as a transformative experience that ultimately alienates the Arab from a traditionally Arab space.

Sayed Kashua's *Second Person Singular* (2010) and Ayman Sikseck's *El-Yafo* (*To Jaffa*, 2010) explore the role of language and the construction of a complex and distinct Arab-Israeli identity. In his first two novels, *Dancing Arabs* and *Let it be Morning*, and his television series "Arab Labor," Kashua presents Arab protagonists copying the language, dress, politics, and cultural attitudes that they believe will help them succeed in Israeli society. This platform (in a conventional exploration of mimicry) offers an opportunity to ridicule the petit bourgeois Arab-Israeli who seeks entry into a society from which he is excluded. Yet *Second Person Singular* moves beyond these acts, which may or may not lead to the successful passing characteristic of his earlier works, and explores the complete metamorphosis of an Arab-Israeli. His novel traces the psychological and social developments that two Arab-Israelis experience as they transform themselves in order to be accepted into Israeli society. As their separate lives weave throughout the novel, the lawyer stands for the imposter grasping at advancement, mimicking the ways of those he perceives to be superior to him. By contrast, Amir La'ab, a social worker, turns into Yonatan Forschmidt. Stripped of his former Arab identity, he becomes the Jew. In its final rendering, the possibility of total transformation both threatens the apparent segregation of Arab and Jew in Israeli society and points to the Arab's assimilation into Israeli society.

Likewise, Sikseck offers a study of the Arab-Israeli raised in a society where Zionist cultural and linguistic codes are learned from childhood. His nameless protagonist aimlessly wanders the streets of Jaffa, looking for a direction in life, constantly moving between both a Jewish and an Arab world. As these two young writers show, the Arab-Israeli is no longer aping the colonizer, but has internalized the colonizer's codes of behavior, language, and dress, thereby accepting the existing cultural structures while adopting the external trappings of a Jewish cultural and political identity, including mastery of Hebrew. Simultaneously, for both Kashua and Sikseck, their protagonists must reject, disguise, or subsume the manifest traits of Arab identity when in the public sphere, and disguise their desires, interests, and modes of thinking when in an Arab sphere.

The texts' consciousness of the process of assimilation and integration suggests the sublimation of Arabness. But in a post-modern meta-consciousness that reflects the distance between a writer and a text, in constructing works that emphasize the loss of Arab identity, the writers make this loss, or at least the process of loss, present. Sikseck and Kashua highlight the tensions Arab-Israelis face between the desire to integrate, often resulting in passively accepting the subordination of their own Arab cultural inheritance, partly as the result of Israeli cultural imperialism, and partly due to the active pursuit of this erasure so that they may become insiders within Israeli society. As with previous Arab writers, including Habiby, Shammas, and Mansour, who have used Hebrew to express the Arab-Israeli struggle, by co-opting the language of Judaism and Zionism, these writers subvert the meaning of Israeli-ness, thereby rejecting the very submission their characters appear to accept. At the same time, these writers diverge from previous generations of Arab writers for whom Hebrew served as a weapon that emphasized their alienation from Israel (and its Jewish Zionist values), offering them the capacity to critique the society they found oppressive and exclusionary. Whereas once Arab writers enacted a Hebrew-speaking identity within the traditions of minor literature—thereby establishing two conflicting poles: Arab or Israeli (implying Jewish/Zionist)—Kashua and Sikseck now explore an alternative cultural hybrid identity that distinguishes Arab-Israelis from both Jewish-Israeli and Arab-Palestinian society. For today's generation of Arab-Israeli writers and their Arab-Israeli characters, though Arabic remains the informal vernacular, Hebrew is not an alien tongue made foreign in the hands of the outsider, but the insider's formal literary language.

Kashua and Sikseck can be viewed in light of recent scholarship on Anglo-Arab writing that has pointed to a second generation in immigrant and post-colonial literature: writing by the children of immigrants raised within the new host countries and their respective value systems, in which there is a distance from the homeland that only exists as an imagined space.[546] Characterized by skepticism and "two or more looks," this generation questions the myths and values associated with their ethnic origins and emphasized within their close family and social groups, while simultaneously critiquing the promised utopia of the colonial/new world space.[547] Kashua and Sikseck may already be considered a third or even a fourth generation of Arab-Israeli writers of Hebrew. Strong features of this writing—of which Kashua and Sikseck are Hebrew examples of a larger literary trend—reveal meditations on ethnic identity, intergenerational conflict, and the tension between traditionalism and modernization. Nevertheless, this literature cannot be essentialized to these specific motifs since, in the Arab-Israeli context, the tensions are neither the traditional relationship of colonizer to colonized that is characteristic of Anglophone or Francophone immigrant writing, nor the identity confusion found in ethnic writing of immigrants to the United States, France, Germany, or the United Kingdom. Unlike African American, Asian American, British Indian, or Turkish German writing, Arab-Israeli writers also contend with the ongoing state of the conflict and the debate about bi-nationalism or a two-state solution.

"Passing," in Arab-Israeli Hebrew fiction, points to an assimilation that threatens to destabilize the already sensitive social boundaries that exist within a discourse preoccupied with questions of nationhood and nationalism. Despite the public spotlight on some recent Arab writers, actors, and visual artists, Arab-Israelis in general are not integrated into Israeli society, socially or culturally, and traditionally remain apart. However, the current generation, born in the 1980s and 1990s, may be revealing substantial changes in this position. For those raised within the Israeli educational establishment, increased access to modes of cultural capital, such as print and online journalism, literature, and media, has enabled many to flourish within an Israeli society that was once closed to most Arabs. But in adopting many of the trappings of Israeli society, Arab-Israelis have also begun to reject what they perceive to be a problematic Palestinian identity with its attendant conservatism, lack of education, and opportunity.

Faced with a dichotomy of learning to assimilate into the Jewish society for which they have been educated but will remain forever excluded by virtue of religion and ethnicity, or to return to a Palestinian society which seems backwards and stifling, their writing reflects identity ambivalence and a newly developed hybridity. Reflecting on the national elements of an Israeli society in which religious symbols are integrated, along with its Zionist historical narrative, these writers are creating a unique space within Hebrew and Israeli culture that is neither Zionist nor Jewish. As Ami Elad-Bouskila notes, for Arab-Israelis there is a "vacillation between national distinctiveness and their Israeli identity together with, intermittently, their desire for legitimization from both Arabs and Israelis, despite their ongoing process of Palestinization. Awareness of their status as a national minority with ties to the Arab world and to the other branches of the Palestinian people has not resolved their situation but rather enhanced their sense of its uniqueness and complexity."[548] The hybrid existence of the Arab-Israeli's "third way," through which the Arab has hebraicized his identity, suggests constantly shifting boundaries for this society in transition, often represented as moving from a traditional, agrarian, and rural way of life to an urban, affluent, and highly educated community whose moral and religious values are in flux, a situation which may in part be modulated by its relative novelty.

In the past, most Palestinian authors who wrote in Hebrew were Druze (Naim Araidi, Reda Mansour) or Christian (Anton Shammas, Atallah Mansour.) They were perceived to have a higher integration into Israeli society, since their interests were often allied with Israel in opposition to Arab-Muslim interests. Therefore, it has been assumed that they chose Hebrew as a way to engage with their minority status, both within Israeli society and as a minority within Arab-Muslim society.[549] Moreover, stylistically it was poetry rather than prose which was considered the preferred genre for Arab-Israeli writers according to Bouskila, capturing a traditional Arab/Middle Eastern form of writing in the Hebrew language, though Rachel Feldhay Brenner also argues that the confessional was also popular among second-generation Arab writers in Hebrew. The uniqueness of Sikseck is that he describes a protagonist whose traditional Islamic identity (his practice lapses in varying degrees throughout the narrative) is a clear and constant marker. In the same vein, though Kashua's protagonists are generally more secular, in his weekly newspaper columns and in "Arab Labor," there are regular references to traditional Muslim practices. The decision by Arab Muslims to write novels in Hebrew demonstrates a new level of integration into the prevailing social codes of Israeli society. Bouskila has challenged Hever's claim that Arab writers chose Hebrew "to strike the Achilles' heel" and instead argues that Kashua's generation of Arab-Muslim writers have chosen Hebrew in order to be integrated into "Israeli culture and its emerging identity, each author for his or her own reasons."[550] Moreover, these young authors appear to demonstrate a symbiotic rather than oppositional relationship to the Hebrew language and Israeli culture, which they embrace.

If Arab writers in the past recognized the silenced home language within the majority space by writing in Hebrew, and addressed their Arabic audiences in the minority language through other political and literary works to demonstrate their mastery of both worlds, they were able to indicate their opposition to the majority and silencing of the minority. By contrast, these new writers signal a major change as part of a generation of Israeli-Arabs distanced from an Arabic literary heritage, but heirs to a now significant Hebrew Arab-Israeli literary heritage (such as Anton Shammas, Naim Araidi, Emile Habiby, Atallah Mansour and others) that reconfigures the previously established relationship between language and identity. Kashua and Sikseck move beyond Shammas' dejudaizing of Hebrew, and instead experience it as their only literary language.[551] The permanent presence of young Arab authors within Hebrew literature lies between the heritage of Bialik and the Bible (with their respective Zionist and religious traditions), and Christian and Druze Hebrew authors with their oppositional writing.[552]

The duality that characterized past writers but seems to be disappearing from the new hybrid Arab-Israeli identity is explored repeatedly throughout Sikseck's novel. The protagonist's proficiency in Hebrew is contrasted with his (and his peer group's) lack of skill in Arabic. At the Hebrew book fair, the unnamed protagonist begins talking to two Arab men standing in line for ice cream when they cannot decipher the words for the flavors. They are surprised to find that he is an Arab and his answer to their question of his origins elicits a response that conveys their sense of alienation from him: "Now it's clear why every second word you utter is in Hebrew."[553] Though he always attends the Hebrew book fair, he is not even aware of the Arab book fair in Haifa, and when he does learn about it, forgets to attend—denoting a subconscious level of cultural sublimation. This theme recurs when the protagonist tries unsuccessfully to read the Arabic letters on the side of a novel in a little shop in the Jaffa flea market. For the aging shopkeeper this failure represents the decline of a Palestinian identity and culture among Arab youth.

'Of course you don't know who that is,' he said. 'Who your age knows who Ghassan Khanafani is? You're just—' he stood up to raise his voice but then he stopped and changed his mind and sat down on the chair opposite us, 'But you aren't to blame.'[554]

In evoking Ghassan Khanafani—not only a renowned Arab writer, but often considered the literary father of Palestinian nationalism—Sikseck highlights an assumed Arab/Palestinian cultural and political heritage. Yet in the same moment the protagonist exhibits his detachment from Kanafani's name, his language, and his writing, thereby signaling a break with his traditional legacy. By contrast, he is well versed in Bialik and the icons of Hebrew literature. "I remember the date of Bialik's death, but I've forgotten most of the stories [in Kanafani's] 'In the Land of Sad Oranges.'"[555] Hebrew literature is second nature for the protagonist, who is versed in its linguistic, cultural, historical, and textual dimensions and therefore the Zionist ideals that led to the establishment of the State of Israel, while Arab literature struggles to establish a position in his cultural knowledge and remains ethereal.

For generations of Arab-Israeli writers, Hebrew was a foreign language, a symbol of the occupation they challenged. Sikseck and Kashua write in Hebrew because it is the language in which they were raised; if not in their home, certainly in schools, media forms, and popular culture. Furthermore, where once Arab writers were polylingual, this generation is no longer as comfortable writing in Arabic as Hebrew, thus the implied dissidence of Arab writers using Hebrew, which was a powerful element for previous generations of writers, is immaterial for these two men. As Gil Hochberg reminds us, Kashua, who was raised in a prestigious Jewish boarding school in Jerusalem, lacks the mastery of written Arabic (*fusha*) that he has of Hebrew. For Kashua, "Hebrew is *not* the language of the other/master, no more so than it is the language of Kashua and his narrators. In Kashua's own words 'Hebrew and I chose each other.'" ("My French Boycott").[556] Or as he claims in his *Ha'aretz* column of September 12, 2012, "Hebrew is the language of building bridges," thus using it offers a way to be heard in Israel. Writing in Hebrew never represents for Kashua and his narrators simply a movement away from the self (or "true identity") and toward assimilation into the culture of the other. Nor does Hebrew represent a space of liberation. More accurately, it functions as a means for coming to terms with the very idea of "the self" as a cultural product—one that is already written from the outside by others. This is no less true for Sikseck, whose protagonist moves between spoken Hebrew and Arabic fluidly but who writes in Hebrew because this is his literary language.

It is undeniable that Arab writers using Hebrew have developed their discourse from the focus on Palestinian and Arab nationalism that dominated the writing of previous generations. Kashua and Sikseck bring a new sense of identity to the Hebrew language they use; they are no longer battling or subverting the language as their predecessors had done, but instead inhabiting it from within. These authors belong to a new, popular, and prolific cohort of Israeli writers whose narrative style draws on surrealistic elements in an otherwise realist narrative that seeks to represent in stark terms the absurdities, violence, and fear that pervade the Israeli reality. This continues to reflect the disempowerment of minority groups, including Arabs within the Israeli establishment. Constructed as a foreign element from within, their references to Arabic language, literature, and customs (food, dress, music) within their fiction nevertheless continue to pose a threat that offers to destabilize the normative order and its Jewish Zionist identity.

Ayman Sikseck's *El-Yafo*

Sikseck's debut novel *El Yafo* is a meditation on the condition of an Arab-Israeli student from Jaffa studying in Jerusalem. The protagonist transitions smoothly between Arab and Jewish cultures without attracting attention by either group. "Passing" disrupts the "accepted systems of social recognition and cultural intelligibility. It also blurs the carefully marked lines of race, gender and class, calling attention to the ways in which identity categories intersect, overlap, construct, and deconstruct one another."[557] The effortlessness with which Sikseck's protagonist appears to perform the different identities he adopts denies their falsity, highlighting his integration rather than pointing to his exclusion or marginalization. The very title of the novel—*Yafo*, instead of *Yaffa*— conjures up the Jewish rather than Arab terminology for the city, indicating total acceptance and assimilation into Hebrew cultural hegemony. The student's act of passing is so complete that he does not articulate it as a formal process, in contrast to the protagonist of Sayed Kashua's first novel, *Dancing Arabs*, whose transformation is articulated as a conscious journey, one which has been much discussed by critics. Rottenberg notes:

> Immediately following his arrival in Jerusalem, he buys himself clothes in a 'Jewish store,' as well as a Walkman and some cassettes in Hebrew. During his second week of school the narrator decides that he must get rid of his Arabic accent in Hebrew. In order to do this, however, he needs to learn how to pronounce the letter "p" correctly. Arabs frequently have trouble with the letter "p" because the sound does not exist in Arabic; they usually pronounce it "p" as if it were "b." While Adel, another Arab student at the boarding school 'was convinced there was really no difference between "b" and "p,"' the narrator who is determined to speak Hebrew like an Israeli Jew, begins to practice by holding up a piece of paper to his mouth and telling himself: 'If the paper moves you've said a "p."'[558]

This performance of cultural difference serves for Rottenberg as a recurring motif for an Arab-Israeli identity anxiety. Attempts at mimicry, such as learning to assimilate culturally, and perfect pronunciation or accent, are frequent among Kashua's protagonists, since only mastery offers the possibility of "passing" in Israeli society. Acceptance offers physical safety, freedom from harassment, and increased opportunity for advancement, yet it becomes a tortuous mask that might be removed at any moment. Thus many of Kashua's characters live in a constant state of tension, afraid of being exposed, humiliated, and exiled. Instead, Sikseck's protagonist exudes a calmness and confidence in his cultural knowledge, which suggests his almost total assimilation into Israel society.

> When I passed through the alleyway that comes out of the station, a guy wearing a kippah came towards me, with a backpack that was almost identical to my own and held out a little booklet; on either side it was bound by pieces of unpainted cardboard.
>
> "A book of psalms, buddy," he explained and pointed with his free hand towards his feet at the sign resting against the electricity pole nearby. "Five shekels to save the Synagogue. Go on, what do you say?" A mitzvah.
>
> I looked ambivalently at the sign and recognized the synagogue he was talking about. I dug my hand into the pocket of my pants and pulled out a few coins to give him.
>
> "Thanks buddy, thanks a lot," he said, and introduced himself as Yigal, shook my hand and gave me the book. I took off my backpack so that I could put the book inside, but my fingers wouldn't work and kept sliding off the zipper.
>
> "Here let me try." Yigal unzipped the bag and opened the largest pocket wide. "It's exactly like mine." His sudden approach to my bag made me nervous, as if he'd entered through a door that I made sure to lock, but suddenly found open, and without answering his smile, I lifted up my bag and turned to go.[559]

Asked to contribute to the building of a local synagogue, the Arab-Israeli protagonist offers up a few shekels and is given a book of psalms in return. In age, look, dress, manner, and behavior he resembles the youth collecting charity and his act of "passing" as an Israeli-Jew is complete even at the narrative's start. Because the Jewish Yigal has mistaken the identity of the Arab protagonist, he is willing to offer him the opportunity for a mitzvah (good deed) symbolizing the Jewish cultural underpinnings that are constantly encoded in even the simplest interactions within Israeli society. In turn the

Arab protagonist reveals that he is familiar with the synagogue mentioned, denoting his connection to the Jewish landscape of Jaffa, challenging readers' expectations about the Arab Muslim's alienation from Jewish sites. In *El Yafo*, despite the anticipated rupture between Arab and Jew, Sikseck suggests that Arab integration has already taken place—notwithstanding the fact that there is further differentiation between ethnic positions along the hierarchical social spectrum, both among Palestinians and Israel's Arabs, and between Jews from different geographic locations. Despite the resemblance between the two men, and the possibility of friendship that arises when Yigal introduces himself, the Arab-Israeli remains suspicious—an inversion of the Jewish suspicion of the Arab, characteristic in Hebrew writing and played out within the novel in the Jewish suspicion of an old Arab woman, seated on a bus with a large shopping bag. Sikseck confronts the Jewish readers' expectations and prejudices, normalizing the Arab-Israeli, and making the Jewish Israeli's reactions seem aberrant.

The Arab protagonist's nerves are evident when he is unable to work the zipper, and Yigal's offer of help only provides further anxiety since he fears that he may finally be exposed. The Arab can transcend social boundaries with ease but his skill is not matched by a concomitant confidence that he will pass, thereby undermining the very act of passing he has just performed. Rottenberg has claimed that the oppression Kashua's characters experience by Israeli authorities and by society at large are what "spur him to attempt to 'pass as a Jew,' taking on the habits of the Jewish population by correcting speech patterns, and buying clothes, books and cassettes." For her, the ability to pass "unnoticed" or be mistaken for a Jew demonstrates "passing" not as integration but as falsity, a mask that can be assumed. However, Sikseck's protagonist never appears to "learn" the rules for "passing," since he was raised with them. Moreover, Kashua's latest novel, *Second Person Singular*, moves beyond this process of mimicry, as previously mentioned.

Arab protagonists who have contended with constant suspicion in Israeli society litter the annals of Arab-Israeli and Palestinian fiction (both in Hebrew and Arabic), most famously in Emile Habiby's *The Secret Life of Sayeed: The Pessoptimist* (1974), which established a tradition that Sikseck bucks against in creating a character not considered threatening for Jews. Sikseck's anti-hero understands the social codes, in terms of dress, language, accent, and education, marked by his ability to pass safely and with ease. This is contrasted with the ways in which other Arabs, who do not "pass," are treated. Ethnically marked and therefore visible as the subaltern and suspicious other, the attack on an old Arab woman highlights the self-affirming relationship between racism and fear that saturate Israeli society. Moments before her wares are upended by a terrified and suspicious passenger, who suspects the old woman of being a suicide bomber, the protagonist's Jewish girlfriend, Nitzan, has already expressed her own apprehension and barely suppressed terror of the old woman.

> Next to the driver stood a woman around my mother's age, wearing a traditional Islamic headscarf and holding a large bag in her hand.
> "Are you thinking what I'm thinking?" Nitzan took my hand and intertwined her fingers in mine.
> "What are you thinking?" I murmured.
> "It looks suspicious to me."
> " What are you talking about, suspicious?" I felt my cheeks turning red. "Because she's Arab she looks suspicious?"
> Nitzan looked at me shocked and went quiet for a while. "What?!" she finally said. "Did you see the bag she's holding? That's why she looks suspicious, anyway look around, everyone is frightened."
> "Nobody is frightened," I tried. The driver silenced the radio so that he could concentrate better on the bag in her hands.
> "But I'm frightened!" she replied angrily.[561]

The nameless protagonist does not experience the fear of the other passengers. He sees a woman much like his mother, rather than the suspicious suicide bomber that the other passengers identify. Though he attempts to calm his girlfriend's panic, he cannot alleviate her fear. His silence in the face of the woman's attack might be read as a symbol of his complicity with Israeli hegemony, and as a sign of his ongoing fear of discovery that will expose the falsity of his acculturation.

In *El Yafo*, the Jewish girlfriend represents the Arab protagonist's desire for total assimilation, but his failure to share her fear marks him out from the Jewish population, and this emotional division ultimately separates them. Though he may pass in Israeli society, he has not become Jewish with its legacy of suspicion and anxiety. Rottenberg has claimed that the acquisition of a Jewish girlfriend for Kashua's protagonist in *Dancing Arabs* symbolizes his most intense "reward" for his attempts to assume "Jewishness," and that it is by virtue of this relationship that he is initiated into mainstream Jewish culture.[562] Sikseck's protagonist is not in need of this initiation or education, he is already part of Jewish culture, exemplified by his Jewish girlfriend's ease, and her role as a member of the security services. At the same time, his identity as an Israeli-Arab, and the constant tension between the societies, of which he is never fully a part, comes to the fore. Shamed by his failure to defend the Muslim woman, who is then assaulted, as her bag is overturned and ransacked, he nevertheless cannot identify with the other passengers' terror.

The impossibility of truly connecting with Israeli Jews forces him to connect with his hybrid identity in its purest form, among others who are like him, a fusion of Arab and Jewish society. The attack on the old woman is sufficient to prevent the protagonist from enjoying the film, and he leaves Nitzan at the cinema and returns to Jaffa, where he is supposed to attend the dedication ceremony of a local mosque. Just as he was unable to enter the cinema, however, he is unable to enter the mosque. He neither belongs to this traditional religious Arab world, nor to the secular Jewish world he just left. When his father exits the mosque and sees him outside, they embrace, which we later learn was the last time they truly hugged. Mistaken in believing his son entered the house of prayer, the father's misunderstanding serves as an allegory for the protagonist's political situation: he is "close enough" and able to "pass" in Palestinian society, just as he passes in Jewish society.

Deviating from the norms of passing, which usually denotes acceptance in one community and alienation if unmasked in the "other" community in which one passes, Sikseck's protagonist engages in "passing" in both Jewish and Arab society, only safe within his new complicated and hybrid identity. Seated outside on a bench, he meets another Arab-Israeli who had also been on the same bus moments earlier. Not recognizing this man as Arab on the bus, demonstrating the absolute success at passing, the characters now share their mutual recognition of one another, leading to a deep friendship. These youths might be considered trapped in a limbo, in which they fit in neither world; yet in their finding of one another and their shared understanding of the Jewish and Arab obligations and moral values that impact their lives, they reflect not the isolation of a liminal and transforming protagonist, one who belongs neither in an Arab nor in a Jewish world, but the creation of a third and clearly demarcated identity. That they use both Hebrew and Arabic together, and are able to discuss their connection to both Jewish and Muslim experiences, suggests that this third way is fixed, and not simply a pendulum oscillating between inaccessible extremes.

Sikseck addresses the flourishing of religious practice and expectation within Palestinian society in recent years through the protagonist, who examines his childhood experiences and reveals that his memories were of the Jewish festivals that took on a nationalist rather than simply a religious identity.

> "Hag Sameach?!" I asked, surprised. "But since when does Ramadan interest—"

"Not Ramadan, idiot," he cut me off with his laughter. "Succot. It's only a few more days, have you forgotten? How is that possible?"

"I remember," I said.

"In high school we were made to feel that it was our holiday as well," he continued, "Maybe enjoyment, maybe resentment. Who thought about Ramadan at all back then?"

Each year, towards the end of the summer, Samahar and I used to build a succah in the yard behind our house.[563]

Jewish culture is transformed into a universal Israeli identity that includes the Arab-Israeli while no strong counter-identity (Ramadan) exists. Similarly, his later attempt to resist the Hannukah delicacy of hot jam-filled doughnuts, which are being distributed freely at the bakery, represents the extent to which he is compromised by Jewish Israeli society; though the woman in front of him refuses the pastry he consumes, he remains torn between the desire to resist, and the pleasure of the steaming, sugary luxury: "The dough was oily and there was almost no jelly, but I swallowed the bite and thanked the girl with a broad grin."[564] Finally, even the woman who has turned down the free sample finds herself browbeaten at the counter into accepting the forced purchase of doughnuts. Neither Arab nor Jew is immune to the pressure to conform. In turn, Judaism becomes a cultural symbol within a secularized Israeli culture applicable to all its citizens, not a separate religious practice. Even while Sikseck's character merges into Israel and its codes, his very presence interrupts their presumed religious authenticity, highlighting his disruption of the very values that underscore Israeli culture.

The protagonist's clear comfort within Israeli culture is a metaphor for his acceptance and understanding of Israelis, which colors his engagement with Israeli security. Broadly, he fights within the system but does not resist it. He easily passes through security barriers and responds politely and graciously, such as his answers to the security guards who approach him at the book fair. Finally when asked for his ID card, his security-guard girlfriend removes him from the interrogations. Pronouncedly, he is only marked out in Israeli society when he associates with Arabs from elsewhere, whereby his cultural camouflage is compromised. By contrast with his behavior, the Arabs with whom he is standing refuse to answer, and the security guard with "a shrug of his shoulders, because he had no choice" requests their ID. The protagonist's respectful engagement is contrasted with the other Arabs' rebelliousness. Sikseck's protagonist is complicit in the oppression of the peripheral Arabs, who are alienated, while the protagonist views this same complicity as an avenue to free movement that is incomprehensible for them.

In his afterword to Sikseck's novel, Hever claims that the protagonist, with his hybrid identity, is engaged in an internal battle, that "of someone who cannot find a place, either national or personal."[565] Just as the protagonist's linguistic and literary heritage now belongs to the culture of Hebrew Israel, rather than an Arab Palestine culture, the protagonist's inability to resist the doughnut suggests the threatening of his Arab identity, as he merges into the dominant social discourse, although the novel repeatedly returns to the possibility of resisting this cultural imperialism. In a surreal search, the protagonist prowls the night looking for "Keren Palastin!" which he finds marked on a sewer cover in Roman and Arabic letters.

This quest he undertakes repeatedly becomes the symbol of his search for a Palestinian identity. While "keren" often refers to a "fund" or "foundation," being a play on the Israel Fund (*Keren Kayemet LeYisrael*; KKL), it also translates as "power" or "prestige," thus his attempt to find a Palestinian identity, a compulsion that drives him increasingly, remains a pursuit conducted under the cover of darkness, without direction or focus. "In my blindness I've passed here over and over, as if it wasn't here at all, and who can know how many times I've trampled it under foot."[566] Yet despite this hint at a sense of a Palestinian nationalism it is already clear that at a family celebration the 1948 Arabs from within Israel already distinguish themselves from those on "the other side of the fence." Seeing Palestinian Arabs as people who can never have "good taste explained to them," the two groups seem separated by more than just distance.[567] Though the specter of ideological solidarity looms, reality demonstrates the increasing misunderstanding and disconnectedness between Palestinians and Arab-Israelis.

The protagonist's attempts to reclaim a fading and vanishing Arab identity manifest in his involvement with protests against the treatment of Palestinians and more broadly Muslims. He refers to protests against the publication in Denmark of a cartoon about Muhammed, to which he responds: "Their indignation aroused my envy, and my heart was embittered because I hadn't known about the protests beforehand."[568] The specific references to protests by Israeli-Arabs in Haifa first appear in the conversation about Arab book week and his failure to attend. Thus his very inclination to participate in protests is tempered by his removal from Arabic culture.

> "Are you helping me with the sign?" called Muhammed from his nest in the sand. A large placard lay before him.
>
> "What's the problem?" Narmin got up and went over to him.
>
> "No problem, I've nearly finished," he said. "I wrote the slogans the way you requested, in Arabic, Hebrew, and English. The problem is I've forgotten how to say 'transfer' in Arabic."

A big laugh broke out among the group.

"You call yourself Arabs?" said Hani, and rejoiced in sharing the word. "In Al Kuds you wouldn't pass the entrance exam."

Despite attempts to reconnect to an Arab identity in which "Al Kuds" rather than Jerusalem (the Hebrew term) becomes the reference point, Sikseck points to the impossibility of stemming the process of assimilation into Hebrew culture. Furthermore, language becomes a framing for the politics of the peace process. While the term population "transfer"—and by extension the peace process—exists in Hebrew as active vocabulary, he cannot summon it in Arabic, suggesting the failure of Palestinian activism and of Arab participation in the future of Palestinians.

While the novel is critical of Israeli society's treatment of Arabs and the erasure of Palestinian identity, it views this cultural destruction as a responsibility that belongs to Arabs as much as it is the fault of Israeli Jews. Similarly, Sikseck is equally critical of an outmoded Arab moral code, which is no longer in keeping with the lives of Arab-Israelis. Though the hero and his paramour Sarihan can conduct an illicit sexual affair, they must do so in secret and she must marry according to the rules of their society, just as his sister must. Though the men have freedom of movement and education, the women remain trapped in a patriarchal system that no longer reflects their own values or desires. Sayed Kashua has been repeatedly criticized for depicting Arab-Israelis negatively by creating Arab stereotypes of traditionalism and backwardness that purportedly fit the pictures Jews already accept as true, and Sikseck's critique is no less pointed at precisely those self-same issues. He is arguing, moreover, that the Israeli Arab's traditional way of life no longer accords with any of the other continually moving goal posts for Arab-Israeli identity.

The impact of Hebrew as a culturally imperialist force has permanently dislocated the Israeli Arab from an Arabic past. The protagonist's continued efforts to record his own identity, through constant acts of writing in his notebook, is a move to construct his self not as either Palestinian or as the "wannabe Jew" of Sayed Kashua's literature, but as a way to create his own distinct Arab-Israeli identity, that passes in both worlds, but exists only in its purest form in the liminal hybrid space of contact with other Arab-Israelis. Hebrew has become the Arab's language and *El Yafo* demonstrates the ultimate failure to maintain the purity of a minority culture. Finally, the novel presents the gradual erosion of Arabic and Palestinian identity that has already taken place for a young generation of Arabs embedded within Israeli culture.

Sayed Kashua—Second Person Singular

Sayed Kashua, columnist, dramatist, short-story writer, and novelist is acclaimed in Israel and abroad. His first two novels, *Dancing Arabs* and *Let it Be Morning*, have received much critical and scholarly attention.[570] These novels, like the early series of his popular television program "Arab Labor," have presented the Arab-Israeli as a figure caught between two worlds, both of which accept his presence with suspicion and ridicule. Accused of creating Arabs who want to be Jews, but can never be accepted as such, Kashua's characters are held back by their own ethnic identity. Constant attempts to pass in both worlds ultimately fail.

Kashua's third novel *Second Person Singular* moves from the act of passing and engages with the possibility of full metamorphosis. He weaves together the stories of two men, a lawyer, who remains nameless, and a social worker, Amir, whose attempts to pass in Israeli society explore the role of education in this process of assimilation and integration. Though both men have degrees from elite institutions, their academic knowledge does not compensate for gaps in cultural education. Their attempts to overcome these handicaps in order to pass within the societies in which they exist lead to fervent attempts to educate themselves in the culture and customs of the world in which they hope to belong. Moreover, writing "passing" highlights the very manner in which identity is constructed. "[B]ringing together two seemingly incompatible identities—Israeli and Arab—only to reinforce, validate, and naturalize the current dominant national ideologies of inclusion and exclusion that inevitably render this identity incomplete: Israeli but Arab, Palestinian but Israeli" creates a split identity:

> It is precisely through the impossibility of the Israeli Arab that we are invited to rethink our notions of (ethnic/national) identity and to envision new possibilities of being that are articulated beyond and across current (and prevailing) ethno-national political maps.[571]

Though Rottenberg argues that in *Dancing Arabs* Kashua's protagonist "not only has always wanted to be a Jew, but that he has pulled off becoming one,"[572] she claims that he nevertheless fails to depict "his full integration into Jewish society. Rather, the novel constantly underscores Jewish Israeli society's ambivalent relationship to him as well as his own ambivalent relationship to this dominant society. He never does become a Jew." In *Second Person Singular*, the transformation from Arab to Jew becomes complete. Unlike the lawyer, who is parodied for his petit bourgeois aspirations manifested in his social climbing, the adoption of a socially superior accent, his self-education, and social acculturation; Amir the Arab metamorphoses, becoming Yonatan the Jew. This act, which is the most extreme of the many characters in Kashua's oeuvre of short stories, his regular column for *Ha'aretz*, and his novels, no longer explores the possibility of the "wannabe Jew" (the passing evident in other cultures) that Hochberg identifies in Kashua's writing, but presents the Arab caterpillar as he becomes a Jewish butterfly. Moreover, the transformation from Arab Palestinian to Ashkenazi Jew disrupts Carol Bardenstein's claim that in the Israeli context there is a racial/ethnic spectrum of transformation, but characters rarely move by significant leaps.[574] Kashua's novel offers a change beyond that of mimicry, impersonation, or passing.

The incentives that the transformation offers are clearly outlined in Amir's extended monologue in which he claims that, more than anything else, Israelis are liberated—a freedom that not only speaks to a security situation, but a social and intellectual liberation that is blocked for the Israeli Arab. As an Arab, he is caught in a culture that maintains tribal codes of family and group, and invariably the accompanying pressures to conform. Trapped by his social culture, experiences of guilt, and barred from the free world available to Israeli-Jews, Amir's claustrophobia is emblematic of the Arab-Israeli condition:

> Today I want to be like them. Today I want to be one of them, to go into the places they're allowed to go, to laugh the way they laugh, to drink without having to think about God. I want to be like them. Free, loose, full of dreams, able to think about love. Like them. Like those who started to fill the dance floor with the knowledge that it was theirs, they who felt no need to apologize for their existence, no need to hide their identity. Like them. Those who never looked for suspicious glances, whose loyalty was never questioned, whose acceptance was always taken for granted. Today I want to be like them without feeling like I'm committing a crime. I want to drink with them, dance with them, without feeling as though I'm trespassing in a foreign culture. To feel like I belong, without feeling guilty or disloyal. And what exactly was I being disloyal to?[575]

Israeli society, with its lack of inhibition and its sense of confidence and ownership, is alluring for the Arab-Israeli protagonist who remains unable to participate because of his own inhibited self. Nevertheless, the apparently liberal Ashkenazi represented in the students' open-minded views and relaxed attitude to integration between Arabs and Jews is shown as hypocrisy, and disappears when the group is in the privacy of what they assume is a likeminded social circle, where they demonstrate racism and bigotry. The same qualities that pervade Arab society and that the Arab-Israeli is attempting to escape are no less evident within the Jewish-Israeli sphere.

During the entire process of Amir's transformation, he is supported in each of his acts by Rochaleh, the liberal, educated, Ashkenazi mother figure who slowly adopts him as her own son. She helps him to gain an education, first by borrowing Yonatan's books, and later by helping him assume her son's identity in order to study at the Bezalel art school. Finally, she encourages Amir to switch the ID cards and, with Yonatan's death, to assume his identity completely—a process she refers to as an organ transplant that "could very well save your life."[576] For Rochaleh, enabling Amir to change his identity is part of her belief that national boundaries are inherently destructive:

> I gathered from our conversations that she had nothing but scorn for tradition, nationalism, religion, roots, roots trips, and sentences like, "He who has no past, has no future." She believed that the Arabs did a bad job of impersonating the Zionists, who did a bad job of impersonating the European nationalists of the early twentieth century. Nor did she believe in identity, certainly not the local nationalistic version of it. She said that man was only smart if he was able to shed his identity.

Rochaleh's notions of identity fluidity are at odds with the nationalism that characterizes the Arab-Israeli conflict. However, this instability is not a solution for Amir, for at the very moment in which Amir has become Yonatan, the Ashkenazi son, his mother Rochaleh abandons their home. Sent out to find another new home, the presumed shelter of an Ashkenzi identity is revealed to be ultimately flawed. Unmarried, Rochaleh is abandoned by her son's father, who ceases to visit after Yonatan's accident and is no less isolated than Amir. The "accident" that serves as the central motif of the novel is Yonatan's attempt at suicide, which is replayed repeatedly in the further imagined attempts at suicide that Yonatan enacts even in his vegetative state. Finally, Rochaleh ends Yonatan's life. The incapacitated Yonatan serves as a metaphor for Israeli-Jewish society's determined self-destruction. At the same time, Amir, having abandoned his Arab identity—first by leaving his mother and by refusing to claim his ancestral land, later by changing his clothes, his hair, his behavior, his language and his ideals, and finally by burying Yonatan with his own Arab identity card as a symbolic burial of himself—is also engaged in a process of self-annihilation. The parallels between these young men, including their interests, physical resemblance, and rejection of home and family mock Amir's metamorphosis. For in becoming the Israeli, he has embarked on a journey of his own obliteration.

Ultimately, the novel's exploration of the polarizing effects of ethnic identity and the attempt at its obliteration can be seen in Amir, who as he becomes the artist Yonatan is caught up in a process whereby he works constantly to maintain the act of erasure. When the lawyer sees the final art exhibition (a series of images that erase ethnic boundaries), he comes to understand the mission that has become Amir/Yonatan's way of seeing Israel: "The lawyer, who was always proud of his ability to discern between Arab and Jew at a glance, had a hard time determining the ethnicity of these people."[578] The images in which it is impossible to distinguish those differences, which are markers of daily Israeli experience, become the articulation of the lawyer's own struggle.

The lawyer's attempts to become invisible to Israeli security reveal a constant process of adaptation and transformation. When he first left his parents' home, "He was stopped practically every time he boarded a bus."[579] He struggles to master a system that will allow him to escape detection and thereby avoid the constant oppression and humiliation that being marked out affords him.

It had taken him some time, but he had finally figured out that the border police, the security guards, and the police officers, all of whom generally hail from the lower socioeconomic classes of Israeli society, will never stop anyone dressed in clothes that seem more expensive than their own.[580]

His superficial transformations of hair and clothing become increasingly more sophisticated:

"What's up?" a security guard asked him near a bus stop, and the lawyer, who knew that the security guards checked the Hebrew of passersby, and who always answered crisply and with a generous smile, now merely nodded, but that too, sufficed. The guard did not ask to see his papers.[581]

The act of passing through checkpoints with ease confounds the Arab-Israeli's bounded situation and supports passage from marginalized to integrated. Karen Grumberg explains in her discussion of his earlier novels:

The Israeli Palestinian…has not been forced to relinquish his spatial rights. Through an intricate and sometimes absurd color-coded system that classifies identification cards, license plates and maps, he is allowed to continue living in his home, and to move about the country relatively freely."[582]

Grumberg's assertion that Kashua's characters daily experience "social, cultural, and spatial 'in between-ness,' to the point that, metaphorically or literally, they cannot move" leads to a process whereby the "character's paralysis asserts the fallacy of their designation as Israelis even as it denounces the futility of their identification with Palestinians and Palestinian nationalism."[583] Accepting Kashua's rendition, that having understood the codes of Israeli-Jewish society his characters are able to operate, supports a charming if simplistic rendition of the divisions within Israel. The lawyer's constant attempts to educate himself and transform his person reflect a destabilizing of identity that leads to a state of incompleteness. He changes his accent from that of the Triangle and "he adopted the more refined, less threatening accent of the Galileans. They seemed more enlightened, more educated, better dressed, better off, the products of superior schools."[584] Though as he later learns, when he meets his wife, a Galilean, despite his assumptions, these people are not wealthier or more educated. He moves to an office in West Jerusalem, even though his clientele continues to come from the Eastern side, since both they and he believe it will make him more authoritative, and it raises his status in their eyes. Even the act of taking a wife is seen in relation to the ways that it improves his social standing. This is so marked that when he suspects his wife's infidelity and questions whether he would have married her if she were not a virgin, he concludes that what matters is whether the other wives in his social circle had previous sexual partners. He remains Arab because his wife is a possession not an equal. He sleeps alone because he is isolated in his quest to fully integrate and become the ideal Israeli he imagines, a dream already undermined by his previous illusions, while his family is able to dwell in the ambiguities of the Arab-Israeli.

For the lawyer, auto-didacticism is an ongoing task, as it is for his entire social group, which, aware of the knowledge they lack, have a monthly meeting in order to educate themselves. But though he represents a generation in transition, the lawyer can never complete the assimilation that Amir accomplishes. Kashua satirizes the lawyer and his unending quest to understand the Israeli psyche. The security guard's simple "what's up" becomes a test of nationality and identity, rather than a greeting. In this novel, Kashua emphasizes "The limits of masquerade and 'passing' as viable political instruments for fighting discrimination," as Hochberg has claimed, "by further calling attention to the violence involved in uncritically internalizing the very illusion of a real unmediated and unmasked identity, itself carried through the promise of a coherent and authentic national subjectivity: Israeli, Palestinian, Arab, or Jewish."[585]

Kashua's constant mockery of the lawyer and his group's attempts at improvement (no one reads the books assigned, a single person dominates talk because of their pet subject, the food and its provenance are the real social measure of the meetings) reminds us that the Arab-Israeli remains forever excluded as much through his own cultural baggage as his alienation from Israeli and Western culture. Ultimately, Kashua despairs that this first generation who aims to assimilate can never succeed. Only their children will know enough about the social codes to be accepted in Jewish-Israeli society.

> The lawyer was certain that the other members of the group had also been made aware of their shortcomings and that they realized that they, too, had to close the gap. If they were unable, then they had to ensure that their children were given the tools to do so. ... the Arab parents simply wanted their children to soak up Western culture, for their children to learn from the Jews that which they themselves could not provide."[586]

The children of the next generation will understand the cultural languages and social codes that remain elusive and unknowable for the lawyer. In his regular column published in *Ha'aretz*, Kashua presents a discussion with his own child who is unclear about her ethnic identity—"'Language is identity,'" I found myself shouting in a whisper. "'Language is belonging.'" The child wisely retorts that Kashua writes in Hebrew; is this then his identity, she asks. As an adult, he has consciously chosen to adopt Hebrew as his literary language in order to connect through his writing with the Israeli culture in which he lives. As an Arab father, his inclination is to find his daughter an Arabic tutor because her increasing integration into Israeli society threatens to remove her from an Arab ethnicity and past. Like the protagonist of Sikseck's novel, there is a growing alienation from an Arab and a Palestinian identity for those who accept Israeli culture in order to assimilate within it. Finally, Kashua comments on his relationship between his identity and the Hebrew language in his response to questions posed by a French literary prize:

> I learned your language at the expense of my mother tongue so I could address you in a language I thought you could understand. So I don't want someone who isn't fluent in the language to speak to me in flawed and slow Arabic. I'm at work, I'm not standing at some checkpoint. And maybe I learned Hebrew just for this moment, when I could use it to shout eloquently at a worker who tried to slight me and remind me of my place. So, "Get out of my office!" I shouted. "And I don't ever want to see your face again!"
>
> Time went by and no one came into my office to request an explanation for my behavior. I went back to the questions for the French prize and answered the one about language: For me, language is merely a tool for writing stories. Hebrew for me is a bridge between cultures.

And as to the second question, about what it means to be an Arab in a Jewish state, I wrote: This question should be referred to Jews, they're the ones who decide.[587]

Kashua aspires to a perfect hybridity, which takes on the best elements of Jewish and Arab society, but liberates Arab-Israelis from the constraints they face in both realms. Like Sikseck, he offers characters who model this possibility even as both writers simultaneously lament the loss of Palestinian language and culture. Kashua, raised within an Arab community that lives separately from the Jewish world, experienced his acculturation through his time at a prestigious Jewish boarding school where the memory of adaptation exists as a trauma, though one now assimilated into his identity. But Sikseck, raised in Jaffa in a "mixed" city where Arabs and Jews live, work, and learn together, imbibed the Jewish-Israeli system at so early an age that he had to "learn" Palestinian Arab traditions more consciously than Jewish religion and culture. It was Succot and not Ramadan that framed his childhood memories. This education may ultimately explain their different positions, but Kashua's children, now raised in Jerusalem with Hebrew as their dominant language, may come to see themselves in light of Sikseck's absolute hybridization. Ultimately, isolated from both traditional Arab and national Jewish worlds, his children's identity may reflect this new, third way. ■

SHIRA WOLOSKY

Teaching in Transnational Israel:
An Ethics of Difference

Prolegomena

The slogan of the BDS movement is that Israel is an apartheid state, an unjust state, indeed, an unjustified state. And yet: Salim Joubran is a justice of the Israeli Supreme Court. Hossam Haick, a Professor at the Technion, Israel's prestigious university of science and technology, will teach the first MOOC—massive open online course—on nanotechnology in Arabic. As he puts it: "If the Middle East was like the Technion, we would already have peace. In the pure academy, you feel totally equal with every person. And you are appreciated based on your excellence."[588] Omar Barghouti, a leading activist of BDS and of the Academic Boycott resolution recently passed by the American Studies Association, has his M.A. from Tel Aviv University.

Israel is not an apartheid state. BDS, in its apartheid slogan, represents itself as a movement for human rights. In fact it is a political movement whose goal is not the righting of human wrongs, or even righting the human rights wrongs suffered by Palestinians. If that were the case it might make mention in its resolutions of the fact that today, every day, thousands of Palestinians are under attack and siege in Syria, caught in the civil war where tens of thousands of civilians are being displaced, wounded, and killed.[589] As Norman Finkelstein, a vocal critic of Israel, states, the BDS movement is masking its intentions. "At least be honest what you want—'we want to abolish Israel and this is our strategy for doing it.'"[590] Omar Barghouti has openly declared that the two-state solution "was never a moral solution to start with." Of BDS he says: "The current phase has all the emblematic properties of what may be considered the final chapter of the Zionist project." His express goal of a one-state solution is one in which "by definition, Jews will be a minority."[591] As Roger Cohen, a writer strongly critical of Israel, concludes, what this means is the end of Israel altogether. Of BDS, he writes:

> Its stated aim is to end the occupation, secure "full equality" for Arab-Palestinian citizens of Israel, and fight for the right of return of all Palestinian refugees. The first objective is essential to Israel's future. The second is laudable. The third, combined with the second, equals the end of Israel as a Jewish state. This is the hidden agenda of BDS, its unacceptable subterfuge: beguile, disguise, and suffocate.

The anti-Apartheid movement in South Africa contained no such ambiguity. As Diana Shaw Clark, an activist on behalf of a two-state solution, wrote to me in an email, "People affiliated with divestment in South Africa had no agenda other than the liberation and enfranchisement of an oppressed majority." This is not the case in Israel, where the triple objective of BDS would, in Clark's words, "doom Israel as a national home for the Jews." Mellifluous talk of democracy and rights and justice masks the BDS objective that is nothing other than the end of the Jewish state for which the United Nations gave an unambiguous mandate in 1947.[592]

The call for Israel to become a democratic state for all its citizens is tautological. Israel is today a democratic state for all its citizens. This is not to claim complete social justice across all sectors, or to disclaim the urgent need for greater opportunity, access, and investment across all sectors. In terms of education, Arabic is an official language of Israel; Arabs run their own educational system, teaching their own cultures in their own language. This system does not receive equal investment. Nor is the access of Arab students to higher education yet equal. Yet a fifth of Israel's medical students are Arab, as are a third of the students at the University of Haifa. In Tel Aviv, 30% of Israeli universities' medical school students are Arab. However, overall only 9% of university students are Arab. In the West Bank as well, there are a respectable number of institutions of higher education: the Arab American University, Al-Quds Open University, Al-Quds University, An-Najah National University, Bethlehem Bible College, Bethlehem University, Birzeit University, Edward Said National Conservatory of Music, Hebron University,

Ibrahimieh College, Khodori Institute, Tulkarm, Palestine Polytechnic University, Al Ahlia University of Palestine.[594]

Discrimination, lack of equal opportunity, and lack of equal investment should and must be addressed within Israeli democratic society. Nonetheless, Israeli democracy is committed to minority rights, in ways that are outstanding in the Middle East. This is one context in which the extraordinary self-subversion of the academic boycott of Israel is apparent. Besides the self-contradictory and self-defeating nature of any academic boycott—how can a boycott for freedom of speech itself boycott freedom of speech?—one directed against Israel attacks the very place where freedom of speech is most intense.[595] Academic boycotts institute the very transgression they are protesting—restriction of freedom and rights of expression.[596] As I will go on to discuss in describing my own experience teaching in Israel, targeting Israeli universities is especially damaging, self-contradictory, and ironic. The university is a protected place for free exploration and expression of ideas, a true public sphere (which Israel provides and protects, unlike, one must add, the Palestinian and other Arab countries surrounding it, where Christians are under assault, rival members of militias silence and attack each other, women are restricted or worse, and gays are outcasts. Saudi Arabia restricts entire areas to Muslims only. On March 25, 2014, they barred an American-Jewish journalist from accompanying President Obama on a visit there. If the claim is that universities supported by governments whose policies are objectionable should be boycotted, then the boycotters of Israel should be boycotting themselves. American universities, whose salaries and other support they accept, are funded by a government whose policies around the world, such as supporting Israel, they protest and reject.[597]

But universities, and in Israel very vehemently, provide scenes of open argument from many varying viewpoints, among faculty and students. Inside Israel, universities constitute a core arena in which Arab and other students are able to encounter each other in a sphere of free discourse exchange, critical thinking, and access to multiple viewpoints. Indeed, Israeli universities provide a rare place and time in which students from different backgrounds are together in a common endeavor, that of learning and earning a degree. This offers an opportunity for intersection that should be commended and supported, not resolved against. Any interruption or condemnation of such a scene closes and devalues the very ethics that are the supposed aims of the boycott in the form of interchange, multiplicity of viewpoints, recognition, and respect.

The legitimacy of Israel proper remains contested, both besides and because of the status of the West Bank, which represents a tragic and recalcitrant battlefield of conflicting narratives. In my mind there is no question that Israel must withdraw from the West Bank, since we do not want to govern people who do not want to be governed by us. A majority of Israelis agree with this, although certainly some resist this recognition. How to pursue a politics that accomplishes withdrawal is a serious problem internal to Israel. As of now, Israel is caught in the terrible vise of attempting to respect democratic norms and human rights in the face of ongoing assaults on its security.[598] Rockets from Gaza, attacks on civilians, all with the express intent of causing harm and destruction to ordinary people, are something Israelis (Arab and Jew) daily face. Nonetheless, I and most other Israelis see the only path for ourselves in order to uphold our own democratic and moral values is withdrawal.

Boycott supporters—in their failure to acknowledge the severe complexity and conflict as the context for Israeli actions; or the continuing attacks on Israel and the denial of its fundamental legitimacy—practice distortion to the point of fabrication.

Internal conflict, reluctance to cede territory for both security and ideological reasons, and distrust of the partner all contribute to the failure to achieve withdrawal from the West Bank on the part of the Israelis. But the looming obstacle above all others is the refusal to recognize the legitimacy of Israel on the part of (some) Palestinians. As Omar Barghouti has said expressly, and what remains the underlying motive of the boycott of Israel among those in its vanguard, is that Israel itself is not a legitimate country. The boycott, and Palestinian politics itself, want to claim a right to self-determination that they deny to Israel as a Jewish State. To be a state with a cultural identity is not anti-democratic—Norway and Denmark, The Netherlands and France, Germany and Britain all are democracies with specific cultural identities. As Michael Walzer has repeatedly argued, one project of Norway is to promote Norwegians and Norwegian culture: its language, its way of life.[599] Arab countries and Palestinians themselves are committed to the continuity and heritage of Islam, as of Arab social forms and language. They militantly claim this right to be who they are in a variety of forums, including political ones. What then makes them deny this right to Israel? The claim to accept Israel as one state so as to create a true democracy is basely prevaricating. Aside from the fact that today there are no examples of multicultural Arab democracies that grant equal rights to minorities (Turkey struggles with its Kurds, has a violent history with its Armenians, and is now in a state of internal struggle over its democratic norms; Lebanon, which long was offered as the model for peaceful and respectful co-existence, experienced a fifteen year civil war and today sees its Shia and Sunni populations on the edge of violence; Iraq is a riven place; throughout the middle east, minorities are under threat, including whatever Jews remain after their expulsion). Most importantly, democracy does not necessarily prevent the suppression or denial of cultural identities. Even the United States as a "nation of immigrants," undefined by exclusionary ethnicity, has a decided cultural identity of shared history, values, political forms, and norms. The denial to Israel of its right to self-determination, while claiming such a right for the Palestinians, gravely contributes to the conflict between them rather than toward its solution. A narrative that denies the legitimacy of Jews to self-determination is one that cannot be reconciled to a two-state solution or to the mutual respect for difference which alone, I believe, can be the basis and foundation of peaceful co-existence and positive recognition.

I. Transnational Israel

Among those who initiate, those who support, and those who are concerned about the issues raised by the academic boycott initiatives against Israel, few, I suspect, have a very vivid picture of what academic life in Israel is like. Since I am the one being boycotted, I would like to share my experience there.

About one third of the students in the classes I teach in the English Department of the Hebrew University are Arab, mainly women: Christian and Muslim and secular, studying with other Israelis who are Russian, American, British, French, Ethiopian, and/or whose parents arrived from European and Arab countries at various times and in various ways, including expulsion or flight. My first point, then, is that Israel is a transnational state.

By transnational I do not mean postnational, a term with which it is often associated but which I think points in a different direction. Transnationalism, I would argue, allows continued recognition of the national polity, which in fact has been the only political format for democracy to date. It also recognizes, however, that, especially today, many individuals claim more than one national affiliation. This situation is best described as *multiple memberships.* Each person may affiliate with, identify with, participate in, and belong to more than one community, in varying ways and degrees, and with varying and at times shifting priorities. Among these memberships there can be—inevitably are—tensions and conflicts. To be Arab/Israeli, Jewish/woman, Arab/woman, traditional/modern is no easy feat. What is called identity is, I propose, much better conceived in terms of membership. Identity as a term implies something static, self-same, unified, fixed, essentialist (identity from *idem*: Latin for same). Membership instead emphasizes active affiliation and participation in a culture or group with which you identify, in ways that are not static but shifting, slackening and strengthening, altering in balance and tension and confirmation with each other. This is especially the case in today's globalized world. As membership, identity involves more than self-description or self-conception, more than an open performative selfhood such as Judith Butler theorizes. Membership is not only self-referring as the term "identity" often seems to be, as if one were autonomously self-identical. Instead, membership acknowledges how people other than yourself partly shape who each self is and becomes; and that selves emerge out of interactions with others both in a past and toward a future. Free self-performance is an abstraction not unlike the liberal self it critiques. It is, moreover, an abstraction that is ethically bereft. It admits no obligations to others, no continuity of ties, no past or future for memory or hope in a shared world where each person, through individual choice as well as obligation, seeks to contribute to ongoing projects that create a world for that self and also for others.

To speak of national polity today is not to speak of unitary ethnicity, which few nations have ever been or had anyway. Claiming such a unitary existence would, moreover, betray the difference that ethnicity both represents and requires, as I shall argue below. Such a unitary ethnicity is certainly not now and has never been the case in Israel. Israel is an immigrant nation, whose citizens come from many places, cultures, and languages. It is a multiethnic and pluralist society (much more, alas, than are the Arab societies which surround it). Besides Jews, there are Druze and Bahai and Arab Christians and Arab Muslims. Each of these transnational identities has in formal terms equal legal rights, if not fully social and economic equality (although all enjoy universal health coverage, something that can't be said for Americans). Each has full cultural rights, to speak and study and dress and marry and celebrate and mourn in its own cultural way (much more than, for example, in France). But the Jews are themselves an intense variety of backgrounds, kinds, customs, and beliefs. The majority of Israeli Jews in fact come from Arab countries, often as a result of expulsion from them. To be Jewish is almost by definition to be transnational, composite in identification and memberships, perhaps one reason that they remain so uncannily at the center of the news preoccupied today with questions of identity. To be transnational is to belong to and identify with a variety of communities, in multiple affiliations and memberships.

In my view, transnationalism is a far better way of positing membership issues today than are more familiar and traditional concepts. It is more apt than diaspora or exile. With regard to Jews, transnationalism acknowledges the age-old fact that Jews, historically as well as today, were members not only of their local communities and polities but also had relationships to other Jewish communities in the world and also to Israel, as a religious center of reference and today as the Jewish national polity. These relations can be considered lateral rather than hierarchical. The Jewish national polity has, however, the distinctive claim of allowing Jews for the first time in two millennia to be self-governing as Jews, with their culture the public (although not exclusive) culture, speaking a language, observing a calendar, and celebrating holidays according to Jewish cultural forms. This is no more than Norwegians do, or French, or Germans in their democratic polities in which a specific culture is the public one. As to what makes Jewish culture Jewish, the answer is not only never endingly complex but also immanent and pragmatic: the historical continuity of a set of texts and practices and languages. Jews are those who identify with, belong to, and wish to contribute to the continued existence of just those texts, practices, and languages as an ongoing historical project. To claim that a national polity provides a unique and desired mode for doing this is to claim for Israel no more than would be claimed for Poles, Latvians, or Palestinians in each of their homelands.

II. The Classroom as Public Sphere

Transnational Israelis, each with multiple memberships that orient them both toward themselves and toward others with whom they share (and also do not share) various forms of membership—gender, religion, heritage, locality, ethnicity: these are the students whom I meet, and who meet each other, in my classes. These students do, and should, each keep their own commitments, their affiliations and participation in their several cultures. Such self-formation through affiliations is especially pronounced among the Arab women I teach. They identify themselves as and with their communities. But this is not to say that their, or anyone's, membership identifications need be unitary, self-enclosed, or intolerant. What can offset the danger of such enclosure is exactly multiplicity itself. Through multiple memberships individuals can resist being determined and controlled by any one identification or group. Diverse memberships can provide critical stances toward each other. Interchange, reciprocity, argument, conflict, subversion, and confirmation are among the ways in which multiple memberships can bear on each other. The result can be confusion, doubt, excruciating conflict, and also renewed commitment, ethical sensitivity, experienced by strengthened, enlarged, complex selves who refer beyond their own private existence into public concerns that shape their world. Such engagement can lead to transformation as well as critique, renewed commitments as well as renegotiations.

My own teaching has centered mainly in courses on American literature and culture; on feminist theory; and also on religion and theory. Each of these topics opens to cultural adventure, as the diverse students of my classes encounter each other. In my experience, the Israeli university especially should be supported and praised as a public sphere in which different sectors who otherwise have few social spaces for doing so can meet each other, all pursuing a common project of education in whatever different fields and ways, and before or outside the structure of lives that will soon be separated by work, family, locality, and sectorial pressures.

Certainly that is how I view my own classroom: as a civic scene, beyond whatever material is under discussion. I see student engagement in the class as civic training for democratic participation and cultural activism. Critical analysis of texts, however canonical; considered debate of positions, however apparently authoritative; perhaps above all, the ability and the desire to address each other in ways that respect difference but also explore terms and seek accommodation: these are the educational opportunities I see the classroom offer. Class discussions become intense scenes of exchange and debate, where persons from and within very distinct contexts are invited and pressed to address and attend to each other.

Especially my class on Feminist Theory is an extraordinary experience. Together my students and I discover a language that names and places our own lives, revealing issues and situations we did not even know were there. It is especially challenging for women to learn to use their voices, to project their voices into the public sphere, to participate in discussion and debate. Doing critical thinking and bringing it to expression runs counter to women's social roles, often working against religious norms, although not—as we also explore—necessarily dictated by religious texts themselves as examined through different modes of interpretation and different (women) interpreters. Such issues of speaking and being heard, of resisting both external and internal silencing, are core concerns throughout feminist theory.[600] In the classroom there are women with covered hair and without covered hair, Muslim and Jewish, Christian and many other sorts of transnational Israelis, traditional to many varying degrees. My goal is to create the classroom itself as a public sphere. It is the chance for women to develop analytical and critical skills for interpreting texts and claims, however sacred or standard, for examining and becoming conscious of their own narratives, and to learn that there are different ones. The class is driven by the attempt to open speaking space to those unfamiliar to it. I try to slow discussion down, to open time for each person to speak despite often deeply ingrained hesitation. I try to ask questions that will invite other questions. I try to create an atmosphere and ethos in which students will speak to each other.

Topics in my feminism course include body image and comportment as forms of social coercion; the political theories of liberalism and communitarianism, weighing how selves conceived through private self-determination compare with selves conceived as embedded in culture. Women's history provides a powerful entry into old recognitions, revealing ways in which one's own experience is not one's own only, not limited to the specific contexts which each woman herself inhabits. Legal, economic, and social histories and debilities are examined, most crucially the very lack of access to public discourse denying women the possibility of shaping the laws under which they live. Women's invisible work in the home, the continued inequalities of work opportunities and conditions, but also continued commitments to family and community are discussed, as is the question of how to balance them. Not least, histories of religious institutions in America, of access to sacred texts, of debates about how these are interpreted and perhaps most urgently by whom—with women's emergence as interpreters of their own religious traditions and claim to religious authority—has special resonance in this Middle Eastern classroom.

Some texts open extraordinary scenes of cultural encounter and confrontation. The portrait of a young girl in Henry James's *Daisy Miller,* who, defiant of social convention, dies from the malaria she contracts when she visits the Roman Forum unchaperoned at night with an Italian man, splits the class among those who sympathize with her independence and those who see her end to be a fit warning against wildness. Most women in the classes, however, are riveted by the women's points of view we uncover, the social, political, historical, and psychological attempts to bring the hidden, which is to say publicly and privately ignored lives of women into the light of record and recognition. Yet most women in my classes, Jewish and Arab Christian and Muslim, identify themselves closely with the tradition(s) and communities they see themselves to a be part of. Theirs is not a performative individualism, answerable only to themselves. There is no "identity" apart from their memberships, to which on the whole they remain deeply attached. To address them and to listen to them is to respect these community memberships, while also developing critical perspectives on them, and discovering the terms and norms of other communities in which other students are members in ways that are both critical and respectful. This means exploring the resources within the cultures themselves for recognizing and respecting other cultures, for upholding one's own particularity while also upholding the other's.

This is the university world that is now under attack and boycott. From a feminist stance I wonder: in these discussions of human rights, are women human? The many places in which women are severely constrained do not occasion calls for boycotts and are not condemned by resolutions. Instead, it is the academy in Israel that boycotts denounce, where women have what for many is their most dramatic and self-conscious opportunity to emerge into voice and participation.

III. An Ethics of Difference

What approach might help move toward reconciliation between Israelis and Palestinians? Boycotts, and indeed most negotiations, derive from and reflect conflicting narratives, each claiming its own right to history, to justice, to self-determination. But approached as a conflict of rights, what often results is denial of rights of the other: denial of the history, justice, and self-determination of the other. The two remain conflictual and apparently incompatible. Recent moral theories, however, particularly feminist ones, propose a different approach: that of responsibility rather than of rights.[601] This is also the moral theory of Emmanuel Levinas, who is perhaps more than any other philosopher the source of discourses of the Other that have become so pivotal and prominent in ethical-political debates. But far from betraying his own ethic of the other in his support of Israel, as is often argued, Levinas offers a path through conflicting rights towards responsibility and respect of difference, including the difference of a Jewish-cultural (democratic) Israel in the Middle East.[602]

Levinasian philosophy opens with a notion not of sameness, which paradoxically generates conflict as claims to identical rights compete with each other; but rather with difference, both as a fact and as a norm. Difference, particularity, especially in the form of nationality, has become the term of suspicion, as the source of conflict in the world. There are many histories to this discourse against nationality. What is very odd, however, is how the historical Other of Western discourse, the Jew, has now become the enemy and oppressor of an otherness now claimed for post-colonial peoples. The granting of peoplehood to post-colonials is upheld due to their prior suffering and domination, but denied to Jews seeking self-determination in Israel. Yet this in fact has reaffirmed Jewish Otherness: the Jew has simply become the Other of the Other. Israel is the Other of and, as nationhood, against whom all the discomfort, suspicion, guilt, and blame directed towards national particularity is now focused and finds expression.

Yet what is at fault and dangerous in national formation is not its recognition of the value of difference and particularity, but their denial. Respect for difference instead would promote respect for other national formations. Asserting one's own rights and rightness against those of others often results in a denial of difference, not its affirmation. Often it results in occluding the narratives of others, claiming one's own formation as the only or most valid one. This is not an assertion of difference but one of formation as the only justified one, amounting to a hegemony of sameness, not a respect of otherness. The refusal to leave or make room for others, inside one's own polity or against the polity of others, is not an assertion of difference but only of one's own sameness.

Levinasian ethics recognizes difference and otherness as a good. Not only does difference in fact constitute the world we live in, but it is a good that it does so. Reversing millennia of philosophical preference for unity as what bestows order, truth, and meaning on the world, but which in practice has led to efforts of domination of one apparently superior form over others, Levinas declares the good of multiplicity.

Multiplicity is first premise. It is both the ultimate and the desirable condition of the world we inhabit, despite centuries of lament at the absence of unity, concord, and consensus, against the fragility, change, and disagreement that multiplicity entails. Yet, as Madison wrote in *Federalist* 10, the remedies for faction—destroying liberty or imposing sameness—are worse than the disease.[603] Upholding difference does not justify any mode of politics that claims its own difference to permit the suppression of the difference of others, in one's midst or outside it. Upholding difference instead calls for arrangements that respect and sustain difference, resisting any claim to its suppression, whether for a group or for individuals. It involves what might be called a mode of positive negative liberty: enacting respect for the difference of others as long as that difference respects difference.

Recognizing the legitimacy, not to mention wealth, of difference is an entirely different premise for negotiation than that of competing demands, each of which claims its own exclusive right at the expense of others. In the Israel/Palestine conflict, respecting difference would require each side to acknowledge, if not the correctness of the narrative of the other, at least the validity that the other has a narrative. The Palestinians and Israelis would each accept the legitimacy of the other's narrative, of each one's historic tie to the land, rather than rejecting the notion of the Jews as a people (rather than only a religion) as is too often the case among Arabs; or claiming a greater Israel that displaces Palestinians, as is the case on the Israeli political and religious right. Each would admit the other to have attachments to the land the other also claims. Arabs would admit the validity and indeed value of cultural and religious difference in a region until now considered Muslim. Israelis would accept (as a majority, polls show, in fact have done) the legitimacy of a Palestinian attachment to the same land, the validity of a national state in which they can determine their own lives; also of the Palestinian narrative, which sees the arrival of the Jews as catastrophe, causing their displacement and challenging long held views of religious history. Mutual recognition and respect for difference would still involve difficult negotiations about how to make room for each other's version of history and claims from it even when it impinges on and challenges one's own. Only then is co-existence, even positive responsibility, in a shared world of differences imaginable. Only then can different narratives reside together. Each would have to cede something to the other, in respect of the other's existence as other, as different; and in responsibility to the lives and welfare of each as living together as others in a world irreducibly multiple. ■

RACHEL FISH

The Bi-nationalist Fantasy within Academia

This essay examines the historical transformation of the idea of bi-nationalism in Palestine and, later, Israel. Tracing the changes in meaning associated with the concept of bi-nationalism highlights the intentions of those who advocate for a bi-nationalist platform. Thus one can interrogate where and how bi-nationalist claims remain part of discourse about Israel and among those for whom bi-nationalism is attractive. The academy is one notable environment in which the bi-national framework continues to be seductive. The last part of this essay explores the cultural and political contexts of the university that enable the bi-national fantasy to entice idealistic hearts and minds.

The dissolution of the European empires in the early modern period and the growth of nationalism posed existential challenges for Jews. By the nineteenth century, Jews in Eastern Europe faced serious distress and persecution. In Western Europe, Jews were enticed by assimilation and acculturation, which weakened the grip of traditional religious practice. Secularization and individual emancipation began to erode traditional Jewish life, ultimately raising the question of whether Judaism could survive there. Both as individuals and as a collective, Jews had to navigate the predicament of their acceptance, or lack thereof, by their host societies. If the Jews were part of the indigenous populations, then why were they different? And if they were unique from other peoples, then why did they continue to live among them?

365

The ideology of nationalism provided Jews with a means to create and maintain a Jewish identity within the modern context.

Jewish nationalism encouraged Jews to attain collective emancipation as a historical nation. Yet this transformation of the Jewish people into a nation was disputed, as Jews were perceived primarily as a confessional or religious group, perhaps even as an ethnic cluster, but not necessarily as a nation. With the Balfour Declaration and its call for the establishment of a "Jewish National Home," however, Jews were recognized as a people claiming sovereignty, and Zionism was set on the path to international legitimacy.

Zionism was a nineteenth-century European project; it encouraged a transformation of the Jewish people from objects of history to subjects. Zionism reflected a realization that emancipation was inherently flawed, indeed in many ways was a failure. Emancipation did not overcome all individual limitations placed upon Jewry and often required Jews to relinquish their distinctive collective identity. Zionism as a form of Jewish activism called for Jews returning as agents to their own history and narrative. It was a revolt against past Jewish passivity, inspiring many to begin imagining what it would mean to chart their own future. Many early immigrants to Israel saw themselves as rebels, for they were unwilling to remain passive during waves of pogroms and increased anti-Semitism and discrimination. Many of the early pioneers harbored anger at Jewish passivity, along with the Jewish leadership and religious institutions that accepted the realities of the European context. Many Zionists felt Jewish values ought to be expressed in collective action, rather than in reliance on either divine intervention or the host societies. Indeed, Zionism preached rebellion as much against the shackling of Jews by the agents of Jewish religion as by alien rulers. Independence meant Jews would be liberated from the rule of rabbis no less than from that of the Czars.

Yet there was no one unified or homogenous Zionist vision. Rather, competing visions of Zionism were expressed in terms of secularism, politics, religion, socialism, and spiritualism. Each of the Zionist camps revitalized a particular mythical past and applied it to the present with the purpose of refashioning Jewish history and identity for the sake of cultivating a new reality expressed in a shared narrative, history, culture, tradition, government, and language. The Zionist leadership was thus challenged to make this plural kaleidoscope functional. This diversity was inherent in Jewry's varied European experience. So it was no surprise to have this cacophony transplanted to the *Yishuv*. The Zionist movement, *Yishuv* politics, and Israeli governments have all been governed by coalition politics. Divisions within the strains of Zionism are rooted in ideology and belief. All the Zionist perspectives sought to influence the shape of the movement, the driving forces that compelled the nation, and the principles to be articulated as motives for a functioning sovereignty. The process of navigating between ideas, ideals, and realities determined the success or failure of each Zionist stream.

The Zionist ideas vying for traction were all involved in the early stages of Israel's inception. Prior to the establishment of the Israeli state, Zionist leaders engaged and debated one another to advance their particular visions for the future. One camp within the movement was that of the cultural/spiritual Zionists. They were interested in recovering and renewing Judaism's spiritual character, but anti-Semitism did not play a role in their perspective. Indeed, the cultural/spiritual Zionists were not interested in Herzl's articulation of political Zionism and sought to counter his vision of creating a sovereign nation-state without particular Jewish content.

Spiritual Zionist Ahad Ha'am (1856-1927) was interested in accommodating the Diasporic existence and not relegating Jews in exile to a subordinate position. For Ahad Ha'am there was no comparability between Palestine and Diaspora. Palestine was considered the geographical and spiritual center, for only in Palestine could Judaism radiate its vitality by developing a rejuvenated religion and culture. The purpose of the state, according to Ahad Ha'am, was to help facilitate a cultural and linguistic renaissance. Cultural Zionists were interested in reviving Hebrew culture and language and these efforts should spread from Palestine throughout the Jewish Diaspora. Their central focus was not the mere creation of a political entity but the spiritual growth of individuals and the development of Jewish content and literacy. Spirituality, however, did not necessarily refer to God; rather belief in God was replaced with an emphasis on peoplehood.

For cultural Zionists, the models for ethical behavior were based on the Biblical prophets. The prophets evoked notions of equality and justice and emphasized these values as prerequisites for creating community. The cultural Zionists appropriated these ideas as the defining qualities of a nation-state. Their litmus test was to judge how equality and justice would be realized in interaction between the Jewish and Arab peoples in the land of Palestine. Thus cultural Zionist warnings about Arab-Jewish relations in Palestine were recognized as issues Zionism had to confront. The manner in which Jewish nationalists approached the Arabs would determine the fate and success of Palestine. Prior to the establishment of the state of Israel, many cultural Zionists advocated the formation of a bi-national state in which there would be cooperation and coexistence between Jewish and Arab populations throughout Mandatory Palestine.

The idea of a bi-national state is not unique to Palestine/Israel. It has been considered and even adopted in other nation-states that confront contested claims to land, questions regarding the identity of the polity, and tensions between two or more ethnic or religious populations. In its most neutral meaning, bi-nationalism designates a nation-state framework wherein two national groups coexist and where each can express its national identity and have some autonomy in matters of culture, politics, education, and religion. But in the discourse of the critique of Zionism, the term bi-nationalism is not neutral. The individuals who first advanced the idea of bi-nationalism as an alternative to Herzlian Zionism, or political Zionism, comprised a small group of intellectuals who rejected the idea of nationalism that dominated European thought and the *Yishuv*.[604] They imagined a new form of nation-state, and envisioned Israel as both democratic and pluralistic, founded on and exemplifying universal moral principles.

The bi-national idea as a theoretical construct is appealing to some Jews and Arabs alike, as it attempts to deemphasize differences between peoples and in principle creates a united society, but in practice the establishment of a bi-nationalist state faces many challenges. Since no bi-national polity for the state of Israel was created, it has been possible for the term to be employed by those with a variety of perspectives and goals. From the 1920s through the present, Zionist theoreticians, Palestinian intellectuals, political activists and academics—Israeli, Arab, Jewish, and non-Jewish—have used the term to advocate very different political goals and visions. Indeed the meanings associated with bi-nationalism have changed, from early Zionist proposals for a bi-national state to the way it is used in twenty-first century non-Zionist and anti-Zionist calls for the dissolution of Zionist society and the Jewish state. The implications of these changes are both immediate and long-term, for they impact public discourse, relations between Israeli Jews and the Palestinian Arab minority, and the persistent debate on how Israel can maintain its identity as both a Jewish and a democratic state.

The idea of a bi-national state was advocated by members of Brit Shalom[605] and certain faculty from the Hebrew University of Jerusalem during the 1920s and the first years of the 1930s. During this period contending Zionist perspectives vied for their particular position. The individuals who advanced these ideologies (cultural, political, religious) were in active dialogue with one another.

During this period, the political leadership of the *Yishuv* was also criticized and questioned openly over its relationship to the Arab community of Palestine. The leadership of the *Yishuv* was not oblivious to the challenge posed by the Arab population. Proponents of the various Zionisms advocated multiple approaches to the question of how best to develop those relationships. Cultural Zionists understood the Arab revolts of 1929 and 1936-1939 as critical turning points that were not properly heeded or recognized by the Yishuv leadership. The small circle of Jewish intellectuals who advocated for a bi-national polity contended that the Zionist leadership was ignoring or marginalizing the nationalist elements within the Arab population and missing an opportunity for serious engagement with the Palestinian Arabs. They envisioned one state based on a type of federation system that would accommodate two peoples. The needs of each community within the sovereignty would be acknowledged and addressed, whether by organizing cantons or institutionalizing governmental autonomy in matters related to personal and national identity, culture, and language.

Jewish proponents of bi-nationalism genuinely believed they could develop a type of nationalism that would avoid the pitfalls of the other nationalistic movements sweeping Europe. Repudiating particularism and chauvinism, they envisioned a form of nationalism instead based on universal values and ideals. Jewish bi-nationalists in the 1920s were attempting to transplant the bi-national framework, borrowed from Western European multi-cultural, multi-linguistic, and multi-religious societies (such as the Hapsburg Empire), onto the Middle Eastern landscape. In this way, the context and essence of a bi-nationalist approach was already transformed across space and time.

The Zionists who espoused such positions rarely found serious Arab counterparts with whom they could partner. In the 1920s and 1930s, the Arabs in the region were not inclined to build bridges with the Jews in Palestine or to pursue mutual cooperation. Among the Arabs both inside and outside of Palestine, the prevailing opinion was that the Zionists were merely temporary residents, and there would be dire consequences if they became permanent. Only a small handful of Arabs were willing to consider a bi-national framework, and they were viewed as traitors to the Arab nationalist cause and, in several instances, were murdered.[606]

It was the 1947 call for partition by the United Nations Special Committee on Palestine, in conjunction with the aftermath of the Holocaust that gave priority to Jewish statehood. Political Zionism was finally able to achieve its goal of a sovereign nation-state when Jews accepted and Arabs rejected partition and the state of Israel was officially declared; once that state existed, advocates of a bi-national polity became even more marginal in mainstream Zionist discourse.

Support for bi-nationalism was then voiced from left of the center. The 1948 war was the defining moment when those bi-nationalists saw interactions between Jews and Arabs in Israel that required immediate redress. Proponents of bi-nationalism exhorted the Jewish leadership to tackle the problem of Palestinian Arab refugees and confront the wrongs inherent in Jewish settlement of *Eretz Yisrael*.[607] A new bi-nationalist group emerged which envisioned a Hebrew identity for Jews and Arabs alike, with the two Semitic peoples constructing a shared narrative based upon geography, language, and culture, rather than religious or nationalist connections. This group, known as the Canaanites, was founded in 1939 and maintained through the 1940s by Yonatan Ratosh.[608] The movement was quite small in number, but it was nonetheless part of the literary and cultural scene. Participants argued that the Land of Israel was that of ancient Canaan, and the emergence of a Hebrew people would reconstitute that ancient people and culture. Judaism was not the primary anchor for the Canaanites; indeed, it was important to them to dissociate both Judaism and Zionism from this proposed Hebrew-Israeli identity. The supporters of this newer version of bi-nationalism aspired to a federated Hebrew state within a larger regional Semitic Mideast federation. Yet they found no serious counterparts, for neither Arab nor other Jewish movements for self-determination shared their enthusiasm for the idea[609] of a federated state or cantonization.

The Canaanite concept of a Hebrew nation projected a strong historical and cultural identity onto the state of Israel, but inherently posed challenges that were not directly addressed by its proponents. Their vision assumed that the state of Israel would separate religion and religious symbols from its foundational principles, but it is questionable how secular, liberal ideals would be able to take precedence in a nation with such deep associations with Judaism's religious heritage and culture. Nor did their approach take into account whether the Arabs of Israel were likely to want to identify as citizens of a Hebrew nation. In sum, this alternative vision seems to have ignored the reality of tribal affiliations among both Jewish and Arab populations.

The 1967 war—when Israel gained control over areas of the West Bank, Gaza Strip, East Jerusalem, Golan Heights, and Sinai Peninsula—was a direct assault against the principles of bi-nationalism in that it exemplified and exacerbated accusations of colonialism. Non- and anti-Zionist supporters of bi-nationalism—as well as many Zionists—argued that controlling another people was unjust and would eventually erode and corrupt Israel's values. This criticism was of serious concern, and not only among the proponents of bi-nationalism. Recalibrating the perceived victims and the victimizers—the David and the Goliath in this equation—resulted in a new paradigm. Unease over how Jews, particularly Israelis, held and used power became an accepted trope in the debate over Israel's territorial conquests and ultimate relationship with the Palestinian Arab communities.

Bi-nationalist discourse had evolved from emphasizing coexistence and cooperation to focusing on deconstructing the Jewish character of the state as the way to ensure equality for all citizens irrespective of national identity, ethnicity, or religion. The model of a homogenous ethnic nation-state was now deemed abhorrent and was to be rejected in favor of a multi-national, multi-ethnic community where each ethnic or national group has its own political structure and framework. This was the new bi-nationalist position post-1967 that persists today.

If we skip ahead to twenty-first-century bi-nationalist discourse, we find but a skeleton of the original bi-national idea. Employing the language of democracy and multiculturalism, the Palestinian Arabs of Israel, particularly the elite and intelligentsia, condemn Israel for representing and thereby ultimately privileging one people's identity, religion, language, and culture over another. Claiming that the nation-state cannot allow a specific identity to be institutionalized by governmental authorities, some Palestinian Arabs of Israel advocate a bi-nationalism they refer to as the "One State" solution and demand the status of a recognized minority. Specific political parties, such as Balad,[610] seek to guarantee equality for the Palestinian Arab sector by erasing the Jewish identity of the state and ensuring that the voice of the Palestinian Arab citizen of Israel is not heard through a "Jewish" or "Zionist" political mouthpiece.

The emergence of post-Zionist ideology and critical rethinking of the founding narratives and myths upon which Israel was established also affected bi-national discourse. Supported by a number of post-Zionist Israeli academicians, the Palestinian Arabs want to replace Israel with a bi-national state, a single state shared by Arab and Jewish citizens, and one that has no identifying Jewish characteristics marking the public sphere. In contrast to the bi-national state imagined by the members of Brit Shalom (with a universal Jewish character), the one imagined by the Canaanites (where Jews and Arabs would share a joint Hebrew culture), and the one envisioned by Balad (with cultural autonomy for the Arabs in Israel and Jewish populations), the current bi-nationalist vision prioritizes the desires of the Palestinian Arab community. It emphasizes and gives expression to Palestinian identity while de-emphasizing the role and concerns of the Israeli Jewish population.

By expressing their own Palestinian Arab political perspectives, they seek to overcome a sense of marginalization and create a more equitable polity. All of this serves as the backdrop against which Palestinian intellectual elites and activists convened to develop their vision and ideal for the state of Israel, as expressed in the *Future Vision*[611] documents. Their collective thinking was based not only in the particular realities of the Palestinian community in Israel, but in the wider context of minority concerns in the international arena. In approaching the matter with language and foundational documents formulated in the international community, Israeli-Palestinian leaders sought to apply international theories, developed in reference to other minorities in the world, to the Israeli-Palestinian experience.

The bi-nationalism of today focuses on the dismantling of the Zionist and Jewish nation-state as it exists and seeks to replace it with a bi-national arrangement (for which, it should be noted, there are no currently successful long term working models) that goes beyond the territory of Israel proper[612] to incorporate the West Bank and Gaza Strip. While, within this imagined polity, Palestinian Arab public intellectuals imagine a framework of two national groups—Jews and Arabs—their bi-nationalist vision does not provide a solution to the fundamental challenges and needs of the Jewish people that the Jewish state was intended to address (i.e. security and self-determination). The *Future Vision* authors' approach inevitably calls for Jewish Israelis to relinquish their aspirations of establishing a sovereign state in the territory of ancient Palestine. Additionally, it goes further than any previous bi-national visions in its embrace of an envisioned polity devoid of Jewish content and collective identity. Their approach amounts to an articulation of Arab nationalism through the discourse of human rights and liberal ideals.

The idea of bi-nationalism has shifted its focus from coexistence and cooperation to asserting the claims of Israel's Arab citizens. As a result, bi-nationalism has become a euphemism for a one-state solution or a "state of all its citizens" that effectively calls for the end of a state with any Jewish character or commitment to the development of Jewish culture. The contemporary discussion of bi-nationalism has thus devolved into a continuation by other means of the conflict between Arabs, Israeli Jews, Jews and non-Jews alike.

This bi-national delusion has received a warm embrace from the academy, largely due to the political and cultural context of the university. Although each university campus environment is unique, there is a set of factors present on many campuses that has become a systemic, structural feature of modern university life and that forms the core of the problem facing Israel today.

On the majority of campuses, throughout North America, there is a small group of Israel detractors, comprised of students and faculty, who are extremely vocal and are supported and facilitated by national, and in some cases international, and well-funded networks of supporters. The majority of the university community is intimidated by, or simply disinterested in, the noise and remains silent. Most students on campus are politically apathetic and disengaged. Nevertheless, the campus is the incubator of American leadership and much of American thought regarding the Middle East. There is a handful of vocal faculty, mostly located in the humanities, who abuse the classroom for their political purposes. Most painful are the Jewish professors who tout their Jewish backgrounds as credentials for their anti-Israel attitudes. These faculty members are the most significant loot captured by the Palestinian cause. Their views have become the litmus test on campus for how progressive one is. Many of these faculty members frame the conversation in favor of the phantasmal bi-nationalist conception.

The assault against Israel on campus has two overriding features. First, campus discourse takes place in a political culture defined by a set of post-modern ideas, which have become the commonly accepted ideological basis for the assault on Israel. Second, as a result of the near-complete victory of this political culture, today's university now comes with inbuilt structures and systems that perpetuate that culture and make it extraordinarily difficult for students to respond to or resist it.

So, what are the cognitive elements that make up a culture hostile to the Jewish state? This is a cursory overview that deserves deeper examination but provides a framework for understanding the phenomenon.

First, Orientalism and the influence of Edward Said[613] have helped shape the discourse not only in Middle East studies specifically but in the humanities in general. Its core teaching is that Westerners cannot understand, explain, or indeed properly study the Islamic world. All truth about that realm must come from people within it. Western critical thought about the Islamic world must not be tolerated, as it can only be racist or supremacist.

Second, post-modernism is the idea that there is no objective truth and all facts are debatable. Post-modernism infiltrated the university communities of Western Europe and America beginning in the late 1970s. History was dismantled as an academic discipline to serve the purpose of an assortment of narratives, each being ascribed equal value. The post-Zionist aims, which emerged within a post-modernist climate, were to expose the past and present sins of the West—colonialism, Orientalism, imperialism, capitalism, particularism, nationalism, etc.—by applying these ideologies and world outlooks against the backdrop of Israeli history. Through these tactics, history is abused in order to undermine a collective Israeli memory and identity. What originated as a historical claim or argument became ultimately a political and ideological assault against the state of Israel. The war of 1948 is the starting point and the original sin of the Zionist and Israeli leadership. This moment in time inaugurates the onslaught against Zionism.

Third, Marxism promotes the themes of domination and resistance. Wealth and power are inherently evil; the poor are inherently more moral, and the ideal of the intellectual is to weaken the powerful and empower the weak.

Fourth, post-colonialism is a view that condemns all actions of the Western world and lionizes and privileges the natives as being the only ones able to understand the local and to dismantle the effects of the colonial. Israel, in this context, is seen as a white imperial outpost.

Fifth, post-nationalism blames the nation-state for the problems of the world while lauding internationalism.

Sixth, is the celebration of the therapeutic where feelings trump facts. Truth is a secondary goal and is usurped by sensitivity, particularly sensitivity for the "other".

Seventh, are universalism and the seduction of multiculturalism. These ideas call for Jews to be for the "other" rather than merely being for themselves and their own particular tribe. Within the university context, Jews are viewed as part of the white majority and should not advocate for particularisms, such as the Jewish nation-state. In comparison, all other minority groups (women, African Americans, gays and lesbians) have the right and responsibility to advance their particular causes and identities. This does not hold for Jews who desire to speak in support of Israel.

Lastly, is the formation of area studies within the academy. Area studies as a discipline has become the study of identity politics and claims. This is most evident within Middle East studies programs. Many faculty members within these programs abuse their positions as educators to use their classrooms as bully pulpits advocating specific positions and calling for actions under the guise of academic freedom.

Taken together, in combination, these ideas form the dominant political culture that permeates the university environment and creates fertile ground for the demonization of the state of Israel. It is within this landscape that one hears the echoes and reverberations of bi-nationalist discourse. Appealing to young hearts and minds, those individuals' ultimate goal is to advance the fantasy of a bi-nationalist framework, which is the sanitized version of de-legitimating the state of Israel. Without dismantling this reigning cognitive paradigm, or at least mounting a credible, serious assault upon it, the chances for defending Israel successfully within the academy are dimmed. ∎

ILAN TROEN

The Israeli–Palestinian Relationship in Higher Education:
Evidence from the Field

Introduction

Most arguments against the movement to boycott Israeli higher education have been cast in terms of the principle of academic freedom and American academic practice. I am an American and an Israeli and have spent most of my career in Israel, which is my permanent home. My task is to present relevant evidence from the field to more fully contextualize the issues and to explain why we should challenge the charges made against the Israeli academy. The call to boycott Israeli universities declares they are directly engaged or are complicit in denying Palestinians the right to an education and that they hinder the functioning of Palestinian universities. These allegations are not supported by facts on the ground as I have learned from experience and observation.

I want to develop three relevant arguments:

1) The allegation that Israel excludes foreigners, including Americans of Palestinian descent from participating in the education of Palestinians is false;

375

2) The Palestinians living in Israel have access to and are integrated in the national system of higher education;

3) There is ongoing cooperation between Israeli and Palestinian universities, and research based in the Israeli academy serves Palestinian society at large.

All three arguments bear on the proposals for boycott and on the alleged wrongs they purportedly seek to right.

My argument is this: Israeli higher education makes a large and significant contribution to the education of Palestinians and to coexistence, notwithstanding a protracted, bitter, and sometimes violent national conflict. Palestinian academics and students inside Israel, and in the Palestinian Authority and the territories under Israeli control are not boycotting Israeli Universities. Palestinian universities are growing at a rapid rate and the number of Palestinians involved as students and faculty in Israeli higher education is similarly expanding. The proponents of the boycott are not speaking on behalf of the large numbers of Palestinians, inside Israel and on the West Bank/Occupied Territories, who are participating in Israel's national system of higher education and associated research centers. Indeed, at least in Israel, the Palestinian community is advocating greater engagement, not disassociation.

I. The Visa and Entry Issue

In another essay in this volume, "The Campaign to Boycott Israeli Universities: Historical and Ideological Sources," I argue that the boycott movement fundamentally opposes the existence of a Jewish state between the Jordan River and the Mediterranean. Sporadic economic boycotts have been attempted for nearly a century, initially prior to Israel's establishment and then after 1948, as an organized international campaign. Note that these had nothing to do with alleged violations of Palestinian rights by Israel's border policies or with academics who wished to enter Israel or the West Bank and Gaza. International pressure against using the boycott to isolate the Jewish state led to its rejection, although, for some Arab countries, the boycott against Israel is still formally intact. Indeed, with the signing of peace treaties with Israel by Egypt (1979) and Jordan (1994), many earlier proponents of economic and political boycotts formally renounced them. In practice, a growing number of Arab countries engage in trade with Israel, if not directly, then in transshipment of goods through third parties.

Israel's economy has demonstrated enormous strength and consistent growth; in 2010, Israel was welcomed into the OECD (Organization for Economic and Cultural Development), the club of the 30-plus most economically advanced and politically progressive nations. Israel currently maintains relations with more than 160 countries around the world. In other words, the economic and political boycott of Israel failed. It was a gesture born of utter rejection and recognized as such. The proposed academic boycott is also likely to fail.

The first charge is that Israel deliberately limits the success of Palestinian universities by denying entry to American citizens of Palestinian descent who wish to teach there. This accusation is made on the basis of a couple of anecdotes but unsupported by actual numbers, names, and dates. Here are some facts: It is actually easier for an American to enter Israel and the West Bank than for Israelis to enter the United States. In 2012, Israel denied entry to a total of 142 Americans; 626,000 entered the country. This puts the Israeli refusal rate that year at about 0.023%, which is more or less the annual average. In 2012, the American refusal rate for Israelis who applied for "B" visas (business and pleasure) was 5.4%. That is, an Israeli who wants to enter the United States is about 200 times more likely to be denied entry than an American who wants to enter Israel, including those whose destination is the West Bank.[614]

The relevant U.S. State Department website referenced by the MLA boycott proponents explicitly advises American citizens not to go to Gaza, since it is under the control of Hamas, defined there as a terrorist organization. It similarly cautions against entering areas in the West Bank, since Americans are likely to encounter violence from Palestinian radicals and experience Israel army closures made in response. There is no blanket accusation that Israeli authorities hinder access to the region. On the contrary, in the most recent advisory of February 2014, Israel is presented favorably, as it has been in previous ones.[615]

Since the State Department recognizes that circumstances may impinge on entry and travel, it is unreasonable to expect Israeli border authorities to ignore these contingencies. Yet the same advisory notes that over three million foreign citizens, including hundreds of thousands of U.S. citizens, safely visit Israel and the West Bank each year for study, tourism, and business. It recognizes both Israel and the Palestinian Authority for their "considerable efforts to protect U.S. citizens and other visitors to major tourist destinations."

The fact is that hundreds of foreign teachers successfully enter Palestine. My own American university, Brandeis, regularly sends faculty and students to Al-Quds in the West Bank. We also have both faculty and students from Palestine at Brandeis. The same is true for other exchange programs. Such two-way activities are expanding. Israel is not closing them.

International organizations that monitor the situation do note that Palestinian universities have difficulty recruiting foreign academics for permanent positions. However, this is not attributed to Israeli border policies. Rather they fault low salaries, poor working conditions, and political pressures that limit academic freedom. The documents presented to the MLA and other professional academic associations blame Israel.[616] The pertinent circumstances that adversely affect the educational opportunities and achievement of Palestinian youth are nowhere to be found.

II. Palestinians in Israeli Higher Education

Israeli youth, including Palestinians, have access to one of the most advanced and distinguished university systems in the Middle East and beyond. Israeli scholars have been awarded Nobel Prizes in such areas as chemistry, economics, and medically related sciences. Israeli universities have outstanding departments in Law, the Humanities—including studies of Islam and the history and culture of Israel's neighbors—the Social Sciences, Agriculture, Engineering, and High-tech.

This helps explain why Israeli Arabs are not calling for BDS. On the contrary, the numbers of Israeli-Palestinian students enrolled in Israeli universities and colleges is steadily increasing. There is a new Arab language college in Nazareth for which a segment of the Israeli Arab community successfully lobbied. But the majority study at Hebrew-language institutions together with Israeli Jews.

Here are some figures: At Haifa University, the institution with the largest proportion of non-Jewish Israelis, 3,000 Israeli Arabs/ Palestinians and Druze comprise 1/3 of the University's 9,000 undergraduate students; another 1,200 are enrolled in graduate and professional programs; 3,000 are in pre-academic programs that prepare them for the university. The numbers are so significant that Haifa University has established a Jewish-Arab Center that sponsors numerous programs to advance mutual recognition and respect.[617] At the same time, the university has altered its academic calendar to accommodate Jewish, Christian, and Muslim holidays. Both the numbers and growing experience with catering to a student body of growing diversity lead to increasing sensitivity and desire to accommodate. Thousands more Palestinian/Israeli Arabs are enrolled in virtually all institutions of higher education throughout Israel and at all degree levels.

Israeli universities' successful inclusion of the Palestinian community has occasioned a revolution. Prior to the establishment of the State in 1948, there was near universal literacy among Jews, as well as perhaps the highest proportion of doctors—medical and Ph.D.s—in any population in the world. At the same time, only 25% of the total Arab population of Palestine was literate, and literacy among Palestinian women was considerably lower. Today illiteracy has been largely erased and Arab women, including women dressed in keeping with the Islamic code, attend Israeli universities.[618]

In Israel's medical faculties, where places are highly prized, 22% of all medical students in Israel are now Palestinians. Please note that 22% is about the proportion of Palestinians in the general population. More than 40% of pharmacology students are Arab. Large numbers have also chosen the human services, from education to social work. This reflects communal needs and empowerment as well as employment opportunities.

My own institution, Ben-Gurion University of the Negev, attracts many Bedouins, a population that was perhaps the most in need of schooling at Israel's founding. More than a thousand Arabs, including some 680 Bedouins, now study at the university. Many come through pre-collegiate enrichment programs designed to bolster success in matriculation exams. Most are granted university scholarships. More than half of Bedouin students are now women. While the majority are undergraduates, more than 30% are in graduate or professional programs.[619]

These numbers reflect years of active recruitment and programs to advance this population through pre-collegiate programs; the outreach efforts of the university have made a demonstrable difference. Note that all this activity is funded by the university out of a sense of responsibility for the role it must serve in addressing needs and contributing to the integration of all sectors of Israeli society into national life.

Today, Arab and Bedouin scholars and researchers are an integral part of the BGU faculty. They currently chair departments of social work, electrical engineering, and Middle East Studies, and direct programs in education, electro-optic engineering, computer sciences, chemistry, creative writing and comparative literature, and medicine. The first Bedouin woman M.D. has been recruited to the Faculty of Health Sciences. Professor Alean Al-Krenawi, formerly Chair of the Department of Social Work at Ben-Gurion, has been appointed president at "Achva," a BGU-affiliated college which like other such institutions serves both Jews and Palestinians. Achva is the Hebrew word for brotherhood, comradeship, amity, and solidarity.

This is a record that is being replicated throughout Israel. It probably helps explain another fact that initially seems surprising: Even leftist Israeli Arabs who identify themselves as Palestinian and who are sharply critical of the state do not include boycotting the Israeli academy in their political programs. This group includes the intellectual elite and signers of the *Future Vision* (2007) documents that call for the disestablishment of a Jewish state in favor of a denationalized polity. They seek more, not less, access to education and integration.[620]

A significant exception is Omar Barghouti—a key MLA panelist and leader of the BDS movement. Barghouti was born in Qatar and educated at Columbia University before coming to Tel Aviv University for graduate studies. His field is ethics. Despite a petition signed by 184,000 individuals demanding the university rescind his degree for advocating boycott of his own institution, Tel Aviv University's president refused; to do so would have been an infringement of academic freedom.[621]

III. Israeli cooperation with Palestinians on the West Bank

Finally, there is incontrovertible evidence of active cooperation between Israeli institutions and those in the Palestinian Authority. During the British Mandate and under Jordanian rule, foreign Christian groups typically supported small Palestinian educational institutions. It was not until after 1967 under the Israeli administration and with its encouragement that these were transformed into public universities.

Enrollment and graduation rates have grown exponentially with more than 200,000 students in the PA's 49 recognized higher education institutions, 34 of which are in the West Bank. Higher education in the PA is growing at such a rate that it intends to capitalize on this success and convert this sector into a "Palestinian Export," bringing in students from all over the region.[622]

Jewish outreach to Palestine's Arabs began well before Israel's establishment, when individual Jewish physicians set up clinics to treat diseases like trachoma. Perhaps the best-known example of Israeli inaugurated medical cooperation is the Hebrew University's affiliated Hadassah Medical Center in Jerusalem that serves the city's Jewish and Arab populations, and well beyond. It is an integrated institution with Arab and Jewish medical staff, support workers, and patients.

There are other examples. Specialized trilateral programs bring together Israeli, Palestinian, and Jordanian health professionals to target cerebral palsy. This largely forgotten population would not likely receive care were it not for the involvement of Israeli researchers. Emergency Medicine is another area of cooperation. Israel has among the most skilled personnel anywhere, due in large measure to the need to respond to terrorist attacks. These painfully acquired skills are shared with Jordanians and Palestinians, with expenses often entirely underwritten by Israeli institutions.

From cerebral palsy and cancer to public health and drug-abuse, Israeli academics engage with Palestinian counterparts to address problems across the Green Line. Professor Khulood Dajani, Vice-President and Founding Dean of Public Health at Al Quds University, holds a doctorate in this area from Ben-Gurion University. Her observation, made during the last Intifada, bears quoting here: "The Israeli-Palestinian experience in collaborative projects in public health has demonstrated that, despite tragic hostile events and marked fluctuations in the political atmosphere, cooperation could be carried on. Thousands of people of both sides were involved and vital health services were provided to populations in need."[623]

Palestinians who work with colleagues at the Technion, the Weizmann Institute, Ben-Gurion, and Hebrew Universities have expressed similar appreciation for what has been achieved through joint projects. A succinct summary of the ongoing significance of cooperation between Palestinians and Israelis was brought before the American Public Health Association (APHA) meetings in Boston in November 2013 where a precursor to subsequent BDS resolutions was presented. The APHA rejected the boycott resolution by a 2-1 margin when confronted with these substantial facts, an impressive selection of which bear quoting. They included referencing the "long history of formal and informal collaboration between many Israeli and Palestinian public health and medical communities in service, training and research"; "substantial Israeli-Palestinian collaborations and Israeli contributions to progress in public health, preventive medicine, water and sanitation, nutrition, agricultural irrigation, immunization—notably polio, detection and prevention of lead poisoning, and medical care and education and training"; "the data on the huge numbers of Palestinians receiving medical care in Israeli hospitals and other care facilities over the years—over 200,000 in 2012 alone, an 11% increase from the previous year"; "the implications of time trends in improvement in public health indicators, notably for children between 1967 and 1995. Since Palestinian administration began, these indicators have remained stable. The lack of major continued improvement since 1995 [when the PLO took control] appears to be attributable to waste, misuse of funds, and mismanagement."[624]

In addition to medicine, I would mention two other essential and active areas of cross-border collaboration. The first is the struggle with desertification. The inhabitants of Palestine/Israel/Jordan and Egypt share a similar arid or semi-arid climate. The most significant place for combating desertification—outside the American Southwest—is in the research spearheaded at Israeli universities. Zionism *has* made the desert bloom. Collaborators from China (the Gobi is larger than the Negev), across Africa and elsewhere come to Israel. This includes Palestinians and Arabs from neighboring countries. Jewish and Arab scientists and students work together in research and the transfer of technologies. A sampling of the collaborative research projects between Arabs and Israelis—beyond public health—clearly illustrates the fact that problems of natural disaster, water supply, and pollution do not recognize geo-political borders and therefore neither do the scientists who contend with them to make a better world. A sampling of such projects includes:

- Collaboration with the PA on Water Research with a grant from MERC (Middle East Regional Cooperation, a US funded agency) to increase the clean water supply around Israel and the Middle East. This study brings together Israelis and Palestinians to address clean water issues in the West Bank area of Nablus over a five-year period. Additionally, a group of Israeli and Palestinian environmental researchers are working together to test the area's water supply for potentially health-altering endocrine-disrupting chemicals.
- A Bi-Annual Conference on Drylands, Deserts, and Desertification sponsored by Ben Gurion University's Blaustein Institute to deal with desertification. More than 500 people from 50 countries—including presenters from American universities and U.S. government agencies—attend, as do Palestinian and Jordanian delegates. The conference is held in cooperation with the United Nations Educational, Scientific, and Cultural Organization (UNESCO).
- Desalination; solar energy; desert architecture; arid zone agriculture; animal husbandry; ensuring the viability of the Dead Sea (a body of water that Jordan, Palestine, and Israel share)—are but a few among many others.

These life-sustaining projects are supported not only by the participating institutions but also by the international community, especially Europe, the United States, and Arab countries such as Oman, which is particularly interested in desalination. These collaborations not only result in new technologies to afford a better life for millions who live under harsh climate conditions, but serve to promote mutual respect, shared understanding, and peaceful coexistence.

The second area is close to my own areas of academic interest that some members of the MLA may share: the construction of narratives. For approximately 20 years, scholars at Israeli and Palestinian universities have attempted to contribute to mutual understanding by sharing our national narratives. We initially imagined we might construct one inclusive narrative out of the conflicting claims and interpretations of the Arab/Israeli conflict and then integrate it into Palestinian and Israeli education. That strategy proved misguided, as Sami Adwan of Bethlehem University and the late Dan Bar-On of Ben-Gurion University explained. Instead of a unitary, homogenized narrative, they suggested, there are parallel ones. In human discourse, as in nature, these parallel lines do not meet. Nevertheless, Adwan and Bar-On deemed the exercise essential, for it has the potential of engendering empathy—a quality that can diminish even if it cannot eliminate conflict.[625]

In 2013, *Israel Studies*, an Israeli-based journal I co-edit for Indiana University Press, published a special issue on "Shared Narratives" that brought together the work of scholars from Israel and Palestine. Our project will now be republished by a Palestinian research center for even wider distribution in the Arab world. Such shared enterprises mitigate the prolonged conflict that has so diminished our lives. Significantly, similar projects are taking place in many Palestinian and Israeli universities and colleges.

To conclude

The dissemination of knowledge should have no boundaries. Israeli and Palestinian scholars and students, who are so vocal in so many areas, are not clamoring before the MLA or any other academic association for support of an academic boycott of Israel. On the contrary, Israeli and Palestinian Jews and Arabs want and need more, not less, of Israeli science and higher education. Both within and across the border, cooperation between Israeli and Palestinian institutions and academics is ongoing and fruitful. It should not be diminished but encouraged for the benefit of all.

A small, politically motivated coterie is attempting to hijack academic associations with false slogans, incomplete data, and distorted information. The proposal to boycott Israeli academic institutions is misinformed and maliciously misleading. It should be identified as such and rejected outright. ■

PART V

A CONCISE HISTORY OF ISRAEL

CARY NELSON, RACHEL S. HARRIS, AND
KENNETH W. STEIN

The History of Israel

Eretz Yisrael, the Land of Israel, was the birthplace of the Jewish people. Here their spiritual, religious, and political identity was shaped. Here they lived as a nation and created cultural values of national and universal importance and gave to the world the eternal Book of Books.

After being forcibly exiled from their land, the people kept faith with it throughout their Diaspora. They never ceased to pray and hope for their return to the homeland where they could restore their political freedom.

Impelled by this historic and traditional attachment, Jews strove in every successive generation to reestablish themselves in their ancient homeland. In recent decades, they returned en masse. Pioneers, immigrants, and defenders, they made deserts bloom, revived the Hebrew language, built villages and towns, and created a thriving community with its own economy and culture. Loving peace but knowing how to defend themselves, the Jewish people brought the blessings of progress to all the country's inhabitants, while aspiring toward independent nationhood.

The opening of the Israeli Declaration of Independence (1948)

As early as the tenth century BCE, Israelite kings ruled in Canaan, a territory that stretched from the Mediterranean Sea to beyond the western banks of the Jordan River. Archeological evidence confirms biblical accounts of a Temple in Jerusalem, constructed about 960 BCE during

King Solomon's reign. After its destruction in 586 BCE, Jews were exiled to Babylon but returned and rebuilt a second temple in 535 BCE that stood until the Romans razed Jerusalem in 70 CE and expelled Jews from their native land. It is this religious and political legacy that forms Jewish historical claims to a region with which the world has associated the Jewish people since ancient times, and with which they have maintained a spiritual and physical connection, despite centuries of exile, persecution, and domination by foreign powers within the area, and within the countries to which they have been dispersed.

As a minority that kept its own customs and traditions, Jews lived at the favor of local religious and political leaders. At times they would flourish under benevolent rulers, but in a moment, they might find themselves subject to cruel tyranny and excessive taxation, often becoming victims of violence and murder. Casualties of world history, Jews were left with little political agency and few methods of defense when Christian and Muslim society turned against them. The inventory that follows is but a partial account.

For the Christians of Medieval Europe, Jews were the killers of Christ; virulent myths about child kidnapping and blood libel were propagated, triggering violent anti-Jewish riots that led to massacres and expulsion from communities that Jews had for a time been able to consider home. By the end of the Middle Ages, Jews had lived in and been expelled from Carthage, England, France, Spain, Germany, Bavaria, Italy, Belgium, Hungary, Slovakia, Austria, the Netherlands, Warsaw, Portugal, Prussia, Lithuania, Bohemia, and Prague, sometimes on multiple occasions, and later from Ukraine, Poland, and Russia. Between the 11th and 19th centuries, Jews were repeatedly massacred; they were expelled more than 30 times from major European cities and states. They lost their property, they were murdered, they were accused of blood libels (kidnapping and murdering Christian children in order to obtain blood for use in preparing Passover matzoh), they experienced forced conversions often at the point of a sword, they were accused of spreading the plague and poisoning wells, and during the crusades they were repeatedly attacked by Christian armies on their way to fight Muslims in the Holy Land. In 1096 more than 5,000 Jews were murdered in Germany. In 1290, King Edward I issued an edict expelling all Jews from England, following 200 years of persecution, including the massacring of 100 Jews in York (1190), when they were burned to death after taking shelter in a tower. Five thousand Jews were killed in France in 1321 after they were accused of prompting lepers to poison wells. Thousands were killed in riots in Germany in 1389. Over 10,000 Jews were massacred in Spain in 1391. Following the wishes of Father Tomas de Torquemada, head of the Spanish Inquisition, 200,000 Jews were expelled from Spain on July 30, 1492, under an edict issued by

King Ferdinand and Queen Isabella, and tens of thousands died in the effort to reach safety while fleeing from Spain. While Jews were tolerated to a greater extent under Muslim rule—as people who shared a holy book and as "dhimmis" ("protected" infidels) were not persecuted for their religious beliefs—they still experienced discrimination, taxation, and at times faced violent prejudice that again led to massacre and expulsion.

The beginning of the Modern period, the end of feudal Europe, and the rise of the nation state opened new opportunities for Jews. While many continued to live a backward, almost medieval existence in parts of Eastern Europe, those in western cities could take advantage of booming industrialization and the rapid development of major European cities. Two clear paths presented themselves for those who sought new opportunities for economic and intellectual growth: assimilation or emancipation. For those who chose assimilation, conversion to Christianity and marriage to a Christian were the most radical choices, but others chose to modernize their dress, habits, and religious practices to be more like the Christians among whom they lived. The development of Reform and later Conservative Judaism were movements designed to shift the lines between the modern world and the ancient religion by finding new interpretations that accorded with the contemporary settings. But Orthodox Judaism would also evolve in this period, with a split forming between the Hassidic sects in Eastern Europe, who embraced spiritual devotion, and the *Mitnagdim* (the "opposers"), who favored intellectual engagement with the text and correct behavior (*derekh eretz*—"good manners"). In both cases, orthodoxy was responding to the modern world, either by avoiding it or by engaging with it intellectually.

The Jewish Enlightenment (the Haskalah) which developed during the 18th and 19th centuries in keeping with European Enlightenment ideals, frightened the traditional orthodox groups by calling for greater integration into modern secular society. As the map of Europe was rapidly transforming, Jews who had embraced Enlightenment ideals saw an alternative to conversion and the abandonment of Jewish faith, instead identifying a place for Jews within the broader brotherhood of man. This belief in the possibility of Jewish emancipation led to political efforts throughout the 19th century to have Jews included as equal citizens within continental European countries, and particularly in the newly created states emerging from the former Ottoman Empire. In Eastern Europe, these same ideals translated into political activism, and Jews believed that in a new Russian democracy they would be free from the violent prejudices of the past. But for many, the dream that Jews would finally be treated as equals in a new modern Russian republic was shattered with the anti-Semitic violence that erupted in the wake of the failed Russian revolution of 1905.

The combination of Haskahlah ideals, the relentless violence against Jews in late nineteenth-century Russia through a series of pogroms, and the increasing manifestations of anti-Semitism in the press of apparently enlightened Western European societies, provided strong impetus for a Jewish national movement—one that believed the only truly safe haven for Jews would come through Jewish self-determination. Thus arose the political movement to establish Jewish sovereignty in the ancestral homeland, a movement we know today as Zionism. This essay offers a compact history of the movement's activities to create what would eventually become the State of Israel, and examines the social, economic, cultural, political, and military challenges that Zionists have faced since the 19th century, and on to the present day.

Ottoman Palestine and Jewish Settlement— the Old Yishuv

From Roman times, Palestine proved a prime battleground; it lay at the meeting point of Asia, Europe, and Africa, which exposed it to warring empires from Assyria, Egypt, Sassania, and Byzantium during the first millennium of the Common Era. Jerusalem as a result was repeatedly under siege. By the Middle Ages, especially during the crusades, as Christian and Muslim armies raged against each other for hundreds of years, the region was left in ruins. The conflict over Jerusalem as a Christian holy site threatened Islamic rule in the region and led to prolonged violence. The Jews of Palestine who lived in the four holy cities—Jerusalem, Hebron, Tiberias, and Safed—as well as in such coastal towns as Jaffa, had established self-contained, self-managed communities, but they were nonetheless often caught up in regional warfare.

When Palestine came under Ottoman rule in 1517 the region experienced a period of relative tranquility. Under Suleiman the Magnificent, who ruled from 1520 to 1566, Palestine regenerated and became affluent. The Jews of Palestine, whose numbers had swelled in the 1490s after Jewish expulsions from Spain and Portugal, revived as well. The walls of Jerusalem were repaired (1535-38), as was the remaining Western Wall of the Temple. This time of social and religious tolerance led to a boom in religious academies in Jewish communities and fostered the growth of Kabbalistic writing and thought. The economy was fairly strong and Jews engaged in trades, crafts, and worked as merchants. But during the 17th and 18th centuries a steady decline took place, as Palestine increasingly became a municipal backwater of a declining Ottoman Empire. With little investment, few local resources, and an impoverished community often racked by plagues and illness, there was little to recommend the area. Moreover, a series of earthquakes in Tiberias and Safed destroyed homes and displaced Jewish communities and led to further overcrowding in the already jam-packed city of Jerusalem. The Jewish community was made up mostly of Sephardic Jews who followed Jewish customs from around the Mediterranean, including Spain. That community, which had lived in the region for hundreds of years, was bolstered by an immigration of roughly 1500 Ashkenazi Jews (Jews from Europe, originally from lands near the Rhine) in 1700. Another 300 Ashkenazi migrated from Europe in the 1770s, picking up other travelers on their routes from Poland and Lithuania. With the exception of these groups, most of the immigrants to Palestine were elderly, making the pilgrimage in order to die in the Holy Land. The Old Yishuv (the Jewish community in Palestine) was now impoverished, with many living in derelict homes and relying on charitable money collected in Europe to maintain themselves.

In 1831, Egypt conquered Palestine in a bid to free itself from Ottoman rule, but in 1840 the Ottomans suppressed the Egyptian uprising and reclaimed their territory. The competing powers left the landscape scarred and further impoverished local communities. Moses Montefiore (1784-1885), a wealthy British Jew who served as Sheriff of London to Queen Victoria, made seven visits to Palestine during his lifetime. Appalled by the barbaric conditions, he built the first Jewish settlement beyond the walls of Jerusalem, using funds from the estate of a New Orleans American Jew, Judah Touro. Mishkenot Sha'ananim, an almshouse built in 1860, could actually be seen from the walls of Jerusalem; that was intended to encourage the new inhabitants to feel safe, but it took a while before they were willing to stay at night, given the marauding bandits and raiding Bedouins roaming the territory beyond the city's gates. With its iconic windmill, this settlement became the first of several built to house the Old Yishuv's Jews; it was swiftly followed by Meah Shearim in 1864, and Nachlaot, a cluster of several neighborhoods that include Mishkenot Yisrael, Ohel Moshe, and Mazkeret Moshe. Numbering approximately 27,000, the religious Jews of the Old Yishuv continued to develop new settlements, not only outside of Jerusalem but also beyond Jaffa and other cities where Jews lived during the 1870s and early 1880s. In many cases, these fledgling communities, such as Petach Tikva (1878), would be augmented by the influx of a new, often secular Jew from Europe— the Zionist pioneers of the First Aliyah (wave of immigration).

The Rise of Zionism

The first traces of modern Zionism emerged among British Protestant supporters of Judaism in the first half of the 19th century. After the establishment of a British Consulate in Palestine in 1838, the Church of Scotland commissioned a report on the condition of the Jews; widely disseminated, it was followed by *Memorandum to Protestant Monarchs of Europe for the Restoration of the Jews to Palestine.* Moses Montefiore (1784-1885), in his role as President of the Board of Deputies of British *Jews*, entered into a correspondence with Charles Henry Churchill (1807-1869), then British consul in Damascus in 1841-42; that correspondence produced the first recorded proposal for political Zionism. The British, particularly under Prime Minister Benjamin Disraeli (1804-1881), imagined a Jewish country that would operate as a British Protectorate, much like Egypt, which accorded with their larger plans for wresting control of the region from the Ottomans. In 1891, American Protestant William Eugene Blackstone (1841-1935) would present U.S. President Harrison with a petition signed by political, business, and religious leaders calling for the return of Palestine to the Jews, echoing a sentiment expressed by the Mormon Church in 1842.

These events, though momentous in their way, were distinct from the grassroots activism taking place among Jews in central and Eastern Europe. In 1834, Rabbi Judah Alkali (1798-1878) of Sarajevo called for Jews to return to the Land of Israel and to establish Jewish organizations to oversee national activities there, including a fund to purchase land for settlement. In 1862, in Prussia, Avi Hirsch Kalischer (1795-1874) published "Seeking Zion" and Moses Hess (1812-1875) published "Rome Jerusalem," both urging Jews to move to the land of Israel, buy property, and settle there. These calls heralded the rise of many small Zionist organizations which began to consider a return to Zion as a political option for Jews. According to Kalischer, "the redemption of Israel, for which we long, is not to be imagined as a sudden miracle . . . [that redemption] will begin by awakening support among the philanthropists and by gaining the consent of the nations to the gathering of some of the scattered of Israel into the Holy Land" (Hertzberg 111). These political murmurings reflected the increasing concern that Jews would never be free of the anti-Semitism that continued to thrive in Europe. As Hess observed, "we shall always remain strangers among the nations." "My nationality," he declared, is "inseparably connected with my ancestral heritage, with the Holy Land." Reflecting on the paradoxes of nationalism, he warned that "anti-national universalism is just as unfruitful as the anti-universalist nationalism of medieval reaction" (Herzberg 121, 119, 129). When Dr. Yehuda Leib

Pinsker (1821-1891), a Russian physician who founded the Hovevei Zion (Lovers of Zion) movement, published *Auto-Emancipation: A Warning to His Kinsfolk by a Russian Jew*, a pamphlet analyzing anti-Semitism in the wake of a series of pogroms in Russia in 1881, his call for the establishment of a Jewish homeland found an audience receptive to a new solution to European intolerance.

The 1881-1884 wave of pogroms (violent riots aimed at persecuting Jews) that swept across southwestern Russia's "Pale of Settlement," the area where Jews were forced to live, came at the end of a century of anti-Semitic government policies that had isolated Jews. Russia forced Jews into military conscription, often for long periods and from an early age. It controlled all aspects of Jewish dress, education, and the ritual slaughtering of meat; and it demonstrated that Russian Jews could not depend on the protection of the Russian government or police forces in the face of local violence. In response, Jews emigrated West to the New World, including the United States, Canada, and South America, as well as to agricultural projects in North and South America and Palestine, where Jewish benefactors created new opportunities for the destitute refugees, funded by the Jewish Colonization Association (JCA) established by Baron Maurice de Hirsch (1831-1896).

The First Aliyah (1881-1904)

The ancient term for going up to the Temple in Jerusalem, *aliyah* ("ascent"), has come to refer to the Jewish immigration from the Diaspora to the land of Israel. The Jews who migrated to agricultural colonies in the late 19th century are described as the First Aliyah of Zionist immigration. In contradistinction to those Jews who had moved to the Old Yishuv over the centuries, the migration that took place in the wake of the Russian pogroms brought young ideologues to Palestine, and that impulse intensified as persecution increased. The 1903-1906 pogroms were more lethal than those of the 1880s. The 1903 pogrom in Kishinev was publicized in dramatic terms by the international press, including the *New York Times*: "There was a well laid-out plan for the general massacre of Jews on the day following the Orthodox Easter. The mob was led by priests, and the general cry, 'Kill the Jews,' was taken up all over the city. The Jews were taken wholly unaware and were slaughtered like sheep . . . . The scenes of horror attending this massacre are beyond description. Babies were literally torn to pieces" (*NYT*, April 2).

Interested in agricultural endeavors, members of Hovevei Zion (Lovers of Zion) groups and BILU (an acronym based on a verse from the Book of Isaiah 2:5, "House of Jacob, Let us ascend") were supported in their pioneering endeavors by the Odessa Committee; officially known as "the Society for the Support of Jewish Farmers and Artisans in Syria and Palestine," this was a charitable organization with roots in Europe and the United States which helped organize immigration to Palestine. With little to no experience of working the land, many enrolled in Mikveh Yisrael, an agricultural school established outside Jaffa in 1870, which equipped the new inhabitants with some of the basic skills they would need to survive. But they remained dependent on the largess of rich benefactors to make the pioneering projects succeed, and Montefiore, Baron Edmond De Rothschild (1845-1934), and Baron Hirsch were key figures in facilitating these dreams. Rothschild would fund settlements and their key needs, from land purchases to well drilling and seed acquisition—often from wealthy Arabs who functioned as absentee landlords. Zionist land purchases from 1880-1914 were concentrated in the coastal plain south of Haifa and in the Jezreel and Jordan valleys, areas largely swampy, uncultivated, and sparsely inhabited. Between 1878 and 1908, Jews purchased about 400,000 dunams, or 100,000 acres. Land purchases often resulted in the dispossession of the tenant farmers, though they received monetary compensation and usually resettled in the immediate environs. Though substantially more land was available for sale, funds were limited and land speculation soon drove up prices significantly.

The Eastern Europeans built early settlements in Rishon le-Tzion (1882), Rosh Pinna (1882), Zikhron Ya'akov (1882), and Gedera (1884)—agricultural farm holder villages (moshavot) that relied on Rothschild's patronage. Yet the inclement climate, disease, and prohibitive Ottoman taxation soon alienated many of the young Zionists. At the same time, Jewish migrants from Yemen arrived in the country, spurred by the messianic promise of a return to the ancestral homeland; they moved mainly to the cities or worked as laborers on the newly created citrus groves of the subsidized farms. Of the 35,000 Jews who arrived with the First Aliyah, 15,000 would leave or die. By 1903, the Jewish population in Palestine numbered 55,000.

European Anti-Semitism and the Rise of the Zionist Movement

During 1894-95, a scandal erupted in France whose repercussions were to shape the future of the Zionist movement and determine its historical course. Alfred Dreyfus (1859-1935), a French Jewish artillery captain on the French general staff, was wrongly convicted of treason and sentenced to Devil's Island. Though the military was relatively open to Jews, Dreyfus had repeatedly experienced anti-Semitism and, when he reported it, was judged to be "unlikeable," which limited his professional advancement. Evidence identifying the real traitor came to light but was suppressed; when it was leaked to the press, Dreyfus' supporters, including Emile Zola (1840-1902), cried out against the endemic anti-Semitism in the country. Though these efforts led to Dreyfus receiving a pardon in 1899, he was not exonerated until 1906. The trial, and the virulent anti-Semitism which accompanied it, showed that even France, the very incubator for the belief that all men were equal, was subject to unremitting prejudice toward Jews.

Among the crowd of journalists who reported on the event was an assimilated Jew who would become the figurehead for the coalescence of the disparate Zionist groups under a single umbrella. Realizing that Zionism offered the only real political solution for a Jewish people who would forever be considered pariahs within other nations' states, Theodor Herzl (1860-1904), convened The First Zionist Congress in Basel, Switzerland, in 1897. His 30,000-word pamphlet *Der Judenstaat: Versuch einer modernen Lösung der Judenfrage* ("The Jewish State: Proposal of a Modern Solution to the Jewish Question") offered a concrete consideration of Zionist aspirations, and the Congress issued a call to establish a Jewish homeland in Palestine.

With Herzl's guidance, Zionism became an internationally recognized political movement. But among its detractors were "ultra-Orthodox and assimilationists, revolutionaries and capitalists, dreamers and pragmatists" (Shapira 5). Some traditionalists considered Zionism a threatening secular movement seeking to supplant God's role in bringing about the redemption of the Jews. Some assimilated Jews felt Jewish nationalism would threaten their status in the countries in which they lived. "A central aspiration of Zionist ideology was the attainment of honor and respect in place of the shame and contempt that were the hallmarks of Jewish life in the Diaspora, especially in the Czarist Empire" (Morris 21). "No longer abject victims, middlemen, peddlers, protected moneylenders, rootless, soft-skinned intellectuals, the Jews were to change into hardy, no-nonsense farmers, who would take abuse from no one" (Morris 45).

But Palestine was not operating in a vacuum. For the Ottoman Turkish authorities who had been at war with the Russian Empire for two hundred years, the sudden influx of Russian immigrants in the late 19th century appeared as a new tactic for Russian authorities to use in seizing control of the dying empire. But with additional and increasingly violent pogroms erupting (1903-6), the tide of Jewish migration from Russia would continue to burden the concerned Ottoman authorities, and when World War I broke out, with Russia and Turkey on opposing sides, entry permits for Russian Jews were stopped. Taher al-Husseini (1842-1908), the Mufti of Jerusalem, urged in 1899 that Jews who had recently settled in the area since 1891 be pressed into leaving or be expelled, and he awakened concerns among the authorities that stretched beyond the new inhabitants' Zionist aims, back to their land of origin.

Meanwhile Arabs were also becoming aware of the national aspirations that had rocked the stability of the Ottoman Empire since Greece first sought independence (1821-32). Egypt's attempts to gain sovereignty had failed, but Arab nationalism spread as a movement from Egypt throughout the Levant and Iraq, and raised new fears for the Ottomans. In 1904-1905, Najib Azouri (c. 1873-1916), a Maronite Christian, published two pamphlets denouncing the Ottoman Empire and calling for an independent Arab state from the Euphrates to the Suez Canal. Though his call met with little enthusiasm, the end of the Ottoman Empire in 1922 created new opportunities for Arab nationalists.

The Second Aliyah, The First World War, and the End of the Ottoman Empire

The Second Aliyah (1904-1914) embraced a new Hebrew ideology that moved beyond the purely agricultural aspirations of their predecessors. Building on the work of Eliezer Ben Yehuda (1858-1922), who had arrived with the First Aliyah and was the guiding spirit behind the revival of the Hebrew language, members of the Second Aliyah rejected Yiddish and the Diasporic languages of their countries of emigration. They embraced the Hebrew language and Hebrew culture, which they saw as powerful manifestations of their connection to the historic homeland. "Converting Hebrew from the language of prayer and sacred texts into the language of Hebrew culture, and beyond that into the language of the street and home, was one of the Zionist movement's most magnificent achievements" (Shapira 57).

Ahad Ha'am (Asher Zvi Hirsch Ginsberg, 1856-1927) had preached cultural Zionism in arguing that Jews should create "a Jewish State" and not just "a State of the Jews." Rather than dreaming that all Jews would migrate to Palestine, cultural Zionism would serve as a rallying cry for Jews everywhere. His ideology offered a powerful alternative to Herzl's political Zionism at a time when few chose the harsh conditions of the pioneer life over the more popular and financially promising option of migration to the United States. But, ultimately, members of the second and Third Aliyah sought to unite both ideals, creating folk music, dances, and Hebrew literature celebrating a Jewish State.

Zionist economic development in the first years of the 20th century continued to focus on agriculture and the building of new communities. In 1907-1908, the Palestine Office, headed by Arthur Ruppin (1876-1943), was established in Jaffa to coordinate Zionist activity in Palestine. In 1909, the same year that Tel Aviv was founded as a suburb of Jaffa and lauded as the first Jewish city built in 2000 years, Degania was established—offering a new kind of collective agricultural settlement built on socialist values. This was the kibbutz:

> From the 1880s until the First World War, Jewish settlement was con-
> centrated almost exclusively in the *moshava*, a traditional kind of colony
> whose members farmed their land independently. The early *moshavoth*
> (plural of *moshava*) failed to achieve economic independence and did
> not develop quickly enough to enable large-scale colonization within
> a reasonable time. Attempts at reform and experimentation led to the
> design of the *kibbutz*, or *kvutza* (collective settlements), and the moshav
> (cooperative farming village). (Troen 4)

But these agricultural settlements were often victims of theft and sometimes local violence. In response, *HaShomer* ("the watchman") was created as a defense system with guards who drew on the customs and dress of local Bedouins, Druze, and Circassians. The Second Aliyah's focus on using only Jewish laborers and guards led to ongoing conflict with private plantation owners who often preferred the cheaper and more experienced labor of local Arabs. Hiring *Hashomer* led to repeated conflict where "mixed" Arab and Jewish employment occurred. By the end of the first decade, signs of Arab discomfort with the Jewish settlements were increasingly apparent. In 1911, Najib al-Khuri Nassar, who had been a land purchasing agent for the Jewish Colonization Association, published a critique of Jewish ambitions in the region; *al-Sihyuniyaa* (Zionism) was the first Arab book to examine the new forms of Jewish immigration.

On the eve of World War I, the Jewish community in Palestine numbered 85,000, more than half living in Jerusalem, though there were also 45 agricultural settlements whose total population exceeded 12,000. But the war was to have a devastating effect on the Yishuv's economy, enough in fact to threaten famine. The community only survived with the arrival of money and supplies donated by American Jews and delivered on American warships. Hundreds of Arabs drafted into the Ottoman Turkish army died in battle or from disease, along with thousands more who were non-combatants. After repeatedly appealing to the British to serve in the army in order to liberate Palestine from the Ottomans, 650 Jews were at first recruited into the Zion

Mule Corps and served in the Gallipoli campaign; later five battalions of Jewish volunteers became the Jewish Legion (1917-1921). Around 91 died in action, but among the survivors were future Israeli members of Knesset, prime ministers and presidents, leading thinkers, artists and writers, and several pioneers from the First Aliyah.

On June 4, 1917, Jules Cambon (1845-1935), director general of the French Foreign Ministry, issued a statement declaring that "it would be a deed of justice and reparation to assist, by the protection of the Allied Powers, in the renaissance of the Jewish nationality in that land from which the people of Israel were exiled so many centuries ago." His comments followed from member of Parliament Winston Churchill's claims in 1908 that Jews must have their own homeland in Palestine. On November 2, British foreign secretary Arthur Balfour (1848-1930) issued a Declaration on behalf of the government, with strong concurrence of prime minister Lloyd George (1863-1945), stating that "His Majesty's Government view with favour the establishment in Palestine of a national home for the Jewish people, and will use their best endeavours to facilitate the achievement of this object, it being clearly understood that nothing shall be done which may prejudice the civil and religious rights of existing non-Jewish communities in Palestine, or the rights and political status enjoyed by Jews in any other country." Britain thereby strengthened its own interests, for "by endorsing Zionism, Britain was legitimizing its own presence there as the protector of Jewish self-determination" (Morris 73). The British were also influenced by Chaim Weizmann (1874-1952), a University of Manchester chemist who helped encourage what amounted to a pro-Zionist lobby among British leaders. Weizmann would become president of the Zionist Organization and later the first President of Israel.

The issuing of the Balfour Declaration helped consolidate and solidify Arab nationalism around the rejection of Zionism. From the Arab perspective, the world powers had no right to award territory that was not theirs to give. As a matter of principle, therefore, the promise to the Jews was without validity. The Jews, on the other hand, maintained that they had a historical right to the land of their ancestors, that they were righting a two-thousand-year injustice, and that Palestine already had a Jewish community residing on legally purchased property.

In December 1917, British General Sir Edmund Allenby (1861-1936) entered Jerusalem with his army and ended four centuries of Ottoman rule. Palestine had been left in ruins, with crops destroyed, trees uprooted, and village life economically devastated. Zionist anticipation that British rule would lead to Jewish self-governance met with disappointment when the military administration revealed a distinctly anti-Zionist outlook. Yet the

Zionists continued to invest and in 1918 laid the cornerstone of the Hebrew University in Jerusalem that would open in 1925.

The British Mandate

On April 18, 1920 the San Remo Convention of the victors in World War I granted Britain a Mandate for Palestine and turned the Balfour Declaration into the official policy of the Entente Powers, thereby granting the Declaration international legal status. Article 4 of the Mandate instrument states: "An appropriate Jewish agency shall be recognized as a public body for the purpose of advising and cooperating with the Administration of Palestine in such economic, social and other matters as may affect the establishment of the Jewish national home and the interests of the Jewish population in Palestine." Herbert Samuel (1870-1963), whose son had served in the Jewish Legion, became the first of nine High Commissioners overseeing Britain's control of Palestine, a mandate that lasted until Britain's physical withdrawal at midnight May 14, 1948, the same day that Israeli statehood was declared. Samuel catered to both Arab and Jewish/Zionist interests by allowing them to develop separate social and religious institutions. While not following an overt policy of divide and rule, Britain's policies established a framework for the Jewish and Arab communities to achieve autonomy. Yet while the Zionists continued to build state institutions for self-governance, including trade unions, welfare services, hospitals and health care, nurseries, and business and industry, the Arab elite continued to view their future self-determination within the feudal leadership systems of the past. They also saw working through the British to build self-governing institutions as a dangerous endorsement of British authority. The Jewish population in Palestine regularly made substantial contributions to British government revenue: in 1928, while only 17% of the population, the Jewish contribution to British administration coffers was 44% of its total revenue; in 1944/45, when Jews constituted 32% of the total population, they contributed 65% toward British administration revenue (Parliamentary Debates, Commons, November 17, 1930 and Report of the Zionist Executive to the 22nd Zionist Congress, 1946, p 6.).

In 1917, pogroms broke out in Russia after the Bolshevik Revolution, killing as many as 60,000 Jews and displacing hundreds of thousands more. In the wake of this terror, thousands of Jews fled. After the hiatus of the war years, the establishment of the British Mandate in Palestine made it possible for Jewish immigration to resume. The Third Aliyah (1919-1923) brought up to 40,000 Jews to Palestine, mainly from Eastern Europe; it was more successful than earlier waves, with most new settlers staying in Palestine, rather than moving on to more hospitable locales. If the Second Aliyah had brought many Hebrew writers and political activists to Palestine, the Third Aliyah would confirm Tel Aviv as the center of Hebrew letters and cement the leadership of the Yishuv that, over the succeeding decades, would pilot the Jewish settlement to statehood. David Ben Gurion, Golda Meir, Levi Eshkol, Moshe Sharett, H. N. Bialik, Saul Tchernikovsky, Haim Brenner, Natan Alterman, and Rachel Bluwstein were just a few of the major political and cultural figures who moved to Palestine in this socially formative period.

In 1924, new immigration restrictions limited Jewish entry to the U.S. An improving economic situation in Palestine attracted more immigrants to the growing urban centers. An influx of middle class families who founded small businesses and light industry arrived in the Fourth Aliyah (1924-1929). This bourgeois class was interested in leisure and recreation and threatened the earnest pioneering folk culture of the agriculturalists with the establishment of new cinemas, cafés, dance halls, and theatres that served the Jewish immigrants, British forces, and the Arab middle class alike. These new activities soon found a successful, if at times tense, place alongside the more conservative labor-driven Zionist culture. Some 67,000 immigrants arrived during this five-year period, but a sudden downturn in the economy in 1927 forced thousands to leave. For those who stayed, investing in new enterprises heralded a self-managed economy that would become increasingly less dependent on imported foreign goods and materials and eventually lead the community in Palestine to self-sufficiency.

Yet this period of boom was also plagued by increasing Arab hostilities. Jewish authors Hans Cohn and Arthur Ruppin noted candidly in a Berlin newspaper, Der Jude (1918-1920), that Zionism would face increasing opposition or enmity from Arabs, but claimed that there was enough room for both peoples in the area. Not all Arabs shared this perspective and in 1919 the King of Greater Syria and of Iraq, Emir Feisal, a leading pan-Arabist, signed an understanding with Chaim Weizmann that sanctioned Jewish immigration to Palestine on condition that Arab tenant farmers' rights were protected, validating religious preference without discrimination and calling on Zionists to assist the "Arab State" in economic development. These gestures did little to quell the bloodshed that would recur periodically throughout the 1920s.

On March 1, 1920, Arab forces attacked three Jewish settlements, including Tel Hai, built by HaShomer in the Galilee Panhandle north of Lake Hula. The Galilee Panhandle, an area abandoned by the British, had become a virtual no-man's land lying between the British and the French. The defenders of Tel Hai and the other two settlements, numbering 30-35 at each site, faced several hundred Arabs. Yusef Trumpeldor, a one-armed veteran of the Russo-Japanese war and Gallipoli who had helped organize the Zion Mule Corps, was mortally wounded in the Tel Hai assault, but the settlement held. Dozens of Arabs died in the assault, but during the night, a relief column reached the settlement. With their ammunition depleted, the settlers burned the settlement and retreated. The battle was thereafter commemorated as a founding story of courage under fire and achieved mythic status in Israeli culture.

In 1920-21, Arab riots led to assaults on Jewish settlements, towns, and cities. The violence convinced many Jews that their Palestinian existence was precarious, and though the rest of the decade would prove to be relatively peaceful, these attacks led to increasingly separate economic development among Jewish and Arab residents. In turn, this separation would ultimately persuade the British that their mandate to produce self-governing entities would best be achieved through partition and the creation of two separate states. Aware of the need for Jewish self-defense in the face of Arab violence, *HaShomer* was succeeded in 1920 by a more developed defense group, the *Haganah*, which was founded as a civil militia or paramilitary organization.

Arab attacks also led to Vladamir Jabotinsky's creation of the largest right wing political party, *Hatzohar* (The Union of Revisionist Zionists), along with Betar, a youth movement and feeder program for the revisionist political agenda. Jabotinsky had been a war hero of the Jewish Legion; his party would serve as the ideological precursor for today's Herut and Likud right-wing political parties. Taking the view that Jews and Arabs would have to be separated in Palestine, Jabotinsky criticized the Zionist leadership for passivity and lack of aggression in dealing with Britain, and his network of political, military, and youth movements helped enact these views through both violent and non-violent means.

In 1922, in an attempt to suppress the Arab uprising, the British Colonial Office, under Winston Churchill, issued a White Paper seeking to reassure the Arabs they had nothing to fear from Jewish interests. Public opinion had begun to shift toward Arabs, and the Paper declared that the Balfour Declaration "does not contemplate that Palestine as a whole should be converted into a Jewish National Home, but that such a Home should be founded in Palestine." Britain concluded that Jewish immigration to Palestine should be defined according to the "economic capacity" of the country to absorb newcomers. Zionists sought to broaden the interpretation of this amorphous term, but Arabs in Palestine opposed both the British presence and the idea of a Jewish national home. An Arab boycott of official association with British rule enabled the Zionist leadership to have an enormous influence over the writing of local ordinances and laws. They did so through the Jewish Agency, organized to serve as Zionism's governing authority under the British Mandate. Only limited funds and the low numbers of immigrants constrained the growth of the Jewish community in Palestine.

Though the 1920s had proved economically and politically constructive for Jews, for Arabs it had been a decade of increasing frustration, and in 1929 Arab violence escalated during a week in August when much of the British leadership was overseas, resulting in the deaths of 133 Jews and 116 Arabs. Arab frustration also reflected the absence of effective Arab leaders and institutions to turn to as a route to change. Learning from the riots in 1920-21, the *Haganah* was able to protect many Jewish residents in places where it had trained groups with weapons. Following the Arab riots, in 1930-31 some *Haganah* officers would found the *Irgun* (a paramilitary group that broke off from the Haganah and was called Haganah Bet or referred to by its initials as Etzel or IZL) to achieve a more aggressive, rather than defensive, military posture.

In late August 1929, Oxford students of religion visiting Palestine as part of their summer abroad program soon found themselves drafted as reserve policemen to help the understaffed local British forces maintain the peace. Belatedly, the British appointed a commission of inquiry, headed by Sir Walter Shaw, which recommended curtailing Jewish immigration. From this point on, British policy in Palestine reflected a gradual effort to disengage from the commitments articulated in the Balfour Declaration.

In October 1930, following the findings of a commission of inquiry, the British government issued the Passfield White Paper. Lord Passfield, the anti-Zionist Colonial Secretary Sidney Webb (1859-1947), recommended restricting Jewish immigration and land acquisition counter to the Mandate. After protests, Britain reversed the Passfield conclusions in a public 1931 letter from Prime Minister Ramsey MacDonald to Chaim Weizmann, which stated that the British had no intention of limiting Jewish immigration. For the next decade immigration to Palestine and land purchase would reach their peak, and Zionist geographic and demographic growth would create the nucleus for a state.

The immigration quotas imposed by the British following the Passfield White Paper could have had a devastating effect on the attempted migration of Jews during the Fifth Aliyah (1929-1936). The U.S. and Canada had closed their borders to those escaping the rise of Nazism in Europe, allowing only a small trickle to enter. Thus 250,000 immigrants arrived in Palestine in this time period, with more than a quarter coming from Germany and Austria. Most of these immigrants settled in urban areas and contributed significantly to business, medicine, education, literature, and music, though 20% of this Aliyah settled in kibbutzim and moshavim. A further 150,000 acres of land were bought, mostly from Palestinian Arab owners. Over the course of this decade, the Jewish community was "largely responsible for the industrialization of Palestine." (Smith, 178-179).

The passive response of the old Palestinian leadership, and the rising power of the new Grand Mufti of Jerusalem, Hajj Amin al-Husseini (c. 1897-1974), disappointed Arabs who wished to modernize and become self-governing like the Jews. Historically, a few important Arab families had competed for control through the Ottoman and British administrative regimes, providing the area's civil servants, judges, and religious officials, and eventually occupying national leadership positions. In a changing political landscape, these families would establish political parties, starting with the Nashishibi's in 1934, who created the National Defense Party in December and rejected the Balfour Declaration as part of their mandate. Considered less extreme than the more popular Palestine Arab Party formed by the Husseini family the following year, the Arab Higher Committee (AHC) was created under the leadership of the Mufti in 1936; all the Arab political parties were members, and the AHC became the official body for negotiating Arab wants and needs with the British authorities. Among its very first actions, the AHC called for the general strike that initiated the Arab Peasants' Revolt of 1936-39. The strike was called off in October, while Arabs waited a year for the conclusions of a new Commission headed by Lord William Robert Peel (1867-1937), but the Arabs rejected the resulting British proposal that Palestine be partitioned into Jewish and Arab states with an independent zone for Jerusalem. Peel believed a one-state solution would be unworkable and proposed that the Jewish state be established where Zionists had concentrated their population and economic development. The 404-page report included a recommendation for an "exchange of population" between the prospective Jewish and Arab states, transferring 225,000 Arabs and 1,250 Jews so as to establish ethnic/religious majorities in each state. Behind the recommendation was the recognition that Transjordan, Syria, and Iraq had "vast uninhabited areas and required additional inhabitants for their own development" (Morris 140). But as Husseini stated in 1936, "there is no place in Palestine for two races. The Jews left Palestine 2000 years ago. Let them go to other parts of the world, where there are wide vacant places." Believing that Arabs had been betrayed by the British, who had failed to give them complete sovereignty over the region, the AHC stepped up its activities. However, when the Acting British District Commissioner of Galilee was assassinated in Nazareth in 1937, the AHC was immediately outlawed.

The Peasants Revolt of 1936-1939 was directed against both the British and the Jews in Palestine. In 1937, the rebels launched 109 attacks against the British and 143 against Jewish settlements. Late that year Jabotinsky's military wing, the Irgun, which, like his political wing, wished to push the Zionist leadership to greater resistance against the British, responded with several bombings of Arab crowds and buses. Between the violence of the Irgun and that of the Arabs, some 986 attacks on British targets and 651 on Jewish targets took place in 1938. Deaths included 77 Brits, 255 Jews, and perhaps 1,000 Arabs. Early in the following year, the revolt began to disintegrate. Some armed bands of Arabs crossed the border into Jordan, where the Arab Legion killed or captured them, and there were clashes between rival groups. Most of the Arabs killed during this period died in inter-factional Arab fighting; the majority of the Arab population, which was rural and agricultural, suffered enormous economic setbacks as a result of the violence and Arab terrorist intimidation (Stein 1987, 25-49). If the peasants were condemned to their fate, the Arab elite were less willing to suffer and as many as 30,000 members fled for the duration. The British suppressed the remainder of the revolt by May 1939. On the eve of World War II, Hitler declared Palestine to be "suffering the cruelest maltreatment for the benefit of Jewish interlopers" (Morris 157).

This statement followed from the growing relationship between Arabs and Germans that had developed steadily during the 1930s. After the AHC was outlawed for contributing to escalating regional violence, Hajj Amin al-Husseini was forced to flee Palestine in 1937 to escape an arrest warrant, eventually taking refuge in Lebanon, Iraq, Rome, and, during World War II, Berlin, where he was welcomed by Hitler. Arab alliances with the Germans posed a serious threat for the British during the war. Protecting British interests in Egypt took precedence over managing intergroup tensions in the Palestine Mandate. In an attempt to lessen Arab hostilities, Britain altered its two-year policy of allowing the development of the Jewish national homeland when it issued yet another policy statement, the White Paper of May 17, 1939, putting several restrictions on Jewish immigration and land purchases. But the Permanent Mandates Commission of the League of Nations rejected this White Paper as a betrayal of the Mandate's terms. Meanwhile, with the demise of the AHC, and no clear leadership, Arab politics would remain paralyzed and fragmented during the war years.

By 1939, the population of Palestine had grown through both births and sixty years of Jewish immigration. Improved life expectancy, better medical facilities, lower infant mortality, clean drinking water, and modernized sanitation led to a demographic boom among Arabs, who now numbered 1,070,000, while Jews made up a third of Palestine's population at 460,000.

World War II (1939-45)

While most of Europe and North Africa was in armed conflict during the war period, life in many ways continued as normal in Palestine; though geographically strategic, the region was out of the line of fire. The Arab leadership, divided and living mostly in exile, used this time to ingratiate themselves with British officials, often under the direction of al-Husseini, even though he was barred from attending the conferences convened to discuss the Palestine Question. Simultaneously some Arab leaders worked with the Nazis, particularly al-Husseini, who promised Arabs independence when the Germans defeated Britain and even went so far as to recruit Muslims for the Waffen-SS to hasten this end. "As of late 1943, [al-Husseini] became increasingly linked to the S.S. and attempts to prevent deals to exchange Jews from the German-occupied Central European countries for lorries and other material resources" (Sela 66).

Zionists focused on bringing Jews to Palestine, legally when possible and illegally when immigration quotas were so limited that it was impossible to gain access by other means. In prewar Palestine (1934-1939), 50,000 Jews had entered illegally, but during the war Britain adopted a brutal policy of capturing and deporting Jewish immigrants. During 1939, the Haganah formed a small offshoot to smuggle Jews out of Europe, but these efforts were increasingly restricted as the war spread. In Palestine, the Haganah developed the Palmach, an elite military strike force with a subdivision, the Palyam, responsible for preparing potential Jewish refugees in areas of crisis to emigrate, arranging for their transport and initial settlement in Palestine.

As early as 1941, the West received news of large-scale Jewish killings by the Nazis. In 1942, the Polish government in exile in London reported that 700,000 Polish Jews had already been murdered by the Germans and, in December of that year, the allies formally announced that Hitler had embarked on the mass murder of Jews. But immigration quotas to Palestine held, and, with most international borders closed to Jews, the progress of the "final solution" through which Jews would be rounded up and sent to camps "in the East" for extermination continued unabated. In 1943, amidst mass extermination of Jews, representatives of the U.S. and Great Britain concluded a meeting in Bermuda where the issue of the disastrous European Jewish condition was debated, but neither country was willing to open its doors to Jewish refugee settlement.

Jews were vulnerable not only in Europe. As a 1941 anti-Semitic outburst in Baghdad showed, when 200 Jews were killed and homes and businesses destroyed, Jews could have no security within other nations. Using the partition plan as a template, Ben Gurion, head of the Jewish Agency, used the war years to build support among American Jews and the Zionists for the establishment of a Jewish state in Palestine. But in Palestine Zionists were less patient and military activities continued. In 1944, five years after the war had started, Menachem Begin (1913-1992) assumed command of the Irgun; concluding that Germany's defeat was imminent, the group returned to the earlier priority of driving the British from Palestine. The Irgun began attacking British targets, activities which the Haganah and Palmach opposed. But by war's end, the Haganah would side with the Irgun to launch the Hebrew Rebellion Movement and attack British targets. In that effort, the Irgun followed the same policy as LHI, a paramilitary group that had split with the Irgun in 1940 so as to begin assaults on British targets then. LHI (or Lehi) was also known as the Stern Gang, after its founder Abraham Stern (1907-1942). Simultaneously, the Haganah stepped up its illegal immigration activities, assisting nearly 71,000 Jews to settle in Palestine between August 1945 and May 1948. Mostly war refugees and Holocaust survivors, many of these Jews were now trapped in internment camps in Germany and Eastern Europe, where they continued to face mass murder by the local populations. In response to the illegal immigrations, the British began a campaign to destroy Haganah ships in European harbors, and from 1946 on forcibly detained the passengers of ships they intercepted in holding camps in Cyprus. Famously, passengers of the *Exodus* were returned to a British-controlled area of Germany and then removed to displaced persons camps, making the Jewish refugees return to the source of their persecution. Despite U.S. president Harry Truman's (1884-1972) support for increased Jewish immigration, which became public knowledge in 1945, international borders remained closed to Jews, and Arabs rejected proposals for a single binational state that would be jointly governed by Arabs and Jews.

In 1944, after repeated pressure from the more moderate Jewish leaders who wished to support the British in their fight against the axis powers, Churchill established the Jewish Brigade. Some 25,000 to 28,000 Palestinian Jews volunteered to serve in the British army, and the Jewish Brigade with its distinctive blue-and-white flag saw action in Italy. After the war, this military training would help Jewish immigration activities, and later would furnish military leaders in the battle for Israel's independence in 1948.

After repeated attempts by Britain to find a compromise for the two warring factions, the British proposed the Morrison-Grady (or Provincial Autonomy) Plan for a binational state in 1946. It was the product of an Anglo-American Committee of Inquiry tasked with studying the problem. The twelve Committee members toured the Middle East in February-March 1946. Documents were submitted from both sides, a three-volume survey (*The Problem of Palestine*) from the Arabs and a 1,000-page report (*The Jewish Case Before the ACC of Inquiry on Palestine*) from the Jewish Agency. The Committee also toured Displaced Persons centers, especially in Poland, where over 1,000 Jews had been murdered since the war's end. The refugees in the DP centers made it clear they wanted to live in Palestine. In May 1946 the Committee recommended that immigration be increased but rejected partition. Both Arabs and Jews rejected the report, and Truman announced U.S. support for the partition of Palestine into two states, thereby further undermining a one-state (binational) solution. By then, Britain concluded it could no longer manage the situation in Palestine. In May 1946, Transjordan, previously part of the British Mandate, was recognized as an independent sovereign kingdom, constituting 75% of the territory for which Britain was responsible. The following year, in the wake of devastating losses to British military and administrative personnel when the King David Hotel was blown up by Irgun forces—killing 91 people, including Britons, Arabs, and Jews, and destroying the southern wing of the hotel, where the British administration was based—Britain turned over the Palestine problem to the United Nations.

In response, the UN General Assembly established the UN Special Committee on Palestine (UNSCOP) to study the matter and make recommendations. The Arabs were hostile and demanded a state that would expel the illegal immigrants and grant no political rights to the remaining Jews. In 1947, Azzam Pasha (1893-1976), the head of the Arab League, told three Jewish Agency representatives that "the Arab world is not in a compromising mood. You won't get anything by peaceful means or compromise. You can perhaps get something, but only by force of arms. We shall try to defeat you. I'm not sure we'll succeed, but we will try. The Arab world regards you as invaders. It may be that we shall lose Palestine. But it's too late to talk of peaceful solutions" (Horowitz 232-235). Jews, by contrast, welcomed UNSCOP and led the delegations on impressive tours of energetic settlements. In comparison, the Arab villages seemed backward, and the Arab leadership and local economic development offered little to recommend itself to governance of the entire remaining area of the Mandate. A majority of eight of the eleven UNSCOP members endorsed a September 1, 1947, report recommending partition of Palestine into an Arab and a Jewish state, with an economic union and independent regime for the Jerusalem/Bethlehem areas. But the Arab states were unwilling to compromise with a Jewish state. The local Arab leadership in Palestine was more open to avenues for compromise, willing to cooperate and even work with the Zionists, though the Mufti, in exile, adamantly opposed Zionism and Jews. Local collaborations with Jews occurred in many ways: Palestinians provided key information to Zionists about Arab strengths, aided in the acquisition of military supplies, sold land to the Zionists, and cooperated on commerce and trade (Cohen 259-268).

On November 29, 1947, the UN adopted a Partition Resolution sanctioning the creation of a Jewish state. The Soviets supported it, briefly reversing their long-standing anti-Zionism with the goal of diminishing British influence in the region. Pressure from Jewish Agency lobbyists at the United Nations significantly contributed to the vote for partition; American Jews thus helped keep the U.S. aboard. The voting at the UN was broadcast live on radio worldwide. Listeners were tense in Palestine, as the UN charter required a two-thirds majority for passage. Thirty-three nations voted yes, thirteen voted no, and ten (including Britain) abstained:

> What appeared to the Jews as a divine miracle, a sign that a global system of justice existed, was perceived by the Arabs as a flagrant wrong, a miscarriage of justice and an act of coercion. They were being called upon to consent to the partitioning of a country that only 30 years earlier had been considered Arab, and to the establishment of a Jewish state in it. To them recognition of the Jews' national rights in Palestine was insufferable, and the only possible response was armed resistance (Shapira 156).

1947-1949—Two Nations at War

Even before the British had withdrawn from Palestine, Jewish and Arab forces were at war. The local Palestinian Arab militia was supported by a military coalition of neighboring Arab states, though never with sufficient arms. While the Arab countries were united in their determination to push the Jews out of Palestine, they largely distrusted one another. The one Arab nation with a clear goal was Jordan; it aimed to annex the West Bank. The character of postwar settlements suggests that the Arab countries overall viewed Palestine either as a possible extension of a pan-Arab nation that included Syria and Jordan, or as an opportunity to add to their own sovereign territory. Nothing suggests they aimed to create an independent Arab nation for Palestinians. In time, however, the Arab states would adopt the Palestinian cause because they realized it would help them to secure both domestic and regional legitimacy. In the final resolution to the war, Israel set up an independent state, while Egypt, Jordan, and Syria annexed different portions of Palestine. The Arab armies had acted separately, without overall coordination, and in 1949 the UN armistice agreements were negotiated separately as well, primarily by the U.S.-provided mediator, Ralph Bunche (1903-1971). Egypt signed first, followed by Jordan. The agreements created new boundaries that came to be known as the Green Line, but they amounted to armistice lines, rather than recognized borders. The state of war between the Arab states and Israel continued, with Arab attacks on Jewish citizens persisting after the war was over.

When floods of Arab refugees arrived in these countries, only Jordan would offer the Palestinians citizenship, while in Gaza (held by Egypt) and Greater Syria (including modern day Lebanon) the migrants were held in refugee camps and granted neither civil rights nor nationality. Palestinian refugees were trapped in a cycle of poverty and suffering, with little reason to imagine a viable future for themselves. Although World War II in Europe produced population transfers numbering in the millions, the Arab states uniquely refused to absorb the Palestinian refugees. Instead, a myth was promoted by the Arab governments that all the displaced and exiled Palestinians would return home once Israel was destroyed, thereby perpetuating the refugee problem and making permanent peace with Israel politically impossible. Those Arabs who remained within the newly formed state of Israel were held under martial law, and were often viewed as a fifth column by successive Israeli governments, but in 1966 they were granted full citizenship, receiving equal treatment under the law. Many have acquired college degrees and become accomplished professionals.

Between 583,000-609,000 Palestinians left their homes (Karsh 264-267). This migration is known to Palestinians as the Nakba ("catastrophe") and formed a central narrative in the creation of Palestinian national identity. Exactly why so many Palestinians fled remains a subject of continuing debate in the scholarly literature, partly because there are competing preferences for uniform, simplified narratives both within and outside the scholarly community. In truth there seem to be multiple causes. The urban Arab elite left early on; the departure of upper-class Arabs, along with professionals and the intelligentsia, delivered an unspoken message that others should leave as well. Some villages were forced out, though the reasons were often strategic. Other villages fled in fear, responding to stories of real, exaggerated, or fabricated violence. An Arab strategy of encouraging Palestinian women and children to leave Israel so men would be free to fight predictably backfired when men left with their families. In the cities, "conflicting economic interests, political differences, and social and interdenominational schisms diminished the appetite for fighting, generated successive waves of evacuees, and prevented national cooperation. There was no sense of an overarching mutual interest or shared destiny" (Karsh 240).

One pivotal event that triggered Palestinian flight was the April 9, 1948, massacre at Deir Yassin, a Jerusalem area Arab village. Fighters from the Irgun and the Stern Gang entered the village to clear it—with Haganah approval—ostensibly as part of an effort to secure the Western approaches to Jerusalem.

When they encountered unexpected armed resistance, they reacted brutally, killing about 107 men, women, and children, partly by blowing up houses. Several captured men were then executed. All parties to the conflict then overstated the number of deaths—the Irgun to sow fear and demonstrate their prowess, the Arabs to rally support for the invasion. Arab propagandists also fabricated and broadcast stories of widespread rape as part of the massacre. While the stories did build support for the invasion, they also drove thousands of Palestinians to flee. The furor raised also led to an Arab massacre carried out for revenge. On April 13, hundreds of Arab militiamen attacked a largely unarmed convoy that was taking students, faculty, doctors, and nurses to the Hadassah Hospital at the Hebrew University campus. After the few defenders ran out of ammunition, the Arabs moved carefully to the line of buses, wet them with gasoline, and set them alight. All told, 78 Jews died, many burnt alive, most of them students and medical personnel.

Given that a roughly equivalent number of Jews fled Arab countries, gave up all their property, and came to Israel, the Israeli government argued that a population transfer had taken place. "Throughout history, problems created by similar population movements had been solved not by repatriation and the creation of large hostile and disruptive national minorities, but by resettlement in the countries chosen by the refugees in the hour of decision" (Sela 78).

As war loomed, there was little confidence in the world that Israel could prevail. In February, the U.S. State Department sought to have the U.S. government rescind its support for partitioning Palestine into Arab and Jewish states. Policy Planning Staff member George Kennan (1904-2005) told Secretary of State George Marshall (1880-1959) that a Jewish state would offend Arab interests and hurt U.S.-Arab relations. He feared that the Zionists would be overwhelmed in a war with the Arabs, forcing the Americans to send troops to defend the Jews, in turn causing the Soviets to dispatch troops to the Middle East, which would put Washington and Moscow in armed confrontation. The U.S. tried but failed to have UN trusteeship established for Palestine's future in hopes of preventing the Jewish state from emerging. Among the groups rallying to Israel's support that year was the National Lawyers Guild, reflecting American progressive support for partition. The Guild resolved that the U.S. State Department "permit American volunteers to go to the aid of those who are defending and complying with the dictates of the UN in the enforcement of the Partition Plan," and called upon the UN Security Council to "equip the Haganah," "defend the Jewish State," and "prevent Arab infiltration of men and arms into Palestine for the purpose of creating strife and the defeat of the Partition Plan."

In April 1948 the Zionist Executive established a People's Council to serve as an embryonic parliament and a People's Administration to function as an embryonic government, and on Friday, May 14, David Ben Gurion (1886-1973), soon to be Israel's first Prime Minister, gathered the People's Council in Tel Aviv and read the Declaration of Independence, establishing the State of Israel. One of the first acts of the new Israeli government was to revoke the immigration and land purchase restrictions imposed by the May 1939 British White Paper.

At that point in 1948, the first phase of the war, an internal civil war between the Yishuv and the Palestinian Arab community, essentially ended. Israel now faced a conventional war with the surrounding Arab nations and Palestinian irregulars. Each Arab country had its own agenda. The fall of Haifa to the Israelis, for example, deprived Iraq of what, at the time, was its primary access to oil terminals and refineries with a seaport. Arab armies invaded across every land border. The Arab Legion moved from Transjordan toward Jerusalem. Two columns of Egyptian troops crossed into the Sinai from the south. In June, a UN-brokered truce went into effect for a month. After fighting resumed, the Israeli Defense Forces were better organized. Syrian forces in the north disintegrated under fire, and the Israelis destroyed the southern arm of the Egyptian army.

By the summer of 1948, the U.S. State Department had come to accept Israel as a reality, yet the celebration in Israel was short lived as riots broke out in many Arab capitals against Jewish citizens who had lived there for centuries. Jews were forced to flee Arab countries for Israel, leaving homes, property, businesses, and synagogues. Between 1948 and 1951, Israel accepted 700,000 new immigrants, doubling the Jewish population. Many of these Jews from Middle Eastern and North African countries arrived stripped of their worldly possessions. Their numbers were approximately equivalent to the number of Palestinians displaced by the 1948 war. After the war, the Israeli government slowly expropriated much of the land in Israel previously owned by Arabs who had fled or been expelled, often to help settle the new immigrants. To decrease the feasibility of a large-scale Palestinian return, they also bulldozed abandoned villages and gave Jewish immigrants access to abandoned Arab homes in city neighborhoods.

The war cost 6,000 Jewish lives, 1% of the Jewish population in Palestine, and many more were injured. But Jews had held onto enough land to establish a state, viewing this War of Independence as a battle for survival. Under the partition plan, the Jews were to receive 14,900 square kilometers, the Arabs 11,700. As a result of the war, Israel's territory grew by 37%, to 20,770 sq. km. Egypt and Jordan occupied Gaza and the West Bank respectively, a total of 5,500 sq. km., until the 1967 war. The war also heightened inter-Arab divisions and produced internal upheavals in Arab countries. The comprehensive failure of the Arab armies, in company with earlier predictions of victory, triggered ultra-nationalist sentiment in several Arab states.

The Making of a Jewish State

The State-building years reveal concerted efforts to unify and assimilate the new Jewish immigrants into the established Zionist ideologies and apparatus. In 1949, the first Knesset was elected and Israel was admitted into the United Nations. After unifying the disparate paramilitary forces in Palestine under the banner of the IDF (Israel Defense Forces) in June, the Knesset passed a national service law stipulating that men and women fit to serve (with some exceptions) were required to be available for military service at age 18, though national service was available as an option for some. After the regular period of enlistment, soldiers remain active in the reserves for 20 to 30 years. With the army largely demobilized after the 1948 war, Israel faced the need to create a force that could defend the country in the event of renewed attacks. Unable to maintain a standing army of the size necessary to meet wartime challenges, Israel adopted a model based on the Swiss military: 30% of the army is kept on active duty, with the remainder held in reserve in civilian life, subject to rapid mobilization when needed. A skilled intelligence service also became a requirement, so that impending attacks could be predicted and, where possible, prevented:

> It was the establishment of a military system where almost every citizen—male and female—was a trained soldier and a reservist, that transformed these disparate groups of people—the Israeli-born *Sabra*, the Orthodox Jew from New York, the scientist from London, the silversmith from Yemen, the lawyer from Egypt, and the small shopkeeper from Morocco—from individuals into a society and one nation under arms. And above all, what kept this Israeli organism together and helped rally Israelis around the flag and their leadership, was a deep sense of external danger" (Bregman 295-96).

In 1950, the Law of Return was adopted, guaranteeing Jews worldwide the right to immigrate to Israel, codifying a benefit announced in the Declaration of Independence and an immigration practice that had become a necessity both for Jews facing persecution and for the new country's demographic requirements. The following year, Israel adopted a national development plan that departed from its established ideology and practice of investing in agricultural and communitarian settlements . . . . The plan assumed that the majority of Israel's population, approximately 80%, would live in towns and cities. Its adoption signified that the initial Zionist dream of renaissance in a physiocratic utopia of Jewish peasants had been supplanted by a vision of a modern, urban, technologically advanced society modeled on Western Europe and Japan. In large measure, the face of Israel at the beginning of the twenty-first century has been determined by this plan (Troen 167).

Austerity and Disease: The Problems of Creating a New State

Following the State's establishment and the influx of immigrants, the new country faced starvation. With exports funding less than a third of the country's necessary imports, Israel was in short supply of food, raw materials for industry, clothes, shoes, and the necessary foreign funds to purchase these goods. Credit at international banks had expired and still new citizens poured into the country. In a coordinated measure to ensure that the population would have necessary supplies, rationing was instituted from 1949-1959. Limiting citizens to 1600 calories a day, in line with British models of rationing (though more was available for the elderly, sick, children, and pregnant women), put pressure on the post-war veterans, as well as both long-time and newly arrived immigrants. Though the program experienced widespread political support, in time the population would begin to push against the restrictions, which for many dated back to 1939 and the shortages of WWII. A thriving black market developed which officials worked hard to suppress but were unable to eradicate.

The arrival of many new immigrants who had often suffered hardship and malnutrition on their journeys also brought such diseases as typhus, tuberculosis, and leprosy, along with scabies, ringworm, and lice; and a polio epidemic broke out which devastated the country's children. Medical efforts for these conditions, which were exacerbated by poor housing and malnutrition, included disinfection by DDT powder, scalp radiation, and isolation. The association of disease with the immigrants from North African and Arab countries, the population that came to be known as *Mizrachim* (Orientals) reinforced the European immigrants' and descendants' prejudice and racism. That they too had experienced disinfection and medical treatment when they arrived or in the detention camps in Europe seemed to play little part in gaining sympathy for the latest Aliyah. Moreover, many of the new arrivals were confined in temporary camps (*ma'abarot*), at first made of tents and later corrugated metal huts that further heightened their association with dirt, squalor, and degradation. By 1956, the Jewish population of Israel had tripled and poverty, overcrowding, and illness had become priorities for a government desperate to establish new housing, schools, and industry to help settle the new immigrants.

When Israel signed a controversial reparations agreement with West Germany in September 1952, known as the Shilumin Agreement, the economic survival of the country depended on this new source of foreign currency. Over the decade it played a large role in securing Israel's economic stability and ending rationing. In the immediate post-independence years, however, contributions from and bond sales to world Jewry were the single largest source of foreign capital:

> In the course of Israel's first decade, then, only one-twelfth of the nation's foreign currency expenditures were paid through 'earned' income. The rest derived from American, German, and other overseas sources. During the 1950s, world Jewry covered 59 percent of the balance of payments deficit, the United States government 12 percent, and West Germany 29 percent. Quite literally, these funds sustained Israel's economy, gave the nation breathing room in the unprecedented task of tripling, feeding, housing, and employing its population and defending its borders. (Sachar 426)

Experiencing multiple economic and social hardships on the home front, the new Israeli government also had to contend with ongoing bloodshed. In the mid-1950s, Arabs infiltrating through the porous borders with Egypt and Jordan continued to kill Israeli civilians. Israel responded by carrying out reprisals against villages suspected of harboring and assisting the terrorists. The aim was not only to convince villages not to harbor terrorists but also to get the Arab countries to police their own borders, but the attacks and reprisals continued. In 1953, Arab women and children were killed in Kibya when houses were blown up by the Israeli military. In 1954, Arab terrorists attacked a bus on the Arava road. Eleven Israelis were killed, three living to report what had happened. In 1955, fighting along the Gaza Strip border intensified, creating mounting pressure with Egypt, with the IDF claiming 180 incidents in four months. These tensions were exacerbated by Israeli concerns over armaments. Having signed a deal with Czechoslovakia, Egypt effectively achieved a military advantage over Israel, but in 1956 Israel was finally able to purchase French aircraft and tanks, thereby rebalancing their military power.

Tensions in the region escalated, partly framed by the cold war, as Egypt allied with Russia, potentially jeopardizing British, French, and American economic and political interests. All this exploded in 1956 after Egypt's Gamal Abdel Nasser (1918-1970) nationalized the Suez Canal. The response proved to be the first and only war Israel fought in collaboration with its allies, but the allied attack designed to "protect" the international waterway was a catastrophe for France and Britain, who lost the canal and their public standing as world powers. Israel, the only party to gain significantly from the Sinai Campaign, took the entire Sinai Peninsula, until it was occupied the following year by a UN international force charged with preventing another war between Egypt and Israel. The conquest had proved Israel's strength to the world.

Nasser had become a hero for Arab nationalists, a unifying symbol of the Arab determination to throw off the yoke of foreign oppression. For Israel's neighboring Arab countries, this served as a rallying cry, which increased wartime strains along the border with Jordan. Israel imposed a curfew on Arab-Israeli border villages, but on the first evening (October 29, 1956), before villagers were aware of the new rule, a group returning home after curfew were shot. "Of the battalion's eight platoon commanders, seven made sure that the inhabitants were allowed to return safely to their homes, but one obeyed the order to the letter, and that evening in Kafr Kassem forty-seven men, women, and children were killed" (Shapira 198). In response to this massacre, eleven Israeli officers and men were tried and eight were convicted. Their sentences were commuted, but a legal precedent was set in Israel making it unacceptable to follow an illegal order.

The 1960s and the Ghosts of the Past

In 1953, Yad Vashem was established as Israel's official memorial for the commemoration of the Holocaust through education, research, documentation, and remembrance. But while the Holocaust was commemorated publicly, in reality the difficulties of the 1950s obscured the survivors' suffering; they were encouraged to adopt the national ethos and forget the past. Little historical material or literary fiction was written about the Holocaust, survivors were marginal characters in the nascent film industry, and psychological services were minimal. This changed in 1960 when Mossad agents in Argentina captured Adolph Eichmann (1906-1962) and brought him back to Israel to stand trial. Though he would be found guilty and sentenced to be hanged (Israel's only death sentence), the significance of his trial extended far beyond the discussion of his complicity. Rather, it opened the way for public conversations about survivor suffering, the Zionist leadership's activities during the Holocaust, and the treatment of survivors in postwar Israel.

During the late 1950s, Palestinians began to mobilize clandestinely, though no clear political leadership emerged. Believing in the larger goal of Arab nationalism, Palestinians placed their hope in the Arab nations. In 1959, Fatah, a Palestinian paramilitary and political group, was founded with the aim of winning its demands through terrorist acts and, in 1964, the Palestine Liberation Organization (PLO) was founded in Jordanian-controlled East Jerusalem. In 1967, following the Six Day War, Israel's defeat of Egypt, Syria, and Jordan resulted in the end of Arab nationalism for Palestinians and made them finally understand that they could only depend upon themselves for political liberation. Along with Fatah and the PLO, the creation of the Popular Front for the Liberation of Palestine (PFLP) in 1967 and the breakaway Democratic Front for the Liberation of Palestine (DFLP) in 1969 produced the first groups to coordinate armed struggle for Palestinian interests. PLO activities from Jordan included a series of raids on Israel, which culminated in a school bus hitting a mine, and resulted in a reprisal attack by the IDF, The Battle of Karameh (1968). Surprisingly, the Jordanian army fought alongside the PLO, turning what was meant to be a small operation into a full-scale battle, but the events were to raise concerns for the Jordanians. The Palestinians were essentially a "state within a state" that was beginning to threaten Jordanian sovereignty and, by the end of the 1960s, King Hussein had instigated the forceful suppression of PLO activities. The Palestinian Arabs, who were "accustomed to vigorous, volatile political activity and factionalism, fermented conflict in the Kingdom. While many of them were prominent in public positions at all levels, many others were active in opposition as agitators" (Sela 673). In two costly battles (September 1970 and July 1971), the Palestinian guerrilla groups were routed by the Jordanian forces.

After these defeats, the PLO leadership fled to Lebanon, where again Palestinians were isolated. It was during this period that the different Palestinian groups engaged in recruitment campaigns within the refugee camps, efforts which were strengthened by high-profile Palestinian airline highjackings and broad spectrum terrorist activities. These included the 1972 murder of eleven Israeli athletes at the Munich Olympic Games by the Black September group and the 1976 highjacking of an Air France plane with over 200 passengers and crew who were held hostage in Entebbe until rescued dramatically by the IDF. A 1972 attack at Tel Aviv's international airport left 26 people dead, many of them Christian pilgrims from Puerto Rico. The terrorists were 3 Japanese gunmen recruited by the Popular Front for the Liberation of Palestine from the Japanese Red Army. They arrived on an Air France flight, carrying violin cases containing assault rifles. In May 1974 a PFLP assault team wearing IDF uniforms crossed the border from Lebanon and took 115 hostages at the Netiv Meir Elementary School in Ma'lot in Israel's Western Galilee region. When an elite Israeli force stormed the building, the terrorists used machine guns and grenades to kill 22 high school students who were staying in the building overnight. These actions led the world media to delegitimize Palestinian claims and discredit the PLO, but they nevertheless put the Palestinian situation on the world political agenda. The Lebanese civil war (1975-1990), growing out of mutual Christian-Muslim hatred, offered Palestinians the opportunity to shoot rockets into Northern Israel in the late 1970s. In response the IDF invaded the south of Lebanon, ultimately forcing the PLO leadership to relocate to Tunis in 1982, but leaving the more radical Hezbollah (backed by Iran) to take its place in Lebanon.

The Six Day War, which proved a catalyst for Palestinian political mobilization, took place from June 5 to 10, 1967. When the Soviets erroneously informed Syria and Egypt that Israel was amassing troops for an attack in the north, Nasser demanded that the UN withdraw from Gaza, Sinai, and the Straits of Tiran. The UN complied and Nasser blocked the Straits, preventing Israel's access through the Red Sea to the Gulf of Aqaba, a major trade route. It amounted to an act of war. The public rhetoric that followed—which included calls on Nasser to drive the Jews out of Israel and PLO chairman Ahmed Shukeri's (1908-1980) boast that "no Jew whatsoever will survive" in the event of war—evoked memories of the Holocaust for Israelis. When Jordan's King Hussein then flew to Egypt to sign a mutual defense pact, Israel reacted to the threat implied in the military alliance and launched a preemptive strike. Within three hours, the IDF had destroyed the entire Egyptian air force on the ground. The felling of Syrian and Jordanian air forces followed swiftly. Over land, IDF forces reached the banks of the Suez Canal and reclaimed the Sinai Peninsula, chasing out the Egyptian army. Though Israel had hoped to avoid conflict with Jordan, Jordanian shelling of West Jerusalem and the Ramat David air base led Israel to respond, eventually taking East Jerusalem and the West Bank, which had been under Jordanian control since 1948. Israel also occupied the Golan Heights, taking this strategic military site from Syria, while capturing the Gaza strip from Egypt.

But with these new territories came a million Palestinians. Unlike the Arab citizens within Israel who had received full and equal rights, Palestinian residents in these new territories would be governed under martial law and Israel would become an occupying power. The early dream of a Greater Israel—a Jewish state occupying all of Palestine—had long lain dormant, but now it rose again to play a significant role in the Israeli polity for the first time since independence.

High Culture at the Center and Territorial Expansion at the Margins

After the 1967 war two Israels seemed to emerge. In the country's center the population was becoming increasingly affluent. Israeli literature of the period ridicules a new decadent class that had radically rejected the pioneering ethos at the heart of the country's foundation. But this transformation also signified the normalization of the country and its recovery after the period of austerity.

In 1964, the Batsheva Dance Company, based in Tel Aviv, was founded by Martha Graham (1894-1991) and Baroness Batsheva de Rothschild (1914-1999) and rapidly established itself to international acclaim. In 1965, the Israel Museum, Israel's national art and archeology museum, was founded, based in part on the collection from the Bezalel art school in Jerusalem opened by Boris Schatz in 1906. In 1966, S. Y. (Shmuel Yosef) Agnon (1888-1970) won the Nobel Prize for literature, sharing it with poet Nelly Sachs. Born in what is now the Ukraine, Agnon had settled permanently in Palestine in 1924. His fiction and poetry embodies the cultural conflicts between tradition and modernity, which characterized the development of Zionist literary and artistic culture.

Tel Aviv café culture, restaurants, hotels, dance venues, and shops reflected a buoyant society, and international tourism flourished. Along with economic liberation came sexual liberation, and though conventional Israeli society continued to be characterized as old-fashioned and traditionalist, post-war euphoria revealed significant social changes in Tel Aviv and its nearby cities. The arrival of French artists and Italian cinema, the introduction of rock music, and the rise of a new youth culture signaled the casting off of the old conservatism.

One of the notable Tel Aviv developments was the growth of a vibrant gay community. Israel inherited anti-sodomy rules from the British Mandate period, but the Israeli Supreme Court ruled in 1963 that they should not be enforced against consenting adults acting in private. The age of consent in Israel for both heterosexuals and homosexuals is 16. The ban was formally repealed by the Knesset in 1988. Discrimination on the grounds of sexual orientation was prohibited in 1992. Although Israel today has not yet approved same-sex marriages being performed in country, despite national support for doing so, it has long honored those performed elsewhere. Meanwhile, the Civil Service Commission extends spousal benefits and pensions to partners of gay employees. Gays can serve openly in the Israeli military.

The vibrant coastal culture, however, did not extend everywhere. In the country's periphery, a different story was unfolding. Many of the new

immigrants were being housed in development towns outside main population centers and often in the newly conquered territories. These projects,
which were frequently built around a single industry upon which the area
would depend, offered new hope for the refugees, but by the 1980s it had
become clear that the social and economic limitations of these neighborhoods had created an uneducated and impoverished underclass of Mizrachi
Jews, often held hostage by appalling working conditions and low factory
wages. Inspired by the American Black protest movements of the 1960s,
Mizrachim created their own Black Panther movement (1971) to protest the
social injustices and discrimination that faced them. The issues they raised
were sidelined by the Yom Kippur War, leading the Mizrachi Jews to mobilize
and making them a significant political force in the 1977 elections.

The territories taken by Israel in 1967 offered political challenges but
also economic advantages, particularly for a country with limited territory
and increasing numbers of immigrants. Despite secret talks in which the
Israeli government offered to return parts of its land in exchange for peace
and recognition, at a summit in Khartoum the Arab States publicly refused to
recognize Israel or to negotiate. In an attempt to resolve problems acquired
with the occupation of the West Bank, Israeli Minister of Labor Yigal Alon
(1918-1980) presented a strategic plan which included a partition in which
Israel would retain control over the Jordan River areas to protect Israel from
Jordanian (and Palestinian) incursions, and the more populated hill areas and
a corridor that included Jericho would be under Jordanian control. Though
Jordanians rejected the plan, Israelis saw opportunities in moving to settle this
newly acquired land. While the government planned to settle Jews in desert-
ed agricultural landscapes, in 1968, for the first time, Jewish settlers defied
the Israeli government and occupied space in Hebron in the heart of the
Arab population. The government's decision to allow them to stay—despite a
1967 opinion by Theodor Meron (1930-), legal counsel to the Israeli foreign
ministry, that civilian settlement in the administered territories would violate
the Fourth Geneva Convention—proved a watershed moment. Settlement
policy became increasingly more aggressive under Menachem Begin's
Likud government after his election in 1977. By July 2012 Israeli Interior
Ministry figures would acknowledge 350,150 Jewish settlers living in 121
officially recognized West Bank settlements, along with 300,000 living in East
Jerusalem. The international community broadly condemned the settlements
as illegal, and the Palestinians have regularly declared them an impediment
to peace negotiations, lodging protests at the addition of any housing units
whether in existing settlements or new locations. Some of the settlements
constitute farming communities or frontier villages, while others amount
to city neighborhoods or suburbs reflecting normal urban expansion. The

largest of the settlements—Ariel, Beitar Illit, Ma'ale Adumin, and Mod'in Illit—constitute cities in their own right. The first disengagement of settlers occurred in 1982 when eighteen Jewish settlements were disbanded in the Sinai Peninsula, including Yamit, upon the return of territory to Egypt. But more significantly, the 2006 disengagement from Gaza, which included a much larger Jewish population, occurred at the instigation of Prime Minister Ariel Sharon, a notorious right-wing hawk who had previously supported the settlement movement. This withdrawal, which had none of the quid pro quo advantages that the Egyptian deal had included, revealed that the government recognized the cost of defending the settlers was ultimately too high a price for the country to pay. Moreover, the disengagement from Gaza demonstrated that Israel had come to accept the principle of Palestinian sovereignty.

Arab Violence and the End of the Old Ways

Despite the resounding defeat of the Arab countries during the 1967 war, hostilities continued, culminating in the 1969-1970 War of Attrition, an escalating series of border clashes with Egypt. The IDF reduced cities along the Suez Canal to rubble and Egyptian refugees flooded into Cairo. U.S. interventions set in place a ceasefire when in 1970 Nassar died suddenly, to be succeeded by Anwar Sadat (1918-1981).

In 1973, The Yom Kippur War (the October War) took place from October 6-24. The conduct of the war was initially shaped by the failure of Israeli intelligence to recognize the extent of Egypt's humiliation in the 1967 war, the political pressure for revenge and the reacquisition of lost territory it created, and the ongoing violence that followed. Thus they failed to pay attention to the heavy buildup of Egyptian troops along the Suez Canal, the massing of Syrian troops at the border, and even disregarded a September 25 warning from King Hussein to Prime Minister Golda Meir (1898-1978) that a coordinated Egyptian-Syrian attack was forthcoming. Meir had become Prime Minister in 1969 upon the sudden death of Levi Eshkol (1895-1969). Complacency about the condition of the Egyptian army, given their easy thrashing in 1967, lessened the motivation of the intelligence services to react and made it possible to accept the idea that Egyptian troop buildups were merely evidence of military exercises. Israel also felt, incorrectly, that its defensive Bar-Lev line on the Suez Canal could not be breached by Egypt. In consequence, the Israeli air force took heavy losses from SAM missiles, while Russian anti-tank missiles destroyed a number of Israeli tanks on the Egyptian front. In the first two days of the attack, top Israeli officials believed the entire country could be lost. The Israelis counterattacked in the Golan Heights on October 11 and within days advanced toward Damascus. Meanwhile, U.S. President Richard Nixon (1913-1994) agreed to an emergency airlift of military equipment to Israel, beginning October 14. That same day the Egyptian army launched a disastrous assault that cost it 250 tanks, compared to an Israeli loss of 20. Soon the IDF crossed the canal and encircled Egypt's Third Army. What began as a rout of Israeli forces ended in a major victory for them, but 2,500 Israeli soldiers died, the highest toll since the 1948 war. Combined Egyptian and Syrian combat deaths approached 15,000, and the two countries had lost 1800 tanks and 400 aircraft. But Israel's confidence was shaken by its intelligence failures and lack of preparation. Then, too, the recent introduction of television in 1969 meant that the Yom Kippur war was the first war to be televised and to appear in people's homes. The sight of bound and blindfolded soldiers being led across the screen reinforced the Israeli public's sense of existential threat.

The Yom Kippur war shook confidence in the government. In the 1960s and 1970s, the citizenry was also rocked by a series of public scandals, including the revelation of Leah Rabin's illegal bank account in the US and Moshe Dayan's sexual escapades and personal possession of national archeological treasures. Political infighting in the Labor party and the demographic rise of the Mizrachi voting bloc then combined to put an end to 30 years of Labor dominance of Israeli political institutions. In the spectacular election of 1977, in an upset Haim Yavin spontaneously called a *ma'apach* ("political revolution"), Begin and the right-wing Likud party came to power. The election permanently changed the landscape of Israeli politics. On the other hand, the early Arab victories in 1973 had made it possible for Sadat to contemplate an alternative to war as a way of solving Egypt's conflict with Israel.

In November 1977, Anwar Sadat flew to Israel and spoke before the Israeli Knesset. His visit revealed the ongoing secret international efforts to lead Israel and Egypt into an agreement offering principles for managing the autonomy of the Palestinians and negotiating a peace treaty between the two warring countries. In 1979, Sadat and Begin signed an agreement at the White House following the Camp David Accords (1978), a series of meetings between Egypt and Israel facilitated by U.S. President Jimmy Carter. Sadat and Begin shared the Nobel Peace Prize that year. Though Israel withdrew from the Sinai, returning the territory to Egypt and dismantling eighteen settlements in the process, the Arab nation was barred from the Arab League for ten years for signing the peace agreement. That was part of an effort to persuade other Arab countries not to make similar agreements. In 1981 Sadat was assassinated during an annual Egyptian victory parade.

Lebanon from Litani (1978) to Withdrawal (2006)

In 1978, in response to terrorist attacks, Israel first crossed the Litani River into Southern Lebanon to drive out the Palestinians shooting at Northern Israel. In March 1978, a Fatah raiding party hijacked an Israeli bus and 32 Israelis died. Though the Israelis pushed the Palestinians back from the border, they invaded again in 1982, after responding to requests for aid and military training from the Lebanese Maronite Phalange Party headed by Bashir Gemayel (1947-1982). Begin was moved by the Maronite appeal, for in his mind the Lebanese civil war was a battle between Muslims and Christians. "For millennia the Christian world had oppressed and killed the Jews. Now a Christian community was appealing to the Jews for succor— after Europe, particularly France, had turned its back. Begin was not one to resist the opportunity of showing the world how his people, in their magnanimity and humanity, would help and protect the Christians of Lebanon from Muslim 'genocide' as Europe and the United States had failed to do for the Jews" (Morris 404-5).

As Muslim Syrian forces advanced into Lebanon, Gemayel responded by sending his own fighters into Syrian dominated territory in 1981, but his militia was overextended and Syrians launched an artillery barrage that killed hundreds of Christian civilians. In a curious alliance, the IDF had become partners with the Maronite Lebanese, if only to protect Israel's northern borders from Palestinian violence. Their air attacks on Palestinian-controlled Lebanese towns reached as far as Beirut, where they destroyed PLO buildings and killed several hundred people. Israel believed that by eliminating the PLO and restoring Christian dominance to Lebanon, they would be able to negotiate a peace treaty with the new government. Their aims tallied with Gemayal's own desires for Christian political rule, though he was not as comfortable admitting his association with Israel publicly as he had been in receiving aid. Despite a slowdown in Palestinian provocations by the end of 1981 and into the spring of 1982, Minister of Defense Ariel Sharon (1928-2014), who would serve as Prime Minister from 2001 to 2006, pressed for the 1982 invasion of Lebanon. When the Israeli ambassador to London, Shlomo Argov (1929-2003), was shot in the head and badly wounded, Sharon had the provocation he needed, and despite PLO condemnation of the assassination attempt (and their denials of involvement in its orchestration), Israel bombed several PLO targets in retaliation, and the Israeli cabinet agreed to a limited invasion of Lebanon. Sharon, with more expansionist ideas, manipulated and misled the cabinet to give piecemeal approval for further steps; they finally agreed to put the IDF into armed conflict with the Syrian forces in Lebanon. After a two-month siege of the city, the IDF entered West Beirut.

Ongoing skirmishes between the PLO and the IDF on the ground and the brutality of urban guerilla warfare left innocent victims in the line of fire. The local PLO militias dug in to fight, using the refugee camps as shelter. Hundreds of Palestinians were killed, and though the IDF sought not to fire on civilians, only a heavy bombing campaign forced the PLO to evacuate. Though the Lebanese Army refused to empty the refugee camps, the Phalangists agreed to take on the job. On the evening of September 16, 1982, Phalangist men moved into the Sabra and Shatilla refugee camps with Israeli approval, presumably also believing they had the IDF's tacit approval for what they were about to do. Two days earlier, Gemayal, already elected president, had been assassinated. Eager for revenge, the Phalangists moved from house to house, killing whole families. The Phalangists were out of sight of the Israelis, who were stationed beyond the walls of the camp, and the Israelis thus did not see what was happening or intervene, ultimately failing in their responsibility to care for the residents' safety.

Yet the Israeli military leadership, under Sharon's authority, certainly had ample reason to be wary of the Phalangists' intentions. After the brutality of the bombings, the massacres "sparked a conflagration among the Israeli public. The possibility that the IDF was even indirectly responsible because it stood aside and did not intervene . . . subverted the army's image as moral in the eyes of civilians and soldiers alike" (Shapira 384). "Intellectuals, media figures, and writers felt that 'their' country was disappearing and being replaced by a country that was not theirs" (Shapira 387). The war was the first time Israel had gone beyond gestures of self-defense to invade another country; accordingly, the government lost public support for the war. Officers signed a letter of protest that became a powerful symbol for Israel's early peace movement, and hundreds of thousands of civilians demonstrated in Tel Aviv against the Sabra and Shatilla refugee camp atrocities, demanding an Israeli commission of inquiry be formed. Begin resisted at first but was compelled to concede and finally resigned in 1983.

Having forcibly expelled the PLO, whose leaders now fled to Tunis, Israel withdrew to a slim borderland buffer zone policed by the Southern Lebanon Army (SLA) where Israel also maintained a military presence of its own. Meanwhile, however, the PLO had been replaced by Hezbollah, an Iranian-backed Palestinian terror group that would use the next twenty years to wage guerilla warfare against the SLA and IDF. In 1996, after constant low-level conflict, Israel and Hezbollah signed a ceasefire treaty agreeing to forgo attacks on civilians. But Israeli soldiers continued to remain targets and Hezbollah adopted a policy of killing or kidnapping them and releasing them in exchange for Palestinian political prisoners held in Israel. Israel continued to fund the SLA, but in 2000 the Southern Lebanese Army collapsed under an onslaught from Hezbollah and from concern the Israelis might abandon the SLA as part of a peace agreement with Syria.

After becoming Prime Minister in 1999, Ehud Barak sought to fulfill a campaign promise to withdraw all troops in Lebanon, but a hope that this might be part of an agreement with Syria faded. Then, in elections, the political wing of the terrorist organization won all the Parliamentary seats allotted for Southern Lebanon. An Israeli withdrawal might have eliminated Hezbollah's legitimacy as a force opposing an occupying power, but it could also have destroyed the SLA. In 2004, the UN called for a dismantling of militia groups and a withdrawal from Lebanon by foreign powers. Syria withdrew in 2005, but Hezbollah refused to lay down its weapons and continued attacking Israeli targets. Tensions in the area led to constant accusations of terror actions by both Hezbollah and Israel, and though Israel had expressed a desire to sign peace accords with Lebanon, the possibility now seemed unlikely. When word of Barak's plans to withdraw leaked, SLA forces began to desert, leaving Israeli troops dangerously exposed in many places. On May 24, 2006, the IDF completed a withdrawal and Israel ended an eighteen-year presence in Lebanon.

Assisted by Iranian and North Korean instructors, Hezbollah thereafter began building an elaborate system of concealed bunkers connected by tunnels throughout what had been the security zone. The bunkers were stocked with sufficient supplies and weapons to survive a siege. Rocket launchers were established underground and mounted on lifts that could raise them into firing position. In July 2006, Hezbollah attacked a patrol on Israel's side of the border. Israel responded with air strikes. Hezbollah then began an aggressive campaign of rocket launches into Israel. An extensive air campaign proved effective in eliminating Hezbollah's medium- and long-range missiles, but had little effect on its 10,000 to 16,000 short-range missiles with a range of 18 to 28 km that could be fired from mobile launchers. From July 12 until August 14, when a ceasefire went into effect, over 4,000 rockets struck Israel, killing and wounding ordinary citizens and substantially disrupting daily life. Just before the UN-brokered ceasefire went into effect, Israel sent in ground troops, but the bunker system, like that used by the North Vietnamese, proved resilient. "Hezbollah had embraced a new doctrine, transforming itself from a predominantly guerila force into a formidable quasi-conventional army . . . . A semi-military organization of a few thousand people, carrying relatively primitive weapons, was able to survive against what was regarded as the strongest army in the Middle East" (Bregman 292). This, the second Lebanon War, displaced a million people in Lebanon and half a million in Northern Israel. The UN finally brokered a ceasefire and since then there have been only limited outbreaks of violence.

The World's Conscience, Economic Growth, and Popular Culture

While Begin was charged with the disasters of the first Lebanon war, the same principle behind the desire to help Maronite Christians was at play when he offered asylum to 300 Vietnamese refugees ("boat people") in 1977-1979. Recalling the world's failure to offer safe haven for Jews during the Holocaust—and citing the example of the *St. Louis* which sailed to Cuba where the passengers were unable to disembark and were finally returned to Hamburg where most died in concentration camps—Begin articulated what had become a fundamental belief about Israel's responsibility to help those in need. In 1958, Israel had adopted an official humanitarian aid agenda as a principal element of the country's international cooperation program. These efforts began formally following Golda Meir's first visit to Africa and the establishment of MASHAV, the Foreign Ministry's Center for International Cooperation, which provides technical training and shares technology with countries striving to alleviate global problems of hunger, disease, and poverty. Over the years, Israel extended humanitarian aid and assistance to more than 140 countries, whether or not they maintained diplomatic relations with the Jewish state. The countries helped included Japan, the Philippines, Haiti, Myanmar, the Democratic Republic of Congo, El Salvador, Sri Lanka, Indonesia, India, Turkey, and Kosovo. Israel responded to such humanitarian disasters as war, famine, earthquakes, and typhoons. Along with providing medical supplies, disaster relief, and support staff during the 1970s, this agenda was expanded to granting safe haven to refugees; along with the Vietnamese, Israel took in foreign nationals from Bosnia, Kosovo, and more recently Darfur.

Yet this pattern also led to condemnation of the government's treatment of African asylum seekers in South Tel Aviv in the 2010s who entered the country illegally through the border between Israel and Egypt. An influx of thousands of refugees from Eritrea and Sudan during the mid-2000s put pressure on local services, but the government failed to coordinate a plan that would give refugees access to work permits, resources, and the opportunity to integrate into society. That created a climate of despair that erupted into violence and local riots in 2012 and 2013. That violence led right-wing Israelis to protest the presence of the Africans as "infiltrators," so labeled because they had crossed the border illegally.

This history of rescuing Jewish refugees, including those from Africa, is part of the founding myths of the State of Israel. Though immigration slowed compared to the massive waves of the 1950s and early 1960s, Israel continued its efforts to save persecuted Jews, wherever they were in the world. Following the 1967 war, the Soviet Union broke off diplomatic relations with Israel and embarked on a policy of renewed discrimination against and persecution of Jews. This treatment, coupled with a sense of pride in the Zionist victories, encouraged many Russian Jews to request visas to leave the USSR. But most were denied on the grounds that, if during their lives they had possessed information vital to Soviet national security, they could not be allowed to leave the country. Known as the "refusnikim," those who were denied continued their struggle to immigrate to Israel, which resulted in a peak 1969-1973 immigration of around 165,000, while approximately another 100,000 would emigrate to the US, Germany, and Australia in the following years. Those who were religiously motivated or impelled by Zionism typically went to Israel; others with larger economic motivations often chose other destinations.

But the window of opportunity for leaving the USSR soon closed, and almost no Jews were able to leave for the following two decades. The sudden and rapid collapse of the USSR in the 1990s, however, led to open borders, and almost a million Russian Jews arrived in 1989-2006. Around one quarter were not Jewish according to Orthodox interpretations of Jewish law, but they were eligible to immigrate to Israel under the rules of the Law of Return, which recognizes patrilineal descent or marriage to a Jew. For many, their high level of education and Ashkenazi background made it easy to integrate into Israeli society, and today they are considered to share a standard of living with native born-Israelis. But the immigration also brought significant cultural changes, including the public presence of Hebrew-speaking Christians, the public celebration of Christmas, and the desire for a wide array of Russian and non-kosher food items. These preferences put Russians into conflict with religious Jews, but the Russian tendency towards right-wing politics has in many ways protected them from the wrath that other immigrant groups have experienced.

Meanwhile, the Ethiopian immigration, which occurred mainly through Operation Moses (1984) and Operation Solomon (1991), rescued many Jews from Sudanese refugee camps to which Ethiopians in the North of the country had fled. These operations were considerably more challenging, equally so when it came to settling these refugees in Israel. The color of their skin, the primitive conditions of their homeland, their low education levels, and the diseases rampant among them evoked the issues that had characterized Mizrachi immigrations in the 1950s and 1960s. Around 121,000 descendants of the Beta Israel, as the Ethiopian Jews are known, now live throughout the country, and while many have integrated, many still face discrimination, poverty, and limited opportunities for advancement. In recent years, Israel has seen large migrations from Latin America and France, where rising anti-Semitism has motivated many to seek shelter in Israel.

The multi-cultural history of Israel, characterizing both its Jewish and non-Jewish populations, was thrown into stark relief following the first Intifada when use of the Palestinian labor force was discontinued. For the first time, Israel invited large numbers of foreign workers from China, the Philippines, Poland, Thailand, and Romania. Though the government was resistant at first, afraid of bringing in large numbers of foreign workers who might settle in the country and undercut the Jewish majority, the economic pressure from the booming Israeli economy demanded a new labor force.

The Russian Aliyah, with its high educational levels, doubled the number of engineers and doctors in Israel, an influx of talent that helped fuel a high tech revolution that dramatically changed the character of the Israeli economy and the nature of its exports. Though Israel had been involved in industry and agriculture since the early years, the restriction of supplies during the Second World War led to increased production, as local manufacturers had to fill supply orders that had previously been imported. The post-war economy benefited from this industry, but Israel's lack of foreign cash reserves, massive immigration, and high level of imports left the economy struggling. By the 1960s the economy had stabilized and reflected strong internal growth, and Israel's international efforts helped produce new market relations, including with developing post-Independence states in Africa and East Asia.

Israel's defense industry also became an important player, serving as a large employer and a strategic national enterprise, making up around 10% of weapons manufacturing in the world. The defense industry originated in the need to have a secure internal source of weapons and only later became a source of export income. In 1982, the *New York Times* reported that Israel had become a major source of arms sales to Costa Rica, El Salvador, Guatemala, and Honduras. Such sales to Central and South American countries, from Somoza's Nicaragua to Pinochet's Chile, dated to the 1970s and served not only to boost Israel's economy but also to support US foreign policy commitments. Israel has also sold arms to the US, Europe, and India. By 2012, Israel had become the world's 11th largest arms exporter.

On October 11, 1961, Israel joined other nations in voting to censure the South African Foreign Minister, Eric Louw (1890-1968), for a speech defending apartheid delivered to the UN General Assembly. Two years later, Israel recalled its ambassador to SA. Like many Western nations at the time, however, Israel combined public condemnations with confidential relations. After Israel's October 1973 war, however, when most African countries publicly severed their relations with the Jewish state, Israel's commercial and military ties to SA increased, partly, at least as Israel asserted, because it was worried about the status of South African Jews and partly because it felt itself too vulnerable and isolated to refuse potential arms and other trade deals. Thereafter Israel, along with France, became major sources of arms for the South African Defense Force, though other nations, including Britain and Saudi Arabia, sold arms to Pretoria as well. In the 1970s Israel and South Africa became partners in construction projects in both countries, and in some efforts in joint nuclear weapons testing and development. By 1987, Israel was the only developed nation maintaining strategic relations with the apartheid regime; that year Israel announced it would approve no new military agreements with SA. That embargo was lifted in 1991, after the US lifted its own sanctions.

Despite the strength of certain industries, such as arms manufacturing and diamond processing—the latter dating from 1937 when refugees expert in diamond cutting and polishing arrived from the Netherlands— after the 1970s the economy began to choke and by 1984 inflation was at 450%. Fearing that the entire system would collapse, the government in 1985 developed a revised economic plan that restructured by introducing financial prudence and market-oriented reforms; the revised plan paved the way to the economic boom of the 1990s. In the past few years, there has been an unprecedented influx of foreign capital as Israel has become a hub for technology and real estate investment; it serves as a net lender on international credit markets. Israel withstood the worldwide crash of the 2000s, partly because of its conservative banking industry, which left it less open to the risks that toppled other nations. It also maintained low unemployment during that period, further complicating the presence of illegal and undocumented foreign workers and asylum-seekers, though they have proved a necessary part of the modern Israeli economy. These macroeconomic developments have moved Israeli society from the collectivist ideology of the 1950s to one committed to private enterprise and free markets. Though the standard of living has risen significantly, Israel has paid a social and political price for its economic success. From "one of the world's more egalitarian societies in the 1960s, Israel turned into one of the least egalitarian in the 1990s. The two main pockets of poverty were the ultra-Orthodox, whose 'society of learners' members did not enter the labor market, and the Arabs, who were subject to social and security restrictions on their integration into the Israeli economy" (Shapira 451). It is these inequities which led to social protest movements in 2012, when tent activists took over Rothschild Boulevard, a main thoroughfare in Tel Aviv, calling on the government to provide low income housing and undo the cuts to social welfare programs which remained a necessary part of life for low income families across the ethnic and religious spectrum.

Many of the nation's young writers and culture-makers could be found speaking out in support of the tent protestors. This commingling of culture and politics has long been a hallmark of Zionist history, and demonstrated the cultural capital that writers, filmmakers, and visual artists have in Israeli society. These artists also gained an increasingly significant international reputation, as Israeli literature was translated into numerous languages and Israeli films and Israeli artists were exhibited throughout the world, often winning important awards, prizes, and recognition. While these artists, including dancers and theatre companies, serve as cultural ambassadors for the country, they also operate as a critical, often left-wing, anti-government voice within the country. Though in Israel's early years, culture had been dominated by the white, male, labor elite, today it encompasses Israel's rich multiculturalism and ethnic diversity.

The Intifadas, The Peace Process, and Palestinian State Building

In December 1987, a grassroots Arab uprising that began with a campaign of civil resistance, including strikes and commercial shutdowns, grew into stone throwing, hurling Molotov cocktails, and assaults with knives—the weapons of an unarmed popular insurrection. Known as the Intifada ("shaking off" in Arabic) this insurgency began as a reaction to Israeli control of Gaza and the West Bank, the persistent and ongoing state of economic deprivation for Palestinians in refugee camps, and the widespread use of Israeli checkpoints at roads and bridges, limiting access to Israel for Palestinians from the occupied territories. While the PLO had done much to raise the public profile of Palestinians, the organization had done little in a practical sense to improve the lives of Palestinians within the West Bank and Gaza. Alienated from these impoverished communities, the PLO would have little impact: in the opening months of the Intifada.

Yet the explosion of anger also turned inward, and many of the Palestinian deaths during the Intifada were caused by intra-ethnic violence, as widespread executions of alleged Israeli collaborators took place. By the end of 1992, approximately 1,800 Palestinians had died during the Intifada, about 800 of those being at the hands of other Palestinians. The Israeli army responded to the uprising with a large show of military strength, but the images of young stone throwers operating against tanks severely damaged Israel's public image and did little to quell the uprising, and even less to mitigate the economic damage caused by a series of strikes called by Palestinian organizations. The Intifada forced the IDF into a policing role for which it was not trained. And the IDF's tactical decisions were sometimes counterproductive. Thus, for example, the decision to close down West Bank and Gaza schools and universities during the 1987-1988 school year simply sent unsupervised students into the streets.

Along with increasing public media support and rising international attention for the Palestinian cause, the Intifada enhanced Palestinian self-esteem and demonstrated that Palestinians were no longer relying upon help from other Arab countries for their own survival; they would negotiate for their own political future. As the PLO worked to direct events, its status as the Palestinians' political representative increased. Yet the single most significant result of the Intifada was no doubt King Hussein's July 31, 1988, announcement that Jordan was relinquishing all claims to the West Bank and instead honoring a Palestinian State. That legitimated a Palestinian place at the table in the peace negotiations of the 1990s. The Intifada lasted at least until 1991, though some historians date its end to 1993 and the signing of the Oslo Peace Accords. It also had serious repercussions for Israel, including the loss to its public image internationally and the intensification of powerful internal criticism. The loss of public support for past expansionist policies pushed the country toward revising its legal position on administering the territories and made it increasingly willing to trade land for peace.

Though Yasser Arafat (1929-2004) ambitiously declared Palestinian independence and a virtual Palestinian state as early as 1988, his refusal to renounce terrorism against Israel abruptly ended US efforts to open a dialogue with the PLO leadership. Moreover, the Intifada had opened the way for other political groups including Hamas, the Palestinian wing of the militant Muslim Brotherhood who dominated Gaza. Notoriously anti-Semitic, Hamas proclaimed its plans for an Islamic State free of both Jews and Christians, vilifying Jews in its charter which cited the infamous anti-Semitic forgery "The Protocols of the Elders of Zion" as evidence of a Zionist plot of world domination. Advocating Jihad against Zionism and refusing any negotiation or recognition of Israel, Hamas took a position more extreme than that of the PLO, which by the 1990s had come to see political maneuvering as a more effective strategy for nation building than terrorism.

But the Palestinian cause was sidelined in the winter of 1990-1991 when Saddam Hussein invaded and annexed Kuwait, and allied forces responded with Operation Desert Storm, which resulted in the Gulf War. Asked by the U.S. to stand down, Israel waited while Tel Aviv and northern Israel were shelled by Iraqi scud missiles. International sympathy returned for the besieged Jewish state. Meanwhile, the Palestinians unwisely threw their support behind the show of Iraqi Arab militarism and lost some of the ground they had worked so hard to gain. The regional conflict soon silenced quieter struggles at home. Meanwhile, at the 1991 Madrid Peace Conference Israel for the first time engaged in direct, face-to-face negotiations with all of its immediate neighbors and their political rulers, also launching a multilateral process that brought Israeli diplomats into contact with representatives of Arab states from North Africa and the Persian Gulf. Though these interactions would lead nowhere, the increasingly stable relationship between Israel and Jordan would be formally recognized through the signing of a peace treaty in 1994.

The growth of the peace movement in Israel and the changing political temperature heralded promise for an era of reconciliation and security. In recognition, the Knesset in 1993 repealed a law banning Israeli-PLO contacts, thereby enabling potential agreements between Israelis and Palestinians to be signed. On September 9, the PLO and Israel mutually recognized each other, and on September 13, the Oslo Peace Accords were signed in Washington by Prime Minister Yitzhak Rabin (1922-1995) and Arafat, with American President Bill Clinton as witness. The Oslo Accords, or the Declaration of Principles on Interim Self-Government Arrangements (DOP), provided for Palestinian self-rule. Following months of negotiations, initially between nongovernmental parties, an agreement was signed that gave Palestinians control over most of Gaza and of the West Bank city of Jericho, and set a timetable for negotiations to enable further transfer of authority.

Though both the Israeli and Palestinian public broadly supported these efforts, both also possessed a strong rejectionist minority. On Israel's right, resistance to the peace process would become increasingly vocal and, with the subsequent death of the Oslo process, dominate Israel's political landscape in the twenty-first century. In the early 1990s, the Palestinians who rejected the accords noted that East Jerusalem remained under Israeli control, that the settlements remained in place, and that Palestinians had gained authority over only a tiny portion of the West Bank. These Palestinians also rejected the PLO's secular apparatus. Hamas and Islamic Jihad opted to undermine the process with terrorist attacks. At first, Israel maintained its determination to continue with the process, and the IDF withdrew from Jericho and most of Gaza in 1994. By mid-May, Arafat had arrived in Gaza and declared Gaza City the capital of the Palestinian Authority (PA), the political body that served as an embryonic government for a future independent Palestine.

In response, on October 19, 1994, a Hamas suicide bomber killed 21 and wounded 23 on a bus in Tel Aviv. This would be part of a wave of suicide bombings—including a Palestinian Islamic Jihad attack by two suicide bombers on January 22, 1995, that killed 21 soldiers at a crossroads bus stop in central Israel—that would terrorize Israel over the coming decade and erode public support for the peace process among the Israeli public. Nevertheless, in an attempt to resist the pressures of a minority, in 1995, the two sides signed the "Israeli-Palestinian Interim Agreement on the West Bank and Gaza Strip," which provided for the election of an 82-person Palestinian Council and a head (Ra'is) of an Executive Committee. The West Bank was divided into three categories of territory. Area A, which includes West Bank cities, was evacuated by the Israelis, with the Palestinian Authority responsible for security and policing. Area B, including most Arab towns and villages, would be controlled by the PA, which would be responsible for civil authority and normal policing, while Israel would retain ultimate responsibility for security. Area C, encompassing unpopulated territory and Israeli military outposts as well as Jewish settlements, would be shared, with the PA overseeing health, education, and other public services for Arabs and Israel doing the same for Jews. Israel would also control security and public order. Later that year, the IDF withdrew from Bethlehem, Jenin, Nablus, Qalqila, Ramallah, and Tulkarm.

Hopeful for the positive outcomes that the new autonomy would provide, Palestinians were eager about the future, but Arafat, a successful wartime leader, lacked the skills needed to be an effective nation builder. The anticipated economic benefits that self-determination was supposed to provide never materialized, as the Palestinian Authority was compromised by bribes and political corruption. The Legislative Council and Presidential elections in the West Bank and Gaza, as prescribed in the Oslo Accords, proved hollow, as Arafat, once elected president, ignored the will of the Legislative Council and operated by fiat and tribal allegiances. The democracy that Israelis enjoyed failed to become a reality for Palestinians, while the Palestinian economic situation deteriorated as travel between the different zones and cities, with their delays and checkpoints, proved burdensome, time consuming, and humiliating. Moreover, the Intifada eliminated work in Israel for many of the Palestinians in the West Bank; they were replaced by a foreign labor force, further limiting their economic opportunities.

Despite the terrorist bombs during the 1990s, in 2000 Prime Minister Ehud Barak (1942-) moved forward with final stage negotiations. Arafat, Clinton, and U.S. Secretary of State Madeleine Albright (1937-) met with Barak at Camp David to pursue a definitive peace treaty. Israel offered to divide Jerusalem, giving the PA sovereignty over most of the East Jerusalem neighborhoods, and to cede 84-90% of the West Bank overall. With Barak having taken office after defeating the incumbent Benjamin Netanyahu (1949-) in 1999 on a peace platform, the potential for success seemed high. But Arafat, attempting to seize on this apparent goodwill, held firm to a demand for PA control of all of the Old City and the entirety of Temple

Mount. Moreover, he insisted on a Palestinian Right of Return, which would offer all Palestinians who left, and all of their descendants, the right to live in Israel. For Israel, acceding to such a request would be a demographic, political, cultural, religious, and financial disaster, not only burdening Israel with the potential immigration of millions of new citizens, but also transforming the makeup of the country, already with a population of one million Arabs, into an Arab country with a Jewish minority. With such a move, Israel would become an Arab country, and the only country where Jews have a sovereign right of national self-expression would disappear overnight. In a symbolic gesture Barak offered to accept several thousand Palestinian refugees, but this was rejected by Arafat as well. In a final attempt to resolve the disputes, Barak offered Arafat 90-95% of the West Bank and expressed his willingness to place the Temple Mount under UN control. Arafat rejected all offers, but in the West Bank, the Arab press claimed that it was Barak who refused to compromise.

Arafat thus rejected not only the best offer Israel had ever made, but also quite possibly the best offer the Palestinians will ever receive. "Some argue that his years at the Palestinian Authority demonstrated to Arafat that what awaited him at the end of the road was a relatively small, poor state burdened with economic and social problems, and that he preferred the romanticism of the struggle rather than the dejecting routine of being president of the Palestinian state. So long as there was no peace, he was a national hero, a media figure at whose door the world's luminaries came calling" (Shapira 445-46). Many observers consider the Second Intifada the substantive Palestinian response. It may reflect a conclusion, based on Hezbollah's success in Lebanon, that a dispersed low-tech policy of violence can defeat a sophisticated modern army.

With Palestinians frustrated and no nearer to independence, the second Intifada erupted in 2000 in the wake of Camp David's failure. It was named for the Al-Aqsa mosque where the first violent uprising broke out in response to an ill-timed and ill-conceived visit by Ariel Sharon. Unlike the First Intifada, which was directed at the Israeli military, this second Intifada targeted Israeli civilians within Israel. Restaurants, markets, shops, and buses were targeted in Jerusalem and Tel Aviv. Israel faced an onslaught of suicide bombers; Jews, Arabs, Christians, and tourists alike were caught up in the violence. On May 25, 2001, two Palestinians drove a car full of dynamite into a bus in the coastal town of Hadera, killing 4 plus themselves and wounding 63. On June 1, a suicide bomber detonated his bomb at the Dolphinarium, a popular seaside Tel Aviv discotheque, killing 21 and wounding more than 80, most of them teenagers. That August, targeting the summer vacation crowds, a Palestinian teenager blew himself up in a Jerusalem pizzeria, killing 6 children and 13 adults and injuring 90 others. Three days later a Haifa café was the target, this time with 20 casualties. On the November 29 anniversary of the UN Partition Resolution, a Palestinian detonated his suicide vest on a bus traveling from Netania to Tel Aviv, killing four and injuring nine. That attack turned out to be a combined Fatah/Islamic Jihad operation. On December 1, powerful bombs in Jerusalem's main pedestrian mall killed 11 and wounded 180. Twelve hours afterwards, a suicide bombing on a Haifa bus took 16 lives and injured 45 more. The following March, 25-year-old Muhammad Abd al-Basset Oudeh, a Hamas recruit, videotaped his plan, donned a wig and dressed as a woman, then walked into the dining room of the Park Hotel in the seaside town of Netanya. The explosion he triggered killed 29 and wounded 150. A June 18 Jerusalem bus bombing, one of 47 bombings that year, killed 19. On July 31, a Hamas-organized blast in the Hebrew University of Jerusalem cafeteria killed nine, four American students among them, and injured approximately 100. Between September 29, 2000, and June 4, 2003, 820 Israelis were killed and nearly 5,000 wounded. Two thirds of the dead were civilians. That said, although the many suicide attacks in Israel proper are the hallmark of the Second Intifada, a large number of other attacks, like randomly shooting into crowds, took place in the occupied territories.

In a particularly disturbing harbinger of future strife, Palestinian Israeli citizens staged demonstrations throughout northern Israel in solidarity with the occupied West Bank from October 1 to 9. The demonstrations moved to civil disobedience, then turned violent. Hundreds of Jews rioted in response. The Israeli police trying to quell the escalating riots faced gun-fire and Molotov cocktails. In the course of the week, the police shot and killed twelve Israeli Arabs. "Although the struggle was broadly directed by Palestinian Authority Yasser Arafat and his associates, the actual operations were carried out by members of the Palestinian security forces and of the many other organizations that had formed in the territories. Attacks were planned and prepared without co-ordination or centralized control, and the relation of individual terrorists to their nominal groups was often vague to the point of being arbitrary" (Herzog 428). Though Israel was hesitant to carry out military operations in the areas for which the PA was responsible, and in which many of the terrorists and agitators were sheltering, the inter-national political climate changed after the September 11, 2001, attacks on the United States, and Israel mounted retaliatory attacks.

In April 2002, a battle took place in the Jenin refugee camp. It was esti-mated to be the source of at least 28 suicide attacks, so neutralizing the threat from the area became a military priority for the IDF. Since Jenin was heavily fortified with booby-traps and snipers were positioned throughout, the Israeli army was reluctant to enter the area and was forced to reject air bombardment for fear of causing civilian casualties. So the IDF entered on foot, conducting house-to-house searches through the narrow alleys. When 13 Israeli reservists were trapped in an ambush and killed, the army was forced to change tactics in order to preserve lives and began bulldozing houses to flatten access routes and clear the way. In total, 23 Israelis and 52 Palestinians died, but news reports photographed bodies and made much of the event, accusing the Israelis of conducting a massacre. "These scenes of death and destruction had a strong effect on Palestinians, galvanizing many of the younger generation to join the ranks of the militants ready to fight the Israelis" (Bregman 242).

Though President George W. Bush called for the establishment of a Palestinian state, reinforcing Clinton's commitment, it was unclear how such an endeavor could proceed. The following year UN Resolution 1397 was the first Security Council Resolution calling for a two-state solution to the Palestinian-Israeli conflict, and in 2003 the Quartet (the US, European Union, UN, and Russia) proposed a performance-based, goal-driven road-map for a negotiated Palestinian-Israeli agreement.

But as the violence continued, persistently terrorizing the whole Israeli population, Israel began building a security fence to reduce the infiltration of Palestinians from the West Bank and Gaza into Israel. In July and August of 2003, the first continuous segment of Israel's security fence was constructed. Most of the fence consists of multi-layered wire, but about 10% is constructed as a concrete wall (in areas where civilians might be vulnerable, for instance, from gunfire). It is one of many border fences in the world, some of the others constructed for security reasons as well, but this one is politically implicated in the Israeli-Palestinian conflict and proves endlessly controversial. It has helped reduce suicide bombings by 80 to 90%, but its administration causes hardships to Palestinians who must regularly negotiate the checkpoints controlling passage through the wall. Moreover, the location of parts of the fence has provoked accusations that Israel is annexing Palestinian land. As we went to press with this book, at the end of May, 2014, Israel intercepted yet another suicide bomber with explosives strapped to his torso at a checkpoint just south of Nablus in the northern part of the West Bank.

The hostility and conflict of the mid-2000s suggested that all hope for peace had disappeared, while Yasser Arafat was besieged. He was pursued by Israel for orchestrating the violent attacks on Israelis, while losing popularity with many of his own citizens for what amounted to the increased corruption of the economy and national politics. In 2004, Arafat died, and the Intifada began to lose some of its energy; though it had at least one decisive long term effect on Israel—the substantial weakening of the Israeli left.

Violence and Extremism—The Israeli Right and Religious Settler Politics

When the first religiously-driven Jewish settlers established themselves in Hebron, it was with a deep sense of homecoming. They believed they were reversing a Diaspora that had exiled them from where they belonged. Possessing a messianic sense of destiny, "they return to Hebron like Abraham, reside in Tekoah like the prophet Amos, and live in Beit Horon where the Maccabees have fought" (Feige 49). "The Bible is omnipresent in the settlers' world; many of their villages have biblical names, as do their children" (Feige 48). They were fulfilling a divine promise. "In other words, the connection between the people and the land is metahistorical; it precedes history and constitutes it" (Feige 43). Accordingly, they felt any compromise with the Palestinians or withdrawal from the occupied territories constituted a severe religious transgression. Even today, many settlers view their actions as realizing the true meaning of the State of Israel.

When the settlers noticed Palestinians at all, they thought of them fundamentally as Arabs, not as Palestinians, and thus as part of that larger people, not a group meriting their own independent homeland. "Like the pioneers, the settlers went to live on a dangerous frontier to fulfill their ideas of a better society. Both groups of settlers regarded themselves as avant-garde, hoping that others would follow once they 'saw the light' or realized the success of the colonization project" (Feige 54). Like some early Zionists they also embodied the Orientalist assumption that the local Arabs would benefit economically and culturally from their arrival and thus should welcome it. The more religiously-driven settlers tend to view Israelis in the coastal plain who criticize them as weak and fearful of non-Jewish opinion.

The ideologically oriented settlements tend to be physically isolated, located farthest from the Green Line and surrounded by Palestinians. The settlers living close to the 1967 borders are more likely to have come for good jobs, better and more affordable housing, and other economic benefits, rather than out of religious conviction. They are also therefore likely to be living on the Israeli side of the wall. The religious settlers are very much aware that this physical barrier puts them on the wrong side of what seems to be a de facto national border. The majority of Israelis, moreover, do not identify with the religious settlers' sense of mission. Palestinians and their allies criticize the wall unsparingly, but it actually offers the potential for a unilateral Israeli withdrawal from 90% or more of the West Bank, effectively establishing a Palestinian state.

The fate the isolated religious settlers face, therefore, may be decisive. Most problematically of all, the Palestinians see themselves as inheriting hundreds of years of history in the land. Yet "the area ceded to the Palestinian Authority was chopped up into a bizarre archipelago to accommodate the needs of the settlers" (Feige 35). Though some Palestinians have gained economic opportunities through the occupation, others find their lives disrupted intolerably. Paradoxically, however, the Palestinian project of disrupting the settlers' daily lives had the effect of hardening their hearts, rather than persuading them to leave. "As the ability to go shopping or take a bus became a declared act of bravery and a national achievement, the banality of normal life became consecrated" (Feige 259). Meanwhile, the extremist elements among the settlers have their own history of violence. Members of a "Jewish Underground" attempted to assassinate several mayors of Arab towns and were planning to bomb the Dome of the Rock until the plot was uncovered and they were arrested in 1984.

On February 25, 1994, Baruch Goldstein (1956-1994), a Jewish doctor from the settlement community of Kiryat Arba, entered nearby Hebron's Ibrahimya Mosque during morning prayers and massacred 29 Muslim worshippers and wounded dozens of others. The survivors proceeded to beat him to death. In the riots that followed, the IDF killed about 30 Arabs and injured hundreds. Goldstein was born in New York and immigrated to Israel in 1983. He was a member of the racist and extremist Jewish Defense League. As a physician, he was also among the first to minister to settler victims of violence, and that may have helped drive him insane.

In 1995, fringe groups on the Israeli far right ramped up zealous, extremist agitation in response to Prime Minister Yitzhak Rabin's (1922-1995) peace initiative, describing him as a traitor and calling for his death. The extremist incitement to violence produced results. On November 4, Rabin was assassinated by Yigal Amir, a 27-year-old law student at Israel's religious university, Bar-Ilan. The assassination took place at a peace rally designed to show support for Rabin. Amir was a graduate of Orthodox and ultra-Orthodox schools and yeshivas. After his arrest, he declared that he aimed to derail the peace process. For many right-wing supporters who had opposed the peace movement, seeing it as a betrayal of Zionist values, these actions had gone too far, and many worked to distance themselves from this extremism, including rabbis who saw that their comments against the government had spilled over from political protest to violence and even treason.

But the failure of the peace negotiations in 2000 and the outbreak of the second Intifada, with its constant suicide bombs, also persuaded many Israelis that the peace camp had decisively failed. That led to Israelis choosing a right-wing government which they thought would be better able to suppress the constant daily violence. In 2001, Ariel Sharon was elected Prime Minister. The Palestinians regarded his election as the equivalent of a declaration of war.

The latest chapter in the Arab-Israeli conflict, 2005-2014

In 2005, several factors seemed to bring significant change to the political landscape. With Arafat's death, the election of Mahmoud Abbas as chairman of the PLO in 2005, and the sudden stroke that left Sharon in a coma until he died nine years later, the traditional positions on the conflict could be rethought. In one of his final acts in office, Sharon had ordered a unilateral withdrawal (and evacuation) from the Gaza Strip and the removal of its 21 civilian settlements. A movement in support of the settlements sprang up through the country, but despite the government's worst fears of a Jewish civil war, the disengagement was ultimately peaceful and conducted ahead of schedule. Israel's withdrawal from Gaza was intended to facilitate the PA's sovereignty as part of the Oslo Accords, but almost immediately—in what began with a Hamas victory in parliamentary elections and evolved into armed conflict after Fatah refused to cede control of the government— Hamas routed Fatah militarily and assumed political power in Gaza and thus divided the Palestinian community into separate ideological as well as geographic entities. Great animosity has permeated the PLO/PA relationship with Hamas and its leadership. For Hamas, the secular nature of the PA and the extensive financial and political corruption that characterized Arafat's nation-building years have cast doubt on the PA's capacity to govern and promoted the assumption that they betrayed the Palestinians by agreeing to a peace process. For the PA and Fatah, the largest party within the confederated multi-party PLO, Hamas' political and religious extremism, their refusal to recognize Israel and renounce terrorism, and their isolation by the international community have so far made them a political liability for Palestinians in their attempts to create an independent state. Whether anything real or long lasting will come of the alliance they announced in 2014 remains to be seen.

In 2008, Israel launched Operation Cast Lead, which lasted from December 27, 2008, to January 18, 2009. This return to Gaza in a military operation was intended to stop the rocket and mortar launches from Gaza to Israel (over 1500 were fired at the Israeli city Sderot in an eight month period from mid-2007 to February 2008, for example) and end weapons smuggling into Gaza. Aerial bombardment of weapons caches, police stations, and political and administrative buildings took place in Gaza, Khan Yunis, and Rafah, all densely populated cities, followed by a ground campaign. After having accomplished its mission, Israel declared a unilateral ceasefire and withdrew its forces. The international Boycott, Sanctions, and Divestment movement would embrace and promote hyperbolic characterizations of Operation Cast Lead as genocidal. Yet the rocket attacks had turned Israeli towns within range into environments of unremitting stress. Every public setting, even bus stops, were hardened against rockets and air raid shelters were added to every apartment, a necessity given that some communities had only seconds' warning of an attack. Those strategies severely curtailed civilian deaths in Israel, but not the grave psychological trauma of living under bombardment, a price particularly unsettling to see children pay. Nonetheless, when Israel entered Gaza, BDS could play up the disparity between Israeli and Palestinian military power and death rates to garner international support.

In 2009, on a visit to Egypt, the recently elected President Barack Obama affirmed the strong bonds of the US-Israeli relationship but criticized Israel for continuing to build settlements that served as an impediment to peace. In June the same year, Israeli Prime Minister Benjamin Netanyahu gave a historic speech where he offered a five-point plan for a negotiated agreement with the Palestinians that included the establishment of a demilitarized Palestinian state on condition that Israel would be recognized as a "Jewish state."

The Palestinian leadership rejected his terms. With no changes in the status quo, and Hamas continuing to fire rockets into Southern Israel, the IDF launched Operation Pillar of Defense (November 2012) with the killing of Ahmed Jabari (1960-2012), chief of the Gaza military wing of Hamas. Just days before, 100 rockets had been launched into Israel. During the operation, nearly 1,500 more rockets fell. Egypt mediated a ceasefire, announced a week after the operation began. Afterwards, Human Rights Watch accused both sides of violating the rules of war. In December, maintaining its bravura in the face of IDF attacks, Hamas leader Khaled Mishal (1956-) called for Israel's elimination.

Despite intensive efforts during 2013 and 2014 by President Obama and the US government to lead Israelis and Palestinians into an agreement, little progress has been made between the PA and Israel. Moreover, Hamas was left out of these negotiations, as were the other Arab countries who continue to maintain populations of Palestinian refugees with few rights and opportunities. Ultimately, any real solution will need to reflect a regional consensus that recognizes Israel's legitimate security concerns and accommodates the Palestinian drive for self-determination, but limits it to the West Bank and Gaza.

Another major outbreak of violence occurred in summer 2014. Three West Bank Israeli teenagers were kidnapped and summarily executed. Extremists kidnapped a Palestinian boy in revenge and burned him alive. Seeing an opportunity to retake center stage and extract concessions, a diplomatically marginalized Hamas launched a massive rocket assault from Gaza, extending as far as Tel Aviv and Ben Gurion Airport. Israel launched Operation Protective Edge in response, in the course of which over 30 deep underground Hamas assault tunnels reaching into Israel itself were discovered. Two thousand Gazans died amidst extensive aerial and artillery bombardment, and Israel lost more of its soldiers in combat than it had in years.

Looking back over all of Israel's history from the vantage point of 2014, the series of short wars and discrete military actions amount, in effect, to one long war that has sometimes paused but never really stopped. The number of belligerent states, combined with paramilitary or terrorist organizations, means that no one nation seems able to prevent the region slipping into war repeatedly. For Israel itself, with the most powerful military and non-oil dependent economy in the Middle East, the risks of terrorism and of Iran's obtaining nuclear weapons loom large. Hamas and Hezbollah are insurgent groups who openly seek Israel's destruction. Israeli governments to date have not been willing to risk temporary or permanent withdrawal from the West Bank over concern for security, and the possibility that a West Bank Palestinian state would be similar to the Hamas-dominated Gaza Strip that makes a true peace process impossible. For now, Israelis seem more willing to accept responsibility and criticism for retaining control over the West Bank than to confront a potentially radical new Palestinian state. Yet the demographic challenge posed by large numbers of Palestinians under Israeli control is equally real. And the restrictions on Palestinians in the West Bank are incompatible with Israeli democracy. As it has since the end of the June 1967 war, the overarching premise of Arab-Israeli negotiations remains: under what conditions and over what period of time will Israel relinquish territories won in the 1967 war and what will Israel receive in terms of a treaty or promise of non-war in return for territorial concessions? ■

Note: Some topics—like the 1982 war in Lebanon and the Second Intifada—are given more space because they remain current subjects of controversy. Our thanks to Asaf Romirowsky, Martin Shichtman, Randy Deshazo, and Ken Stern for their comments on earlier drafts.

Sources

Bartram, David B. "Foreign Workers in Israel: History and Theory." *International Migration Review* 32: 2 (Summer, 1998), pp. 303-325.

Bregman, Ahron. *Israel's Wars: A History Since 1947.* New York: Routledge, 2010.

Cohen, Hillel. *Army of Shadows: Palestinian Collaboration with Zionism, 1917-1949.* Berkeley: University of California Press, 2008.

Feige, Michael. *Settling in the Hearts: Jewish Fundamentalism in The Occupied Territories.* Detroit: Wayne State University Press, 2009.

Herzberg, Arthur. *The Zionist Idea: A Historical Analysis and Reader.* Philadelphia: The Jewish Publication Society, 1997.

Herzog, Chaim. *The Arab-Israeli Wars: War and Peace in the Middle East from the 1948 War of Independence to the Present.* Updated by Shlomo Gazit. New York: Vintage Books, 2010.

Horowitz, David. *State in the Making.* New York: Knopf, 1953.

Khalaf, Issa. *Politics in Palestine: Arab Factionalism and Social Disintegration 1939-1948.* Albany: State University Press of New York, 1991.

Karsh, Efraim. *Palestine Betrayed.* New Haven: Yale University Press, 2010.

Morris, Benny. *Righteous Victims: A History of the Zionist-Arab Conflict, 1881-2001.* New York: Random House, 2001.

Sachar, Howard M. *A History of Israel: From the Rise of Zionism to Our Time.* 3rd Edition. New York: Alfred A. Knopf, 2010.

Schiff, Ze'ev and Ehud Ya'ari. *Israel's Lebanon War.* New York: Simon and Schuster, 1984.

Sela, Avraham. Ed. *The Continuum Political Encyclopedia of the Middle East.* New York: Continuum, 2002.

Shapira, Anita. *Israel: A History.* Waltham, MA: Brandeis University Press, 2012.

Smith, Barbara. *The Roots of Separatism in Palestine: British Economic Policy, 1920-29.* Syracuse: Syracuse University Press, 1993.

Stein, Kenneth. *The Land Question in Palestine, 1917-1939.* Durham: University of North Carolina Press, 1984.

Stein, Kenneth. "Palestine's Rural Economy, 1917-1939." *Studies in Zionism* 8:13 (1987), 25-49.

Stein, Kenneth. *Heroic Diplomacy: Sadat, Kissinger, Carter, Begin and the Quest for Arab-Israeli Peace.* New York: Routledge, 1999.

Stein, Kenneth. *History, Politics, and Diplomacy of the Arab-Israeli Conflict: A Source Document Reader for College Courses and Adult Education.* E-book: www.israel.org, 2013.

Troen, Ilan S. *Imagining Zion: Dreams, Designs, and Realities in a Century of Jewish Settlement.* New Haven: Yale University Press, 2003.

PART VI

A BOYCOTT DOSSIER

Boycott Resolutions by Academic Associations

1. Association for Asian American Studies

Proposal to Boycott Israel Academic Institutions

April 20, 2013

Resolution: for AAAS to honor the call of Palestinian civil society for a boycott of Israeli academic institutions; and to support the protected rights of students and scholars everywhere to engage in research and public speaking about Israel-Palestine and in support of the boycott, divestment and sanctions (BDS) movement

Whereas the Association for Asian American Studies is an organization dedicated to the preservation and support of academic freedom and of the right to education for students and scholars in the U.S. and globally;

and
Whereas Arab (West Asian) and Muslim American communities, students, and scholars have been subjected to profiling, surveillance, and civil rights violations that have circumscribed their freedom of political expression, particularly in relation to the issue of human rights in Palestine-Israel;

and
Whereas the Association for Asian American Studies seeks to foster scholarship that engages conditions of migration, displacement, colonialism, and racism, and the lives of people in zones of war and occupation;

and

Whereas the Association for Asian American Studies seeks to advance a critique of U.S. empire, opposing US military occupation in the Arab world and U.S. support for occupation and racist practices by the Israeli state;

and

Whereas the United Nations has reported that the current Israeli occupation of Palestine has impacted students "whose development is deformed by pervasive deprivations affecting health, education and overall security";

and

Whereas Palestinian universities and schools have been periodically forced to close as a result of actions related to the Israeli occupation, or have been destroyed by Israeli military strikes, and Palestinian students and scholars face restrictions on movement and travel that limit their ability to attend and work at universities, travel to conferences and to study abroad, and thereby obstruct their right to education;

and

Whereas the Israeli state and Israeli universities directly and indirectly impose restrictions on education, scholarships, and participation in campus activities on Palestinian students in Israel;

and

Whereas Israel imposes severe restrictions on foreign academics and students seeking to attend conferences and do research in Palestine as well as on scholars and students of Arab/Palestinian origin who wish to travel to Israel-Palestine;

and

Whereas Israeli institutions of higher education have not condemned or taken measures to oppose the occupation and racial discrimination against Palestinians in Israel, but have, rather, been directly and indirectly complicit in the systematic maintenance of the occupation and of policies and practices that discriminate against Palestinian students and scholars throughout Palestine and in Israel;

and

Whereas Israeli academic institutions are deeply complicit in Israel's violations of international law and human rights and in its denial of the right to education and academic freedom to Palestinians, in addition to their basic rights as guaranteed by international law;

and
Whereas the Association for Asian American Studies supports research and open discussion about these issues without censorship, intimidation, or harassment, and seeks to promote academic exchange, collaboration and opportunities for students and scholars everywhere;

Be it resolved that the Association for Asian American Studies endorses and will honor the call of Palestinian civil society for a boycott of Israeli academic institutions.

Be it also resolved that the Association for Asian American Studies supports the protected rights of students and scholars everywhere to engage in research and public speaking about Israel-Palestine and in support of the boycott, divestment and sanctions (BDS) movement.

2. American Studies Association:

Council Resolution on Boycott of Israeli Academic Institutions

December 4, 2013

Whereas the American Studies Association is committed to the pursuit of social justice, to the struggle against all forms of racism, including anti-semitism, discrimination, and xenophobia, and to solidarity with aggrieved peoples in the United States and in the world;

Whereas the United States plays a significant role in enabling the Israeli occupation of Palestine and the expansion of illegal settlements and the Wall in violation of international law, as well as in supporting the systematic discrimination against Palestinians, which has had documented devastating impact on the overall well-being, the exercise of political and human rights, the freedom of movement, and the educational opportunities of Palestinians;

Whereas there is no effective or substantive academic freedom for Palestinian students and scholars under conditions of Israeli occupation, and Israeli institutions of higher learning are a party to Israeli state policies that violate human rights and negatively impact the working conditions of Palestinian scholars and students;

Whereas the American Studies Association is cognizant of Israeli scholars and students who are critical of Israeli state policies and who support the international boycott, divestment, and sanctions (BDS) movement under conditions of isolation and threat of sanction;

Whereas the American Studies Association is dedicated to the right of students and scholars to pursue education and research without undue state interference, repression, and military violence, and in keeping with the spirit of its previous statements supports the right of students and scholars to intellectual freedom and to political dissent as citizens and scholars;

It is resolved that the American Studies Association (ASA) endorses and will honor the call of Palestinian civil society for a boycott of Israeli academic institutions. It is also resolved that the ASA supports the protected rights of students and scholars everywhere to engage in research and public speaking about Israel-Palestine and in support of the boycott, divestment, and sanctions (BDS) movement.

---

3. Native American and Indigenous Studies Association

Declaration of Support for the Boycott of Israeli Academic Institutions by the Council of the Native American and Indigenous Studies Association

December 15, 2013

The council of the Native American and Indigenous Studies Association (NAISA) declares its support for the boycott of Israeli academic institutions.

A broad coalition of Palestinian non-governmental organizations, acting in concert to represent the Palestinian people, formed the Palestinian Campaign for the Academic and Cultural Boycott of Israel. Their call was taken up in the United States by the US Campaign for the Academic and

Cultural Boycott of Israel. A NAISA member-initiated petition brought this issue to NAISA Council. After extensive deliberation on the merits of the petition, the NAISA Council decided by unanimous vote to encourage members of NAISA and all who support its mission to honor the boycott.

NAISA is dedicated to free academic inquiry about, with, and by Indigenous communities. The NAISA Council protests the infringement of the academic freedom of Indigenous Palestinian academics and intellectuals in the Occupied Territories and Israel who are denied fundamental freedoms of movement, expression, and assembly, which we uphold.

As the elected council of an international community of Indigenous and allied non-Indigenous scholars, students, and public intellectuals who have studied and resisted the colonization and domination of Indigenous lands via settler state structures throughout the world, we strongly protest the illegal occupation of Palestinian lands and the legal structures of the Israeli state that systematically discriminate against Palestinians and other Indigenous peoples.

NAISA is committed to the robust intellectual and ethical engagement of difficult and often highly charged issues of land, identity, and belonging. Our members will have varying opinions on the issue of the boycott, and we encourage generous dialogue that affirms respectful disagreement as a vital scholarly principle. We reject shaming or personal attacks as counter to humane understanding and the greater goals of justice, peace, and decolonization.

As scholars dedicated to the rights of Indigenous peoples, we affirm that our efforts are directed specifically at the Israeli state, not at Israeli individuals. The NAISA Council encourages NAISA members to boycott Israeli academic institutions because they are imbricated with the Israeli state and we wish to place pressure on that state to change its policies. We champion and defend intellectual and academic freedom, and we recognize that conversation and collaboration with individuals and organizations in Israel/ Palestine can make an important contribution to the cause of justice. In recognition of the profound social and political obstacles facing Palestinians in such dialogues, however, we urge our members and supporters to engage in such actions outside the aegis of Israeli educational institutions, honoring this boycott until such time as the rights of the Palestinian people are respected and discriminatory policies are ended.

Letter from ASA Members

November 18, 2013

To Members of the National Council of the American Studies Association:

As members of the American Studies Association (ASA), including several former presidents, Council members, and ASA award winners, we are deeply committed to the values of academic freedom and the free exchange of ideas. **Given these priorities, we are troubled by the attempt of a vocal minority amongst the ASA's membership to force the entire association to enact a boycott of Israeli academic institutions.** The "Proposed Resolution on Academic Boycott of Israeli Academic Institutions" sponsored by the ASA Caucus on Academic and Community Activism does not further, but rather harms, the general interests of the association. If upheld, it would set a dangerous precedent by sponsoring an inequitable and discriminatory policy that would punish one nation's universities and scholars and restrict the free conduct of ASA members to engage with colleagues in Israel.

Collectively, we, the undersigned, represent a wide range of views on the Israeli-Palestinian conflict and how it should be resolved. While we can and should vigorously discuss these differences there is one issue on which we all agree; **We oppose all academic boycotts, including the idea of an association-imposed boycott against Israeli academic institutions.**

A fundamental principle of academia is academic freedom; the belief that scholars must be free to pursue ideas without being targeted for repression, discipline, or institutional censorship. The adoption of an academic boycott against Israel and Israelis would do violence to this bedrock principle. Scholars would be punished not because of what they believe—which would be bad enough—but simply because of who they are based on their nationality. **In no other context does the ASA discriminate on the basis of national origin—and for good reason.** This is discrimination pure and simple. Worse, it is also discrimination that inevitably diminishes the pursuit of knowledge, by discarding knowledge simply because it is produced by a certain group of people.

The notion of an academic boycott has been raised by ASA members in the past and was rejected by the ASA's Committee on Programs and Centers for this very reason. **The ASA should not set policies that would impose on or restrict our academic right to research, and collaborate with colleagues as we see fit.**

In 2005, the American Association of University Professors (AAUP) issued a strong statement expressing opposition to academic boycotts. AAUP maintained neutrality in a complex and multi- layered conflict by neither supporting nor opposing the policies of the Israeli government or the Palestinian Authority. In May 2013, AAUP released a *Statement on Academic Boycotts* saying, "In view of the association's longstanding commitment to the free exchange of ideas, we oppose academic boycotts. On the same grounds, we recommend that other academic associations oppose academic boycotts. We urge that they seek alternative means, less inimical to the principle of academic freedom, to pursue their concerns."

Academic boycotts are not only anathema to academic freedom, but they undercut the important role of academics as thought leaders in both critiquing and evaluating government policies. Similarly, the proposed boycott resolution unjustly holds Israeli academics responsible for policies put in place by the Israeli government. Israeli professors—just like professors in the U.S. or elsewhere—are politically independent and enjoy the right to express opposition to their government and any of its policies. If an academic boycott were imposed, it would collectively punish every Israeli (Muslim, Christian, Druze, Jewish and Atheist) regardless of their political views including those Israeli academics who are instrumental thought leaders in the movement for a just peace. In 2006, Sari Nusseibeh, President of Al Quds University, the Arab university in Jerusalem, publicly condemned academic boycotts, telling *The Associated Press,* "If we are to look at Israeli society, it is within the academic community that we've had the most progressive pro-peace views and views that have come out in favor of seeing us as equals. If you want to punish any sector, this is the last one to approach."

Healthy, constructive debate on the Middle East and other complex topics is most welcome within our association and the academy. We believe the ASA should permit its members to address these issues freely, including between ASA members and Israeli colleagues. **Squelching dialogue and cultural exchange through a boycott is not a constructive way to advance political concerns.**

Peace for both Israelis and Palestinians depends on both parties working together towards a negotiated, mutually agreeable solution. In contrast, an academic boycott is divisive and undermines this objective. We must instead encourage constructive efforts to bring Israeli and Palestinian academics together on joint projects, including those that foster reconciliation and promote understanding and trust—all critical factors that will enable Israelis and Palestinians to coexist in peace and security. The call for an academic boycott of Israel is a destructive attempt not only to silence, but also punish those involved in this important and potentially transformative academic work.

Since its founding, the objective of the ASA has been to promote "the study of American culture through the encouragement of research, teaching, publication, the strengthening of relations among persons and institutions in this country and abroad devoted to such studies." We urge the ASA to uphold these values by rejecting an academic boycott on a single group of people.

Letter from Former ASA Presidents

December 11, 2013

To: Members of the American Studies Association

As eight former presidents of the American Studies Association (ASA), we write to urge members to reject the "Proposed Resolution on Academic Boycott of Israeli Academic Institutions," which the ASA's National Council recently approved and has put to a membership vote.

We believe academic boycotts to be antithetical to the mission of free and open inquiry for which a scholarly organization stands. For all the reasons outlined in a letter to the Council signed by many ASA members including the eight former presidents writing you today, we see an academic boycott as setting a dangerous precedent by sponsoring an inequitable and discriminatory policy that would punish one nation's universities and scholars. Our task is to open conversation, not to close it off, and to do so with those who reflect ideas (and support policies) with which many of us may strongly disagree.

We are also deeply concerned by the process by which the ASA Council has put this decision to the membership. ASA Members were provided only the resolution and a link to a website supporting it. Despite explicit requests, the National Council refused to circulate or post to the ASA's website alternative perspectives.

That the membership vote is being undertaken with only one side of a complex question presented seems to us to amplify the profound contradictions of the academic boycott strategy, and to compound its potentially pernicious consequences. This can only damage the ASA and further deflect attention from the serious moral and political issues proponents seek to raise. We believe there are far more effective and constructive ways than a hollow, divisive academic boycott for ASA to engage these important concerns.

We provide here links to documents opposing an ASA academic boycott, and urge members to study them carefully: A letter to the Council by ASA members opposed to academic boycotts, a solidarity letter signed by

Americanists who also oppose academic boycotts, and the AAUP's Open Letter to ASA members urging them to reject this and all academic boycotts.

Members have until 11:59PM on Dec. 15th to vote. You need your ASA membership number (provided on the ASA e-mail announcing the vote) to cast your vote. If you cannot find it, e-mail Kathy Gochenour (KAG@press.jhu.edu). Vote here: http://asa.press.jhu.edu/cgi-bin/2013_israel_asa_vote.cgi.

The National Council has agreed to reject this resolution if less than 50% of voting members explicitly approve it. We urge ASA members to vote to reject this divisive and discriminatory resolution. If members remain uncertain, we urge them to register their votes as abstentions. Sincerely,

- -Shelley Fisher Fishkin, Joseph S. Atha Professor of Humanities Professor of English Director of American Studies, Stanford University, ASA President 2004-2005
- -Michael Frisch, Professor of American Studies and Senior Research Scholar, University at Buffalo, State University of New York, ASA President 2000-2001
- -Karen Halttunen, Professor of History, University of Southern California, ASA President 2005-2006
- -Mary Kelley, Ruth Bordin Collegiate Professor of History, American Culture, & Women's Studies, University of Michigan, ASA President 1999-2000
- -Linda K. Kerber, May Brodbeck Professor in the Liberal Arts Emerita, University of Iowa, ASA President 1988-1989
- -Alice Kessler-Harris R., Gordon Hoxie Professor of History, Columbia University, ASA President 1991-1992
- -Patricia Limerick, Professor of History, Faculty Director and Chair of the Board of the Center of the American West, University of Colorado, ASA President 1996-1997
- -Elaine Tyler May, Regents Professor, Departments of American Studies and History, University of Minnesota, ASA President 1995-1996

An Open Letter to a University President

December 17, 2013
University of Maryland

To: President Wallace Loh, Provost Mary Ann Rankin, Vice-Provost Juan Uriagereka and Dean Bonnie Thornton Dill:

As a historian of anti-Semitism and a U.S. historian who is also an affiliate of the American Studies Department respectively, we are writing to you about a matter of urgent concern to the University of Maryland. As you probably know, two weeks ago the National Council of the American Studies Association unanimously approved a resolution to boycott Israeli universities and decided to put it to a vote of the full membership. Yesterday the results were announced: 66% in favor. However, since apparently only about 1,200 of the 5,000 members cast a ballot, that 66% percent represents only about 16% of the total membership. In other words, less than 20% of the membership has succeeded in gaining a majority for a resolution that attacks the most basic norms of the community of scholars, rests on false assertions about the state of Israel, and is, in fact, a blatant act of anti-Semitism.

Indeed, this resolution amounts to a blacklist of Israeli scholars, most of whom are Jews. Though its advocates celebrate themselves as great champions of the fight against racism and Zionism—they equate the two, they are, in fact, advocates of one of the oldest and longest- lasting forms of hatred: hatred of the Jews and of the Jewish state. No matter how many anti-Israeli Jews they can produce to support their action, the boycotters' obsessive focus on Israel's alleged sins in the midst of a world of sinners indicates that this very old prejudice is at work here in a new guise.

The late Mancur Olson, the University of Maryland's Nobel Prize-winning economist, would have seen this event as a classic example of the logic of collective action in which an organized minority was able to achieve its goals against an indifferent or uninvolved majority. After all, most professors, most of the time, focus their efforts on their jobs, that is, on teaching, research and service to the university. The politically engaged minorities who push resolutions such as the present one devote their efforts to politics. As Olson argued, the less committed majority whose interests are multiple often loses out to the committed vanguard. As leaders of our academic community, you are in a position to speak out against the resolution and give the heretofore silent majority a voice.

Many scholars from around the country, including eight past presidents of the ASA, urged the organization not to proceed with this resolution. We pointed to the American Association of University Professors' official opposition to academic boycotts. We argued that the American Studies Association is a scholarly, not a political organization. We stressed that a boycott of institutions and people constitutes a form of blacklist, since it is directed against particular people because of their affiliations with Israel. We pointed out that in its consequences this is an act of anti-Semitism—that is, a racist act. We argued that, while as individuals, professors could certainly express whatever opinions they wished to about Israel, an effort to break links with Israeli academic institutions was incompatible with the norms of the academy.

None of these very good arguments made any difference to the committed and well-organized groups that pushed this resolution through.

It is the policy of this University to support diversity and reject all forms of discrimination based on racial, gender, ethnic, religious or national grounds. In defense of norms that all scholars should respect and support, we ask, therefore, that the senior administrative officers of the University denounce the ASA resolution. If you do not, your silence can plausibly be interpreted as acquiescence in this one form of discrimination. It would be tantamount to saying that discrimination against Jews, and this ill-considered attack on Israeli universities, are compatible with upholding the banner of diversity. In fact, it is nothing of the sort. If you do not speak out against this resolution, your credibility to speak out in favor of diversity and inclusion in other areas will be destroyed. Who will care what you think about the conventional notions of diversity and inclusion if you won't raise your voice against attacks on Israel and on Jewish scholars? Within the left-wing of academia you will find apologists for such double-think, but in the wider world of politics and journalism—and among the majority of the faculty within the University— such a double standard would not stand the test of public discussion.

Moreover, what began with a leftist vanguard in American Studies could expand. Flushed with its victory in this field, anti-Israeli activists may aim more broadly. They may attack programs such as Jewish Studies and Israel Studies, which cannot, of course, function effectively without ongoing contact with Israeli scholars. They may set their sights on even bigger fish, such as the cyber-security research that goes on here at Maryland. Indeed, UMD's contacts with Israeli universities and scholars in the STEM fields may be even more extensive than those in the Humanities and Social Sciences. We can imagine that accusations of collaboration with "US imperialism" and "the Zionist occupation regime" could be extended to natural scientists and engineers who work with Israeli colleagues and universities. If you don't speak out now against this measure, a witchhunt against all those who held to be "guilty of complicity" in "Israel's crimes" is not beyond the realm of possibility.

Accordingly, we urge you to:

1. publicly reject and denounce the American Studies Association boy-cott/blacklist resolution. Remind the campus of the ethical norms of the community of scholars and of the principles that the AAUP has clearly articulated.
2. reaffirm that support for diversity and inclusion is incompatible with advocacy of anti-Semitism.
3. as the ASA is now on record as supporting this boycott, make it University policy to refuse to allow any funds to be used to pay for faculty or graduate student membership in that organization or participation in its activities as long as the boycott resolution remains in place.

We thank you for considering this matter. We would, of course, be happy to discuss it with any of you in person.

Sincerely,

Jeffrey Herf
Professor, Department of History

Sonya A. Michel
Professor, Department of History

MICHAEL C. KOTZIN

Politics and the Modern Language Association:
Reflections Before and After the MLA Vote

The recent passage by the American Studies Association (ASA) of a resolution declaring an academic boycott of Israeli universities alerted many members of the American Jewish community to the troubling views held by numerous activist faculty members on campuses throughout North America. Even though only some 800 ASA members voted for that resolution, in taking into account the motives of those behind the global Boycott, Divestment, and Sanctions (BDS) movement which has called for such steps and which in truth constitutes an assault on Israel's legitimacy, concerns about this development are understandable. Equally understandable in their own way are the concerns of many communal organizations about what happened when the Modern Language Association—a group some six times the size of the ASA—held its annual convention in Chicago on January 9-12. But as important as the upcoming meeting and the resolution that will be introduced there are, it is equally important to keep in perspective what actually is on tap to happen at the MLA meeting, and to understand what it all means. For though what will be happening indeed matters to the Jewish community, what is going on most centrally is an internal battle regarding the meaning and purpose of the MLA itself, and it is that body which is about to face its moment of truth.

My own familiarity with this organization goes back over five decades, to a time when I was a graduate student in English at the University of Minnesota. The annual MLA convention is, among other things, a major job-hunting venue, and I lined up my first academic position at the 1967 meeting, also held in Chicago, where I was offered a position at Tel Aviv University. That led to my teaching there for eleven years, after which I returned to the States and began a very different kind of career in Jewish communal service. If no longer as central to my professional pursuits, my interest in literature continued. So it made sense when, two years ago, as I cut back my hours at the Jewish Federation of Metropolitan Chicago, I used some of the time made available to return to the classroom as a Visiting Professor at the University of Illinois for a semester and to begin to publish in scholarly journals once more. And when the program for this year's MLA convention was announced in early November, I renewed my membership and registered for the conference.

I continue to feel attachments to the historic purposes of the association. And I share the views of its members that the Humanities, which today suffer from decreasing support on the American educational scene, are of great value in general and in a democratic society in particular. Additionally, I have an ongoing interest in several of the fields the conference covers, and among this year's over 800 sessions, a number have topics that sound attractive to me. But at the same time, I have been troubled by the way that Israel has been treated at other academic conventions, and what I saw in this year's program led me and a number of longstanding members of the MLA with whom I have been in contact to have deep concerns about what was about to happen here.

While this year's MLA program does not include consideration of a resolution calling for an academic boycott of Israel like the one passed by the ASA, it does include a roundtable discussion session on the topic of academic boycotts whose panelists have all have gone on record in support of such boycotts or have otherwise demonstrated an animus for Israel. The line-up includes Omar Barghouti, identified in the conference program as an "independent scholar" but far better known for having founded the Palestinians' BDS movement. Another of the panelists is David Lloyd, a professor of English at the University of California's Riverside campus who wrote a column for the *Electronic Intifada* supporting the ASA vote and attacking what he called "the nightmare hidden within liberal Zionism." His primary target in that piece was the commentator Peter Beinart, whom he condemned for writing a column for the *Daily Beast* which, while criticizing Israel's settlements policy, also strongly affirmed the need for a two state solution to the Israel-Palestinian conflict. For Lloyd, who describes Israel as an "exclusively racist state," the "two state solution threatens Palestinians," and he decidedly rejects that solution himself.

In addition to that panel discussion, this year's MLA program also includes a resolution on Israel which, though not on the subject of academic boycotts, is troubling in its way. It calls for the association to urge the U.S. State Department "to contest Israel's arbitrary denials of entry to Gaza and the West Bank by U.S. academicians who have been invited to teach, confer, or do research at Palestinian universities." While on its face such language may sound reasonable to members of the MLA's Delegate Assembly who will vote at the end of this week, if examined carefully the resolution proves to be based on flimsy, limited evidence presented in a one-sided background report, and the resolution's charges are made without any suitable context. The resolution's insistence that measures taken by Israel in determining the implementation of its policies regarding foreign visitors are merely "arbitrary" is blind to the realities Israel faces, and the resolution's bias is evidenced in its unfairness in singling out Israel alone for engaging in a widespread global practice and in the assumptions it implies about Israel's motivation.

My early years as a member of the MLA took place in the '60s, a politically volatile time in America when I myself, outside of the classroom, was involved in the anti-Vietnam war movement. Despite whatever may have gone on in MLA conventions at that time, and although through the years various political causes may have been supported by the association, the MLA has continued to have the core identity of an academic and scholarly enterprise. What is happening now has the potential of changing that utterly. Accordingly, the central issue that is currently in play is not about a conflict of some sort between the Jewish community and the MLA, as some have suggested. Instead, the conflict which is unfolding is within the MLA itself.

Yes, the attempt to delegitimize Israel might get a bump if the supporters for implementing an academic boycott against Israel in the Roundtable discussion gain adherents. But that activity has never caught on in America as it has in England and Europe, and it remains unlikely to. Though Omar Barghouti may have called what happened at the ASA conference a "tipping point," the rejection of a boycott and strong criticism of the ASA for endorsing that position from one university president after another, and many faculty members as well, proves the contrary. Indeed, what the ASA did may have actually made the BDS movement weaker and less credible in America than it had been.

And yes, if the proposed MLA resolution passes despite its inherent flaws and despite the well-substantiated opposition of key MLA members, that probably would be portrayed by the resolution's supporters as a major victory, and some damage would indeed be done. In that regard, some members of the MLA opposed to this resolution suspect that it is a "stalking horse" which, if passed, could lay the groundwork for the introduction of a boycott resolution next year, and the anti-boycott momentum created recently by the sharp negative response to the ASA's action throughout the country could be blunted somewhat. But the resolution still is significantly weaker than what the ASA passed.

So as much as supporters of Israel are right to take seriously what is happening at the MLA convention, that concern should be kept in perspective. At this point it is not the MLA as an organization but some of its members who are creating a problem, and what is really at stake in these meetings is the future of the MLA itself. The key question at hand thus is whether the MLA will continue to be a body defined by its proclaimed mission of serving as an organization with the purpose of "promoting the teaching and study of language and literature" which embraces academic ideals and the advancement of scholarly pursuits. The stark alternative, which would follow if the MLA chooses to enter on the path which the ASA has taken, is that it can come to be regarded the way the ASA is today—as a fringe organization more concerned with the advancement of a one-sided, unfair, ideology-driven foreign policy agenda—rather than as a credible scholarly association. What is at stake in these meetings is the very soul of the MLA.

On January 11, the Delegate Assembly of the Modern Language Association (MLA) meeting in Chicago voted 60 to 53 to support a resolution which urged the U.S. State Department "to contest Israel's denial of entry to the West Bank by U.S. academics who have been invited to teach, confer, or do research at Palestinian universities." To become adopted by the organization as a whole, the resolution will next have to be approved by the MLA's Executive Council, scheduled to meet in late February, and if it passes it would face a vote of the total membership.

While the resolution passed by the MLA's Delegate Assembly thus has yet to be adopted, it still is a matter of concern and merits scrutiny. A useful way to approach it would be to apply a variation on the analytic terms first developed by medieval Kabbalists for reading the Torah—starkly different though the nature of these texts may be.

This approach proceeds by considering four levels of meaning, the first of which deals with the literal meaning of the text. Looked at on its face, the resolution thus is simply calling for certain State Department action. This reading is in tune with the claim made by one of the drafters of the resolution in opening the discussion at the MLA session where it was voted on, who asserted that the resolution should be taken only in the narrow sense of coming to the support of fellow academics.

But looked at only in this way, the resolution has hardly any value. It is hard to imagine the State Department truly "contesting" Israel's application of its security policies regarding academic visitors—especially because, as research done by a newly formed group called MLA Members for Scholars' Rights showed, the proponents of the resolution could identify only one person who might have faced the problem, which is cited as the purported basis of the resolution.

Looking then for other meanings to this resolution, we can next see it as a symbolic statement of solidarity with the Palestinian people, whom the drafters and supporters of the resolution clearly regard as an oppressed people. If the resolution is seen this way, what matters is not what it calls for directly but how it could be taken by the Palestinians. Their sense of grievance and victimhood was validated by the language of the resolution's backers, who repeatedly spoke about Israel's "racist" system and "apartheid" regime when they took the floor at the MLA meeting. Given that approach, this resolution and other statements like it can be seen as perpetuating the situation the Palestinians currently face, ultimately hardening both sides of the Israel-Palestinian conflict instead of advancing reconciliation and hastening the coming of the day when the Palestinians could have self-determination in a state of their own next to the state of Israel.

Moving on to the third level of meaning, the resolution can be seen as advancing a narrative which, as supporters of the resolution demonstrated, sees Israel as being a racist country practicing apartheid and using chemical weapons. As we dig deeper and get closer to the true meaning behind a resolution like this, we recognize that the rhetoric of its supporters is the rhetoric of the delegitimizers of Israel, of those who would marginalize the state for what they portray as its gross violations of human rights. This resolution may not go as far as the one passed by the members of the American Studies Association, whose right to call for an academic boycott was defended in an "emergency resolution" that failed to achieve consideration by the MLA. But the resolution's defenders talked about Israel with the same animosity as do the boycotters. The hostility of one speaker after another at the MLA session was tangible.

And this brings us to the resolution's deepest, fourth level of meaning, to what Cary Nelson, Professor of English at the University of Illinois at Urbana-Champaign, calls "the elephant in the room." That is anti-Semitism.

Those of us who talk about these matters need to use the anti-Semitism charge with care—both because its seriousness needs to be respected and also because, in attempting to pre-empt consideration of this issue, Israel's enemies are always quick to claim that Israel's friends use the term indiscriminately when talking about any critic of any of Israel's polices or actions. Though one of the supporters of the resolution at the MLA meeting attacked what he called the "rhetorical ploys" and "suppressive rhetoric" of Israel's supporters, it is in fact the enemies of Israel who try to suppress exposure of the anti-Semitism that often suffuses their own rhetoric and approach.

Thus, though we should be careful about using the term anti-Semitism, when anti-Semitic concepts can be identified within the verbal attacks on Israel, it is far from improper to point that out. So when one of the supporters of the resolution who took the floor during the Delegate Assembly meeting talked about financial contributions to political candidates in America by a "pro-Israel lobby," which, he implied, corrupt American foreign policy, the anti-Semitic reverberations were surely there.

That speaker, along with several others, was opposing the charge that there is something wrong with "singling out" Israel as does this resolution. In fact, the pattern of singling out at the least raises the possibility that there is something off-kilter in such treatment of Israel, and those who do the singling out don't like to be put on the spot about that. They talk about the amount of financial aid that Israel has received from the U.S. through the years and things like that as justifying particularist criticism of it. But with the proponents of a resolution that singles out Israel rejecting the replacement of it with a resolution that calls for freedom of movement for all academics, as was the case at the MLA meeting, it's hard not to suggest that the secret is out and that something is at play that is not just about the rights of traveling academics.

The introducer of this resolution, who spoke first at the meeting and who two days before had been a panelist on a discussion session that supported academic boycotts of Israel, said he was insulted by the claim that this resolution was seen by some as laying the groundwork for a boycott resolution in the future. Whether or not that was the intent, there clearly is an affinity between the backers of this resolution and the supporters of such a boycott. Their shared methods, it has increasingly been recognized, marginalize Israel through a strategy of demonization and delegitimation which ultimately, it can be suggested, is intended to lead to Israel's elimination as a Jewish state, just as apartheid-ruled South Africa was brought down. And as much as the proponents of the boycott and other such measures may not like to have it said, the denial to the Jewish people of the right of national self-determination in their ancient homeland is an act of discrimination equivalent to the kinds of bigotry-driven acts carried out against Jewish individuals and Jewish communities in past eras.

So as much as it would be wrong in many ways to reduce everything to anti-Semitism, neither should we fail to identify what much of all of this is about. What we are witness to within the MLA and one academic association after another is the application of an anti-colonial ideology which in the name of helping the Palestinians does quite the opposite and which unfairly vilifies Israel as a racist violator of human rights that does not deserve to exist. Given the rhetoric with which these concepts are advanced, this ideology has become a key transmitter of the anti-Semitic virus in our time. That needs to be seen, and that needs to be called attention to. ■

Note: These pieces were published, respectively, in *The Times of Israel* and JUF News as the events described unfolded. The MLA resolution was not ratified by the organization's membership. The vote was announced on June 4, 2014.

JEFF ROBBINS

MLA Vote:
Will Bias Beat Scholarship?

There is a scene in *Guys and Dolls*, the Damon Runyan-inspired tale about entertaining mobsters, in which a thug nicknamed Big Julie From Chicago lays down the law: he will not be shooting craps unless the outcome is safely rigged in advance. He announces to Nathan Detroit, who has beaten him until then using actual dice, that they will now be using his own "specially made" dice.

"I do not wish to seem petty," Detroit offers, "but your dice ain't got no spots on them. They're blank."

"I had the spots removed for luck," replies Big Julie From Chicago, "but I remember where the spots formerly were."

The meeting of the Modern Language Association in Chicago earlier this year featured a resolution censuring Israel for applying visa restrictions to four individuals whom it regarded as a security threat, promoted by academics who pronounced themselves motivated by their passionate support for the free exchange of ideas. But the promoters deployed tactics aimed at preventing those with a dissenting view from being heard with a lack of sheepishness that would have made Big Julie From Chicago proud, and the late Chicago Mayor Richard J. Daley positively beam.

Even so, the anti-Israel measure barely passed the MLA's Delegate Assembly, eking out only a narrow 60-53 margin. It now goes to the MLA's

28,000 members, who began voting on it this week, with on line balloting set to conclude on June 1.

There is considerable concern on the part of scholars that the MLA is in danger of being hijacked by a relatively small cadre whose hatred of Israel has become so unhinged that they care less about the MLA than they do about having their agenda serviced. The anti-Israel crowd's focus on squelching dissent, on one hand, while holding themselves out as devotees of the open exchange of ideas, on the other, has not reassured the skeptics.

The less-than-inspirational commitment to encouraging the expression of dissenting views was on display from the beginning of the MLA session. The organization had 799 panels on academic topics, and exactly one non-academic panel, entitled "Academic Boycotts: A Conversation About Israel and Palestine." Despite a promise from the MLA's president that the panel would present a "diversity" of views, a diversity of views was precisely what there was not. Each of the panelists had publicly called for boycotts of Israel. No opponents of boycotts were invited to present a dissenting view.

Indeed, in a scene reminiscent of the 1968 Democratic National Convention in Chicago, opponents of a boycott were obliged to hold an "alternative panel" off-site, at a nearby hotel. Those who wished to distribute materials opposing boycotts at the MLA meeting found themselves impeded from doing so. Meanwhile, the stalwart defenders of the free exchange of ideas denied press credentials to two journalists who wanted to cover the meeting, but who represented press outlets that MLA officials regarded as unlikely to fawn over what was unfolding.

When they introduced their resolution censuring Israel for denying entry to four American academics, the proponents stumbled. Having styled their resolution as one urging the State Department "to contest Israel's arbitrary denials of entry to Gaza and the West Bank," the anti-Israel academics muffed matters badly. Far from engaging in "arbitrary denials," it emerged that Israel provides due process and substantive standards consistent with the world's liberal democracies, notably the United States—whose State Department was being urged to "contest" the Israeli decisions. It emerged further that the United States was approximately 200 times likelier to deny a visa to an Israeli than Israel was to deny a visa to an American. As for the resolution's criticism of Israel for refusing entry into "Gaza," the proponents had failed to inform themselves that Egypt controlled the Gaza border, not Israel.

All of this required the sponsors to rapidly amend their resolution in order to jettison the patent errors, but not before their credibility and that of the resolution had taken a sizable hit. It was, observed Professor Cary Nelson, former President of the American Association of University Professors and a leading opponent of the anti-Israel measure at the MLA, "like a circus, with a surfeit of clowns."

With MLA delegates showing some discomfort at a resolution whose bias outstripped its scholarship, the proponents had an ally in the Chair. Maggie Ferguson, the incoming President of the MLA and thus entitled to preside over the proceedings, was not what one would call an impartial arbiter of procedural disputes: she had formally, publicly endorsed boycotting Israel. Those who assumed she would feel honor-bound to recuse herself from ruling on disputes as a matter of fundamental integrity, however, were to be disappointed. She perceived no conflict in both advocating for anti-Israel boycotts and ruling from the Chair on challenges to the anti-Israel resolution, and when an alternative resolution was proposed designed to be "more inclusive and less partisan," Ferguson ruled it "out of order."

By the time the vote on the censure resolution was called, mayhem and disgust had taken their toll, and more than half of those eligible to vote had either left or disassociated themselves from the process. After it passed by seven votes, the anti-Israel crowd took one more opportunity to remind everyone what they were really after: a vote to boycott Israel altogether. Because the MLA had gone on record opposing boycotts and because they had represented that the censure resolution was in no way a stalking horse for a boycott, this required some thought—but not much. The adherents of freedom of expression settled on a second, "emergency resolution" which "condemned" those who had expressed their criticism of anti-Israel boycotts. Condemning others for dissenting from the call for boycotts seemed a bit too much like the actions of fledgling counselors at Stalinist summer camp for the Assembly, which soundly defeated the "condemnation resolution" by a 59-41 vote before leaving Chicago.

Over the next 6 weeks, the MLA members will vote to either ratify or reject the anti-Israel resolution. The proponents have continued to do their best to prevent their fellow academics from hearing views dissenting from their own.

Thus, when the MLA Members for Scholars' Rights that had been formed by opponents sent fact sheets to the MLA membership demolishing the resolution, the MLA website erupted with howls of protest from those accusing them of "invad[ing] the privacy of members of the MLA" in a fashion that was "highly problematic." When it was pointed out that the MLA directory was part of the public domain, resolution supporters changed their attack, warning darkly that the "funds" that must have been necessary to distribute the fact sheet strongly suggested "undue influence."

That, too, was nonsense: the cost of sending the fact sheet was approximately 800 dollars, and was cheerfully borne by MLA members who wanted their fellow academics to have the facts. Resolution backers declined to apologize for the false charges, hewing to the remarkable line that there was something "unethical" about getting information that had been largely excluded from the MLA convention out to members, who might actually read it and conclude that they did not wish to be had.

As the MLA vote has neared, the ugliness of the comments posted by resolution supporters has gotten more pronounced. "This resolution rightly targets only Israel," one backer posted, "given the humungous [sic] influence that Jewish scholars have in the decision-making process of academia in general." Not a single supporter of the resolution posted anything critical of this fairly egregious bit of anti-Semitism. Opponents, however, noted that the resolution's promoters had lost their way. "Only against Israel can we feel ourselves so powerful," one wrote. "Such is the provocation of vulnerability. We have, let us face it, no shame."

The MLA vote will determine whether the organization's future lies in promoting the free exchange of ideas or in preventing it. Opponents of the resolution are placing their faith in the idea that a majority of academics prefer scholarship over partisanship, and will on that basis reject the ride offered them by the resolution's backers. The vote will also say a lot about whether the kind of bare-knuckled blocking of dissent at the MLA will make Big Julie From Chicago the poster boy for future academic battles. ■

Note: This piece was first published in *The Times of Israel*. The MLA resolution was not ratified by the organization's membership. The vote was announced on June 4, 2014.

ROBERT FINE

Speaking in Opposition

This is not the first time I have been embroiled in a boycott debate. In the 1980s I was involved in solidarity work with the fledgling independent trade unions in South Africa. They were a living expression of non-racial democracy across so-called national lines. Solidarity included establishing direct links between South African and British unions at official and rank and file levels. As a result of our solidarity activities we were pilloried by leading figures in anti-apartheid, the ANC and the South African Communist Party for breaking the boycott! When we invited a South African academic, a leading advocate of the new unions and anti-apartheid scholar, to speak at our Comparative Labor Studies program at Warwick University, a demonstration was organized by a couple of SACP stalwarts to prevent him from speaking. When we wrote a trade union solidarity pamphlet, we were told that unions could only be legal in South Africa if they collaborated with the regime and that we were in effect collaborationists.

Beneath the argument about boycott what was also going on was a political battle between a progressive socialist politics and a quite reactionary nationalist politics. It is a battle that has not stopped and is rising to the surface in contemporary South Africa. I grant there is no direct analogy between the boycott of apartheid South Africa and that of Israeli academic institutions, but I contend that a similar political battle is taking place. It is a battle over the future of our own political life.

465

The normal practice of international solidarity is to make contact with and support individuals and associations that are critical of an oppressive power. Depending on the circumstances, I am thinking of trade unions, women's movements, community organizations, peasant associations, some religious institutions, human rights activists, individual writers and academics—all who find themselves oppressed by and / or in struggle against oppressive powers. As far as Israeli and Palestinian academics are concerned, we should find ways of speaking to one another more, not less. We can do this in the normal way: by establishing links between our professional and union organizations, supporting campaigns for decent conditions, defending academic freedom and freedom of movement, by facilitating academic links across the national divide, and so forth. A boycott directed at Israeli academic institutions and Israeli academic institutions alone shifts our focus away from international solidarity and toward a refusal to have anything to do with one nationally defined section of our fellow academics.

The academic boycott fails to make a distinction crucial to all radical political thought: that between civil society and the state. The academic boycott punishes a segment of civil society, in this case Israeli universities and their members, for the deeds and misdeeds of the state. The occupation of Palestine and the human rights abuses that flow from the occupation are to my mind simply wrong, but there is something very troubling in holding Israeli universities and academics responsible for this wrong. Israeli academics doubtless hold many different political views, just as we academics do in the UK, but the principle of collective responsibility applied to Israeli academe as a whole sends us down a slippery path. The motion calls for Israel—and I would hope all other parties to conflict in the Middle East—to abide by international law, but the essential point of international law is to get away from categories of collective guilt and affix personal and political responsibility where it is merited. It is wrong to hold academic institutions and academics responsible for the actions of the Israeli state—even if many of the universities in question are, like most British academic institutions, rather lacking in political bottle.

It is as discriminatory to boycott any academic institutions or any academics on the basis of nationality, as it would be to boycott on the basis of race, religion or gender. This would be true not only of Israel but of any other country. It is wrong to penalize academics because of the nation to which they or their universities belong. It is also discriminatory to impose a political test that academics of one particular nation must pass in order to be allowed to speak and work with us—as if we are arbiters of all that is allowed to pass muster. Worst of all, I am sure we would agree, would be to base a decision to boycott or not to boycott Israeli academics on whether they are deemed

Jewish, Arab or Muslim, but the cases I know of actual boycott have been directed against Jewish Israeli academics.

A selective academic boycott aimed only at Israeli academic institutions and not at universities and research institutes belonging to other countries with equally bad or far worse records of human rights abuse, is also discriminatory. I admit that the wrongs done by 'my own people', in this case fellow Jews, grieve me more than the wrongs done by other peoples, but this is a confession, not a principle of political action. An academic boycott directed exclusively at Israeli academic institutions generates a quite realistic sense that Israel is being picked on—not because it is different from other countries but because it is the same. Given the slaughter currently occurring in Syria, including that of Palestinian refugees, given the repression currently imposed by the military government in Egypt, given the slave-like conditions currently endured by migrant workers in Qatar, it is increasingly eccentric to select Israel alone for boycott. This is not to say that the Israeli occupation should be normalized, certainly not, but it is all too easy to hold some other category of people, the larger and the further away the better, as the embodiment of absolute culpability.

The absence of good reasons to boycott Israeli academic institutions has led to ever more wild and hyperbolic depictions of Israel itself. Pascal once said: if first you kneel, then you will pray. Marx translated this aphorism into the notion that being determines consciousness. In this case, those who call for an academic boycott of Israel end up offering increasingly Manichaean images of Israel's evil essence in order to justify their practice. We are told that Israel is just like the apartheid state in South Africa, that Israel treats Palestinians just like Nazis treated Jews, that Gaza is just like the Warsaw ghetto, that the Israel lobby controls American foreign policy just like antisemites used to say that the Jewish lobby controlled the nations of Europe, that Zionism is responsible for all that is wrong in Palestine or the Middle East or the world. The existence of these projections of course preceded the boycott, but the boycott encourages us to search everywhere for evidence of Israel's criminality that will then justify the boycott itself.

Let us turn to the controversial antisemitism question. We should be able to agree that antisemitism is like any other racism something that progressive movements must be against. In my union, UCU, proponents of an academic boycott of Israel always couple their calls with more or less categorical declarations that criticism of Israel is not or not 'as such' antisemitic. Supporters of BDS in the States declare categorically that the charge of 'antisemitism', when leveled against them or other critics of Israel, is not only mistaken but also raised for dishonest reasons. I have often heard it said—look for example at Alain Badiou's recent polemics on antisemitism—that while antisemitism was a real problem in the past, it is no longer a problem of the present and has now been converted into a mere ideology of Zionism. What I see is a disturbing reluctance on the part of proponents of boycott to take seriously the problem of antisemitism. To reduce concern over antisemitism to a way of censoring critical thought about Israel is insulting to those of us who are concerned about antisemitism and have no wish to censor critical thought. We should surely understand by now that it is racism and antisemitism, not opposition to racism and antisemitism, which constitute the restriction of free speech.

Criticism of any country can be racist—whether it is criticism of Zimbabwe on the grounds that Africans cannot rule themselves, or criticism of India on the grounds that Asian values are essentially authoritarian, or criticism of the Arab Spring on the grounds that democracy and human rights are foreign to the Arab mindset, or criticism of Ireland on the grounds that the Irish are not intelligent, or even criticism of apartheid South Africa on the grounds that whites are genetically primed to infantilize Blacks. Criticism of Israel is no exception. It can be antisemitic and it is a moral obligation we ought to honor post-MacPherson to take very seriously the fear that the academic boycott encourages antisemitism because its effect is to exclude Jews and only Jews from the global community of academe.

I am not against all boycotts, but I am against an academic boycott linked to a political doctrine that treats Zionism as a dirty word. Zionism is a kind of nationalism. Like other nationalisms it has many faces—at times socialist, emancipatory, in search of refuge from horror; at other times narrow, chauvinistic, exclusive and terroristic. It depends which face we touch. For most Jews, Zionism simply means commitment to the existence of a Jewish state and is compatible with a plurality of political views. Zionism is not fundamentally different in this respect from other national movements born out of opposition to colonial and racial forms of domination. Most show the same Janus-face. Consider, for example, the ANC's African nationalism: on the one hand, it has overthrown apartheid and achieved constitutional revolution; on the other, it reveals its own proclivity to authoritarianism, corruption, violence and class politics. The murder of 34 mineworkers at Marikana was only the most visible sign of a new order in which profits are still put before people. What I object to is heaping onto 'Zionism' all the wrongs of nationalism in general, as if this nationalism were all bad while other nationalisms are off our critical hook. It is deeply regressive to turn 'Zionism' into an abstraction—abstracted from history (the Holocaust in Europe), abstracted from politics (conflict over land with Arab countries and Palestinians), abstracted from society (including the exclusion of most Jews from Middle East and Maghreb societies). It seems to me that there is some line of continuity between the abstraction of 'Zionism' today and the abstraction of 'the Jews' in the past.

The argument is put forward that Palestinian civil society has called for a blanket boycott of Israeli academic institutions. There is an empirical question concerning how true this is—to the chagrin of BDS this call is not supported by Mahmoud Abbas and the Palestinian Authority—but the more fundamental problem is present in the idea that Palestinian civil society is one homogenous bloc with one opinion. To work on this assumption is to diminish the subjectivity of Palestinians, to deny plurality within the Palestinian people, to attribute to Palestinians a single voice that is in fact an echo of your own voice. Palestinians are certainly victims of Israel but they are not only victims and they are not only victims of Israel. Racism is a versatile beast and I would contend that most Palestinians have no more interest in antisemitism than do Jews. Usually it is fellow Palestinians, not Jews, who are the first and main victims of antisemitic political forces within Palestinian society. The academic boycott offers little tangible support for Palestinian academics.

Israel has a definite political responsibility that goes with its current power, and like many other Jews in Israel and the diaspora I feel a frustrated yearning for Israel to fulfill its responsibilities. However, Israel's power is relative, not absolute. It looks like Goliath when compared with the Palestinian David, but it looks more like David when compared with other state powers. There is something very disturbing in the totalizing images of Zionist power associated with the boycott movement and in the innocent vision of peace and harmony that will prevail once this power is broken. Closer to home this self-same image of Zionist power manifests itself in the repeated refrain of resisting 'intimidation' we hear from advocates of the boycott.

Solidarity with Israeli and Palestinian academics should have as its aim the building of trust, the surrender of the occupied territories, the establishment of an independent Palestine alongside the Jewish and other Arab states, and above all the humanization of all parties. In this spirit I would offer our solidarity to the 165 Israeli academics who support a boycott of Ariel University in the occupied territories and the 11 academic institutions that have publicly condemned giving Ariel University status. The problem with 'the academic boycott', however, is that it blocks our ears to points of view we don't want to hear, or don't want to admit might exist, or indeed to anything that questions our own self-certainty. It grants us license to invent what we assume others think, in this case Israeli academics, rather than hear what they actually say. The principle of academic freedom is not absolute but it is something. It contains norms of openness, understanding, inquiry, criticism, self-criticism and dialogue, which we abandon at our peril. In any event, we in Europe must face up to our particular responsibility not to project onto one side or the other all the sins of racism, imperialism, ethnic cleansing and genocide of which Europe itself has been so very guilty. The boycott of Israeli academic institutions is by contrast the tip of a reactive and regressive political turn. ■

Robert Fine delivered this speech at Leeds University in March 2014. He spoke in opposition to the following motion: "This house believes that UK academics should boycott Israeli academic institutions until Israel ends the occupation and abides by international law." First published on the *Engage* website by David Hirsh.

ONLINE RESOURCES
(in alphabetical order)

1. Anti-BDS Sites

The AMCHA Initiative
http://www.amchainitiative.org/academic-boycott-of-israel-map/
A non-profit organization dedicated to investigating, documenting, educating about, and combating antisemitism at institutions of higher education in America. (AMCHA is the Hebrew word meaning "Your People.) The link above takes you to an online map documenting faculty support of BDS at over 300 U.S. universities.

Anti-Defamation League
www.adl.org
If you type BDS into the site's search engine, you will be taken to an extensive set of BDS updates and news stories.

BDS Cookbook
www.bdsisrael.com
A compilation of strategies to use in combating BDS on campus.

BICOM—Britain Israel Communications & Research Centre
http://static.bicom.org.uk/wp-content/uploads/2014/02/BICOM_Apartheid-Smear_FINAL.pdf
The link above is to "The Apartheid Smear," a detailed critique by Alan Johnson of the claim that Israel is an apartheid state.

Boycott Watch
www.boycottwatch.com
This site deals with all kinds of boycotts, including those against a wide range of consumer products. It can help in comparing BDS strategies with other boycott efforts.

Boycotted British Academic
http://boycotted-uk-academic.blogspot.com
An older site that documents effects of British BDS efforts to 2009.

Buycott Israel
www.buycottisrael.com
This is the site that helped launch the counter-boycott movement to organize efforts to buy Israeli products. It includes updates, strategies, definitions, and useful links.

CAMERA—Committee for Accuracy in Middle East Reporting in America
www.camera.org
Extensive reporting on all Israel-related issues, including BDS.

Divest This
www.divestthis.com
The site includes ongoing blog posts on BDS, fliers, strategy suggestions, and a colorful and graphically inventive brochure "Divest This."

Divestment Watch
www.divestmentwatch.com
Although this site has not been updated in some time, it has useful information on earlier divestment campaigns.

Engage
www.engageonline.wordpress.com
Founded by British sociologist and activist David Hirsh, *Engage* is perhaps the single best archive of academic essays on BDS and anti-Semitism. You can sign up for email notices of new posts.

Israel Action Network (The Jewish Federations of North America)
www.israelactionnetwork.org
The Israel Action Network (IAN) is the strategic initiative of The Jewish Federations of North America, in partnership with the Jewish Council for Public Affairs, created to counter assaults made on Israel's legitimacy. The

IAN was created to educate, organize, and mobilize the organized North American Jewish community to develop strategic approaches to countering these assaults and developing innovative efforts to change the conversation about Israel and achieve peace and security for two states for two peoples. The IAN website provides information and resources on key issues central to debates about Israel, news updates, links to recommended readings, and data on IAN's projects to counter BDS initiatives. IAN has a special commitment to help academic organizations deal with boycott initiatives.

Israel On Campus Coalition (ICC)
www.israelcc.org
ICC is a national network of students, faculty, and professionals dedicated to strengthening the pro-Israel movement on campus. The site, which serves as a connecting point for individual activists to access pro-Israel resources from ICC and its coalition partners, also features an Israel opportunities board for community postings.

The Israel Project
www.theisraelproject.org
Issue oriented coverage of a wide range of news stories related to Israel.

Legal Insurrection
http://legalinsurrection.com
A general political website that maintains a section devoted to academic boycotts at
http://legalinsurrection.com/2013/12/list-of-universities-rejecting-academic-boycott-of-israel/. It has lists of academic associations and universities rejecting academic boycotts of Israel and links to related documents.

The Meir Amit Intelligence and Terrorism Information Center
http://www.terrorism-info.org.il/en/article/20634
The link above is to a detailed overview of the BDS movement.

NGO Monitor—Making NGOs Accountable
www.ngo-monitor.org
The web site includes an extensive BDS resource page. It is particularly useful in tracking BDS funding.

SPME—Scholars for Peace in the Middle East
www.spme.org

The toolbar includes a BDS link with multiple resources. The site also covers numerous other Mideast issues.

StandWithUs
www.standwithus.com
The site provides news updates, fliers, brochures, lesson plans, and other resources covering BDS and many other topics related to Israel. There are still more resources on their password-protected site: http://www.standwithus.com/divestment/#.U2p4T158vnc

The Third Narrative
http://thirdnarrative.org/get-involved/academic-advisory-council
The website of a group of progressive academics, opposed to BDS, who support a two-state solution and seek justice for both Israelis and Palestinians.

Tulip—Trade Unions Linking Israel and Palestine
http://www.tuliponline.org
A British site supporting a two-state solution that reports on BDS.

2. Pro-BDS Sites

The Electronic Intifada
www.electronicintifada.net
An extensive anti-Israel pro-BDS site, including essay-length commentary.

Jewish Voice for Peace
http://www.usacbi.org
The website for a Jewish organization critical of Israeli policies that endorses boycotts as a strategy; it includes detailed commentaries advocating its positions.

Mondoweiss—The War of Ideas in the Middle East
www.mondoweiss.net
An ongoing collection of opinion pieces critical of Israeli policies and supportive of BDS.

PACBI—Palestinian Campaign for the Academic & Cultural Boycott of Israel
www.pacbi.org

A comprehensive pro-boycott site, with statements, resources, guidelines, and opinion.

Palestinian BDS National Committee
www.bdsmovement.net
A good source for pro-BDS takes on the news, along with a list of official statements.

USACBI—US Campaign for the Academic & Cultural Boycott of Israel
http://www.usacbi.org
In addition to a mission statement, a speakers bureau, FAQs, and guidelines, this site has an essential list of over 1,000 US faculty endorsements, along with lists from abroad and a means to connect with PSCABI, the Palestinian Students' Campaign for Academic Boycott of Israel.

3. Debates

The AAUP *Journal of Academic Freedom*
http://www.aaup.org/reports-publications/journal-academic-freedom/volume-4
In 2013 this peer reviewed online journal published six essays supporting academic boycotts and one mildly critical of them. A debate followed with sixteen responses from multiple points of view.

Los Angeles Review of Books
https://lareviewofbooks.org/academic-activism
In March 2014 LARB published a forum with eight essays, divided between supporters and opponents of academic boycotts.

Bitterlemons
http://www.bitterlemons-dialogue.org/archive.php
http://www.bitterlemons-books.org/index1.php
Until it ceased operating in 2012, Bitterlemons provided a forum for Israeli/Palestinian debate and dialogue. Its archive offers ten such dialogues. Its book section offers downloadable PDFs of collections of Bitterlemons essays and interviews.

Endnotes

NOTES TO THE INTRODUCTION

1.   Here is the final text of MLA's Resolution 2014-1:

Whereas Israel has denied academics of Palestinian ethnicity entry into the West Bank;

Whereas these restrictions violate international conventions on an occupying power's obligation to protect the right to education;

Whereas the United States Department of State acknowledges on its Web site that Israel restricts the movements of American citizens of Palestinian descent;

Whereas the denials have disrupted instruction, research, and planning at Palestinian universities;

Whereas the denials have restricted the academic freedom of scholars and teachers who are United States citizens;

Be it resolved that the MLA urge the United States Department of State to contest Israel's denials of entry to the West Bank by United States academics who have been invited to teach, confer, or do research at Palestinian universities.

After we pointed out that Egypt controlled the main access to Gaza, the resolution's supporters deleted references to Gaza from the text. They also dropped the word "arbitrarily" as a modifier before "denied" in the first Whereas clause, after Martin Shichtman asked what "arbitrarily" meant in this context. But that deprived the resolution of any claim that Israel's actions were not motivated by security concerns.

2.   Comments from MLA members through March 23 are available at http://pastebin. com/index/HyJtnBeC. Comments continued to appear online at MLA's website through April 15. Although I only provide names for comments in the portion of the debate that was copied onto the pastebin website, it is more than a little unrealistic for MLA members to assume confidentiality will apply to a site available to 28,000 people.

3.   The MLA member list used to be printed, sent to all members, and included in library subscriptions to the organization's lead journal, *PMLA*. It has thus traditionally been a public document. Now it is made available online instead. Members, however,

can still buy a paperbound version for $20. It is an opt-in list; members can withdraw their information if they so choose. Notably, only 20,000 of MLA's 28,000 members provide their email addresses for this purpose. We had no way to reach MLA's other 8,000 members, but Feal likely did. Members have always been free to assemble group email lists from the Directory to notify people about professional opportunities or provide information of potential interest. We did so on a larger scale, but there are no organizational rules prohibiting that. On April 9, 2014, Rosemary Feal wrote to us to quote the policy of the email distribution service we used, which was to "only use permission based lists." Instead of simply neutrally requesting information, she then leveled a hostile accusation: "MLA members deserve to know why you violated the terms of the company you used to send your message." As it happened, we had told the company how the MLA list was compiled, and they had no problem with its use. It is a permission-based list. We also included an opt-out button when we sent our email. Of the 20,000 MLA members, 55 opted out, including one of the resolution's cosponsors and Rosemary herself. For the record, though RF always referred in anonymous, neutral terms to "member" requests for information, we assumed that MLA leaders like its anti-Israel 2013 and 2014 presidents, Marianne Hirsh and Margaret Ferguson, might well be advising the staff, especially since it would be both unusual and unwise for an Executive Director to take such aggressive actions against members without consulting the top elected leaders. If MLA has taken any further "steps" regarding our effort to educate its members, they must be treading lightly, since we've not heard of them. No MLA leader or staff member has expressed any thanks for our work in sending out a fact sheet that gave some balance to the MLA's information packet. It would seem that the MLA needs to rethink and reform its procedures for informing members about the issues at stake in resolutions distributed for a vote so that both pro and anti positions are represented. In this case not even the Israeli government was given the opportunity to respond to accusations made against it. Feal repeatedly sent out the anti-Israel packet, always referring to it as "the" background information for the resolution.

Because MLA rigidly adhered to its rules about what documents were required to be distributed to the membership, it gave the impression it was urging a vote to approve the resolution. Looking back on more than six months of MLA executive decisions, all of them siding with the BDS constituency, it becomes difficult to ignore what has changed in an organization that now has a significant presence of BDS advocates in its leadership. Years ago, when MLA's Radical Caucus proposed boycotts of Israel, Feal and the rest of the MLA staff made multiple special efforts to help me defeat the proposals— from providing me with open-ended free photocopying at the annual meeting to helping reword alternative resolutions and interpreting the rules to get them considered. Now, with the political climate in the leadership having changed, the staff was working the other side of the issue. The Radical Caucus was still considered an unreliable fringe group; but now MLA presidents were BDS advocates. Thus the "rules" were rigidly applied to deny us an anti-BDS session because the application deadline had passed.

Notably, the anthropologists' association staff waived its deadlines to get us an alternative session in 2014 because they realized the Association would present a more neutral political profile that way. Not MLA. Then two reporters likely to be critical of BDS were denied press credentials to cover the January 2014 annual MLA meeting because they didn't personally evidence a history of writing about higher education. The record of the publications they represented was deemed irrelevant. Then Margaret Ferguson, incoming MLA president, was allowed to chair the discussion of the resolution without revealing that she had signed a public pro-BDS petition. The staff knew, but chose to keep the news to itself. Feal would later make the absurd argument that Ferguson's bias was irrelevant because she had signed the petition before taking office. Ferguson proceeded to rule as "out of order" exactly the sort of alternative resolution the staff would have facilitated only a few years earlier. Given the amount of time Feal, Ferguson, and others spent consulting with one another in onstage huddles, there was plenty of opportunity to advise Ferguson to rule differently, but Feal knows what side of the political bread her salary is buttered on. That said, both then and now the advantage of alternative resolutions was that they gave the members of the Delegate Assembly more options and more flexibility, thereby enhancing the Association's posture of neutrality. For Feal, so I believe, the only calculation to be made was narrowly political.

4.   The fact sheet we distributed is available at http://scholarsrights.files.wordpress.com/2014/01/oppose-resolution-2014-1_postconvention.pdf. The letter to MLA members is available at http://scholarsrights.wordpress.com

5.   For Palumbo-Liu's detailed BDS advocacy see his *Los Angeles Review of Books* essay in my Works Cited list. Deprived of his conspiracy-theory funding complaint, Palumbo-Liu then decided to express his grave concern over whether we had paid the student workers a sufficient hourly wage.

6.   On April 22, 2014, Feal wrote to Shichtman turning down his request to send our critique of the resolution to MLA's members: "I do not see any justification for privileging your comments over those from other members in the way you have requested." Of course our fact sheet was signed by several of us and was an express product of our new coalition, plus, unlike any other "comments," it had been distributed to the Delegate Assembly prior to their vote on the resolution.

7.   In his *Hidden Histories: Palestine and the Eastern Mediterranean*, Basem L. Ra'ad details his assertion that our understanding of the Middle East is "distorted by absolutist unhistorical claims" (1), specifically by "an inflated exploitation by the Zionists of dominant accounts related to ancient times" and (2) "the Israelis construct their identity and history on the basis of misleading ties to ancient idealized entities like 'Hebrews' and 'Israelites,' and use other biblical justifications" (197). In fact, he concludes, there was "no Israelite conquest, no dispersion, no Diaspora, no 'Jewish people.'" (3). This is basically anti-Semitism masquerading as scholarship.

Although beliefs of this sort—when added to a conviction that Israel has no right to exist and is a fundamentally oppressive state—can lead to very aggressive campus activism and strong feelings for some that the campus environment has become decidedly hostile, many of us opt for corrective speech, rather than the application of federal law as a remedy. Ra'ad's views, for example, are protected by academic freedom. On April 20, 2011, I (in my capacity as AAUP President) and Kenneth Stern (in his capacity as a staff member at the American Jewish Committee) issued the following Open Letter on Campus Antisemitism:

Recently, there have been allegations of antisemitism at three universities—the University of California at Berkeley, the University of California at Santa Cruz, and Rutgers. Any claim of bigotry must be treated with the utmost seriousness, not only because hatred harms its victims, but also because it can undermine academic freedom: students become afraid to be who they are and thus say what they think. Conversely, a climate which values academic freedom can unleash the best responses to bigotry, by promoting critical thinking and clear ideas.

Yet some, in reaction to these recent incidents, are making the situation worse by distorting the provisions of Title VI of the Civil Rights Act of 1964, and what has been called the "working definition of antisemitism." Opposing anti-Israel events, statements, and speakers, they believe the only way to "protect" Jewish students is by imposing censorship.

There has been a debate in recent years about whether Title VI, which prohibits discrimination on the basis of race, color or national origin in federally-funded programs, extends to Jewish students when antisemitic intimidation or harassment is directed at them based on the perception of ethnic, as opposed to religious, identity. In October 2010, the Office for Civil Rights of the Department of Education issued a letter clarifying that in certain limited contexts, antisemitic behavior or intimidation (the letter gave examples of swastika daubings and Jew-baiting bullying) is clearly based on a perception of ethnicity or national origin and is therefore covered by Title VI. "Harassment" encompasses both "different treatment" and the "existence of a racially hostile environment," meaning that the offending conduct is so severe or pervasive that, in order to continue their education, students have to suffer an educational environment that a reasonable person would consider intimidating, hostile, or abusive.

While some of the recent allegations (such as charging pro-Israel Jewish students admission to a university event while allowing others to attend for free) might well raise a claim under Title VI, many others seek to silence anti-Israel discourse and speakers. This approach is not only unwarranted under Title VI, it is dangerous.

Six years ago the European Monitoring Centre on Racism and Xenophobia (EUMC) created a "working definition" of antisemitism. Some European countries had no definition of antisemitism, and the few which did had different ones, so it was very difficult for monitors and data collectors to know what to include or exclude.

The "working definition," while clearly stating that criticism of Israel in the main is not antisemitic, gives some examples of when antisemitism may be in play, such as holding Jews collectively responsible for acts of the Israeli state, comparing Israeli policy to that of the Nazis, or denying to Jews the right of self determination (such as by claiming that Zionism is racism). In recent years the US Department of State and the US Commission on Civil Rights have embraced this definition too.

It is entirely proper for university administrators, scholars and students to reference the "working definition" in identifying definite or possible instances of antisemitism on campus. It is a perversion of the definition to use it, as some are doing, in an attempt to censor what a professor, student, or speaker can say. Because a statement might be "countable" by data collectors under the "working definition" does not therefore mean that Title VI is violated. To assert this not only contravenes the definition's purpose (it was not drafted to label anyone an antisemite or to limit campus speech), it also harms the battle against antisemitism.

The purpose of a university is to have students wrestle with ideas with which they may disagree, or even better, may make them uncomfortable. To censor ideas is to diminish education, and to treat students as fragile recipients of "knowledge," compromises their development as young critical thinkers. When the disquieting ideas are bigoted, it is incumbent on others on campus to speak out. University leadership should say something when appropriate too (not in every instance, because its role is not to be a quality control on campus debate).

Universities can do many other things to combat bigotry, from surveying students to see if and how they are experiencing bigotry, to offering courses on why and how people hate, to bringing in outside scholars and others to speak on relevant topics. Title VI is a remedy when university leadership neglects its job to stop bigoted harassment of students; it is not a tool to define "politically correct" campus speech.

Antisemitism should be treated with the same seriousness as other forms of bigotry. But one should not, for instance, suggest that a professor cannot make an argument about immigration simply because some might see any such argument as biased against Latino students. Nor was Title VI crafted with the notion that only speakers who are "safe" should be allowed on campus.

By trying to censor anti-Israel remarks, it becomes more, not less, difficult to tackle both antisemitism and anti-Israel dogma. The campus debate is changed from one of exposing bigotry to one of protecting free speech, and the last thing pro-Israel advocates need is a reputation for censoring, rather than refuting, their opponents.

The "working definition" is a useful tool to identify statements that merit attention on campus, but deciding whether a given remark is antisemitic can require careful attention to rhetoric, context, and even intent. As the AAUP has suggested, even objectionable statements can have content worthy of debate. Most individual remarks, moreover, do not rise to the level of creating hostile environments.

AAUP ACADEMIC BOYCOTT STATEMENT NOTES

8.   The full text of the statement is in *Academe: Bulletin of the AAUP* 91 (July–August 2005): 57. On June 1, 2006, AUT merged with the National Association of Teachers in Further and Higher Education to form the University and College Union.

9.   The United Nations Educational, Scientific, and Cultural Organization (UNESCO) advances the same principle as the AAUP: "[H]igher-education teaching personnel should be enabled throughout their careers to participate in international gatherings on higher education or research, [and] to travel abroad without political restrictions. . . . [They] are entitled to the maintaining of academic freedom, that is to say, the right, without constriction by prescribed doctrine, to freedom of teaching and discussion, [and] freedom in carrying out research and disseminating and publishing the results thereof." UNESCO, *Recommendations Concerning the Status of Higher-Education Teaching Personnel* (November 11, 1997).

10.   AAUP, "Statement on Collective Bargaining," *Policy Documents and Reports*, 9th ed. (Washington, D.C., 2001), 252.

11.   See *AAUP Bulletin* 56 (Spring 1970): 11–13; (Summer 1970): 123–29, 257; (Fall 1970): 346–47.

12.   *Academe: Bulletin of the AAUP* 71 (July–August 1985):4. In 1977, the Rev. Leon Sullivan initiated a program to persuade companies in the United States with investments in South Africa to treat African employees as they would their American counterparts. The program included several specific courses of action, or principles, for the companies to follow.

13.   *Academe: Bulletin of the AAUP* 74 (July–August 1988): 6.

14.   Nelson Mandela, *No Easy Walk to Freedom* (London: Heinemann Educational, 1990), 63.

15.   Omar Barghouti and Lisa Taraki in *PalestineChronicle.com*.

RUSSELL BERMAN NOTES

16.   Judith Butler, "Academic Freedom and the ASA's Boycott of Israel: A Response to Michelle Goldberg," *The Nation*, December 8, 2013.

17.   http://www.thenation.com/article/177512/academic-freedom-and-asas-boycott-israel-response-michelle-goldberg#

18.   http://www.theasa.net/what_does_the_academic_boycott_mean_for_the_asa/

19.   Butler, "Academic Freedom"

20.   Ibid.

21.   Edward H. Kaplan and Charles A. Small, "Anti-Israel Sentiment Predicts Anti-Semitism in Europe," *The Journal of Conflict Resolution*, Vol. 50 (2006), No. 4, pp. 548-561.

22.   Rania Khalek, "Does *The Nation* have a problem with Palestinians?", *The Electronic Intifada*, December 19, 2013 http://electronicintifada.net/content/does-nation-have-problem-palestinians/13022. Cf. Philip Weiss and Adam Horowitz, "'*The Nation*' and the privileging of Jewish voices on Israel/Palestine," *Mondoweiss*, December 23, 2013, http://mondoweiss.net/2013/12/privileging-voices-israelpalestine.html. One could point to examples in Europe: Günter Grass' 2012 public poem where he struggles to overcome German taboos on anti-Semitic discourse. Or in France the perfomer Dieudonné, who, as an anti-Zionist and anti-Semite, cultivates ties with the National Front of holocaust-denier Jean-Marie Le Pen. His political gesture, the *quenelle*, is spreading in popular culture; and Jean-Loup Amselle speaks of the phenomenon of a "post-colonial anti-Semitism."

BRAHM/ROMIROWSKY NOTES

23.   Scott Jaschik "Taking Israel to Task," *Inside Higher Ed*, January 13, 2014, http://www.insidehighered.com/news/2014/01/13/mla-delegate-assembly-narrowly-votes-criticize-israel#sthash.JOfjdn4e.dpbs; Jennifer Howard, "MLA Delegates Narrowly Approve Controversial Resolution on Israel," *Chronicle of Higher Education*, January 13, 2014, https://chronicle.com/article/MLA-Delegates-Approve/143985/

24.   Natan Sharansky, "3D Test of Anti-Semitism: Demonization, Double Standards, Delegitimization," *Jewish Political Studies Review* 16, no. 3-4 (Fall 2004): http://jcpa.org/phas/phas-sharansky-f04.htm

25.   This vision of a Greater Palestine saturates, for example, a recent manifesto-like volume, Laura Lim, ed., *The Case for Sanctions Against Israel* (New York: Verso 2012), and is widely recognized as at the heart of Omar Barghouti's public statements in any number of settings. Moreover, the overriding "justice" of a "one state solution" (minus Israel as a Jewish and democratic state) features centrally in not only the rhetoric of BDS's most visible spokesperson, but also in the more refined writings of its prime philosopher, Judith Butler. See Butler's *Parting Ways: Jewishness and the Critique of Zionism* (New York: Columbia University Press, 2012), where she makes her own vision of "justice" as "bi-nationalism" abundantly, unabashedly clear. An even worse mishmash of anti-Semitic anti-Zionism typical of BDS philosophy is Gianni Vattimo and Michael Marder, eds., *Deconstructing Zionism: A Critique of Political Metaphysics* (New York: Bloomsbury Academic, 2014). In it, Vattimo, a leading Heideggerian philosopher, stakes out fresh grounds for an "ontology" of anti-Semitism today by writing as follows, in support of Iran's policies toward the Jewish state, "When Ahmadinejad invokes the end of the State of Israel, he merely expresses a demand that should be more explicitly shared by democratic countries that instead [sic] consider him an enemy" (19). What, one

wonders, ought to be the thoughtful BDSer's position on an Iranian nuclear bomb—aimed squarely at Palestine?

26. That's our emphasis. See Chaim Seidler-Feller "Omar Barghouti at UCLA: No to BDS, no to occupation," *Jewish Journal*, January 23, 2014, http://www.jewishjournal.com/opinion/article/omar_barghouti_at_ucla_no_to_bds_no_to_occupation

27. Rachel Hirshfeld, "Finkelstein: BDS Movement is a 'Cult,'" *Arutz Sheva*, February 15, 2012,

28. http://www.israelnationalnews.com/News/News.aspx/152799#.U1MW-vldV8E

29. It's a problematic book but far from devoid of valid insights. One could say the same of all Arendt's writings on Jewish questions—problematic, wrong sometimes and right others, but always interesting and illuminating if taken with a grain of salt.

30. Vijay Prashad, "Understanding the Boycott of Israel's Universities," *Washington Post*, January 24, 2014, http://www.washingtonpost.com/opinions/understanding-the-boycott-of-israels-universities/2014/01/24/ecbc1064-7f05-11e3-93c1-0e888170b723_story.html

SHARON MUSHER NOTES

I want to thank Cary Nelson for his patience. David Greenberg's support and editorial acumen made this a much stronger piece. Simon Bronner provided key leadership at the time, and insightful comments on an early draft. Additional feedback from Alice Kessler-Harris and Linda Gordon was extremely helpful, as was a roundtable discussion, entitled "Beyond the Resolution," at the Eastern American Studies Association. All mistakes in this piece are mine alone. My activism would not have been possible without my husband Daniel Eisenstadt's encouragement. He has been my rock through this and all other struggles.

For the full statement of ASA goals quoted in my opening paragraph, see ASA Constitution and Bylaws, http://www.theasa.net/about/page/constitution_and_bylaws/#article-1.

31. Gene Wise, "'Paradigm Dramas' in American Studies: A Cultural and Institutional History of the Movement," *American Quarterly*, vol. 31, no. 3 (1971): 313.

32. Alice Kessler-Harris to author, e-mail, 4/30/14; Linda Kerber to author, e-mail, May 2, 2014.

33. Barbara Tomlinson and George Lipsitz, "American Studies as Accompaniment," *American Quarterly,* vol. 65, no. 1 (March 2013): 9.

34. US Campaign for the Academic and Cultural Boycott of Israeli

(USACBI) Academics, Endorsers, November 1, 2013, http://web.archive.org/web/20131101002249/http://www.usacbi.org/endorsers/.

35. USACBI Advisory Board, November 1, 2013, http://web.archive.org/web/20131101001704/http://www.usacbi.org/advisory-board/. USACBI. Organizing Collective, November 1, 2013, http://web.archive.org/web/20131101195437/http://www.usacbi.org/about-us/.

36. Elizabeth Redden, "American Studies and Israel," *Inside Higher Ed*, 11/25/13, http://m.insidehighered.com/news/2013/11/25/american-studies-association-meeting-scholars-debate-proposed-academic-boycott#sthash.u8KP0aSM.dpbs; "Caucus on Academic and Community Activism: Academic and Cultural Boycott Campaign," http://www.theasa.net/caucus_activism/item/academic_and_cultural_boycott_campaign/.

37. "Resolution Proposed: Support Boycott of Israeli Academic Institutions," Association for Asian American Studies, Annual Conference April 2013, http://web.archive.org/web/20130805055711/http://www.aaastudies.org/content/images/files/aaas%204_20_13%20-%20conference%20resolution%20to%20support%20the%20boycott%20of%20israeli%20academic%20institutions.pdf.

38. Change.org Petition, https://www.change.org/petitions/to-the-council-of-the-native-american-and-indigenous-studies-association-please-support-the-resolution-to-boycott-israeli-academic-institutions.

39. Caucus on Academic and Community Activism: Academic and Cultural Boycott Campaign, http://www.theasa.net/caucus_activism/item/academic_and_cultural_boycott_campaign/.

40. "Council Statement on the Boycott of Israeli Academic Institutions," http://www.theasa.net/from_the_editors/item/council_statement_on_the_academic_boycott_of_israel_resolution/.

41. Caucus on Academic and Community Activism: Academic and Cultural Boycott Campaign, http://www.theasa.net/caucus_activism/item/academic_and_cultural_boycott_campaign/.

42. ASA program description, https://convention2.allacademic.com/one/theasa/theasa13/.

43. Simon Bronner to author, e-mail, April 22, 2014.

44. Opposition letter, http://www.scribd.com/doc/187635747/Letter-in-Opposition-to-the-ASA-s-Proposed-Resolution-on-AcademicBoycott-of-Israeli-Academic-Institutions.

45.   Change.org petitions, http://www.change.org/petitions/to-national-council-of-the-american-studies-association?share_id=cRUFrLXymg&utm_campaign=signature_receipt&utm_medium=email&utm_source=share_petition; http://www.change.org/petitions/members-of-the-asa-support-resolution-to-boycott-israeli-academic-institutions.

46.   David Greenberg, "The ASA's Boycott of Israel is Not as Troubling as it Seems," *New Republic*, December 19, 2013.

47.   Michael Kazin to author, e-mail, November 20, 2013.

48.   David Hollinger to author, e-mail, December 16, 2013.

49.   Miles Orvell, "Beyond the Resolution: The Future of American Studies," roundtable discussion, Eastern American Studies Association, La Salle University, March 28, 2014.

50.   ASA Solidarity Letter, http://www.scribd.com/doc/189318253/Solidarity-Letter-by-non-ASA-Member-Americanist-Scholars-in-Opposition-to-the-ASA-s-Proposed-Resolution-on-AcademicBoycott-of-Israeli-Academic-Instit.

51.   Author to ASA national council, e-mail, November 20, 2013.

52.   ASA official to author, e-mail, November 21, 2013.

53.   Sharon Ann Musher, "Why I left the American Studies Association," *Times of Israel*, January 17, 2014, http://blogs.timesofisrael.com/why-i-left-the-american-studies-association/.

54.   Ibid., "A Host of Problems with the American Studies Association's Boycott of Israel," *Times of Israel*, December 19, 2013, http://blogs.timesofisrael.com/a-host-of-problems-with-the-american-studies-associations-boycott-of-israel/.

55.   Revised versions of some of these talks can be found here: Noura Erakat, Alex Lubin, Stene Slaita, J. Kehaulani Kauanui, and Jasbir Puar, "Substantive Erasures: Essays on Academic Boycott and the American Studies Association," *Jadaliyya*, December 23, 2013, http://www.jadaliyya.com/pages/index/15697/substantive-erasures_essays-on-academic-boycott-an.

56.   Ibid.

57.   Henry Reichman to ASA national council, e-mail, November 15, 2013.

58.   Lena Ibrahim, "'What Happened There Was Historic': A Report from the American Studies Association Boycott Debate," *Mondoweiss*, November 27, 2013; Sunaina Maira, "The BDS Movement and the Front Lines of the War on Academic Freedom," University of Minnesota Press, April 9, 2014.

59. ASA member to author [e-mail], November 25, 2013.

60. ASA member to author [e-mail], November 24, 2013.

61. US Campaign for the Academic and Cultural Boycott of Israeli (USACBI) Academics, Endorsers, November 1, 2013, http://web.archive.org/web/20131101002249/http://www.usacbi.org/endorsers/.

62. Ilan Troen, "De-Judaizing the Homeland: Academic Politics in Rewriting the History of Palestine," *Israel Affairs,* vol. 13, no. 4 (Oct. 2007): 872-884.

63. Eric Aronoff to author, e-mail, November 23, 2013.

64. Simon Bronner to author, e-mail, December 3, 2013.

65. "What does the Boycott of Israeli Academic Institutions Mean for the ASA?" http://www.theasa.net/what_does_the_academic_boycott_mean_for_the_asa/.

66. See the reference to the USACBI's mission statement (http://www.usacbi.org/mission-statement/) in "What Does the Academic Boycott Mean for the ASA?" http://www.theasa.net/what_does_the_academic_boycott_mean_for_the_asa/ US Campaign for the Academic and Cultural Boycott of Israeli (USACBI) Academics, Endorsers, November 1, 2013, http://web.archive.org/web/20131101002249/http://www.usacbi.org/endorsers/.

67. Jonathan Marks, "To Professors of Asian American Studies," *Inside Higher Ed*, May 16, 2013.

68. Opposition letter, http://www.scribd.com/doc/187635747/Letter-in-Opposition-to-the-ASA-s-Proposed-Resolution-on-AcademicBoycott-of-Israeli-Academic-Institutions; ASA Solidarity Letter, http://www.scribd.com/doc/189318253/Solidarity-Letter-by-non-ASA-Member-Americanist-Scholars-in-Opposition-to-the-ASA-s-Proposed-Resolution-on-AcademicBoycott-of-Israeli-Academic-Instit.

69. Rudy Fichtenbaum and Henry Reichman, "Open Letter to Members of the American Studies Association," December 6, 2013, http://www.aaup.org/file/OpenLettertoASA.pdf .

70. "What Does the Academic Boycott Mean for the ASA?" http://www.theasa.net/what_does_the_academic_boycott_mean_for_the_asa/.

71. ASA Former Presidents' Letter, http://www.scribd.com/doc/190932504/Letter-from-ASA-Presidents-in-Opposition-to-Proposed-Boycott-of-Academic-Institutions.

72. Ibid.

73. Patricia Limerick to former ASA presidents, e-mail, December 15, 2013.

74. Anonymous former ASA president to other former ASA presidents, e-mail, December 14, 2013.

75. Linda Kerber to former ASA presidents, e-mail December 13, 2013.

76. Richard Pérez-Peña and Jodi Rudoren, "Boycott by Academic Group Is a Symbolic Sting to Israel," *New York Times,* December 16, 2013.

77. Cynthia Ozick to author, e-mail, December 17, 20/2013.

78. "ACE President Molly Corbett Broad's Statement on Boycotts of Israeli Academic Institutions," 12/29/13, http://www.acenet.edu/news-room/Pages/ACE-President-Molly-Corbett-Broad-Statement-on-Boycotts-of-Israeli-Academic-Institutions.aspx; "APLU Statement in Opposition to Boycott of Israeli Academic Institutions," 1/2/14, http://www.aplu.org/page.aspx?pid=2857; "AAU Statement," https://www.aau.edu/WorkArea/DownloadAsset.aspx?id=14859; AAUP Statement on ASA Vote, http://www.aaup.org/sites/default/files/AAUPStatementASAVote_0.pdf; William A. Jacobson, "List of Universities Rejecting Academic Boycott of Israel (Update—250)," 12/22/13, http://legalinsurrection.com/2013/12/list-of-universities-rejecting-academic-boycott-of-israel/.

79. Ibid., "Catholic U 100th University Rejecting Israel Boycott, in Blistering Statement," *Legal Insurrection*, 1/1/14, http://legalinsurrection.com/2014/01/catholic-u-100th-university-rejecting-israel-boycott-in-blistering-statement/.

80. Ibid., "List of Universities."

81. Jacobson, "California Chapter of ASA Refuses to Apply Anti-Israel Academic Boycott," *Legal Insurrection*, 2/25/14, http://legalinsurrection.com/2014/02/california-chapter-of-asa-refuses-to-apply-anti-israel-academic-boycott/.

82. Michael Frisch to author, e-mail, April 21, 2014.

83. "ASA Increases Membership and Support in Wake of Academic Boycott of Israel Endorsement," April 10, 2014, http://www.theasa.net/from_the_editors/item/american_studies_association_increases_membership_and_support/.

84. Adam Horowitz, "Judith Butler, Rashid Khalidi and Over 150 Other Scholars Condemn Censorship," Intimidation of Israel Critics, Mondoweiss, March 5, 2014, http://mondoweiss.net/2014/03/scholars-censorship-intimidation.html.

85. David Hirsch, "Opposing the Campaign to Exclude Israelis form the Global Community," *Engage*, January 21, 2014, http://engageonline.wordpress.com/page/3/?archives-list=1.

86.   Linda Gordon, Alice Kessler-Harris, and Elaine Tyler May, "Don't Cut Off Debate With Israeli Institutions—Enrich it Instead," *The Chronicle of Higher Education*, December 31, 2013.

DAVID HIRSH NOTES

87.   From the ASA resolution and from the PACBI "call" and "guidelines" which it resolves to endorse and to honor. See appendix for relevant excerpts from the ASA resolution and the PACBI documents to which the resolution refers.

88.   Civil Society is specified because there is no "call" from the official institutions of the Palestinian Authority or from the Presidency or from the PLO. President Mahmoud Abbas told South African journalists in December 2013: "No, we do not support the boycott of Israel." See Yoel Goldman, " Abbas: Don't Boycott Israel," *Times of Israel*, December 13, 2013, http://www.timesofisrael.com/abbas-we-do-not-support-the-boycott-of-israel/

89.   From the ASA resolution and from the PACBI "call" and "guidelines" which it resolves to endorse and to honor. See appendix for relevant excerpts from the ASA resolution and the PACBI documents to which the resolution refers.

90.   Michael Yudkin, "Is an Academic Boycott of Israel Justified?" special issue, *Engage* (2007): http://www.engageonline.org.uk/journal/index.php?journal_id=15&article_id=61

91.   Bencie Woll and Wendie Sandler, "'Sign Language Translator and Interpreter: Another Mona Baker Journal Boycotting Israeli Scholars," *Engage* (blog), August 9, 2007, http://www.engageonline.org.uk/blog/article.php?id=1336

92.   Steve Cohen argued that to require Jews to disavow was itself reminiscent of previous campaigns to exclude Jews. See Steve Cohen, "I Would Hate Myself in the Morning," *Engage* (blog), May 29, 2006, http://www.engageonline.org.uk/blog/article.php?id=444

93.   British Campaign for the Universities of Palestine.

94.   Scottish Palestine Solidarity Campaign.

95.   Jon Pike, "The Myth of the Institutional Boycott," *Engage* (blog), February 13, 2006, http://engageonline.wordpress.com/2013/02/27/the-myth-of-the-institutional-boycott-jon-pike/

96.   Picket lines were set up against Jews outside universities in Nazi Germany; Jewish quotas were still in place in some elite American universities into the 1960s.

97.   "Council Resolution on Boycott of Israeli Academic Institutions," American

Studies Association, last modified December 4, 2013, http://www.theasa.net/american_
studies_association_resolution_on_academic boycott_of_israel

98. "Call for Academic and Cultural Boycott of Israel," Palestinian Campaign for the
Academic and Cultural Boycott of Israel (PACBI), last modified July 6, 2004, http://
pacbi.org/etemplate.php?id=869

99. "Guidelines for Applying the International Academic Boycott of Israel," PACBI,
last modified October 1, 2009, http://www.pacbi.org/etemplate.php?id=1107

CARY NELSON NOTES

100. I want to thank Michael Bérubé, Gabriel Brahm, Sam Fleischacker, Todd Gitlin,
Rachel Harris, Jeffrey Herf, Michael Kotzin, Jonathan Marks, Sonya Michel, Alexis
Pogorelskin, Kenneth Stern, Paula A. Treichler, Ilan Troen, Kenneth Walzer, and the
audience members at February 2014 presentations at Yale University and University of
Minnesota Duluth for their immensely helpful suggestions. An earlier version of this
essay appeared March 16, 2014 *LA Review of Books*, followed by a revised version in *The
Journal for the Study of Antisemtiism*. This version includes further revisions.

101. My review of the Bruce Robbins film appeared in 5:2 2013 issue of the *Journal for
the Study of Antisemitism*.

NANCY KOPPELMAN NOTES

102. Thanks to Steve Blakeslee, John Howard, Andy Koppelman, David Marr, John
McLain, Trevor Speller, and Michael Zimmerman for helpful readings of an earlier draft
of this essay.

103. Examples of earlier efforts include Jesuit education and the founding of land-grant
universities in the 19th century and the emergence of the field of social work during
the late years of the Progressive Era. For contemporary examples, see Campus Compact,
founded in 1985, "a national coalition of more than 1,100 college and university
presidents—representing some 6 million students—who are committed to fulfilling
the civic purposes of higher education," at http://www.compact.org; and the Bringing
Theory to Practice Project of the American Association of Colleges and Universities at
http://www.aacu.org/bringing_theory/index.cfm.

104. W. E. B. DuBois, *The Souls of Black Folk* (1903; repr., Mineola, NY: Dover, 1994),
52-53.

105. Scientists rarely participate in the BDS movement, so the exceptions prove the
rule. When world-renowned theoretical physicist Stephen Hawking announced that he
would not attend the fifth annual Israeli Presidential Conference because Palestinian
colleagues convinced him not to, supporters called it a significant political breakthrough

for precisely this reason. See Isabel Kershner, "Israel: Hawking Joins Academic Boycott," *New York Times*, May 9, 2013.

106. Mark Bauerlein, "Social Constructionism: Philosophy for the Academic Workplace," in *Theory's Empire: An Anthology of Dissent,* ed. Daphne Patai and Will H. Corral (New York, NY: Columbia University Press, 1995), 341-353. See also Nancy Easterlin, "Making Knowledge: Bioepistemology and the Foundations of Literary Theory," 621-35. For more recent interventions into the viral nature of constructionist and contingency theories, see Bruno Latour, "Why Has Critique Run out of Steam? From Matters of Fact to Matters of Concern," *Critical Inquiry* 30 (Winter 2004): 225-248; and Stephen Best and Sharon Marcus, "Surface Reading: An Introduction," *Representations* 108, no. 1 (Fall 2009): 1-21.

107. A most troubling example was the March 2014 conference at New York University entitled "Circuits of Influence: U.S., Israel, and Palestine." At first, Lisa Duggan, current president of the American Studies Association, advertised the conference on Facebook for all the world to see. But when anti-boycott students and colleagues got wind of it and tried to participate, Duggan pulled the Facebook page and backpedaled, working hard to keep the conference under the radar. As the day of the conference drew near, it was clear that it was not academic in nature and careful efforts were made to keep the press out. See "From UCLA to NYU, BDS Supporters Struggle with Dialogue," *New York Observer*, February 27, 2012, http://observer.com/2014/02/from-ucla-to-nyu-bds-supporters-struggle-with-dialogue/. This kind of behavior is an extreme version of the tendency for academics to seek control of conversations about ideas that matter to them. See Burton Bledstein, *The Culture of Professionalism: The Middle Class and the Development of Higher Education in America* (New York, NY: W.W. Norton, 1978).

108. For instructive examples, see Neve Shalom/Wahat al-Salam (the "Oasis of Peace" in Hebrew and Arabic), founded in the 1970s and the only Israeli community where Jews and Palestinians choose to live, work, and raise their children together, at http://www.oasisofpeace.org/; Rabbis for Human Rights, an association founded in 1988 to promote the human rights of marginalized peoples in Israel and Palestine, at http://rhr.org.il/eng/about/; and B'Tselem, founded in 1989 and the most prominent human rights organization in Israel, at http://www.btselem.org/. None of these organizations promotes boycotts. For a practical, long-term effort at decolonization in Kenya, see the Maasai Community Partnership program at Prescott College, at http://www.prescott.edu/learn/campus-community-resources/maasai-community-partnership.html. For an excellent study of the history and complexities of directly alleviating human suffering through humanitarian efforts, see Michael Barnett, *Empire of Humanity: A History of Humanitarianism* (Ithaca, NY: Cornell University Press, 2013).

109. There are too many to list, but a dozen American social history scholars whose work illustrates this insight through a wide range of topics include Nancy Cott, Tom

Dublin, Eugene Genovese, Philip Greven, James Henretta, Rhys Isaac, John Kasson, Michael Merrill, Edmund Morgan, Jonathan Prude, Dan Rodgers, William Rorabaugh, and Susan Strasser.

110. Fernand Braudel, *Afterthoughts on Material Civilization and Capitalism* (Baltimore, MD: Johns Hopkins University Press, 1977); Greg Mullins, "Paradoxes of Neoliberalism and Human Rights" (unpublished manuscript).

111. A popular incarnation of this idea is Francis Fukuyama's argument that the hegemony of neo-liberalism bespeaks an end to many kinds of heretofore intractable political conflicts; *The End of History and the Last Man* (1992; repr., New York, NY: Free Press, 2006).

112. See, for example, "Some say natural disaster was 'divine judgment,'" *The Washington Post*, September 4, 2005, http://www.chron.com/news/hurricanes/article/ Some-say-natural-catastrophe-was-divine-judgment-1938772; "Punish Them for Their Sins," *The Economist*, November 7, 2012, http://www.economist.com/blogs/ pomegranate/2012/11/divine-wrath-and-hurricane-sandy.

113. See Richard White, *"It's Your Misfortune and None of My Own": A New History of the American West* (Norman, OK: University of Oklahoma Press, 1991), 26. For only one example of brutality among legions across centuries and continents, see an account of the seventeenth-century battles among the Iroquois, Algonquians, Huron, Miami, Seneca, and other native peoples of North America, including accounts of torture, cannibalism, slavery, and forced starvation, in Richard White, *The Middle Ground: Indians, Empires, and Republics in the Great Lakes Region*, 1650-1815 (Cambridge, MA: Cambridge University Press, 1991), 1-5.

114. Although many scholars have panned Jared Diamond's work, their criticism says more about the constructionist bent, and particularly its commitment to human agency, than it does about the soundness of Diamond's research and analysis. Diamond offers a challenge that his detractors have yet to take up: integrating a geographical analysis of inequality into a historical understanding of justice. See *Guns, Germs, and Steel: The Fates of Human Societies* (New York, NY: W.W. Norton, 1999).

115. For a fresh perspective about the potential of the human sciences for understanding the human condition, see Wilhelm Dilthey, *Introduction to the Human Sciences, Vol. 1*, ed. Rudolf Makkreel and Frithjof Rodi (1883; repr., Princeton, NJ: Princeton University Press, 1989).

116. For an account of how the early social science disciplines shaped higher education, see Dorothy Ross, *The Origins of American Social Science* (Cambridge, UK: Cambridge University Press, 1990).

117. Immanuel Kant, *Groundwork of the Metaphysics of Morals* (1785; repr., Cambridge, UK: Cambridge University Press, 2012).

118. For a robust attempt to manage this contradiction through scholarship, see Linda Tuhiwai Smith, *Decolonizing Methodologies: Research and Indigenous Peoples* (London, UK: Zed Books, 2012).

119. Lynn Hunt, *Inventing Human Rights: A History* (New York, NY: W.W. Norton, 2007). On *Uncle Tom's Cabin*, see Philip Fisher, *Hard Facts: Setting and Form in the American Novel* (Oxford, UK: Oxford University Press, 1987), 87-127. On sentimental fiction, see Jane Tompkins, *Sensational Designs: The Cultural Work of American Fiction* (Oxford, UK: Oxford University Press, 1986); and Shirley Samuels, ed., *The Culture of Sentiment: Race, Gender, and Sentimentality in 19th Century America* (Oxford, UK: Oxford University Press, 1992).

120. The German philosopher Odo Marquard calls this chronic inability to meet the demands of a rapidly changing world "tachogenic unworldliness"; see *In Defense of the Accidental* (Oxford, UK: Oxford University Press, 1991), 71-90.

121. Elaine Scarry, *Thinking in an Emergency* (New York, NY: W.W. Norton, 2011); Stephen Kern, *The Culture of Time and Space, 1880-1918* (Cambridge, MA: Harvard University Press, 1986), 65-67.

122. Jewish immigration to British-controlled Palestine was illegal during World War II, when the British Mandate restricted Jews from fleeing there. Some survivors of Buchenwald were arrested by the British when they arrived in Palestine in 1945. Nevertheless, over 100,000 Jews managed to travel by boat to Palestine, thereby saving their own lives.

123. Samuel Moyn, *The Last Utopia: Human Rights in History* (Cambridge, MA: Belknap, 2010), pp. 3-4, 231.

124. George Mosse, *Toward the Final Solution: A History of European Racism* (Madison, WI: University of Wisconsin Press, 1985).

125. G. W. F. Hegel, *The Philosophy of History* (1837; repr., Mineola, NY: Dover, 2004), 21.

126. Louis Menand, *The Metaphysical Club: A Story of Ideas in America* (New York: Farrar, Straus and Giroux, 2001), xi-xii.

127. Phillip Ariès, *Centuries of Childhood: A Social History of Family Life* (New York, NY: Vintage, 1965). See also Steven Mintz, *Huck's Raft: A History of American Childhood* (Cambridge, MA: Belknap, 2006), for a generous dose of other scandalous facts about childhood. (Interestingly, Mintz concludes that for generations of children in North America, geography shaped the experience of childhood more than any other factor.)

128. See FN 100. Anecdotal evidence of this habit of mind abounds. For example, in

spring of 2013, I invited a guest speaker from the North American Conference on Ethiopian Jewry to my campus to talk about Ethiopian Jewish immigration to Israel, which began in the 1950s and has accelerated since the 1980s through the efforts of the Israeli government. The talk was supported by the President's Diversity Fund and advertised widely. Faculty who are hostile to the state of Israel broadcast campus-wide email messages to delegitimize the speaker and dissuade people from attending.

BDS academics have been surprised when their own invited speakers don't support the boycott movement. For example, local BDS academics and activists sponsored talks by Yehuda Shaul, Foreign Relations Director of Breaking the Silence, an organization of former IDF soldiers, and Terje Carlsson, Swedish director/producer of the film *Israel vs. Israel*. During each guest's presentation, the audiences discovered that they reject boycotts of Israel, they recognize the legitimacy of the state of Israel, and they are nevertheless highly critical of Israel. These nuances obviously escaped the understanding of the people who planned these events, but may be crevices from which real dialogue and change might develop.

129. Curtis Marez, "In Defense of an Academic Boycott of Israel," *The Chronicle of Higher Education*, December 31, 2013, http://chronicle.com/blogs/conversation/2013/12/31/in-defense-of-an-academic-boycott-of-israel/.

130. F. W. Lancaster and Lorraine Haricombe, "The Academic Boycott of South Africa: Symbolic Gesture or Effective Agent of Change?," *Perspectives on the Professions* 15, no. 1 (Fall 1995).

131. One of the most important criticisms of such compromises was put forth by W. E. B. DuBois, who took Booker T. Washington to task for sacrificing thought in favor of "doing" at the Tuskegee Institute, which Washington helped found and steward for 34 years until his death; see "Of Mr. Booker T. Washington and Others" and "Of the Wings of Atalanta," in *The Souls of Black Folk* (1903; repr., Mineola, NY: Dover, 1994), 36-48, 59-67.

132. See the first three citations in FN 101.

133. Rami Almeghari, "Chomsky In Gaza," *The Electronic Intifada*, October 20, 2012, http://electronicintifada.net/content/chomsky-gaza-academic-boycott-will-strengthen-support-israel/11795; and Jeffrey Blankfort, "Damage Control: Noam Chomsky and the Israel-Palestine Conflict," http://www.leftcurve.org/LC29WebPages/Chomsky.html.

134. "CJPME Interview with Norman Finkelstein" at http://www.cjpme.org/DisplayDocument.aspx?DocumentID=2306&SaveMode=0; and Gabriel Ash, "Norman Finkelstein's Disinformation about BDS," *Mondoweiss*, July 7, 2012 http://mondoweiss.net/2012/07/norman-finkelsteins-disinformation-about-bds.html.

135. Susan Sontag, *Styles of Radical Will* (1969; repr., New York, NY: Picador, 2002), 18.

TAMMI ROSSMAN-BENJAMIN NOTES

136. http://www.amchainitiative.org/academic-boycott-of-israel-map/

137. http://www.theasa.net/american_studies_association_resolution_on_academic_boycott_of_israel

138. http://amchainitiative.us2.list-manage2.com/track/click?u=0beb330b057061522b be22a7f&id=9a76f2fa86&e=af475dce6a

139. http://naisa.org/node/719

140. For example, see: http://pacbi.org/etemplate.php?id=2293

141. For example, see: http://electronicintifada.net/blogs/nora/bds-roundup-new-year-and-new-boycott-campaigns-ahead

142. For example, see: http://www.csun.edu/~vcmth00m/studyabroad.html

143. For example, see: http://boycottzionism.wordpress.com/2010/03/10/a-joint-letter-to-the-international-society-of-iranian-studies-on-ariel-university-of-samaria-israel/

144. For example, see: http://www.insidehighered.com/news/2012/05/31/boycott-kills-u-texas-project-women-writers-middle-east#sthash.0TKAD3wt.dpbs

145. http://www.usacbi.org/mission-statement/

146. http://www.pacbi.org/etemplate.php?id=1801

147. http://archive.adl.org/terrorism/symbols/palestinian_national_islamic_front.html

148. http://www.state.gov/j/ct/rls/other/des/123085.htm

149. http://jcpa.org/article/what-is-the-real-bds-endgame/

150. http://www.usacbi.org/about-us/

151. http://www.amchainitiative.org/organizations-universities-condemned-american-studies-associations-academic-boycott-israel/

152. http://www.amchainitiative.org/wp-content/uploads/2014/02/asa+nyu.jpg

153. http://ethnicstudies.sfsu.edu/content/news-events

154. http://www.amchainitiative.org/wp-content/uploads/2014/01/UCR-Omar-Barghouti-event-announcement.pdf

155. https://www.facebook.com/events/410982679004835/?source=1

156. http://www.amchainitiative.org/wp-content/uploads/2014/04/Petitions-calling-for-academic-boycott.doc

157. In a survey of 21 campuses with English departments that have one or more faculty members who have endorsed the academic boycott of Israel, English faculty made up an average of 5% of the total faculty at any institution, with a low of 1% and a high of 13%.

158. Research activity of all faculty in the English Departments of the following universities was surveyed: Bates College, College of Staten Island, Cornell University, Florida State University, Fordham University, Hofstra University, Indiana University South Bend, Indiana University Bloomington, Michigan State University, Middlebury College, Ohio State University, Pace University, San Jose State University, University of California Davis, University of California Los Angeles, University of Chicago, University of Hawaii, University of Massachusetts Boston, University of Pennsylvania, University of Vermont, West Chester University.

159. http://www.english.ucr.edu/people/faculty/index.html

160. http://www.amchainitiative.org/wp-content/uploads/2014/01/UCR-Omar-Barghouti-event-announcement.pdf

161. http://sca.as.nyu.edu/object/LisaDuggan

162. http://www.amchainitiative.org/wp-content/uploads/2014/02/asa+nyu.jpg

163. http://www.csun.edu/~vcmth00m/

164. http://www.csun.edu/~vcmth00m/studyabroad.html

165. http://www.csun.edu/~vcmth00m/boycott.html

166. https://asa.ucdavis.edu/faculty/sunaina-maira

167. http://mesa.ucdavis.edu/faculty/me-sa-faculty/sunaina-maira

168. https://www.facebook.com/events/410982679004835/?source=1

169. http://www.sfsu.edu/~amed/faculty.html

170. See for instance Abdulhadi's talk at a student-organized conference at University of British Columbia entitled "Return and Liberation" in May 2013, which was attended by some GUPS students: http://www.youtube.com/watch?v=A0vSYbScWAs.

171. http://www.amchainitiative.org/wp-content/uploads/2014/01/Leila-Khaled-GUPS-.jpg

172. http://www.amchainitiative.org/wp-content/uploads/2013/11/GUPS1.jpg

173. http://www.amchainitiative.org/mohammad-g-hammads-tumblr-postings-about-sfsu-professor-rabab-abdulhadi/

174. http://www.amchainitiative.org/mohammad-h-hammads-tumblr-

postings-5713-111013/

175. http://cla.calpoly.edu/hist_foroohar.html

176. http://www.amchainitiative.org/pappe_at_csu/

177. http://www.amchainitiative.org/wp-content/uploads/2014/04/Foroohar-Academic-Senate-Resolution-on-Academic-Freedom-.pdf

178. http://www.jns.org/news-briefs/2012/12/11/bds-linked-professor-to-chair-california-university-anti-sem.html#.UzwRm4WU6Hk

179. http://www.calstate.edu/AcadSen/documents/DRAFT_January_2014_Plenary_Minutes.pdf

180. http://web.international.ucla.edu/cnes/person/61

181. http://normanfinkelstein.com/2009/another-important-initiative/

182. http://cascholars4academicfreedom.wordpress.com/about/

183. See for example: http://cascholars4academicfreedom.wordpress.com/2014/03/13/letter-to-dr-leslie-wong-president-sfsu-re-amcha-letter/ and http://cascholars4academicfreedom.wordpress.com/2013/09/26/letter-to-president-of-sdsu-re-ghassan-zakaria/

184. http://cascholars4academicfreedom.wordpress.com/2012/08/14/letter-to-uc-president-yudof-regarding-campus-climate-report-on-situation-of-jewish-muslim-and-arab-students/

185. http://cascholars4academicfreedom.wordpress.com/2012/09/24/an-open-letter-from-california-scholars-for-academic-freedom-to-california-assemblymembers-linda-halderman-bonnie-lowenthal-and-66-co-authors-of-california-house-resolution-35/

186. http://cascholars4academicfreedom.wordpress.com/2014/01/09/letter-to-chancellor-white-re-response-to-asa-resolution/

187. http://ethnicstudies.sfsu.edu/home3

188. http://www.albany.edu/womensstudies/ws-mission.shtml

189. See: http://www.soc.ucsb.edu/graduate-studies

190. http://www.asianam.illinois.edu/about/

191. http://www.international.ucla.edu/person.asp?Facultystaff_ID=61

192. www.universityofcalifornia.edu/regents/policies/6065.html

193. http://law.onecle.com/california/government/8314.html

194. http://www.dhr.ny.gov/law#296

195. http://www.bis.doc.gov/index.php/enforcement/oac

196. See note 7 (Introduction) for an alternative view [Editor's note].

197. See: www.nas.org/images/documents/A_Crisis_of_Competence.pdf

198. http://pulsemedia.org/2009/01/19/open-letter-to-obama/

199. https://docs.google.com/spreadsheet/viewform?formkey=dERVMFdtcGR4UG5L
N045ZFJQTnlLa1E6MA#gid=0

200. http://www.jadaliyya.com/pages/index/5010/debating-palestine_representation-
resistance-and-l

201. http://laborforpalestine.net/2011/07/14/u-s-trade-union-statement-in-support-
of-palestinian-call-for-full-and-immediate-arms-embargo-against-apartheid-israel/

202. http://boycottzionism.wordpress.com/category/international-bds-actions/page/29

203. http://www.al-awda.org/pou.html

204. http://www.al-awda.org/geneva.html

205. https://www.facebook.com/note.php?note_id=295686450465836

206. http://electronicintifada.net/content/why-americans-should-oppose-
zionism/9003

SAMUEL AND CAROL EDELMAN NOTES

207. Statistics collected by the Israel on Campus Coalition.

208. Transcriptions of the conference from audio recordings provided to the authors by audience members.

209. Fern Oppenheim et al., "American Views of Israel: The Great Divide & How To Overcome It," Applied Marketing Report summary, July 31, 2011. Unpublished report.

210. Josh Nathan-Kazis, "Survey of Campus BDS Finds Few Serious Cases," *The Forward*, May 4, 2011, http://forward.com/articles/137518/survey-of-campus-bds-finds-few-serious-cases/#ixzz30EMT88hi.

211. Students for Justice in Palestine—UC San Diego's Twitter page, accessed May 2, 2014, https://twitter.com/sjpucsd; Students for Justice in Palestine—UC San Diego's Facebook page, accessed May 2, 2014, https://www.facebook.com/sjpucsd.

212. "UC San Diego Response to AS Council Resolution on Divestment," last modified March 14, 2013, http://ucsdnews.ucsd.edu/pressrelease/uc_san_diego_

response_to_as_council_resolution_on_divestment.

213. Oberlin College Students for a Free Palestine's Facebook page, accessed May 2, 2014, https://www.facebook.com/pages/Oberlin-Students-for-a-Free-Palestine/296899357104981; Oberlin College Students for a Free Palestine's Twitter page, accessed May 2, 2014, https://twitter.com/OberlinSFP.

214. Ed Wittenberg, "Oberlin College Rabbi Downplays Impact of Divestment Resolution," *Cleveland Jewish News*, May 7, 2013, http://www.clevelandjewishnews.com/news/local/article_5e71bbc0-b777-11e2-b41b-0019bb2963f4.html.

215. Randall L. Bytwerk, *Julius Streicher: The Man Who Persuaded a Nation to Hate Jews* (New York: Stein and Day, 1983), 22-26.

KENNETH MARCUS NOTES

216. The author benefited from comments by the editors, Doron Ben-Atar, and participants in the Indiana University Institute conference on "Deciphering the New Antisemitism." Nevertheless, fault for any remaining errors remains with the author.

217. Kenneth L. Marcus, *The Definition of Anti-Semitism* (Oxford: Oxford University Press, forthcoming). This forthcoming volume provides the source for much of the analysis in this chapter.

218. David Hirsh, "Accusations of Malicious Intent in Debates about the Palestine-Israel Conflict and about Antisemitism: The Livingstone Formulation, 'Playing the Antisemitism Card' and Contesting the Boundaries of Antiracist Discourse," *Transversal* 1 (2010): 47-76; Lesley Klaff, "Political and Legal Judgment: Misuses of the Holocaust in the UK," *Journal for the Study of Antisemitism* 5, no. 1 (2013): 45, 53-54.

219. Hannah Arendt, *The Origins of Totalitarianism* (New York: Schocken, 2004), 21-25.

220. Walter Laqueur, *The Changing Face of Anti-Semitism: From Ancient Times to the Present Day* (Oxford, U.K.: Oxford University Press, 2006), 71-89.

221. Ibid., 73.

222. Theodor Herzl, *Der Judenstaat*, trans. Sylvie d'Avigdor (New York: Dover Publications, 1882), Kindle edition.

223. "Boycott of Jewish Businesses," *Holocaust Encyclopedia*, http://www.ushmm.org/wlc/en/article.php?ModuleId=10005678. Although the boycott was officially called for three days, April 1-3, 1933, the boycott is generally associated with the events of April 1.

224. Lucy S. Dawidowicz, *The War Against the Jews: 1933-1945* (New York: Bantam, 1986), 52.

225. "Boycott of Jewish Businesses," *Holocaust Encyclopedia.*

226. Harold Brackman, *Boycott Divestment Sanctions (BDS) Against Israel: An Anti-Semitic, Anti-Peace Poison Pill* (Los Angeles: Simon Wiesenthal Center, 2013), http://www.wiesenthal.com/atf/cf/%7B54d385e6-f1b9-4e9f-8e94-890c3e6dd277%7D/REPORT_313.PDF

227. "Boycott of Jewish Businesses," *Holocaust Encyclopedia.*

228. Laqueur, *The Changing Face*, 108-109.

229. On the connections between Nazis propaganda and the modern ideologies of the Middle East, see Matthias Küntzel, *Jihad and Jew-Hatred: Islamism, Nazism, and the Roots of 9/11*, trans. Colin Meade (New York: Telos, 2009); Paul Berman, *The Flight of the Intellectuals* (New York: Melville House, 2011).

230. Jeffrey Herf, *Nazi Propaganda for the Arab World* (New Haven: Yale University Press, 2009).

231. Ibid., 13.

232. Barry Rubin and Wolfgang G. Schwanitz, *Nazis, Islamists, and the Making of the Modern Middle East* (New Haven: Yale University Press, 2014). Moreover, new research indicates that German foreign policy towards the Middle East continued to bear the imprint of Nazi ideology during the Cold War era. Ulricke Becker, "Post War Antisemitism: Germany's Foreign Policy Toward Egypt," in *Global Antisemitism: A Crisis of Modernity* ed. Charles Asher Small (Leiden, The Netherlands: Brill, 2013), 283-296.

233. Mitchell Bard, "Arab League Boycott: Background & Overview," Jewish Virtual Library, last modified September 2007, http://www.jewishvirtuallibrary.org/jsource/History/Arab_boycott.html.

234. Ibid.

235. Rubin and Schwanitz, *Nazis, Islamists*, 246.

236. Martin A. Weiss, *Arab League Boycott of Israel* (Washington, D.C.: Congressional Research Service, 2013), http://www.fas.org/sgp/crs/mideast/RL33961.pdf.

237. Klaus-Michael Mallmann and Martin Cüppers, *Nazi Palestine: The Plans for the Extermination of the Jews in Palestine*, trans. Krista Smith (New York: Enigma Books, 2005), 211.

238. Bernard Lewis, *Semites & Anti-Semites* (New York: W.W. Norton, 1986), 223-224.

239. Ibid., 224-226.

240. Weiss, *Arab League Boycott*, 3.

241. Alan Baker and Adam Shay, "Manipulation and Deception: The Anti-Israel 'BDS' Campaign (Boycott, Divestment, and Sanctions)," *Jerusalem Issue Briefs*, Vol. 12, No. 2 http://jcpa.org/article/manipulation-and-deception-the-anti-israel-bds-campaign-boycott-divestment-and-sanctions/#sthash.y5wtaqkC.dpuf.

242. Brackman, *Boycott Divestment Sanctions*, 9.

243. Mitchell G. Bard and Jeff Dawson, *Israel and the Campus: The Real Story* (Chevy Chase, MD: The American-Israeli Cooperative Enterprise, 2012), 16.

244. Brackman, *Boycott Divestment Sanctions*, 9.

245. "Palestinian Civil Society Calls for Boycott, Divestment and Sanctions against Israel Until it Complies with International Law and Universal Principles of Human Rights," last modified July 9, 2005, http://www.bdsmovement.net/call.

246. Ibid.

247. Abraham H. Foxman, "An Open Letter on Academic Freedom and University Responsibility," *Commentary*, February 2013, http://www.commentarymagazine.com/wp-content/uploads/2013/02/adlletterbds.pdf.

248. Natan Sharansky, "Anti-Semitism in 3D," *Jerusalem Post*, February 23, 2004, http://www.foiwa.org.au/sites/default/files/pdf/Anti-Semitism-in-3D.pdf; Natan Sharansky, "3D Test of Anti-Semitism: Demonization, Double Standards, Delegitimization," *Jewish Political Studies Review*, 16 (Fall 2004): 3-4, http://jcpa.org/phas/phas-sharansky-f04.htm.

249. "Statement of Jewish Organizations on Boycott, Divestment and Sanctions (BDS) Campaigns Against Israel," *Jewish Virtual Library*, http://www.jewishvirtuallibrary.org/jsource/IsraelonCampusReport2012.pdf.

250. Kenneth L. Marcus, "Anti-Zionism as Racism: Campus Anti-Semitism and the Civil Rights Act of 1964," *William and Mary Bill of Rights* 15, no. 3 (February 2007): 837-891.

251. Sina Arnold, "Antisemitism and the Contemporary American Left: An Uneasy Relationship," (paper presented at "Deciphering the 'New' Antisemitism," Institute for Contemporary Antisemitism, Indiana University at Bloomington, April 2014).

252. European Union Monitoring Center, "Manifestations of Antisemitism in the EU 2002–2003" (Vienna: European Union Agency for Fundamental Rights, 2004), http://fra.europa.eu/sites/default/files/fra_uploads/184-AS-Main-report.pdf.

253. Charles Y. Glock and Rodney Stark, *Christian Beliefs and Anti-Semitism* (New York: Harper & Row, 1966), 102.

254. These examples are drawn from reports that Jewish university students have

recently made to attorneys at the Louis D. Brandeis Center for Human Rights Under Law (www.brandeiscenter.com).

255. Hannah Weisfeld, "When BDS And Anti-Semitism Meet," *The Daily Beast*, December 14, 2012, http://www.thedailybeast.com/articles/2012/12/14/when-bds-and-anti-semitism-meet.html. It should be noted that the Palestine Solidarity Campaign issued a statement in opposition to the incident that Weisfeld reported.

256. Steven K. Baum, *Antisemitism Explained* (Lanham, MD: University Press of America, 2012), 160-161.

257. Ibid.

258. Florette Cohen, Lee Jussim, Gautam Bhasin, and Elizabeth Salib, "The Modern Anti-Semitism Israel Model: An Empirical Relationship Between Modern Anti-Semitism and Opposition to Israel," *Conflict & Communication Online* 10 (2011):1; Florette Cohen, Lee Jussim, Kent D. Harber, and Gautam Bhasin, "Modern Anti-Semitism and Anti-Israel Attitudes," *Journal of Personality and Social Psychology* 97 (2009): 290-306.

259. Edward H. Kaplan and Charles A. Small, "Anti-Israel Sentiment Predicts Anti-Semitism in Europe," *Journal of Conflict Resolution* 50 (2006): 548-561.

260. Steven K. Baum and Masato Nakazaw, "Antisemitism and Anti-Israeli Sentiment," *Journal of Religion & Society* 9 (2007) 1:9; Steven K. Baum, "Christian and Muslim Antisemitism," *Journal of Contemporary Religion* 23 (2009): 77-86.

261. Günther Jikeli, "Discrimination Against Muslims and Antisemitic Views Among Young Muslims in Europe," Papers on Antisemitism and Racism, last modified February 2013, http://www.kantorcenter.tau.ac.il/sites/default/files/jikeli.pdf, citing Andreas Zick and Beate Küpper, "Traditioneller Und Moderner Antisemitismus" Bundeszentrale für politische Bildung, last modified November 28, 2006, http://www.bpb.de/politik/extremismus/antisemitismus/37967/traditioneller-und-moderner-antisemitismus?p=all.

262. NGO Monitor, "Antisemitic Ideology," http://www.ngo-monitor.org/article/antisemitic_theology.

263. Judith Butler, *Parting Ways: Jewishness and the Critique of Zionism* (New York: Columbia University Press, 2012), 116.

264. Bernard Harrison, *The Resurgence of Antisemitism* (Lanham, MD: Rowman & Littlefield, 2006), 108.

265. Ibid.

266. Omar Barghouti, "Why Israel Fears the Boycott," *The New York Times*, Jan. 31, 2014.

267. Judith Butler, "Remarks to Brooklyn College on BDS," *The Nation*, Feb. 7, 2013. For a more detailed response to Butler, see Cary Nelson, "The Problem with Judith Butler: The Political Philosophy of the Movement to Boycott Israel," *Los Angeles Review of Books*, March 16, 2014, https://lareviewofbooks.org/essay/problem-judith-butler-political-philosophy-movement-boycott-israel. Nelson's essay is substantially revised and expanded in the present volume.

268. Hernandez-Montiel v. INS, 225 F.3d 1084, 1093 (9th Cir. 2000).

269. "FAQs," U.S. Campaign for the Academic Boycott of Israel (USACBI), http://www.usacbi.org/faqs/.

270. Others take the opposite approach, charging the Jewish community with a failure to engage in self-criticism.

271. Emanuele Ottolenghi, "Present-day Antisemitism and the Centrality of the Jewish Alibi," in Alvin H. Rosenfeld, *Resurgent Antisemitism: Global Perspectives* (Bloomington, IN: Indiana University Press, 2013), 425.

272. Yitzak Santis and Gerald M. Steinberg, "On 'Jew-Washing' and BDS: How Jewish anti-Israel activists are gaining influence among Christian groups," *The Jewish Week*, July 24, 2012, http://www.thejewishweek.com/editorial-opinion/opinion/jew-washing-and-bds.

273. Arye L. Hillman, "Economic and Behavioral Foundations of Prejudice," in *Global Antisemitism: A Crisis of Modernity*, ed. Charles Asher Small (Leiden, The Netherlands: Brill, 2013), 62.

274. Shulamit Volkov, "Readjusting Cultural Codes: Reflections on Anti-Semitism and Anti-Zionism," *Journal of Israeli History: Politics, Society, Culture* 25, no. 1 (2006): 51-62.

275. Arnold, "Contemporary American Left."

276. Sander Gilman, *Jewish Self-Hatred: Anti-Semitism and the Hidden Language of the Jews* (Baltimore: Johns Hopkins University Press, 1986).

277. Anthony Julius, *Trials of the Diaspora: A History of Antisemitism in England* (Oxford: Oxford University Press, 2010), 67.

278. Gordon Allport, *The Nature of Prejudice* (New York: Doubleday, 1958), 147.

279. Robert S. Wistrich, *A Lethal Obsession: Anti-Semitism from Antiquity to the Global Jihad* (New York: Random House, 2010), 515.

280. Gilman, *Self-Hatred*, 2.

281. Julius, *Trials*, 34.

282. Léon Poliakov, *The History of Anti-Semitism*, vol. 1, *From the Time of Christ to the Court Jews,* trans. Richard Howard (New York: Vanguard, 1974), 52.

283. Julius, *Trials*, 34-37.

284. Gilman, *Self-Hatred*, 391.

ALAN JOHNSON NOTES

285. Louis Althusser and Etienne Balibar, *Reading Capital* (London: Verso, 1970) p.141.

286. Ilan Pappe, "Two lectures by the Israeli historian Ilan Pappe, Part 1, recorded at the University of Amsterdam," (Stan Van Houcke Audioblog, 2007). Accessed March 12, 2014. http://www.stanvanhoucke.net/audioblog/lectures/Ilan%20Pappe%201.mp3

287. YouTube, "BDS Bullies at NUI Galway." Accessed March 12, 2014. http://www.youtube.com/watch?v=1gkiGUBAM7g

288. Alan Johnson, "BDS bullies at Galway University". *Times of Israel* (blog), March 10, 2014, accessed April 24, 2014. http://blogs.timesofisrael.com/bds-bullies-at-galway-university/ and Alan Johnson, "On Israel, the intellectuals are driving the students mad," *The Daily Telegraph* (blog), 13 March, 2014. Accessed April 24, 2014. http://blogs.telegraph.co.uk/news/alanjohnson/100263386/on-israel-the-intellectuals-are-driving-the-students-mad/

289. Louis Althusser, *Philosophy of the Encounter: Later Writings, 1978-1987.* (London: Verso, 2006), 281.

290. As a down-payment, this much can be said here. The Boycott Divestment and Sanctions (BDS) movement, and other anti-Israel organizing efforts and practices, are central to the process of attracting individuals to the AZI and forming the individual's subjectivity and identity *in the terms of the ideology*—"interpellating" them, to use Althusser's term. If an individual is to embrace the ideology and its practices, and so become subjectivized, then he must "identify with an 'other' who is his peer [*semblable*]" until he "recognises himself as existing through the existence of the other and through his identification with him." Subjectivity is constructed in ideology, but ideology is, in turn, "inseparable from the institutions by means of which it is manifested, with their codes, languages, customs, rites and ceremonies." See Althusser, *Encounter*, 283-4.

291. Althusser, *Encounter*, 283.

292. Distinct ideologies, thought Althusser, have a history of their own. The AZI certainly does. It has developed in waves—Jewish, Arab, Old Left, New Left, Islamist, and today's mélange. To grasp each in its specificity we will need the resources of (something like) Gaston Bachelard's concept of "historical epistemology" as well as an intimate knowledge of the two shaping social contexts of each wave—first, the relation of the

wave to wider social structures; what Althusser called the "historical relations (both theoretical, ideological and social) in which it produces" and, second, the "practico-social function" that the ideology performed in that given society at that given moment. (See Gregory Elliot, *The Detour of Theory*, 97.) The goal of this essay is much more modest: to begin the work of mapping contemporary left-wing academic anti-Zionism.

293. See the discussion in Gregory Elliot, *Althusser: The Detour of Theory* (London: Verso, 1987), 99.

294. Ilan Pappé, *The Idea of Israel: A History of Power and Knowledge* (London: Verso, 2014), 75.

295. Pappé, *Israel*, 125.

296. Pappé, *Israel*, 78.

297. Yitzhak Laor, *The Myths of Liberal Zionism* (London: Verso, 2009), 100, 109.

298. Jacqueline Rose, *The Last Resistance* (London: Verso, 2007), 44-45.

299. 'Foreword' to Laor, *Myths*, vii.

300. Ilan Pappé, in Noam Chomsky and Ilan Pappé. *Gaza in Crisis: Reflections on Israel's War Against the Palestinians* (London: Penguin, 2010), 58-9, 61, 65.

301. Pappé, *Two Lectures*.

302. Elliott, *Althusser*, 131.

303. David Hirsh, "Rebels Against Zion," *Fathom Journal* 5 (2014), 68. http://www.fathomjournal.org/reviews-culture/rebels-against-zion/

304. Pappé, *Israel*, 10.

305. Quoted in Rose, *Resistance*, 194.

306. Gianni Vattimo and Michael Warder, ed. *Deconstructing Zionism: A Critique of Political Metaphysics* (London: Bloomsbury, 2014), xvi.

307. Hirsh, "Rebels," 68-69.

308. Steve Cohen, *That's Funny, You Don't Look Anti-Semitic.* (London: Beyond the Pale Collective, 1984). http://www.engageonline.org.uk/ressources/funny/contents.html Accessed April 24, 2014.

309. Norman Geras, "Alibi Antisemitism," *Fathom* 2 (2013). Accessed April 24, 2014. http://www.fathomjournal.org/policy-politics/alibi-antisemitism/

310. Moishe Postone, "Zionism, anti-semitism and the left: an interview with Moishe Postone," Workers' *Liberty*, 5 February, 2010. Accessed April 24, 2014. http://www.

workersliberty.org/story/2010/02/05/zionism-anti-semitism-and-left

311. Elliott, *Althusser*, 153.

312. Elliott, *Althusser*, 125.

313. Elliott, *Althusser*, 100.

314. Isaac Deutscher, *The Non-Jewish Jew and Other Essays* (London: Merlin Press, 1981).

315. Ariella Azoulay and Adi Ophir. *The One-State Condition: Occupation and Democracy in Israel/Palestine*. Translated by Tal Haran (Stanford: Stanford University Press, 2013), 261.

316. Rose, *Resistance*, 200-201.

317. Shlomo Sand, *The Words and the Land: Israeli Intellectuals and the Nationalist Myth*. (Los Angeles: Semiotext(e), 2011), 107.

318. Sternhell, "Defence," 62.

319. See the exchange in *Democratiya* between Shalom Lappin and Jacqueline Rose. Shalom Lappin, "The Question of Zion," *Democratiya* 6 (2006): 11-36. http://www. dissentmagazine.org/democratiya_article/the-question-of-zion; Jacqueline Rose, "The Question of Zion: A Reply to Shalom Lappin," *Democratiya* 7 (2006): 94-115, http://www.dissentmagazine.org/democratiya_article/a-question-of-zion-a-reply-to-shalom-lappin; Shalom Lappin, "A Question of Zion: A Rejoinder to Jacqueline Rose," *Democratiya* 7 (2006). Accessed April 24, 2014. http://www.dissentmagazine.org/democratiya_article/a-question-of-zion-a-rejoinder-to-jacqueline-rose

320. Rose, *Resistance,* 53-54, 55-56, 217-18.

321. John J. Mearsheimer and Stephen M. Walt, *The Israel Lobby and US Foreign Policy* (London, Penguin, 2007) 229-262.

322. Robert Fine, "The Lobby: Mearsheimer and Walt's conspiracy theory," *Engage* (blog), 21 March 2006. Accessed 24 April 2014. http://www.engageonline.org.uk/blog/article.php?id=310 and Walter Russell Mead, "Jerusalem Syndrome: Decoding The Israel Lobby", *Foreign Affairs*, November/December 2007. http://www.foreignaffairs.com/articles/63029/walter-russell-mead/jerusalem-syndrome

323. Pappé, *Israel*, 118.

324. Pappé in Chomsky and Pappé, Gaza 35. Note what is being claimed. Although America was the victor of World War Two, a superpower on the threshold of "The American Century," it nonetheless "succumbed to the power" of the Jews. And this just three years after six million of the said Jews had been murdered in Europe. In what terms can we possibly understand such a power?

325. Pappé in Chomsky and Pappe, *Gaza*, 41.

326. Quoted in Alan Johnson, "Parting Ways" *Fathom* 2, (2013), 71. http://www. fathomjournal.org/reviews-culture/parting-ways/ Accessed April 24, 2014.

327. Pappé, *Israel*, 43, 47, 127, 132.

328. Norman G. Finkelstein, *Image and Reality of the Israel-Palestine Conflict* (London: Verso, 1995), 2-3.

329. Sand, *Words*, 35, 43, 65, 42.

330. Tikva Honig-Parnass, *False Prophets of Peace: Liberal Zionism and the Struggle for Palestine* (Chicago: Haymarket Books, 2011), 49.

331. Laor , *Myths*, 47, 71, 55, 57, 97.

332. Vattimo, *Deconstruction*, 15.

333. David Hirsh, *Anti-Zionism and Antisemitism: Cosmopolitan Reflections.* Working Paper (Yale Initiative for the Interdisciplinary Study of Antisemitism, Yale University, 2007), 20, 27.

334. Laor, *Myths*, 130-31.

335. Omar Barghouti, "A Secular Democratic State in Historic Palestine: Self-Determination through Ethical Decolonisation" in Anthony Loewenstein and Ahmed Moor, eds., *After Zionism: One State for Israel and Palestine* (London: Saqi Books, 2012), 195.

336. Yehouda Shenhav, *Beyond the Two State Solution: A Jewish Political Essay* (Cambridge: Polity Press, 2012), 21, 181.n51, 191.n76, 48, 84, 3.

337. Lesley Klaff, "Holocaust Inversion," *Fathom* 5, 2014. Accessed April 24, 2014. http://www.fathomjournal.org/policy-politics/holocaust-inversion/

338. Lesley Klaff, "Political and Legal Judgment: Misuses of the Holocaust in the UK," Social Science Research Network, 8 May 2013. http://papers.ssrn.com/sol3/papers. cfm?abstract_id=2284423

339. Chomsky, in Chomsky and Pappé, *Gaza*, 8.

340. Rose, *Resistance*, 131. Rose's claim is completely false. Israeli Prime Minister Rabin condemned Goldstein unequivocally: "You are not part of the community of Israel . . . You are not part of the national democratic camp which we all belong to in this house, and many of the people despise you. You are not partners in the Zionist enterprise. You are a foreign implant. You are an errant weed. Sensible Judaism spits you out. You placed yourself outside the wall of Jewish law . . . We say to this horrible man and those like

him: you are a shame on Zionism and an embarrassment to Judaism." As for the shrine that extremists built for Goldstein, it was demolished by . . . the IDF.

341. Shenhav, *Beyond*, 99.

342. Honig-Parnass, *Prophets*, 9.

343. Sand, *Words*, 167.

344. For a critique of the work of Lenni Brenner, see Gerry Ben-Noah, "Brenner on the Nazi Massacre" and John O'Mahony, "Lenni Brenner's Fake Internationalism," both in *Arabs, Jews and Socialism* (London: Alliance for Workers Liberty, 1993), 37-38, 52-54. http://www.workersliberty.org/system/files/Arabs%20Jews%20and%20 Socialism-04072011125617.pdf.

345. Rose, *Resistance*, 47.

346. Hazem Saghiyeh and Saleh Bashir, "Universalizing the Holocaust: How Arabs and Palestinians relate to the Holocaust and how the Jews relate to the Palestinian victim," *Palestine-Israel Journal*, Vol.5 Nos. 3 & 4, 1998.

347. Pappe, *Israel*, 177, 166.

348. Vattimo, *Deconstructing*, 21.

349. Sternhell, "Zionism," 111.

350. Lucy Winkett, "Bethlehem Unwrapped is about 'beautiful resistance' not taking sides," *Guardian Comment is Free*, 2 January 2014. http://www.theguardian.com/ commentisfree/2014/jan/02/bethlehem-unwrapped-not-taking-sides-israel-security-wall. See also Alan Johnson "This barrier stops fascists: A response to Bethlehem unwrapped," *The Times of Israel* (blog), 8 January 2014. http://blogs.timesofisrael.com/ this-barrier-stops-fascists-a-response-to-bethlehem-unwrapped/.

351. Laor, *Myths*, 126.

352. Shenhav, *Beyond*, 113. About the PLO's insistence that "not one Israeli" will remain in a new Palestinian state there is another symptomatic AZI silence.

353. Steve Cohen, *That's Funny, You Don't Look Antisemitic. An Anti-Racist Analysis of Left Antisemitism* (Manchester: Beyond the Pale Collective, 1987) Accessed on 24 April 24, 2014. http://www.engageonline.org.uk/ressources/funny/contents.html.

354. Quoted in Pappe, *Israel*, 134.

355. Honig-Parnass, *Prophets*, 9.

356. Rose, *Resistance*, 50.

357. Pappé, *Israel,* 182.

358. I adapt the dichotomy from Rosalind Sydie, *Natural Women / Cultured Men: A Feminist Perspective on Sociological Theory* (New York: NYU Press, 1994).

359. Hirsh, *Anti-Zionism*, 9. Material factors boosted the appeal of reactionary anti-imperialism, including Israeli collusion with the UK and France (during the Algerian War) at Suez; the emergence of two super-power backed blocs in the Middle East, with Israel in the western camp and the radical Arab states in the Soviet camp; the political alignment of radical Arab states with the radical post-colonial Arab states, and with the southern African liberation movements; the creation of a second wave of Palestinian refugees in 1967 and the election of a right wing Israeli government a decade later. Thanks to Dave Rich for discussion on this point.

360. Alan Johnson, "More Palestinian than the Palestinians," *World Affairs* (blog) 16 October 2012. http://www.worldaffairsjournal.org/blog/alan-johnson/judith-butler-more-palestinian-palestinians.

361. Pascal Bruckner, *The Tyranny of Guilt: An Essay on Western Masochism* (Princeton: Princeton University Press, 2010), 6, 13, 2, 60-2.

362. Laor, *Myths*, 65.

363. Honig-Parnass, *Prophets*, 49.

364. Rose, *Resistance*, 135.

365. Shenhav, *Beyond*, 121, 122, 136.

366. Pappé, *Israel,* 138.

367. Pappé, *Israel*, 176.

368. Sand, *Words*.

369. Pappé, in Chomsky and Pappé, *Gaza*, 82.

370. Honig-Parnass, *Prophets*, 212.

371. Laor, *Myths*, 42-43.

372. Rose, *Resistance*, 167.

373. Jean Bethke Elshtain, *Just War Against Terror: The Burden of American Power in a Violent World* (New York: Basic Books, 2004).

374. Rose, *Resistance*, 11.

375. Sand, *Words*, 76-77.

376. "To critique Zionism is not . . . anti-Semitic," objects Jacqueline Rose. The objection is intellectually lazy, refusing the labor of discernment that would establish when anti-Zionism is, and when it *is not*, antisemitic. (Another symptomatic AZI evasion.) A few lines after her imperious fiat, Rose tells us that "the task of criticism is to be able to make distinctions." *Resistance*, 195.

377. Pappé, *Israel*, 37, 175-6.

378. Christopher Mayhew, a civil servant who worked closely with Bevin, confided to his diary in May 1948: "Must make a note about Ernest's anti-semitism . . . There is no doubt in my mind that Ernest detests Jews. He makes the odd wisecrack about the "Chosen People"; explains Shinwell away as a Jew; declares the Old Testament is the most immoral book ever written . . . He says they taught Hitler the technique of terror—and were even now paralleling the Nazis in Palestine."

379. Pappé, *Israel*, 74-75.

380. Pappé, *Israel*, 188-89.

381. Azoulay and Ophir, *One-State*, 256.

382. Postone, "Zionism."

383. Alan Johnson, "What a one-state solution really means," *The Jewish Chronicle*, 17 October 2012. http://www.thejc.com/comment-and-debate/comment/86919/what-a-one-state-solution-really-means.

384. Rose, *Resistance,* 44.

385. Omar Barghouti "A Secular Democratic State in Historic Palestine: Self-Determination through Ethical Decolonisation," in *After Zionism: One State for Israel and Palestine*, edited by Anthony Lowenstein and Ahmed Moor (London: Saqi Books, 2012), 198.

386. Ali Abunimeh, "ICAHD endorses one-state solution, warns against 'warehousing' of Palestinians," *The Electronic Intifada* (blog), 14 September 2012.

387. http://electronicintifada.net/blogs/ali-abunimah/icahd-endorses-one-state-solution-warns-against-warehousing-palestinians

388. Sternhell, "Zionism," 114.

389. Shenhav, *Beyond*, 9.

390. Saree Makdisi, "The Power of Narrative: Reimagining the Palestinian Struggle," in *After Zionism: One State for Israel and Palestine*, edited by Anthony Lowenstein and Ahmed Moor (London: Saqi Books, 2012), 96-97.

391. Butler, "The End of Oslo."

392. Adam Shatz, "Is Palestine Next?" *The London Review of Books*, 14 July 2011, http://www.lrb.co.uk/v33/n14/adam-shatz/is-palestine-next

393. Benny Morris, "The Liar as Hero," *The New Republic*, March 17, 2011. http://www.newrepublic.com/article/books/magazine/85344/ilan-pappe-sloppy-dishonest-historian.

394. Saree Makdisi "Narrative," in *After Zionism: One State for Israel and Palestine*, edited by Anthony Lowenstein and Ahmed Moor (London: Saqi Books, 2012) 90.

395. Honig-Parnass, *Prophets*, 211, 77.

396. Chomsky, in Chomsky and Pappé, *Gaza*, 9.

397. Makdisi, "Narrative," 93.

398. Pappé, in Chomsky and Pappe, *Gaza*, 72.

399. Shenhav, *Beyond,* 193.

400. Azoulay and Ophir, *One-State*, 247.

401. Judith Butler, *Parting Ways: Jewishness and the Critique of Zionism* (New York: Columbia University Press, 2012), 208, 16.

402. Azoulay and Ophir, *One-State*, 263-4.

403. Shenhav, *Beyond*, 34, 38.

404. Honig-Parnass, *Prophets*, 211-212.

405. Hirsh, *Anti-Zionism*. See also his "Hostility to Israel and Antisemitism: Toward a Sociological Approach," *Journal for the Study of Antisemitism* 5, 1401-1422.

406. Vattimo, *Deconstructing*, 19-20.

DAVID CAPLAN NOTES

407. Derek Walcott, *Collected Poems: 1948-1984* (New York, Farrar, Straus, and Giroux, 1986), 17.

408. Sharon Olds, *The Unswept Room* (New York: Alfred A. Knopf, 2002), 61.

409. Sharon Olds, *Satan Says* (Pittsburgh: University of Pittsburgh Press, 1980), 7.

410. Vivian Gornick, "Saul Bellow, Philip Roth, and the End of the Jew as Metaphor," in *The Men in My Life* (Cambridge, MA: MIT Press, 2008), 85-129.

411. As will be clear, I take my title from Berryman's story, not Alain Finkielkraut's book

that shares the same title, though some of its concerns intersect with those my essays explores. See Alain Finkielkraut, *The Imaginary Jew*, trans. Kevin O'Neill and David Suchoff (Lincoln, NE: University of Nebraska Press, 1994).

412. John Berryman, *Recovery/Delusions, Etc.*, 248.

413. Berryman, *Recovery/Delusions, Etc.*, 251.

414. Nat Hentoff, *Boston Boy* (New York: Alfred A. Knopf, 1986), 16-17.

415. Berryman, *Recovery/Delusions, Etc.*, 252.

416. See Andrew Gross, "Imaginary Jews and True Confessions: Ethnicity, Lyricism, and John Berryman's *Dream Songs*," *Journal of Transnational American Studies* 1, no. 1 (2009): E1

417. See Eileen Simpson, *Poets in Their Youth: A Memoir* (New York: Vintage Books, 1983) 165.

418. R. P. Blackmur, "The Jew in Search of a Son: Joyce's Ulysses," *Virginia Quarterly Review* 24 (January 1948): 96-116; reprinted in *Eleven Essays in the European Novel* (New York: Harcourt, Brace, and World, 1964), 39.

419. Anne Sexton, *The Selected Poems of Anne Sexton*, ed. Diane Wood Middlebrook and Diane Hume George (New York: Mariner Books, 2000), 5 and Sylvia Plath, *Ariel* (New York: HarperCollins, 1999), 57.

420. For two retrospective perspectives on this issue, see Helen Vendler, *Last Looks, Last Books: Stevens, Plath, Lowell, Bishop, Merrill* (Princeton, NJ: Princeton University Press, 2010), 50-53 and Adam Kirsch, *The Wounded Surgeon: Confession and Transformation in Six American Poets* (New York: W. W. Norton and Company, 2005), 267-268.

421. Jeffrey Meyers, ed., *Robert Lowell: Interviews and Memoirs* (Ann Arbor, MI: University of Michigan, 1988), 94.

422. Ian Hamilton, *Robert Lowell: A Biography* (New York: Random House, 1982), 5.

423. Robert Lowell, *Life Studies and For the Union Dead* (New York: Farrar. Straus, and Giroux, 1989), 11.

424. Berryman, *Recovery/Delusions, Etc.*, 240, 241.

425. John Berryman, "The Art of Poetry," interview by Peter A. Stitt, *The Paris Review*, 1972, http://www.theparisreview.org/interviews/4052/the-art-of-poetry-no-16-john-berryman.

426. Tess Gallagher, *Dear Ghosts* (Saint Paul, MN: Graywolf Press, 2006), 41.

427. Paul Fussell, *Poetic Meter and Poetic Form* (New York: McGraw-Hill College, 1979), 81.

428. Sherman Alexie, *The Summer of Black Widows* (Brooklyn: Hanging Loose Press, 1996), 117.

429. Alexie, *The Summer of Black Widows*, 117.

430. Ibid, 121.

431. Ibid, 54.

432. Randall Jarrell, *Selected Poems*, ed. William Pritchard (New York: Farrar, Straus and Giroux, 1990), 23.

433. Ibid, 24.

434. "[B]y the late sixties," Leslie Fiedler notes, "Jewish-American writers had ceased to seem central." See Leslie Fiedler, *Fiedler on the Roof: Essays on Literature and Jewish Identity* (Boston: David R. Godine, 1991), xii.

435. Terry Eagleton, *Reason, Faith, and Revolution: Reflections on the God Debate* (New Haven, CT: Yale University Press, 2010), 3.

436. Terry Eagleton, "Occupy London are True Followers of Jesus, Even if They Despise Religion," *Guardian*, November 3, 2011, http://www.theguardian.com/commentisfree/belief/2011/nov/03/occupy-london-jesus-religion

Later in the article, Eagleton does refer to Karl Marx as "a later Jewish prophet," although this reference barely disguises the article's anti-Jewish animus.

437. See Robert Michael, *A Concise History of American Antisemitism* (New York: Rowman & Littlefield Publishers, 2005), 180.

438. Chris Elliott, "The Readers' Editor on… Averting Accusations of Antisemitism," *Guardian*, November 6, 2011, http://www.theguardian.com/commentisfree/2011/nov/06/averting-accusations-of-antisemitism-guardian

439. Terry Eagleton, *After Theory* (New York: Basic Books, 2004), 147.

440. Eagleton, *Reason, Faith, and Revolution*, 23-24.

441. In another example of Eagleton drawing a parallel to associate Jews with Wall Street, Eagleton observes, "So it is that those who cannot conceive of an end to Wall Street are perfectly capable of believing in Kabbalah." See Terry Eagleton, *Culture and the Death of God* (New Haven, CT: Yale University Press, 2014), 191.

442. Elliott, "The Readers' Editor on… Averting Accusations of Antisemitism."

443. Jonathan Franzen, *Freedom* (New York: Farrar, Straus, and Giroux, 2010), 265. For two considerations of this passage, see Marc Tracy, "A Quibble With a Magnificent Novel," *Tablet*, August 25, 2010, http://www.tabletmag.com/scroll/43539/a-quibble-

with-a-magnificent-novel# and Adam Kirsch, "Jonathan Franzen, the Iraq War, and Leo Strauss," *New Republic*, September 22, 2010, http://www.newrepublic.com/blog/foreign-policy/77838/jonathan-franzen-the-iraq-war-and-leo-strauss.

444. Franzen, *Freedom*, 266.

445. Ibid, 266-277.

446. Ibid, 270.

447. T.S. Eliot, *Collected Poems: 1909-1935* (New York: Harcourt, Brace, and World, 1971), 21. For an overview of Pound's anti-Semitism, including vivid examples, see Alex Houen, "Pound and Anti-Semitism," in *Ezra Pound in Context*, ed. Ira Nadel (Cambridge: Cambridge University Press, 2010), 391-401.

448. Edward Said, *Power, Politics, and Culture: Interviews with Edward Said*, ed. Gauri Viswanathan (New York: Pantheon Books, 2001), 458.

RICHARD LANDES NOTES

449. A serious examination of the validity of the accusations used by BDS advocates against Israel would probably find over 85-90% of them either untrue or seriously distorted.

450. Landes, *Heaven on Earth: The Varieties of the Millennial Experience* (New York: Oxford, 2011), chaps. 7 (Taiping), 11 (Communism) and 12 (Nazism). Estimates for deaths resulting from Soviet and Maoist efforts to complete the "revolution" range from 50 to over 100 million dead, Jean-Louis Panné et al., *The Black Book of Communism* (Cambridge MA: Harvard University Press, 1999).

451. Ironically, for all the calls "to listen to what the 'terrorists' [sic] have to say," pronounced by open-minded Westerners (here, Neal Ascherson, "September 11," *London Review of Books*, 23:19 [October, 2001]; http://www.lrb.co.uk/v23/n19/nine-eleven-writers/11-september), this call has served mostly as an occasion to project one's own critiques of America onto the Jihadis. Most people, especially on the GPL, have no idea what the 'terrorists' have to say. See, e.g., Ross Caputi, "The Vicious Cycle of Jihadism and Patriotism," *Common Dreams*, May 2, 2012; https://www.commondreams.org/view/2012/05/02-1. This is true on the "right" as well as the "left", Dinesh D'Souza, *The Enemy at Home: The Cultural Left and its Responsibility for 9-11* (New York: Doubleday, 2007).

452. The following discussion is based on the following works on the apocalyptic dimension of Islam in the current period: Timothy Furnish, *Holiest Wars: Islamic Mahdis, Their Jihads, and Osama bin Laden* (New York: Praeger, 2005); Laurent Murawiec, *The Mind of Jihad* (New York: Oxford, 2006); David Cook, *Contemporary Muslim Apocalyptic*

Literature (Syracuse: Syracuse University Press, 2008); Landes, *Heaven on Earth*, chap. 14; Jean Pierre Filiu, *Apocalypse in Islam* (Los Angeles: University of California Press, 2011).

453. *Dar al Islam* means the land/realm of submission to Allah, i.e., lands where Muslims rule and Sharia governs the lives of both Muslims and *Dhimmi* ("protected" infidels); *Dar al Harb* means the land/realm of the sword, i.e., the land of war, where *Kufar* (infidels) are independent (*harbi* = inhabitants of Dar al Harb, destined to the sword). Although these concepts and their view of the world are already implied in many Qur'anic surahs and hadith, they only become formalized in the writings of al-Hanafi, in the early 2nd century of Islam (8th century CE). Despite ups and downs throughout Muslim history, Jihadis have revived them in our day.

454. For a recent case of Jihadis imposing the dhimma contract on kufar, see the case in Northern Syria: Mark Mouvsesian, "In Syria, the Dhimma Returns," *First Things,* March 2014; http://www.firstthings.com/blogs/firstthoughts/2014/03/in-syria-the-dhimma-returns.

455. The words of Bassem Jarrar, Palestinian apocalyptic writer, immensely popular with Hamas, on Yusef al Qaradawi's website, cited in Dore Gold, *The Fight for Jerusalem: Radical Islam, the West and the Future of the Holy City* (Washington DC: Regnery, 2007), p. 237.

456. Role of women in "signs of the end," see Cook, *Contemporary Muslim Apocalyptic*, 52-54. For a current example, see the writings of Imran Nazar Hosein, "Ten Major Signs of the Last Day—Has One Just Occurred," http://www.imranhosein.org/articles/signs-of-the-last-day/76-ten-major-signs-of-the-last-day-has-one-just-occurred.html.

457. H. Abd al-Hamid, 1996, 64; Cook, *Contemporary Muslim Apocalyptic*, 199-20. Cook points out how modern Muslim apocalyptic literature borrows extensively from Christian apocalyptic literature from the Bible to Hal Lindsay.

458. Arif, Nihayat al-Yahud, 85, cited in Cook, *Contemporary Muslim Apocalyptic*, 220.

459. For the best description of this apocalyptic matrix for shahidah, see Anne-Marie Oliver and Paul Steinberg, *The Road to Martyrs' Square: A Journey into the World of the Suicide Bomber* (New York: Oxford University Press, 2005).

460. Hamas MP Al-Astal, March 6, 2014, on the Hamas-owned Al-Aqsa TV, broadcasting from Gaza, MEMRI translation; http://www.memri.org/clip_transcript/en/4202.htm.

461. "Islam is the religion that will dominate over all others," Quran Tafsir Ibn Kathir: http://www.qtafsir.com/index.php?option=com_content&task=view&id=2563&Itemid=64. Not all Muslims believe this, and still fewer believe that dominion should come about through violent imposition, but it is unquestionably a belief within Islam, and lies

at the heart of the current Muslim millennial dream: global Sharia. The belief that there is no such thing as an innocent infidel, and that terrorism can legitimately target infidel civilians, derives from this teaching of absolute superiority. See Anjem Choudhary in response to the BBC's Steven Sackur's attempt to get a condemnation from him of the London 7-7 bombings: "Look, at the end of the day, when we say 'innocent people' we mean Muslims. As far as non-Muslims are concerned they have not accepted Islam and as far as we are concerned that is a crime against God"; http://keeptonyblairforpm. wordpress.com/2008/09/09/transcript-anjem-choudary-hardtalk-interview-77-london-bombings/#transcript.

462. In the period just before the "conversion" of the Roman Empire to Christianity, one of the major ideologues of that development, Eusebius of Caesaria, wrote a book called *Praeparatio Evangelici*, the preparation of the Gospels, in which he argued that the Roman Empire, traditionally viewed as an apocalyptic enemy (The Whore of Babylon), was actually, unwittingly, the vehicle for the spread of Christianity: its 'global' imposition of 'peace' allowed the salvific message to spread to the four corners of the world, and set up the Christian take-over of the very empire that persecuted it. On the notion of hostile outside forces proving to be vehicles for one's own redemptive movement, see Sefi Rachlevsky, *Hamoro shel Meshiach* [Messiah's Donkey] (Tel Aviv: Yediot Aharonot, 1998), where he analyzes both Rav Kook's attitude towards secular Zionism, and Christian premillennialists' view of Jewish Zionism.

463. Cook, *Contemporary Muslim Apocalyptic*, 49-58.

464. Cook, *Contemporary Muslim Apocalyptic*, chap. 2, 9 (Israel) and chap. 7 (U.S.).

465. For a tragic example, see the case of the Xhosa "cattle slayers," in Landes, *Heaven on Earth*, chap. 4.

466. Yusuf al-Qaradawi, Speech at Muslim Arab Youth Association, Toledo, Ohio, 1995; http://www.investigativeproject.org/profile/167. On Da'wa, a term most Westerners do not know, see David Bukay, "Islamic Da'wah for Dummies," *American Center for Democracy*, March 5, 2014; http://acdemocracy.org/islamic-dawah-for-dummies/. See also, McCarthy, *The Grand Jihad*, chap. 5.

467. Landes, "From Useful Idiot to Useful Infidel: Meditations on the Folly of 21st Century 'Intellectuals,'" in *Intellectuals and Terror: the Fatal Attraction*, ed. Anna Geifman and Helena Rimon, special issue of the journal *Terrorism and Political Violence*, 25:4 (2013): 621-34.

468. In the following discussion, I will refer in this essay to the broad range of groups that engage in apocalyptic Jihad, whether overt or covert, as the Global Jihadi Right (GJR), since their values correspond closely to what we in the West consider extreme "right-wing" tendencies—killing, domination, hatred and contempt for the "other". In

the same vein, I refer to the Global Progressive Left (GPL) to designate that cluster of progressive groups who treasure the opposite values—nurturing, egalitarian freedoms, empathy for and openness to the "other."

469. Most of the documentation of this alliance is profoundly hostile to it (understandably), and too easily dismissed by progressives as "right-wing." Whatever one feels about the conclusions, however painful the material and occasionally grating some of the rhetoric, these studies are important to read for their extensive documentation. See David Horowitz, *Unholy Alliance: Radical Islam and the American Left* (Washington DC: Regnery, 2004); Jamie Glazov, *United in Hate: The Left's Romance with Tyranny and Terror* (New York: WND Books, 2009); Andrew McCarthy, *The Grand Jihad: How Islam and the Left Sabotage America* (Encounter Books, 2010); Richard Cravatts, *Genocidal Liberalism: The University's Jihad Against Israel & Jews* (Shermon Oaks, CA: David Horowitz Freedom Center, 2012).

470. Landes, "Final Battle," *Tablet Magazine*, August 21, 2011; http://www.tabletmag. com/news-and-politics/76511/final-battle/.

471. Jean Baudrillard, "The Spirit of Terrorism," *Le Monde*, November 2, 2001 (tr. Rachel Bloul (http://www.egs.edu/faculty/baudrillard/baudrillard-the-spirit-of-terrorism.html). Richard Wolin, "September 11 and the Self-Castigating Left," *South Central Review* 19 (Summer, 2002), pp. 39-49. John Miller, "When terrorist response is justified—an interview with Osama Bin Laden"; http://www.justresponse.net/Bin_Laden3.html.

472. See, for example, the series of responses to 9-11 in the *London Review of Books*, summed up by one reader as "America had it coming." "11 September," Vol. 23 No. 19 · 4 October 2001; http://www.lrb.co.uk/v23/n19/nine-eleven-writers/11-september. Olivier Roy argued that Bin Laden "Islamized a latent anti-Americanism," cited in *Taguieff, Nouvelle judéophobie*, p. 116, n. 185.

473. The literature on Anti-Americanism is vast, in particular since 2000. For a good bibliography, see Keith Beattie and Ian Gordon, "Anti-Americanism: Recent Sources," *Australasian Journal Of American Studies*, 2004; http://www.anzasa.arts.usyd.edu.au/a.j.a.s/Articles/2_03/Beattie%20Gordon.pdf. See also Andre Markovics, *Uncouth Nation* (Princeton University Press, 2007). Recent sober reflection by John Loyd, "How anti-Americanism betrays the left," *The Guardian* (March 16, 2014); http://www.theguardian.com/politics/2002/mar/17/world.comment.

474. The tale of Western "left" conspiracy-thinking about 9-11 is long and complex. On the spread of the Protocols analog thinking, see Chip Berlet, "Protocols to the Left, Protocols to the Right: Conspiracism in American Political Discourse at the turn of the Second Millennium," in *Paranoid Apocalypse: A Hundred Year Retrospective on The Protocols of the Elders of Zion*, ed. Richard Landes and Steven Katz (New York: NYU Press, 2011),

chap. 14; more broadly, Landes, "Jews as Contested Ground in Post-Modern Conspiracy Theory," *Jewish Political Studies Review*, Vol. 19:3-4 (2007): 9-34.

475. *The Workers Revolutionary Party* remarked, "Another banner on the march proclaimed 'We are Hamas', demonstrating the mass support for the elected Palestinian government in Gaza by both the Palestinian people and people all over the world."; http://www.wrp.org.uk/news/3873; and by George Galloway: https://www.youtube.com/watch?v=pJcclllxeEU. Speakers on the podium shouted, "Victory to Hamas!" to rounds of applause: Peter Tatchell, *Guardian*, February 18, 2009; http://www.theguardian.com/commentisfree/2009/feb/18/hamas-palestine-israel-human-rights.

476. Norman Cohn, *Warrant for Genocide: The Myth of the Jewish World Conspiracy and the Protocols of the Elders of Zion* (Oxford: Oxford University Press, 1970), 14; cited by Nick Cohen, *What's Left? How Liberals Lost their Way* (London: Fourth Estate, 2007), 17. For an excellent analysis of the moral disorientation of the "anti-war" rally of 2003, see Cohen's discussion, *What's Left?*, chap. 7.

477. "The Jews whom the Messiah [Jesus] will kill on that day are those who come with the Antichrist… at that time al-Aqsa Mosque will be in the hands of the Muslims and Jerusalem will be the capital of the Caliphate, all of which is incompatible with the present situation." *Hawwa*, 1985, 6:3041; Cook, *Contemporary Muslim Apocalyptic*, 111-12.

478. Stephanie Gutman, *The Other War: Israelis, Palestinians and the Struggle for Media Supremacy* (New York: Encounter Books, 2005); Landes, "Meditations on Reutersgate: What's Going on in the Media," *Augean Stables*, August 10, 2006; http://www.theaugeanstables.com/2006/08/10/meditations-on-reutersgate-whats-going-on-in-the-msm/; Landes, "Lethal Journalism and Al Durah Journalism," http://aldurah.com/lethal-journalism/.

479. Early examples of secular replacement theology arise within the context of Soviet-Palestinian coordination: Joel S. Fishman, "The Big Lie And The Media War Against Israel: From Inversion Of The Truth To Inversion Of Reality," *Jewish Political Studies Review* 19:1-2 (Spring 5767/2007); http://www.danielpipes.org/rr/4465.php; Robert Wistrich, *From Ambivalence to Betrayal: The Left, the Jews, and Israel* (Lincoln, University of Nebraska Press, 2013), chap. 14.

480. During the Israeli siege of southern Beirut in 1982, *Newsweek* compared Beirut to the Warsaw Ghetto, Joshua Muravchik, "Misreporting Lebanon," *Policy Review*, 23 (Winter 1983): 14.

481. This is not the place to explore the extensive evidence that this scene was staged, hence pure war propaganda, and the role of journalists in not only spreading it but resisting any criticism as an infringement on the "freedom of the press." For evidence, see Aldurah Project: http://aldurah.com/the-al-durah-incident/the-evidence/; for lethal

journalism, see http://aldurah.com/lethal-journalism/.

482. No single piece of evidence better illustrates the gap between the principles of Western and Palestinian journalism than the response of the news editor responsible for this "editing": "it's an artistic way to tell the truth, and we never forget our journalistic commitment to tell the truth and nothing but the truth"; http://youtu. be/E2xHB35umcU. Some Western "progressives" defended this "higher truth," see Jeff Weintraub's critique: "The Truth of Mohammed al-Dura—If iconic imagery makes for powerful propaganda, should we treat questions of historical truth or falsehood as irrelevant?" May 20, 2013; http://jeffweintraub.blogspot.co.il/2013/05/the-truth-of-mohammed-al-dura-if-iconic.html.

483. *Messages to the World: The Statements of Osama bin Laden*, ed. Bruce Lawrence (London: Verso, 2005), 147-8. The brackets fill in the gaps between reality and dream state so easily jumped over by apocalyptic thinkers. The core of the blood libel, whether a ritual murder done in secret or a murder done by armed soldiers in public, is the claim that this story is part of a larger project of mass murder.

484. Sheikh Ibrahim Madhi at the Sheikh 'Ijlin Mosque in Gaza City, broadcast live on April 12, 2002, PA TV.

485. See Dore Gold, "Jerusalem as Launching Pad for Future Global Jihadism," *Fight for Jerusalem*, 239-43.

486. Pierre Andre Taguieff, *Rising from the Muck: The New Anti-Semitism in Europe* (Chicago: Ivan Dee, 2004); Shmuel Trigano, "Les juifs de France visés par l'Intifada?" *Observatoire du monde juif*, 1 (November 2000); http://obs.monde.juif.free.fr/pdf/omj01. pdf, and subsequent issues treating various aspects of the phenomenon.

487. After a decade of lethal journalism, almost half the population of Germany and Great Britain believes that Israel is committing genocide against the Palestinians: *Intolerance, Prejudice and Discrimination: A European Report* (Forum Berlin, 2011), 57; http://library.fes.de/pdf-files/do/07908-20110311.pdf.

488. Farhad Khosrokhavar, *Quand Al-Qaïda parle: Témoignages derrière les barreaux* (Paris: Grasset & Fasquelle, 2006). A large body of Muslims in the diaspora "alienated and alone, bonded over a feeling of Muslim victimhood as observed on television and in pictures of wars involving Muslims." Marc Sageman, *Understanding Terror Networks* (Philadelphia: Penn Press, 2005), chap. 3. See also: "Identification with the traumas of others and secondary traumatization occurring by 'witnessing,' over the internet or television, vivid images of injustices enacted on others with whom one identifies as fictive kin, (i.e. the brotherhood of Muslims) may also resonate with individual feelings of being disaffected." Anne Speckhard, "Understanding Suicide Terrorism: Countering Human Bombs and Their Senders" in *Topics in Terrorism: Toward a Transatlantic Consensus on the Nature of*

the Threat" (Volume I), Eds. Jason S. Purcell & Joshua D. Weintraub Atlantic Council Publication, 2005 [http://www.uwmc.uwc.edu/alumni/news_items/speckhard/uanderstanding%20_suicide.pdf].

489. Gerald Steinberg, "The Durban Strategy," *Jerusalem Post*, September 11, 2005; http://www.ngo-monitor.org/article/_the_durban_strategy.

490. Gerald Steinberg, "The Centrality of NGOs in the Durban Strategy," *Yale Israel Journal*, Summer, 2006; http://www.ngo-monitor.org/article/_the_centrality_of_ngos_in_the_durban_strategy.

491. Among the many examples, Adam Kredo, "Pro-Israel Students Called 'Kike,' 'Dirty Jew' at University of Michigan," *Washington Free Beacon*, March 24, 2014; http://freebeacon.com/issues/pro-israel-students-called-kike-dirty-jew-at-university-of-michigan/.

492. Douglas Davis, "The BBC is quickly becoming one of the world's 'kosher' purveyors of hate," *Jewish World Review*, July 24, 2002; http://www.jewishworldreview.com/0702/davis_bbc.html.

493. Most recently, David Nirenberg, *Anti-Judaism: The Western Tradition* (New York: W.W. Norton, 2013).

494. Robin Shepherd, *A State Beyond the Pale: Europe's Problem With Israel* (London: Orion Books, 2009).

495. For a list of such intimidating tactics on campus, see "A Toxic Campus Environment," *BDS Cookbook*, http://www.stopbds.com/?page_id=4. The response has been to invoke academic freedom and accuse those who object to these tactics as racists and censors.

496. "The reason the BDS strategy should be tried against Israel [i.e. first] is practical: in a country so small and trade-dependent, it could actually work." Klein, "Israel: Boycott, Divest, Sanction."

497. Sander Gillman, *Jewish Self-Hatred* (Baltimore: Johns Hopkins University Press, 1986); Barry Rubin, *Assimilation and Its Discontents* (New York: Times Books, 1995), chap. 6. See also Robert Wistrich, *From Ambivalence to Betrayal*.

498. *Alter-Juif*, ed. Trigano; also known as "asajew", or "Theobald Jew" (for the Jewish convert who first promoted the blood libel in 12th century England); see "*The Guardian's* anti-Israel Jews, and a letter to my teenage nephew," CiF Watch, August 11, 2010; http://cifwatch.com/2010/08/11/the-guardians-anti-israel-jews-and-a-letter-to-my-teenage-nephew/. For the prominent role of such anti-Zionist Jews in promoting BDS, see Gerald Steinberg and Yitzak Santis, "On Jew-Washing and BDS," *The Jewish Week*, July 24, 2012; http://www.thejewishweek.com/editorial-opinion/opinion/jew-

washing-and-bds.

499. For a description of this at work, see the sardonic novel of Jacobson, *The Finkler Question* (London: Bloomsbury, 2010); and more analytically in Nidra Poller, *Al Dura: Long Range Ballistic Myth* (Paris: authorship international, 2014).

500. See the remarkable case of Alain Finkielkraut who had the nerve to question the orthodoxy that the riots of 2005 had *nothing* to do with Islam: "Finkielkraut's Plain Talk On Race," *New York Sun*, November 29, 2005; http://www.nysun.com/opinion/finkielkrauts-plain-talk-on-race/23689/.

501. On the controversy concerning Butler and the Adorno Prize in 2012, see Landes, "Judith Butler and the Adorno Prize: A Preliminary Annotated Bibliography," *Augean Stables*, September 13, 2012: http://www.theaugeanstables.com/2012/09/13/judith-butler-and-the-adorno-prize-a-preliminary-annotated-bibliography/. See also climate-change activist Naomi Klein, endorser of BDS, "Israel: Boycott, Divest, Sanction," *The Nation*, January 26, 2009; http://www.thenation.com/article/israel-boycott-divest-sanction.

502. For a critique of "tikkun olam," see Landes, "Does Burston really think it's legitimate to view BDS as Tikkun Olam?" *Augean Stables*, December 18, 2010: http://www.theaugeanstables.com/2010/12/18/does-burston-really-think-its-legitimate-to-view-bds-as-tikkun-olam/. A good illustration of this phenomenon is the "Jewish Voice for Peace" (http://jewishvoiceforpeace.org/), prominent proponents of BDS.

503. Note that while these critics of Israel invoke their role as modern-day prophets, they do what no prophet would have done, which is take their scathing criticism of their own people, itself a form of flagellating rhetoric (you are as bad as Sodom), and publish it among their people's enemies. For a good discussion of the phenomenon and its effects, see Alvin Rosenfeld, "Progressive Jewish Thought and the New Anti-Semitism." AJC, NY, 2006; http://www.ajc.org/atf/cf/%7B42D75369-D582-4380-8395-D25925B85EAF%7D/PROGRESSIVE_JEWISH_THOUGHT.PDF); for a critique of the liberals who attacked Rosenfeld and defended the radicals, see Landes, "Jewish Hypercritics of Israel Criticized: How Dare You?" *Augean Stables*, February 1, 2007; http://www.theaugeanstables.com/2007/02/01/jewish-hypercritics-of-israel-criticized-how-dare-you/.

504. One of the more interesting cases of this phenomenon is Phillip Weiss, one of the most prolific injection points of lethal narratives about Israel into the public sphere. Having witnessed the behavior of the BDS supporters at Vassar, he wrote: "No, the spirit of that young progressive space was that Israel is a blot on civilization, and boycott is right and necessary," Weiss, "Ululating at Vassar: the Israel/Palestine conflict comes to America," *Mondoweiss*, March 20, 2014; http://mondoweiss.net/2014/03/ululating-israelpalestine-conflict.html.

ILAN TROEN NOTES

505. Nancy Turck, "Arab Boycott of Israel," *Foreign Affairs* 55, no. 3 (April 1977): 472-493.

506. "Arab League Boycott: Background and Overview," last modified September, 2007, http://www.jewishvirtuallibrary.org/jsource/History/Arab_boycott.html.

507. An excellent review of UNGA Resolution 2279 is found in Gil Troy, *Moynihan's Moment; America's Fight Against Zionism as Racism* (Oxford University Press: New York, 2013).

508. http://unispal.un.org/UNISPAL.NSF/0/2FCA2C68106F11AB05256BCF007BF 3CB.

See article 4: "An appropriate Jewish agency shall be recognized as a public body for the purpose of advising and co-operating with the Administration of Palestine in such economic, social and other matters as may affect the establishment of the Jewish national home and the interests of the Jewish population in Palestine, and, subject always to the control of the Administration, to assist and take part in the development of the country…"

509. Boaz Neumann, *Land and Desire in Early Zionism* (University Press of New England: Waltham, MA, 2011).

510. The term "imagined communities" derives from Benedict Anderson, *Imagined Communities: Reflections on the Origins and Spread of Nationalism* (Verso: New York, 1991). My understanding of the relevance of this term for the Zionist experience is found in S. Ilan Troen, *Imagining Zion; Dreams, Designs, and Realities in a Century of Jewish Settlement* (Yale University Press: New Haven, 2003), pp. 141-162.

511. The historical background for changing the names into Hebrew as well as a criticism of the practice may be found in Meron Benvenisti, *Sacred Landscape: The Buried History of the Holy Land Since 1948* (Berkeley, CA: University of California Press, 2000). A more favorable appreciation as well as additional information may be found in Imanu el Hare uveni, *Yi ra el : ha-yishuvim e-atare ati otehem*. [The Settlements of Israel and Their Archaeological Sites](Givatayim-Ramat Gan: Masadeh, 1979)(Hebrew) and Ze'ev Vilnay, *ha-Yishuvim be-Yi ra el : arukhim be-seder alef-bet be-li yat tsiyurim e-tarshimim*. [The Settlements in Israel] (Hebrew) (Tel-Aviv, 1951).

512. George Antonius, *The Arab Awakening: The Story of the Arab National Movement* (Simon Publications: New York: 1939).

513. Nathan Rotenstreich, "The Revival of the Fossil Remnant: Or Toynbee and Jewish Nationalism," *Jewish Social Studies* 24, no. 3 (July 1962): 131-143.

514. Edward Said, *Culture and Imperialism* (Vintage: New York, 1993). This trope was

first espoused to enthusiastic acclaim in his *Orientalism* (Vintage: New York, 1978) and is reiterated in his many writings.

515. Edward Said, *Blaming the Victims: Spurious Scholarship and the Palestine Question* (Verso: New York, 2001), 235.

516. Ivan Davidson Kalmar and Derek J. Penslar, eds., *Orientalism and the Jews* (University Press of New England: Hanover, NH, 2005).

517. Naim Ateek, *Justice and Only Justice: A Palestinian Theology of Liberation* (Orbis Books: Maryknoll, NY: 1989). Ateek not only removes Jews from the ancient past and dispenses with their claims in the Christian era, he erases them from much of Palestine. See his description of his birthplace, Beit Shean, where the presence of Jews in that town and, most importantly, in the proximate region is ignored. For him, Palestine is a land in which there are but Christians and Muslims. *Idem*. pp. 7 and ff. For the ongoing infiltration of this stream of Liberation Theology into mainline American Protestantism see Lazar Berman, "Presbyterian Church Group: Zionism is the Problem," *Times of Israel*, February 11, 2014. http://www.timesofisrael.com/presbyterian-church-group-zionism-is-theproblem/?utm_source=The+Times+of+Israel+Daily+Edition&utm_campaign=97a135d5b3-2014_02_11&utm_medium=email&utm_term=0_adb46cec92-97a135d5b3-54589553.

518. Leading works of this school include Thomas L. Thompson, *Early History of the Israelite People from the Written and Archaeological Sources* (Brill Academic Publishers: Leiden, 1992) and Philip Davies, *In Search of Ancient Israel* (T&T Clark: Sheffield, 1992). A perceptive review and criticism of this scholarship is found in Marc Brettler, "The Copenhagen School: The Historiographical Issues," *Association for Jewish Studies Review* 27 (2003): 1-21.

519. Keith Whitlam, *The Invention of Ancient Israel: The Silencing of Palestinian History* (Routledge: London, 1996), 3-4 and 225.

520. S. Ilan Troen, *Imagining Zion; dreams, designs and realities in a century of Jewish settlement* (Yale University Press: New Haven, 2003), ch. 3.

521. Gershon Shafir, *Land, Labor, and the Origins of the Israeli-Palestinian Conflict, 1882-1914* (Berkeley, CA: University of California Press, 1989).

522. Dennis K. Fieldhouse, *The Colonial Empires: A Comparative Survey from the Eighteenth Century* (Weidenfeld and Nicolson: London, 1966).

523. John. A. Hobson, *Imperialism: A Study* (J. Nisbet: London, 1902) and V. I. Lenin, *Imperialism, the Highest Stage of Capitalism: A Popular Outline* (International Publishers: New York, trans., 1939). Unlike Hobson and Lenin, Fieldhouse does not view European colonial expansion as the latest stage of the capitalist revolution. Nor does he believe

Europe or capitalism will collapse after de-colonization.

524. See Barch Kimmerling, *Zionism and Territory: The Socio-Territorial Dimensions of Zionist Politics* (Berkeley, CA: University of California Press, 1983); Simon Schama, *Two Rothschilds and the Land of Israel* (Knopf: New York, 1978); and Ran Aaronsohn, "Settlement in Eretz Israel—A Colonialist Enterprise? 'Critical' Scholarship and Historical Geography," *Israel Studies*, 1:2 (Fall 1996), 214-229.

525. Fieldhouse, *The Colonial Empires*, 239 and 250.

526. Ibid, 318.

527. National Committee for the Heads of the Arab Local Authorities, "The Future Vision of the Palestinian Arabs in Israel," *Electronic Intifada*, last modified January 12, 2007, http://electronicintifada.net/content/future-vision-palestinian-arabs-israel/3054

528. Havatzelet Yahel, Ruth Kark, and Seth J. Frantzman, "Are the Negev Bedouin an Indigenous People?" *Middle East Quarterly* (Summer 2012): 3-14; Seth Frantzman, "The Politicization of History and the Negev Land Claims: A Review Essay on Indigenous (In)justice," *Israel Studies* 19, no. 1 (2014): 48-74.

529. See for example "Apartheid, Colonisation, and Occupation," BDS Movement, http://www.bdsmovement.net/apartheid-colonisation-occupation

RACHEL HARRIS NOTES

An earlier version of this article was published in the *Journal of Jewish Identities*. With thanks to Phyllis Lassner and Adriana X. Jacobs for their helpful comments. Unless otherwise noted, translations are by the author.

530. Sammy Smooha concluded that in 1980 (the decade that Kashua was in school and Sikseck was born), "over 75% of [Arab citizens of Israel] were born, reared, and educated in Israel, thereby shaped by the realities of Israeli society." Sammy Smooha, *The Orientation and Politicization of the Arab Minority in Israel*, Monograph Series on the Middle East, No. 2 (Haifa: Institute of Middle East Studies, Haifa University, 1984), 7.

531. Lital Levy, "Exchanging Words: Thematizations of Translation in Arabic Writing from Israel," *Comparative Studies of South Asia, Africa and the Middle East* 23, no. 1 and 2 (2003): 106–127, 107.

532. This essay examines characters who are Arab-Israeli, Jewish-Israeli, and Palestinian. I have avoided using the term "Palestinian" for Arab citizens in Israel (or Palestinians of '48), and have instead used "Arab-Israeli" or Israeli Arab to avoid confusion when referring to those living within Israel's borders and who have Israeli citizenship by contrast with those living in Gaza, the West Bank, or elsewhere, to whom I refer as "Palestinians."

533. Hannan Hever and Orin D. Gensler, "Hebrew in an Israeli Arab Hand: Six Miniatures on Anton Shammas's *Arabesques*," in "The Nature and Context of Minority Discourse," ed. Abdul R Jan Mohamed and David Lloyd, special issue, *Cultural Critique* 7 (1987): 47–76, 74, 76. Published in Hebrew as 'Ivrit Be'hoshet 'arati Shisha Prakim 'al arabsekot Me-et Anton Shammas' *Te-oriya U-vikoret* 1 (Summer 1991): 23–38.

534. Gilles Deleuze and Felix Guattari, *Kafka: Toward a Minor Literature*, trans. Dana Polan (Minneapolis: University of Minnesota Press, 1986).

535. Na'im Araidi, "Sifrut 'Ivrit Ma Na'amt'" *Moznayim* 65, no. 4 (1991): 41; Ami Elad-Bouskila, *Modern Palestinian Literature and Culture* (London: Frank Cass, 1999); Rachel Feldhay Brenner, "The Search for Identity in Israeli Arab Fiction: Atallah Mansour, Emile Habiby, and Anton Shammas," *Israel Studies* 6, no. 3 (2001): 91–112, 103–104; Mahmoud Kayyal, "Arabs Dancing in a New Light of Arabesques: Minor Hebrew Works of Palestinian Authors in the Eyes of Critics," *Middle Eastern Literatures* 11, no. 1 (2008): 31–51; Lital Levy, "Literature in Conflict," *Journal of Palestine Studies* 39, no. 2 (Winter 2010): 131–132; Reuven Snir, "Petza' Me Ptza'ar: HaSifrut Ha'Aravit HaFalastinit Be Yisrael," *Alpayim* 2 (1990): 244–68; and Reuven Snir, "'Hebrew as the Language of Grace': Arab-Palestinian Writers in Hebrew," *Prooftexts* 15 (1995): 163–183; Ranen Omer-Sherman, "Longing to Belong: Levantine Arabs and Jews in the Israeli Cultural Imagination," *Michigan Quarterly Review* 49, no. 2 (Spring 2010): 254–291.

536. Hannan Hever and Yael Shapira, "Yitzhak Shami: Ethnicity as an Unresolved Conflict," *Shofar: An Interdisciplinary Journal of Jewish Studies*, 24 no. 2 (Winter 2006): 124–139, 135.

537. Lawrence Silberstein, *Mapping Jewish Identities* (New York: New York University Press, 2000), 17.

538. Rachel Feldhay Brenner, *Inextricably Bonded: Israeli Arab and Jewish Writers Re-Visioning Culture* (Madison: University of Wisconsin Press, 2010), 126; referring to Yael Feldman, "Postcolonial Memory, Postmodern Intertextuality: Anton Shammas's *Arabesques* Revisited," *Publication of Modern Language Association* 114:3 (May 1999): 373–89.

539. Rachel Feldhay Brenner, "The Search for Identity in Israeli Arab Fiction," *Israel Studies* 6, no. 3 (2001): 91–112, 103–104.

540. Catherine Rottenberg, "Dancing Arabs and Spaces of Desire," *Topia* 19 (2008): 15; referring to Hannan Hever, *Producing the Modern Hebrew Canon: Nation Building and Minority Discourse* (New York: New York University Press, 2002). Emphasis in original.

541. Orna Sasson-Levy and Avi Shoshana, "'Passing' as (Non) Ethnic: The Israeli Version of Acting White," *Sociological Inquiry* 83, no. 3 (August 2013): 448–472, 456.

542. These divisions may be further subdivided, with Ashkenazi Jews being categorized as Anglo-Saxon, German, Polish, Russian, and Hungarian, for example, and Mizrachi Jews referring not only to those from North Africa, as the term originally implied, but also including Yemenite, Syrian, and Iraqi, as well as those not from Arab lands who might also be deemed "black," such as Indian, Persian, and Bukharian.

543. Carol Bardenstein, "Cross/Cast: Passing in Israeli and Palestinian Cinema," in *Palestine, Israel, and the Politics of Popular Culture*, ed. Rebecca L. Stein and Ted Swedenburg (Durham, NC: Duke University Press, 2005), 100.

544. Maria C. Sanchez and Linda Schlossberg, eds., *Passing: Identity and Interpretation in Sexuality, Race, and Religion* (New York: New York University Press, 2001), 3.

545. See the Bourekas films *Kazablan, Salah Shabbati, and HaShoter Azulai* to name but a few. The political and social reality were different and Mizrachi Jews experienced certain kinds of discrimination, disadvantageous settlement policies, poverty and other social, medical, educational and economic problems, but the very suggestions of cultural harmony and equality suppressed the visibility of economic and social realities in Israeli society for decades, in contradistinction to the presentation of race, ethnicity and colonialism in other contexts which maintained separation as a cultural standard.

546. See Samaa Abdurraqib, "Making it Survive Here and 'Dreams of Return': Community and Identity in the Poetry of Mohja Kahf," in *Arab Voices in Diaspora: Critical Perspectives on Anglophone Arab Literature*, ed. Layla al Maleh (New York: Rodophi BV, 2009), 449–463.

547. Evelyn Shakir, "Arab-American Literature," in *New Immigrant Literatures in the United States: A Sourcebook to Our Multicultural Literary Heritage*, ed. Alpana S. Sharma (Westport, CT: Greenwood Press, 1996).

548. Ami Elad-Bouskila, *Modern Palestinian Literature and Culture* (New York: Routledge, 1999), 27.

549. Elad-Bouskila, *Modern Palestinian Literature and Culture*, 39.

550. Ibid.

551. In *Arabesques*, Anton Shammas presents the character of Yehoshua (Yosh) Bar-On, a thinly disguised depiction of the Israeli-Jewish author A. B. Yehoshua, whose representation of Arabs in fiction were lauded for their authenticity, and for the representation of the Arab voice such as the Arab monologue in *The Lover*. Among these texts, "Facing the Forests" actually depicts a mute Arab. For Shammas, his critique of this writer and Shammas's own attempt to write his personal history instead become a multilayered and complicated family saga in which identity becomes impossible to pin down, reflecting his notion that it is for the Arab to tell his own story, with whatever

difficulties may be entailed.

552. Hannan Hever comments on Shammas's attempt to de-Judaize Hebrew from its Jewish identity in "Ivrit be-eto shel aravi," *Teoria Ubikoret* 1 (Summer 1991): 23–38; and "Hebrew in an Israeli Arab Hand: Six Miniatures on Anton Shammas's *Arabesques*," in *The Nature and Context of Minority Discourse*, ed. Abdul R. JanMohamed and David Lloyd, (Oxford: Oxford University Press, 1990), 264–93.

553. Ayman Sikseck, *El Yafo* (Tel Aviv: Yediot Aharonot, 2010), 114.

554. Sikseck, *El Yafo*, 39–40.

555. Ibid.

556. Gil Hochberg, "To Be or Not to Be an Israeli Arab: Sayed Kashua and the Prospect of Minority Speech-Acts," *Comparative Literature* 62, no. 1 (2010): 82–83.

557. Maria C. Sanchez and Linda Schlossberg, introduction to *Passing: Identity and Interpretation in Sexuality, Race, and Religion* (New York: New York University Press, 2001), 2.

558. Rottenberg, "Dancing Arabs and Spaces of Desire," 100; Kashua's *Dancing Arabs* is quoted on 102.

559. Sikseck, *El Yafo*, 9.

560. Rottenberg, "Dancing Arabs and Spaces of Desire," 106.

561. Sikseck, *El Yafo*, 55.

562. Rottenberg, "Dancing Arabs and Spaces of Desire," 107.

563. Sikseck, *El Yafo*, 20.

564. Ibid., 45.

565. Ibid., 139.

566. Ibid., 25.

567. Ibid., 11.

568. Ibid., 60.

569. Ibid., 74.

570. Kashua's work has received much scholarly attention for these two books, and for his creation of an Arab-Israeli "space." See Karen Grumberg, *Place and Ideology in Contemporary Hebrew Literature* (Syracuse: Syracuse University Press, 2011.)

571. Hochberg, "To Be or Not to Be an Israeli Arab," 70

572. Rottenberg, "Dancing Arabs and Spaces of Desire," 91.

573. Ibid., 107.

574. Bardenstein, "Cross/Cast: Passing in Israeli and Palestinian Cinema," 100.

575. Sayeed Kashua, *Second Person Singular* (New York: Grove Press, 2012), 304.

576. Ibid., 291.

577. Ibid., 290.

578. Ibid., 345.

579. Ibid., 20.

580. Ibid., 21.

581. Ibid., 156.

582. Karen Grumberg, *Place and Ideology in Contemporary Hebrew Literature* (Syracuse: Syracuse University Press, 2011), 125.

583. Ibid.

584. Kashua, *Second Person Singular*, 143.

585. Hochberg, "To Be or Not to Be an Israeli Arab," 78. Emphasis in original.

586. Kashua, *Second Person Singular*, 39.

587. Kashua, "Language is Identity," *Ha'aretz*, Sept 6, 2012, English edition.

SHIRA WOLOSKY NOTES

588. Tom Friedman, "Breakfast Before the MOOC" *New York Times*, February 18, 2014.

589. With Israel providing medical care to Syrian wounded.

590. "Arguing the Boycott Divestment and Sanctions (BDS) with Norman Finkelstein" Huffpomonitor: interview at Imperial College London http://vimeo.com/36854424#sthash.Wy4XBGnC.dpuf

591. Omar Barghouti, "Relative Humanity: The Fundamental Obstacle to a One-State Solution in Historic Palestine," January 6, 2004, http://electronicintifada.net/content/relative-humanity-fundamental-obstacle-one-state-solution-historic-palestine-12/4939. Other statements by BDS activists include: As'ad Abu Khalil, "Justice and freedom for the Palestinians are incompatible with the existence of the State of Israel;" Ahmed Moor: "OK, fine. So BDS does mean the end of the Jewish state....I view the BDS movement as a long-term project with radically transformative potential....In other words, BDS is

not another step on the way to the final showdown; BDS is The Final Showdown," April 22 2010, http://mondoweiss.net/2010/04/bds-is-a-long-term-project-with-radically-transformative-potential.html.

592. Roger Cohen, "The B.D.S. Threat" (*NYTimes* Feb 10 2014). Cf. Leon Wieseltier, who remarks on the boycott claim that "Israeli academic institutions are part of the ideological and institutional scaffolding of the Zionist settler-colonial project." "That is not anti-occupation, it is anti-Zionist; it is the foul diction of delegitimation," "The Academic Boycott of Israel is a Travesty," *New Republic*, Dec 17 2013.

593. In 2007/08 of the applicants who were accepted and studying, 83.3% were Jews, and 13.4% were Arabs. Of all applicants for second-degree studies at universities, of those who were accepted and studying, 93.2% were Jews and 4.9% were Arabs; and of the applicants who were rejected, 82.8% were Jews, and 15% were Arabs. The proportion of Arabs among all students at colleges of education was 28.5%, compared with 11.8% of the students in universities, 5.9% at the Open University, and 5.7% at academic colleges. Of the Arab first-degree recipients, 42.8% were enrolled in colleges of education, and 40.3% were enrolled in universities. The share of Arabs out of all first-degree recipients was 31.8% in colleges of education, compared with 8.7% in universities, 4.7% in academic colleges, and 3.7% in the Open University.

594. "List of Palestinian Universities" Wikipedia http://en.wikipedia.org/wiki/List_of_Palestinian_universities_and_colleges.

595. The statement on the American Studies website that "We are now witnessing accelerating efforts to curtail speech, to exercise censorship, and to carry out retaliatory action against individuals on the basis of their political views or associations," by "Scholars Condemn[ing] Censorship and Intimidation of Israel Critics" calls for the writers, as Leon Wieseltier puts it, to pick up their Orwell: "The Academic Boycott of Israel is a Travesty," *New Republic*, Dec 17 2013.

596. See for example Stanley Fish "Academic Freedom Against Itself," *New York Times*, October 28, 2013 and November 11, 2013. Cf. Richard Slotkin, "Richard Slotkin Bashes the Boycott," a lengthy critique of the ASA boycott resolution posted on the association's website. Declaring himself "strongly opposed to the Israeli government's policies in the Occupied Territories, and (in other forums) supporting a call for 'disinvestment' by universities as a way of directly pressuring the Israeli government. But this call for boycott is wrong in principle, politically impotent, intellectually dishonest, and morally obtuse. The boycott is, first and foremost, a violation of the principles of academic freedom, free association and open inquiry that are the essence of scholarly life. . . The ASA cannot credibly accuse Israeli universities of systematically violating the canons of academic freedom. Israeli universities are one of the primary loci of opposition to government policies, and of joint projects in aid of Palestinian scholars,

students and educational institutions. . . Finally, the boycott is morally obtuse. Asked why Israel is singled out, when so many other states are worse violators of human rights and UN resolutions, ASA President Curtis Marez answered "one has to start somewhere." So Israel—not Bashar Assad's Syria, or Khamenei's Iran; not the People's Republic of China which commits cultural genocide in Tibet; or Cuba, which remains a police state and persecutes dissidents and homosexuals; not even North Korea, most people's notion of hell on earth. The choice seems either arbitrary, or a reflection of ideological bias. http://www.theasa.net/from_the_editors/item/asa_members_vote_to_endorse_academic_boycott/; http://thefutureofamericanstudies.wordpress.com/2013/12/18/richard-slotkin-bashes-the-boycott/

597. The claim, as for example in an Open Letter in Defense of Academic Freedom in Palestine/Israel and the United States posted on the ASA official website (which reads like a BDS site), that the ASA "resolution did not call for the boycotting of individual scholars or termination of collaborations between Israeli and U.S. scholars and students. Nor did it call for the cessation of dialogue with these scholars; in fact the ASA is inviting Palestinian and Israeli scholars to its conference in November. What the resolution calls for is the boycott of Israeli academic institutions because they have been directly or indirectly complicit in the systematic maintenance of the illegal occupation of Palestinian territory." This is disingenuous. Most Israeli scholars travel to conferences on funding from their universities. To boycott university-funded projects is to boycott them. And to hold academic institutions directly (or indirectly for that matter) complicit in government policies is to breach every protection of or respect for academic autonomy.

598. Here may be the place to mention that many specific details of both fact and interpretation can be challenged re boycott claims. The MLA resolution now pending, for example, condemns the "denials of entry to the West Bank by U.S. academics who have been invited to teach, confer, or do research at Palestinian universities." But according to a report issued by MLA members opposing this resolution, in 2012, only 142 Americans were denied entry to Israel and the disputed territories out of 626,000 who wanted to enter, a refusal rate of about 0.023 percent. The U.S. restricts entry to its own borders at a much higher rate—5.4 percent in 2012 for Israeli applications for "B" visas, as reported by both the Israeli embassy in the U.S. and the U.S. State Department. 25 Cubans were just denied visas to the U.S. One needs to add that no Israeli academics are permitted to travel freely to Arab Countries; these countries are closed to people with Israeli entry stamps on their passports.

599. Michael Walzer, e.g. in "The State of Righteousness," April 24, 2010, www. huffingtonpost.com/michael-walzer/liberal-zionists-speak-out-state-" What the most oppressed and impoverished people in the world today most need is a state of their own, a decent state acting on their behalf. I feel some hostility, therefore, toward people who

want to 'transcend' the state—and I am especially hostile toward those who insist that the transcendence has to begin with the Jews."

600. Shira Wolosky, *Feminist Theory across Disciplines: Feminist Community and American Women's Poetry* (New York: Routledge, 2013).

601. Carole Gilligan, *In a Different Voice* (Cambridge: Harvard University Press, 1984) and the many writings that have built upon it.

602. Judith Butler, *Parting Ways* (NY: Columbia University Press, 2012); Shira Wolosky, "Cosmopolitanism vs. Normative Difference: From Habermas to Levinas," *The Israeli Nation State: Political, Constitutional and Cultural Changes* ed. Yedidya Stern and Fania-Oz Salzberger, Academic Studies Press, forthcoming.

603. James Madison, *Federalist* 10: as he continues, "As long as the reason of man continues fallible, and he is at liberty to exercise it, different opinions will be formed." http://avalon.law.yale.edu/18th_century/fed10.asp

RACHEL FISH NOTES

604. The term *Yishuv* literally means settlement. The *Yishuv* refers to the period in history in which Jewish residents settled within the land of Palestine prior to the creation of the state of Israel. From the 1880s until the creation of the state in 1948, the term Yishuv denotes pre-state Jewish residents in *Eretz Yisrael*.

605. Brit Shalom was a political organization founded in 1925 predominantly by Jewish German intellectuals. It sought to create a bi-national state for Palestine and foster coexistence between the Jewish and Arab populations.

606. Throughout the period of Mandatory Palestine, one of the weakest aspects of those advocating bi-nationalism was the inability to find, until 1946, a serious Arab leader willing to accept the bi-national blueprint. The most notable Arab to engage in serious discussion of constructing a bi-national framework in the land of Palestine was Fauzi Darwish el-Husseini (1896-1946), organizer of '*Falastin al-Jedida*, "A New Palestine." Darwish el-Husseini, along with four other members of his organization, in partnership with the League for Arab-Jewish Rapprochement, signed a document on November 11, 1946 endorsing the concept of a bi-national Palestine. "The agreement spoke of Arab-Jewish 'cooperation,' political equality, Jewish immigration limited only by the country's economic absorptive capacity, and the inclusion of Palestine in a league of neighboring Arab states." Benny Morris, *One State, Two States: Resolving the Israel/Palestine Conflict* (New Haven, CT: Yale University Press, 2010), 95. An unknown Arab nationalist murdered Fauzi on November 23, 1946. It is worth mentioning that Fauzi was a cousin of the Grand Mufti of Jerusalem, Haj Amin al-Husseini. Martin Buber, *A Land of Two Peoples: Martin Buber on Jews and Arabs*, ed. Paul Mendes-Flohr

(Gloucester, MA: Peter Smith, 1994), 252. Another Arab who was willing to cooperate with members of Brit Shalom was Sami Taha (1916-1947), though he held no serious clout politically or intellectually within his own community. Taha was involved with the Palestine Arab Workers Society, and was ultimately appointed as the labor representative of the Arab Higher Committee. Tensions between Taha and members of the al-Husseini family increased. Taha was believed to be insufficiently anti-Zionist and anti-British in his outlook and policies, resulting in his murder on 12, 1947. The murderer was not apprehended and was believed to be following the orders of the Grand Mufti of Jerusalem. Tamar Hermann, "The Bi-National Idea in Israel/Palestine: Past and Present," *Nations and Nationalism* 11, no. 3 (2005): 385.

607. The term *Eretz Yisrael* refers to the Biblical geographical territory of the Land of Israel—not to the political landscape of Mandatory Palestine under the British authority.

608. Ratosh was the pseudonym for Uriel Heilperin, born in Warsaw Poland in 1908 to a Zionist family. Ratosh embraced Revisionist Zionism. Ratosh tried to synthesize the political views of Revisionist Zionism while embracing the Semitic character of Hebrew identity.

609. In Ben Gurion's book, *My Talks with Arab Leaders*, he enumerates his various encounters with Arabs both inside of Palestine (and later Israel) and throughout the Arab world. He discusses potential frameworks for the future state of the Jewish people, bi-nationalism among them. However, for Ben-Gurion, a bi-national state was merely a tactical means to gain political autonomy for the Jews, and political parity with the Arabs while Jewish immigration continued. He reported that despite his engagement with various Arabs, he was unable to locate an Arab leader who was interested genuinely in political parity with the Jews. Ben-Gurion was unable to locate Arab partners who would agree to the idea of a bi-national arrangement in Palestine. David Ben-Gurion, *My Talks with Arab Leaders*, trans. Areyh Rubinstein and Misha Louvish (Jerusalem: Keter Books, 1972).

610. Balad is a political party comprised primarily of support from the Palestinian Arab citizens of Israel. Balad is an acronym for *B'rit Le'umit Demokratit*—National Democratic Assembly. Balad opposes Israel as a Jewish state and seeks to transform it into a bi-national state. Balad was formed in 1995 under the political leadership of Azmi Bishara.

611. The *Future Vision* documents includes: *The Future Vision of the Palestinian Arabs in Israel* (Nazareth: National Committee for the Heads of the Arab Local Authorities in Israel, 2006), http://www.adalah.org/newsletter/eng/dec06/tasawor-mostaqbali.pdf; *The Haifa Declaration* (Mada al-Carmel, The Arab Center for Applied Social Research, 2007), http://www.mada-research.org; and *The Democratic Constitution*, (Haifa: Adalah, The Legal Center for Arab Minority Rights in Israel, 2007), http://www.adalah.org/eng/democratic_constitution-e.pdf. If an individual document is analyzed here, the

specific document will be named. If all three of the documents or the overarching ideas expressed in all three manifestos are discussed, they will be referred to as the *Future Vision* documents.

612. The phrase "Israel proper" refers to the territorial demarcations as outlined by the 1949 Armistice Agreements between Israel and its neighbors after the events of the 1948 war. The exception to this is the inclusion of the Golan Heights which Israel annexed after it captured this territory in the 1967 war.

613. Edward Said's work *Orientalism* is utilized as a foundational text in the academic field of post-colonialism. For Said, the term "orientalism" is a Eurocentric understanding of the Middle East and Arab and Islamic societies. He argues that the prejudices of Europe inform their perception of the "orient" falsely. Edward Said, *Orientalism* (New York: Vintage Books, 1979).

ILAN TROEN NOTES

614. Israel Diplomatic Network, "Border Security: Entry into Israel." *The Embassy of Israel to the United States*, 2014. See: http://www.israelemb.org/washington/ConsularServices/Pages/Entry-to-Israel.aspx.

615. "Israel, the West Bank, and Gaza Travel Warning," *United States Department of State*, last modified February 3, 2014, http://travel.state.gov/content/passports/english/alertswarnings/israel-travel-warning.html.

616. David Robinson, *The Status of Higher Education Teaching Personnel in Israel, the West Bank and Gaza* (Canadian Association of University Teachers: Ottawa: 2010). Can be found at http://www.google.com/url?sa=t&rct=j&q=&esrc=s&source=web&cd=1&ved=0CCgQFjAA&url=http%3A%2F%2Fdownload.ei-ie.org%2FDocs%2FWebDepot%2FThe%2520Status%2520of%2520Higher%2520Education%2520Teaching%2520Personnel%2520in%2520Israel%2C%2520the%2520West%2520Bank%2520and%2520Gaza.pdf&ei=F-BKU6bjAbDKsQTqyIIY&usg=AFQjCNEflZB_GBq2hcmIr1aCOv8ANk0WqA&bvm=bv.64542518,d.cWc . See, too, *6th EI International Conference on Higher Education and Research* (Malaga: Nov. 14, 2007).

617. http://en.wikipedia.org/wiki/Jewish-Arab_Center.

618. S. Ilan Troen, *Imagining Zion: Dreams, Designs, and Realities in a Century of Jewish Settlement* (Yale University Press: New Haven, 2002), 47-53.

619. Statistics and information derive from correspondence with the Office of the President of Ben-Gurion University of the Negev.

620. National Committee for the Heads of the Arab Local Authorities, "The Future Vision of the Palestinian Arabs in Israel," Electronic Intifada, last modified January 12,

2007, http://electronicintifada.net/content/future-vision-palestinian-arabs-israel/3054.

621. "Expel Omar Barghouti," Petition Online, http://www.petitiononline.com/expelOB/petition.html; and "Omar Barghouti," Wikipedia, last modified March 7, 2014, http://en.wikipedia.org/wiki/Omar_Barghouti.

622. European Commission, *Higher Education in the Occupied Palestinian Territory* (Ramallah, 2012). See: http://eacea.ec.europa.eu/tempus../participating_countries/overview/oPt.pdf.

623. Khuloud K. Dajani and Rafael S. Carel, "Neighbors and Enemies: Lessons to Be Learned from the Palestinian-Israeli Conflict Regarding Cooperation in Public Health," *Croatian Medical Journal* 43, no. 2 (2002): 138-140.

624. "Victory for Israel at APHA," *Hebrew University of Israel Faculty of Medicine*, last modified November 19, 2013, https://medicine.ekmd.huji.ac.il/schools/publichealth/En/newsandEvents/news/Pages/APHA.aspx.

625. Sami Adwan, Dan Bar-On, Eyal Naveh, eds, *Side by Side: Parallel Histories of Israel-Palestine* (New York, 2012); Paul Scham, Walid Salem, Benjamin Pogrund, eds. *Shared Histories: A Palestinian-Israeli Dialogue* (Walnut Creek, CA, 2005); Paul Scham, Benjamin Pogrund, and As'ad Ghanem, eds., special issue, *Shared Narratives—A Palestinian-Israeli Dialogue, Israel Studies* 18, no. 2 (Summer 2013).

Notes on Contributors

Paul Berman, a senior editor of *The New Republic*, writes widely about politics and literature. His books include *Terror and Liberalism*, *The Flight of the Intellectuals*, *A Tale of Two Utopias,* and *Power and the Idealists*.

Russell A. Berman, Walter A. Haas Professor in the Humanities at Stanford University and Professor of Comparative Literature and German Studies, is the author of *The Rise of the Modern German Novel: Crisis and Charisma; Modern Culture and Critical Theory: Art, Politics and the Legacy of the Frankfurt School; Enlightenment of Empire: Colonial Discourse in German Culture; Anti-Americanism in Europe: A Cultural Problem; Fiction Sets You Free: Literature, Liberty and Western Culture* and other books. He is a former president of the Modern Language Association.

Michael Bérubé, Edwin Erle Sparks Professor of Literature and Director of the Institute for the Arts and Humanities at Pennsylvania State University, is the author or editor of nine books, including *The Left at War*, and is a former president of the Modern Language Association.

Gabriel Noah Brahm, Associate Professor of English at Northern Michigan University, is coauthor of *The Jester and the Sages: Mark Twain in Conversation with Nietzsche, Freud and Marx* and coeditor of *Prosthetic Territories: Politics and Hypertechnologies*.

Emily Budick, Ann and Joseph Edelman Professor of American Studies and Director of the Center for Literary Studies at the Hebrew University of Jerusalem, is the author of the forthcoming *The Subject of Holocaust Fiction* and eleven other books.

David Caplan, the Charles M. Weis Chair in English at Ohio Wesleyan University, is the author of four books, most recently, *Rhyme's Challenge: Hip Hop, Poetry, and Contemporary Rhyming Culture.*

Donna Divine, Morningstar Professor of Government at Smith College, is the author of *Politics and Society in Ottoman Palestine: The Arab Struggle for Survival and Power*; *Postcolonial Theory and The Arab-Israeli Conflict*; and *Exiled in the Homeland: Zionism and the Return to Mandate Palestine.*

Carol F. S. Edelman is CSU Chico Emerita Professor of Sociology and former Associate Dean of Behavioral and Social Sciences.

Samuel M. Edelman is CSU Chico Emeritus Professor and former Dean of Undergraduate Education at the American Jewish University.

Robert Fine, professor emeritus of sociology at Warwick University, is the coauthor of *Beyond Apartheid: Labour and Liberation in South Africa*, and the author of *Political Investigations: Hegel, Marx, Arendt* and other books.

Rachel Fish is a recent PhD and associate director of the Shusterman Center for Israel Studies at Brandeis University.

Rachel S. Harris teaches Israeli and comparative literature at the University of Illinois at Urbana-Champaign. She is the author of *An Ideological Death: Suicide in Israeli Literature* and the coeditor of *War: Dissent and Narrative in Israeli Culture and Society.*

Jeffrey Herf, Professor History at the University of Maryland, is the author of *The Jewish Enemy: Nazi Propaganda During World War II and the Holocaust*; *Divided Memory: The Nazi Past in the Two Germanys* and other books.

David Hirsh, Lecturer in Sociology at Goldsmiths College, University of London, is the founder of Engage, a campaign against academic boycotts of Israel. He is the author of *Law Against Genocide: Cosmopolitan Trials.*

Alan Johnson is the Editor of *Fathom: for a deeper understanding of Israel and the region.* A professor of democratic theory and politics, he is a Senior Research Associate at the Foreign Policy Centre, an editorial board member at Dissent, and co-author of the 2006 "Euston Manifesto," a modern statement of social democratic antitotalitarianism. He blogs at *World Affairs.*

Nancy Koppelman is professor of American Studies and Humanities at Evergreen State College. She creates and team-teaches full time interdisciplinary undergraduate academic programs with colleagues from the humanities, the sciences, and the social sciences, all based on the pedagogy of learning communities. For four years, she was the Lead Faculty for the Teaching American History Project serving school districts in South Puget Sound, WA.

Michael C. Kotzin is Senior Counselor to the President of the Jewish Federation of Metropolitan Chicago. He has taught at Tel Aviv University and has more recently been a Visiting Professor at the University of Illinois in Urbana-Champaign. He is the author of *Dickens and the Fairy Tale*.

Richard Landes, Professor of History at Boston University, is the author of *Relics, Apocalypse, and the Deceits of History*; *Heaven on Earth: The Varieties of the Millennial Experience*, and other books.

Sonya Michel, Professor of History at the University of Maryland, is the author of *Children's Interests / Mothers' Rights: The Shaping of America's Child Care Policy* and the editor of several other books.

Cary Nelson, Jubilee Professor of Liberal Arts and Sciences and Professor of English at the University of Illinois at Urbana-Champaign, is the author or editor of 30 books, including *Manifesto of a Tenured Radical*; *No University is an Island: Saving Academic Freedom*; and *Revolutionary Memory: Recovering the Poetry of the American Left*. He was president of the American Association of University Professors from 2006-2012 and is currently co-chair of The Academic Advisory Council of The Third Narrative. His work and career are the subject of the edited collection *Cary Nelson and the Struggle for the University*.

Sharon Ann Musher, Associate Professor of History at Richard Stockton College of New Jersey, is the author of *Democratic Art: The New Deal's Influence on American Culture*.

Martha Nussbaum, Ernst Freund Distinguished Service Professor of Law and Ethics at the University of Chicago, is the author of eighteen books.

Asaf Romirowsky is a fellow at the Middle East Forum, coauthor of *Religion, Politics, and the Origins of Palestine Refugee Relief*, and Executive Director of Scholars for Peace in the Middle East.

Jeff Robbins is a Boston-based lawyer who served as a United States delegate to the United Nations Human Rights Commission in Geneva, Switzerland. He was first appointed to this position by President Clinton in March 1999 and then reappointed in March 2000. He served as Board Chair of ADL's New England Region from 2012-2014.

Tammi Rossman-Benjamin is a lecturer at University of California Santa Cruz and the co-founder of AMCHA Initiative, an organization that investigates, documents, educates about, and combats campus antisemitism in institutions of higher education in America.

Sabah A. Salih, professor of English at Bloomsburg University, is the author of *Modernism or Art Under the Watchful Eyes of Art*.

Kenneth W. Stein, Professor of Contemporary Middle Eastern History, Political Science and Israeli Studies at Emory University, is the author of *Heroic Diplomacy: Sadat, Kissinger, Carter, Begin, and the Quest for Arab-Israeli Peace*; *Making Peace Among Arabs and Israelis: Lessons from Fifty Years of Negotiating Experience*; and *The Land Question in Palestine, 1917-1939*. He is the president of the Atlanta based Center for Israel Education.

Ilan Troen, Stoll Family Chair in Israel Studies and Director of the Schusterman Center for Israel Studies at Brandeis University, is also Lopin Professor of Modern History, emeritus, Ben-Gurion University of the Negev. He is the author or editor of eleven books, including *Imagining Zion: Dreams, Designs and Realities in a Century of Jewish Settlement*; and, with Jacob Lassner, *Jews and Muslims in the Arab World*; *Haunted by Pasts Real and Imagined*.

Shira Wolosky, professor of American Studies and English at Hebrew University, has written *Poetry and Public Discourse in Nineteenth Century America*; *Language Mysticism: The Negative Way of Language in Eliot, Beckett, and Cela*; *Feminist Theory across Disciplines: Feminist Community and American Women's Poetry* and other books.

Along with Martin Schictman, Russell A. Berman, Rachel S. Harris, and Cary Nelson are on the executive committee of MLA Members for Scholars' Rights. MMFSR is not affiliated with the Modern Language Association.

Index